Practical Trust Administration

Practical Trust Administration

The Law and Practice of Wills,
Estates and Trusts

Third Edition

Michael Sladen LLB, FCIB
of Lincoln's Inn, Barrister

The Chartered
Institute
of Bankers

First published by Europa Publications Ltd, 1977
Second edition, 1983
Third edition published by The Chartered Institute of Bankers, 1993

BANKERS BOOKS LIMITED
c/o The Chartered Institute of Bankers
10 Lombard Street
London EC3V 9AS

CIB publications are published by The Chartered Institute of Bankers, a non-profit making, registered educational charity, and are distributed exclusively by Bankers Books Limited which is a wholly-owned subsidiary of The Chartered Institute of Bankers.

© M Sladen, 1977

 British Library Cataloguing-in-Publication Data

Sladen, Michael
   Practical Trust Administration: Law and Practice of
   Wills, Estates and Trusts
   3 rev ed
   I. Title
   344.20659

ISBN 0 85297 328 4

Typeset in 10/11 pt Times, by Style Photosetting Ltd, Mayfield, East Sussex
Printed by Staples Printers Rochester Ltd, Rochester, Kent;
on 80 gsm paper; cover on 240 gsm

Cover illustration: Thomas Braithwaite of Ambleside making his will (artist unknown). Reproduced by courtesy of Abbot Hall Art Gallery, Kendal, Cumbria.

Contents

Preface

There is a considerable difference between the contents of this edition and those of the two previous editions. Because of changes in the examination structure for trustee candidates of The Chartered Institute of Bankers, it is necessary to cover as fully as possible the law relating to wills, the administration of deceased estates and trusts. Previous editions certainly contained *some* of the law but the main emphasis was on the practice of personal representatives and trustees. I have now tried to retain this practical content but at the same time to increase considerably coverage of the relevant law. The result is a bigger book and, as a result of pressure on the available space, I have omitted the middle tax section which appeared before; tax matters are still dealt with at appropriate points in the text, but a basic knowledge of taxation is assumed. One thing I have not tried to do is to elucidate the general relationship between trustees and the provisions of the Financial Services Act; it seems that, in one respect at least, trustees do come under the Act's umbrella but I have chosen not to enquire into this. Notwithstanding the change in character, my hope is that the book will continue to be of use to those professionally engaged at all levels in the administration of estates and trusts. The law stated is generally as at 30 April 1992 but reference is made to the second of the 1992 Finance Acts, together with one or two other very recent developments in the courts.

I have had a lot of help in preparing this edition. I am glad to acknowledge this and must give pride of place to my friend Ron Coker. Not only has he produced an impeccable typescript via his word processor but his own great experience and knowledge has been brought to bear on the content of the text. As I fed material to him he reviewed it, criticised it and suggested improvements and remedied omissions; in a number of places he contributed valuable new passages so that, virtually, he is a co-author. Certainly the book is altogether broader and deeper in scope than it would have been without his massive contribution, and I am correspondingly grateful.

Another friend, Tony Sherring, also deserves a deep vote of thanks, for he has been kind enough to advise and comment on some of the tax problems which I found particularly baffling. His generous help with these has been invaluable. I owe a debt of gratitude to Graham Lane of The Law Debenture Corporation for giving me the benefit of his expertise concerning current pension fund law and practice and the controversies in which it is at present enveloped. Ron Porter of the National Westminster Bank has been equally generous with his expert advice about the intricacies of the modern unit trust world. Robert Anstice and David Macreavy, also the National Westminster Bank, have been most helpful in supplying information and advice. My grateful thanks also to John Gorham of The Royal Bank of Scotland for his most helpful contribution to the section dealing with the Scottish law of wills and intestacies. Lastly, but by no means least, I come to The Chartered Institute of Bankers; without their constant support and encouragement I would not have got to the point where this preface is needed and there would be no third edition of *Practical Trust Administration*. So, my deepest thanks to the Institute of which I had the honour of becoming a member rather more than 50 years ago!

I would repeat my previous request to be informed of errors as and when these are discovered.

Michael Sladen
Shimpling
December 1992

Table of Cases

The cases listed below are to be found under the chapter and section given in the right-hand column; 6.45 refers to Chapter 6, section 45, and 9.38n10 means note 10 of Chapter 9, section 38.

Table of Statutes

The statutes listed below are to be found in the chapter and section given in the right-hand column; 3.13 refers to chapter 3, section 13, and 8n4 means note 4 of chapter 8.

Table of Statutory Instruments

The statutory instruments listed below are to be found under the chapter and section number given in the right-hand column; 3.44 refers to chapter 3, section 44.

List of Abbreviations

STATUTES AND STATUTORY INSTRUMENTS

Administration of Estates Act 1925	AEA
Administration of Estates Act 1971	AEA 1971
Administration of Justice Act 1982	AJA 1982
Administration of Justice Act 1985	AJA 1985
Family Law Reform Act 1969	FLRA
Income and Corporation Taxes Act 1988	ICTA
Inheritance Tax Act 1984	IHTA
Land Registration Act 1925	LRA
Law of Property Act 1925	LPA
Married Women's Property Act 1882	MWPA
Non-Contentious Probate Rules 1987 & 1991	NCPR
Perpetuities and Accumulations Act 1964	PAA
Settled Land Act 1925	SLA
Taxation of Chargeable Gains Act 1992	TCGA
Taxes Management Act 1970	TMA
Trustee Act 1925	TA
Trustee Investments Act 1961	TIA
Wills Act 1837	WA
Wills Act 1963	WA 1963
Wills Act 1968	WA 1968

JOURNALS, ETC.

Conveyancer	Conv
Current Law	CL
Current Law Year Book	CLYB
Inland Revenue Booklet	IR
Law Quarterly Review	LQR
New Law Journal	NLJ
Solicitors' Journal	SJ
Statement of Practice	SP

OTHER ABBREVIATIONS USED

Capital Gains Tax	CGT
Capital Transfer Tax	CTT
donatio mortis causa	*dmc*
Extra Statutory Concession	ESC
Income Tax	IT
Inheritance Tax	IHT
Personal Representatives	PRs
Potentially Exempt Transfer (for IHT)	PET
Statement of Practice	SP
Statutory Instrument	SI

Bibliography

Throughout the text, these books are referred to by their author(s), in the form *Hanbury*. Where an abbreviated form is used (e.g. *W & S-B*), this is indicated at the end of each entry.

Brighouse (1986), *Precedents of Wills and Life Transfers*, 11th edn., Sweet & Maxwell.

Dicey and Morris (1987), *The Conflict of Laws*, 11th edn., Stevens.

Dymond (1991), *Capital Transfer Tax*, Longman Law, Tax and Finance.

Eastaway and Booth (1990), *Practical Share Valuation*, 2nd edn., Butterworth.

Hanbury and Maudsley (1989), *Modern Equity*, 13th edn., Stevens (*Hanbury*).

Heywood and Massey (1985), *Court of Protection Practice*, 12th edn., Stevens.

Hill and Redman (1988), *Law of Landlord and Tenant*, Butterworth.

Inland Revenue (1991), *Inheritance Tax* (IHT 1), HMSO.

Keeton and Sheridan (1983), *The Law of Trusts*, 11th edn., Professional Books.

Lewin (1964), *Trusts*, 16th edn., Sweet & Maxwell.

Megarry and Wade (1984), *The Law of Real Property*, 5th edn., Stevens.

Mellows (1983), *The Law of Succession*, 4th edn., Butterworth.

Miller (1977), *The Machinery of Succession*, Professional Books.

Morris and Leach (1962), *The Rule against Perpetuities*, Stevens.

Oakley (1987), *Constructive Trusts*, 2nd edn., Sweet & Maxwell.

Parker and Mellows (1983), *The Modern Law of Trusts*, 5th edn., Sweet & Maxwell.

Pettit (1989), Equity and the Law of Trusts, 6th edn., Butterworth.

Ray and Redman (1991), *Practical Inheritance Tax Planning*, 2nd edn., Butterworth (*Ray*).

Sherring (1991), *Tolley's UK Taxation of Trusts*, 2nd edn., Tolley.

Snell (1990), Principles of Equity, 29th edn., Sweet & Maxwell.

Theobald (1982), *Wills*, 14th edn., Stevens.

Tolley's Tax Havens (1990), Tolley.

Tristram and Coote (1989), *Probate Practice*, 27th edn., Butterworth (*T & C*).

Underhill and Hayton (1987), *Law of Trusts and Trustees*, 14th edn., Butterworths (*Underhill*).

Vaughan (1990), *The Regulation of Unit Trusts*, Lloyd's of London.
Whitehouse and Stuart-Buttle (1991), *Revenue Law*, 9th edn., Butterworth (*W & S-B*).
Williams (1987) *Wills*, 6th edn., Butterworth.
Williams, Mortimer and Sunnucks (1982), *Executors, Administrators & Probate*, 16th and 4th edns, Stevens (*W,M & S*).
Winfield and Curry (1991), *Success in Investment*, 4th edn., John Murray.
Winfield and Jolowicz (1989), *Textbook of the Law of Tort*, 13th edn., Sweet & Maxwell (*Winfield*).
Wolstenholme and Cherry (1972), *Conveyancing Statutes*, 13th edn., Oyez.
Wylie (1986), *Irish Land Law*, 2nd edn., Professional Books.

PART I

WILLS, INTESTACIES AND DECEASEDS' ESTATES

1 Wills (1)

1.1 WHY MAKE A WILL?

Under English law the general freedom of disposition of property includes
the right to direct the way in which such property is to devolve on one's
death, by means of a will. If a will is not made, the rules for distribution on
intestacy apply; these are inflexible and may be unsatisfactory in practice.
Making a will allows one to choose executors – persons in whom the
testator has confidence and who will be available for duty as soon as death
occurs, with no hiatus. Guardians of infant children may be appointed.
Funeral wishes may be expressed. Special provisions for the conduct of any
business owned can be inserted. Charitable legacies and gifts of specific
items of property may be bequeathed. Substitutional gifts can be made to
cover the possibility of a beneficiary predeceasing the testator or dying as
the result of a joint catastrophe. Trusts for the benefit of dependants may
be created. Moreover, a will is 'ambulatory' by nature – it 'walks' during
the testator's life but is of no effect until his death, unlike a gift *inter vivos*,
which takes effect as soon as it is completely constituted. Consequently, a
will cannot be made irrevocable – it may be revoked at any time before
death occurs and its contents updated by execution of either a codicil or a
new will; indeed, it is very desirable that a will should be reviewed both at
intervals and when a change in the testator's circumstances occurs.

1.2 TAXATION ON DEATH

Death results in a deemed transfer of the value of the deceased's property
for IHT purposes (s. 4(1) IHTA); when making a will it is therefore sensible
to estimate the potential tax bill which one's executors are going to have to
meet. This requires a valuation in round terms of the current value of one's
estate, including trusts in which a life interest is held and the value of any
potentially exempt transfers made within the past seven years. This exercise
may well show that it is both desirable and possible to carry out a
tax-saving operation at once – in simplest terms, by making lifetime gifts
which will be free of tax if the donor survives for seven years. In any case,
a will should be drawn so as to minimise the tax bill on death, so far as is
consonant with the testator's objectives. Will-making not only involves the
making of directions for the disposition of one's property but also may
constitute a tax-saving exercise and a general taking stock of one's personal
financial affairs.

1.3   NATURE OF A WILL: REQUIREMENTS OF AN ENGLISH OR WELSH WILL

A will is the expression by a person of his intentions regarding the disposition of his property on, and only on, his death. It is, therefore, the final transaction by which a property-owner exercises his freedom of disposition. *Inter vivos* dispositions may be effected in different ways and with greater or lesser formality according to the form of property being disposed of, but in England and Wales the form and execution of a will are strictly controlled by the provisions of the Wills Act 1837; apart from these formal requirements it is essential that a testator should have capacity to make a will.

1.4   CAPACITY TO MAKE A WILL

For a testamentary disposition of movables, capacity is governed by the law of the testator's domicile, probably that which existed at the date of the will; capacity to dispose of immovable property is governed by the *lex situs*. If the domicile so established is English, the testator must be at least 18 years old (s. 7 WA), unless the will is of the 'privileged' variety (see *post* 1.31). Otherwise, the test to be applied to ascertain whether or not capacity exists is well described in the words of Cockburn CJ in *Banks* v *Goodfellow* (1870):

'It is essential . . . that a testator shall understand the nature of the act and its effects; shall understand the extent of the property of which he is disposing; shall be able to comprehend and appreciate the claims to which he ought to give effect; and, with a view to the latter object, that no disorder of the mind shall poison his affections, pervert his sense of right, or prevent the exercise of his natural faculties – that no insane delusion shall influence his will in disposing of his property and bring about a disposal of it which, if the mind had been sound, would not have been made.'

One can paraphrase the above passage as follows: firstly, a testator must know that he is expressing his intentions as to the disposition of his property on his death (not necessarily that he is making a *will*); secondly, he must appreciate the extent and value of the property he is capable of disposing; thirdly, he must understand the claims of those he includes and excludes from benefit.

1.5   MENTAL AND PHYSICAL DISABILITY

A patient for the purposes of the Mental Health Act 1983 is not necessarily incapable of making a will. There may be a presumption that mental illness deprived such a patient of capacity, but this may be rebutted by showing that the will was made during a lucid interval (see *post* 1.10 for the making

4

of statutory wills for the mentally disabled). The passage quoted in 1.4 refers to 'insane delusion': such a delusion may deprive a testator of capacity, but will not do so if the delusion in question could not have influenced him in connection with the making of his will. It will be understood from the above that there are no hard-and-fast rules for capacity – each case is judged on its merits. Eccentricity, irrationality and caprice are not necessarily signs that a testator lacked capacity, although they are grounds upon which a successful action to have a will set aside may be founded. When a former Master of the Rolls, Sir Joseph Jekyll, left his fortune to pay the National Debt, Lord Mansfield said, unsympathetically, that he might as well have attempted to stop the middle arch of Blackfriars Bridge with his full-bottomed wig; the will was set aside on the ground of imbecility.

Mental instability is not the only reason for a testator's lack of capacity. A testator who is either blind or illiterate is handicapped by his disability; in these circumstances (and in other doubtful cases) a will is not admitted to probate until the registrar has satisfied himself that the testator had a proper knowledge of its contents at the time of execution (NCPR 13). It is therefore desirable for such wills to end with an attestation clause which states that the will was read over to the testator and that he appeared to understand it. It is essential that the testator knows and approves the contents of his will when he executes it, but the fact that he may be mistaken as to its legal effect is immaterial: *Re Horrocks* (1939).

1.6 PRECAUTIONS FOR ENSURING FULL KNOWLEDGE AND APPROVAL

Precautions should be taken in any case where either the mental or the physical condition of the testator may call his capacity into question when the will has to be proved. In such circumstances the will should be 'witnessed or approved by a medical practitioner, who ought to record his examination of the testator and his findings. That was the golden, if tactless, rule.' However, this advice, given by Templeman J. (as he then was) in *Kenward* v *Adams* (1975) is not always easy to follow; for instance, there is evidence that doctors prefer not to be involved in this way. One should add, perhaps, that the person responsible for drafting the will and getting it executed should take particular care to satisfy himself that the testator has the essential capacity; a note recording the circumstances and the reasons for believing capacity to exist may be useful at a later date. Precautions of this sort may prevent the development of a possibly ill-judged and expensive dispute. A bank manager will often be responsible for setting in train the drafting and execution of a will; he, too, should bear in mind the question of capacity and issue a suitable warning to the solicitor in appropriate cases.

Particular care to ensure that capacity, in the sense of full knowledge and approval, exists is also necessary in cases (known as 'suspicious circumstances') where the will is prepared by someone who, or whose close relation, benefits under it. The best-known case on this subject is probably *Wintle* v *Nye* (1959), in which a solicitor drew up a will for an elderly 'unintelligent' lady which gave him the residue of her estate. But see also *Re A Solicitor* (1975) where the Disciplinary Committee of the Law Society held that a solicitor in whose favour a client wishes to make a will was bound to tell her that she must be separately advised and, if she refused to go to another solicitor, it was his duty to decline to act. This is 'an exceptionally high standard . . . probably higher than that imposed in the probate courts when the validity of the will is in question' (*per* Lord Widgery CJ).

Where the circumstances are sufficiently suspicious to throw doubt on the testator's knowledge and approval of the contents of his will, the burden of proof will be on the executor propounding the will to remove that doubt; contrast this with the situation where undue influence is alleged – see below.

1.7 UNDUE INFLUENCE AND COERCION

Even if capacity exists, a will may be invalid because it was signed under significant pressure, either mental or physical. Clearly a will which is signed under duress will not stand up. Undue influence is equally pernicious, but more subtle. It can occur wherever there is a special relationship between testator and beneficiary, e.g. householder and housekeeper, bank manager and customer, doctor and patient. For *inter vivos* transactions, where such a special relationship exists, undue influence may be presumed, leaving the opposition with the task of rebutting it, but with a will a presumption of undue influence does not arise automatically – those who allege it must prove it.

1.8 UNDUE INFLUENCE IN LIFETIME TRANSACTIONS

Recent cases about undue influence have tended to be concerned with bank loans; *National Westminster Bank* v *Morgan* (1985) is helpful because the decision emphasises that, before a transaction can be set aside on the ground of undue influence, it must be shown to have been disadvantageous to the person influenced, as happened in *Goldsworthy* v *Brickell* (1987), where the transaction complained of was so improvident as not to be accounted for by ordinary motives. It is not essential in such cases for the victim to have been 'dominated' by the other party, as seems to have been the case in *Re Craig* (1971) (an elderly widower and his secretary); the essential element is the existence of a confidential relationship. [1]

1.9 QUESTIONING THE DECEASED'S CAPACITY TO MAKE HIS LIFETIME GIFTS

Lack of capacity may have to be considered by PRs in connection with lifetime gifts made by the deceased; see, e.g., *Simpson* v *Simpson* (1989) where certain substantial transfers of property effected by the deceased shortly before his death in favour of his wife were held to be invalid because he lacked the capacity to make them effective; although the question of undue influence did not arise, in certain circumstances its existence between husband and wife could be presumed, but generally the marital relationship does not give rise to this presumption: see *Midland Bank* v *Shephard* (1988) where the Court of Appeal declined to regard a wife's signature of a loan agreement as being made under the influence of her husband. Regarding *inter vivos* gifts in general, see *Re Beaney* (1978); the degree of understanding required varies according to the circumstances – the greater the gift in proportion to the donor's fortune, the greater the degree of understanding needed to satisfy the capacity test.

1.10 STATUTORY WILLS FOR THE MENTALLY DISABLED

Section 96 Mental Health Act 1983 authorises the Court of Protection to order the execution of a will for an adult person whom a judge has reason to believe is incapable of making one for himself. Although the section refers to the order of a judge, his functions are exercisable by the Master or designated officers of the Court of Protection. The Court has published rules, SI 1984/2035, and a Practice Direction (1983) concerning the procedure; there is also a procedure note (PN9), available from the Court of Protection. Section 97 contains provisions concerning the execution of a will made under s. 96. Applications for the making of such a will may be made either by the patient's receiver or by one or more persons seeking to benefit under it, and be sent to the Public Trust Office, Protection Division, Kingsway, London WC2B 6JX. Subsequently, if the Court approves, the will is drafted and executed by a duly authorised person on behalf of the patient. Note that such a will cannot dispose of immovable property outside England and Wales, but otherwise can do anything which the will of a testator having full capacity could do. See *Re D.(J.)* (1982) for a discussion of the principles applicable to the drafting of a statutory will, and also *Re C* (1991); the assumption, in the absence of evidence to the contrary, was that the patient for whom a will was to be made was a normal, decent person acting in accordance with contemporary standards of morality.

Section 96 also contains power for the judge to order the making of a settlement of a patient's property and, indeed to order the making of outright gifts, provided it can be accepted that such transaction would have been carried out by the patient himself, had he been fully capable.

1.11 FORMAL REQUIREMENTS FOR A VALID WILL

The crucial provision is s. 9 WA as amended by s. 17 AJA 1982; in its amended form the section applies to the wills of persons dying after 31 December 1982:

9. No will shall be valid unless
   (a) it is in writing, and signed by the testator, or by some other person in his presence and by his direction; and
   (b) it appears that the testator intended by his signature to give effect to the will; and
   (c) the signature is made or acknowledged by the testator in the presence of two or more witnesses present at the same time; and
   (d) each witness either
      (i) attests and signs the will; or
      (ii) acknowledges his signature,
      in the presence of the testator (but not necessarily in the presence of any other witness),
   but no form of attestation shall be necessary.

Although a will must be in writing (apart from the exception of the privileged will – see *post* 1.31) this provision is interpreted broadly; a will may be handwritten, typed, printed or a combination of any of these methods. If written, ink should be used, not pencil. Home-made wills are sometimes made on printed will forms – not always with satisfactory results: see 1.13. If more than one page is used it is desirable for the pages to be securely attached together. There is no legal necessity for a will to be on paper – in one case an empty eggshell was used. In another, dispositions written on a piece of cardboard and executed and witnessed during a snooker game were held to constitute a valid will: *Re Murray* (1963).

1.12 NOMINATIONS

Certain assets, e.g. moneys due from Friendly Societies and trade unions, may be nominated by their owner to pass to a specified person on his death. For National Savings Certificates and National Savings Bank accounts, nomination has not been possible since 1 May 1981, although nominations made before that date remain valid. The authority for such nominations is statutory and there is some resemblance to testamentary disposition, especially in the fact that, like wills, nominations are ambulatory (see *ante* 1.1), have no effect until the nominator dies and may be revoked at any time until death occurs. But the formal requirements for the two concepts are different. It is said that there is some danger in making a nomination as it tends to be overlooked later on, perhaps when a will is being made; in such circumstances, the nomination survives the execution of the new will until revoked by its own prescribed method. A nomination in accordance with the rules of a pension scheme is not a will: *Re Danish Bacon Co Staff Pension Fund Trusts* (1971).

1.13 PLACING OF TESTATOR'S SIGNATURE

It is no longer essential for the signature to be 'at the foot or end' of the will as was the case before 1983. Instead it must *appear* that the testator *intended* by signing the will to give effect to it – presumably external evidence could be adduced to prove this intention. Reference has already been made to the need for care where more than one sheet of paper is used – a signature on one document will not necessarily be treated as executing another. *Re Bean* (1944) is a case where a home-made will went wrong; a will form was used but the testator did not sign it. Instead he wrote his name and address and the date of the will on the *back* of the form and again on an envelope which was used for the completed will form. Neither signature qualified as a signature to the will. Contrast *Re Mann* (1942) where again the testatrix wrote her name on the envelope containing the will and asked the witnesses to sign the will itself, pointing out that the two documents constituted her will. In the second case the court clearly assumed that the signature on the envelope was *intended* by the testatrix to give effect to her will – in the former case this assumption could not be made. It seems that the main risk of making a will without professional advice may well lie in the possibility of failure to carry out the execution of the document in accordance with the rules. See, for instance, *Wood* v *Smith* (1992) where the testator signed his home-made will at the beginning and before making any dispositions. At first instance, the court held that this was not a valid signature – he could not have intended to give effect to a will which did not yet exist. However, the Court of Appeal disagreed; if the writing of the will and the appending of the signature were all one operation it did not matter whereabouts on the document or when in the course of writing the signature was appended (the will was, however, invalid on grounds of lack of capacity). The testator in this case had written his will out by hand; such a document is termed a 'holograph' will; in some countries, including Scotland, a holograph will, provided it is signed by the testator himself, is valid without having been witnessed (see Appendix 5). It has no special status of this kind under English law.

1.14 NATURE OF TESTATOR'S SIGNATURE

Like 'writing', the word 'signature' is interpreted widely; a signature may be a mark, a thumbprint, the impression of a rubber stamp. It may be a form of words which is not a signature in the accepted sense – in one case the testatrix wrote 'Your loving mother' at the end of the will and the court accepted this as satisfying the need for a signature.

1.15 THE WITNESSES

There must be at least two witnesses and they must both be present when the testator either signs the will or acknowledges his signature. Subsequently, each witness must either add his own signature or acknowledge it in the presence of the testator, but in this respect it is not necessary for all the witnesses to be present. The ability of witnesses to acknowledge a previous signature *after* the testator has signed or acknowledged in their joint presence is an innovation introduced by the revised s. 9 in 1982 and will prevent failure on grounds of faulty attestation as in *Re Colling* (1972). As with the testator's signature, 'signature' by a witness is capable of being interpreted broadly. It seems that the position of the witness's signature is immaterial, provided it can be shown that it was intended to be an attestation of the testator's signature.

1.16 CAPACITY OF WITNESSES

The only reference to the capacity of witnesses is in s. 14 WA, which merely says that if a witness is found incompetent to prove the execution of the will, it is not necessarily invalid. The moral is to ensure that those who act as witnesses will be competent, efficient and credible if called upon to prove execution. Note that a blind person cannot be a witness – *Re Gibson* (1949). Attestation of a will should not be treated simply as a formality. Incidentally, it is always better for there to be an attestation clause; if there is none (or if it is insufficient) the validity of the will must be proved by an affidavit of due execution made by one or more of the witnesses (NCPR 12).

1.17 POSSIBLE RELEVANCE OF A THIRD WITNESS

Mention should perhaps be made of WA 1968, amending s. 15 WA. Section 15 makes void any gift to a witness or a witness's spouse. The 1968 Act (unchanged by the AJA 1982) provides that such a gift shall not be void if the will was validly executed without having to rely on the attestation of the beneficiary-witness. (See also *post* 6.33.)

Although there may be a theoretical risk to a professional executor's remuneration (which has the character of a legacy) when it is authorised by a will witnessed by an employee of the executor, the practical risk of its being successfully attacked under s. 15 appears to be a remote one: compare *Re Ray* (1936). But a solicitor-partner must be careful not to witness a will which includes authority for his firm to charge.

1.18 WILL-MAKING FORMALITIES – EXCEPTIONS

In spite of the heavy emphasis placed by English law on the absolute necessity for will-making formalities to be accurately observed (except in the cases of privileged wills, to be dealt with later in this chapter, and the doctrine of incorporation by reference, *post* 3.41), two equitable doctrines exist which enable such rules to be comprehensively bypassed. The first of these is the doctrine of secret trusts, the second that of mutual wills.

1.19 SECRET TRUSTS

Testator A makes a will which includes a legacy of £10,000 to his friend B; later on, he tells B that he wants him to hold this legacy for the benefit of C, A's illegitimate daughter. B agrees to do this. A dies. Who is entitled to the £10,000? There is no trace of C in the will. If there is, indeed, a testamentary gift to her, it certainly does not comply with s. 9 WA. Should B, therefore, keep the £10,000 for himself? No, says Equity; this would be tantamount to using the statute as an engine of fraud. B must hold the legacy on trust for C. The equitable doctrine of secret trusts is applicable. In fact, modern theory inclines to the view that such trusts are enforced not so much to prevent fraud, though this must still be true, but because they are valid express trusts which operate quite outside (*dehors*) the will; hence they do not need to comply with the Wills Act.

It should be emphasised that, in order to be enforceable, secret trusts of all kinds must be communicated to the beneficiary/trustee under the will and accepted by him; silence, it seems, may be taken to indicate acceptance: *Moss* v *Cooper* (1861). Such communication and acceptance must occur before the death of the testator. If B first hears about C's possible interest (in the above example) after A dies, he may keep the legacy for himself. His conscience is not affected.

1.20 ARE SECRET TRUSTS EXPRESS OR CONSTRUCTIVE?

Are secret trusts express creations, as suggested above, or are they perhaps constructive trusts – see *post* 8.22? There is some debate about this; *Snell* deals with them under the express heading, as does *Underhill*, and this seems to be the better solution. There is a little awkwardness because of the statutory requirement of evidence in writing for an express trust of land – see *post* 7.4 – but the absence of such writing seems to be no inhibition:

> In *Ottoway* v *Norman* (1972) the testator had made a will devising his bungalow to H absolutely. There was evidence that the testator and H had agreed that the latter would leave the bungalow in her will to X and Y. There was no writing to support this trust of land and its absence seems to have been simply ignored by the court. Presumably if this point had been raised it would have been defeated as a technical defence which would amount to making use of the statute for a fraudulent purpose. The other extraordinary feature of this case was the assumption, in the words of Brightman J., that if property is given to the primary donee on the understanding that the primary donee will dispose by his will of such assets, if any, as he may have at his command at his death in favour of the

secondary donee, a valid trust is created in favour of the secondary donee which is in suspense during the lifetime of the primary donee, but attaches to the estate of the primary donee at the moment of the latter's death. The concept is a curious one of a secret trust that is left to float until the death of the trustee-beneficiary.

Interestingly, Brightman J. based his assumption on the Australian case of *Birmingham* v *Renfrew* (1937) – see *post* 1.29. The doctrine of mutual wills rests in contract, in contrast to the secret trust which owes its origin to the communication and acceptance of a trust. If that trust is immediately operative on the death of its creator upon clearly defined assets, the solution is clear but, if not, the details of the express trust need piecing together almost as if it were in the same league as a mutual will, or indeed a case of proprietary estoppel – see *Re Cleaver* (1981) in 1.28 below which did much to help along the decision in *Re Basham* (1986) in 8.28 *post*.

That secret trusts do operate independently of the will and the formal requirements of the Wills Act is emphasised by the case of *Re Young* (1951):

> The testator in that case had made a will which contained a gift to his widow subject to certain directions already communicated to her; one such direction was that she should give a legacy of £2,000 to the testator's chauffeur in her own will. The chauffeur in question witnessed the testator's will, bringing into play s. 15 WA: *ante* 1.17. Danckwerts J. held that the chauffeur did not forfeit his right to the £2,000 given to him by the secret trust, which was a separate entity from the will, and not subject to the provisions of the statute. (The same result, it is submitted, would be produced if the chauffeur had witnessed the *widow's* will containing the actual gift in his favour, since although that gift would be revoked as a legacy, the executor would still be bound to fulfil the obligation under the secret trust.)

1.21 HALF-SECRET TRUSTS

Re Young is, in fact, an example of a secret trust which was not entirely concealed from view, since the testator had made it plain in his will that *some kind* of commitment was attached to the gift to the widow. As Professor Pettit remarks, there are rather more difficulties in the relevant law about half-secret trusts than about fully-secret ones. Their validity was not fully established until *Blackwell* v *Blackwell* (1929) was decided by the House of Lords; there, the testator made a codicil leaving a legacy of £12,000 to legatees upon trust 'for the purposes indicated by me to them'. This trust the legatees had accepted before the codicil was executed. The House of Lords held that the trust must be enforced.

1.22 DISTINCTION BETWEEN SECRET AND HALF-SECRET TRUSTS

The most important distinction is that, in the case of fully secret trusts, the trust may be communicated and accepted at any time up to, but not after, the date of death. In the case of half-secret trusts, the trust must be communicated and accepted before or at the execution of the will – not afterwards. The difference in the rule is tiresome and seems illogical. It may be that, as there can be no question of fraud in the half-secret cases, the courts feel that there is no need to extend the exemption from s. 9 WA unnecessarily; moreover:

> A testator cannot reserve to himself a power of making future unwitnessed dispositions by merely naming a trustee and leaving the purposes of the trust to be supplied afterwards. Viscount Sumner in *Blackwell* v *Blackwell*.

Whatever the reason, we have to accept the fact that, as between secret and half-secret trusts, there are different rules as to the timing of communication and acceptance.

1.23 CONFLICT OF WORDS AND EVIDENCE IN A HALF-SECRET TRUST

Another problem may arise in connection with half-secret trusts; by definition, there are words in the will indicating that a trust exists. All secret and half-secret trusts must be proved by external evidence, written or oral. If this evidence, in the case of half-secret trusts, contradicts the terms of the will it will be inadmissible:

> In *Re Keen* (1937) the testator included in his will a gift to X and Y, 'to be held upon trust and disposed of by them among such person, persons or charities as may be notified by me to them or either of them *during my lifetime*' [emphasis supplied]. One of the trustees had, before the will was made, been given a sealed envelope containing the name of the beneficiary of the trust. It was held that this form of communication was acceptable in itself but that, as it took place before the date of the will, it was inconsistent with the terms of the will referring to future communication and was therefore unacceptable evidence of the trust. The trust would have failed anyway as a half-secret trust, because its terms permitted contravention of the rule against communication after the date of the will.

Where a half-secret trust fails, for whatever reason, the trustee holds the gift in trust for the residuary legatees or next-of-kin, as the case may be; he may not keep it for himself.

1.24 PLURALITY OF TRUSTEES — COMMUNICATION PROBLEM

Secret trusts: it will sometimes happen that a testator makes a gift to X and Y and communicates to X only the fact that he wants the gift held in trust for Z. The result depends upon whether the gift is to X and Y as joint tenants or as tenants in common, and also upon whether the communication is made before or after the execution of the will:

> If the gift is to X and Y as tenants in common and only X is told about and accepts the secret trust, then, provided Y hears nothing about the matter until after the testator's death, X is bound by the trust but Y may take beneficially.
>
> On the other hand, if X and Y are joint tenants, the answer depends upon whether X was told about and accepted the trust before or after the date of the will; if told before, both X and Y will be bound by the trust. If told after, then only X will be bound, provided, as before, that Y hears nothing about the matter until after the testator's death.

These rules were reviewed by Farwell J. in *Re Stead* (1900). It is difficult to see the logic of the distinction between communication to joint tenants before and after the date of the will or, indeed, why there should be any distinction between the rules for tenants in common and joint tenants. In this, as in other matters, the law relating to secret trusts is not an unqualified success; a short statute, codifying an improved set of rules, would be welcome.

Half-secret trusts: trustees under this head will always be joint tenants, so the rule mentioned above for communication before the will is executed will apply (communication after that event would be ineffective anyway).

1.25 FURTHER APPLICATION OF THE SECRET TRUST PRINCIPLE

There need not necessarily be a will for the principle or doctrine to apply; suppose that A refrains from making a will, relying on the promise of B (entitled on A's intestacy) that B will leave his estate in turn to C? If this agreement can be proved, B must make a will in favour of C, or, if he does not, then B's PR will hold B's estate in trust for C: see *Re Gardner* (1920).

1.26 MUTUAL WILLS

Mutual wills arise in the following circumstances; two persons (usually husband and wife, but not necessarily) make wills in favour of each other, with provision that the estate of the survivor should go to a nominated beneficiary or beneficiaries. These wills are made pursuant to an agreement that such wills should not be revoked by one party without the consent of the other. Assuming that the agreement is adhered to during the joint lives, on the first death the agreement becomes binding on the survivor. Although this survivor cannot be stopped from revoking his will (no will can be made irrevocable) his PR will have to deal with his estate in accordance with the agreement – a constructive trust is imposed by the court in favour of the beneficiary or beneficiaries under the revoked will.

1.27   THE CONTRACTUAL NATURE OF MUTUAL WILLS

Although the doctrine of mutual wills is commonly dealt with under the general heading of constructive trusts, it seems that its true nature is contractual; the position was concisely stated by Lord Camden in *Dufour* v *Pereira* (1769):

> A mutual will is a revocable act. It may be revoked by joint consent clearly. By one only, if he gives notice, I can admit. But to affirm that the survivor (who has deluded his partner into this will upon the faith and persuasion that he would perform his part) may legally recall his contract, either secretly during the joint lives, or after at his pleasure, I cannot allow.

1.28   IDENTICAL WILLS ARE NOT NECESSARILY MUTUAL WILLS

It should be emphasised that the mere existence of two wills in more or less identical terms does not mean that they are mutual wills and enforceable as such. There must be enough evidence (up to the ordinary civil standard of proof, i.e. balance of probabilities) to convince the court that there was an agreement between the two testators. This was found to be the case in *Re Cleaver* (1981); a husband and wife made wills in similar terms in 1974, the effect of which was to leave their estates to each other and for the survivor to leave his or her estate to their three children; one child (Martha) was to have only a life interest. The husband died and the widow took his estate. She then made further wills, the last of which gave the residue of her estate to Martha and her husband. The court was able to find sufficient evidence of an agreement between husband and wife to make it right to enforce the terms of the 1974 will upon the widow's PRs, who thereupon became constructive trustees.

1.29   THE ASSETS TO WHICH THE MUTUAL WILLS AGREEMENT ATTACHES

The question of what property is subject to the constructive trust in these circumstances is not easy to answer, but the court in the *Cleaver* case took the view that the surviving partner to the agreement could enjoy property received from the first to die as an absolute owner (if an absolute interest was given) subject only to a prohibition on the making of gifts intended to defeat the agreement for mutual wills. This is based on an Australian decision, *Birmingham* v *Renfrew* (1937) and is probably the best solution available to this particular problem.

Are mutual will agreements something to be 'avoided like the plague' (see R Burgess in 34 Conv 230), or do they meet a real need for some testators (see F H G Sunnucks in *NLJ* 20 May 88 at p. 351)? I believe the latter view may be the better one, but only if testators enter into such agreements under professional advice.

1.30   JOINT WILL

That is, one document executed as a will by two or more persons – an excessively inconvenient concept. The main advantage of such a will seems to be that it can effectively exercise a power given to two or more persons jointly to appoint by will. Possibly also it might be thought useful to deal with jointly owned property. But both these situations can be dealt with quite satisfactorily by sole wills.

A joint will is treated as if it were the separate will of each of the parties. The joint will can always be revoked, either during the joint lives or by the survivor. An unrevoked joint will is admitted to probate on the death of the first to die, just as if it were his sole will, and if still unrevoked on the death of the survivor, it will again be admitted to probate as if it were the survivor's sole will. But it is possible for a joint will also to be a mutual will, and then the contractual aspects of mutual wills will apply:

> In *Re Hagger* (1930) husband and wife made a joint will in 1902 by which they gave their Wandsworth properties, owned jointly and beneficially, to the survivor of them for life with remainder to a number of beneficiaries, of whom Eleanor was one. The will contained a declaration that it should not be changed except by mutual agreement. The effect of this arrangement was to sever the joint tenancy, so that henceforth their beneficial interest in the properties was as tenants in common. The wife died in 1904 and the widower started to enjoy his life interest in her share of the properties. Eleanor died in 1923 and the husband in 1928, having made a different will in 1921 which deprived Eleanor of her interest in remainder in *his* share. It was held that from the wife's death in 1904 the husband had held his own share upon trust to give effect to the provisions of the joint will. Thus Eleanor had a vested interest in the husband's share as well as the wife's share and her PRs were able to claim it on behalf of her estate.

1.31   PRIVILEGED WILLS

The rules for form under s. 9 WA do not apply to this special category; neither does the capacity rule requiring a testator to be at least 18 years old. Section 11 WA reads:

> Provided always . . . that any soldier being in actual military service, or any mariner or seaman being at sea, may dispose of his personal estate as he might have done before the making of this Act.

This provision was extended and explained by the Wills (Soldiers and Sailors) Act 1918; as a result it extends to both real and personal estate and covers not only soldiers and sailors but also members of the RAF. It entitles such persons to make completely informal, even oral, wills, whether or not they are under or over 18.

1.32   MEANING OF 'SOLDIER' AND 'ACTUAL MILITARY SERVICE'

The term soldier 'includes not only the fighting men but also those who serve in the Forces, doctors, nurses, chaplains, WRNS, ATS, and so forth' said Lord Denning in *Re Wingham* (1949) and went on to add that 'actual military service' means service in the armed forces 'in connection with military operations which are or have been taking place or are believed to be imminent'. Service on internal security operations as in Northern Ireland qualifies as 'actual military service' – *Re Jones* (1981), where an oral declaration 'If I don't make it, make sure Anne gets all my stuff' was admitted to probate as a privileged will.

1.33   MEANING OF 'ANY MARINER OR SEAMAN BEING AT SEA'

This expression covers both members of the Royal Navy and members of the Merchant Marine; in this latter category, a typist and a barman on an ocean liner have both been held to qualify. 'Being at sea' has been liberally interpreted to include, for example, (a) service on a ship permanently stationed in Portsmouth Harbour and (b) being under orders to join a ship, even though on dry land at the time. *Re Rapley* (1983) drew a distinction, however, between being under orders and waiting for a new posting. An apprentice to a shipping company qualified as a seaman but could not make a privileged will during the interval between being discharged from one ship and posted to another. But there must be a testamentary intention, and *Re Knibbs* (1962) is useful as a reminder that, however informal a privileged will may be, it must have this feature. 'The mere exchange of family gossip, of opinions and information about family matters . . . cannot be regarded as a testamentary act'.

1.34   FORMALITIES OF INTERNATIONAL WILLS

Section 1 WA 1963 reads:

A will shall be treated as properly executed if its execution conformed to the internal law in force in the territory where it was executed, or in the territory where, at the time of its execution or of the testator's death, he was domiciled or had his habitual residence, or in a state of which, at either of those times, he was a national.

These provisions apply to all deaths occurring on and after 1 January 1964, even though the will was executed before that date. The object is to give the widest possible recognition to a will executed in accordance with the internal law of any territory with which the testator could claim a connection of one kind or another. One or two other alleviating rules are also provided; where a will has been made on a ship or aircraft, it will additionally be treated as properly executed if it conforms with the internal law of the country with which the ship or aircraft is taken to have been most closely connected. And where a will disposes of immoveable property, then so far as that property is concerned, there is the additional option of treating it as properly executed if made in accordance with the internal law of the country in which the property is situated.

There is also an overriding rule that advantage can be taken of retrospective alterations in the chosen law, if favourable to the will's formal validity; otherwise those alterations can be ignored.

A form of international will was provided for in a Convention on International Wills concluded in Washington in 1973; this has been given the force of law by s. 27 AJA 1982, but that section has not yet been brought into effect. When it is, a will made in accordance with the Convention will be admissible for probate in this country even if it cannot be validated under the WA 1963.

2 Wills (2)

2.1 MAKING THE WILL

Wills should be professionally drafted; home-made wills are a fruitful source of disputes and litigation. Consider, for instance, *Re Barnes* (1972) where the testatrix made her will without professional assistance. She left 'one half of any *money* I may leave' to her brother and the other half to two nieces and a nephew. The use of the word 'money' in what may be termed a lay will is fairly common. Recourse is usually had to the leading case of *Perrin* v *Morgan* (1943) – see *post* 2.24. Apart from the inevitable sloppiness in terminology there is also the risk that home-made documents will not be properly executed.

2.2 THE AIM OF THE WILL

A will must be designed to function effectively – it must be a sufficient answer to the human problems that are likely to arise and it must achieve this answer without running into the more disastrous consequences of modern taxation. The contents and wording of a will are primarily a matter for the drafter and testator, but the latter may wish to discuss it with the proposed executor. A trust corporation, such as the Public Trustee or one of the clearing banks, will expect to be informed when it is appointed and will be available to discuss things beforehand and to consider the will in its draft form.

2.3 THE DRAFTER'S RESPONSIBILITY

There are an infinite number of variations possible in the contents of a will. What is desirable in a particular case will depend on (a) the personal circumstances of the testator and (b) his dispositive wishes. A proposed executor, given the chance, will look at a draft will to see whether the ways in which the benefits are defined make sense so that there is no room for argument and doubt when it is too late to put things right, i.e. after death. One hopes, for example, that a professional executor might have noticed (and had corrected) the typist's omission of 33 words which necessitated reference to the court in *Re Reynette-James* (1976), although rectification of a mistake in a will occurring as a result of a clerical error has since become an available remedy under s. 20 AJA 1982 – *post* 2.30. Incidentally, a beneficiary who suffers loss as the result of negligence by one who drafts a will or oversees its execution may now have a right of action against the negligent person, following the decision of the Vice-Chancellor in *Ross* v *Caunters* (1980), where there was a failure to warn the testator against using a witness who was also married to a beneficiary, followed by a failure to notice this serious flaw when the will was seen after its execution. That there is no *general* duty of care towards a beneficiary is made clear by the Court of Appeal's decision in *Clarke* v *Bruce Lance & Co* (1988) where the will contained the gift of a service station and subsequently, under the guidance of the solicitors who had drawn the will, the testator gave the tenant of the service station an option to buy it from his executors for £28,000, thus imperilling the gift under the will; held that the solicitors owed no duty to the beneficiary to dissuade the testator from granting the option.

2.4 ESTABLISHING THE TESTATOR'S CIRCUMSTANCES AND WISHES

A testator may, of course, have only the roughest of ideas about what he wants to do. He may have been told (e.g. on marriage) that he ought to make a will but, apart from a general desire to do his best for wife and family, knows no more than that. Before a will can be drafted, a 'drawing-out' process is required, the object being to establish in as much depth as possible the testator's circumstances and wishes. *Mellows* suggests that the following considerations be taken into account by an intending testator and his professional advisors:

(a)   The persons to be benefited;
(b)   the circumstances in which they are to be benefited;
(c)   the amount of that benefit;
(d)   the type of benefit; and
(e)   the means by which that benefit can be conferred with the greatest taxation advantage.

2.5 A SPECIMEN WILL

What follows is the skeleton of a will for a married man who wishes to give the residue of his estate to his wife and his children. The fiscal advantage of a life interest to a surviving spouse applies only to cases created during the estate duty era, before the introduction of capital transfer tax, but, where the estate is of sufficient size, this form of gift (linked with a power to use capital for the widow's benefit) may still be acceptable if an outright gift to the widow is not. A testator may feel that his widow will appreciate the guidance and advice of sympathetic trustees; also, he can determine the ultimate destination of the capital. Nevertheless, in many – perhaps most

– cases, an outright gift of residue to the surviving spouse will be all that is required. The alternative to the life interest is the inclusion of a discretionary trust provision, which can either be retained during the life of the surviving spouse or can be wound up by the executors within two years of death, so as to take advantage of s. 144 IHTA.[1] The following layout was originally based on 'Wills of Married Persons' in *Brighouse*, but there is no shortage of alternative published advice in this field. For a very useful guide to taking instructions for a will see *Ray*, Appendix 6. As a matter of interest, the Statutory Will Forms should be mentioned here; these are published by the Lord Chancellor in accordance with s. 179 LPA; reference to one or more of these forms will certainly shorten the text of a will, but they are not much used in practice.

(a) *Revocation of all previous wills.*
(b) *Appointment of executors* (and trustees where appropriate). Trust corporations will have their own clause, authorising fees and importing standard conditions. Professional men will need a clause authorising them to charge profit costs.
(c) *Funeral wishes* – instructions, for example, for cremation or for removal of parts of the body for research. It is perhaps better to have such wishes expressed in a separate letter to a close relative; whatever may be done, the testator's wishes should be discoverable *immediately* after death occurs.
(d) *Appointment of guardians*, where appropriate.
(e) *Gift to wife of furniture and personal effects.* The only caveat which needs to be entered under this head concerns any item or collection of special value or interest, e.g. a stamp collection. A testator should give such an asset some thought before including it in a general gift of personal effects – perhaps by inadvertence. Similarly, consider the need to refer specifically to any motor car owned by the deceased at the date of his death (see *post* 6.4); it may be of considerable value and, if used for business purposes, will not pass under the statutory definition of 'personal chattels' contained in s. 55(1)(x) AEA – see *post* 4.5. (There should be a specific reference to this provision in the will if it is to be used to define the expression 'personal chattels'.)
(f) *Pecuniary legacy to wife*, given priority. Useful in the early days and essential if legal apportionment (see *post* 5.21) not negatived.
(g) *Specific devises and bequests* (including testator's interest in matrimonial home to wife if not in the name of husband and wife as beneficial joint tenants). Care will be needed concerning the incidence of charges where the assets have been mortgaged or charged (see *post* 6.14); in the case of foreign assets, the question of relieving the beneficiary of (i) IHT as well as foreign imposts should be considered (see *post* 5.42) and (ii) costs of transfer to the beneficiary (see *post* 5.44).
(h) *Pecuniary legacies.* Care is needed over freedom of tax where there are both exempt and non-exempt gifts for IHT purposes; the grossing-up calculations in such circumstances can be of impressive complexity (see, e.g. the Inland Revenue IHT booklet, pp. 22–4). According to *Ray*, the golden rule is to ensure that all gifts indicate *expressly* whether they are free of or subject to IHT. The simplest

solution, so far as IHT is concerned, is to make *all* non-residuary non-exempt gifts subject to payment of IHT. Turning to other considerations, it is often convenient to give the executors authority to accept the receipt of parents as a full discharge for legacies given to infants, at any rate where the amounts are not substantial. In general, legacies payable upon a contingency should be worded to carry the intermediate income: see *post* 10.15. Where there are gifts to charities, care should be taken to describe the donees with complete accuracy. Check either with the charities themselves or by reference to the annual *Charities Digest*. If still in doubt, check registration with the Charity Commissioners (see *post* 12.15). The testator may wish, in the event of failure of a charitable gift, that the legacy be applicable for charitable purposes generally (see *post* 12.16). Gifts to unincorporated associations need particular care (see *post* 7.36); avoid any wording which might be construed as imposing a purpose trust. Authorise the executors to accept a receipt from the Treasurer or other officer purporting to have authority to provide it and state that such a receipt shall be a full discharge.

(i)   *Gift of residue* (subject to payment of debts, expenses and legacies) upon trust for sale and conversion, with power to postpone such sale; the trust for sale is unnecessary if the beneficial interests in the residue are absolute and immediate: see *Williams*, p. 1197. Care needs to be taken, where husband and wife make similar wills, that payment of pecuniary legacies is not duplicated. Such legacies should be restricted to the estate of the first to die; for a form of wording to achieve this, see *Williams*, p. 1366.

(j)   *Division of residue* between wife and children (with or without life interest to wife; if with, possibly terminating on remarriage). The way in which the division is effected will depend upon (i) the testator's view of his wife's financial needs after his death and (ii) the tax implications, e.g. the advantage of using up some or all of the nil rate band with legacies to taxable beneficiaries such as the children. It is desirable to make a substitutional provision in respect of the interest of a residuary legatee who predeceases the testator – see *post* 6.27. As to the use of *conditional* gifts, see *post* 2.31.

(k)   *Administrative powers*. It is assumed here that a trust is involved – either a life interest to the wife, or during the infancy of children. There is no point in overloading a will with administrative powers where it is clear that the executors will be able to distribute the whole estate at the end of the administration period; if there is any chance that this will not be the case (as where the residuary legatees will be infants), then the extended administrative powers outlined below should be incorporated.

(i)   *Investment*. Power for executors and trustees to invest as if they were beneficial owners, *plus* power to purchase, improve, etc., real or leasehold property as a residence for a beneficiary, *plus* power to purchase non-income-producing assets. Investment powers are discussed in detail in Chapter 11.

(ii)   *Apportionment*, legal and equitable. Except where income is taxable in the hands of a beneficiary at a high rate (in which case the priority pecuniary legacy referred to at (f) above can be given), apportionment under the Apportionment Act 1870 should be excluded, both on the death of the testator and on the subsequent death of any life tenant – see *post* 5.21. So far as the rules of equitable apportionment (see *post* 6.44) are concerned, it has been said that there are few cases in which the requirements of convenience do not outweigh the need to retain them.

(iii) *'Emergency' clause* giving trustees power at their absolute discretion to raise and pay capital to or for the benefit of the wife – probably essential where there is a life interest. Extending this power so as to give the trustees power to *lend* capital to the wife is useful.

(iv) *Maintenance and advancement.* It is customary to extend the statutory powers found in ss. 31 and 32 Trustee Act 1925 by deleting the proviso to s. 31(1) and giving trustees an absolute discretion thereunder and by extending the power to advance under s. 32 to the whole of a presumptive share instead of one-half. See Chapter 10 for a full description of these powers.

(v) *Appropriation, power of.* The statutory power in s. 41 AEA is helpful (see *post* 6.35) but it should be extended so that it can be used by trustees as well as by executors and should be exercisable by them without the necessity of obtaining consents.

(vi) *Power to insure.* The power to insure conferred by s. 19 Trustee Act 1925 is unsatisfactory. The Law Reform Committee has made a recommendation regarding it, but this has not yet been implemented. Until the statutory authority is amended, wills and trust deeds should include a power to insure property comprehensively and to charge premiums to income or capital at the discretion of the PRs or trustees.

(l) *Survivorship clause.* For example, 'No person shall take any benefit under this my will unless he or she survives me by at least one calendar month' (*Brighouse*, p. 45). It is probably more usual to restrict such a clause to a surviving spouse or persons living together such as two sisters. Under s. 92 IHTA the survivorship period needs to be restricted to six months or less, to avoid the risk of *two* charges to the tax arising, one on the testator's death, the other at the end of the period – see *post*, 6.27.

(m) *IHT, payment of.* The testator may wish to relieve the donee of a gift made within the last seven years of liability, either for additional tax (in the case of a chargeable transfer) or for the tax on a PET. The direction to pay such tax will itself amount to a legacy and have to be grossed up for the calculation of IHT, unless expressed to be subject to the payment of IHT.

(n) *Professional charging clause* – where appropriate.

(o) *Corporate trustee, power to appoint and to pay its fees.* It may be useful to include this where private executors are appointed in the first place. Should they later (as trustees) wish to appoint a trust corporation, the question of authority for its fees may otherwise be difficult to resolve (except in the case of the Public Trustee – see *post* 12.1).

2.6 SPECIAL PROBLEMS

(i) *Interests in unincorporated businesses.* Where the testator is either a sole trader or has a share in a partnership, some thought needs to be given to the administration and disposal of the asset after death. The executors will not normally be concerned with the running of a partnership business after death, because the responsibility for it will devolve on the surviving partners. They will, however, inevitably have to step into the testator's shoes where the latter was a sole trader (see *post* 3.23). Corporate executors such as banks will not usually carry on such a business for longer than is necessary to wind it up, or to find a buyer or to transfer it to a beneficiary. It may be, of course, that the testator will be happy for his business to devolve absolutely on a surviving widow or child, but where he wants it to continue in trust over a longer period he should make specific provision for this. He could, for instance, authorise conversion into a limited company and retention of its shares or, alternatively, authorise the transfer of the business to a beneficiary trustee who is to carry it on independently of the main trustees during the trust period. Or he can appoint as a separate executor of his business interests a person willing to accept full responsibility over an extended period.

(ii) *Unquoted shares* (see also *post* 5.24 to 5.30). Three points: if such shares are specifically given, is the testator satisfied that the then directors will register the beneficiary? It is no longer a statutory requirement that a private company shall restrict the right of transfer of its shares, but many, if not most, of them will continue to have such a provision in their Articles of Association. If the shares are to be held in trust, has the testator considered exonerating the trustees from responsibility for the holding, since it is often difficult for them to exert any influence in this kind of situation? Lastly, if the testator is a significant figure in the company's affairs, has he considered grooming someone to succeed him? This last point is not strictly germane to the will, but can conveniently and suitably be discussed with it.

(iii) *Interests in other estates and trusts.* Is the testator himself acting as an executor or trustee? The point is that a sole executor who dies having appointed an executor himself, has also appointed an executor by representation – see *post* 3.13. At least the testator and his own executors should be aware of the possibility that the latter will end up administering two estates instead of one. The problem is not so acute where the testator is a trustee; s. 36(1) TA gives the PRs of a deceased sole trustee the power to appoint new trustees, but the executor will become involved in some responsibility for the trust fund between death and new appointment and the testator should consider appointing a new trustee or trustees to act with him and after he dies.

(iv) *Powers of appointment.* Any connection between the testator and an existing trust raises the possibility that he has a power of appointment exercisable by will. This should be investigated. Indeed, the terms of the trust itself may well have a considerable bearing upon the way in which the testator frames his own dispositions. The potential liability for IHT in such circumstances will need to be considered. Under s. 52(1) IHTA, if the testator has an interest in possession, the value of the trust fund at his death will be aggregated with his own free estate to arrive at the average rate of tax applicable to both.

(v) *Settled Land Act 1925* (see *post* 11.16). The executor will be interested to know whether the testator is a tenant for life under this Act. If the trust will continue after the death of the tenant for life, there will be a special grant limited to the settled land to the persons who are trustees of the settlement at that time. If, on the other hand, the trust ends with the death of the tenant for life the legal estate vests in his general PRs, whether they like it or not. They may not like it very much if the former settled land is of substantial value and complexity, thus imposing on them an additional burden over and above that anticipated. At least if the situation is disclosed when the executors are appointed they have advance warning of the problem.

2.7 CHOOSING EXECUTORS

This is a matter of some consequence. Executors may have in their charge substantial funds, which will be at their absolute disposition although they will, eventually, be called on to account for the funds they have administered. The welfare of the testator's dependants may well hang upon the good sense or otherwise of their actions. On the other side, the office of executor is in all cases a burden, sometimes a heavy one, and the responsibilities can be severe. A testator must, therefore, not make an idle selection and those advising him should be prepared to take an objective view on his behalf.

Roughly speaking, the choice lies between a private individual such as a relative or friend, a professional man such as a solicitor or accountant, and a trust corporation such as one of the clearing or merchant banks, an insurance company or the Public Trustee. A combination of these is quite in order and may be the better solution, especially if either the administration is to be of unusual complexity or if a trust is to follow. It must be remembered that where a will does create a trust it is usual to appoint the executors to be trustees after the administration period, and an appointment must therefore have an eye to the future – the end of the trust may well be many years away.

2.8 TRUST CORPORATIONS

Reference is made in the previous paragraph to trust corporations; some words about this term may be helpful at this point. It has been well said that the path to the definition is tortuous. One starts with s. 68(18) TA (there are alternatives), which runs as follows:

> 'Trust corporation' means the Public Trustee or a corporation either appointed by the court in any particular case to be a trustee, or entitled by rules made under subsection (3) of section four of the Public Trustee Act 1906, to act as custodian trustee.

The definition is extended by s. 3 Law of Property (Amendment) Act 1926, but the extensions are not relevant in this context. The rules in question are the Public Trustee Rules 1912; rule 30, as substituted by SI 1975 No. 1189 (subsequently amended), lays down the following basic conditions required of commercial concerns before they can act as custodian trustee:

1. The company must be constituted under the Law of the UK or under the law of any other member state of the EEC and, so far as UK companies are concerned, must be registered under the Companies Act 1985 or under the Companies Act (Northern Ireland) 1960. All must have one or more places of business in the UK.

2. Its constitution must authorise it to undertake trust business in England and Wales.

3. It must have an issued capital of not less than £250,000, of which not less than £100,000 must have been paid up in cash.

For an example of a foreign company qualifying as a trust corporation and therefore being entitled to obtain a grant of probate in this country, see *Re Bigger* (1977), in which the Bank of Ireland was the successful applicant.

Companies qualifying to act as custodian trustees are therefore trust corporations and may obtain a grant to a deceased's estate in their own name, whereas companies which are not trust corporations must proceed through a nominee. Although certain public offices and bodies (e.g. the Treasury Solicitor, the Official Solicitor) are trust corporations, when choosing executors one thinks of the Public Trustee (a corporation sole), the leading banks and the major insurance companies (corporations aggregate).

2.9 TRUST CORPORATIONS AS EXECUTORS AND TRUSTEES

The merits and demerits of trust corporations as executors and trustees are as follows. On the credit side, expertise acquired through specialisation over a number of years, impartiality, continuity, the security of a strong balance sheet and the advantages of an efficient record-keeping and book-keeping system. On the debit side, cost and what may be described, tentatively, as a reluctance to cut corners; this last is not always to the liking of beneficiaries. A testator should be allowed to make up his own mind about this question. Is he prepared to pay a premium for a service which, inevitably, will sometimes be less than perfect but which, overall, can be relied on to reach a consistently high standard? Where, for instance, complications are foreseen (such as a family dispute), and where limited interests are being created, the case for the appointment of a trust corporation is a strong one.

2.10 AFTER EXECUTION

A will, once executed, should be kept in a safe, *known* place. To lose a will through faulty execution is exasperating; to suspect strongly that a will exists but not to know where to find it is even worse. It is possible to obtain proof of a missing will (see *post* 3.41), but the formalities and expense involved are unattractive. Moreover, a presumption may arise that the testator has destroyed the will with the intention of revoking it (see *post* 2.15). Many wills are, of course, lodged with the solicitors who drew them, but it is suggested that the better course is to leave the executed document with the testator's bankers, not because it will necessarily be any safer there but because the existence of the bank account is likely to be common knowledge within the testator's family circle. (Some banks are said to refuse deposit of a will in a *sealed* envelope – this point will need to be settled before deposit.) The same cannot always be said of the solicitor who drew the will. Great care should be taken not to fasten anything to the document, by any means, at any time. If, when the time comes to prove the will, there are signs that this has been done, the Probate Registry will want an explanation of the circumstances.

Another good reason for making sure that the will comes to light immediately after death is the risk that the estate may be administered in ignorance of its existence, from which – if the missing document eventually comes to light – may follow revocation of the original grant and a complete recasting of the administration. Finally, the will may contain wishes regarding disposal of the body and about funeral arrangements – all of which makes it highly desirable for the document to be available within a short time of death.

At this stage, a testator may be recommended to complete the Law Society's Personal Assets Log which records, amongst other things, the place where the original will is kept, the names and addresses of the executors, and details of assets owned. (The Public Trustee provides a similar record form for his clients.)

2.11   DEPOSITING A WILL WITH THE COURT

There is provision for a will, when executed, to be deposited with the Principal Probate Registry, pursuant to The Wills (Deposit for Safe Custody) Regulations SI 1978 No. 1724. It is now possible for a will deposited under these provisions to be withdrawn by the testator – see *T & C*, pp. 486–8. Sections 23–5 AJA 1982 have made it possible for the UK to ratify the 1972 European Convention for Establishment of a Scheme of Registration of Wills but, like the international form of will (see *ante* 1.34), have yet to be brought into effect. When they are, wills deposited with the Principal Registry will become registrable compulsorily under the Convention.

2.12   REVISING A WILL

A will is always revisable and revocable. Minor revisions can conveniently be dealt with by means of a codicil, which will be proved jointly with the last will. It is better, though, not to let the parent will give birth to a multitude of children; once the number is above two or three the room for error increases and the problem of elucidating the precise meaning of a number of related documents, all with cross-referenced additions and deletions, makes life difficult for the executors. It should also be borne in mind that a codicil which refers to a will republishes the latter as at the date of the codicil – s. 34 WA – so that the will takes effect as if executed on the later date and will be interpreted accordingly (unless to do so would defeat the testator's intention).

2.13 THE OCCASIONS FOR REVISING A WILL

Some testators take delight in continually adding to and revising their dispositions, and the difficulty is to restrain their enthusiasm for what is, after all, a fairly innocent occupation. Others – the majority – forget about their wills as soon as executed and give them not another thought. A testator should reconsider his will when any substantial change occurs in his personal connections – such as marriage, which may revoke a will (see below), or the birth or adoption of a child. He should also reconsider it when external conditions change, e.g. when any substantial changes occur in the laws of capital taxation and when there is any significant change in the nature and value of his assets. It is not a responsibility of the executors to prompt such a review but, as their work will be affected by any changes made, they are entitled at least to take an interest.

2.14 REVOCATION OF WILLS

Revocation of a will requires the same standards of capacity and intent as does the execution of the document – see *ante* 1.4 to 1.8. Reference to ss. 18–22 WA will indicate the ways in which revocation can take place. After the earlier sections dealing with revocation by marriage and divorce, s. 20 goes on to say:

> No will or codicil, or any part thereof, shall be revoked otherwise than as aforesaid, or by another will or codicil executed in manner hereinbefore required, or by some writing declaring an intention to revoke the same, and executed in the manner in which a will is hereinbefore required to be executed, or by the burning, tearing, or otherwise destroying the same by the testator, or by some person in his presence and by his direction, with the intention of revoking the same.

Most wills – at least if professionally drawn – contain a revocation clause which will be effective to revoke all previous wills and codicils made by the testator. If no such clause is included, then the provisions of any previous and unrevoked wills and codicils will be revoked insofar as they are inconsistent with the provisions in the later document. If there is any dispute about what is and is not revoked, the court will ask itself, as a matter of construction, which provisions the testator intended to take effect upon his death. It may be noted that it is not necessary for a revocation to be incorporated in a new will or codicil – 'some writing declaring an intention to revoke' will suffice; in *Re Spracklan* (1938) a letter signed by the testatrix ('Will you please destroy the will already made out') and duly attested by witnesses was held to satisfy the provision just quoted.

2.15 REVOCATION BY DESTRUCTION

This method of revocation causes some problems, both under the heading of intention and where the destruction is only partial or even trifling. So far as intention is concerned, *Re Everest* (1975) is instructive; the testator cut off part of his will, leaving the beneficial dispositions incomplete. Nevertheless, it was held that he had not intended to revoke completely, and the mutilated will was admitted to probate. A testator's intention to revoke may be absolute or conditional; in the latter case, revocation will not take effect until the condition is satisfied. *Re Jones* (1976) is another case where a will had been mutilated, but here the question was whether the revocation was conditional upon execution of a new will – should the doctrine of dependent relative revocation,[2] not considered in the Court of Appeal since 1925, be invoked? The court held that the act of revocation was not dependent upon the testatrix's intention to make a new will – it was complete and effective in itself. See also *Re Carey* (1977); the testator destroyed his will, believing that he had nothing to leave, whereas he had in fact inherited an estate of £4,000. The court held that the destruction of the will was conditional upon the testator's belief being true, which it was not, and the will was admitted to probate. Like an act of destruction, an express revocation may be either expressly or impliedly conditional:[3]

In *Re Finnemore* (1991) a testator had made three wills in succession, each containing a revocation clause. Each also contained a gift to Mrs C of a house and a share in the residue. Unfortunately, the lady's husband witnessed wills two and three; ordinarily this would deprive the lady of her benefit: see *ante* 1.17. However, the court found that the testator's revocation of previous wills in wills two and three was conditional upon the effectiveness of the gift to Mrs C in the last will. As it was not, the revocation was ineffective so far as it related to that gift and the lady took, in fact, under the first will. Otherwise, the dispositions in the third will were effective.

For a case involving destruction (the will was torn into more than 40 pieces) without intention to revoke and therefore ineffective, see *Re Aynsley* (1973). Where a will which was in possession of the testator cannot be found on his death, there is a presumption that it has been destroyed with intention to revoke; however, this presumption can be rebutted, as in *Re Davies* (1978), and the missing will can be proved from extrinsic evidence, e.g. from a completed draft in a solicitors' office.

2.16 IMPERFECT DESTRUCTION

Two cases on destruction of a partial nature: in *Cheese* v *Lovejoy* (1877) a testator took his will, drew his pen through some of its lines and then wrote on the back 'All these are revoked'. He then threw it on a heap of waste paper, from where it was retrieved by his housekeeper who kept it in the kitchen until the testator died some years later. The Court of Appeal held that the will was not revoked, as there was no act of destruction. In *Re Adams* (1990) the testatrix had scribbled with a ballpoint pen over her own signature to her will and also over those of the witnesses, so that they became illegible. Was this 'destruction' within the meaning of s. 20 (which refers, it will be remembered, to 'burning, tearing, or otherwise destroying')? In deciding that the will was revoked, the court had recourse also to s. 21 which says that 'no obliteration, interlineation, or other alteration' in a will shall have effect 'except so far as the words or effect of the will before such alteration shall not be apparent'. As the signatures on Mrs Adams's will were not apparent, even with the use of a magnifying glass, they were revoked (the testatrix's intention to revoke being accepted) and consequently so was the whole will. As was remarked by the learned Casenote Editor of *The Conveyancer* (1990) 391, this is not a method of revocation to be recommended. 'The intention of the testatrix prevailed, but not without the expense of a visit to the High Court'. Do testators generally use the revocation by destruction method without first consulting their solicitors? The cases seem to indicate that this is so. The wisdom of having a will drafted professionally has already been mentioned (*ante* 2.1) and reference to one's legal advisor before revocation is also prudent. The one act warrants as much care as the other.

2.17 OBLITERATION, INTERLINEATION, OR OTHER ALTERATION

Section 21 WA makes it clear that, if made after execution of the will, obliterations, interlineations, or other alterations must be executed in the same way as the will itself, i.e. by having the testator and witnesses place their signatures or initials opposite or near to the alteration. Otherwise those alterations will only be effective if they make it impossible to read the obliterated or altered material, as in *Re Adams supra*.

The testatrix in *Re Itter* (1950) had pasted slips of paper over the amounts of certain legacies in her will; these alterations were not properly attested and so were ineffective. Evidence was given that it was impossible to decipher the original amounts beneath the slips of paper except by taking infra-red photographs. The original amounts were therefore not 'apparent' within the meaning of s. 21, which allowed only 'natural' means to be used to decipher the words, such as the use of a magnifying glass. The result was that the original amounts were revoked, but the court applied the doctrine of dependent relative revocation and admitted the original will to probate *in toto*.

When it comes to applying for probate of a will, any alterations in it are presumed to have been made *after* execution unless they are accompanied by the signatures or the initials of the testator and the witnesses. It is therefore very desirable that this procedure is followed – otherwise an affidavit from an attesting witness may be needed to authenticate the existence of any alterations made before the execution of the will. For a curious failure to carry out this procedure correctly, see *Re White* (1990) where a properly executed will made in 1981 was altered by the testator in 1984. Two witnesses then signed the end of the document but the alterations themselves were not signed or initialled either by witnesses or by testator. The result was that the original unaltered will was admitted to probate.

2.18 REVOCATION ON MARRIAGE

Section 18 WA, as substituted by s. 18(1) AJA 1982 reads:

(1) Subject to subsections (2) to (4) below, a will shall be revoked by the testator's marriage.
(2) A disposition in a will in exercise of a power of appointment shall take effect notwithstanding the testator's subsequent marriage unless the property so appointed would in default of appointment pass to his personal representatives.
(3) Where it appears from a will that at the time it was made the testator was expecting to be married to a particular person and that he intended that the will should not be revoked by the marriage, the will shall not be revoked by his marriage to that person.
(4) Where it appears from a will that at the time it was made the testator was expecting to be married to a particular person and that he intended that a disposition in the will should not be revoked by his marriage to that person -
(a) that disposition shall take effect notwithstanding the marriage; and
(b) any other disposition in the will shall take effect also, unless it appears from the will that the testator intended the disposition to be revoked by the marriage.

These revised provisions apply only to wills made after 1982; s. 177 LPA is repealed. It will be seen that the basic rule as to revocation by subsequent marriage remains, as does the provision saving such a will if it is made in contemplation of a particular marriage, which duly takes place. However, there is now a rebuttable presumption that, where *part* of a will is expressed to be made in contemplation of marriage and nothing to show that other gifts are to be revoked by the marriage, the whole will survives the marriage. The use of the words 'fiancé' or 'fiancée' is a sufficient indication that a marriage is contemplated for the purposes of this provision. Section 18(2) preserves from revocation by subsequent marriage the exercise of a power of appointment in a will, unless the property so appointed would in default of appointment pass to the testator's PRs (previously the appointment was also revoked if the gift over was to the heir or statutory next-of-kin). Note that a voidable marriage (but not a void one) will be an effective marriage for the purposes of these provisions – see *Re Roberts* (1978).

2.19   EFFECT OF DIVORCE OR ANNULMENT ON A WILL

The AJA 1982 added a new s. 18A to Wills Act 1837, which applies to deaths occurring after 1982:

(1) Where, after a testator has made a will, a decree of a court dissolves or annuls his marriage or declares it void –
(a) the will shall take effect as if any appointment of the former spouse as an executor or as the executor and trustee of the will were omitted; and
(b) any devise or bequest to the former spouse shall lapse except in so far as a contrary intention appears by the will.
(2) Subsection 1(b) above is without prejudice to any right of the former spouse to apply for financial provision under the Inheritance (Provision for Family and Dependants) Act 1975.
(3) Where –
(a) by the terms of a will an interest in remainder is subject to a life interest; and
(b) the life interest lapses by virtue of subsection (1)(b) above,
the interest in remainder shall be treated as if it had not been subject to the life interest and, if it was contingent upon the termination of the life interest, as if it had not been so contingent.

Thus, if a marriage is ended by divorce, annulment or declaration that it is void, any will made by a party to that marriage is read as though (a) an appointment of a former spouse as executor is omitted and (b) any gift to a former spouse lapses, unless a contrary intention appears in the will. Section 18A(3) covers the situation where the interest of the remainderman is either vested or contingent upon outliving the wife; so, if a life interest to a spouse is ended in accordance with s. 18A(1)(b), the remainderman's interest is accelerated to fill the vacuum created, even if made contingent upon survival of the spouse. (The principle of acceleration is discussed *post*, 4.24.)

2.20   MEANING OF 'LAPSE' IN S. 18A(1)

The court decided in *Re Cherrington* (1984) that 'predeceased' in the will could be equated with 'lapse' in s. 18A(1)(b), so that alternative provisions in the will came into effect. However, this decision was swiftly set aside by the Court of Appeal in *Re Sinclair* (1985), where the will was in similar terms, the alternative provision in the event of the wife predeceasing the testator being in favour of the Imperial Cancer Research Fund. The court held that 'lapse' in s. 18A(1) could not be read so as to cover a reference in the will to the wife predeceasing the testator – it was not the natural meaning of the word, and the court could not rewrite the will on the basis of intelligent guesswork about what the testator might have wanted to happen. It is clearly important for those just divorced to consider whether they need to make new wills – it will be dangerous to rely on s. 18A to produce a desired result. It is probably not going to be easy to persuade a happily married testator or testatrix that he or she should make alternative provisions in a will to take into account the possibility of divorce.

2.21 *DONATIONES MORTIS CAUSA (DMC)*

A *donatio mortis causa* (a gift anticipating death) has been described by one judge as having an amphibious nature (*Re Beaumont* (1902)); it is neither a lifetime gift nor a legacy, but a bit of both. Not surprisingly, such an amorphous concept causes trouble.

Snell lists three conditions which must be satisfied if there is to be an effective *dmc*:

(a) The gift must be made in contemplation of death in the near future; normally, perhaps, when the donor is very ill but it seems that the imminence of a major operation would suffice or if the donor is to be involved in hostile military operations. A death satisfying this condition need not be the one which the donor had in mind.

(b) The gift must be conditional on death occurring. If the donor does not die, the gift is ineffective and revocable so long as he lives.

(c) Delivery of the subject-matter to the donee, or something representing it, is essential. The donor must have the intention of parting with 'dominion' over the subject-matter – not, for instance, simply of passing it over for safe-keeping. A chattel is easily disposed of by delivery; choses in action can be delivered so as to satisfy this condition if a document representing the chose is parted with – e.g. a bank deposit passbook, National Savings Certificates, a cheque payable to the donor (but *not* the donor's own cheque).

2.22 *DMCs* OF LAND AND SHARES

It is said that stocks and shares cannot be the subject of a *dmc*. The authority for this is doubtful and may be unreliable. It used to be said with equal conviction that land could not be the subject of a *dmc* but we now know that this is wrong – see *Sen* v *Headley* (1991) – in which case it was accepted that constructive delivery of the title to a house had taken place, apparently evidenced by the fact that the donee had the keys in her possession. In the High Court the judge followed the accepted rule that land could not be the subject-matter of a *dmc*; the Court of Appeal stood this rule on its head and said that land was capable of passing by way of *dmc* and that the three conditions stated above had been satisfied. (The land in question was unregistered; the decision must surely also apply to registered land, 'dominion' being parted with when land certificate, plus keys perhaps, is handed over to donee.) The court accepted the fact that the doctrine was anomalous, 'but anomalies did not justify anomalous exceptions'. It seems likely that there is now no restriction as to the type of property that can be given in this way; we have a bigger and better anomaly. See also *Woodard* v *Woodard* (1991) in which a *dmc* of a car was effected by the words 'You can keep the keys, I won't be driving it any more'.

2.23 CONSTRUCTION OF WILLS

Even professionally drawn wills sometimes contain obscure passages; home-made wills (and quite a surprising number come to light) frequently need elucidation before their provisions can be carried into effect. In such cases, it is necessary to *construe* the will, hence the principles of construction evolved by the courts to assist them in reaching the correct solution. They form a substantial body of law which it is impossible even to summarise here. A PR faced with a construction problem will need legal advice; the more difficult case will have to go to the Chancery Division to be solved. (The Chancery Division of the High Court deals with problems of interpretation in wills already proved; questions of formal validity are dealt with in the Family Division.) Some initial help can be got from the recognised authorities on the construction of wills, e.g. *Hawkins & Ryder* and *Theobald*. However, it has been suggested that there is now less judicial enthusiasm for the traditional rules of construction than there was.* If this is true, it may be that they will no longer apply in such a way as to defeat the testator's intention and that there will be a perceptible fall in the number of ghosts of dissatisfied testators who, it has been said, wait on the other bank of the Styx to receive the judges responsible for misconstruing their wills (*per* Lord Atkin in *Perrin* v *Morgan* (1943)).

2.24 ILLUSTRATION – THE MEANING OF 'MONEY'

Perrin v *Morgan* is, in fact, a useful case to illustrate the more liberal approach to problems of construction. The home-made will contained a gift of 'all my money'. In deciding that this meant all the testator's estate, the House of Lords restated its basic philosophy in such matters, here expounded by Lord Simon (my emphasis):

---

*C H Sherrin, *The Wind of Change in the Law of Wills*, 40 Conv 66.

'The fundamental rule in construing the language of a will is to *put on the words used the meaning which, having regard to the terms of the will, the testator intended.* The question is not, of course, what the testator meant to do when he made his will, but what the written words he uses mean in the particular case – what are the "expressed intentions" of the testator.'

So the court deduces the testator's intention from the will itself; it will not try to remake a will to produce a better result. 'It is not the function of a court of construction to improve upon or perfect testamentary dispositions' – Jenkins LJ in *Re Bailey* (1951). The only circumstances in which the court will interfere with dispositions occur where an application is made to it under the Inheritance (Provision for Family and Dependants) Act 1975: see *post* 4.30 *et seq.*

2.25 CIRCUMSTANTIAL EVIDENCE (THE 'ARMCHAIR PRINCIPLE')

If the above philosophy is generally adopted, the rules or principles of construction will not be disregarded, but will not be rigidly applied, and where it is clear from the will what the testator's intention was, having regard to the language used and the circumstances in which it was used, then no rule should be allowed to override it. As Lord Evershed MR remarked in *Re Levy* (1960) 'I do not accept the view that there is any rule of law which in such cases overrides intention'. The need to have regard to the circumstances in which the will was made is sometimes called the 'armchair principle', from the words of James LJ in *Boyes* v *Cook* (1880):

'You may place yourself, so to speak, in the testator's armchair and consider the circumstances by which he was surrounded when he made his will to assist you in arriving at his intention.'

2.26 OTHER RULES OF CONSTRUCTION

Other rules include the so-called 'golden rule', i.e. that a will should be construed so as to lead to testacy rather than intestacy (*Re Harrison* (1885));[4] and the rule that non-technical words should be given their plain, ordinary meaning and technical words their technical meaning; but always subject to the testator's expressed intention decreeing otherwise. It may be clear from the will and other admissible evidence that the testator has used a word or phrase in a different sense from that which is generally accepted; in such cases, the testator's meaning is accepted – the so-called 'dictionary principle' is applied, the testator being taken to have supplied his own dictionary for the purposes of interpretation. If the literal interpretation produces an untoward result then, in Lord Denning's view at least 'you should reject that interpretation and seek for a sensible interpretation' (see his judgment in *Re Allsop* (1968)). For the class-closing rules, see *post* 6.30.[5]

2.27 SECTION 24 WILLS ACT 1837

Although the basic rule of construction requires reference to the will and nothing but the will to find out what the testator intended, there are occasions when other evidence is admissible – for instance armchair (or circumstantial) evidence is admissible to prove the existence and identity respectively of the subject and object of a gift. In this connection, one has to remember that by s. 24 WA every will is to be construed, so far as the property disposed of is concerned, as though it had been executed immediately before the testator died. So a description of the subject-matter of a gift will, unless a contrary intention appears, comprise all relevant property owned at the date of death, including property acquired after the will was made. A gift of 'all my shares in ICI' will include not only shares owned at the date of the will but also shares subsequently bought. For an example of a contrary intention excluding s. 24, see *Re Sikes* (1927), where a gift of 'my piano' was held to apply to the one owned at the date of the will, not to the different one owned at the date of death: see also *post* 6.4.

2.28 PATENT AND LATENT AMBIGUITIES

The gift of money in *Perrin* v *Morgan* (see *ante* 2.24) is an example of a patent ambiguity, because the will itself employed ambiguous phraseology. Latent ambiguities fall into two categories. Firstly, there is the situation where the ambiguity does not surface until the will is considered in the light of the armchair evidence, as in *Charter* v *Charter* (1874), where there was a gift in the will (drawn by the local vicar!) to Forster Charter and neither of the two surviving sons fitted that description. Evidence of the state, circumstances and habits of the family was admissible. An example of a similar ambiguity in relation to subject-matter would be a devise of 'my seaside cottage Channel View' when the only two cottages owned by the testator are 'Atlantic View' and 'Ocean View'. If the armchair evidence provides no clue to enable the correct beneficiary or the correct subject-matter to be identified, the courts have been loth to go further and call for evidence of the testator's intentions.

Secondly, there is the situation where the armchair evidence reveals two beneficiaries or two subject-matters which fit perfectly the description in the will. This kind of ambiguity has been called an equivocation and is one that the courts have been prepared to resolve by calling for direct evidence of the testator's intentions. Thus, in *Re Jackson* (1933) the testatrix had given property to 'my nephew Arthur Murphy'; use of the armchair principle made it clear that there were two legitimate nephews called Arthur Murphy and one illegitimate one of the same name. Direct evidence was admissible (from outside both the will and the armchair) to show that the testatrix's intention favoured the illegitimate nephew.

2.29 STATUTORY EXTENSION OF ADMISSIBILITY OF EVIDENCE OF INTENTION

For testators dying after 1982, s. 21(1) AJA 1982 has increased the admissibility of extrinsic evidence in connection with the construction of wills; in future such evidence (including evidence of the testator's intention) can be used where any part of the will is (a) meaningless, (b) ambiguous on the face of it, and (c) ambiguous in the light of the surrounding circumstances. It is not easy to envisage a situation fitting s. 21(1)(a), unless the testator takes the extraordinary course of using a private code, which actually happened in *Kell* v *Charmer* (1856) where two legacies were stated as sums of 'i.x.x.' and 'o.x.x.' Evidence showed that these were coded expressions for £100 and £200 (the testator was a jeweller). Section 21(1)(b) covers the *Perrin* v *Morgan* and other situations of patent ambiguity. Section 21(1)(c) codifies the already existing rule of construction that direct evidence of intention is admissible where there is an equivocation, as in *Re Jackson (supra)*. It also removes any doubts about the admissibility of such evidence to resolve other kinds of latent ambiguity, such as the one in *Charter* v *Charter (supra)*.

Section 21(1)(b) was invoked in *Re Williams* (1985) where the testatrix had died in 1983, leaving a home-made will which listed 25 individuals and organisations to share in her estate, but without indicating the shares which they were to take. She had written to her solicitors the day before she made the will and her letter was admitted as evidence by the court, under s. 21(1)(b) rather than under s. 21(1)(a). Unfortunately, it proved to be of no help and the court ordered that the gift must be taken as being made to all 25 beneficiaries as tenants in common in equal shares.

2.30 RECTIFICATION OF WILLS

In the case of testators dying before 1983, the Probate court could omit any part of the will which was inserted by fraud or coercion, or without the testator's knowledge and approval, leaving it to the Chancery Division as the court of construction to make the best job it could of the blanks left in the will. Omission was generally the sole weapon of rectification; words could not be altered or inserted, unless it was clear from the will itself that a clerical error had been made, in which case the court of construction took upon itself a very limited power to make changes.

In the cases of testators dying after 1982, s. 20 AJA 1982 provides a limited statutory power to rectify a will, if the court is satisfied that the will fails to carry out the testator's intentions in consequence (a) of a clerical error; or (b) of a failure to understand the testator's instructions. The clerical error could be that of the testator himself or of his amanuensis; or, more usually, of the person drafting or typing the will. In *Wordingham* v

Royal Exchange Trust Co (1992) a drafter's mistaken exclusion of a clause exercising a power of appointment was held to be a clerical error, and so rectifiable.

The failure to understand the testator's instructions can apply only where there is an intermediary (amanuensis, solicitor, bank manager or other lay person) and would have no application to a will made by the testator himself. Nor can it be of any help where a solicitor or anyone else preparing the will arrives at the wrong result for the testator through a misunderstanding of the legal effect of his draftsmanship. Furthermore, if rectification is sought for failure to understand the testator's instructions, it will be necessary, in the process of establishing how the will falls short, to prove what the testator's instructions were.

The application for rectification under s. 20 must be made within six months of the date of the grant, unless the court permits an extension. After six months the PRs are excused from liability for distributing the estate.

The rectification of deeds is on a different footing – see *post* 8.19.

2.31   CONDITIONS AND CONDITIONAL INTERESTS

It is a favourite gambit of testators (and for that matter of settlors too) to seek to attach conditions to their gifts. There is some well-mapped territory where it is safe to do this, and other situations where it becomes a hazardous pursuit.

(a)   A general restraint on marriage is acceptable, if imposed by a husband on his wife or vice versa. As the law does not permit the attachment to an absolute gift of any conditions, the gift to the spouse must be of a limited interest, e.g. to W for life until remarriage with remainder to the children (or to W for life but if she remarries, to the children).

(b)   Provided that the gift takes the form of a determinable interest, the determining event in the case of any disposition can be marriage in general (for life until remarriage) or marriage to a particular person (for life until marriage to a non-Jew). But for historical reasons if the gift is on a condition which wholly restrains marriage (to Ann for life but if she marries, then to X) the law will regard this as promoting celibacy and will strike out the condition, leaving Ann with her life interest intact. A partial restraint is usually acceptable (to Ann for life but if she marries a non-Jew, then to X).

(c)   The law dislikes conditions which infringe family obligations. In *Re Caborne* (1943) the testatrix gave her son a conditional gift of residue which was to enlarge into an absolute interest, if his wife should die or the marriage be otherwise terminated and it was held by the House of Lords that the condition was void as inducing an invasion of the sanctity of the marriage bond. On the other hand, in *Re Lovell* (1920) the testator gave an annuity to his mistress who was a married woman living apart from her husband, provided that she did not return to her husband or remarry. This was held to be a provision for her pending her return to her husband or remarriage, rather than an incentive to stay away from him and not to remarry.

(d)   A condition subsequent can easily fail for uncertainty unless it is precise in its operation, but a more lenient view may be taken of conditions precedent (although there are situations in which the event that cuts down a preceding gift is also the event which triggers the commencement of the gift over). In *Clayton* v *Ramsden* (1943) the beneficiary's interest was to be forfeit on marriage with a person 'not of Jewish parentage and of the Jewish faith' and the House of Lords decided that both limbs of this condition were void for uncertainty. But in *Re Allen* (1953) a gift to the eldest son of X 'who shall be a member of the Church of England and an adherent to the doctrine of that church' was held to be sufficiently certain; here there was a condition precedent but the courts appear to adopt in modern times a more benevolent view of conceptual difficulties about belonging to a particular religion, whether the condition is precedent or subsequent: see *Re Tuck* (1978).

(e)   Residential restraints are acceptable provided the condition is phrased with sufficient precision. In *Re Gape* (1952) a condition for forfeiture on failing to 'take up permanent residence in England' was held by the Court of Appeal to be sufficiently certain. The clue here is the use of the word 'permanent'; without it the condition would have failed for uncertainty.

(f)   A forfeiture clause for a legatee who fails to claim his legacy within a specified time (coupled with an express gift over to indicate that time is of the essence) is valid, as is a condition requiring the donee to use and continue to use a certain name and arms. Names and arms clauses went through a rough patch in the courts at one time but were firmly re-established in *Re Neeld* (1962).

(g)   A trust which attempts to deny to the beneficiary the natural consequences of the ownership of the interest conferred upon him is void. Thus, if the enjoyment of his interest is made subject to a condition that he must not give his future income away or that it is to be preserved from the claims of his trustee in bankruptcy, the condition is of no effect. But the gift of a life interest to someone else (never for the settlor himself) which comes automatically to a premature conclusion by bankruptcy is valid. So, in a gift by S to L for life, *but if* he become bankrupt, then to R absolutely, the condition is void and L obtains an unconditional life interest from the outset. On the other hand, if the gift is to L for life *until* he becomes bankrupt, L has a *determinable* life interest, which will be destroyed quite spontaneously, not only by L's death but also by an act of bankruptcy, thus leaving his trustee in bankruptcy with nothing to lay hands on.

(h)   A settlor can impose upon his own life interest a condition against assigning or charging the income with a gift over, for example, to his wife should he do so. There is also no objection to the inclusion of himself in his own discretionary settlement as a possible beneficiary. But there must not be any intention to escape creditors (see *post* 7.37 *et seq.*) and the tax implications may present an insuperable barrier to such a course – see *post* 8.10.

(i)   If a testator or settlor has reason to doubt the ability of a particular beneficiary to look after his money properly, the protective trust giving him the income only and taking it away from him if he tries to anticipate it is particularly useful. An ideal version of it is enshrined in s. 33 TA. If the beneficiary kicks over the traces, he does not necessarily lose all benefit; a discretionary trust comes into operation for the benefit of himself and his family. (See also *post* 13.5.)

3 Death and probate

3.1 DISPOSING OF THE BODY

Although no one can own a dead body, the deceased's executors are entitled to possession of it and are primarily responsible for making the funeral arrangements – see *Williams* v *Williams* (1882). If there are no executors, the duty to bury or cremate falls on others, and they too have the right to possession.* In practice, it is quite usual for the funeral arrangements to be left to relatives and friends. Any wishes expressed by the deceased should be observed as far as possible. In *Re Grandison* (1989) the court held that it probably had power to control an executor's decision regarding a funeral, but would not normally interfere with the honest exercise of a discretion of this kind. It should be noted that any directions given by the deceased as to funeral arrangements are not *binding* on his executors. In any event the wishes of close relatives should be given every consideration. It is important to make sure that notice of the time and place of the service is given to all persons who may be interested in attending.

3.2 FUNERAL EXPENSES

The expense of the funeral should be confined to what is reasonable, according to the circumstances. If an unreasonable amount is spent, the executors may have difficulty in persuading the Capital Taxes Office to allow the complete bill as a deduction under s. 172 IHTA. They may also get into trouble with the beneficiaries. 'Reasonable funeral expenses' for the purpose of s. 172 now includes the cost of a tombstone or gravestone, as well as a reasonable amount of mourning for family and servants.

3.3 USE OF BODY FOR ANATOMICAL OR THERAPEUTIC PURPOSES

Reference has already been made (see *ante* 2.5) to the possibility of the deceased making provisions of this kind – and urgent action is needed in such cases; this fact underlines the importance of such provisions being immediately discoverable on death. The statutory provisions relating to the use of the deceased's body in this way are found in s. 4 Anatomy Act 1984 and s. 1 Human Tissue Act 1961. There is a very helpful note on the subject

---

*'Whose Body?' by Paul Matthews, *Current Legal Problems*, 1983.

in *Williams*, pp. 1035–8. Notwithstanding use of the body for these purposes, it must eventually be the subject of a funeral, either by burial or cremation; this fact should not be overlooked.

3.4   ACTION TO BE TAKEN ON DEATH

A useful guide to all necessary action on death appears in *What to do when someone dies*, published by the Consumers' Association. Note in particular the requirements of the statutory forms prior to cremation. In practice, the funeral director employed will be able to advise on procedure. The death has to be registered; again, this action is often carried out by a relative but the executor will certainly want one copy of the certificate as soon as possible and may need more than one at a later stage.

If there is no close relative or friend to whom registration of death and funeral arrangements can be delegated, the executor must deal with these essentials personally. In such circumstances it is often also necessary to take urgent action to protect and secure the deceased's property – especially the residence and personal effects. An executor may want to take care to avoid, at this stage, accepting office by implication – anyone other than an executor should consider the risk of becoming an 'executor *de son tort*' – see *post* 3.10.

3.5   ACCEPTANCE AND RENUNCIATION

An executor cannot be compelled to act, even if he has, during the testator's lifetime, agreed to do so. After the death of the testator he therefore still has the option to decline office. Some quick thinking may be needed in marginal situations. A private executor can renounce office without necessarily having to produce a reason for doing so; a professional executor such as a bank trustee department is in business to act, and should not renounce without being able to show good cause. In some cases, of course, the beneficiaries themselves ask an executor to renounce, perhaps to save expense; if all the beneficiaries are of age and *sui juris* it will usually be reasonable to comply with this request. Where minority interests or a trust are involved a decision to renounce is less easy to take; it is wrong to renounce if the administration during either a minority or a life interest will be imperilled. Particular care should therefore be taken in such cases to ensure that the administrators who are to act in place of the renouncing executor (or the other executor or executors where more than one is appointed) can be relied on to do so responsibly and efficiently. The problem is not unlike that which occurs when trustees retire and appoint others in their place (see *post* 9.13). It may be noted here that a PR in whom settled land becomes vested on the death of a tenant for life (and it continues to be settled) may renounce his right to a settled land grant

41

without losing the right to a general grant: s. 23 AEA. Where the land ceases to be settled under the SLA, the deceased's executors cannot avoid responsibility for both the general estate and the trust fund.

An executor who has intermeddled (see *post* 3.9) may not renounce, although a very trivial act of intermeddling may not make a renunciation invalid. Renunciation by an executor does not affect his right to a grant of administration with will annexed, and if he has this right it should be expressly renounced to clear him out of the way completely – NCPR 37(1).

Renunciation is effected by signature (or by sealing in the case of a corporation) of a document in one or other of a number of standard forms – see *T & C*, pp. 1095–97 for examples. When complete, the sensible practice is to send the renunciation (with the will) to the solicitors acting for the remaining executors or the administrators who are to take out a grant of letters of administration. However, a renouncing executor should bear in mind that renunciation is not final until it is filed, and there may be occasions when it should be at once lodged by him at a probate registry – again, accompanied by the will. This course can be followed where the executor has made an independent decision to renounce in advance of any plans being made by other interested parties for an application for a grant of letters of administration. Even after a completed renunciation has been lodged with the probate registrar, it may be retracted, with the registrar's leave – NCPR 37(3); it must be shown that retraction would be for the benefit of the estate and its beneficiaries.

3.6 OCCASIONS FOR RENUNCIATION UNILATERALLY

The most obvious case, perhaps, where an executor may wish to renounce unilaterally is where he discovers that the estate is insolvent. This not only involves an executor in administration problems of some delicacy but will also imperil any remuneration which the testator may have authorised him to take, since it will have to take its place as a legacy behind the creditors: see *post* 5.7. A professional executor who is faced with an insolvent estate will usually feel impelled to renounce unless his fees are underwritten by a third party; exceptionally, he may wish to act in order to preserve a personal interest in the estate, e.g. if he is a creditor. The Public Trustee (see *post* 12.1), incidentally, is not allowed to administer an insolvent estate – s. 2(4) Public Trustee Act 1906. In a solvent estate a similar problem arises where the will lacks authority to charge the executor's fees against the estate. It is then usual to ask the beneficiaries to authorise the fees and to indemnify the executor. An executor may be prepared to accept such an authority and indemnity from those representing less than the complete beneficial interest in the estate – it is a question of deciding for himself the extent of the risk involved and whether he is prepared to accept it, bearing in mind that fees taken by him which are not authorised either by the testator or by the beneficiaries are refundable to the estate. The only alternative to authorisation of fees by beneficiaries is to go to court for authority, but this must be a remedy of last resort. Another factor which will influence an executor in deciding whether or not to accept office is the existence of connected estates and trusts – see *ante* 2.6 and *post* 3.13 *et seq.* Remuneration which is authorised by the will under which he is appointed is very unlikely to be applicable also to the connected cases.

3.7 THE MAKING OF SMALL PAYMENTS WITHOUT A GRANT

In small cases, where it is decided to keep the cost of administration to a minimum, one should bear in mind the provisions based on the Administration of Estates (Small Payments) Act 1965, enabling sums not exceeding £5,000 to be paid to the person entitled, without production of a grant.[1] The subject is discussed in *T & C*, pp. 11–18, but typical items which may be dealt with in this summary fashion are National Savings Certificates, National Savings Bank accounts and Premium Savings Bonds. It is thought that clearing banks follow a similar practice with regard to small balances in their hands. Whilst the power to dispense with a grant in suitable cases is a discretionary one, and therefore cannot be invoked as of right, its existence may be a helpful factor when consideration has to be given to the administration of a small estate.

3.8 APPLICATION FOR GRANT WITH POWER RESERVED

In general, an executor should make up his mind quickly when it comes to deciding whether or not to act. In many cases immediate action is required to deal with the estate assets and liabilities – see *post* 3.18 *et seq.* Apart from this, the slower the start, the greater the delay before the beneficiaries are paid. If there is one single criterion by which beneficiaries measure the success or failure of an administration, it is the speed with which the PRs discharge their legacies or account to them for their shares of residue. An executor also needs to bear in mind that, if he takes a long time to make up his mind, he may receive a citation requiring him either to prove or renounce; see *post* 3.12.

However, where several executors are appointed, it is not necessary for *all* to apply for a grant initially. One or more may apply on their own, power being reserved to grant 'double probate' to the executor or executors not proving in the first instance. Where one executor out of several is unavailable or undecided, this rule does enable a grant to be issued quickly so that the administration can proceed. Note, however, that notice must be given to the non-proving executors by the one applying for a grant (NCPR 27(1)), though the registrar may dispense with such notice if it would be impracticable or unduly expensive (NCPR 27(3)). Note also the requirement in s. 114(1) Supreme Court Act 1981 that probate or administration shall not be granted to more than four persons for the same part of the estate.

3.9 INTERMEDDLING

Acceptance of office can easily be inferred from conduct. Describing oneself as 'executor' is an obvious example of such conduct. Paying the deceased's debts is another, and opening an executor's bank account yet another. Advertising for claims against the estate will be conduct implying acceptance of office if there is a specific reference to the executor (more discreet enquiries should be published if they are intended to be non-committal). What are called 'acts of mere humanity' such as arranging the funeral or feeding children or animals are not in themselves acts from which acceptance of office can be inferred. Simply protecting the assets of the estate is equally inoffensive in this context, as are administrative acts of so trivial a character as to be merely 'technical' intermeddling – so described in *Holder* v *Holder* (1968) at p. 392, but the dividing line between acts which will commit an executor and those which do not is often difficult to draw in practice. An executor who makes the initial decision to preserve temporarily his freedom of choice will move with discretion and refrain from acts which may, albeit inadvertently, commit him to act.

3.10 EXECUTOR *DE SON TORT*

A distinction should, perhaps, be drawn between the executor who accepts office by implication and the non-executor who intermeddles and thereby becomes an executor *de son tort*. The former can subsequently be compelled to take out a grant, the latter cannot. Section 28 AEA restricts the liability of the executor *de son tort* 'to the extent of the real and personal estate received or coming into his hands, or the debt or liability released', allowance being made for any debt validly due to the intermeddler and to any payments made by him which might properly have been made by an accredited PR. An individual or corporation not nominated executor may be asked by an interested party to act as administrator and, while investigating the proposal, inadvertently become executor *de son tort*. Even so, the situation is not fatal; they cannot be compelled to take out a grant and are only liable to account to the extent of the assets actually handled – or, in the case of a debt, actually released. That the risk is a real one, however, is made clear by the case of *New York Breweries Co Ltd* v *Attorney-General* (1899) where an English company which permitted a transfer of shares to be registered by American executors without having produced to it an English grant was held liable as executor *de son tort* for the payment of the estate duty on the shares in question.

3.11 INTERMEDDLING BY A NON-RESIDENT

In *IRC* v *Stype Investments (Jersey) Ltd* (1982), after the death of Sir Charles Clore in 1979 the defendant Jersey company directed that £20m., being the proceeds of sale of land in England held by it as bare trustee for Sir Charles's estate, should be paid to its account in Jersey. The Court of Appeal held that this was intermeddling with Sir Charles's English estate and that the defendant had constituted itself executor *de son tort* liable to pay CTT; the court also confirmed a grant of letters of administration *ad colligenda bona* to the Official Solicitor on the grounds that special circumstances made it desirable not to issue a grant to the named executors. Such a grant empowers the administrator to get in the estate but not to distribute it, and is made when the court thinks the assets need protection. Both the Revenue and the Official Solicitor were given leave to serve writs on *Stype* outside the jurisdiction (i.e. in Jersey) in accordance with RSC Order 11. In such circumstances, an executor *de son tort* is liable for tax only to the extent of the deceased's assets coming into his hands; a properly constituted PR is liable to the extent of the assets he has received 'or might have so received but for his own neglect or default': s. 204(1)(a) IHTA. See also *IRC* v *Stannard* (1984) in which the court held that an executor resident in Jersey was *personally* liable for CTT arising on the death of a testator resident and domiciled in England.

3.12 CITATIONS

In 3.8 mention was made of citing an executor to accept or renounce probate (a procedure, incidentally, which is equally applicable to a would-be administrator who is dragging his feet). An executor (but not an administrator, because he falls under the executor *de son tort* rules) who is thought to have intermeddled may also be cited. A citation is an instrument issued from either the Principal Registry of the Family Division or a district probate registry; before it is issued, the citor must enter a caveat – NCPR 46(3). Subsequently, a citation may take one of three forms:

(a) To accept or refuse a grant; this is issued at the request of a person with an inferior right to a grant and calls upon a person with a superior right either to apply for a grant or to renounce it. If the person so cited still fails to act, his rights as executor cease and the citor may obtain a grant – or some other person may do so, if the citor himself is unwilling to act (NCPR 47).

(b) To take probate; when an executor has intermeddled and has not applied for a grant within six months of death, he may be cited to apply for probate by anyone beneficially interested in the estate. If he fails to do so, the citor may apply for an order either *requiring* the executor to apply for a grant or for a grant to be made to himself or some other person (NCPR 47).

(c) To propound a will; when a person knows of the existence of a will, as yet unproved, which will affect him adversely, he may cite the executors and beneficiaries named in the will to prove it. This will have the effect either of clearing the will out the way (if the persons cited take no action) or of submitting it to proof in solemn form (NCPR 48).

Note that before any citation can be issued, every will referred to in it must, if possible, be lodged with a probate registry: NCPR 46(5).

3.13 CHAIN OF REPRESENTATION

Although an executor may neither assign his office nor retire and appoint another in his place (as may a trustee – see *post* 9.5 *et seq*.) he can well be responsible for having the administration carried on after his own death by his own executor – who may have been entirely unknown to the first testator, or who may even have been actively disliked by him. This follows from s. 7 AEA which reads:

1. An executor of a sole or last surviving executor of a testator is the executor of that testator.

This provision shall not apply to an executor who does not prove the will of his testator, and, in the case of an executor who on his death leaves surviving him some other executor of his testator who afterwards proves the will of that testator, it shall cease to apply on such probate being granted.

2. So long as the chain of such representation is unbroken, the last executor in the chain is the executor of every preceding testator.

3. The chain of such representation is broken by
    (a) an intestacy; or
    (b) the failure of a testator to appoint an executor; or
    (c) the failure to obtain probate of a will;
but is not broken by a temporary grant of administration if probate is subsequently granted.[2]

4. Every person in the chain of representation to a testator
    (a) has the same rights in respect of the real and personal estate of that testator as the original executor would have had if living; and
    (b) is, to the extent to which the estate whether real or personal of that testator has come to his hands, answerable as if he were an original executor.

A few simple examples will serve to illustrate the principles contained in this section:

(a) A appoints B to be his executor. B appoints C. A dies first and B proves A's will. B then dies and C proves B's will. C is executor of both A and B. This 'chain' can be extended indefinitely.

(b) The same facts, except that B does not prove A's will. The chain's first link is never formed and neither C nor any subsequent member of the chain can be A's executor.

(c) The same facts, except that A does not appoint an executor and B takes out a grant as administrator. Neither C nor any subsequent member of the chain can be A's executor. If, when B dies, part of A's estate remains unadministered, a grant of letters of administration *de bonis non* will be needed.

(d) The same facts, except that A appoints *two* executors, B and BB. BB survives B. C (nor any subsequent member of the chain) is not A's executor. Note that if it were B who appointed two executors, C and CC, they would both be executors of A. Suppose that, after A's death, B alone took a grant, with power reserved to BB; on B's death, C could cite BB to obtain double probate, which would break the chain and release C from responsibility for A's estate.

It is impossible to escape the effect of the chain; if, in the first of the above examples, C wants to prove B's will he cannot avoid taking on responsibility for A's administration as well. The administration may, of course, be 'dead' – nothing, in fact, to be done. Should some matter in connection with A's estate arise in the future, however, C (or his successor in the chain) will have to deal with it. Note that a grant limited to settled land does not act as a link in a chain. The consequences of acting as the last link in a chain are obviously considerable and merit serious consideration by an appointed executor at an early stage – particularly where the testator was a person more likely than not to have been acting as executor – e.g. a solicitor or an accountant.

Under s. 1(3) AEA 1971 a Scottish confirmation (the equivalent to an English grant of probate) cannot constitute or continue a chain of representation; no such disapplication applies to Northern Irish grants.

3.14   NO CHAIN OF REPRESENTATION FOR TRUSTEESHIPS

Some care should be taken to distinguish between those cases where the testator was acting as executor and those where he was acting as a trustee. There is no chain of representation with regard to the office of trustee; PRs may assume the responsibilities of deceased sole trustees, but need not do so: s. 18(2) TA. Equally, they need not exercise the power given to them under s. 36(1) TA (see *post* 9.7) to appoint a new trustee or trustees, although it is usually desirable that they should. Until such time as they make an appointment, PRs may exercise or perform any power or trust which was exercisable by the former trustee. Being the executor of a last surviving trustee does not, therefore, involve quite such an inevitable burden as does becoming the executor of an executor.

3.15   ADMINISTRATORS

Where either no executor has been appointed or none is willing to act, an administrator must be found to deal with the estate. The orders of precedence to be used when choosing an administrator are set out in NCPRs 20 and 22, to which reference should be made for the details. Broadly speaking, the first choice will be the person with the most immediate interest in the estate. Where there is a will to be proved, but no executor exists or comes forward, the first in line is any trustee of the residuary estate, followed by any other residuary legatee or devisee, including a life tenant. In the case of a complete intestacy, the surviving spouse has the first right to a grant, followed in turn by the children and issue of any child who died during the lifetime of the deceased, the deceased's father and mother and brothers and sisters of the whole blood (or issue of any deceased brother or sister who predeceased the intestate). The order of priority therefore corresponds to the rules for distribution in such circumstances – as to which, see ch. 4 and Appendix 4.

3.16 PROFESSIONAL ADMINISTRATORS

Notwithstanding the existence of NCPRs 20 and 22, letters of administration can be granted to an individual or corporation not first entitled to act – or, indeed, to someone without a beneficial interest of any kind. No one can be compelled to take out a grant as administrator – not even after having intermeddled in the estate. The right to a grant of administration can be renounced in the same way as can the right to a grant of probate. This opens the door for the professional administrator to act in cases where none of the persons entitled to benefit wishes to take out a grant.

The decision to renounce the right to an administration grant and to have the administration handled by a third party such as a solicitor or trust corporation is one for the beneficiaries to take; they therefore have more control over the destiny of an administration than in cases where executors are appointed. Questions of complexity and cost will have to be considered. An independent judgment may be just as useful in this sort of case as in any other – perhaps more desirable when the alternative is to have the beneficiaries themselves dealing with the estate. It must be borne in mind that, if a minority or life interest arises, s. 114(2) Supreme Court Act 1981 requires the grant to be made either to a trust corporation (with or without an individual) or to not less than two individuals, unless it appears expedient to appoint an individual as sole administrator. Under s. 116 of the same Act the court has considerable discretionary powers; it can pass over persons with a prior right to a grant in favour of those with a lesser right or even those with no right at all. For an example of the exercise of this discretionary power, see the involved story of the Clore English estate, *ante* 3.11. It is normal practice to accept as administrator a person or trust corporation to whose appointment the persons interested in the estate have given their consent.

It only remains to add that the choice of an administrator and his acceptance of office should be dealt with expeditiously. An executor's authority derives from the will; the grant of probate confirms it. An administrator, on the other hand, has no authority until it is given to him by the court in the grant of letters of administration – see *post* 3.27. An administrator is, therefore, less well-placed to make a prompt start with his duties. Wrangling over his identity wastes time. The matter is one which should be attended to and resolved as soon as it becomes clear that no executor is going to extract a grant.

3.17 FIRST STEPS

As soon as an executor or administrator-elect has decided to commit himself, he can take the first step towards the eventual goal of a completely administered estate. It may be useful, at this point, to summarise the main stages involved in this operation.

(a) Ascertainment of the deceased's assets and liabilities followed by their valuation.
(b) Obtaining a grant, securing control over assets, payment of taxes and liabilities, realisation of assets for this purpose.
(c) Having cleared the estate of liabilities, payment of legacies and distribution to the beneficiaries.

Often one stage will not have been cleared before the next is embarked on – in a complex estate, a PR may, for instance, still be seeking to establish the value at death of unquoted shares whilst carrying out a partial distribution to beneficiaries. Nevertheless, it is important to keep the identity of these three stages clearly in mind and not to embark upon a new one without being reasonably satisfied that there are no extensive unknown areas in the previous one. It would be foolish, for instance, to start paying debts (stage (b)) without having established with a reasonable degree of confidence that one had discovered and valued with a reasonable degree of accuracy all the estate's assets and liabilities.

As we have seen *ante* in 3.9, certain activities are not in themselves such as to commit an executor to acceptance of office. What follows is based on the assumption that the die has been cast, the executor or administrator is committed to going ahead and need not have any reservations in his dealings with the estate, its beneficiaries and the outside world. The first stage is to discover, to list and to value all the assets and liabilities of the estate. It is not usually necessary, however, to defer lodging an application for a grant until a complete and detailed valuation of *all* assets and liabilities is available. It is always desirable to get a grant without delay; see *post* 3.46.

3.18 PERSONAL EFFECTS

These must be secured. Small, portable items of value should be deposited with the bankers of the estate. This may not be feasible for larger objects, which must therefore be made as secure by an alternative method as is conveniently possible. If the deceased was the owner of an authorised firearm, the local police should be advised of this; Chief Officers of Police may authorise PRs to hold firearms for the purpose of sale or other disposition: s. 7 Firearms Act 1968. Consideration should be given to having an inventory prepared; for instance, where it is not at once possible to put the effects in the hands of agents for sale or to hand them to a beneficiary. Where there is no risk of insolvency, no risk that a grant will not be obtained and the estate assets are obviously sufficient to satisfy prior and concurrent beneficial interests, then the sensible course is to release the personal effects at once to the beneficiary entitled to them and to take his receipt (having first, of course, established their value for insertion in the Inland Revenue Account).

3.19 INSURANCE

This should be considered at the earliest opportunity. Existing policies should be endorsed with the PR's interest. If, as is often the case, the deceased was under-insured, the cover should be raised to a proper level. There may be a problem about insuring the deceased's home, if it is unoccupied. Insurers' practice varies in such cases and will need to be checked; there may be no problem, so far as insurance is concerned, if the property is only unoccupied for a short period but the insurer may want the water supply turned off and reasonable precautions taken to secure the property. Personal Representatives will want to take such precautions, whether the property is furnished or not, to make sure that the property is secured against illegal entry, and perhaps to ask the police to keep an eye on it and to arrange regular inspections themselves.

3.20 INSURANCE OF BUSINESSES AND MOTOR CARS

Where the PR is responsible for carrying on a business for the time being, he should take particular care to ensure that there is adequate insurance against all business risks, including, in the case of professional practices, claims for breach of the duty of care. Professional indemnity insurance is increasingly difficult to effect. Personal Representatives should consult either their insurers or a member of one of the leading insurance broking associations about all aspects of insurance. The insurance of motor vehicles needs special care. Section 143 Road Traffic Act 1988 makes it an offence to use a motor vehicle or *to allow one to be used* unless there is a third party policy in force for its use by the driver in question. It is therefore essential not to allow any vehicle belonging to a deceased to be used until the insurers have been informed of the death, have been told by whom it is to be driven in future, and have issued a new or amended certificate of insurance to cover the new situation.

3.21 STATUTORY POWERS OF INSURANCE

As mentioned *ante* in 2.5 regarding administrative powers, the theoretical basis for insurance by PRs and trustees is unsatisfactory. Section 19 TA authorises them (but does not require them) to insure against loss or damage by fire 'any building or other insurable property to any amount, including the amount of an insurance already on foot, not exceeding three fourths parts of the full value of the building or property' and to pay the premiums out of income. The restrictions to cover against fire and to three-fourths of the value are out of accord with modern practice. So far as land and buildings are concerned there is a further power in s. 102(2)(c) SLA which is not restricted as to amount but which is again confined to cover against fire and it applies only to land in which an infant has a beneficial interest in possession or to land held for a person contingently entitled. In these days it is customary to insure against a greater range of risks than fire alone, and insurers usually require the insured sum to represent the replacement value; no prudent PR will want to effect insurance on any other basis. Section 30(2) TA authorises both PRs and trustees to reimburse themselves for all expenses properly incurred and this provision could, perhaps, be pressed into service if needed. Alternatively, the beneficiaries can be asked to approve arrangements for sensible insurance cover.

3.22 RUNNING A BUSINESS

If the deceased had shares in a limited company, the responsibility for continuing its business rests with the surviving directors. The executors may wish to take part in the appointment of one or more directors to ensure that there is no hiatus at board level. Later it may be desirable to appoint a director who will act as 'nominee' of the estate, especially where the shareholding is substantial; see *post* 5.30. Where the deceased was a partner, the surviving partners are legally responsible for continuing the business; the executors should obtain copies of the partnership agreement and up-to-date partnership accounts as soon as possible, so as to establish and quantify the rights of the estate in the partnership property. In neither of these cases do the executors become personally involved in the business.

3.23 SOLE PROPRIETOR'S BUSINESS (SEE ALSO 5.31)

Where the deceased was a sole trader, the situation is different. Unless the business can either immediately be transferred to a beneficiary, or unless there is no point in seeking to continue trading, the executors must perforce accept responsibility, if only for a restricted period during which a buyer can be found or arrangements made for transfer to a beneficiary.

Acceptance of responsibility will usually mean the imposition of direct financial control, although one would expect any manager employed to be given limited discretion for items such as payment of wages. (Unless the PR is proposing to run the business personally, employment of a manager will be essential, and priority must be given to finding and securing a suitably qualified person for this job.) In addition to imposing control, financial and otherwise, PRs must be prepared to make periodic full reviews of the state of the business – perhaps at quarterly intervals. A weekly perusal of the business bank account and scrutiny of monthly figures for purchases, sales, creditors, debtors and stock should enable them to prevent anything going seriously wrong. It is by no means always easy to do this. Any licensing requirements (whether relating to consumer credit, heavy goods vehicles or any of the other rules and regulations affecting different types of business) should be considered. Existing stocks of stationery may have to be modified to comply with the Business Names Act 1985. As regards VAT, see Regulations 11(2) and 63 VAT (General) Regulations 1985 (SI 1985 No. 886).

Although there is no general rule of law authorising PRs to carry on the deceased's business, they may do so with a view to sale, if a sale as a going concern is the right option. The testator may have given his executors and trustees authority to run the business in his will (and should have done so, if the circumstances demand this). A power to postpone sale gives PRs power to carry on a business during postponement; *Re Crowther* (1895) illustrates this vividly, the trustees in the case having postponed sale for 22 years, carrying on two businesses for the benefit of the life tenant. Chitty J. held that they were in order to do this. It is better, however, for there to be express authority, and this should specify which assets may be employed for business purposes – if this is not mentioned, PRs will probably be confined to the business assets at the date of death. Personal Representatives will, of course, be *personally* liable for business debts which they contract while carrying on a business; however, they have a right of indemnity out of the estate assets. If carrying on with a view to realisation, they have a prior right of indemnity over both beneficiaries and creditors at the date of death. If not carrying on for this purpose, their right of indemnity is good against the beneficiaries only, unless a creditor has assented to the carrying on of the business, in which case the right extends to that creditor also. These questions of authority, personal liability and indemnity can, of course, be resolved by turning the unincorporated business into a limited company; the will should authorise this where it may be the sensible course to take.

3.24   INFORMING THE BENEFICIARIES

A beneficiary under a will or intestacy should be told of his interest in the estate (whatever may be the theoretical position about his rights in this respect). Reading the will after the funeral is a custom not now observed except, perhaps, in one or two of the more remote parts of the country. As soon as the executor has decided to act – or so soon as the administrator is selected – he should write to beneficiaries to inform them of their interest. Residuary legatees should have copies of the will and should also be given details of the assets and liabilities, when assembled. Having thus started off on the right foot, the competent PR keeps his beneficiaries informed, according to the degree of their respective interests; nothing is more destructive of a happy relationship between the two sides than lack of communication.

3.25   NOTICES FOR CLAIMS

It is usually easier to establish the liabilities of an estate than its assets. Creditors are not slow to notify PRs of claims against them. Nevertheless, for their own protection, they should seriously consider advertising for claims, in accordance with s. 27 TA. Summarised, this section authorises PRs to give notice by advertisement in the *London Gazette* and in a daily or weekly newspaper circulating in the district in which any land is situated, such notices for claims against the estate as would have been directed in a special case by the court in any action for administration. Irrespective of the existence or non-existence of any land in the estate, the usual media for insertion of the statutory notices for claims are the *London Gazette* and a local newspaper or newspapers circulating in the district or districts with which the deceased was principally connected. National papers are not much used, and only on rare occasions is it necessary to seek the directions of the court. At the end of the period fixed by the notice the PRs may then distribute the property to which the notice relates, having regard only to the claims of which they then have notice. The period of the notice must not be less than two months.

3.26   PROTECTION AFFORDED BY S. 27 TRUSTEE ACT 1925

A PR is normally liable for any debts due from the estate whether or not he had notice of them, but always provided the estate has sufficient assets to pay the debts. Section 27 provides an escape from the dilemma produced by this rule. It also protects PRs and trustees from claims by illegitimate beneficiaries whose existence does not come to light during the administration period or, in the case of trustees, during the period following upon the event giving rise to the distribution. The expense of the necessary advertisements is not usually significant. Private PRs, it is true, often waive insertion of notices, but one wonders whether they really understand the implications of inactivity, particularly as the Trustee Act has the useful attribute of binding the Crown – s. 71(4). Note that s. 27 also refers to the publication of notices 'elsewhere than in England and Wales'; PRs dealing with an estate with connections outside these countries need to consider what notices would, in such circumstances, be 'directed by a court of competent jurisdiction in an action for administration'. Difficult cases of this kind may make it desirable to seek the directions of the court.

Having advertised for claims before distribution will not, of course, protect a PR who has *notice* of a claim. The advertisements should be directed at 'any person interested' and are therefore intended to catch not only creditors but anyone who considers himself to have a claim against the estate, e.g. a claimant under the Inheritance (Provision for Family and Dependants) Act 1975 (see *post* 4.30 *et seq.*) or an illegitimate descendant of the deceased.

3.27 THE DOCTRINE OF RELATION BACK

There is no reason why an executor should not publish the above notices as soon as he has accepted office. An administrator is in a different position; he lacks authority until he has a grant, and notices inserted by him before he has a grant are possibly not efficacious. It is recommended that an administrator-elect waits until he has a grant before advertising under s. 27. Subject to this point, however, notices should always be published as soon as possible.

The position of an administrator generally is rather curious. Whilst all the deceased's real and personal property vests in his executor (if of full age) as from the date of death, the property of an intestate (which for this purpose appears to include a testator who leaves no executor of full age) vests in the President of the Family Division of the High Court until such time as a grant of administration is made – s. 9 AEA. In order to protect the estate during this interregnum the fiction of 'relation back' has been created; it is asserted that, when the grant *is* made, the title of the administrator relates back to the date of death, so that he may, for instance, sue for any injury to the property caused after death but before grant. Similarly, acts done by the administrator before he gets his grant may be validated under the fictitious doctrine, but only if to do so will be for the benefit of the estate – an administrator is not estopped from denying acts which would not benefit the estate – *Mills* v *Anderson* (1984), where it was held that settlement of a claim by the estate before grant for a lesser sum could not be validated.

3.28 DOMICILE

It is assumed that the law and practice discussed here and in other chapters relate to the estate of a deceased person who was domiciled in England and Wales. The applicant for a grant will include in his oath a statement as to domicile. The vast majority of grants issued in England and Wales are for deceased persons formerly domiciled therein. If there is any doubt on this score, care needs to be taken; a foreign domicile may affect the application for the grant in the first place and, subsequently, the administration of the estate. Note that 'foreign' in this context may mean domicile in another part of the United Kingdom, such as Scotland or Northern Ireland.

3.29 MEANING OF 'DOMICILE'

Rules 4 to 7 in *Dicey & Morris* read as follows:

4.(1) A person is, in general, domiciled in the country in which he is considered by English law to have his permanent home.

(2) A person may sometimes be domiciled in a country although he does not have his permanent home in it. ['Country', according to *Dicey & Morris*, means the whole of a territory subject under one sovereign to one body of law.]

5. No person can be without a domicile.

6. No person can at the same time for the same purpose have more than one domicile.

7. An existing domicile is presumed to continue until it is proved that a new domicile has been acquired.

Thus, every person has a domicile (but not more than one at the same time); it may be a domicile of *origin*, i.e. that which he acquired on birth, or it may be a domicile of choice, i.e. that which he acquired subsequently by residence in another country accompanied by a conscious intention to reside there permanently. Most of us maintain our domicile of origin throughout our lives and this, in the case of a legitimate child, will be that of the father at the time of birth; an illegitimate child takes his mother's domicile.

3.30 DOMICILE OF CHOICE NOT EASILY ACQUIRED

It is often difficult to establish whether or not a domicile of choice has been acquired and, if so, where. It is notorious that a domicile of origin is of some tenacity, and it is less easy to prove that it has been abandoned than it is to prove abandonment of a domicile of choice. An illustration of the problems involved is contained in *IRC* v *Bullock* (1976):

There the taxpayer was born with a Canadian domicile of origin but from 1932 onwards lived in England and married an Englishwoman. Nevertheless, he visited Canada several times and said that eventually he meant to return there to live. He claimed that he had never acquired a domicile of choice in England (thereby relieving him of income tax on his unremitted Canadian income) and the Court of Appeal agreed with him; the taxpayer had established a permanent matrimonial home in England but he had never abandoned his intention of returning to Canada in the event of his surviving his wife. This was not an unreal possibility. The decision is similar to the earlier one in *Jopp* v *Wood* (1865) where residence in England of 25 years' duration was not accepted as establishing domicile here because of an intention eventually to return to Scotland.

3.31 DOMICILE OF CHOICE ACQUIRED

For a case running the other way from the *Bullock* decision, see *Re Furse* (1980):

> There the testator was born in Rhode Island, USA, his father being domiciled there. He served in the British Army in the 1914–18 war. In 1923 he and his wife came to England and, in 1924, his wife bought an English farm where the testator lived for the rest of his life. He and his wife did think about going back to the USA but he finally decided not to do so as long as he could lead an active life on the farm; he died in 1963 at the age of 80. His executors asked the court whether, for estate duty purposes, the testator was domiciled in England or in New York state. The court said that the testator's intention of returning to the USA was vague and indefinite and that he had acquired a domicile of choice in England. The facts showed a man 'deeply settled' here, wanting to go on living here till the end of his life. It may be noted here that one may be domiciled in a territory which is not a separate entity for the purposes of public international law.

The question in *Re Furse* was whether the testator died domiciled in New York state, not whether he was domiciled in the USA. So also one may be domiciled in a Canadian province (not Canada), an Australian state (not Australia) or in one of England and Wales, Scotland or Northern Ireland (not the United Kingdom, which these three countries comprise, although it is correct to speak of a non-UK domicile for tax purposes, since they all share the same fiscal regime).

3.32 TENACITY OF DOMICILE OF ORIGIN

Two other modern cases emphasise, however, the tenacity of the domicile of origin. To acquire a domicile of choice, clear evidence of a firm decision to establish permanent and indefinite residence has to be produced. In a further instalment of the 'Clore Saga' (see *ante* 3.11), Nourse J ruled that Sir Charles Clore had not abandoned his domicile of origin in England: *Re Clore* (1984). Under advice, Sir Charles had moved to Monaco in 1977 and spent £2m on an apartment there, but there was not enough evidence to show that he had formed a settled intention to stay there permanently. As a result, CTT was charged on the worldwide estate of Sir Charles, who died in 1979. In *Plummer* v *IRC* (1988) the taxpayer's domicile of origin was England. In 1979, her grandmother bought a house in Guernsey. The taxpayer, who was either at school or university in England for all the relevant years, visited Guernsey for holidays and weekends. Not surprisingly, the court held that she had not acquired a domicile of choice in Guernsey, the element of residence being insufficient (see below).

3.33 THE ELEMENT OF RESIDENCE

The obvious conclusion to draw from the cases on this subject is that the acquisition of a domicile of choice is not a precisely definable procedure and much will depend on the individual facts of each case. There seems to be no limit to the kind of facts which may be considered; amongst those which have been taken into account are membership of clubs, director-ships, development of business interests in a new country, marrying a native of that country and buying a grave space there. There must always, however, be an element of *residence* in the new country – defined in *IRC* v *Duchess of Portland* (1982) as 'physical presence in that country as an inhabitant of it' – not, e.g. as a traveller or holiday-maker. Such residence need not be lengthy – an immigrant into a new country would be domiciled there even if he died the day after he landed.

3.34 DOMICILE OF A MARRIED WOMAN

Before 1974 a married woman acquired the domicile of her husband on marriage; since then s. 1 Domicile and Matrimonial Proceedings Act 1973 enables her to acquire an independent domicile, as may any other person (except children under the age of sixteen and the mentally disordered), and she will not automatically, on marriage, acquire her husband's domicile. Where the marriage took place before 1974 the wife retains the husband's domicile until she either acquires a domicile of choice of her own volition or her domicile of origin is for any reason revived: see the *Duchess of Portland* case *supra*.

3.35 OTHER ASPECTS OF DOMICILE

This extremely brief survey of the law relating to domicile has done no more than scratch the surface of the subject; for a full discussion, reference should be made to one of the standard textbooks such as *Dicey & Morris*.

In July 1987 the English and Scottish Law Commissions published a joint report recommending reform of the rules for determining domicile, together with a draft Domicile Bill; this includes a new definition of domicile, whilst abolishing the concepts of domicile of origin and of choice. The new definition consists of two elements: 'presence' and 'intention to settle for an indefinite period'. It seems doubtful whether the proposals, in their present form, will be an improvement on the present state of affairs. As the late Astbury J. is alleged to have remarked, 'Reform, reform; aren't things bad enough already?'.

Since November 1986 the Hague Conference on Private International Law has been working on the law applicable to Succession to the Estates of Deceased Persons. The draft completed in October 1988 and embodied in a Consultation Paper of February 1990 envisages the replacement of domicile as the connecting factor by the 'dominant law', this being either (a) the law of a state designated by the testator to govern the succession to his estate, provided that at the date of the will or the date of his death he was a national of that state or was habitually resident there or, in the absence of an effective designation, (b) a choice of law determined by a cascade of three rules: – (i) habitual residence at time of death, if conforming with nationality; (ii) habitual residence for no less than five years immediately preceding death, but yielding to nationality if that is manifestly the closer connection; (iii) nationality at time of death, unless at that time the deceased was more closely connected with another state, in which case the law of that other state applies. This new doctrine, if eventually taken on board by English legislation, would apply only to the ascertainment of the law applicable to the devolution of the estate, often called its essential validity; the ordinary principle of domicile would continue to apply in ascertaining the law relevant to (a) capacity to make a will, (b) the formal validity of a will, and (c) the construction of a will.

For IHT purposes there are special rules which may require the substitution of a 'deemed domicile' for a domicile ascertained in accordance with the normal principles – see *post* 13.20.

Double taxation conventions have the task of reconciling our legal principles with those of other countries. 'Fiscal domicile', as it is called, is the domicile attributed to the taxpayer by both contracting parties under the convention or, if there is a conflict, the one determined by the rules for establishing fiscal domicile – see *post* 5.42n11.

Section 41 Civil Jurisdiction and Judgments Act 1982 provides a new and complicated definition of domicile (mainly focusing on residence) which is applicable only for the purpose of the Act, the object of which is to facilitate the service of a writ in one of the other European Community countries if, in the case of an individual, the defendant is domiciled in the UK or part of it. Conversely, if the individual is domiciled in another European Community country, the English court cannot exercise jurisdiction over him by virtue of his temporary presence here.

3.36   SIGNIFICANCE OF DOMICILE

What is the significance of domicile to the English PR? Firstly, the law of a testator's domicile at the time he makes a will governs his capacity to make it, at least so far as his moveable property is concerned – see *ante* 1.4. It is true that a will 'shall be treated as properly executed', i.e. formally valid, provided it complies with one of several residential and domiciliary conditions either on execution or on death under s. 1 WA 1963 – see *ante*

1.34. Formal validity must, however, be supported by capacity. Secondly, what is called the 'essential validity' of the contents of the will must be considered.[3] Granted that the will is formally valid and that the testator had capacity at the time it was executed, the dispositions it contains must not offend the relevant law at the date of death. For moveables, this is the *lex domicilii*, i.e. the law of the testator's last domicile; for immoveables, it is the *lex situs*, i.e. the law of the country in which they are situated. If a question of construction or interpretation arises, the law to be invoked will be that of the testator's domicile at the time he made his will, even though he subsequently changes his domicile.[4] The rule is the same for both moveables and immoveables, but the *lex situs* might deny practical effect to the interpretation in the case of immoveables. Lastly, but by no means least, if a deceased person was domiciled, or deemed to be domiciled, in the UK, IHT applies to all his property, wherever situated; if, however, he was domiciled abroad, the tax applies only to UK assets: s. 6(1) IHTA.

3.37 CLASSIFICATION OF MOVEABLES AND IMMOVEABLES

It will be seen, therefore, that, if the domicile of the deceased is not English, the English PR is bound to be concerned with at least one foreign system of law, and should take advice from an appropriate source before implementing any dispositions for which he is responsible. For intestacies, the law of the last domicile applies to moveables, the *lex situs* to immoveables. It should be borne in mind that the distinction between moveables and immoveables does not correspond to that between real and personal property.[5] For instance, the English courts have classified leasehold interests in land, mortgages of land and unsold land held on trust for sale as immoveables for the purposes of English private international law, although English domestic law regards them as personal property. Where it is necessary to establish the *situs* of property, the rule is that choses in action (i.e. personal rights to property enforceable by legal actions) are situated in the country where they are recoverable or enforceable (see *Kwok* v *Commissioner of Estate Duty* (1988), where a promissory note payable only in Liberia was held to be outside the scope of Hong Kong estate duty). Land is situated in the country where it lies and interests in land are situated where the land itself is situated.

3.38 RIGHT TO A GRANT WHERE DECEASED DIES DOMICILED ABROAD

The normal rules for priority of right to a grant do not apply to a person dying domiciled out of England and Wales. The practice in such cases is governed by NCPR 30 and is discussed in detail in *T & C*, chap. 12. To put the matter in the simplest terms, if there is a will which is admissible to proof in this country and it is in either the English or Welsh language, any executor named therein can obtain a grant here, either directly or through an attorney if he lives abroad. In other cases an executor 'according to the tenor' may obtain a grant here and, subject to proof of foreign law in accordance with NCPR 19, so may a person entrusted with the administration of the estate in the country of the domicile or, failing him, a person beneficially entitled to the estate. Where the deceased was domiciled in one of the countries to which the Colonial Probates Acts 1892 and 1927 apply (see *T & C*, pp. 472–3 for a full list) it is usually possible to reseal a grant made in the country of domicile, and this procedure is often simpler than applying for a full grant here. Under ss. 1–3 AEA 1971, where the deceased was domiciled in any part of the UK a grant made by the court of the country of domicile is recognised in the other countries of the UK without the necessity of resealing. It is no longer possible to reseal Republic of Ireland grants.

3.39   UNCONTESTED GRANTS

It is the duty of all PRs to collect and get in the real and personal estate of the deceased and to administer it according to law: s. 25(a) AEA as amended by s. 9 AEA 1971. This duty is expressly sworn to in the Oath required from all applicants for a grant. Except in small cases (see *ante* 3.7) this duty cannot be carried out properly without the issue of a grant. Neither an executor nor an administrator can prove his title without one. The first objective must, therefore, be to get such a grant, without any greater delay than is necessary, for a reasonably true picture to emerge of the deceased's assets and liabilities at the time of his death, together with his interests in trusts, taxable gifts and so on.

What follows consists mainly of a brief discussion of the way in which grants are applied for when there is no dispute about either the validity of the will sought to be proved or about the choice of administrator in intestate cases. Such applications are uncontested – hence the Non-Contentious Probate Rules 1987; these are reproduced in full in *T & C*.

Uncontested grants are said to have been obtained in 'common form'. They are distinguished from those cases where a will is in dispute and is proved in 'solemn form' by means of litigation ending with an order of the court. All grants are, in fact, court orders but the uncontested ones (the vast majority) have more of an administrative flavour than a judicial one. Contentious probate business, including proof in solemn form, is dealt with *post* 3.51.

3.40   APPLICATION FOR A GRANT

No grant of probate or grant of letters of administration with will annexed will be issued within seven days of death, and no letter of administration without will within 14 days of death, except in very special circumstances. In practice, an executor or administrator is not usually ready to proceed within these time limits. Applications for grants of all kinds may be made to (a) the Principal Registry of the Family Division at Somerset House, Strand, London, WC2R 1LP, or (b) one of the 11 District Probate Registries, or (c) one of 18 Sub-Registries which act as satellites to the District Registries (see *T & C*, pp. 26–7). Applications may be made either in person (NCPR 5) or through a practising solicitor (NCPR 4) and applications for all types of grant may be made through the post; a personal applicant may not apply through or with the help of any agent or adviser (NCPR 5(2)). Under s. 23 Solicitors Act 1974 as amended by ss. 54 and 55 Courts and Legal Services Act 1990, an unqualified person (including a corporate body) is precluded from taking instructions concerning an application for a grant and drafting the necessary papers for such an application. From a date yet to be decided by a commencing order, the amending legislation will bring within the range of qualified persons institutions such as banks, building societies and insurance companies, all of whom are bound under the existing law to employ a solicitor to prepare the probate papers. There is the likelihood of the appointment of an Ombudsman to oversee probate matters in the changed environment created by the new legislation.

Although under s. 115(1) Supreme Court Act 1981 a trust corporation has the distinctive ability to obtain a grant in its own name, it is not permitted to obtain a grant by personal application, because a personal applicant is defined in NCPR 2 to mean a person other than a trust corporation.

3.41 DOCUMENTATION

What are the papers that have to be prepared and lodged when applying for a grant? Where there is a will then this, of course, must be submitted; included in this term are any codicils to the will and what is called 'testamentary paper' which can be proved because it is incorporated in validly executed documents through reference therein. For the doctrine of incorporation by reference to apply, the following conditions are required:

(a) The will must refer to an existing written instrument, *not* to a future one (see *Re Smart* (1902)) and
(b) in such terms that the court cannot make a mistake as to the instrument's identity.
A recent case on incorporation is *Re Berger* (1990); the testator had made a will in Hebrew ('the zavah') and also an English will. The former was executed in accordance with the Wills Act, the latter was not. The former was therefore admitted to probate (in translation) and, since the English will was in existence when the zavah was made and was referred to in it, it could be treated as incorporated in the zavah for probate purposes.

This doctrine is not to be confused with the concept of the half-secret trust – see *ante* 1.21. Probate may be granted of a lost will, provided evidence is available of its contents; for the practice in such cases, see *T & C*, p. 538 *et seq*. In all cases the applicant must swear to a document known as the Oath; the basic contents are the same whatever form the application takes. The applicant may have to submit an Inland Revenue Account, the purpose of this being to enable an assessment to be made of the liability for IHT arising on death – if any. Evidence of death will be required.

3.42 RENUNCIATION

Reference has been made (*ante* 3.5) to renunciation by an executor. The completed renunciation will usually accompany any subsequent application for a grant. Similarly, a renunciation of the right to a grant of letters of administration by a person having the prior right to that of the applicant will be filed by that applicant with the rest of the necessary papers. Normally it is not necessary for such an applicant to produce written consents to his acting from those with prior interests, because they can be 'cleared off' through production of their renunciations or by means of citation, as to which see *ante* 3.12. Where a trust corporation is applying for an administration grant, however, it must produce written consents from (a) where there is a will, the residuary beneficiaries; (b) where there is no will, the persons taking under the intestacy. Where, in these circumstances, any beneficiary is a minor, the grant will be limited until the beneficiary in question applies for and gets a grant.

3.43 THE INLAND REVENUE ACCOUNT

This was referred to briefly above. There are at present three forms of account available for initial use in probate cases; IHT200 is the standard form where the deceased was domiciled somewhere in the UK. IHT201 is used where the deceased was domiciled elsewhere. IHT202 is used:

(a) where the deceased was domiciled in the UK leaving an estate not exceeding the threshold at which IHT becomes payable; and
(b) where the estate comprises only property which has passed under the deceased's will or intestacy or by nomination or beneficially by survivorship; and all that property was situate in the UK.

These forms (and a booklet of instructions, CAP213) may be obtained from the Capital Taxes Office, either through the post or personally; also from the Stamps Office in Bush House, Strand WC2 by personal application only; and from most head post offices.

3.44 'EXCEPTED ESTATES' PROCEDURE

The preparation and signature of the appropriate Inland Revenue Account are an essential preliminary to the issue of a grant, other than in cases excepted by The Inheritance Tax (Delivery of Accounts) Regulations 1991, SI 1991/1248; such cases, broadly speaking, consist of estates worth no more than £125,000 gross belonging to a deceased of UK domicile who made no chargeable transfers for IHT purposes during his life or any PETs that have become chargeable. For these excepted estates an Inland Revenue Account need not be delivered.

3.45 PENALTIES

The forms referred to in 3.43 carry a clear warning that failure to make full enquiries, to disclose all information and to answer questions to the best of the applicant's knowledge and belief may make the applicant liable to prosecution and penalties (as to which, see ss. 245–53 IHTA). Personal Representatives must, therefore, be energetic in seeking out and establishing to the best of their ability all the assets and liabilities of the deceased; the nature and extent of his interests in settled property and the deceased's chargeable transfers for IHT purposes contained in his personal 'accumulator' or to be added to it by PETs that have become chargeable – see, for example, Appendix 2. See also the First Check-list for Personal Representatives in Appendix 1. The professional executor will be expected to supply the solicitor responsible for drafting the probate papers (unless they are one and the same) with a schedule of the assets and liabilities and the other information required for the completion of the Inland Revenue Account, including details of exemptions from IHT.

3.46 ASSESSMENT AND PAYMENT OF IHT

A personal applicant will be told how much tax is payable, but in most cases the tax and interest payable will be self-assessed by the solicitor lodging the papers with the Probate Registry, except in the following cases:

(a)   the deceased was domiciled outside Great Britain;
(b)   conditional exemption is claimed for (i) works of art considered to be of national, scientific, historic or artistic interest; (ii) land and buildings of outstanding historic, scenic or scientific interest. See Appendix 3;
(c)   payment of tax is to be made by transfer of deposits in the National Savings Bank or out of the proceeds of National Savings Certificates and Premium Savings Bonds[6] encashed before the grant;
(d)   the grant is required only for settled land, or is to be one of *de bonis non*, double probate or *cessate*.

The professional executor can help by working out the figures himself as a check on those produced for him by the solicitor. Reference can be made to the Capital Taxes Office for advice in difficult cases. An example of an IHT calculation on death is shown in Appendix 2. In subsequent correspondence with the Capital Taxes Office, the file number allocated to the estate should always be quoted.

Under s. 226(2) IHTA payment of the tax calculated to be due has to be made when the Account is delivered, except so far as the instalment option under s. 227 can be exercised; there is provision in the Account for the written election to pay by instalments. If not so elected at the time, the option will be lost. If immediate payment is required, the applicant must therefore either realise assets for this purpose or make arrangements to borrow the necessary sum from the estate's bankers. [7] Although in the normal way a PR must wait until after his grant is available to complete the sale of an asset and obtain the proceeds, he need not be entirely without resources in the interim. Some insurance companies and building societies will release funds before grant for the payment of tax. (Incidentally, there is nearly always a delay in collecting life assurance moneys due to the estate, and the PR should not hesitate to ask for the payment of interest from the date of maturity, i.e. the date of death.) The beneficiaries themselves may have cash available (e.g. from insurance) which they are willing to lend to the estate temporarily.

It is a pity to postpone the application for a grant – which it is nearly always desirable to have without delay – merely because full and accurate details of every last asset and liability are not available. Complete accuracy is not essential at this stage; under s. 216(3)(a) IHTA reasonable provisional values may be inserted and a corrective account submitted later. Delay is, in any case, now ultimately self-defeating. Generally, IHT is due six months after the end of the month in which death occurs, unless paid by instalments: s. 226(1) IHTA. If not so paid, under s. 233 interest is charged at a rate determined from time to time by statutory instrument and starts to run on any tax unpaid. It is not deductible for income tax purposes.

3.47 AFFIDAVITS REGARDING IRREGULARITIES

If all is in order, the grant should issue from the Registry within 10–14 days of lodgment of the papers (sealed copies of the grant are obtainable in addition to the original and will help to get registration work done quickly; they should be ordered when the papers are lodged). Issue of the grant may be delayed if there is some doubt as to the validity of the execution of the will – if, for instance, the attestation clause is either defective or non-existent. An affidavit of due execution from one of the witnesses may be called for under NCPR 12(1). Anticipation of this requirement may reduce or eliminate delay. The existence of marks on the will (e.g. pinholes or the impression of a paper clip) indicating that another document has at some time been attached to it will have to be accounted for (for this reason care should always be taken to avoid attaching the will to any other document for any reason). An explanation of some kind will be called for and the registrar may insist upon an affidavit of plight and condition under NCPR 14.

3.48 CAVEATS

The most likely source of delay, however, to an application for a grant which is otherwise in order lies in the issue of a caveat. This is a notice in writing to a registrar not to seal a grant without notice being given to the person who has entered the caveat (the 'caveator'). It effectively puts a stop to the administrative process by which a grant is issued. A specimen form of caveat is given below.* Generally the objective of the caveator is to gain time to make further enquiries, to take advice and, perhaps, to try to negotiate the settlement of a claim as a *quid pro quo* for withdrawal of the caveat.

(NC Probate Rule 44(2))
In the High Court of Justice.
Family Division
The (Principal) *or* (District Probate) Registry.
Let no grant be sealed in the estate of *(full name and address)*   deceased,
who died on the   day of   , 19   , at   without notice
to *(name of party by whom or on whose behalf the caveat is entered)*.
Dated this   day of   , 19   .
(Signed)   *(to be signed by the caveator's solicitor*
                       or by the caveator if acting in person)
whose address for service is:
Solicitors for the said   *(If the caveator is acting in person, substitute 'In person'.)*
(NCPRs, Form 3)

3.49 CAVEATS – THE WARNING PROCEDURE

It is the duty of an executor appointed under what appears to be a valid last will to propound it for the benefit of the beneficiaries named therein. It is a duty which, as we have seen (*ante* 3.5), can be renounced. In the absence of renunciation the proper course is to proceed firmly with an application for a grant. The entry of a caveat may entail delay, but steps may be taken to minimise this; the first retort of the applicant for a grant is to issue a 'warning' to the caveator. This in turn requires the caveator to

---

*Reproduced from *T & C*, p. 1028 by permission of the publishers, Butterworth and Co. (Publishers) Ltd.

do one of two things within eight days of service of the warning. He must either enter an appearance showing what 'contrary interest' he may have in the estate of the deceased or, if he has no such interest but merely wishes to prevent the issue of a grant to a particular person, he must issue and serve a summons for directions. If the caveator does nothing, the caveat ceases to have effect and the issue of a grant can proceed, but he may feel forced, perhaps prematurely, to respond by either of the available procedures as described above; then the business becomes contentious and both the applicant and the caveator will need legal advice. In any event, the applicant should advise the principal beneficiaries of the incident as soon as he has knowledge of the caveat; it may be that the procedure is being used as a tactic to support a claim against the estate. In the past, claimants for provision from an estate have used the caveat both as a means of making their presence felt and in order to have certain knowledge that an application for a grant is going forward; it is now possible to apply to either the Principal Registry or a District Registry for what is called a 'standing search' to be made – NCPR 43. A person so applying will be sent an office copy of any grant corresponding to the description given and issued within either twelve months *before* the application or six months after. This service will assist persons who have no wish to prevent the issue of a grant but want to know when it is issued, in order, for instance, to commence proceedings under the Inheritance (Provision for Family & Dependants) Act 1975 – *post*, 4.30 *et seq*.

3.50   AMENDMENT AND REVOCATION OF GRANTS

NCPR 41(1) says:

> Subject to paragraph (2) below, if a registrar is satisfied that a grant should be amended or revoked he may make an order accordingly.

Paragraph (2) simply adds that such power should be exercised only in exceptional circumstances, unless it is used with the consent of the grantee.

Unimportant errors may be put right by amendment; substantial errors require revocation and a further grant. Whilst a grant in common form – i.e. uncontested – is conclusive evidence in the courts of England and Wales of the title not only of the grantee but also of all persons the grantee has dealings with in the course of administration, it is by no means invulnerable. It may later be attacked on any of the grounds upon which wills have been known to founder – for instance, lack of capacity of the testator, or irregular execution. An executor who has reason to suspect that such grounds exist will do well to consider proving in solemn form in the first place. Where the court has pronounced in favour of a will in solemn form (involving a trial where the evidence for and against the will is heard and tested), the grant is irrevocable and binding not only upon all the parties to the action but also upon those who could have participated in the proceedings but chose not to do so, despite their known interest; but there are the following exceptions to the inviolability of the solemn form grant:

(a) where a later will is discovered; or
(b) where the grant was obtained by fraud; or
(c) where it is found that the will proved was revoked by the testator's marriage.

With a common form grant, on the other hand, it is open to any interested party subsequently to attack the grant. In the early case of *Re Napier* (1809) the 'deceased' had been left for dead on the field of battle, but was happily able to appear in person at the application for revocation of the grant to his estate.

A grant may also be revoked where it has been made as the result of official error – for instance, where made whilst a caveat is in force. Lastly, a grant may be revoked as the result of subsequent events; in *Re Galbraith* (1951) a grant made to two executors was revoked because they had both become incapable of acting; note, however, the recent new power given to the court to appoint substitute PRs in place of one or all existing PRs – s. 50 AJA 1985 – a provision which should help to avoid the need for revocation of the original grant in circumstances similar to the *Galbraith* case.

When a grant is revoked, for whatever reason, what is the position regarding transactions carried out by the PR acting under the authority of the revoked grant? A purchaser from such a PR is protected by s. 204(1) LPA, which says that a court order (a grant, of course, being such an order) is not invalidated as regards a purchaser in good faith and for valuable consideration, 'on the ground of want of jurisdiction' – so a grant is conclusive authority in such circumstances. Section 37 AEA specifically protects purchasers of any interest in both real and personal estate who deal in good faith and for valuable consideration against subsequent revocation or variation of the grant, always provided that the transaction was effected by a 'conveyance' – a word generously interpreted. Section 27(1) AEA protects PRs making any payment or disposition in good faith 'notwithstanding any defect or circumstance' affecting the grant. Note the reference to 'good faith'; a PR who had notice of a possible defect in his grant and still went on making payments out of the estate would risk being held to lack good faith. Lastly, s. 27(2) AEA protects both those who make payments *to* a PR before his grant is revoked and the PR himself for payments *from* the estate; the latter is entitled to reimburse himself in respect of payments he has made before handing over to the new PR, provided such payments were ones which the new PR might properly have made himself.

3.51 CONTENTIOUS PROBATE BUSINESS

A caveat may turn out to be the start of a full-scale trial in the High Court. If this is so, the executor propounding what appears to him to be a valid will must set about collecting the supporting evidence from the attesting witnesses, the deceased's doctor, close relatives and friends, and so on. It is professional etiquette for a solicitor, where there is seen to be a serious dispute over a will, to provide a statement of his evidence concerning its execution and the surrounding circumstances to anyone concerned either in proving it or challenging its validity. This rule is intended to avoid costly and unnecessary litigation; a solicitor who complies with it may save himself from having to pay his own costs.

3.52 COSTS

The court has an unfettered discretion as to costs in a probate action, as in other areas of litigation; the general rule is that costs follow the event, i.e. loser pays. In two cases the general rule may not be followed. Firstly, if the litigation is due to the conduct of the deceased (or of the residuary beneficiaries), then all costs may be ordered out of the estate, irrespective of the outcome of the litigation. Secondly, if the circumstances are such as to make it reasonable to bring the action – if, for instance, there is some indication of lack of capacity, but the losing party had good reason for arguing otherwise – then the court may decide to make no order as to costs, leaving each party to bear its own. Generally, an executor who successfully propounds a will in solemn form should get his costs out of the estate but there can never be an absolute guarantee either about the outcome of the action or about his costs, and if he is prudent, he will take an indemnity from his beneficiaries before going ahead. He will, in any case, not go ahead without their full and informed agreement and he will further keep them informed throughout the course of the litigation. At all stages the possibility of a compromise should be borne in mind; if one can be agreed, its terms will be set out in a schedule to the court order necessary to end the proceedings. (The subject of litigation costs is also discussed *post*, 4.48.)

As regards compromising probate actions, see s. 49 AJA 1985 which provides that, where all the 'relevant beneficiaries' have consented, the court may pronounce for or against validity of a will without further argument. This sensible provision enables a Master of the court to pronounce in solemn form so long as everyone affected by this order agrees to the compromise. Unfortunately, the definition of 'relevant beneficiary' includes those who might be interested under an intestacy – see s. 49(2)(b) – even if no question of an intestacy arises. It seems that the next-of-kin must be sought out and their agreement obtained – as, indeed, must that of all beneficiaries under the will, even if they are not affected by the proposed compromise.[8]

3.53   ADMINISTRATION PENDING SUIT

It may be useful to end this passage on probate litigation by referring to the invaluable grant pending suit, formerly known as the grant *pendente lite*. When a probate action has started, application may be made for the appointment of an administrator pending suit in accordance with s. 117 Supreme Court Act 1981; where the issue of a full grant is likely to be delayed, the appointment of such an administrator should always be considered, particularly where there are assets which are likely to deteriorate in value if not sold, e.g. empty residential property, stocks and shares. It has been suggested that a person unconnected with the dispute over the will should act but, where the named executor under the last will is not beneficially interested in any event, e.g. a solicitor or a trust corporation, it seems more sensible to have them appointed, and this is quite commonly done. The consent of the parties to the dispute should be obtained. Note that an administrator pending suit is an officer of the court and acts under its directions; apart from being barred from making beneficial distributions he has the same powers as a general administrator. He is entitled to such remuneration as may be awarded by the court; when his duties are complete he produces his accounts and his bill is taxed.

4 Intestacy, rearrangements and family provision

4.1 FROM THE *DAILY TELEGRAPH*, 3 JANUARY 1991

'The late Robert Holmes à Court left no will for his multi-million dollar business when he died of a heart attack last September, the family solicitor said yesterday. Australian media reports have suggested he carried a draft of a will in his briefcase for the 18 months before his death, but never signed it.'

4.2 BASIC INTESTACY PROVISIONS

Notwithstanding the obvious advantages in dying testate (that is, being survived by a valid will) many people still die intestate. This may be simply inadvertence, or because of the mistaken belief that the rules for distribution of estates on intestacy will be entirely satisfactory in one's own case; also, quite probably, there may be a fairly strong feeling that to make a will is the equivalent of signing one's death warrant. This superstition is prevalent amongst rich and poor alike. Making a will is not compulsory – yet – and English law (like that of other countries) has created its own scheme of beneficial interests to take the place of a will where a person dies intestate, either wholly or partially. Partial intestacy occurs where the deceased has left a valid will which fails to dispose of all his assets or all his interest in them; the part undisposed of is dealt with in accordance with the intestacy rules.

The basic intestacy provisions are contained in Part III of AEA, ss. 33 and 46–9, incorporating the amendments made by the Intestates' Estates Act 1952 and the Family Law Reform Act 1969; s. 14 Family Law Reform Act 1969, which still stands alone; and (for deaths after 3 April 1988) ss. 1 and 18 Family Law Reform Act 1987. As regards the rights of the surviving spouse in the matrimonial home, s. 5 Intestates' Estates Act 1952 still stands alone.

4.3 STATUTORY TRUST FOR SALE ON INTESTACY

Section 33 AEA may be summarised as follows: subject to any provisions in the will of a partially intestate deceased, when anyone dies intestate as to any real or personal estate, such property is held by his PRs upon trust for sale, with power to postpone such sale for such period as the PRs think proper; reversionary interests should not be sold before they fall in unless there is a special reason for such sale. Personal chattels also should not be sold unless there is special reason for doing so.

Out of the net proceeds of sale the PRs are directed to pay the funeral, testamentary expenses and debts, having regard to the rules of administration found in Part III of the Act and, in the case of a partial intestacy, to set aside out of the residue of such moneys a fund to pay any pecuniary legacies bequeathed by the deceased – see *post* 4.19 and 6.16 *et seq.*

The residue remaining and any investments representing it are subsequently referred to in Part III of the Act as 'the residuary estate of the intestate'.

4.4 SUCCESSION TO PROPERTY ON INTESTACY – THE MAIN RULES

These are contained in s. 46 and are summarised in the Table of Distribution set out in Appendix 4. Note:
(a) 'Issue' as used in the Table means descendants generally, not just children of the deceased;
(b) 'Personal chattels' are defined in s. 55(1)(x) AEA – see *post* 4.5;
(c) 'Statutory trusts' are defined in s. 47(1)(i) – see *post* 4.6 – and take care of the possibility that there may be beneficiaries who have not reached their majority. Property devolving on intestacy is therefore held on these trusts, not only for issue of the deceased, but also for brothers and sisters and uncles and aunts and their descendants. The Law Commission (Law Com.No. 187 dated 18 December 1989) has made the following recommendations for the reform of the rules:

    (a)   A surviving spouse should in all cases receive the whole estate.
    (b)   The statutory 'hotchpot' rule affecting issue should be repealed (post 4.10).
    (c)   The statutory 'hotchpot' rules affecting issue and spouses upon partial intestacy should be repealed (*post* 4.15 and 4.16).
    (d)   A spouse should only inherit under the intestacy rules if he or she survives the intestate for 14 days.
    (e)   Cohabitants should be able to apply for reasonable financial provision under the Inheritance (Provision for Family and Dependants) Act 1975 without having to show dependence (*post* 4.36).

Legislation to implement these proposals is not yet in sight.

4.5 RIGHTS OF THE SURVIVING SPOUSE

(a) *Personal chattels.* Where the surviving spouse does not take the whole estate, i.e. where issue or near relatives also survive, she is entitled to the personal chattels as defined in s. 55(1)(x) AEA, which reads as follows:

> 'Personal chattels' mean carriages, horses, stable furniture and effects (not used for business purposes), motor cars and accessories (not used for business purposes), garden effects, domestic animals, plate, plated articles, linen, china, glass, books, pictures, prints, furniture, jewellery, articles of household or personal use or ornament, musical and scientific instruments and apparatus, wines, liquors and consumable stores, but do not include any chattels used at the death of the intestate for business purposes nor money or securities for money.

A reference to this definition is sometimes used in wills as a convenient form of shorthand for a gift of personal effects. Where there is a problem in deciding what falls within the definition, the court construes the expression widely.

(b) The fixed net sum or 'statutory legacy', plus interest from date of death to date of payment and interest in residue – for details see Appendix 4. The Lord Chancellor has power, under s. 1 Family Provision Act 1966, to amend the amount of the fixed net sum and last did so by increasing the amounts to £75,000 or (where no issue survive) to £125,000.[1] The current rate of interest is 6%.[2]

(c) Capitalisation of life interest, i.e. where there are issue surviving. The surviving spouse has the right under s. 47A AEA to require the administrators to pay out a capital sum in lieu of the life interest, a right that must be exercised in writing within twelve months of the date of the grant. Calculation of the lump sum must be in accordance with the rules laid down by statutory instrument.[3] Capitalisation of the life interest will be administratively convenient, in that the whole estate is distributed at an earlier stage than would otherwise be the case. Perhaps one should add that where all issue are of full age and capacity, there can be agreement as to the share of the capital to be taken by the surviving spouse and a calculation under s. 47A will not be needed – see *post* 4.25. Note also that under s. 47A(7), where the surviving spouse is the sole PR, notice of an exercise of this right must be given to the Senior Registrar of the Family Division of the High Court.

(d) Right to dwelling-house. Where the surviving spouse was resident in a dwelling-house owned by the deceased at the date of death there is the right to require the PRs to appropriate it in or towards satisfaction of any absolute interest in the estate, including the capitalised value of a life interest: s. 5 and Second Schedule, Intestates' Estates Act 1952. Such a dwelling-house will usually be the matrimonial home, but the intestate need not also have been living there. Like the right to a capital sum in lieu of a life interest, this right must be exercised within twelve months of the issue of a grant, during which period, if the surviving spouse is not the PR or not one of the PRs, the residence cannot be sold without the spouse's written consent.

In *Re Phelps* (1980) the Court of Appeal held that the right to the appropriation of the dwelling-house extended to cases where the value of the surviving spouse's absolute interest in the estate was less than the value (at date of appropriation) of the property, the deficit to be made up by a cash payment from spouse to PRs. It will be gathered that the relevant valuation date is the date of appropriation (the usual rule with appropriation), not the date of death; see *Re Collins* (1975).

4.6 THE STATUTORY TRUST ON INTESTACY

Where property devolving on intestacy descends to issue of the intestate or to brothers and sisters or to uncles and aunts (or to the issue of those relatives), it is held on the statutory trusts which under s. 47(1)(i) AEA as amended by s. 3(2) Family Law Reform Act 1969 require the residuary estate, if held for the intestate's issue, to be distributed as follows:

> In trust, in equal shares if more than one, for all or any the children or child of the intestate, living at the death of the intestate, who attain the age of eighteen years or marry under that age, and for all or any of the issue living at the death of the intestate who attain the age of eighteen years or marry under that age of any child of the intestate who predeceases the intestate, such issue to take through all degrees, according to their stocks, in equal shares if more than one, the share which their parent would have taken if living at the death of the intestate, and so that no issue shall take whose parent is living at the death of the intestate and so capable of taking.

Section 47(3) applies the above scheme to cases where relatives of the intestate, other than issue, benefit.

4.7 DISTRIBUTION *PER STIRPES*

Summarised, this means that, where all or part of the estate is held upon the statutory trusts for issue of the intestate, such whole or part is divided in equal shares between such of the children of the deceased as survive him and reach the age of eighteen or marry under that age. If a child dies before the intestate, leaving children living at the intestate's death, they take in equal shares between them the share which their parent would have taken had he survived – again, subject to their reaching the age of eighteen or marrying under that age.

> *Example.* A died intestate on 1 January 1990 leaving a net residuary estate of £375,000 and was survived by two legitimate children, B and C, aged 35 and 29 respectively and one illegitimate child D, aged 15. He was predeceased by a child, E, whose issue are two children, F (aged 20), G (aged 16) and H (a child of F aged 2). During his life A had made a gift of £25,000 to B to help him buy a share in a business venture. Distribution of the estate is as follows (ignoring IHT):

		Net residue	£375,000	
		Add advance to B	25,000	
			£400,000	divisible into four shares
B takes	*C takes*	*D takes*	*F and G take*	
£100,000	£100,000	£100,000 if he	£50,000 each, in G's case	
Less 25,000		survives to 18 or	contingently on reaching	
£75,000		marries earlier	18 or marrying earlier	

4.8 DISTRIBUTION *PER STIRPES* AND *PER CAPITA*

The method of distribution shown above, resulting from the death of A intestate, is described as being *per stirpes* – according to the stocks; each child of the deceased constitutes a stock and each stock is entitled to an equal share. This method may be contrasted with distribution *per capita*, which results in each member of the class of beneficiaries – in this case issue of the deceased – being entitled to an equal share. Applying the *per capita* method to the above example would, therefore, result in B, C, D, F and G each taking £80,000. It will be noted that the interest taken by issue of the deceased is conditional upon their either attaining the age of 18 or marrying under that age. Should any member of the class fail to satisfy one or other of these conditions, his share fails and is distributed amongst the remaining issue. In the above example, for instance, should D die aged 15, the £100,000 previously allocated to him will become divisible into three shares, one to B, another to C and the third between F and G equally.

It will be recalled that s. 47(1)(i) refers to issue of the deceased 'living at the death of the intestate'; s. 55(2) defines this as including a child or issue *en ventre sa mère* at the death.

4.9 ADOPTED, LEGITIMATED AND ILLEGITIMATE CHILDREN

Under s. 39 of the Adoption Act 1976 a child who has been formally adopted, i.e. by court order, is treated as the legitimate child of the adopting parents, and not as a child of its natural parents. Section 45 of that Act protects PRs who do not have notice of an adopted child and distribute in ignorance of its existence. Under s. 5(3) of the Legitimacy Act 1976 a legitimated person – i.e. a child born illegitimate but whose parents subsequently marry – is entitled to benefit under an intestacy as if born legitimate. Section 7 of that Act protects PRs in the same way as does s. 45 of the Adoption Act. For intestacies arising before 1970 there were reciprocal rights of succession (a) between mother and illegitimate child and (b) between an illegitimate person and his or her spouse and children. Section 14 of the Family Law Reform Act 1969 took the modest step of extending to illegitimate children the right to share in the intestacies of father as well as mother (and gave to father as well as mother the right to share in the intestacy of their illegitimate child). Now, under s. 18 of the Family Law Reform Act 1987, for deaths occurring after April 3, 1988, an illegitimate person has equal rights to share in an intestate distribution with legitimate persons, whatever the relationship. For example, an illegitimate nephew will be entitled to share on the death intestate of an uncle; likewise an uncle will be entitled to share on the death of an illegitimate nephew. Illegitimacy has become an irrelevant factor in an intestate distribution. Unfortunately, the protection formerly given to PRs (of the same kind as that described above for adopted and legitimated persons) was abolished by s. 20 of the 1987 Act. PRs who distribute an estate (whether on intestacy or otherwise) and accidentally overlook an illegitimate beneficiary will be liable to that beneficiary for his share of the estate, even if no fault attaches to them. Personal Representatives should take care to investigate any indication of the existence of adopted, legitimated and illegitimate beneficiaries; subject to this duty, they may protect themselves (especially with reference to illegitimacy) by advertising in accordance with s. 27 TA – see *ante* 3.26.

4.10 HOTCHPOT

In the example of an intestate distribution given above in 4.7, child B received a gift of £25,000 from his father during the latter's lifetime, and this £25,000 was brought into hotchpot when making the distribution, with the result that B received £25,000 less than did the other stocks. The reason for this is the passage in s. 47(1)(iii) AEA:

> any money or property which, by way of advancement, or on the marriage of a child of the intestate, has been paid to such child by the intestate or settled by the intestate for the benefit of such child (including any life or less interest and including property covenanted to be paid or settled) shall, subject to any contrary intention expressed or appearing from the circumstances of the case, be taken as being so paid or settled in or towards satisfaction of the share of such child . . . and shall be brought into account.

For the purpose of this exercise the advance is valued as at the death of the intestate; a cash advance will not increase in value as a result of this, but an advance of shares or land may well be greatly different in value at the date of death from what it was when given.

In the case of total intestacy, the hotchpot rule applies only to the deceased's own children. Where there is a partial intestacy, the rule is extended – see *post* 4.15 and 4.16.

4.11 ADVANCEMENT

The reason for the hotchpot rule on intestacy or partial intestacy is to try to equalise benefits to children. A father who has given substantial sums to one child during his life may be presumed to have wished that such child should have its benefits under intestacy reduced by a comparable amount. Note that it is only gifts to the intestate's children which may qualify as advancements and need to be brought into account. A gift from A to his grandchild F, in the example in 4.7 above, would not need to be considered for this purpose. But had there been an advancement to the parent of F and G, it would have been taken into account in assessing the value of their stirpital share.

What is meant by advancement in this context? A general definition would be a payment or transfer of property to or for a child with the intention of making some permanent provision for it; it is a similar concept to that of the 'portion' which may have to be taken into account in the case of gifts to children in a will: see *post* 6.40. Often such a payment will be made whilst the child is young, but not necessarily. *Hardy* v *Shaw* (1976) is a case in point:

> A mother gave shares in a family company to two (out of three) of her children; the donees were middle-aged and already well established in life. On the mother's death intestate, the third child claimed that the shares should be brought into account. The court agreed and held that there was no evidence of contrary intention – no indication that the mother meant that, on her death, the two donees should be substantially preferred to the third non-advanced child. For a case where the court decided that the lifetime gift was not substantial enough to qualify as an advancement, as defined above, see *Re Hayward* (1957), where £500 had been advanced and the estate at death was £1,800.

There is no question, incidentally, of a refund by the child advanced, if the result of hotchpot is to put the child's share into deficit. (Advancement in this context should not be confused with the use of the same word to describe the presumption which may arise in favour of a wife or child on a transfer of property to them.)

4.12   CADUCIARY RIGHTS OF THE CROWN

If an intestate dies without leaving a surviving spouse, issue or relative within the prescribed range, his estate devolves upon the Crown, the Duchy of Lancaster or the Duchy of Cornwall as *bona vacantia*. It is then open to anyone, related or not, for whom the deceased might have provided, to ask either the Treasury Solicitor or the solicitors for the respective Duchies for provision to be allowed, *ex gratia*, from the estate under s. 46(1)(vi) AEA, bearing in mind also that a claim under s. 1 Inheritance (Provision for Family and Dependants) Act 1975 is a possibility in such circumstances: see *post* 4.30 *et seq*.

Where the deceased has died domiciled abroad and there is a claim from a foreign government to the English moveable estate under the foreign law of succession, unless that claim is by way of succession rather than to ownerless property, the English Crown's claim to the ownerless property will be upheld: *Re Musurus* (1936).

4.13 PARTIAL INTESTACY

This occurs where the deceased person has left a valid will but has made an effective disposition of part, not all, of his property. If, for instance, A dies, having made a valid will which gives his residuary estate to B, C and D in equal shares and D has predeceased A then, unless either A had incorporated alternative provisions in his will to deal with this situation or D was issue of A (in which case the gift may be preserved – see *post* 6.28) D's share is undisposed of and must be dealt with under the intestacy rules. A partial intestacy may also occur where there is a gap in the devolution, as in the case of *Re McKee* (1931), discussed *post* in 4.14.

Special rules apply to partial intestacy cases and are contained in s. 49 AEA. Section 49(1)(a) – see *post* 4.16 – was described, accurately, by Danckwerts, J. as being 'as bad a piece of draftsmanship as one could conceive' (although the draftsman was defended by R E Megarry in (1956) 72 LQR 483).

4.14 THE STATUTORY TRUST FOR SALE UNDER A PARTIAL INTESTACY

By way of preliminary, s. 49 directs that undisposed of property shall be dealt with in accordance with Part IV of the Act, i.e. ss. 45–52, but subject to the provisions contained in the will – for instance, a provision intended to deal with any intestacy which may arise. It is quite probable that a testator will have imposed an express trust for sale on his residuary estate; such an express trust will exclude the statutory trust for sale contained in s. 33 (see *ante* 4.3) regarding undisposed of property – s. 33(7). In *Re McKee* (1931):

> there was an intestacy in respect of the reversion to the residuary estate, of which the testator's widow was life tenant. There was an express trust for sale in the will. The court refused to order an immediate sale of the reversion and directed that the widow was not entitled to any immediate payment in respect of the intestacy which would occur on her death; when that happened, her PRs would be entitled to the statutory legacy plus interest from the date of the testator's death.

4.15 ADDITIONAL HOTCHPOT RULES FOR PARTIAL INTESTACY

The main difficulty in s. 49 arises in cases where one or both of two additional hotchpot rules have to be applied. Firstly, s. 49(1)(aa) –

introduced by Intestates' Estates Act 1952 – requires any surviving spouse of the deceased to bring into account against the statutory legacy 'any beneficial interests received under the will', other than personal effects specifically bequeathed. To take a simple example:

A dies, survived by his widow and children, leaving an estate of £300,000 (including personal effects valued at £10,000). He made a valid will, giving his personal effects and £10,000 to his widow, coupled with a life interest in one half of his residue but failed to dispose of the other half of his residuary estate, which falls to be dealt with under the intestacy rules. The widow becomes entitled to the personal effects (already hers under the will), a fixed net sum of £75,000 and a life interest in one-half of the intestate residue. Her £75,000 will be reduced by the £10,000 received under the will. A life interest received under the will is valued actuarially for the purpose of this hotchpot rule, say, at £70,000. Her statutory legacy, already reduced to £65,000, is now extinguished altogether and she is left with a legacy of £10,000 and a life interest in £140,000, worth, say, £70,000. It would pay her to disclaim (see *post* 4.21) her life interest under the will; she would then get a legacy of £10,000, a statutory legacy of £65,000 and a statutory life interest in one-half of £225,000 worth, say, £55,000.

4.16 ADDITIONAL HOTCHPOT RULE FOR ISSUE UNDER PARTIAL INTESTACY

The other of the two rules has always been in s. 49 and is the one causing the most trouble. It is s. 49(1)(a) and reads:

The requirements of s. 47 of this Act as to bringing property into account shall apply to any beneficial interests acquired by any issue of the deceased under the will of the deceased, but not to beneficial interests so acquired by any other persons;

It will be seen that s. 49(1)(a) extends the scope of s. 47(1)(iii); the latter requires property given to or settled on a *child* of the intestate by way of advancement or on marriage to be brought into account against that child's share. The former adds to this rule the requirement that on partial intestacy any *beneficial interest* received by *issue* of the deceased under the will shall be brought into account also. Nothing is added about the way in which such interests shall be brought into account, so s. 47(1)(iii) applies and such interests are brought in against the relevant child's share, presumably at the date of death value and subject to any contrary intention, either express or appearing from the circumstances.

Example. The testator died on 1 January 1990, having by his will given his estate upon trust for sale and after payment of debts, testamentary expenses and legacies to divide it between A (his son), B (his daughter) and S (his sister) equally. The sister predeceased and as there was no gift over of her share, it was undisposed of. The testator also had a son, C, who had predeceased. The will contained legacies of £20,000 each to D and E (children of A) and legacies of £40,000 and £60,000 respectively to F and G (children of C). B and E had each received an advancement of £30,000 during lifetime but before the date of the will. The residue, net of liabilities, was £710,000, or £570,000 after deducting the legacies, and the amount of the undisposed of share was therefore £190,000. Adding back the advancement to B and the legacies, the gross amount for division under the partial intestacy is £360,000. Distribution of the estate (ignoring IHT) is as follows:

	Intestacy	Under will
To A under the partial intestacy – £120,000 less the legacies of £40,000 to his children (s. 49)	80,000	190,000
To B under the partial intestacy – £120,000 less the advancement of £30,000 (s. 47)	90,000	190,000
To D		20,000
To E (s. 49 does not apply to advancements)		20,000
To F under the partial intestacy – one half of the balance of C's share after deducting both legacies to C's children (s. 49)	10,000	40,000
To G under the partial intestacy – as for F above (s. 49)	10,000	60,000
	£190,000	£520,000

Thus the effect of s. 49 as far as grandchildren or more remote issue are concerned is to leave their relative positions unchanged, G getting £20,000 more than F under the combined operation of the will and the partial intestacy, just as he would have done had S survived and there had been no partial intestacy. But the main objective of s. 49 is to ensure equality of treatment for each family unit. For the relevance of the express trust for sale, see *post* 6.16; and for the significance of the date of the advancement, see *post* 6.40.

4.17   THE STIRPITAL CONSTRUCTION OF S. 49(1)(a) FOR LIMITED INTERESTS

There will obviously be difficulty in some cases in deciding how the provisions of s. 49(1)(a) should be applied. For instance, A dies having made a will leaving one-half of his estate to his son B for life, with remainder to B's children, the other half share being undisposed of. B is clearly entitled to share in the distribution of the undisposed of half. If he is the *only* beneficiary under the partial intestacy, questions of hotchpot do not arise, but, if there are other beneficiaries, how are the interests given to B and his children to be brought into account? The answer provided by Harman J. in *Re Young* (1951) has been called the 'stirpital construction'; in this case, the deceased gave his widow a life interest in the residuary estate and, after her death, a one-seventh share upon discretionary trusts for life for his son Charles and Charles's children. When Charles died, his children were to take the fund absolutely. There was a partial intestacy of another share and the interests of Charles and his issue had to be brought into account against Charles's personal share in the intestate distribution. What was to be brought into account in these circumstances? Harman J. decided that not only Charles's discretionary interest in the fund should be brought in but also his children's interests – in effect, the value of the whole settled share.

4.18 THE DISTRIBUTIVE CONSTRUCTION OF S. 49(1)(a)

The foregoing decision seems to be more in accordance with the wording of s. 49(1)(a) than the alternative, which has been described as the 'distributive construction' and was mooted (but not adopted by) Pennycuick J. in *Re Grover* (1971); applying this construction would require any descendant of the testator who received an interest under the will to bring such interest into account against any interest the descendant receives under the partial intestacy. But reading s. 49(1)(a) in conjunction with s. 47(1)(iii) makes it clear that the combined hotchpot provisions operate against a *child's* share under a partial intestacy. It needs to be kept in mind, of course, that a child's share under a partial intestacy may be subject to *two* accounting operations – firstly, in respect of any advancements made to such child by his parent during the latter's life; secondly in respect of any interests given to him and his issue by the will.

4.19 PARTIAL INTESTACY AND THE MARSHALLING OF ASSETS

To conclude this brief discussion of the rules relating to partial intestacy, it may be helpful to draw attention to Schedule I, Part II AEA which directs that, in the case of a solvent estate, the debts and expenses of that estate shall first be paid out of property undisposed of by will, subject to retention of a fund to pay pecuniary legacies. This matter is dealt with more fully in Chapter 6, where it will become apparent that the payment of testamentary expenses (which term includes IHT – see s. 211 IHTA) out of the undisposed of property (if not obstructed by the will) may have the fortunate effect of swamping the partial intestacy rules out of existence.

4.20 INTESTACY IN SCOTLAND

The intestacy rules we have discussed apply only to the estates of persons dying domiciled in England and Wales. It is interesting to compare the position in this country with that of a person who dies domiciled in Scotland: see Appendix 5.

4.21 DISCLAIMER

Mr Bumble opined that the law was 'a ass – a idiot'; however 'The law certainly is not so absurd as to force a man to take an estate against his will' (Abbot CJ in *Townson* v *Tickell* (1819)). A beneficiary under a will or under an intestacy is, therefore, perfectly free to tell the PRs that he does not want his legacy or other benefit. He may disclaim it, and is free to do so at any time before he has actually accepted some benefit from it or has in some other way expressed his acceptance of the gift. Once the beneficiary has accepted, either expressly or by implication, it is too late to disclaim. In *Re Hodge* (1940) the court had to consider a gift to the deceased's husband of certain properties, charged with the payment of an annuity to the deceased's sister; should the properties be sold the sum of £2,000 was to be invested for the benefit of the sister and her children. The husband accepted the properties and paid the sister the annuity for five years. The properties were then sold and the husband sought to disclaim the gift to avoid payment of the £2,000. The court held that it was too late for him to do this; he had, quite clearly, accepted the gift and the liabilities attached to it. However, it is permissible for a beneficiary to disclaim an onerous gift and to accept another separate gift in the same will, unless the testator has made it clear that he must take both or none at all.

4.22 RETRACTION OF A DISCLAIMER

On the other hand, a disclaimer can be withdrawn if, subsequent to its being made, the beneficiary changes his mind. However, retraction of a disclaimer can be effective only if no one has changed his position to his detriment as the result of the disclaimer. In *Re Cranstoun* (1949) there was a residuary gift to the Home of Rest for Horses. Believing that this gift might be onerous rather than beneficial, the Home executed a renunciation of all claims to the estate. Twenty years later, when the estate was finally cleared, it was found that there was a net residue of some £4,000. The court decided that the Home could withdraw its disclaimer. No one had altered his position to his detriment as a result of the Home's renunciation many years previously.

4.23 FORMALITIES OF DISCLAIMERS

It seems that a disclaimer may be made either formally – by deed – or informally – verbally or by conduct. However, it is prudent for a PR to insist that a disclaimer be evidenced in writing; to rely upon a purely informal disclaimer would be to run the risk of its being disputed later on. In any event, as explained below, if a disclaimer is to be effective for tax purposes, it must be in writing.

4.24   REASONS FOR DISCLAIMERS

Whilst disclaimers are, no doubt, made either because the gift appears to be onerous in some way (for instance, the gift of a business which may or may not be profitable) or because the disclaiming beneficiary genuinely does not want the money but prefers it to go elsewhere, it is probable that most disclaimers are made these days with some tax advantage in mind. To take a simple example; a testator has made a will leaving a legacy of £50,000 to his son and the residue to his grandchildren. If the son is already comfortably off, he may disclaim his legacy so that it falls into the residue, thus avoiding the additional IHT which would be payable on his own death on his augmented estate.

At first sight it would appear that by disclaiming his legacy the son has himself effected a transfer of value for IHT purposes, for example, under s. 3(3) IHTA by omitting to exercise a right. However, s. 142 IHTA positively encourages such tax-saving gestures by stating that where a disclaimer is made within two years of death, the change in the destination of the gift which results from it is treated as having been made by the testator himself – hence no transfer of value occurs, apart from the deemed transfer on death. As stated above, to be effective for IHT purposes, a disclaimer must be in writing, refer specifically to the provision in the will which is being disclaimed and must be signed by the person disclaiming. The Capital Taxes Office will, of course, have to be notified in order that the IHT charge can be recalculated, but it is not necessary for an election to be made, as is the case where a variation occurs: see *post* 4.27. Provided the requirements mentioned above are satisfied, the effect of the disclaimer will be automatically applied for IHT purposes.

A disclaimer needs to be distinguished from (a) an assignment which is the disposition or transfer of an interest, keeping the interest transferred alive; (b) a release, which is the giving up of an interest, usually one that is not yet in possession and usually with an eye to allowing subsequent events to operate under the trust instrument; and (c) a surrender, which is a transfer of an interest in possession to the person next entitled. However, the expressions tend to be used loosely and interchangeably. A disclaimer under s. 142 IHTA is the rejection of an interest before the PR's assent to it but it is not so easy to understand how a so-called disclaimer under s. 93 IHTA – see *post* 4.28 – can be put in the same category, because the reversioner to the settled property as contemplated by the section may well have obtained a marketable interest long before the question of disclaimer comes up. The section clearly contemplates the disclaimer of the interest after the cesser of the limited interest, by which time the reversioner's interest will usually have come into possession and ceased to be excluded property.

The rejection by disclaimer of an interest under a will does not preclude the beneficiary from benefiting either under the residuary gift or under the resulting intestacy; and, on the strength of *Re Scott* (1978), it appears that the rejection by disclaimer of a statutory right under an intestacy allows the intestacy to take effect as if the disclaimed right had never existed, as is apparent from the example given in 4.15 *ante*. One advantage of a disclaimer (in the true sense of the rejection of a proffered gift) over an assignment, a release or a surrender is that it does not constitute a 'settlement' under s. 670 ICTA – important if the accelerated interest belongs to an infant child of the person disclaiming.

One possible result of a disclaimer, which should be considered before it is effected, is the acceleration of interests subsequent to the disclaimed one. If X is given a life interest by will, remainder to Y, and X disclaims, Y's interest immediately vests in possession even if, as may well be the case, the gift in remainder is expressed to take effect on the death of X. The same result may follow without any disclaimer on X's part if X or X's wife has witnessed the will or if X's life interest is revoked by a codicil without any substituted provision.

However, the terms of such a gift may make it plain that acceleration is *not* to take place if the prior interest is terminated prematurely. In *Re Flower* (1957):

> A settlement made in 1936 gave the trustees power to apply the trust income for various purposes during the settlor's life and, after his death, there was to be a life interest to his widow with a gift in remainder to his three children. The discretionary power was held void for uncertainty. Were the subsequent trusts accelerated? The Court of Appeal thought not, the settlor having made it plain that such trusts were only to take effect on his death.

It may be more difficult to show that acceleration is the correct course in the case of an *inter vivos* trust. Acceleration did occur in *Re Harker* (1969):

> The testatrix had given a life interest to her son, with remainder to his children in equal shares at 21. In 1958 the son released and surrendered his life interest; at that time he had three children one of whom had reached the age of 21. Goff J. concluded that their interests were accelerated but that the class of remaindermen was not thereupon closed in accordance with the rule in *Andrews* v *Partington* and would still be determined upon the death of the son, thereby admitting to the class any further children born to him, which meant that the child of over 21 could not demand payment of his share immediately. (Had the gift in remainder been to the son's grandchildren at 21, the rule in *Andrews* v *Partington* – *post* 6.30 – would have been applicable and, logically, the class would similarly have remained open but there is authority for saying that the application of that rule would likewise have been accelerated: see *Megarry and Wade*, p. 534, who add that this seems 'contrary to principle'.)

It should be added that the rule in *Andrews* v *Partington* is designed to deal with an inconsistency between the date fixed for distribution (e.g. the death of the life tenant) and the correct determination of the class. A contingent gift to the life tenant's own children after his death does not throw up any inconsistency, since, while the class is capable of contraction, it cannot expand after the date of distribution, so facilitating immediate distribution to those who have satisfied the contingency.

4.25 VARIATION BY REDIRECTING AND REARRANGING

Section 142's benevolence extends also to the redirection of gifts already received by a beneficiary and the variation of the terms of the will or intestacy before distribution takes place. Alterations to the terms of an *inter vivos* nomination of nominated property and of beneficial joint tenancies are equally acceptable. It is somewhat ironic that, for all the care taken to ensure that a testator's wishes are set out in prescribed form and that the will containing them is executed precisely in accordance with s. 9 WA, a post-death variation is commonplace and may completely frustrate the intentions of the testator. It should be borne in mind, however, that all the affected parties must be of full age and *sui juris*; if not, then an order of the court for consent must be obtained on behalf of the beneficiaries who are not competent to execute the variation.

4.26 ADVANTAGES OF VARIATION OVER A DISCLAIMER

Redirecting and rearranging the gifts allows for a more flexible approach than a simple disclaimer, which cannot influence the destination of the disclaimed gift. For instance, a testator has made a will leaving everything to his wife – a very common testamentary disposition. If the will is left as it is, the testator's nil rate band – £150,000 for 1992/93 – is wasted. Provided the widow has sufficient funds to maintain herself in comfort for the rest of her life she may well wish to redirect at least £150,000 to her children or grandchildren; no IHT will be payable on her husband's death (assuming that there are no lifetime gifts to be taken into account) and there will be a substantial saving on the widow's own death. Because of the provisions of s. 142, she is not treated as having made a lifetime gift of £150,000 – the disposition to children or grandchildren is treated as having been made by the testator himself.

There is a parallel provision to s. 142 in s. 62(6) TCGA; a variation or disclaimer made within two years of the date of death may be treated as having been made by the deceased and will not be a chargeable disposal for CGT purposes. The formalities are the same as for IHT, and an election is necessary in respect of a variation. In most cases an election will be made for both IHT and CGT, but this is not essential – the two elections are independent of each other.

4.27 FORMALITIES OF VARIATIONS

Like a disclaimer, for the purposes of s. 142, a variation or rearrangement must be in writing and signed by the person or persons entitled to redirect (in any event, it is an obvious practical requirement). It is essential to spell out in the document the provisions in the will which are being varied, or, in the case of an intestacy, the particular provisions which are to be redirected. The person or persons effecting such a written variation must, if advantage of s. 142 is to be taken, send a written election to the Capital Taxes Office within six months of the document's execution; where the result of the redirection is to increase the tax charge (and this may be desirable in order to achieve a greater saving at a later date) the PRs must join in the election; they can refuse to do so only on the grounds that they do not have sufficient assets to pay the extra tax. The document itself, or a copy, must accompany the form of election.

Curiously, it seems entirely possible for such a variation (though not a disclaimer) to be carried out even after an estate has been distributed – subject, of course, to its being done within two years of the date of death. Moreover, a beneficiary who has died within the two-year period can, through his PRs, accept a diminished benefit (if necessary, refunding a benefit already received) or accept an enhanced benefit.

Care is needed when framing proposals for a variation to ensure that no outside consideration is introduced. An exchange of inheritances by beneficiaries is in order but if, for instance, cash is brought in to balance the dispositions, the arrangement would not be acceptable under s. 142.

It is also important to ensure that the first attempt at an arrangement is effective, because you cannot have two bites at the cherry. In *Russell* v *IRC* (1988) a deed of variation was made which did not carry out its intended purpose; a second deed (still within the two-year period) was therefore made. The court rejected the second document for the purposes of IHT – it was not a variation of the terms of the will, but a variation of the first document. Note, however, that a deed of variation which contains an error and so does not carry out the parties' intention may be rectified by the court later on, even if more than two years from the date of death has elapsed – see *Lake* v *Lake* (1989).

4.28 SETTLED PROPERTY

Section 142 has no application to settled property in which the deceased had an interest in possession, although it is possible for the succeeding beneficiaries to disclaim their interests under s. 93, even after they have fallen into possession, provided that nothing has been done which indicates acceptance of the benefit; neither does s. 142 have any application to gifts with reservation which remain in the free estate at the date of death.

Reversionary interests retain their status as excluded property (see s. 48(1) IHTA) despite being moved about under a variation, and can enter into an exchange of beneficial interests without running foul of the rule that there must be no monetary consideration passing under the scheme: s. 142(5).

Although PRs cannot be forced to take part in an election which would result in their being forced to pay tax for which they have no funds, the trustees of an associated settlement are not so fortunate. It is quite possible for a variation to raise their tax liability because the aggregation of the settled fund in which the deceased had a life interest with the free estate may involve a sharing of the nil rate band, and their proportion of it will be diluted by an increase in the taxable free estate. Such trustees may think it provident to check on the possibility of a variation of the deceased's dispositions before distributing the settled funds.

4.29 OTHER SIMILAR IHT RELIEFS

(a) Under s. 144 IHTA where distributions are made within two years from a discretionary trust set up by the will. The advantage of the short term or mini-discretionary trust, as it is sometimes called, is that the appropriate variations can be carried out without the consents required under s. 142: see *ante* 2.5 and footnote 1 thereto.

(b) Under s. 143 where a beneficiary within two years of the date of death complies with a non-binding request from the testator to pass property on to a third party; a useful device for a gift of personal chattels to a friend or relative, delegating to him or her the task of distributing individual items in accordance with an informal letter of wishes; but there is no corresponding TCGA provision, so the legatee will have to rely upon the annual exemption or the chattels exemption.

(c) Under s. 145 where the surviving spouse exercises the right to capitalise a life interest under intestacy.

4.30 FAMILY PROVISION

A person domiciled in England and Wales has complete freedom of disposition by will; there is no equivalent in this country to the restrictions which exist in France and Germany in favour of close relatives of the deceased. Even in Scotland a testator may be restrained by the knowledge that his spouse and issue will be entitled to 'legal rights', consisting of shares in his moveable estate, whatever dispositions he makes in his will or leaves under intestacy. Nevertheless, the apparent freedom which the English testator enjoys is illusory and has been so since 1938, when the Inheritance (Family Provision) Act was passed. This statute, based upon a New Zealand model in operation since the beginning of the century, gave the courts a discretionary power to make provision for surviving spouses and (subject to conditions) for children where it was found that the deceased had not made reasonable provision for them in his will.

4.31 THE 1975 ACT

In 1975 the 1938 Act was replaced by the Inheritance (Provision for Family and Dependants) Act, which substantially extended the range of persons who qualified as possible applicants to the court for financial provision out of a deceased's estate. The power of the court to award such provision remained discretionary. In one way it would be better if a system of fixed rights applied (as in Scotland). Since the whole scheme of things under the Act is discretionary nobody can know for certain what the outcome of an application can be although, in many cases, a fairly shrewd guess can be made. The legislation applies only to the estates of persons who died domiciled in England and Wales (see *ante* 3.29 *et seq.*); if there is any doubt about the deceased's domicile, it is up to an applicant to satisfy the court that the deceased was so domiciled.

Unlike the 1938 Act, the 1975 version applies also to intestacies.

4.32 TIME LIMIT

An application to the court under the 1975 Act must be made within six months of the date of the grant to the estate (s. 4). It must be a full or residuary grant. Occasionally there may be successive grants, as in *Re Freeman* (1984) where the original grant of probate was revoked when it was proved that the will was not duly executed. A grant of letters of administration was then made; the court held that the six-month period ran from the date of the *effective* grant – in this case, of course, the second one.

Under s. 4, the court has power to allow an application after the end of the six-month period. An applicant who wishes to apply out-of-time must convince the court that it will be just and proper to allow this. In *Re Salmon* (1981) the applicant asked the court for leave to make an application five and a half months after the six-month period had expired; there had been no warning that an application was in the offing until four and a half months after the end of the period, by which time most of the estate had been distributed. The fault for the delay was entirely with the applicant and her solicitors, and the court refused leave for the out-of-time application to be made. *Re Dennis* (1981) makes it clear that any late applicant must convince the court that he has an arguable case for claiming provision out of the estate. Another factor which the court takes into account in deciding such cases is whether a refusal will leave the applicant without redress against anybody – for instance, it may be possible for the applicant to sue solicitors for negligence where the delay has been due to their faulty advice. Whatever the result of such an application, a PR who has distributed an estate *after* the end of the six-month period will not be liable simply on the ground that the court might give leave for an out-of-time application (s. 20). If the PR is on notice that such an application may be made, then distribution should not be made without care – see *post* 4.45.

4.33   DEATH OF APPLICANT

The right to apply for financial provision out of an estate under the 1975 Act is personal to the applicant – it does not survive for the benefit of the applicant's estate. In *Re Bramwell* (1988) a widow was on the point of commencing proceedings under the Act when she died. Her PRs sought to bring proceedings in her place, but the court ordered them to be struck out. Until an actual order under the Act had been made, no cause of action survived for the benefit of a deceased applicant's estate.

4.34   QUALIFYING APPLICANTS

Listed in s. 1(1) are the five classes of person qualified to make applications under the Act:

(a)   the wife or husband of the deceased;

(b)   a former wife or former husband of the deceased who has not remarried;

(c)   a child of the deceased;

(d)   any person (not being a child of the deceased) who, in the case of any marriage to which the deceased was at any time a party, was treated by the deceased as a child of the family in relation to that marriage;

(e)   any person (not being a person included in the foregoing paragraphs of this subsection) who immediately before the death of the deceased was being maintained, either wholly or partly, by the deceased;

s. 1(3) states:

For the purposes of subsection (1)(e) above, a person shall be treated as being maintained by the deceased, either wholly or partly, as the case may be, if the deceased, otherwise than for full valuable consideration, was making a substantial contribution in money or money's worth towards the reasonable needs of that person.

'Wife or husband' of the deceased includes a party to a void or voidable marriage which had not been annulled during the deceased's life; also a judicially separated spouse (but see *post* 4.39). It also includes one wife out of several in the case of a polygamous marriage – *Re Sehota* (1978). Classes (a) and (b) applicants may be inhibited from making an application if, on the decree of divorce or nullity or judicial separation, the court ordered that such an application should not be made – the intention being that there should be a 'clean break' and that nothing should be done to disturb this. Under s. 25(1) 'child of the deceased' includes children *en ventre sa mère* at the date of death, and illegitimate children; adopted children are also included: s. 39 Adoption Act 1976 but the same provision excludes a natural child of the deceased who has been adopted by someone else – he then becomes a child of the adopter: see *Re Collins* (1990).

4.35 PERSON TREATED AS A CHILD OF THE FAMILY – S. 1(1)(d)

This is a new category and has given rise to some litigation. *Re Callaghan* (1984) concerned an application by an adult stepson of the deceased. When his mother married the deceased he was 35 and clearly had not been brought up as a child of the marriage. However, he had always kept a close relationship with his stepfather and he and his wife looked after the stepfather for several months prior to his death. It was held that the applicant qualified under para.(d). *Re Leach* (1985) may be regarded as making this classification even broader in scope, since the applicant, a woman of 53, had never lived with her father and stepmother and had a close relationship with the latter only after the father's death. Nevertheless, she was held entitled to make an application for provision out of her stepmother's estate and was, in fact, awarded half of it.

4.36 PERSON MAINTAINED BY THE DECEASED – S. 1(1)(e)

This, too, is a new category and has given rise to litigation. In fact, the first reported claim under the Act concerned an application by a 'maintained person' – see *Re Wilkinson* (1978), where a sister of the deceased had taken up residence with her, sharing the housework and the cooking. The deceased, who suffered increasingly from ill-health and subsequently was able to do less and less around the house, paid all the household expenses, including the food bills. The applicant continued to do what she could with housework and provided companionship and personal services to the deceased. When the deceased died in 1976, the applicant did not feel that the will made reasonable provision for her and applied to the court under the Act. On the preliminary point, whether the applicant was in fact being maintained by the deceased other than for full valuable consideration, the court found in the applicant's favour. What the deceased had been providing for the applicant before she died outweighed what the applicant had been providing for the deceased. This is the sort of balancing act which has to be done in all cases where the applicant claims to be entitled to apply as a s. 1(1)(e) person; qualifying in this way does not mean, of course, that the actual application for provision out of the estate will be successful. This will depend upon the objective view taken by the court of the provision made by the deceased for the applicant.

Apart from the special standard for surviving spouses (see *post* 4.39), reasonable financial provision means what it would be reasonable for the applicant to receive for his maintenance: s. 1(2)(b). 'Maintenance' was defined by Brown-Wilkinson J. in *Re Dennis* (1981) as:

'payments which directly or indirectly enable the applicant in the future to discharge the cost of his daily living at whatever standard of living is appropriate for him. The provision that is to be made is to meet recurring expenses of living of an income nature.'

One recent family provision case also concerns an application by a 'maintained person'. This is *Bishop* v *Plumley* (1991); the deceased and the applicant lived together as man and wife, the deceased providing their home. In return the applicant cared for the deceased. His will left his estate to his son and daughter, and the court held that the applicant who had applied for provision out of the estate was entitled to do so. She had not given full valuable consideration for the maintenance she had received from the deceased. Her care of him was 'part of the mutuality of their relationship'. As the court said:

'Is he or she to be in a less advantageous situation ... than one who may be less loving and gave less attention to the partner? I do not accept that this could have been the intention of Parliament in passing the legislation.'

It has been said in the past that the more a maintained person does in return for maintenance, the less likely are they to qualify as a maintained applicant, since they would run the risk of having given full valuable consideration for the maintenance. But the court has said that this balancing act cannot be an exact exercise in pounds and pence, and that it would not be right to deprive a person in the position of the applicant in *Bishop* v *Plumley* of the right to ask for provision – see *Jelley* v *Iliffe* (1981), p. 141. At the same time, it does appear that such applicants survive as claimants only because the court is prepared to take a fairly liberal approach to the interpretation of the relevant passages in the 1975 Act.

4.37 'IMMEDIATELY BEFORE THE DEATH'

It will be recalled that a person who wishes to apply for provision on the grounds that he was being maintained by the deceased must show that maintenance was being provided 'immediately before the death of the deceased'; this does not mean literally what it says; in *Re Beaumont* (1980) the deceased had been in hospital at the date of her death and was clearly not maintaining the applicant at that moment in time. But Megarry VC said that what had to be considered was not the *de facto* state of maintenance at the moment of death, but the *general* arrangement then existing for the maintenance of the applicant.

4.38 REASONABLE FINANCIAL PROVISION

Once an applicant has surmounted the first hurdle, i.e. has satisfied the court that he is indeed qualified to make an application, he has two more obstacles to overcome before he can claim success; in the first place, he has to satisfy the court that the provisions contained in the deceased's will, or under the intestacy rules, are not such as to make reasonable financial provision for him. Secondly, and assuming that he can convince the court that this is so, he must persuade the court that it should exercise its discretion in his favour and order such provision to be made for him out of the deceased's estate.

4.39 TWO STANDARDS OF PROVISION

Section 1(2) of the 1975 Act sets out two different standards of 'reasonable financial provision':

    (a)   in the case of an application made by virtue of subsection (1)(a) above by the husband or wife of the deceased (except where the marriage with the deceased was the subject of a decree of judicial separation and at the date of death the decree was in force and the separation was continuing), means such financial provision as it would be reasonable in all the circumstances of the case for a husband or wife to receive, *whether or not that provision is required for his or her maintenance* [emphasis supplied];

    (b)   in the case of any other application made by virtue of subsection (1) above, means such financial provision as it would be reasonable in all the circumstances of the case for the applicant to receive *for his maintenance* [emphasis supplied].

The court tests the provision (or lack of it) by objective standards – the views, state of mind, motives and so on of the deceased are irrelevant. Section 3(5) directs the court to take into account the facts as known to the court at the date of the hearing, including anything relevant that has occurred since the date of death. One might say that it is the *result* of the dispositions made by the deceased (or derived from his intestacy) viewed in the light of current circumstances which will be tested by the court as reasonable or otherwise.

4.40 THE GUIDELINES

Section 3 of the Act contains a long list of 'matters' which the court, when considering whether provision made for the applicant is 'reasonable' and the exercise of its discretion in favour of the applicant, shall have regard to. Special attention is to be paid in respect of surviving spouses (other than judicially separated ones) to, amongst other things, 'the provision which the applicant might reasonably have expected to receive' if the marriage had been ended by divorce rather than death – in other words, the section is equating provision for the surviving spouse after death with that which a court might have awarded on divorce – not a very apposite comparison. In the case of applications by 'maintained' persons, the court is to have regard to the extent to which and the basis upon which the deceased assumed responsibility for the applicant's maintenance and the length of time for which that responsibility was discharged.

Amongst the general guidelines, note especially s. 3(1)(e) – size and nature of the net estate – and s. 3(1)(g) – conduct of the applicant or any other person which the court may consider relevant. In this connection, Lord Denning once said the question to ask was whether it would be repugnant to anyone's sense of justice if an order for financial provision were made.

4.41   LUMP SUM PROVISION

It is clear from the reports that the fact that an applicant is entitled only to provision for maintenance does not mean that a lump sum cannot be provided; in *Re Callaghan* and *Re Leach* (4.35 *ante*) the applicants were awarded £15,000 and half the net estate respectively. Both cases concerned applications by adults of full capacity. Such applications are not always successful – in *Re Coventry* (1979) an application by a 40-year-old son of the deceased who was in good health and full-time employment was dismissed. It seems probable that applications of this kind will be unsuccessful unless special circumstances exist which will predispose the court in favour of the applicant.

4.42   PROVISION FOR SURVIVING SPOUSE

Re Bunning (1984) is an interesting example of the kind of provision likely to be made for a widow. The net estate was worth some £237,000 and the deceased's will made no provision for the widow, who had helped the deceased substantially with his business affairs. The court awarded her £60,000 which, with her own assets, would roughly equalise her estate with what remained of her husband's. It is clear that regard was being paid to the 'divorce' guide referred to *ante* 4.40. Nevertheless, the suggestion has been made* that the court is not always sufficiently generous to surviving spouses, having regard to the important distinction drawn in the Act between applications by them and applications by other persons. It has to be remembered that under the original legislation of 1938 surviving spouses were entitled to claim maintenance provision out of an estate only on the same level as everyone else.

4.43   ANTI-AVOIDANCE PROVISIONS

Where a deceased has made a disposition not more than six years before the date of his death with the intention of defeating an application for

---

*See 'Provision for a Surviving Spouse' by Professor Miller, (1986) 102 LQR 445.

provision under the Act, the court may make an order requiring the donee to provide such sum of money or other property as may be specified towards any financial provision which the court orders in favour of an applicant – s. 10(2). Dispositions which are caught by this provision are those made other than for full valuable consideration; they include the payment of premiums on a policy but not the exercise of a special power of appointment. Personal Representatives of a donee who have distributed an estate in ignorance of the possibility of an anti-avoidance order are protected by s. 12(4); as are trustees who distribute property put into trust by the deceased – s. 13(2).

Dawkins v *Judd* (1986) is an example of the kind of situation to which these anti-avoidance provisions apply; shortly before he died the deceased transferred the matrimonial home to his daughter. The court found that this transfer was made with the intention of defeating an application under the Act, and ordered that £10,000 from the proceeds of sale of the house should be paid to the widow.

Section 11 additionally attacks contracts entered into by the deceased which bind his PRs to provide gifts from his estate and which are intended to defeat an application under the Act. The contract must have been made after 31 March 1976, but remains vulnerable whenever the deceased dies. There are again protecting provisions for PRs and trustees.

4.44   PRs AND FAMILY PROVISION CLAIMS

The PR who becomes aware that a family provision claim is in the offing should, strictly speaking, preserve a non-committal attitude. It is not for him to take sides in a dispute between the beneficiaries on the one hand and the claimant(s) on the other (the two categories are not mutually exclusive, of course). He should, however, make it his business to see that the interests of infant and unborn children are properly represented. Otherwise, it is his duty to assist the parties impartially by providing information about the estate and its assets as and when this is needed; when proceedings commence, the PR is obliged to lodge an affidavit giving details of the estate and its beneficiaries – RSC O 99 r 5. Where all parties are *sui juris*, any settlement which may be negotiated (it is always desirable for such a settlement to be considered) can be embodied in a deed of family arrangement, and the sanction of the court is not required; if proceedings have actually been started in such a case, the action may be stayed by means of a 'Tomlin' order,[4] the terms of the settlement being embodied in a schedule to the order. If one or more beneficiaries are not *sui juris*, then any proposed arrangement must be referred to the court, which will then make an order. In such cases the provisions of the order (including a consent order) are deemed to have had effect for all purposes (including income tax, CGT and IHT) as from the date of death – see s. 19(1) of the Act and s. 146

IHTA. In effect, the successful applicant becomes the equivalent of a beneficiary under the will or intestacy: *Re Pointer* (1946).

4.45 DISTRIBUTIONS PENDING RESOLUTION OF APPLICATION

It will be understood that until a dispute of this kind is disposed of, the PR is in some difficulty; he is inhibited from making any beneficial distribution because he cannot be certain that the interests provided for in the will or under the intestacy will remain undisturbed. This dilemma has been discussed in *Re Simson* (1950) and *Re Ralphs* (1968). The former case shows that the provision made for an applicant will not necessarily be ordered to be made out of residue only, although this is the usual course. Where a will gives substantial legacies and the residue is relatively small, the legatees may well bear some of the burden of the provision ordered. Thus the PR may seem precluded from distributing any part of the estate. Where, however, the applicant herself (or himself) is given some benefit by the will, *Re Ralphs* makes it clear that this should not normally be withheld. The PR may also at his discretion make other payments, e.g. where there are a few small legacies and a substantial residue, making it safe to pay the legacies. He might probably also pay someone with a high moral claim who is suffering hardship. If he is in doubt about making some payment he may ask any person who might be prejudiced for his consent. In the absence of such consent the PR may apply to the court for authority. If the court thinks that a consent was unreasonably withheld it can throw the costs of the application on the party to blame (see the last paragraph of Cross J.'s judgment in *Re Ralphs*).

4.46 INTERIM PROVISION

The moral of this is that PRs should make it their business to consider whether any beneficiary is likely to suffer by being deprived of his or her benefit under the will or intestacy so long as a claim is pending. If this does appear to be the case they should then assess the risks of providing that beneficiary with interim payments, if necessary with the consent of other parties or perhaps with the backing of the court. An applicant under the Act who is in immediate need may, pending disposal of the application, ask the court to order interim provision under s. 5.

4.47 PRs – PRECAUTIONS PENDING EXPIRY OF TIME LIMIT

The time limit imposed on applicants (*ante* 4.32) prevents the threat of a claim from holding up the distribution for an extended period. Clearly there *is* an impediment during the period running up to the end of the six months subsequent to the grant. Personal Representatives have always (since the 1938 Act came into force) run some risk during this period when distributing capital because of the possibility that a family provision claim might subsequently be made, but at least the class of possible applicants was small and not difficult to identify. It was also not usually a great problem 'to form a view' about the likelihood of a family provision claim. That no reported cases exist of PRs being criticised for distributing an estate in advance of a claim shows that the risk involved is not, perhaps, a very serious one.

The extension of the class of potential applicants effected by the 1975 Act creates a wider area of doubt, and PRs need to exert greater caution. It is difficult to suggest guidelines for them because each estate will have to be dealt with in the light of its own facts. It may be desirable to make enquiries to see whether a claim is likely to be made, e.g. where the deceased was living with someone who could qualify as a 'maintained' applicant. Scrutiny of the deceased's bank accounts during recent years may reveal the existence of maintenance payments to a possible applicant. Publication of the statutory notices for claims (*ante* 3.26) is all the more essential; failure to publish might inhibit the court from granting relief to the PRs under s. 61 TA (see *post* 14.19). The earlier a grant is issued, the shorter the length of time between the date of death and the date when capital distributions become risk-free – so far as the PRs are concerned. Perhaps it might be fair to say that where a small estate is given entirely to a surviving spouse with whom the deceased was living when he died, there is little risk in making a substantial payment on account during the period available for claims – provided, that is, no actual notice of a claim has been received. A PR who receives such notice must then proceed only in accordance with the guidance provided by Cross, J. in *Re Ralphs* (see *ante* 4.45). In the larger estates the cautious approach will be to distribute income where appropriate, but to make only modest payments on account in respect of capital benefits.

It may also be noted here that any order made by the court in favour of an applicant is made out of the 'net estate' of the deceased under s. 2(1) and that 'net estate' is widely defined to include, *inter alia*, nominated property and death-bed gifts (s. 8) and the deceased's severable share of joint assets (s. 9) so, taking into account the 'claw-back' effect of the anti-avoidance provisions (see *ante* 4.43). The court's powers are wide-ranging both as to the form its orders may take and as to the property to which it has access for the purposes of such orders.

Comment here about the possible merits of claims and the way in which the court may interpret them for the purposes of making orders under the 1975 Act would be inappropriate. The role of the PR in this field is a neutral one. The applicant and the beneficiaries are the active participants. The latter should be told to seek advice from their solicitors – the same firm can,

95

if necessary, advise both PRs and beneficiaries, but they will be represented separately in court. Beneficiaries who are minors or under some other disability will need to be separately advised and represented. In all cases, the possibility of compromising the application should be considered; the cost of an action of this kind fought to the end may demolish a small estate (as to PRs' powers of compromising claims, see *post* 5.4).

4.48   COSTS

This may be an appropriate place at which to mention the subject of costs in more detail; where PRs and trustees instruct solicitors to initiate and continue litigation on their behalf then they are, of course, personally liable to the solicitors for costs so incurred. If the litigation is prosecuted to a conclusion, the question of costs of both plaintiff and defendant will normally be decided by the court after the matter is concluded one way or the other. How the burden of costs is to be borne is entirely at the discretion of the court, but the *general* rule (not the inevitable one) is that costs follow the event, i.e. the loser pays both his own costs and those of the other side. He will, of course, be personally responsible for his own costs anyway (ignoring the subject of legal aid); the amount to be paid in respect of the winner's costs is calculated in accordance with rules of court, the basis of taxation and the scale appropriate to the case. The sums allowed for individual items are entirely within the discretion of the Taxing Master of the High Court (or Registrar in a County Court case), to whom the itemised bills of costs are submitted. Such costs will be taxed either on a standard basis, which will cover all costs which are reasonable in nature and amount (the benefit of the doubt being given to the paying party) or on an indemnity basis, which will cover all costs except those of an unreasonable amount or which were unreasonably incurred (the benefit of the doubt being given to the receiving party). Normally a loser will have to pay the winner's costs on the standard basis, but the indemnity basis might be invoked if, e.g., his case were considered wholly unmeritorious.

It follows that a winner who is awarded costs by the court will not necessarily be wholly indemnified by the loser – in fact, it would be unusual if this happened. However, a PR or trustee who has properly fought and won an action should be entitled to defray any costs not paid by the loser out of the estate or trust involved, under the normal rule as to reimbursement of expenses incurred. Where litigation is settled before it gets into court then it is open to the parties to agree between themselves how costs incurred so far should be allocated. Such an agreement can be embodied in the terms of a 'Tomlin' order, see *ante* 4.44 and note 4. Where there is an agreed application to court – as, for instance, for variation of a trust, *post* 13.6 *et seq.* – the order asked for can include a term directing that costs of all parties shall be paid out of the subject-matter of the application.

5 Dealing with the liabilities and the assets

5.1 OBJECTIVES OF PERSONAL REPRESENTATIVES

The first objective of the PR is to obtain his grant, whether of probate or of letters of administration. When this objective is achieved, he moves on to his second, which is to complete the collection and control of the assets, and then to his third, which is to sell so much of the assets as is either necessary or desirable in the particular circumstances of the estate – see *ante* 3.17. He will have begun this process before obtaining a grant but, until his title is established by the court, his actions are necessarily restricted. The adroit administrator of estates, however, maps out his realisation policy at an early stage, reserving to himself the right to make such changes as circumstances dictate.

During this period it is imperative for the PR to keep in mind the requirements and wishes of the beneficiaries. He will probably have already discussed with them the steps to be taken once a grant is issued – whether a property shall be sold or retained, whether stocks and shares should be sold or transferred as part of a distribution. Assets which are the subject of specific gifts should (subject to administration requirements) be dealt with only in accordance with the wishes of the devisee or legatee.

If the PR is to make the speedy progress which is so desirable *after* issue of the grant he must make his plans *before* this happens – in fact, as soon as he has a reasonably accurate picture of the whole estate. At that time he establishes his basic strategy for the whole campaign.

5.2 POWERS OF PERSONAL REPRESENTATIVES

Personal Representatives have always had very wide powers to sell personal property (including leaseholds) for administration purposes, and s. 2(1) AEA extends these powers to real property. Certain powers, such as a power to postpone sale where a trust for sale is imposed, are often found in wills and, where they exist, the PR will note them and use them as occasion demands. He has, in any case, a full range of statutory powers available and it will be recalled that s. 33 AEA imposes a trust for sale on the death of a person intestate as to any real or personal estate (subject to what may be in the will, if any): see *ante* 4.3 and 4.14. There are also the very important provisions of s. 39 AEA, which give to all PRs powers of sale and mortgage of any real or personal estate of the deceased 'for administration purposes' and confer on them the same statutory powers (including SLA powers) in relation to land and the proceeds of sale of land as are given to trustees for sale by s. 28(1) LPA. Sections 36 and 39 AEA, which deal with assents by PRs and their management powers respectively, have been described as perhaps the two most important sections of the Act. Section 39 applies only to the duties of PRs as such but is extended, specifically, to cover the minority of a beneficiary or the subsistence of a life interest. Other important powers dealt with elsewhere in this book are:

— the power to appropriate under s. 41 AEA: *post* 6.35,36;
— the power to employ agents under s. 23 TA: *post* 5.45 *et seq.*;
— the power to compromise and compound liabilities under s. 15 TA: *post* 5.4;
— the powers of investment under the TIA: *post* ch. 11.

It is important to remember the non-statutory power which gives all PRs the same rights of action with regard to assets of the estate as belonged to the deceased; where an asset is improperly withheld from the PR he may sue for it in the courts and should not hesitate to do so if the circumstances demand this in the interests of the beneficiaries (subject to the need to ensure that the costs involved may properly be incurred – see *post* 5.12).

Possession of the grant enables PRs to move forward in earnest. This chapter is concerned with some of the problems which may be met in dealing with particular types of asset, including valuation as at the date of death. The basis of such valuation for taxation purposes is the price which an asset might reasonably be expected to fetch if sold in the open market at that time – s. 160 IHTA – see *post* 5.24.

In exercising a power of sale, a PR should take care to ensure that he is striking a bargain which cannot successfully be attacked. The best way of achieving this is to sell under advice at arm's length in an open market. In the case of quoted stocks and shares, a sale through a member of the Stock Exchange is an example of such a sale. Advice from a properly qualified and independent agent is often desirable and is particularly so where the sale is either not at arm's length, e.g. to a beneficiary (which is not, in itself, improper), or not in the open market, e.g. a sale of unquoted shares.

Both PRs and trustees must bear in mind the necessity of getting the best price on a sale, irrespective of any moral principle which might serve to deter a private individual: *Buttle* v *Saunders* (1950), see *post* 10.5.

5.3 SALES TO THE PRs THEMSELVES

A PR (and a trustee) *may* buy estate or trust assets, but such sales are always liable to be set aside, however fair the price, unless authorised by (a) the court or (b) the trust instrument or (c) the beneficiaries. The reason for questioning them is that neither a PR nor a trustee should place himself in a position where his duty and self-interest dictate opposite courses. For an example of authorisation by the trust instrument of such a sale, see *Re*

Hayes (1971); the testator gave his executors and trustees, one of whom was his son, power to sell certain land to the son at the estate duty valuation. The court upheld the exercise by the executors of this power, notwithstanding complaints by the deceased's daughters. The court added that, when agreeing an estate duty valuation, it is the duty of the executors to consider the interest of the estate as a whole, not the effect between different classes of beneficiaries. The rule against selling to interested parties applies also to persons clearly connected with the estate such as the estate solicitor but not to cases where the contract was made before the fiduciary relationship arose. There may be special circumstances which enable the court to approve a sale to a PR or trustee, as in *Holder* v *Holder* (1968), where the purchaser was technically a PR but his connection with the administration was minimal: see *ante* 3.9 also. As regards authorisation by beneficiaries, if all of them are ascertained and of full capacity, a sale of estate assets to a PR is feasible. A beneficiary who has concurred in the sale cannot afterwards complain of it. However, a PR who wishes to rely on such authority will be sensible if he insists on a formal document to which the beneficiaries are made parties only after having been fully informed and after having received independent advice. The remedy of a beneficiary who has *not* authorised a PR to purchase an estate asset is to apply to the court to have the transaction set aside and for any profit accruing to the PR out of the purchase to be recovered. It must also be remembered that a person who buys such an asset from the PR with notice of the fiduciary office will be affected if the court sets the first sale aside, and fear of such an eventuality could inhibit subsequent transactions. Joining the beneficiaries in the conveyance to the PR is one solution to this problem, but will not necessarily be effective. Trustees are in the same position as PRs so far as this subject is concerned: see *post* 9.34 and 9.38.

A purchase by a PR or trustee of his beneficiary's *beneficial interest* is not so strictly controlled, but is always liable to be set aside if there is any hint of unfair dealing. Note also s. 68 SLA enabling the tenant for life to have dealings with the trust fund – see *post* 11.18.

5.4 PAYING THE DEBTS

Personal Representatives should pay and settle just debts and claims against the estate as soon as convenient. Funeral expenses have priority. Where a residence continues to be occupied, early payment of household bills, e.g. for food and services, is desirable. In other cases payment can wait until cash is available from the sale of assets. When this happens, payment of all outstanding debts should take place. Some debts, e.g. for the tax liability to the date of death, will not be finally established until some time later but a payment on account can be made where interest is mounting up, as will be the case where a tax assessment has been received.

Section 15 TA gives PRs (and trustees) a very wide discretion for the settlement of debts and claims. They may, for instance, pay or allow a debt or a claim on such evidence as they think fit and may compromise, abandon or otherwise settle any debt upon terms and without being liable for loss – provided they act in good faith. The section covers a much wider area than that covered by the ordinary debt incurred for business or household purposes; it is wide enough, for instance, to cover the compromise by PRs of a claim for provision from the estate by a disappointed dependant of the deceased: see *ante* 4.30 *et seq.* It is also wide enough to entitle PRs and trustees to accept a compromise which involves a variation of the beneficial interests over which they preside – see *Re Earl of Strafford* (1980) where Megarry VC said:

> 'The trustees must listen to the beneficiaries and pay attention to their wishes, but even if all of them oppose the proposed compromise, the trustees have power under s. 15 to agree a proposed compromise.'

Personal Representatives and trustees should, however, bear in mind that the section requires an *active* exercise of their discretion – simply failing to collect debts due to the estate would not be a proper exercise of the statutory power.

5.5 UNKNOWN DEBTS AND DOUBTFUL DEBTS

Notwithstanding the existence of this wide discretion, a debt or claim should not be settled without satisfactory evidence of its authenticity. In general, PRs should not pay debts which need not be paid, whether because they are unenforceable or for any other reason; there is one exception to this rule, where the *only* reason for unenforceability is the fact that the debt is statute-barred, e.g. under s. 5 Limitation Act 1980 (action on simple contract barred after six years). Personal Representatives may pay the debt if they wish (but if the court has declared the debt statute-barred it must not be paid).

It must be remembered that, basically, the estate and its PRs are liable for *all* the outstanding debts of the deceased when he died, whether or not they have come to light. Even after having settled all known debts, a PR is still at risk, if he distributes the estate, of being faced with a claim from a previously unknown creditor. The only protection against this risk is to publish notices for claims in accordance with s. 27 TA – see *ante* 3.25. Having done this and waited for expiration of the period of notices (this must be at least two months) the PR may distribute the estate:

> having regard only to the claims, whether formal or not, of which the trustees or personal representatives then had notice and shall not, as respects the property so conveyed or distributed, be liable to any person of whose claim [they] have not had notice at the time.

All professional executors will be familiar with the problems caused by contingent liabilities – possible debts or claims which may or may not crystallise as certainties. It is foolish to ignore their existence, but what can be done? It is not unknown, for instance, for a claim to be made against an estate on account of services rendered to the deceased during his life, and for the PRs to reject the claim on the grounds that its validity has not been proved to their satisfaction. Suppose the claimant then does nothing – he neither prosecutes his claim nor withdraws it. Should the PRs distribute the whole estate in the hope that the claim will not be revived and pursued? They would be running a risk in doing so – possibly one which is judged small enough to be covered by a joint and several indemnity from the beneficiaries. Alternatively, they have the power to retain a reasonable reserve to meet the contingency. This course would not be so popular. If the sum involved is a large one, they would be wise to consider getting the directions of the court.

5.6 GUARANTEES

Frequently the PRs find out that the deceased had guaranteed the banking account of a relative or business concern in which he was interested. Guarantees are potentially dangerous and should be handled firmly but with care. The law is clear enough – where a guarantee secures an immediately enforceable debt the guarantor is entitled to call on the principal debtor to relieve him from his responsibilities by paying off the debt. For an example of the application of this principle in practice, see *Thomas* v *Nottingham Incorporated Football Club Ltd* (1972). The death of the guarantor will not normally end liability; the rights of creditor and guarantor will be regulated by the terms of the instrument creating the guarantee. If the terms permit, PRs should take prompt steps to bring the estate's commitment to an end, firstly by giving notice of termination to the creditor bank, secondly by asking the principal debtor to make other arrangements. How much time may be allowed for this process is a matter for judgment in each case, but to allow negotiations to drag on indefinitely exposes the estate – and the PRs – to risk. On the other hand, too much haste in determining the guarantee may precipitate the bank into calling in the guarantee, leaving the PRs with the dubious privilege of seeking recovery from the principal debtor.

The secondary liability of a guarantor must be carefully distinguished from the liability of an indemnifier as principal. Under a contract of indemnity there is an obligation to take over the liability, when it arises, as principal debtor, with no recourse against the person indemnified.

5.7 INSOLVENT ESTATES

Where the estate is insolvent, the order in which debts are paid becomes extremely important. The rules for priority of debts on bankruptcy are now found in the Insolvency Act 1986 as modified by various orders made under it, including in particular the Administration of Insolvent Estates of Deceased Persons Order 1986, under which the reasonable funeral, testamentary and administration expenses have priority over preferential debts. Preferential debts rank equally amongst themselves and include (a) income tax due to the Revenue under PAYE for one year; (b) VAT, car tax, betting and gaming duties for limited periods; (c) Social Security and pension scheme contributions due for the previous twelve months; and (d) remuneration due to employees for four months, subject to a maximum of £800 for each employee. Non-preferred debts also rank equally amongst themselves. Debts due to a spouse are deferred debts and are thus payable only after the preferential and ordinary creditors have been paid in full, including interest.

If no one has presented a petition for bankruptcy (either the deceased himself when he was alive or a creditor or the PR), an estate may be administered in the ordinary way by the PR, even though it appears to be insolvent or could become insolvent if the assets do not realise as much as expected. Whether there is a formal bankruptcy (for which it is essential to employ a qualified insolvency practitioner) or an informal administration by the PR, the priority rules are the same. So if there is any doubt about the solvency of the estate, the priority rules should be strictly observed; they cannot be varied by the testator. Improper allocation of the resources of an insolvent estate may well result in the PR's becoming personally liable for any resulting deficit. The risk is that a PR may pay a debt 'out of turn', thus implying that he has enough funds to pay (a) all prior debts and (b) all debts of equal degree to the one just paid. It will often be prudent to pay only 'priority' debts in full until the limits of the estate's financial resources are clearly established. Note, however, the protection given by s. 10(2) AEA 1971 to a PR who pays a debt (including one owed to himself) in the honest belief that the estate is solvent. If it subsequently becomes clear that it is insolvent, he is protected against claims by creditors of the same degree as the one paid.

'Testamentary and administration expenses' will include all costs which a PR may properly incur in the course of establishing control over assets, obtaining a grant and managing and realising assets for administration purposes. It will also include the cost of obtaining legal advice on appropriate aspects of the case, such as its insolvency. The phrase will *not* include a professional executor's fee for acting as such.

5.8   SECURED CREDITORS IN AN INSOLVENT ESTATE

The privileged position of the secured creditor should be borne in mind; provided his security is sufficient in value to cover his debt he remains unaffected by the insolvency or its order of priority for payment of unsecured debts. Under the 1986 legislation he can do one of four things:

(a) Rely on his security and not prove for his debt.
(b) Realise his security and prove for the balance.
(c) Surrender his security and prove for the whole of the debt.
(d) Set a value on his security and prove for the balance.

The property on which the debt is secured is, of course, not within the control of the PR.

5.9 CAUSES OF ACTION

Section 1(1) Law Reform (Miscellaneous Provisions) Act 1934 says that, on the death of any person, all causes of action subsisting against or vested in him shall survive against, or, as the case may be, for the benefit of, his estate. If the deceased had a claim either for breach of contract or in respect of a negligent or other tortious act, his PRs may bring the appropriate action on behalf of his estate. Equally, of course, his estate may be sued in either contract or tort. Where an action was in midstream, so to speak, at the date of death then, provided the cause of action survives, the action may proceed; application is made to join in the action the deceased's PRs in place of the deceased. If no such PRs exist the opposing plaintiff or defendant can ask the court to appoint a person to represent the estate for the purposes of the action or, alternatively, for the court to authorise the action to proceed in the absence of any representative of the deceased litigant – see RSC O 15 r 15.

5.10 CAUSES OF ACTION THAT DO NOT SURVIVE

Some causes of action, such as defamation, do not survive death; contracts for personal service (such as authorship) are discharged by death (unless there is express provision to the contrary), but a cause of action over such a contract, which had already arisen before death, will survive either for or against the deceased's estate. (It should, perhaps, be made clear that a PR is bound to honour non-personal contracts entered into by the deceased, such as a contract for the purchase or sale of a house, up to the limits imposed by the size of the estate and the existence of other commitments; if the estate is insufficient to meet all its liabilities it must be dealt with as an insolvent case; see *ante* 5.7.) Exemplary damages are not recoverable in an action on behalf of an estate.

5.11 LITIGATION IN PROGRESS AT DEATH

Where the deceased was already plaintiff or defendant at the date of death his PRs have a major decision to make. Should they continue to prosecute or defend, or should they seek to stop the action? To do the latter may well mean paying both sets of costs and offering a sum to the other side by way of settlement of the dispute. But to proceed with the action will involve further costs which may ultimately fall on the estate. Section 15(f) TA (see *ante* 5.4) is a comprehensive authority for compromise in such circumstances, but it does not absolve the PRs from making up their own minds. Obviously they will rely heavily upon the views of their legal advisers – solicitors and counsel. They will also heed the views expressed by the residuary beneficiaries, who should be told what is happening. They must eschew recourse to sentiment and emotion, since PRs have no right to squander funds on a lost or doubtful cause, or one not affecting the estate. See, e.g., *Re Dunn* (1904) where an administrator was not allowed to charge against the estate costs incurred in successfully defending an action which did not bear upon the estate.

5.12 INITIATING LITIGATION AFTER DEATH

The same criteria apply to those cases where PRs or trustees either are advised to commence proceedings on their own account or have an action started against them e.g. for some debt incurred by or in favour of a deceased person during his lifetime. In all cases they will be well advised to consider applying to the court for leave to bring the action or defend, as the case may be. This is what is known as a *Re Beddoe* (1893) application. The rule, briefly stated, is that a PR or trustee should not bring or defend an action without the court's approval; if he does not get this, he is at risk with regard to any costs incurred, at any rate to the extent to which such costs exceed what would have been the cost of a *Re Beddoe* application. Of course, if all the beneficiaries are *sui juris* and they all authorise the action or defence, an application to the court is unnecessary; equally, if PRs decide to use their powers under s. 15(f) TA to compromise a claim – certainly a course always to be borne in mind.

A *Re Beddoe* order will not *inevitably* entitle PRs to an indemnity for their costs – it all depends on the facts; see *Evans v Evans* (1986) where the plaintiff was claiming the whole estate and if successful could hardly be expected to meet the defendant administrator's costs. The court may take the view that the beneficiaries of an estate, rather than the estate itself, should bear the cost of an unsuccessful defence of a claim against the estate; in the *Evans* case the Court of Appeal directed the beneficiaries to be joined in the action as defendants, and the executors' role became a passive one.

5.13 PERSONAL INJURY CLAIMS

Claims for damages for personal injury sustained by the deceased survive for the benefit of his estate in the same way as other claims in tort preserved by s. 1(1) Law Reform (Miscellaneous Provisions) Act 1934. Such claims are to be distinguished from those made under the Fatal Accidents Act 1976 (incorporating earlier legislation dating back to 1846). Law Reform Act claims are made for the benefit of the deceased's estate; Fatal Accidents Act claims may be made for a specified class of persons connected with the deceased if they have suffered financially from his death, of whom the most significant members are the surviving spouse and issue of the deceased (including adopted, step- and illegitimate children); s. 3 AJA 1982 (revising ss. 1 to 4 of the 1976 Act) introduced a new member of the class – any person who was living with the deceased as husband or wife when he or she died and had been doing so for at least two years previously.

Notwithstanding that a Fatal Accidents Act claim is made for the benefit of the deceased's dependants rather than for his estate, it is primarily to be brought by his PRs on behalf of members of the specified class. However, if either no such PRs exist or, after six months from the date of death, no action has been brought by them, such action may be brought 'by and in the name of all or any of the persons for whose benefit an executor or administrator could have brought it' – s. 2(2) of the 1976 Act.

5.14 NATURE OF FATAL ACCIDENTS ACT CLAIM AND INTERACTION WITH LAW REFORM ACT

In *Davies* v *Powell Duffryn Associated Collieries Ltd* (1942) Lord Wright gave a pithy explanation of the basis for claims under the Fatal Accidents Acts:

'The claim is for injuriously affecting the family of the deceased. It is not a claim which the deceased could have pursued in his own lifetime, because it is for damages suffered not by himself, but by his family after his death. . . . The damages are to be based on the reasonable expectation of pecuniary benefit or benefit reducible to money value. . . . The actual pecuniary loss of each individual entitled to sue can only be ascertained by balancing, on the one hand, the loss to him of the future pecuniary benefit, and, on the other, any pecuniary advantage which from whatever source comes to him by reason of the death.'

Note, however, that the revised s. 4 of the 1976 Act now provides that benefits accruing to the claimant from the deceased's estate or otherwise as a result of his death shall be disregarded in assessing the damages which may be awarded. See *Pidduck* v *Eastern Scottish Omnibuses Ltd* (1990) in which the court held that an allowance paid by the deceased's former employers to his widow should be disregarded in assessing her damages under the Act. There seems to be no end to the number of questions which can be asked about the application of s. 4; see, e.g., *Wood* v *Bentall Simplex Ltd* (1992) and *Hayden* v *Hayden* (1992). In the former, Beldam LJ said:

'No aspect of the law of damages had been found in practice to be *more dependent on the facts* of each particular case than the assessment of loss of pecuniary benefit to dependants under the 1976 Act.' [emphasis supplied].

This important new provision applies to causes of action arising after 1982. Section 4(2) AJA 1982 also makes an important change to the way in which damages are assessed in claims under the Law Reform Act; they are not to include '(i) any exemplary damages (ii) any damages for loss of income in respect of any person after that person's death'.

Apart from damages for loss of financial support from the deceased, damages may also be awarded under the Fatal Accidents Act for funeral expenses and (from 1983) a new head of damages for 'bereavement' is introduced – see s. 1A of the Act – which is available to a surviving spouse and to the parents of a deceased unmarried infant. Currently, the sum to be awarded under this head is £3,500; it is subject to amendment by the Lord Chancellor. Under the Law Reform Act, claims on behalf of the estate may include (a) special damages as a result of the defendant's wrongful act, (b) general damages for pain and suffering, (c) damages for loss of earnings up to the date of death and (d) funeral and medical expenses.

Whereas damages awarded under the Law Reform Act form part of the deceased's estate for IHT purposes, the Fatal Accidents award goes direct to the family without any payment of tax.

5.15   RESPONSIBILITIES OF PRs

It is clear that PRs have serious responsibilities towards both the estate and the deceased's dependants where death was preceded or was caused by personal injury arising out of the fault of another. Advice should be taken without delay as soon as it is realised that the possibility of a claim exists. It is particularly important to consider at an early stage what evidence will be required to support a claim and how this may be acquired. Adult dependants should be consulted and kept informed about the progress of any action. The time limits for actions for damages for personal injuries under the Law Reform Act and for claims under the Fatal Accidents Act need to be borne in mind. These are now set out in ss. 11 to 14 Limitation Act 1980. Broadly speaking, the available period is three years from the date of death or the date when either the PR or the relevant dependant found out that a claim was a possibility. The court can override the time limits at its discretion.

Deaths occurring as the result of accidents to passengers by air, rail and road may require reference to the Carriage by Air Act 1961, the Carriage by Railway Act 1972 and the Carriage of Passengers by Road Act 1974. The Carriage by Road and Air Act 1979 amends the 1961 and 1974 Acts; the 1972 and 1974 Acts appear to be relevant only where international journeys are involved. All four statutes give effect to international conventions and may be said to extend the principles of the Fatal Accidents Act to accidental deaths during journeys without involving the claimant in the necessity of proving negligence on the part of the carrier but, at the same time, limiting the compensation payable unless negligence can be proved. *Goldman* v *Thai Airways International Ltd* (1983) illustrates the severe restrictions on damages resulting from these statutes; damages of £51,163 in the High Court were reduced to £11,700 by the Court of Appeal, since the plaintiff could not prove that his injuries were caused either by an intent to cause damage or by reckless behaviour of the carrier airline. See *Winfield*, ch. 24, for a general discussion of the survival of causes of action on death and claims under the Fatal Accidents Act.

5.16 THIRD PARTY APPLICATIONS FOR A LITIGATION GRANT

Personal Representatives sometimes have to act as such for the estates of two or more members of the same family, killed as a result of a common accident. If the negligence of one such member contributed to the cause of the accident the PRs find themselves needing to act as both plaintiff and defendant. This is not possible and, in order to deal with the situation, a third party must apply for a grant of administration limited to bringing or defending the action on behalf of the estate. The Official Solicitor may be asked to perform this function.

Mention may perhaps also be made of another somewhat similar provision which is useful where the injured party or his PR wishes to bring an action against the estate of a deceased person but no grant for it has been issued. By s. 87(2) Supreme Court Act 1981 and RSC O 15 r 6A the court may make an order appointing a person to represent an estate for the purposes of defending an action in cases where no grant has been taken out. Again, this is a function which the Official Solicitor may be prepared to accept, subject to his receiving an undertaking to indemnify him for his costs.

5.17 VESTING OF ASSETS ON DEATH

On death, all a deceased person's property vests at once in his executor (if of full age), including, since 1925, any landed property that he owned for an interest not ceasing on his death (s. 1 AEA). Because of the decision in *Re Bridgett & Hayes* (1928), settled land vested in the deceased as tenant for life under the SLA will also vest in his executor, if as the result of his death the land ceases to be settled under the SLA; if the SLA continues to apply, it will vest instead in the trustees of the settlement as the deceased life tenant's special executors under s. 22(1) AEA: see *ante* 2.6 and 3.5.

For the position if there is no will or no executor of full age, see *ante* 3.27. The treatment of settled land will again depend upon whether the fetters of the SLA have dropped off.

5.18 QUOTED STOCKS AND SHARES

No problems arise so far as valuation is concerned; the practice built up in estate duty days is used also for IHT purposes. One takes either:

(a) the lower of the two prices shown in the quotations for the shares or securities in the Stock Exchange Daily Official List (SEDOL) on the relevant date plus one-quarter of the difference between those figures, or
(b) half-way between the highest and lowest prices at which bargains, other than bargains done at special prices, were recorded in the shares or securities for the relevant date,
whichever method produces the lower value.

If no bargains were done on the relevant date, then, of course, method (a) must be used. Neither method will be used if it can be shown, for instance, that the official quotation is not a proper measure of the open market value, as it may well not be if no recent business in the shares has been done. If the Stock Exchange was closed on the relevant date the market value is ascertained by reference to the last available date before or the next available date after – whichever produces the lower figure. This is an advantage for IHT purposes but a disadvantage for CGT. Capital Gains Tax has the same valuation code (s. 272(3) TCGA) and on death the valuations for both taxes are the same (s. 274 TCGA). Where investments are quoted ex dividend the whole of the net dividend or interest should be accounted for separately. Gilt-edged securities are always quoted clean of interest and in this case the accrued income (or a rebate of income, if the death occurs after the books are closed for the next interest payment) is separately accounted for under the accrued income scheme – see *post* 5.22. Company debentures and loan stocks are also within the accrued income scheme but the quoted price allows for the apportioned income or the rebate of it. Unit trust holdings are valued on the basis of the manager's 'bid' price on the relevant date or, failing a quotation on that date, on the latest date before.

A stockbroker will value quoted stocks and shares for probate purposes and will charge a fee for doing so. Alternatively, PRs can produce their own valuations by reference to the relevant SEDOL.

5.19 SALE OF INVESTMENTS BEFORE GRANT

Sales of stocks and shares can be made before a grant is issued, although it should be stressed that such a proceeding is sensible only where it is clear that there is no impediment to the prompt issue of a grant. Stockbrokers should be advised that a grant is being applied for and that the sales are to be effected for deferred delivery. The title to securities sold in this way also needs to be carefully checked, since the scrip has not yet been through the hands of the registrars. It is, nevertheless, better to sell too early rather than too late; in other words, once a cash requirement is established it is prudent to provide for it without delay, and not to hang on in the hope, for instance, that the market will turn upwards. In any case, it is always desirable to be in a position to sell and to complete sales as soon as possible after a grant is issued – which means indenting beforehand for a sufficient number of copy grants to enable registration to be completed quickly (see *ante* 3.47).

When discussing with brokers the timing and range of sales of quoted stocks and shares it is necessary to bear in mind the requirements of any trust arising at the end of the administration. If there is to be such a trust and one which will consist largely or entirely of stocks and shares, then some at least of those held by the testator may prove suitable for retention. Equally, others will be seen as quite unsuitable.* It will be necessary to check that there is power to postpone sale or to retain, or, alternatively, that investments to be kept are authorised either expressly or by statute. The prospect of an outright distribution should prompt PRs to consult the residuary legatees about their interests in the portfolio; following this, it may be possible for PRs to draw up a scheme which allocates the investments to individual beneficiaries according to their entitlements to the estate (for appropriation of investments, see *post* 6.35).

5.20 SALE OF QUOTED INVESTMENTS AT LESS THAN PROBATE VALUE

The possibility of a claim for relief under ss. 178–89 IHTA must also be considered. In brief, this permits the sale value of stocks and shares which are quoted on a 'recognised stock exchange'[1] or dealt in on the Unlisted Securities Market (USM) and are sold within 12 months of death to be substituted for the date of death value; likewise with authorised unit trusts whether or not quoted on the Stock Exchange. The relief must be applied to the net loss from *all* sales. It does not appear that relief is restricted to *essential* sales and the residuary legatees may prefer, when stocks and shares due to come to them have lost ground compared with the value at the date of death, to have the securities sold and the cash proceeds paid to them instead. Securities which they subsequently buy do not affect the relief (unlike purchases by the PR – see s. 180 IHTA, which dilutes the relief if these is any reinvestment by the PR at any time between death and two months after the date of the last sale). Securities bought by the beneficiaries may well, of course, have a lower acquisition value for CGT purposes, a disadvantage which must be weighed against the s. 179 relief.

---

*The investment of trust funds is fully discussed in chapter 11.

5.21   LEGAL APPORTIONMENT

Dividends from stocks and shares (and other periodical receipts in the nature of income, such as rents) are apportionable at the date of death in accordance with the Apportionment Act 1870 and unless legal apportionment is barred by the will, it will commonly apply to settled legacies and settled residue as well as to specific gifts of income-bearing investments; inevitably it will apply to a statutory life interest on intestacy, if there is no will to negative its application.

Outgoings of a similar nature are also apportionable – *Re Joel* (1967), a case which also drew attention to the need to apply legal apportionment on the death of a member of a class before attaining a vested interest and on the birth of a new member of a class (many non-apportionment clauses fail to exclude this type of apportionment). Sums already received by the deceased (or already due to him, as in the case of a dividend declared in lifetime but unpaid at death), whether in arrears or in advance, and outgoings already paid by the deceased, whether in arrears or in advance, are outside the scope of the Act but the former may need to be taken into account when apportioning sums received by the PRs after the date of death:

> Example: X died on 30 November 1991. On the preceding 30 October, he had received an interim dividend of £100 from Y Ltd for the company's year ended 31 December 1991. On 30 April 1992 Y Ltd paid a final dividend of £265 to X's PRs. The total dividend of £365 for 1991 is apportioned thus:

Capital – 334 days	£334	
Income – 31 days		£31
365 days		
Less received by deceased	£100	
	£234	£31

Of the final dividend received by the PRs, £234 will be credited to capital and £31 to income. The whole sum will, however, be treated as the income of the PRs for income tax purposes – *IRC* v *Henderson's Executors* (1931).

There is a rule of convenience (stemming from *Scholefield* v *Redfern* (1863)) that there is no apportionment of income on the purchase or sale of investments, provided that it does not produce any glaring injustice as between capital and income. Obviously, if capital and income go in the same direction, there is no need for apportionment at all. When this is *not* the case, as where a life interest is given to the surviving spouse, legal apportionment will be required both on the death of the testator *and* on the death of the life tenant, unless expressly excluded for both events. The rules for apportionment on the life tenant's death were usefully reviewed and summarised in *Re Henderson, Public Trustee* v *Reddie* (1940). See also *Re*

Ellerman (1984) where sale proceeds after the death of the life tenant included £155,000 of accrued income (most of it accruing before death); the decision was to add it all to capital. Nowadays, in the case of fixed interest investments, the accrued income scheme would result in an apportionment as between the vendor trustees and the purchaser but the accrued amount, less tax, would still go to capital as part of the proceeds of sale.

5.22 THE ACCRUED INCOME SCHEME

This came into effect on 28 February 1986 as an anti-'bond washing' measure; the relevant legislation is now found in ss. 710–28 ICTA. It applies to virtually all fixed-interest securities (preference shares and National Savings certificates are amongst those excluded). When such securities are transferred, the accrued interest to the date of transfer, on a day-to-day basis, is charged to the transferor for income tax purposes; relief on the same amount is allowed to the transferee.

'Transfer' in this context can mean a sale, an exchange, a gift (including a settled gift) and a 'deemed' transfer. Death is a deemed transfer and interest accrued to the date of death will be treated as income of the deceased for income tax purposes: s. 721(1); the deceased's PRs can claim relief on a similar amount in respect of the next interest payment. However, if, before such a payment is received, they transfer the security to a beneficiary, that person gets the relief instead: s. 721(2). Otherwise, a transfer to a beneficiary will entail apportionment of interest for income tax purposes at the date of transfer.

Personal Representatives who hold securities of a nominal value of £5,000 or less in the year of assessment in which the interest period ends *and* in the previous year of assessment are exempt from the charge under the Scheme.

So, if T dies owning £4,000 Treasury stock (and no other fixed interest stocks) and his PRs acquire no other such securities during the administration period, there need be no interest apportionment on T's death and none on a transfer to a beneficiary or on a sale: s. 715(1)(c), although apportionment may be required for other reasons – see *ante* 5.21. A similar *de minimis* relief is available to individuals but not, strangely, to trustees – see *post* 11.14.

Where the relief does not apply, PRs are both charged to and relieved from tax at the 25% rate. It appears to be assumed that a transfer takes place when PRs become trustees at the end of the administration period: s. 720(4) and see *post* 7.7.

So far as calculations of residuary income are concerned, if there is an absolute interest, an accrued amount does not increase the income but a rebate amount entitling the PRs to relief from income tax will reduce it. If, on the other hand, the residue is settled, it is for the PRs to determine the amount to which the life tenant is entitled, and rebate amounts could affect the calculation.[2]

111

Deeds of variation effected within two years of death (see *ante* 4.25) have no retrospective effect for income tax purposes; the relief available if a fixed-interest security is transferred swiftly following death under s. 721(2) is not available to a beneficiary under such a deed (unless, presumably, he would have been entitled to the security anyway).

5.23 TREATMENT OF CAPITAL DISTRIBUTIONS BY COMPANIES

The basic principle is that unless a company is either in liquidation or is making an authorised reduction of capital, *any* distribution which it makes will come out of distributable profits and will therefore be income and, as such, will be apportionable under the 1870 Act (unless excluded). Thus in *Re Doughty* (1947) a distribution by the company stated to be out of realised capital profits was held to be tax-free income due to the life tenant of the trust. On the other hand, if a company decides to capitalise its profits by making a free issue of shares to its shareholders (the normal bonus issue), the shareholder will finish up with a greater number of shares of smaller value, leaving his proportionate share of the equity in the company unchanged. Such a capitalisation issue will be capital in the hands of the PRs or trustee. A less obvious example of this principle is to be found in *Re Outen* (1963) where Courtaulds, in fighting off a take-over bid from ICI, capitalised their reserves and made a free issue to their shareholders of a new loan stock; held that the loan stock was capital in the hands of a trustee. For a review of the rules deciding whether such receipts are capital or income, see *Bouche* v *Sproule* (1887) and *Hill* v *Permanent Trustee of NSW* (1930); also *W, M & S*, pp. 514, 515.

It has become a regular practice with many of the larger UK companies to give their shareholders an option to take their dividends either in cash or in the form of an issue of shares. Such shares are income in the hands of PRs or trustees who exercise the option and therefore go to the life tenant, if there is one. The company gets a corporation tax advantage, but there is no income tax advantage for the shareholder: s. 249 ICTA; indeed there is a positive disadvantage for the low taxpayer, as he cannot make a repayment claim for the tax suffered at source.

In recent years problems have arisen where a parent company with reserves of undistributed profit demerges a subsidiary and declares a dividend which is paid to the shareholders of the parent company, not in cash, but in the form of shares in the demerged company. The demerger legislation relieves the shareholder of income tax and CGT (s. 213 ICTA and s. 192, TCGA) but leaves open the question of whether the new shares should be regarded as capital or income. The better opinion appears to be, based on a colliery amalgamation case *Re Thomas* (1916), that they must be treated as income.

5.24 UNQUOTED SHARES

The valuation of this type of asset is not cut and dried as in the case of quoted shares; although a value for an unquoted holding must be inserted in the Inland Revenue Account when applying for a grant, it is unlikely to be a firm figure – more likely to be a reasonable estimate at that stage. The PR will subsequently need to refine (perhaps confirm) his initial estimate before seeking agreement with the Capital Taxes Office. In valuing unquoted shares for IHT, two sections of the IHTA have to be read together:

> Section 160 Except as otherwise provided by this Act, the value at any time of any property shall for the purposes of this Act be the price which the property might reasonably be expected to fetch if sold in the open market at that time; but that price shall not be assumed to be reduced on the ground that the whole property is to be placed on the market at one and the same time.
>
> Section 168(1) In determining the price which unquoted shares or unquoted securities might reasonably be expected to fetch if sold in the open market it shall be assumed that in that market there is available to any prospective purchaser of the shares or securities all the information which a prudent prospective purchaser might reasonably require if he were proposing to purchase them from a willing vendor by private treaty and at arm's length.

Also relevant is s. 171, which not only ensures that an increase in the value of an asset brought about by the death is to be taken into account (as in the case of an assurance policy) but also permits decreases in value attributable to the death, for example, if the deceased shareholder had been providing services of special value to the company. Section 274 TCGA purports to impose the same valuation for CGT purposes as is agreed for IHT, but unfortunately this will not invariably be the case, because a high valuation brought about by the related property provisions in s. 161 IHTA will not apply for CGT, where the concept of related property does not exist.

One therefore has to imagine both a willing seller (who may be anybody, not necessarily the PRs involved) and a willing buyer (who may be an existing shareholder or a complete stranger); between them, these mythical characters agree an open market price for the shares. If the holding is a minority one – say, less than 25% – the price will be established by reference to the required dividend yield, which can be arrived at by selecting several quoted companies in the same business as the unquoted one and averaging their dividend yields. The percentage rate so deduced is then uplifted by 20%–30% for the unquoted concern to compensate for lack of marketability and restrictions on transfer, if they exist. It will be necessary to inspect the company's Articles of Association and to consider also its recent history and future prospects before selecting the appropriate rate of uplift. Holdings of between 25% and 50% of the issued capital may be valued by the same method but, as the size increases, more weight will be given to earnings yield and asset backing. In the case of majority holdings, i.e. over 50%, value will be directly related to either the going-concern value of the business or its break-up value, whichever is the greater, discounted modestly if the holding is over 75% but less than total. If the holding falls within the 51%–74% bracket, the discount will be more substantial – perhaps in the range 10%–20% – to reflect the lack of power to dictate the company's winding-up. There is an interesting example of the substantial gap which can exist between the value of majority and minority holdings in *Lloyds Bank plc* v *Duker* (1987) – see *post* 9.40. *Holt* v *Holt* (1990), a New Zealand appeal to the Privy Council, perhaps improves the hypothetical basis for valuation by referring to 'a willing *but not anxious* seller' and 'a willing *but not anxious* buyer'.

5.25   UNQUOTED SHARES – FINALISING THE VALUATION

Having arrived at a realistic estimate of the open market price in this way (the initial estimate should leave scope for negotiation), the valuation is normally submitted to the Shares Valuation Division of the Capital Taxes Office. The difference between valuations submitted and those actually agreed can be quite significant because there are bound to be honest differences of opinion as to values in an imaginary market situation for which there is no precedent. The examiner dealing with the valuation will expect to see accounts for the three financial years ending prior to death, the Memorandum and Articles of Association and a note of any recent purchases and sales, although they will not necessarily be relevant to the open market valuation on death. One should bear in mind also that neither the Revenue nor the taxpayer is bound by past valuations, although the examiner may try to fit the current negotiation into the pattern of past examples.

Lack of space forbids an extended discussion of this interesting subject which, it has to be said, is an art rather than a science. In substantial cases the PR will, of course, take advice. Often, such advice is obtained from the company's own accountants. This is convenient and, in many cases, without danger; there is a risk, however, of such accountants becoming too inflexible in their ideas about value, particularly if they have a duty to provide a 'fair value' for the purpose of share transactions between shareholders in the company. It is better not to have preconceived ideas about the value of an unquoted holding, whether based on prices for *inter vivos* transactions or on a previous valuation on death.

If the intention is to sell the unquoted holding, then one may assume that the sale price will represent the value at the date of death. This will not, however, necessarily be so because such a sale will almost inevitably be to an existing shareholder or someone selected as specially interested (see *post*

5.27) and will not, therefore, be a genuine open market sale. The Capital Taxes Office may well claim a higher value at death and the converse can also apply. In any event it is sensible to try to establish the value at death, if only for comparison with the proposed sale price. The point has already been made that a sale of unquoted shares should be made under advice, and this is particularly desirable where the unquoted company has contracted an agreed merger or takeover with another company (see *post* 5.29).

The affairs of private companies are not always conducted as they should be; accounts are sometimes years in arrear. This makes it difficult, if not impossible, to make a proper valuation of the shares. The PR must, however, persevere and exert pressure where it will do most good. An early start in collecting the relevant data as already outlined is very desirable in this case as in others. Negotiations with the Capital Taxes Office over the value of unquoted shares tend to be prolonged; a PR will do well to remember two things. Firstly, the Shares Valuation Division has acquired a collective experience and knowledge in this field which is second to none. Secondly, its officers are responsible people and are prepared to listen to a fair argument on behalf of the estate; an apparently unbridgeable difference of opinion can often be resolved by means of a frank discussion across the table at Shepherd's Bush.

5.26 TRANSFERRING UNQUOTED SHARES

Turning to the administration of unquoted shares, the PR will take account of the eventual destination of the asset. If the shares go out absolutely then they must either be transferred to the beneficiary or sold; directors of a private company may have the right to decline to register new members, so a sale may be the only available course. If there is a following trust, incorporating a power to postpone sale with or without a power to retain existing investments, then the holding can, technically, be kept indefinitely, although the Articles may prevent the PRs from being registered as members and may, in fact, require shares of a deceased holder to be offered for sale to the existing shareholders. The Articles of the private company involved in *Safeguard Industrial Investments Ltd* v *National Westminster Bank Ltd* (1982) contained such a requirement, but the court held that it did not apply to shares assented to beneficiaries but retained in the name of the PR as bare trustee. Whether it is wise to hold unquoted shares is a different matter (powers to postpone and retain should be exercised consciously and continuously). A minority shareholder in a private company is *not* in a strong position to influence events and is, of course, locking up trust funds in an asset of an unrealisable nature. The general rule should, therefore, be to sell rather than to retain. If the holding is kept, it may occasionally be necessary to bear in mind ss. 459–61 Companies Act

1985 (power of court to grant relief against company where members unfairly prejudiced[4]) and s. 122(1)(g) Insolvency Act 1986 (empowering the court to order the winding-up of a company where it is just and equitable to do so). See also *Daniels* v *Daniels* (1978); breach of duty by directors and majority shareholders to detriment of the company is actionable by minority shareholders – an exception to the rule in *Foss* v *Harbottle* (1843).

Re a Company No. 005287 of 1985 (1986) makes it clear that the court's powers under s. 461(1) are very wide – it may make such an order 'as it thinks fit' and this includes power to grant relief against a respondent who is no longer a member. In *Re a Company No. 00370 of 1987* (1988) failure to pay reasonable dividends was held to be grounds for ordering a winding-up under s. 122(1)(g) Insolvency Act 1986.[5]

5.27 SELLING UNQUOTED SHARES

How does one go about selling unquoted shares? There is no single answer to this question. One method was described in Lord Reid's judgment in the House of Lords in *Lynall* v *IRC* (1972):

'The case for the Revenue is based on evidence as to how large blocks of shares in private companies are in fact sold. There is no announcement that the shares are for sale and no invitation for competitive bids. The seller engages an expert who selects the person or group whom he thinks most likely to be prepared to pay a good price and to be acceptable to the directors. If that prospective purchaser is interested he engages accountants of high repute and the directors agree to co-operate by making available to the accountants on a basis of strict confidentiality all relevant information about the company's affairs. Then the accountants acting in an arbitral capacity fix what they think is a fair price. Then the sale is made at that price. Obviously the working of this scheme depends on all concerned having complete confidence in each other, and I do not doubt that in this way the seller gets a better price than he could otherwise obtain.'

Lord Reid went on to reject the Revenue's evidence as irrelevant because the kind of sale contemplated was not a sale in the open market, but a sale by private treaty.*

The Lynall case was one concerning estate duty, but the valuation basis was the same as is found in s. 160 IHTA, although there was nothing at the time corresponding to s. 168 for estate duty.

It may be possible in larger cases to make use of the unlisted securities market operated by the Stock Exchange. This avenue, however, is not likely to be available to smaller family companies, the shares of which are tightly held and only offered for sale at longish intervals. Local stockbrokers and accountants may be able to help, as may 3i plc, the successor to EDITH; EDITH was founded to help with cases where an estate duty

---

*See also 'Problems of Transferring Shares in Private Companies' in [1986] 130 SJ 718

liability created problems for shareholders in unquoted companies. 3i will consider buying shares in unquoted companies as an investment; it does not seek a controlling interest and does not require representation on the board. Section 162 Companies Act 1985, re-enacting the provision that first appeared in the Companies Act 1981, enables all companies to buy their own shares, provided their articles authorise this; in the case of a private company, even the company's capital can be used for this purpose. This may be a very convenient solution to the problem *if* the company in question has enough cash to buy shares from the PRs, but the tax consequences of such a transaction need to be carefully considered before it is undertaken.

A personal approach to persons thought to have a possible interest in buying the shares is an obvious possibility, and the comments made by Lord Reid above are significant. Advertising in trade journals is another method which might be considered if all else fails. The sale of the shares to an employee trust is another possible course: see *post* 12.30.

What is vital in all cases is for PRs to seek expert advice on the price at which the shares should be sold. There will almost certainly be nothing like an open market in the shares, and the consideration must be established by negotiation. The PR involved in this must have competent professional help, usually from an accountant used to dealing with such matters. He should be asked to provide a reasoned argument to support a positive recommendation to sell at such-and-such a price. Even this, of course, will not absolve an executor or administrator from applying his own knowledge, expertise and common sense to the matter, and a professional PR will be expected to contribute a higher standard of such expertise than will a layman.

5.28 THE *LYNALL* CASE

The *Lynall* case, incidentally, is an interesting one and should be read by all who are or may be concerned with the valuation of unquoted shares. (It is discussed in some detail in Appendix 6.) It was quite a typical situation, in that the directors of the company (Linread) had an absolute discretion to refuse to register transfers and the company's Articles also provided that no share should be transferable until after it had been offered either to a Mr E H Lynall (a director) or to members of the company at a 'fair value'. The 'fair value' might be fixed by the company in general meeting but, if not so fixed, was to be par, i.e. £1. Two questions had to be dealt with: were the restrictions upon sales in the Articles to be imported into the hypothetical open market price required as at the date of death? And were the hypothetical buyers in that open market to be regarded as having some confidential information about a possible take-over bid known only to Linread's directors? The answer to the first question, following *IRC* v

117

Crossman (1937), was 'yes' to the extent that, although a hypothetical purchaser on the open market would buy the shares irrespective of the restrictions, he would then himself become subject to them. The answer to the second question was 'no' but the decision in this respect was quickly counteracted by legislation, now to be found in s. 168 IHTA – see *ante* 5.24. *Crossman* was followed in *Alexander* v *IRC* (1991); the value of a lease for CTT purposes was the amount for which, on a hypothetical sale, a person would be willing to acquire the lease subject to the obligation to make a repayment to the landlord in the event of a disposal within the meaning of s. 8(3) Housing Act 1980, but on this footing – that the hypothetical acquisition itself did not give rise to such a disposal.

5.29 TAKE-OVER BIDS FOR UNQUOTED COMPANIES

Personal Representatives and trustees are sometimes involved in an agreed take-over bid for an unquoted company in which they hold shares. Not infrequently this is negotiated and settled without their knowledge, and they are then asked to 'rubber-stamp' the deal. This proposition should be resisted. Whether they need independent advice depends upon the quality of the advice being given to the shareholders as a body. If the PRs are not satisfied with it they should not hesitate to instruct their own advisers. The sale will usually be embodied in a formal vending agreement, which all the shareholders will be asked to sign, and this will almost certainly incorporate certain warranties, indemnities and covenants as to the conduct of the company's affairs and potential tax liabilities. PRs usually have no personal knowledge of such matters and the best course is for them to ask to be excepted from giving the warranties etc. If this is not an acceptable proposition (and it usually is not) then their liability under the warranties etc. can be restricted to the assets in their hands (less liabilities) at the date of the agreement. Even this is often unacceptable to a purchaser; a compromise solution is to limit the PRs' liability to the proceeds of sale and to provide in the vending agreement that no claim can be made against them after the end of a specified period. The PRs must then, of course, take care not to distribute the proceeds of sale until the specified period has expired. In any event, the PRs should extract from the directors and auditors of the company a statement that it is in order for them to give the warranties, indemnities and covenants as set out in the vending agreement.[6]

5.30 THE STEWARDSHIP OF UNQUOTED SHARES

If unquoted shares are to be held for any length of time, whether during a protracted administration or in trust, arrangements should be made to be kept fully informed as to the company's progress, results and prospects. Annual accounts and reports must, of course, be obtained. A member of the board may be asked to bear in mind the interests of the estate or trust and to have regular meetings with the PRs and trustees where the holding is of any size – say, more than 15% of the issued share capital. It may be possible to have a director specially appointed to represent the estate. Vigilance over investments is always necessary, but especially so in the case of unquoted shares. Sometimes they are kept, at the request of the beneficiaries, for sentimental reasons; PRs and trustees should take care to prevent this expression of emotion from becoming an expensive luxury.

The trustee in *Bartlett* v *Barclays Bank Trust Co Ltd* (1980) held 99.8% of the shares in a private company which, for many years, operated with reasonable success in the property investment field. Then, in 1961, it decided to invest in property development. As a result of some ill-judged speculative activity it sustained a large loss which reduced the value of its shares, and the beneficiaries sued the trustee for failure to prevent the company from undertaking the loss-making project. The trustee thought that its supervision of the company's activities through attendance at the annual general meeting had been enough, but the court thought otherwise. The prudent man of business holding a controlling interest in a private company will make sure that he can take informed decisions to protect his asset, and a trustee must keep to the same standard. There is no general rule about the way in which such information should be got; it can come through a member of the board or by receipt of copies of the agenda and minutes of board meetings or by receipt of monthly management accounts. Failure to get such information (and act on it) will make a trustee liable if loss ensues; furthermore, a professional trustee is expected to provide a higher standard of care and will fail to do so if it neglects to exercise the special skills which it professes to have. Barclays Bank Trust Co, wrongfully and in breach of trust, had neglected to ensure that it got an adequate flow of information. If it had got such a flow it could, and should, have stopped the loss-making development project – so the trustee was liable to the beneficiaries for the fall in the value of the shares. See also *Re Lucking* (1968) for an earlier example of a trustee being made liable for loss in value of a controlled company's shares (for details see *post* 10.8).

5.31 SOLE PROPRIETOR'S BUSINESS

Valuation of business assets (including goodwill) is dealt with in *Dymond*, ch. 23, which includes a useful note on underwriting interests. Where royalties are payable to an estate, an estimate of value should be obtained from a publisher or literary agent. If a business is shortly to be sold then the proceeds of sale can normally be used for tax purposes.

Where the deceased was a sole trader (a matter that has already been touched on, *ante* 3.23), the position of the PR is simplified by the fact that no other beneficial interests in the business assets and liabilities exist. The objective is to obtain and maintain control until either sale or transfer to a beneficiary takes place. There may, of course, be an early decision to stop trading and to sell off the assets as individual items rather than collectively as a going concern. The main problem is to get a firm grasp on the business and to maintain this for so long as it remains in the estate. The method of disposal will vary according to the circumstances; as in the case of the smaller unquoted companies, the personal approach and advertising in trade publications are possible courses. Trade or professional associations may be able to put the PR in touch with potential buyers. Advertising in the local and national press can be considered.

5.32 PARTNERSHIPS

The position where the deceased was partner in a business is less straightforward in one sense, because, as already indicated *ante* 3.22, the surviving partner or partners are interested parties and the PR has to consider the estate's interest in the business in the general context of the partnership contract. In one way, however, the PR's job is simplified, in that the actual *conduct* of the business henceforth devolves on the surviving partners. The title to the partnership assets vests in the survivors and they have authority to do what is necessary to wind up the affairs of the business following dissolution of the agreement by death. It is perhaps necessary to point out that a partnership is necessarily dissolved by death in the absence of any agreement to the contrary: s. 33(1) Partnership Act 1890. Commonly there *is* agreement to the contrary, but this will not usually affect the rule already stated that control of the business devolves on the surviving partners. A joint decision on the future tax treatment of the business may need to be taken by the PRs and the surviving partners; it is possible for them to elect, within two years of death, for profits to be assessed to tax on a continuing basis instead of on the basis that the business ceased on the death of the former partner: s. 113 ICTA. Where no such election is made, the profits for the first three years of assessment following the year of assessment in which cessation and recommencement took place are all assessed on the actual basis. There is an option for the taxpayer to have the fifth and sixth years also assessed on the actual basis: ss. 61(4) and 62 ICTA.

5.33 PARTNERSHIP ACT 1890

The foregoing does not mean, of course, that the PR need take no steps to deal with the deceased's interest. His first action, on learning of its existence, should be to obtain a copy of the partnership agreement and a copy of the last partnership accounts. Where there is no express agreement, the contract between the partners is governed by the above Act; the emphasis is upon equality without regard to the individual input of capital or effort by them. Section 24 commences as follows:

The interest of partners in the partnership property and their rights and duties in relation to the partnership shall be determined, subject to any agreement express or implied between the partners, by the following rules:
(1) All the partners are entitled to share equally in the capital and profits of the business, and must contribute equally towards the losses whether of capital or otherwise sustained by the firm.

Obviously, the firm's books or accounts may well rebut this presumption of equality. An express agreement will usually contain provisions to deal with events following the death of a partner, and the surviving partners may be given power to purchase the deceased's share at a price calculated in accordance with a stated formula. In the absence of such provision, s. 39 provides a valuable right of enforcement:

On the dissolution of a partnership every partner is entitled, as against the other partners in the firm, and all persons claiming through them in respect of their interests as partners, to have the property of the partnership applied in payment of the debts and liabilities of the firm, and to have the surplus assets after such payment applied in payment of what may be due to the partners respectively after deducting what may be due from them as partners to the firm; and for that purpose any partner or his representatives may on the termination of the partnership apply to the court to wind up the business and affairs of the firm.

5.34 DISSOLUTION OF THE PARTNERSHIP

Whether there is dissolution and winding up in accordance with the statute, or whether there is a sale in accordance with express provisions in the partnership agreement, the PR must keep an eye on progress made towards a settlement and, if necessary, require the surviving partners to complete the transaction in reasonable time. On dissolution one is entitled to see a final account which should, of course, run on from the last previous account. If the process is prolonged it is reasonable to ask for an interim account. Sale to the surviving partners may warrant the taking of separate advice for the PR as to value; the question can be answered only in the light of the precise terms of the sale agreement.

When considering a final account, reference to s. 44 of the 1890 Act may be necessary; this describes the rules for distribution of assets, in the absence of any special agreement. Note also the right of the estate either to share in any profits made after dissolution or to take interest at 5% – in both cases the sum due is calculated on the value of the deceased's interest in the partnership assets – see s. 42(1) of the Act; if a share of profits is taken it may be difficult to resist a claim by the surviving partner for remuneration over and above his own share of profit. If there is a partnership agreement, there may be a provision for the surviving partner(s) to be paid a fee or salary for work done in the winding-up; even if there is no such provision, it seems that there is an entitlement to some form of remuneration for acting in this capacity. In *Barclays Bank Trust Co Ltd* v *Bluff* (1982) the surviving partner of a farming partnership dissolved on death claimed that a very large increase in the value of the former partnership assets since death was profit under s. 42(1) and that, as the deceased partner's PR had elected to take interest at 5%, the estate was not entitled to share in the increase. The court held that profit in this context means profit accruing in the ordinary course of trading pending realisation. The right of the estate to a share in the increase in value was not affected. Until realisation, the surviving partner was trustee of the business (including the increase) for the estate and himself.

5.35   ESTATE'S LIABILITY FOR PARTNERSHIP DEBTS

In all cases the PR should bear in mind the estate's joint and several liability under s. 9 of the Act for partnership debts outstanding at the date of death, which includes the costs of subsequently completing a contract that was then unperformed. The estate is excluded from liability for debts incurred *after* death – ss. 14(2) and 36(3) of the Act – unless, presumably, the PR holds himself out to be continuing the business with the surviving partners – s. 14(1). As regards the debts due at the date of death, the PR should satisfy himself that they have all been paid, or should get a release from outstanding creditors or should get a satisfactory indemnity from the surviving partners. It behoves him to see that the deceased's name is deleted from the firm's stationery, which will forestall any question of holding out and at the same time ensure compliance with the Business Names Act 1985.

5.36   LANDED PROPERTY

In many estates, the only land asset is the family home; if it continues as such, the administrative problems are slight. A provisional valuation may be used at first. Delay is often incurred, subsequently, in agreeing the value for tax purposes. If the property is sold within a reasonable period from death the sale price may be used as the date of death value and it is then unnecessary to instruct an agent to agree a figure with the District Valuer. Where the probate value has been agreed with the Valuation Office it is not the practice of the Capital Taxes Office to reopen the question in the event of a later sale at a higher figure, although the PR may substitute the sale price of land sold at a loss within three years of death: ss. 190–8 IHTA.[7] Where the transfer is from one spouse to another the spouse exemption will make this time-consuming procedure unnecessary. In any event, where no IHT is payable, the Capital Taxes Office will not agree a valuation for this or any other kind of unquoted asset, which may cause CGT problems for a taxpayer who has to try to establish his acquisition price for, say, unquoted shares inherited on a death ten or fifteen years earlier. In such circumstances the PR should think about passing on relevant valuation material to the beneficiary when the asset is transferred to him.

5.37 SALE OF LANDED PROPERTY

Sales of real and leasehold property will normally be carried out through estate agents. Their advice should be taken concerning the mode of sale, bearing in mind always the need to make the property available in the widest market which it is reasonable to use. Accusations are sometimes made that PRs and trustees have not advertised a property sufficiently to produce a satisfactory response. There is always a suspicion that a private sale may not be at the best possible figure. Agents must therefore be instructed to provide very positive advice that a sale in this mode is the most appropriate choice and should always be required to back up advice to accept an offer for property with a definite recommendation to the PR. A properly advertised auction, though it involves extra expense and may prove abortive, is probably the method of sale least open to criticism. The legal advisers should be asked to check title before estate agents are instructed and, subsequently, should be asked to verify the description of the property to be issued to prospective purchasers. In all cases the PR himself should scrutinise this description with care; an error in it can be expensive and may lead to rescission of a subsequent contract for sale.

5.38 LIABILITIES ATTACHING TO LEASEHOLD PROPERTY

Where an estate contains leasehold property PRs should consider (a) what actual liabilities are outstanding and claimed and (b) what potential liability they may incur in respect of the lease in the future.

Technically, the PRs' liability comes under two heads, (a) as assignee by operation of law and (b) under the doctrine of privity of estate. The second head applies only if PRs take possession of the property (*Re Owers* (1941)) but as they can hardly avoid doing so in most cases, e.g. through either collecting or paying a rent, the condition is not of great significance.

So far as (a) is concerned, provided all accrued and claimed liabilities are settled and, where appropriate, a sufficient fund is set aside to answer any future claim in accordance with any provision to this effect in the lease, PRs may distribute the estate (including, of course, the leasehold property itself) and will not be personally liable under the lease afterwards: s. 26(1) TA. This is a particularly useful provision in cases where the deceased was the original lessee, whose liability under the covenants of the lease would persist throughout its term. It appears that it is not unusual these days for a landlord to take action against the original tenant or his PRs. [8]

As regards the *Re Owers* liability, there is no such statutory safeguard. [9] An indemnity can be obtained from the beneficiaries; one will, in any case, be obtained from the purchaser of leasehold property by s. 77(1) LPA and expressly from the devisee in an assent. This may not be regarded as very adequate protection to the PRs, and they may prefer to retain a fund until any claim against them under this head is statute barred. Retaining a fund is, naturally, not popular with beneficiaries and an alternative is to insure against possible claims. The risk is, of course, greatly increased if the lease has only a short time to run and, where this is the case, the precautions must be correspondingly thorough. *In extremis*, the PRs can always apply to the court for directions and can obtain protection from this source if no other is either available or sufficient; such an application may also be necessary where it is desired to retain a fund to meet future liabilities and the beneficiaries oppose this course of action. The possibility that a PR or trustee who is an original lessee might become liable for an assignee's breaches of covenant (including the non-payment of rent and future rent increases) is discussed *post* 11.42.

5.39   JOINT PROPERTY

Strictly, it is illogical to discuss joint property here because the title to it at least will usually devolve upon a surviving joint owner and not on the PRs. Co-ownership in any form of landed property (apart from party walls) is necessarily held, in the absence of an express trust, behind a statutory trust under ss. 34–6 LPA for which there must be two trustees or a trust corporation to confer a valid title on a purchaser. Unless the deceased happened to be the sole surviving trustee, the title to the asset will pass to the other trustee(s). Co-ownership of pure personalty is not dealt with by statute, although in practice there will almost invariably be an express or implied trust behind which it shelters but with no requirement about the number of trustees; again, unless the deceased happened to be the sole or sole surviving trustee, the other trustee(s) will automatically take over, since a joint tenancy is *de rigueur* for trustees. We are talking here of legal title (or equitable title in the case of equitable assets, such as reversionary interests), not the true ownership of the underlying beneficial interests. To determine the latter, the trust document (or the evidence provided by the parties, often aided by equitable presumptions) must be studied (see *post* 8.22 *et seq.* for the informal creation of equitable interests in homes).

To deal with land first, because the co-ownership interests will (one hopes) have been created formally, it is usually evident from an inspection of the deeds, in the case of unregistered land, what beneficial interests have been created; for registered land, if the title of the joint owners is registered without restriction, the inference is that there was a true joint tenancy, i.e. that the beneficial interest as well as the legal title has survived over to the other party. If the beneficial ownership had been shared as tenants in common, there will be a restriction on the register under s. 58(3) LRA in the following form:

No disposition by a sole proprietor of the land (not being a trust corporation) under which capital money arises is to be registered except under an Order of the Registrar or the Court.

Thus, if the deceased was a beneficial joint tenant, he will no longer be interested, although his PRs will have to account for IHT on the value of his severable share;[10] if he was a beneficial tenant in common, his severed share forms part of his free estate.

It should be borne in mind that a beneficial joint tenancy can be severed during life, but not by will; equity's dislike of beneficial joint tenancies has led to its being ready to treat a joint tenancy as severed so as to avoid the operation of the *ius accrescendi*. Severance can take place as the result either of an express intention to effect this, e.g. by notice in writing from one joint tenant to another under s. 36(2) LPA; or of some other act inconsistent with a beneficial joint tenancy, such as the sale by one joint tenant of his interest in the property. In *Burgess* v *Rawnsley* (1975) a property was conveyed into the names of two persons as beneficial joint tenants. They agreed between themselves that one should buy the share of the other and it was held that the joint tenancy was severed by mutual agreement.

But whatever kind of asset is involved, the PRs must ask themselves two questions. Firstly, has the title to the asset vested in us and, if so, what outstanding trusts are there to be performed and what is our deceased's beneficial interest under those trusts? Secondly, if the title to the asset has not vested in us, what claim can we make against the holder of the asset to establish that our deceased had a beneficial interest in it?

Where a share in property has to be valued for IHT, the basis is the open market value under s. 160 IHTA, and the result is usually less than the corresponding fraction of the value of the whole. If the property was a residence for the co-owners, any vacant possession element should be eliminated from the valuation. In husband and wife cases, if the husband leaves his share as tenant in common to his children, there will be no discount for the fraction, because of the related property provisions: s. 161 IHTA.

5.40 COLLECTING THE DECEASED'S SEVERED SHARE

What should be done by PRs who find themselves responsible for an interest in a tenancy in common where the legal title is held elsewhere by a surviving joint owner? The answer must surely depend on the future of the basic asset – is it to be retained or sold? If to be sold, then the title may remain in the survivor's name and he will account to the PRs for the net share belonging to the estate. If the asset is landed property, note the need for two trustees or a trust corporation to give a good receipt for the proceeds: ss. 2 and 27 LPA (although a sole PR *as such* can give a valid receipt for capital moneys – s. 27(2)).

On the other hand, if the PRs are content to retain the interest for some time they may well feel that they should be appointed as additional trustees to act with the survivor of the original joint tenants. If this is done there will, in effect, be a subsidiary trust running alongside their parent trust and, for the professional trustee at least, questions of additional remuneration arise. If landed property is involved, there may be a clash of opinion over the future sale of the property – see *post* 8.29.

5.41 FOREIGN PROPERTY

The existence of foreign assets and liabilities in an estate introduces problems of two different kinds; in the first place, there is the physical problem of administering and collecting the assets and, in the second place, the problem of working out the correct incidence of debts, expenses and taxes incurred in the foreign country.[11] So far as the physical problem is concerned, English PRs will rarely want to exercise direct personal control over foreign assets. The inconvenience of doing so is obvious. Unless a testator has appointed separate executors in the foreign country – and this is sensible where the overseas element is substantial – the English PRs will need to appoint an attorney to represent them there – under s. 23(2) TA – *post* 5.45. It will not be possible to make such a thorough check of the proposed attorney's status and capability as in the case of UK agents, but the appointment should not be made blind. UK bankers can both recommend and report on foreign professional firms. Reference can also be made to UK consular officials in the country involved and to the country's Embassy in London for further help.

It has to be admitted that dealing with foreign agents can be frustrating. Overseas revenue departments seem to move more slowly than those in the UK and the legal procedures on death sometimes seem designed to obstruct rather than to assist. One is largely in the hands of the appointed agent although it is worth pointing out that there are lawyers practising in England who are able to provide advice on specific foreign legal systems and the associated practice. It is prudent to warn beneficiaries that the completion of an administration which includes a foreign element is likely to be protracted.

5.42 LIABILITY FOR TAXES ON FOREIGN ASSETS

Where the deceased was domiciled in England and Wales – which is the assumption throughout this book – his English PRs are liable for IHT on all his assets wherever situate and notwithstanding that separate executors may have been appointed of foreign property – *Re Manchester* (1912). Their liability is, it is true, limited to the assets which they have received or would have received but for their own neglect or default: s. 204(1) IHTA. Nevertheless, this is a rule which may cause liquidity problems where the overseas estate is large in proportion to that in the UK, especially where, for whatever reason, it proves to be impossible to recover the tax paid from either the foreign property itself or from its beneficiary. The combined effect of ss. 211 and 237 IHTA is to make all foreign property bear its own tax; so, if such property is specifically given (or pecuniary legacies are charged on it) the beneficiary takes net of the tax, both UK and foreign (subject to the availability of double taxation relief[11]), unless the testator devices otherwise — see s. 211(?)

5.43 FOREIGN DEBTS

The question of foreign debts may arise (as regards advertising for foreign claims, see *ante* 3.26). In general terms, an English PR is as much liable for such debts as for domestic ones, but whether an English court will impose liability upon him for them depends upon the law of this country rather than upon the law of the country where the debts are domiciled. This is because the payment of debts is an administration matter and, as such, is controlled by the *lex fori* – the law of the country in which the grant was made. So claims against an English PR are decided in accordance with English law. In *Re Lorillard* (1922) a testator died domiciled in New York leaving assets and creditors in both New York and England. The New York assets were exhausted in paying the debts there, leaving unpaid certain creditors whose claims were statute-barred in England but not in New York. The court directed that the English assets be distributed amongst the beneficiaries. The Foreign Limitation Periods Act 1984 now has to be considered in this kind of situation; where the law of a foreign country has to be taken into account in court proceedings in this country, the foreign law on limitation of actions prevails. In a case similar to *Re Lorillard* this would apparently mean that the New York debts would *not* be statute-barred.

Where there is an excess of liabilities over assets in the foreign country there is a strong argument for disclaiming the foreign estate completely – equally so, one would think, where there is no reasonable prospect of ever reducing the foreign estate into possession. In the 'normal' situation, however, the task of the foreign agent is to collect the foreign assets, discharge taxes, debts and expenses, and account to the UK representative for the balance.

5.44 EXPENSES OF FOREIGN ADMINISTRATION

The question does sometimes arise as to the allocation of expenses in respect of foreign assets. Where they fall into residue there is no problem, the expenses being general expenses of administration. Where, on the other hand, there is a specific gift of foreign property, a decision has to be made about dividing the expenses incurred between those required to prove the title and obtain legal dominion over the foreign assets and those further incurred in transferring the asset to the legatee. The former are residuary, the latter should be borne by the legatee. See *Re Fitzpatrick* (1952) where some specifically bequeathed chattels situate in Monaco had to be sent to England where the specific legatee lived. The cost of carriage and insurance was payable by her. Harman J. pointed out that it was not the duty of UK executors to go to a foreign country (where they have no standing) and obtain the specifically bequeathed assets. Their duty is to assent to the legacy, which can be done in the UK; having done this, any further expense involved in getting the asset into the hands of the legatee must be borne by her.

Under s. 173 IHTA an allowance for any *additional* expense incurred in administering or realising property outside the UK is made against the value of such property, up to a maximum of 5% of its value.

5.45   USE OF AGENTS

A PR has always had the power to appoint agents but the statutory power is so wide that it is unnecessary to consider the non-statutory one. Section 23(1) TA reads:

> Trustees or personal representatives may, instead of acting personally, employ and pay an agent, whether a solicitor, banker, stockbroker, or other person, to transact any business or do any act required to be transacted or done in the execution of the trust, or the administration of the testator's or intestate's estate, including the receipt and payment of money, and shall be entitled to be allowed and paid all charges and expenses so incurred, and shall not be responsible for the default of any such agent if employed in good faith.

Perhaps the main innovation in this subsection is that it does away with the former requirement that agents should be employed only in the case where 'prudence or necessity justified delegation'. Nowadays a PR can employ an agent (and pay him) to do any work which he himself is required to do. The only reservation – an important one – is that he should not delegate a discretion to an agent unless either the will expressly allows it or use is made of s. 25 (below). The PR must remain in control of the general conduct of the administration; the only exception to this rule is contained in s. 23(2) which gives a power to appoint agents or attorneys for overseas property of all kinds. This power is all-embracing and includes the delegation of any discretion, trust or power relating to the property in question. Mention must be made in this context of s. 25, which was amended by the Powers of Attorney Act 1971. As amended, it provides for a trustee – including a

PR – to delegate all or any of the trusts, powers and discretions vested in him for a period not exceeding 12 months. Persons who may be donees of a power of attorney under this section include a trust corporation and, where there are only two trustees, one may not delegate to the other unless that other be a trust corporation. There are certain provisions as to notice, and the donor of the power is liable for the acts or defaults of the donee as if they were his own – which means that the donor will need to be satisfied that his delegate will not abuse his temporary office.

5.46 LIABILITY FOR ACTS OF AGENTS

This conveniently brings us to the general question of the liability of a PR and a trustee for the acts of agents appointed by them. The saving phrase at the end of s. 23(1) – 'shall not be responsible for the default of any such agent if employed in good faith' – has to be read in conjunction with s. 30 which says that a trustee (which includes a PR here) shall be 'answerable and accountable only for his own acts, receipts, neglects or defaults . . . [and not] for any other loss, unless the same happens through his own wilful default'.

These two subsections – 23(1) and 30(1) – were considered by Maugham J. in *Re Vickery* (1931); he said that s. 23(1):

'. . . revolutionises the position of a trustee or executor so far as regards the employment of agents. He is no longer required to do any actual work himself, but he may employ a solicitor or other agent to do it, whether there is any real necessity for the employment or not. No doubt he should use his discretion in selecting an agent, and should employ him only to do acts within the scope of the usual business of the agent; but a question arises whether even in these respects he is personally liable for a loss due to the employment of the agent unless he has been guilty of wilful default.'

Maugham J. then went on to define 'wilful default' as 'either a consciousness of negligence or breach of duty or a recklessness in the performance of a duty' – a definition which has met with criticism, but it would seem to be not inconsistent with the general duty of care required of a PR or trustee: that of the ordinary prudent man of business. Failure on the part of a PR to exercise proper control over an agent could well amount to 'wilful default', particularly if the PR in question is of the professional variety, of whom higher standards are expected. In such a case, the fact that the agent was originally appointed 'in good faith' would be irrelevant.

The moral is, therefore, only to appoint agents in whom one has complete confidence and to exercise proper supervision over their activities – and, it may be added, to discard them if they prove unsatisfactory. After all, Lord Denning is on record as saying that, if counsel delays unreasonably, solicitors should withdraw instructions from him and send them elsewhere. The same principle applies to dealings between PR and agent. Failure to observe it could be dangerous. 'Wilful default' may result from leaving funds in the hands of agents for too long; there is statutory authority for leaving cash on deposit or other account with a bank 'while an investment is being sought for' – s. 11(1) TA. Documents of all kinds may also be deposited with a bank whose business includes the undertaking of the safe custody of documents – s. 21 – and bearer securities must be so deposited – s. 7 TA. There is no objection, however, to leaving other documents of title in the hands of one out of several co-executors and title deeds required at frequent intervals for reference may be left in the hands of the estate solicitors.

5.47   DELEGATION TO A BENEFICIARY UNDER LPA

One other power of delegation which trustees for sale of land (including PRs) may find useful is that given by s. 29(1) LPA, which enables them to hand over to a person of full age with a beneficial interest in possession in the income of the land their powers of leasing and management. The delegation must be in writing and revocable; the persons delegating such powers are not liable for the acts and defaults of the delegate.

5.48   LAW REFORM COMMITTEE RECOMMENDATIONS

The Committee, in its 23rd Report, *The Powers and Duties of Trustees* [1982 Cmnd.8733], has recommended that trustees (which term includes PRs) should be entitled to recover the costs of employing an agent only if such costs were reasonably incurred, taking into account the trustee's knowledge, qualifications and experience and the level of remuneration received by him. It also thinks that a trustee should be responsible for the default of an agent unless it is shown that it was reasonable to employ such an agent, that reasonable steps were taken to ensure that the agent was competent and that reasonable steps were taken to ensure that the agent's work was done competently. There is also a recommendation to omit from s. 23(1) TA the words 'and pay' from the phrase 'employ and pay an agent'.

The Committee is quite emphatic that trustees can delegate their discretions (including investment decisions), for a year at a time, under s. 25 but admit some doubt as to whether a delegate under s. 25 can properly be paid for his services.

5.49   ENDURING POWERS OF ATTORNEY

Reference is made to these at the end of the next chapter in connection with the distribution of estates to beneficiaries who may lack capacity. As s. 3(3) Enduring Powers of Attorney Act 1985 authorises the donee of such a power to exercise all powers and discretions vested in the donor as trustee (possibly also those vested in him as PR?), it appears that a trustee executing such a power may delegate his office for an unlimited period, irrespective of the provisions of the TA; and unlike powers granted under that Act, the power would continue after the donor had become mentally incapable.[12]

6 Distributing the estate

6.1 SATISFACTORY PROVISION FOR LIABILITIES

In this chapter it is assumed that the estate's debts have been paid or, at least, that the PRs are satisfied that they know the maximum figure which may be required for this purpose. Basically, debts and claims should be satisfied before any beneficial distribution is arranged.

PRs should bear in mind their *personal* liability whenever they give instructions for anything to be done for the estate. This is not quite so bad as it sounds, as, provided the expenditure is properly incurred, the PRs are entitled to pay the bills out of the estate and furthermore, should the estate turn out to be insolvent, the reasonable funeral and administration expenses rank in front of the preferential debts. Therefore, the PRs could not be personally penalised unless, exceptionally, the estate were so short of assets as to be unable to meet the PRs' expenditure. They are personally liable for the funeral expenses, even if someone else instructed the undertakers. In practice the most important personal liability they shoulder is for IHT, where, however, s. 204(1) IHTA limits their liability to the assets they have received or which they would have received, but for their own neglect or default. So, if there are important overseas assets which are not easily realisable, it may be necessary to suspend the distribution of the UK assets just in case the tax on the world-wide estate exceeds the available assets. Note that the liability for IHT extends overseas; in *IRC* v *Stannard* (1984) the Jersey executor of an English-domiciled deceased was held personally liable for the IHT arising as a result of the death and the executor's UK assets were seizable to defray the liability.

The most treacherous situation for PRs is if they try to run a business otherwise than with a view to its prompt realisation: see *ante* 3.23.

A creditor can sue for a debt immediately after the date of death, but there is no obligation to make any payments to beneficiaries until the 'executor's year' has expired: s. 44 AEA. In practice, exceptions to this rule have to be made. It may not be possible to establish precisely the amounts due and the validity of all claims until some time after the date of death. Tax liabilities, in particular, may remain unquantified for many months – even for years[1]. A reasonable balance must be struck between excessive caution and bravado. It is usually unnecessary to deprive the beneficiaries completely because one or two debts remain outstanding. Personal Representatives must form their own view about the maximum reserve required to meet oustanding claims and may then safely make payments on account from the balance. Exceptionally, it may not be possible to make a reasonable estimate of this kind – for instance, where the Revenue gives notice that a back duty (IT or CGT) claim is to be made. In such cases it is only prudent to 'sit tight'; the beneficiaries should, of course, be kept fully informed. Where substantial sums are involved and the delay looks like being prolonged, an application to court for directions may be considered. Before making any beneficial distribution, PRs should assess not only the maximum sum required for any debts and claims still unpaid, but also the reserve needed to cover administration expenses, which may include IT and CGT, their own fees and expenses and those of any agents instructed.

6.2 OVERPAYING BENEFICIARIES

It is not suggested that PRs should behave otherwise than with reasonable caution when making interim payments from an estate, i.e. before the residue is accurately and finally established. The risk of overpaying beneficiaries is a real one and, if the result in the end is a deficiency, the PRs are primarily responsible – even though the sum involved may also be recoverable from the overpaid beneficiaries – see *post*, 6.11. This is not a situation in which a professional executor will wish to find himself; there is an equal danger in paying the wrong person. The words of Lord Greene MR in *Re Diplock* (1948) should ever be held in view:

> Since the original wrong payment was attributable to the blunder of the personal representatives, the right of the unpaid beneficiary is in the first instance against the wrongdoing executor or administrator: and the beneficiary's direct claim in equity against those overpaid or wrongly paid should be limited to the amount which he cannot recover from the party responsible.

This very significant case is also interesting because it emphasises the right of the unpaid beneficiary to make a claim against third parties, irrespective of whether the PR's mistake was one of law or one of fact – the equitable claim being different in this respect from the common law claim for money had and received, where an action will not lie where money has been paid under a mistake of law: see *post* 14.23.

6.3 LEGACIES AND DEVISES

A legacy, strictly, is a gift of personal property; a devise is a gift of real property. However, the term 'legacy' is loosely used to describe *any* gift made by will. Hence, the person to whom the residue of an estate is left – that is, what is left after payment of debts, taxes, expenses and legacies – is often called the residuary legatee. Legacies and devises which have priority over the residuary gift are termed specific, general and demonstrative.

6.4 SPECIFIC LEGACIES AND DEVISES

Such gifts are of a particular asset or type of asset forming part of the estate at the date of death, e.g. my shares in ICI or all my books or my property Dunromin. The subject matter of a specific gift may be described in such a way as to cover a change in the asset owned between the date of the will and the date of death without this change depriving the donee of benefit through operation of the doctrine of ademption. Section 24 WA reads:

> Every will shall be construed, with reference to the real estate and personal estate comprised in it, to speak and take effect as if it had been executed immediately before the death of the testator, unless a contrary intention shall appear by the will.

A pleasant illustration of this rule was given by Sir Richard Malins VC in *Castle* v *Fox* (1871):

> 'Suppose a man to have a brown horse . . . and bequeath it, and then to sell it, and buy another brown horse, and die, does the horse of which he was possessed at the time of his death pass? I should say, unless he uses other words to describe the brown horse, all I am at liberty to ask is, had he a brown horse when he died? Yes. Then he has said, "I give my brown horse" and that is the one he applies the description to, and it is perfectly immaterial that he had another brown horse when he made his will.'

For 'horse', in these days, substitute 'motor car'. The Vice-Chancellor's words were *obiter* and he did go on to suggest that a gift of 'my brown horse I bought of AB' would express a contrary intention excluding s. 24. Furthermore, in *Re Sikes* (1927), Clauson J. held that a legacy of 'my piano' must be taken to refer to the one owned at the date of the will, not to a later replacement owned at the date of death – the gift was therefore adeemed. A PR faced with a problem of this kind should not jump to conclusions; advice will be needed, perhaps also, if the value of the subject is great, an application to the court for directions.

While a specific legacy is vulnerable to ademption, it will score over a general legacy in being less likely to abate (see *post* 6.11). It should be borne in mind that the court leans against specific legacies and is inclined, if it can, to construe a legacy as general rather than specific: *per* Jenkins J. in *Re Rose* (1949), a case that contains a useful summary of the authorities relating to the distinction between specific and general legacies.

6.5 ADEMPTION

Where the subject-matter of a specific legacy or devise has been disposed of by the testator between the date of the will and the date of death, the gift is adeemed and the beneficiary gets nothing. So, if a testator bequeaths 'all my shares in ICI' to X and subsequently sells the shares, X will receive nothing – not even the proceeds of sale, if traceable. This will be so, even if the contract for the sale has not been completed at the date of death.

This is a convenient point at which to mention the anomalous doctrine established in *Lawes* v *Bennett* (1785); where property is specifically given in a will, and, subsequently, the testator grants an option to purchase it, the exercise of such an option *after* the date of death will adeem the gift. The doctrine applies to any class of property and has been extended to a conditional contract where the sale becomes unconditional after the date of death.

In *Re Sweeting* (1988) the testator devised Blackacre to one of his children. After the date of the will he entered into a contract for the sale of the property conditional upon his wife's waiver of any rights therein. This she did after his death. It was held that the fulfilment of the conditional contract by the executors had the effect under *Lawes* v *Bennett* of converting the devise into residuary personalty.

Turning back to the testator with his ICI shares, suppose that, having sold his ICI shares, he buys some more and owned them at the date of death – would they pass to X in accordance with the gift in the will? Keeping in mind s. 24 WA (*ante* 6.4), the terms of the legacy are such as to cover the shares held at the date of death, although they are not the same shares as those held at the date of the will. But if the testator had referred to 'my 1,000 shares in ICI' the contrary intention, to which s. 24 is subject, has been expressed and the gift could not apply to the holding of ICI shares subsequently acquired – even if the number of shares were the same.

It may be that the subject-matter of the gift has not been sold but has been exchanged for other property; the rule is that a mere change of name or form does not adeem a specific gift. For instance, in *Re Clifford* (1912) twenty-three £80 shares had been bequeathed. Before the testator died, they were subdivided into £20 shares; the court held that the legatee was entitled to 92 of the new shares. Where, however, a company has been taken over and shares in the new company are held in place of those in the old one, the gift of the old shares will normally be adeemed. The test in such cases was stated by Cozens-Hardy MR in *Re Slater* (1907):

'You have to ask yourself, where is the thing which is given? If you cannot find it at the testator's death, it is no use trying to trace it unless you can trace it in this sense, that you find something which has been changed in name or form only, but which is substantially the same thing.'

6.6 INCOME AND OUTGOINGS RELATING TO SPECIFIC GIFTS

Unless the will provides to the contrary, a specific gift carries with it any profit, including income, becoming due *after* the date of death. Dividends declared before death, or rents falling due before death will not be included,

135

even though received after death. Logically, the gift also has to bear any loss in value suffered between death and transfer to the beneficiary. Costs incurred in administering the assets should be borne by the beneficiary, as should the cost involved in the actual transfer to him; see also *ante* 5.44 regarding foreign assets. It is often necessary to apportion both income received and expenses incurred as at the date of death (e.g. rent and outgoings in the case of a house specifically given), so that the beneficiary of the specific gift is affected only by receipts and payments appertaining to the *post*-death period: see *ante* 5.21 regarding legal apportionment. For IT and CGT purposes any income or gains between the date of death and the date of transfer will be that of the specific beneficiary, not of the PRs.

In the common case of a specific gift of stocks and shares the cost of administration and transfer will be minimal and needs no special consideration. Real and leasehold properties and valuable chattels can involve substantial costs and it is desirable for the PR to consider these at an early stage and to discuss them with the beneficiary. If the latter then wishes to object about a particular item, e.g. insurance cover, he has the opportunity to do so before the event rather than after: see also s. 19(2) TA and *ante* 3.21. Prompt consultation also enables the parties to conclude arrangements for payment of costs in advance of the actual demand.

6.7   ASSETS ALREADY IN THE POSSESSION OF THE BENEFICIARY

Where the beneficiary is already in possession of the articles from the date of death (either as a specific beneficiary or as residuary legatee), it is sensible to take a receipt at an early stage – even before probate – unless there is a real risk that recourse may have to be made to such effects for administration purposes. Generally, PRs should use their common sense over gifts of personal articles; they can usually give effect to them long before the administration is complete.

Incidentally, it is possible to allow a beneficiary possession of land to which he is presumptively entitled without going so far as to assent to the gift; the PRs retain power to resume possession if the exigencies of the administration demand it – see s. 43(1) AEA. This provision is useful in cases where it is important for the property to be secured or managed pending assent. On the other hand, most PRs would not welcome the prospect of having to take proceedings against a beneficiary if he declined to give up possession when asked to do so; the power is, therefore, one to be used discreetly.

Conversely, if the PRs hang fire in making an assent when it is practicable for them to do so, the beneficiary can bring pressure to bear through ss. 36(10) and 43(2) AEA, provided that he provides reasonable security for any outstanding liabilities relating to the landed property.

6.8 GENERAL LEGACIES AND DEVISES

These are gifts of property to be provided out of the testator's estate, irrespective of whether the property which is the subject of the gift forms part of the estate or not. Usually such a gift is of money (hence, a *pecuniary legacy*) but it may be any kind of personal property (if a legacy) or of real property (if a devise). A gift is of a general nature if nothing in its terms, or elsewhere in the will, shows that the testator intends to refer to something which he owns. For instance, 'I give 1,000 shares in Marks & Spencer to X'; even if the testator actually owned such a holding when he made his will, the legacy is a general one in the absence of other evidence that the testator intended it to be specific. A non-specific devise is not likely to turn up these days, except in the form of a gift of 'all my real estate' as a component of a residuary clause, when it would probably be construed as a residuary devise rather than a general devise.

6.9 PECUNIARY LEGACIES

Reference was made above to such legacies when a general legacy of money is given; it should be borne in mind, however, that the AEA provides its own definition of this term; s. 55(1)(ix) provides that for the purposes of the Act it includes an annuity, a general legacy, a demonstrative legacy so far as it is not discharged out of the designated property and any other general direction by the testator for the payment of money. This definition is of importance in connection with the statutory application of assets in cases of abatement – see *post* 6.11. It is possible for annuities to be either specific (a gift of an annuity to which the testator is entitled and which continues after his death) or demonstrative (where charged on a specified asset); normally, however, an annuity is a general legacy payable in instalments.

6.10 DEMONSTRATIVE LEGACIES

These are hybrids, partaking of the nature both of specific and general legacies. A legacy is called demonstrative when a particular fund is designated for its payment; e.g. 'I give to X £1,000 out of my account with the ABC Bank'. This legacy is specific to the extent that the account is sufficient to satisfy it and general to the extent that the account is *in*sufficient. If, for instance, the account at the date of death has only £500 in it, X's legacy is specific as to £500, general as to the rest. Again, this characteristic is important in connection with abatement.

6.11 ABATEMENT OF LEGACIES

Take the following situation: Ted Stator has just died leaving an estate of some £250,000 gross. You are his executor. His will bequeaths specific legacies worth about £50,000, an annuity of £1,000 per annum, a legacy of £10,000 payable out of an account which, at death, was worth £5,000, and sundry general legacies totalling £100,000. Debts are estimated at £50,000. There is going to be an IHT liability which cannot be quantified with any accuracy because Stator was the life tenant of a trust, the value of which is not known. The residue of the estate is left to various nephews and nieces.

It is clear that the value of the residuary gift is debatable at this point in time; there are too many unknown factors. There may be no residue at all and inroads may have to be made into the legacies. If this has to be done what is, so to speak, the batting order? In other words, in what order, if any, do the legacies stand to be reduced in value or to abate?

Subject to any contrary intention expressed in the will, general legacies abate before specific and demonstrative legacies. Where there is doubt as to the existence of residue at the end of the day, restraint should be observed when considering payment of pecuniary legacies of a general nature – one may even refrain from paying them at all until the outcome is clear. A PR should bear in mind that, if it turns out that he has overpaid, he cannot exercise a right to recover the excess unless, it seems, the overpayment was made either under threat of proceedings or without knowledge of a debt or claim which subsequently appears, in which case it would presumably also be necessary to show that notices for claims had been published and had expired before the payment was made – see *ante* 3.25. A payment under the directions of the court is, of course, in order whatever the circumstances; in a complex administration, where the PRs are in doubt as to the correct course to take and when, perhaps, they are being pressed by the legatees to pay out, it may well be sensible to seek such directions.

As we have already seen, the unpaid or underpaid beneficiary has a right of recovery, primarily against the PRs and secondarily against those who have been overpaid or wrongly paid – see *ante* 6.2.

6.12 RULES FOR ABATEMENT

In the above example, therefore, if it does transpire that either there is no residue or that it is insufficient to pay all the debts and testamentary expenses, recourse is to be had first of all to the general legacies. An annuity is a general legacy of a special kind – see *post* 6.20 – and there are special rules governing the way in which it should abate. In the example, £5,000 of the demonstrative legacy would abate with the rest of the general legacies. Specific legacies abate last. This is always assuming that Stator has not varied the batting order in his will. Unlike the rules for payment of debts in insolvent estates (see *ante* 5.7), a testator can always make special rules governing the order in which assets should be used for payment of debts and expenses where the estate is solvent. Generally, all legacies within a certain category abate rateably according to value but, again, a testator can make his own rules about this situation. The order of abatement outlined above is based on that contained in Part II, First Schedule AEA; this must now be discussed in a little more detail.

6.13 INCIDENCE OF DEBTS AND LEGACIES IN A SOLVENT ESTATE

Where an estate is insolvent the beneficiaries naturally have no concern with the way in which the debts are paid and the concern of the PRs and of the creditors will be to see that the right priorities are observed. Where, on the other hand, the estate is solvent the *incidence* of the debts and legacies – that is, the source from which they are paid – is a very material factor to the beneficiaries. The creditors, on the other hand, are not concerned about this; so long as they get paid the source of the payment does not matter to them. This subject is perhaps the most obscure of all of those one has to deal with in connection with estate administration. I do not propose to do more here than to sketch in the background; for a full discussion of the problems involved see, e.g. *Theobald*, ch. 59; *W, M & S*, chs. 50, 74.

6.14 CHARGES ORIGINATED BY THE DECEASED ON HIS ASSETS

Fortunately, one can start with a relatively easy concept – the treatment of debts charged on specific assets at the time of death. Section 35 AEA enacts the principle that property charged with the payment of money, whether by way of legal mortgage, equitable charge or otherwise shall, so far as the beneficiaries are concerned, be primarily responsible for payment of the debt so charged. This rule can be negatived by the written expression (either in the will or in another document) by the deceased of a contrary intention, but a general direction in the will for the payment of debts is not in itself regarded as such a contrary intention and neither is a charge of debts by the will upon the estate without the addition of further words identifying the particular charge created by the deceased.

An interesting and fairly typical example of the sort of situation to which s. 35 applies is described in *Re Birmingham* (1959):

On 31 March 1953 a Mrs Birmingham contracted to buy a freehold property for £3,500 and paid a deposit of £350. On 17 April 1953 she made a second codicil to her will specifically devising the property to her daughter 'free of all duties'. Completion was due to take place on 27 April but the testatrix died on the 21st. By arrangement, the property was subsequently conveyed direct to the daughter, the balance of the purchase money being paid by the executors who then asked the court how this balance should be borne as between the residuary legatees and the specific devisee. Upjohn J. held that the unpaid purchase money at the date of death was charged upon the property and the specific devise in the codicil was not evidence of a 'contrary intention'. The solicitors' costs for completing the purchase were administration expenses and came out of residue.

6.15 MARSHALLING OF ASSETS BETWEEN BENEFICIARIES

Having established what property, if any, bears its own debt on account of a charge, PRs may next have recourse to the First Schedule to AEA:

Part II
Order of Application of Assets where the Estate is Solvent
1. Property of the deceased undisposed of by will, subject to the retention thereout of a fund sufficient to meet any pecuniary legacies.
2. Property of the deceased not specifically devised or bequeathed but included (either by a specific or general description) in a residuary gift, subject to the retention out of such property of a fund sufficient to meet any pecuniary legacies, so far as not provided for as aforesaid.
3. Property of the deceased specifically appropriated or devised or bequeathed (either by a specific or general description) for the payment of debts.
4. Property of the deceased charged with, or devised or bequeathed (either by a specific or general description) subject to a charge for the payment of debts.
5. The fund, if any, retained to meet pecuniary legacies.
6. Property specifically devised or bequeathed, rateably according to value.
7. Property appointed by will under a general power, including the statutory power to dispose of entailed interests, rateably according to value.
8. The following provisions shall also apply –
   (a) The order of application may be varied by the will of the deceased.
   (b) This part of this Schedule does not affect the liability of land to answer the death duty imposed thereon in exoneration of other assets. (Under s. 211(1) IHTA, the IHT on all a deceased's real and personal estate in the UK is now a testamentary expense.[2])

These statutory provisions have been criticised, not without reason. It seems anomalous, for instance, that heads 3 and 4, although expressly appropriated for or charged with the payment of debts, should appear in the order *after* the residuary gift. However, in practice, the problems met with in paying debts from a solvent estate are not formidable. It is best to keep first in mind s. 35 (ante 6.14) and then to make sure that any specific legacies and devises are put on one side (no. 6 in the order and therefore of low priority so far as incidence of debts is concerned).

So far as the anomaly referred to above is concerned, the courts have decided that, in order to make property appropriated for or charged with the payment of debts primarily liable, the testator must provide an indication that it was his *intention* that such property should be made so liable and that other property should be exonerated.

The commonest kind of undisposed of property is a lapsed share of residue. A well-drawn residuary clause will make it clear that the residue to be divided is net of the debts and testamentary expenses; the lapsed share is likely to be calculated by reference to the gross residue, if there is either an isolated direction to pay debts or none at all.

The Court of Appeal's decision in *Re Harland-Peck* (1941) is noteworthy for its effort to rationalise the difference between the two types of case. Subject to the payment of funeral and testamentary expenses and debts, the testatrix devised and bequeathed all the rest and residue of her property to two named persons in equal shares as tenants in common, one of whom predeceased, so that his half share lapsed. It was held that this provision varied the statutory order. The whole residue, therefore, not the lapsed share, was primarily liable for the liabilities. The court drew a distinction between a gift, as here, made subject to the payment of debts, thus creating a charge on the property given, and a direction to pay debts followed by a gift of residue. See also *post* 6.16 concerning the use of the word 'after'.

6.16   LAPSED SHARE OF RESIDUE – TREATMENT OF LEGACIES

This very brief examination of a complex subject will at least have made it clear that it needs to be dealt with circumspectly. Where a lapsed share of residue arises, or where there is property appropriated for or charged with the payment of debts, PRs are put on warning and should take advice. So far as a lapsed share of residue is concerned, if there is no trust for sale in the will, s. 33(2) AEA will operate so as to make the legacies payable out of the gross fund before ascertaining the lapsed share, assuming there is no contrary indication in the will. But it cannot be assumed that similar treatment will be accorded to the debts and testamentary expenses.

In *Re Berrey* (1959) there was a will on a printed will form, bequeathing legacies and providing that 'after all my debts, and funeral, and expenses are paid I give and bequeath all the residue of my estate in equal shares' to four named persons, one of whom predeceased. It was held that the legacies were primarily payable out of the share undisposed of by the will because the effect of s. 33(2) AEA, requiring a sufficient fund to be set aside to provide for pecuniary legacies, was to make the undisposed of share the proper fund for payment of these legacies. But it was also held that the debts and expenses were, because of the use of the word 'after', charged on the whole residuary estate before division.

The more tricky situation is where the will contains an express trust for sale, thus supplanting s. 33(2) AEA; see *ante* 4.14. If the will does not make it clear that the residue is to be ascertained after payment of the legacies, it may be necessary to decide whether any pecuniary legacies bequeathed should come from it *after* the residue has been divided up (applying s. 34(3) AEA and its Schedule without regard to pre-1926 law), or whether the legacies should be taken out of the estate *before* the residuary division takes place, as often used to happen in such situations before 1926. *Snell* inclines to the former view, but the cases are irreconcilable. In *Re Midgley* (1955) there was, in the first place, a will which contained pecuniary legacies followed by a residuary gift to six named persons. Later, by a codicil, one of the six residuary legatees was deleted, and her share became undisposed of property. It was held that the pecuniary legacies were payable from this lapsed share. *Re Taylor* (1969) was basically similar in that there was an undisposed of share of residue and some pecuniary legacies were payable, but the court came to the opposite conclusion and decreed that the legacies should be paid out of the whole residue before division, in accordance with pre-1926 law. Salt, QC, Ch, in giving judgment, described the statutory provisions under discussion as 'notoriously obscure' and this seems a very fair comment.

6.17 MARSHALLING (a) IF THERE IS NO INTESTACY AND (b) OF REALTY AND PERSONALTY

Two other questions concerning payment of legacies should be borne in mind. First, does Part II of the First Schedule apply in cases where there is no undisposed of fund? Second, to what extent is real property to be used, compared with personal property, where an estate contains both? The answer to the first question appears to be affirmative.

> *Re Anstead* (1943) was a case where there was no undisposed of property. The will contained no trust for sale or administrative directions. There were pecuniary legacies totalling £45,000 and it was held that the fund for their payment must be set aside from residue under Para. 2 of the First Schedule, but using residuary personalty in preference to realty (following *Re Thompson* (1936)). The nub of the decision was that the legacies were free of estate duty except to the extent that realty had to be used to supplement them. These were the days (which existed right up to 1983) when estate duty (later CTT) was a charge on realty in the absence of exoneration by the testator. The underlying taxation principle in *Re Anstead* can still apply if payment of the legacies is directed to be made out of a residue containing a mixture of UK and foreign assets and the legacies are not given free of tax.

The answer to the second question is that legacies should be paid primarily from personalty, as in *Re Thompson* (1936) where Clauson J. said that the rule established in *Re Boards* (1895) had not been changed. It is open to a testator to vary the rule, by directing that the legacies be paid out of a mixed fund 'in which case they are paid rateably out of realty and personalty'. Note that where the interest in realty owned by the deceased is subject to either a statutory or an express trust for sale it loses its identity as realty and is available for payment of legacies on equal terms with personalty.

6.18 ANNUITIES

People always live for ever when there is any annuity to be paid them; and she is very stout and healthy, and hardly forty. An annuity is a very serious business; it comes over and over every year, and there is no getting rid of it.

(Jane Austen, *Sense and Sensibility*, ch. 2)

A straightforward annuity is not a very satisfactory kind of gift in times of inflation – at any rate if the annuitant may live for a considerable time to enjoy it. The real value of the gift will decline considerably during such a period. The better course may be to give the recipient the option of purchasing an annuity from a first-class insurance company as this should provide the annuitant with a better return than would be the case from an annuity secured on an invested fund. Moreover, there is a tax advantage in this course under s. 656 ICTA, which is not available where the annuity is bought in accordance with a direction in a will.[3] It has to be remembered that an annuitant may be entitled to call for a capital sum in lieu, e.g. where the will directs the executors to purchase an annuity for him without imposing a restriction such as a protective trust. This right is available to him even though the will directs that the capital value shall *not* be paid to him – *Stokes* v *Cheek* (1860). In such cases he must be advised of his rights and allowed to exercise them if he so wishes.

Where a PR has perforce to provide for an annuity he can either appropriate existing investments (see *post* 6.35) or set aside a cash fund and invest it. In either case, the principle is the same. The fund must be so invested as to secure payment of the annuity out of income during the life of the annuitant. The safe course is to assume that the annuitant will live to be one hundred. Investments producing income which may fluctuate, e.g. equities or land, are not satisfactory. The ideal solution for the elderly annuitant is a Government stock with a first redemption date on or near the annuitant's 100th birthday, although undated stocks have their attractions, particularly as they are now priced so low as to carry virtually no prospect of further capital loss.

It is true that many gifts of annuities provide for them to be secured on capital as well as income[4] but it is bad practice to rely on the capital element. Once recourse is had to capital, a vicious circle is entered into and one descends in an ever-narrowing spiral to the point where both capital and income cease to exist. Personal Representatives should bear in mind that residue remains liable to assist with the payments of an annuity after a fund has been set aside to service it *unless* the will contains a provision which exonerates residue from this impediment.

6.19 TAX FREE ANNUITIES

These are a problem. Personal Representatives sometimes set aside a fund which produces an income larger than is immediately necessary so as to give them the ability to cope with any subsequent rise in personal tax rates. Unless this procedure is authorised by the testator it seems doubtful whether it is correct. See, for instance, *Re Williams* (1936) in which Romer LJ said:

'I think their [i.e. the trustees'] duty will be to set aside at the end of a year from the testator's death such an amount as will produce the income of £1,000 after deduction of income tax at the current rate. If the rate of income tax increases after that date so much the worse for the beneficiary.'

Perhaps this problem should be considered in conjunction with the rule that PRs may accumulate surplus income where they foresee a future deficiency and may do so, apparently, without regard to the usual statutory limits imposed upon accumulations – see *Re Berkeley* (1968), a case which is also authority for the anomalous rule that the late payment of an annuity does not bear interest. In paying the annuity, the PRs will gross up the sum stated in the will, deduct income tax at the basic rate and pay the net amount to the annuitant, accompanied by a tax certificate.

A further difficulty arises where the annuitant is personally liable for tax at either *less* or *more* than the basic rate. In the former case he must hand to the PRs so much of any tax repayment he receives as relates to the annuity and in the latter case he is entitled to recover from them the tax at the higher rate payable in respect of the annuity: *Re Pettit* (1922). This complication can be overcome if the will adopts the formula of describing the annuity as such an amount as after deduction of income tax at the basic (or standard or current) rate will leave the stated net amount; *Re Jones* (1933). The same considerations apply to voluntary *inter vivos* dispositions. But separation agreements and the like which purport to confer a tax free annuity come up against s. 106 TMA. However, in *IRC v Ferguson* (1969) the House of Lords was prepared to construe such an agreement along the lines of the *Re Jones* formula, thus getting round s. 106.

From another House of Lords case, *IRC v Cook* (1945), is derived the practice of treating the *Re Pettit* refund as *taxed* income in the hands of the PRs or trustees receiving it from the annuitant, which means that it must be grossed back and certified accordingly to the surplus income beneficiary.

6.20 ABATEMENT OF ANNUITIES

As remarked above (*ante* 6.9), an annuity expressed in monetary terms is classed as a general legacy. If there are insufficient funds in an estate to pay all general legacies, including an annuity, in full, then the annuity must abate *pro rata* with the other legacies unless, indeed, the testator has made it clear that the annuity is to have priority.

The procedure in such cases is to make an actuarial valuation of such annuities. The actuarial value is then abated with the other general legacies and the resulting sum is paid to the annuitant – *Wright* v *Callender* (1852). This method is a rule of practice, not of law. It will not be used if there is only one annuity and no other general legacies. Although it has been used in cases where the estate is actuarially solvent (e.g. *Re Cox* (1938)), it will not be used in such a situation where 'there is no commercial risk of insufficiency'. In *Re Hill* (1944) the testator's will contained a number of pecuniary legacies and annuities and it appeared that there would not be enough money to pay all the legacies in full and to set aside sufficient sums to service the annuities; but, as soon as even the smallest annuity ceased, there would be sufficient funds to proceed in the orthodox way; the Court of Appeal ruled that there should be no abatement; the annuities could be paid out of income and topped up out of capital, if necessary, during the short period which would elapse before income became fully sufficient.

6.21 LEGACIES TO INFANTS

The problem here for the PR is one of making provision for a legacy which cannot be paid for a given number of years. One solution is to appoint trustees of the legacy under s. 42 AEA, after which the PRs are discharged from further responsibility for it, but this course is available only where the legacy is vested. Otherwise, PRs have to work out their own salvation, always bearing in mind that the legatee, whether he has a vested or contingent interest, is going to be disappointed (at least) if the amount paid to him on the due date is less than the amount specified in the will.

6.22 VESTED LEGACY TO AN INFANT

The distinction between vested and contingent legacies needs to be kept in view. A vested legacy to an infant is not paid over because, until the legatee is 18, the PR cannot get a discharge for it. The legacy belongs to the infant and must be set aside *in toto*. As Vaughan Williams LJ said in *Re Hall* (1903):

'The legatee has an absolute right to go to the trustee or executor and say "Although my legacy is payable *in futuro* it is a vested legacy, and I require you to invest the amount of it".'

If the legatee dies before reaching majority the legacy forms part of his estate and will be paid to his own PRs when they can produce a grant. Sometimes PRs are given authority to pay a vested legacy to an infant's parents and to get a good discharge for doing so. The risk in doing so is obvious and so is the convenience. It is suggested that it may sensibly be adopted where the legacy is small in amount – and where the probity of the parents is not in question.

A vested legacy normally earns interest from the first anniversary of death,[5] as in the case of other pecuniary legacies, and also carries the 'intermediate income', i.e. the income earned by the legacy during the time it remains in the hands of the PRs and, subsequently, the trustees, if any. When the legatee comes of age he gets not only the capital of the legacy but also any accumulated income; for the powers of maintenance and advancement see *post* ch. 10.

6.23   CONTINGENT LEGACIES TO INFANTS

Contingent legacies have to be approached rather differently. Typically these take the form of £x to Y if and when he reaches the age of 18 (or 21 or even 25, as some testators prefer). There is no certainty that the legacy will become payable. What the PRs have to do is set aside a fund from which the legacy *can* be paid if necessary. In other words, they provide for a contingency in this respect (just as they are entitled to do for other contingent liabilities). They must bear in mind, when considering what sort of fund to set aside, that the requirement is for £x at some specified date in the future, and not £x at the date when the fund is set up. In the case of both vested and contingent legacies the PRs may be asked to consider using up to one half of the value of the legacy at some intermediate date for the advancement or benefit of the legatee under s. 32 TA – see *post* 10.21 *et seq*. Contingent legacies must be distinguished from legacies which are vested but subject to being divested: see *post* 10.15

6.24   INCOME OF AN INFANT'S CONTINGENT LEGACY

The income of a fund set up for payment of a contingent legacy (whether for an infant or for an adult) belongs to the residuary legatees, unless it is given to a child of the testator or to a child to whom he stood in *loco parentis*, when it automatically carries the intermediate income, as is also the case where the legacy is expressed to be for the maintenance of a child (it need not be the testator's).[6] Unless the intermediate income *is* carried, the statutory power of maintenance is not available.

It is suggested that testators give less attention to this question than they should and that in many cases they would actually prefer such income to go to the contingent legatee rather than to the residuary legatees – if their attention were drawn to the point. Certainly it is more convenient administratively for income and capital to go together and there is the further advantage that there will then normally be an accumulation and maintenance trust (provided the conditions set out in s. 71 IHTA are satisfied) and the question of a contingent claim for IHT that would otherwise have arisen on the determination of the residuary legatee's interest in the income of the legacy fund cannot arise: see *post* 8.11 to 8.13.

6.25 INVESTMENT OF INFANTS' LEGACIES

Probably enough has already been said to indicate that my own preference, so far as the investment of infants' legacies is concerned, is for a cautious approach. Equities should only play a minor role, if any, even when parents of infant beneficiaries ask the PRs to introduce an equity element. It may be better to turn down, politely but firmly, such requests in the case of smaller legacies and to choose stocks with a fixed date of redemption. The choice of coupon may turn upon the likelihood of receiving a request for the infant's maintenance; a high income, if applied for maintenance, may be useful in maximising the income tax repayment, depending upon other sources of income. Index-linked investments are a possible alternative, unless credence is placed on political assurances to squeeze inflation out of the system. Where the legacy is contingent, two interests are being protected, the principal beneficiary's and that of the person who takes on failure of the gift.

Where there is a contingent pecuniary legacy not carrying the intermediate income, the interest of the residuary legatee in the income is probably of lesser importance, as the prime task is to ensure that the capital of the legacy will be intact, either when the contingency is satisfied (or fails) or when capital is advanced (with the consent of the residuary legatee) under s. 32 TA.

6.26 SETTLED FUNDS

This term is used here to describe funds arising out of gifts of a full life interest – whether in a specific asset, such as a house or in a cash sum or residue of the estate (a residuary settled fund will often arise as the result of an intestacy – see *ante* 4.5). Such gifts equate with, and are dealt with at the same time as, absolute gifts of a specific, general and residuary nature. Personal Representatives will find more scope for making use of existing assets where they have to constitute either general or residuary settled funds (powers of appropriation are dealt with *post* 6.35). The possibility of doing so should be borne in mind during the first stages of an administration, when PRs are making plans for sales to meet their cash requirements. In addition, where land is settled, the SLA may apply. If it does, thus constituting the person (of full age) beneficially entitled in possession *tenant for life* under s. 19(1) SLA, the better course is to vest the title in such person in accordance with s. 9(2). The old rule that freehold property bears its own death duties has been abrogated by s. 211 IHTA, subject to any contrary intention shown by the deceased in his will.

Having provided for and constituted a settled fund, provision should be made for:

(a)   Regular payment of income to the person or persons entitled.

(b)   The provision to them of periodic statements of account and of certificates of deduction of tax R185E (in connection with which, Statement of Trust Income R59 and Form 1, which is a statement of untaxed income, must be submitted annually to the trustees' Inspector of Taxes).

(c)   Regular reviews of the fund's investments (see *post* 11.12) and of other assets held, including land other than that vested in a tenant for life under the SLA. In the case of land for which the trustees will (in the future) be responsible, arrangements should be made for collection of any rents due, for rent review and for regular inspection of the properties; also for an annual review of insurance cover.

6.27   FAILURE OF BENEFIT BY LAPSE; *COMMORIENTES*; SURVIVORSHIP CLAUSES

If a beneficiary named in a will predeceases the testator, the general rule is that his gift lapses, unless exceptionally the beneficiary was owed a moral obligation. The rule applies to companies which have been dissolved and to clubs and societies which have ceased to exist. So far as charities are concerned, a gift may be saved from lapse if a general charitable intention on the part of the testator can be presumed; in such a case the gift will be applied *cy-près* (see *post* 12.16).

In *Re Leach* (1948) the facts were that the testratrix made a codicil leaving a legacy of £1,000 to P; there was a recital stating that the testratrix's son (who predeceased her) was indebted to P in the sum of £1,000 when he died. P predeceased the testratrix also. Vaisey J held that the legacy should not lapse but should go to P's estate. There was a moral obligation to leave the legacy to P and this preserved it. The limits of the doctrine are a bit uncertain; it may be confined to cases where an unenforceable debt is intended to be satisfied by a legacy.

A testator should consider whether he wishes to include any substitutional provisions in the event of a beneficiary's predeceasing him. This is certainly desirable in the case of a residuary gift; if the residue is given to A, B and C as tenants in common in equal shares, the previous death of C will leave a gap in the gift which will devolve as on intestacy of the partial kind. This should be avoided. If the residuary gift is to joint tenants, then the *ius accrescendi* applies and there will be no lapse. Nevertheless, a testator may well prefer an alternative to this and should make provision accordingly.

Closely associated with the doctrine of lapse is that of solving the problem of the order of deaths in a case where it is scientifically impossible to tell which person predeceased the other. The first port of call is s. 184 LPA, which reads:

In all cases where, after the commencement of this Act, two or more persons have died in circumstances rendering it uncertain which of them survived the other or others, such deaths shall (subject to any order of the court), for all purposes affecting the title to property, be presumed to have occurred in order of seniority, and accordingly the younger shall be deemed to have survived the elder.

In *Hickman* v *Peacey* (1945) the House of Lords decided, but only by a majority, that simultaneous death in a bomb disaster amounted to circumstances rendering it uncertain who the survivor could be, thus letting in the presumption under s. 184. But if the evidence is able to separate the deaths by even the smallest interval of time, there is no room for the section to operate.

An important exception to the generality of this statutory rule is provided by s. 46(3) AEA (introduced by the Intestates' Estates Act 1952), which reads:

'Where the intestate and the intestate's husband or wife have died in circumstances rendering it uncertain which of them survived the other and the intestate's husband or wife is by virtue of s. 184 LPA, deemed to have survived the intestate, this section [i.e. s. 46] shall, nevertheless, have effect as respects the intestate as if the husband or wife had not survived the intestate.'

In other words if a married couple die together and the older one of the two dies intestate, the other spouse is to get nothing from the intestacy. Section 46(3) will apply only where s. 184 can apply, i.e. where the order of deaths cannot be determined. Note also that s. 46(3) is not so extensive as s. 184. Whereas s. 184 applies wherever the title to property is in question (for example, to settled property and joint property as well as free estates), s. 46(3) is confined to the intestacy of an older spouse.[7]

Under s. 4(2) IHTA, in those cases where either s. 184 LPA or s. 46(3) AEA apply, the rule is that the deaths occurred simultaneously; thus there will be no passing of the assets from the elder person's estate to the younger person's and each estate will be taxed separately without reference to the other. This principle applies also to life tenant and remainderman who happen to die together; the momentary interest in possession of the remainderman (if the younger of the two) will not be taxed. But if the statutory presumptions under s. 184 and s. 46(3) do not apply – in other words, there is an interval of time (however short) between the deaths – the only relief will be under s. 141 IHTA in the form of 100% successive charges relief, which, because of the operation of the nil rate band, will not necessarily give the same benefit.[8]

The *commorientes* rule (i.e. the rule dealing with the situation where there is uncertainty about the order of deaths) can be eliminated by a survivorship clause: see *ante* 2.5, para. (1). For such a clause to be acceptable for IHT purposes the survivorship period must not extend beyond six months; if a longer period is deemed necessary, recourse must be had to the mini-discretionary trust under s. 144 IHTA: *ante* 2.5 and 4.29. The advantages of a survivorship clause are:

(a)   In the case of pecuniary and specific legacies, where the commingling of estates is not an issue, there is an evident advantage in postponing vesting for, say, three months. The bequests are unlikely to be satisfied any sooner and it will help to ensure that only those take who are alive at the time of distribution. Most testators prefer their money to go to those who are alive to enjoy it.

(b)   If a beneficiary dies in a situation where it would otherwise be appropriate to use the statutory presumptions about the order of deaths, the survivorship clause has the advantage of providing an immediate solution to the problem without waiting for a determination of the facts and without the possibility of encountering an argument with the Revenue, bearing in mind that they will refuse to tax the two estates separately without proof of the inseparability of the deaths.

(c)   Where there are parallel wills, with each person in the common disaster liable to share in the other's estate, the survivorship clause has the merit of forestalling the possible commingling of the two estates. This is likely to have dramatic advantages for IHT purposes if the couple concerned are not married, i.e. they are brothers or sisters or otherwise living together. For example, if we take the case of a bachelor brother and his spinster sister who leave their estates to each other with a gift over to charity, a survivorship clause would ensure, if they died closely together, that both estates reached the charity without the payment of any tax. On the other hand, the fiscal advantages for the married couple may be illusory.[9]

(d)   The survivorship clause may be of particular value for a substitutional gift. Thus, if there is a gift to the testator's child with a gift over to that child's issue *per stirpes* in the event of his failing to survive the testator by three months, the result is a refined version of s. 33 WA: see below.

6.28   THE STATUTORY EXCEPTION FROM LAPSE

Section 33 WA deals with cases of gifts to children and other issue of the testator. In its amended form it reads:

(1) Where –
  (a)   a will contains a devise or bequest to a child or remoter descendant of the testator; and
  (b)   the intended beneficiary dies before the testator, leaving issue; and
  (c)   issue of the intended beneficiary are living at the testator's death,
then, unless a contrary intention appears by the will, the devise or bequest shall take effect as a devise or bequest to the issue living at the testator's death.

(2) Where –
  (a)   a will contains a devise or bequest to a class of persons consisting of children or   remoter descendants of the testator; and
  (b)   a member of the class dies before the testator, leaving issue, and
  (c)   issue of that member are living at the testator's death,
then, unless a contrary intention appears by the will, the devise or bequest shall take effect as if the class included the issue of its deceased member living at the testator's death.

(3) Issue shall take under this section through all degrees, according to their stock, in equal shares if more than one, any gift or share which their parent would have taken and so that no issue shall take whose parent is living at the testator's death and so capable of taking.

(4) For the purposes of this section –
  (a) the illegitimacy of any person is to be disregarded; and
  (b) a person conceived before the testator's death and born living thereafter
is to be taken to have been living at the testator's death.

The original s. 33 was amended by s. 19 AJA 1982 in respect of testators dying after 1982 and certainly now operates more sensibly than in its unamended form. In effect, any gift to a descendant of the testator is preserved provided that issue of the deceased beneficiary are living at the date of the testator's death. Where this is the case, the gift devolves on such issue *per stirpes*.

> *Example* – A, by his will, has left his residuary estate to his children B, C and D in equal shares. D predeceased the testator, leaving three children of his own, E, F and G. E died before A but his children H and J are also living at A's death. The gift to D of a third share is preserved and will be divided three ways – a third each to F and G and the remaining third equally between H and J.

The new section applies as much to gifts of life interests and joint interests as it does to gifts of absolute interests. If the original gift contained an age contingency which the original donee had already satisfied in the testator's lifetime, it seems clear that the age contingency will not be imported into the substituted gift; a position which is likely to hold good even if the age contingency had not been satisfied, provided there is no gift over on failure of the contingency to indicate a contrary intention. In the case of class gifts with an age contingency, it is sensible to suppose that a substituted member of the class would enter into it on the same terms as the original members *sed quaere*.

The operation of s. 33 is nullified by a contrary intention in the will, which may be either express or implied. Testators should consider whether they want the section to apply or whether they want to make their own arrangements.

6.29 CLASS GIFTS

The rules as to lapse do not apply to a class gift, i.e. a gift to persons who are included and comprehended under some general description: *Kingsbury* v *Walter* (1901).[10] Clearly, a person within such a description who predeceases the testator cannot qualify as a member of the class at the date of death. The testator can, of course, make provision for this by extending his class definition. Class gifts do give rise to some practical problems arising out of the need to establish membership of the class satisfactorily. There should be some authenticated evidence and the best form of such evidence is a statutory declaration by some person with knowledge of the facts and supported, where appropriate, by certificates of birth, marriage and death. Bear in mind that illegitimate and adopted children (depending

151

upon the date of the trust instrument or the date of its coming into force) are now equally entitled to share with legitimate and natural issue, unless expressly excluded by a testator.

6.30 CLASS-CLOSING RULES

Reference may perhaps usefully be inserted here to the so-called 'class-closing rules', applicable to testamentary gifts to classes (and to similar gifts in *inter vivos* settlements). These have been developed purely as a matter of convenience, in order to speed up the completion of an administration and to prevent beneficiaries from having to wait a long time to receive their shares of a class gift. Under the rule in *Andrews* v *Partington* (1791) membership of a class, for the purposes of a gift, is closed on the date upon which its first member becomes entitled to a vested interest in possession; persons born after that date are excluded from the gift and the maximum number of shares is fixed. On the other hand, where shares are to vest at birth, the class will remain open indefinitely unless a member was born before the testator's death or before the end of some prior limitation such as a life interest.

> *Example* – gift in a will to all the children of A who attain 21. When the testator dies A has two children aged 18 and 15. The class is still open and can admit any further children of A until the time when the first member of the class to reach 21 does so, who will not necessarily be either of the existing children. However, suppose that a third child is born and subsequently the oldest child attains 21, the class will thereupon close and any further child of A afterwards born cannot be admitted to the class.
>
> If, on the other hand, the gift were simply in favour of all A's children without any age contingency, the class would close immediately on the death of the testator in favour of the children aged 18 and 15. If A had no children living when the testator died, the class would remain open right the way through to A's death.

6.31 CLASS-CLOSING – MODERN DECISIONS

The rule in *Andrews* v *Partington* is subject to the expression of a contrary intention by the testator or settlor; deciding whether or not this exists may be regarded as something of a lottery. In *Re Edmondson* (1972) there was, effectively, a gift to 'such of my grandchildren whenever born as shall attain the age of 21'. The Court of Appeal held that the words 'whenever born' were sufficiently emphatic to exclude the rule. On the other hand, in *Re Chapman* (1978) there was a gift to the settlor's grandchildren 'now born or who shall be born hereafter', the vesting age being specified as 25 (subject to reduction) and the Court of Appeal held that these words did not exclude the rule and the class closed when the elder grandchild reached 25. See also

Re Tom (1987) where the settlor defined the objects of a power as his existing and future great-grandchildren, the latter being great-grandchildren born after the date of any appointment and before a specified closing date. When the eldest existing beneficiary reached 18, the trustees asked whether the class-closing rule applied; the Vice-Chancellor said that the presumption in favour of closing could be rebutted only by provisions which were inescapably incompatible with it; such provisions did exist here – the mind of the draftsman had been directed to the composition of the class and the existence of a specified closing date clearly implied that any member of the class born before that date should be entitled to benefit. For application of the class-closing rules on disclaimers and surrenders, see *ante*, 4.24.

6.32 FAILURE OF BENEFIT BY FORFEITURE

There is a rule of public policy, known as the forfeiture rule, which precludes a person who has unlawfully killed another from acquiring a benefit as a result of the deed.[11] Section 2 Forfeiture Act 1982 gives the court wide discretion to modify the effect of this rule where it is satisfied that, 'having regard to the conduct of the offender and of the deceased and to such other circumstances as appear to the court to be material', justice requires some modification to be made. But such modification cannot be in favour of a murderer – s. 5 – and see *Davitt* v *Titcomb* (1990), which decided that a murderer was not entitled to any part of the proceeds of a sale of a house jointly owned by himself and his victim.

> In *Re K* (1985) the husband had behaved violently towards his wife for years and fearing an attack, she had picked up a loaded shotgun to defend herself. She released the safety catch and the gun went off, killing the husband. The wife's plea of manslaughter was accepted. The deceased's estate was a large one and he had given her substantial benefits in his will. 'After anxious consideration', Vinelott J., applying s. 2 of the Act, decided that the wife should not be deprived of any of these benefits and his decision was upheld in the Court of Appeal.
>
> *Re H deceased* (1990) is another manslaughter case, where the court expressed the view that it would not be just to apply the forfeiture rule to *all* manslaughter cases as a matter of course. In this case there had been no 'deliberate, intentional and unlawful violence or threats of violence'. The forfeiture rule did not apply, and there was therefore no need to consider whether or not to apply the Act.

Section 3 of the Act provides that the forfeiture rule shall not preclude any person (except a murderer) from making an application under the Inheritance (Provision for Family and Dependants) Act 1975: see *ante* 4.30 *et seq*. In *Re Royse* (1984) it was held that someone who lost reasonable provision under the deceased's will because of the application of the rule could not make a claim under the 1975 Act, since the absence of reasonable provision for the applicant, as required by s. 2(1) of that Act, was due not to a failure on the part of the deceased but to the application of the forfeiture rule.

6.33 FAILURE OF BENEFIT BY WITNESSING THE WILL

By s. 15 WA, if a beneficiary witnesses a will there is an effective attestation but any gift to that beneficiary or his or her spouse contained in the witnessed document is void. The section was modified slightly by s. 1 WA 1968; where the attestation of the will is complete without having to resort to the beneficiary's part in it, then the gift to the beneficiary is preserved. This can only happen, of course, if there are three or more witnesses, which must be an unusual situation, but the legislation arose as a result of a case of that kind; see *Re Bravda* (1968) where a will was validly executed and attested by two non-beneficiaries. The testator then asked his two daughters, sole beneficiaries under the will, to witness it 'to make it stronger'. They did so and the Court of Appeal held that their gifts failed. There is a rebuttable presumption that anyone, other than the testator, whose signature is found at the end of a will, signed as a witness.

Section 15 cannot apply to privileged wills, since they do not have to be witnessed. Neither does it apply to a will containing an offending gift which is afterwards confirmed by another testamentary document which is *not* witnessed by the beneficiary or his or her spouse – *Re Trotter* (1899). If a will makes a gift to a beneficiary and is not witnessed by that beneficiary, but a subsequent codicil is so witnessed, the beneficiary is not deprived of the gift under the will. The rule does not apply to gifts to a witness as trustee; and a beneficiary under a secret or half-secret trust is not deprived of benefit if he or she witnesses the will through which the trust arises – *Re Young* (1951) discussed *ante*, 1.20.

6.34 TIME FOR PAYMENT OF LEGACIES

A PR need not pay legacies before the first anniversary of the death (not even, it seems, if the testator *directs* payment during this period): see s. 44 AEA. On the other hand, there is nothing to stop him doing so during the 'executor's year' if he considers it safe to do so. Even after 12 months have gone by, circumstances may prevent payment of the legacies but, if this is the case, interest starts to run from the end of the first year, subject to certain exceptions: see *ante* 6.22n5. The rate of interest where an estate is being administered in the High Court is now 6% under RSC O 44 r 10 (since 1 Oct 1983) but only 5% for a parental legacy under s. 31(3) TA. In *Re Pollock* (1943) a legacy of £1,000 to the widow 'to be paid to her immediately after my death for her immediate requirements' was held to carry interest from the date of death. Generally a direction that a legacy be paid as soon as possible does not affect the rule that interest only becomes payable at the end of the first year.

A professional executor will always try to arrange payment of pecuniary legacies well before the end of the executor's year – subject, of course, to his being quite satisfied that he will be left with sufficient funds to defray outstanding claims of all kinds. When, as is often the case, such claims are not yet precisely quantified, the maximum possible cash requirement should be calculated and a margin above this allowed for safety before deciding whether legacies may be paid.

6.35 APPROPRIATION

Instead of realising assets and discharging legacies in cash, it may be possible to satisfy the beneficial interests arising out of the will or intestacy by appropriating specific assets of the estate to satisfy them. Gifts of annuities sometimes have a power of appropriation attached to them, but there are usually practical problems of an almost insoluble kind in exercising such a power in such a situation. The same difficulty applies to the appropriation of assets to satisfy infants' legacy funds. On the whole such a power, whether express or derived from s. 41 AEA, seems most useful when dealing with settled funds and residuary gifts. In the case of settled funds a 'mixed bag' of investments may well not be out of place. Residuary gifts between several people (some absolute perhaps, some settled) can conveniently be dealt with by means of appropriation, although if the division of each investment is not exactly in accordance with the shares given by the will, it will be necessary to inform the beneficiaries that despite the adoption of current prices for the purpose of the scheme of division, for CGT purposes the base value in their hands must be calculated on the probate price: s. 62(4), TCGA. The inequality between probate prices and appropriation prices is a factor for the beneficiaries to consider when approving the scheme of division. Despite this difficulty, it remains important that the appropriation should be fair to all parties, not only those directly concerned with it but also those indirectly affected. Section 41 gives a PR very wide powers so that any asset may be appropriated (with the requisite consent) – but common sense should ensure that only those assets entirely suitable for the purpose are selected. Equally, whilst it is possible to appropriate all the high quality assets and leave behind the second-best for the other beneficiaries, it is not a policy which the conscientious PR will follow.

The overriding principle of fairness is reinforced by s. 41(5) which makes it necessary for the PR to consider the interests of future or unascertained beneficiaries as well as those whose consent is not required. There is also the basic rule that the assets should be revalued at the date of appropriation, a rule that was accepted in *Re Collins* (1975) where the dwelling-house was worth £4,200 at the date of death and had increased to £8,000 in value by the time of appropriation to the intestate's surviving spouse. The unfairness of adopting any other procedure is apparent.

6.36   CONSENTS TO APPROPRIATION

Section 41 requires certain consents to be obtained; some wills authorise PRs to dispense with such consents. This, of course, can be useful – for instance, where there is failure by beneficiaries to agree on a distribution scheme or where simply there is no response to proposals by the PRs. On the other hand, in accordance with the desirable policy of keeping all beneficiaries fully informed, one should advise the person or persons affected of what is being done. In the absence of any express power of appropriation in the will it should be remembered that s. 41 applies only to PRs, not to trustees (although the Law Reform Committee, in its 23rd Report, para.4.42, has recommended that the statutory power should be extended to trustees without, surprisingly, the requirement of consent). Where a trust is created, PRs should at least consider making full use of the present statutory power before the administration period ends.

6.37   DISTRIBUTING THE ESTATE – EQUITABLE DOCTRINES

The following equitable doctrines (satisfaction, election and equitable apportionment) may not be encountered very often in practice but are bound to turn up from time to time, and PRs need to be able to recognise the situations in which they may be relevant and applicable.

6.38   SATISFACTION – OF DEBTS BY LEGACIES

It has to be said first that this particular rule is excluded by a direction in the will to pay the debts, or the debts and the legacies. As most professionally-drawn wills contain such a direction, the rule will not often have to be applied. If there is no such direction in the will, the following conditions must be satisfied for the rule to apply:

(a)   The legacy to the testator's creditor must equal or exceed the amount of the debt and must be as beneficial to the creditor as the debt; for instance, a contingent legacy will not satisfy a debt and neither will a legacy of uncertain amount.

(b)   The will containing the legacy must have been made *after* the debt was incurred.

6.39   SATISFACTION – OF LEGACIES BY LEGACIES

This is not, strictly, a case of satisfaction in the equitable sense, since that sense requires the satisfaction of an *obligation*. However, the cases are usually dealt with under this heading. Suppose a testator leaves a legacy of £5,000 to A in his will and later in the same document leaves another legacy of £5,000 to A; should A get both legacies or only one? Where this situation occurs and the same motive, or no motive, is expressed for the two legacies, the presumption is that only one is payable. Legacies of different amounts in the same instrument are both payable. Where the two legacies are contained in different documents, e.g. will and codicil, then both are payable unless they are of the same amount *and* the same motive is expressed for both. The only exception to this rule will occur where evidence, either in the documents themselves or in the surrounding circumstances, shows that the one legacy was simply a duplicate of the other.

6.40 SATISFACTION – THE PRESUMPTION AGAINST DOUBLE PORTIONS

This may apply in two differing sets of circumstances. In the first place, where a testator has left a legacy to a child of his and subsequently provides that child with a portion, then the presumption is that the legacy is adeemed, *pro tanto*, by the portion; this part of the doctrine is sometimes called the ademption of legacies by portions and it is essential to it that the will should come first. Secondly, if a father covenants to provide a portion for a child (as he might in the child's marriage settlement) and afterwards makes a will leaving that child a legacy (or afterwards makes him a gift in the nature of a portion), there is a presumption that the portion-debt is satisfied, again *pro tanto*, by the subsequent legacy or gift; here the obligation arises first and the will comes later.

It should be emphasised that normally the rule against double portions applies only as between father and child or between child and some other person who has assumed the responsibilities of a father and has undertaken 'the office and duty of the parent to make provision for the child' – the words are those of Lord Cottenham LC in *Powys* v *Mansfield* (1837). Such a person stands in *loco parentis* to the child and could, for instance, be the child's mother or the child's grandfather. Once the legacy is adeemed or partially adeemed by the later *inter vivos* gift, a subsequent updating codicil will not alter the position. The following words of wisdom also emanate from the case of *Powys* v *Mansfield*:

> 'It is very true that a codicil republishing a will makes the will speak as from its own date for the purpose of passing after-purchased lands, but not for the purpose of reviving a legacy revoked, adeemed, or satisfied. The codicil can only act upon the will as it existed at the time; and, at the time, the legacy revoked, adeemed, or satisfied formed no part of it.'

The purpose of the rule is to ensure equality as between children (and those in *loco parentis*); other beneficiaries are not allowed to benefit:

In *Re Heather* (1906) the testator bequeathed £3,000 to his adopted daughter and divided his residue equally between that daughter and a stranger. Subsequently he made a gift of £1,000 to the daughter and it was held that, even if the gift had been a portion, the daughter's legacy would not have been adeemed, as the effect of such ademption would have been to benefit a stranger at the expense of the child.

Equity is full of backwaters and there is case law which says that, even in the case of beneficiaries with no parental connection, a legacy expressly given for a particular purpose or in obedience to a specific moral obligation is *prima facie* adeemed by the payment of money in the testator's lifetime for the same purpose, or in pursuance of the same moral obligation.

6.41 MEANING OF 'PORTION'

The word 'portion' has rather an old-fashioned ring about it in these days. It can have the narrower meaning of the provision in a strict settlement for the younger children but, more broadly, it comprehends both a lifetime advancement made by an intestate under s. 47(1)(iii) AEA – see *ante* 4.11 – and the kind of gift we are now contemplating. Reference to *Taylor* v *Taylor* (1875) provides some help concerning its meaning, the following being extracts from the judgment of Jessel MR:

> 'I have always understood that an advancement by way of portion is something given by the parent to establish the child in life, or to make what is called provision for him – not a mere casual payment.' He went on to say that nothing could be more productive of misery in families than if he were to hold that every member of the family must account strictly for every sum received from a parent. According to his view, nothing was an advancement unless it were given on marriage, or to establish the child in life. *Prima facie*, an advancement must be made in early life; but any sum given by way of making a permanent provision for the child would come within the term establishing for life.

If the testator fails to survive the portion gift by seven years, the benefit to be brought into account by the donee will be reduced by the amount of IHT which the donee incurs, in accordance with the principle in *Re Beddington* (1900); see also *Re Turner* (1968).

It would appear that the subsequent gift or portion must be valued for the purpose of hotchpot at the date when it was made; this is in contrast to the rule for advancements under an intestacy – see *ante* 4.10.

6.42 ELECTION

Where a testator, whether intentionally or not, gives property to X and, in the same instrument (will and codicil counting as one for this purpose), gives property of X to Y, X cannot take his gift from the testator *and* keep his own property – he must elect either to take against the instrument or under it. In the first case he takes the testator's gift for himself and keeps his own property but, out of the former's value, must compensate Y for his loss in not getting X's own property. If X elects to take under the instrument, he takes the testator's gift and hands over his own property to Y. The principle is similar to that doctrine of Scottish Law which declares that a person cannot approbate and reprobate – to put it in homelier terms, one cannot have one's cake and eat it.

Compensation of the disappointed beneficiary is an essential element of the rule, which is illustrated by *Re Gordon's Will Trusts* (1978):

> The testatrix was joint tenant with her son of a house; this devolved on the son absolutely when the testatrix died, though, by her will, he was given only a life interest in the property, subject to which its proceeds of sale were to fall into residue. The son was also given some furniture and effects, a legacy of £1,000 and a protected life interest in one-half of the residue. The son, in effect, elected to take against the will by selling the house and keeping the proceeds. There was no doubt that he had to compensate the other residuary beneficiaries out of the value of the furniture and effects and legacy but the Court of Appeal refused to say that he must also surrender his protected life interest; to do so would destroy the interest, thus making it useless for the purposes of compensation.

So also, where the beneficiary cannot elect because his own property is inalienable, the rule will not apply. Election should not be confused with *disclaimer*; a beneficiary may always effectively refuse a gift provided he does so before accepting benefit from it (for disclaimer generally, including the IHT consequences, see *ante* 4.21 *et seq.*). So, in theory at any rate, a beneficiary could accept a beneficial legacy under a will and disclaim an onerous one; but the will may be so framed as to preclude the beneficiary from picking and choosing in this way, as where there is a composite gift of an onerous leasehold and its valuable contents.

6.43 ELECTION USUALLY ARISES FROM TESTATOR'S MISTAKE

So far as the doctrine of election is concerned, it is assumed that it was the testator's intention in making his will that every part of it should be effective, including a gift of somebody else's property. It seems to be immaterial that he did not know he was giving away property which he did not in fact own or perhaps mistakenly believed it to be his own. As *Snell* remarks 'probably most cases of election arise from a mistake of law or fact'. It has also been said that the equitable doctrine of election is a mischievous doctrine.*

The doctrine of election may apply also (a) where the testator purports to give away the entirety of an asset when in fact he is merely a co-owner

---

*See 'Mistakes in Wills and Election in Equity' by N Crago (1990) 106 LQR 487.

or a life tenant; (b) where the testator purports to give away a foreign asset which he cannot dispose of under the local law; and (c) to those entitled in default of appointment where a testator exercises a special power of appointment in favour of non-objects.

In *Re Dicey* (1956) the testatrix had a life interest in Blackacre with remainder to A, B and C in the proportions of one-half, one-quarter and one-quarter respectively. By her will she devised Blackacre to B absolutely and also gave her own property, Whiteacre, to A absolutely. The Court of Appeal decided that the doctrine of election applied, so that if A elected against the will he must compensate B out of Whiteacre to the extent of a half of the value of Blackacre, with the alternative of retaining Whiteacre and conveying his half share of Blackacre to B.

In *Re Ogilvie* (1918) Margaret died domiciled in England, leaving her English moveable property to her son and her Paraguayan tramway to charity, but under the *lex situs* of the tramway, the charity could not take more than a fifth, as the son was the compulsory heir under the law of Paraguay of the other four-fifths. The son was put to his election – either to give up his interest in the tramway and keep his English bequest or keep his interest in the tramway and compensate the charity out of the English moveable property.

In *Whistler* v *Webster* (1784) the testator had a power of appointment in favour of his children, who were also the beneficiaries in default of appointment. By his will he exercised the power in favour of grandchildren and also gave legacies to his sons. It was held that the sons were put to their election (a) to take their legacies and let the grandchildren benefit under the improper appointment or (b) to take the funds in default of appointment and compensate the grandchildren out of their legacies.

6.44   EQUITABLE APPORTIONMENTS

These rules consist of the application to particular situations of the basic principle that PRs and trustees should behave with complete impartiality to beneficiaries, not favouring the interests of one at the expense of another. It has to be said that applying the rules in practice can be a complex and time-consuming business and they may safely be ignored where their application will produce only a trifling difference. Testators will often expressly negative their application.

(a)   The rule in *Howe* v *Lord Dartmouth* (1802): where in a will there is a residuary gift of personal property (excluding leaseholds) to persons in succession, equity imposes (in the absence of an express trust for sale) a duty to sell wasting, unauthorised and non-income producing assets and to invest the proceeds in authorised securities. Until this is done, the income from the estate or trust should be adjusted so that the life tenant gets a fair but not excessive yield. Generally speaking, a power to *retain* such assets will exclude the rule, a power merely to postpone sale will not.

(b)   The rule in *Re Earl of Chesterfield's Trusts* (1883) is a branch of *Howe* v *Lord Dartmouth* concerning the proceeds of realisation of non-income producing assets. Such proceeds are apportioned between capital and income so as to produce a fair yield for the life tenant for the period up to the date of sale or falling in. As regards intestate estates, the rule will not normally apply to a reversionary interest but it may do so in the case of other non-income producing assets: s. 33(1) AEA.

(c)   The rule in *Dimes* v *Scott* (1828) is a branch of *Howe* v *Dartmouth* which deals with cases where the testator has provided an express trust for sale and conversion of a residuary gift of pure personalty. It needs a power to retain consciously exercised to exclude apportionment. Intestacies are outside the rule: s. 33(5) AEA.

(d)   The rule in *Allhusen* v *Whittell* (1867) is again concerned with gifts by will of residuary property (whether real or personal) to persons in succession and requires the true residuary fund to be ascertained by treating debts, expenses and legacies as having been paid partly out of capital and partly out of the income produced by that capital up to the date of payment. The rule applies also to the residuary estate of an intestate. The rule was applied by *Re Perkins* (1907) to cases where a debt, such as an annuity, is paid by instalments. The rule 'is not to be slavishly followed' (*W, M & S*, p. 914) and, in most cases, 'rough and ready calculations' will suffice – *Re Wills* (1915).

This very short treatment of equitable apportionment may be supplemented, in case of need, by reference to *Snell* pp. 227–231 and 347–8.[12]

There is a line of cases headed by *Re Atkinson* (1904) which deal with the problem of apportionment between life tenant and remainderman where an authorised mortgage is in default (or where a mortgage derived from the testator or settlor is in default) and the amount eventually received is insufficient to cover both capital and arrears of interest. A similar apportionment will be necessary if there is partial repayment of a debenture stock and accrued interest under a scheme of arrangement by the company concerned: *Re Morris* (1960).

6.45   DISTRIBUTION WHERE DECEASED DIED DOMICILED ABROAD

Reference has already been made to the rule that the administration is controlled by the *lex fori* – see *ante* 5.43; however, once the administration is over, the picture changes. The probability is that an English PR will be acting either as the attorney-administrator (*ante* 3.38) of a PR in the country of domicile (sometimes called the 'principal representative') or as an executor appointed in a will of the deceased dealing only with English assets. In the former case, it may seem right for the English PR to account to the principal representative for the net estate in his hands – *Re Achillopoulos* (1928) – but this will not necessarily be so; see *Re Lorillard* (1922), *ante* 5.43. It would certainly not be right to do this if any beneficiary objected and, in case of doubt, application to the court for directions is highly desirable. As an illustration, see *Re Manifold* (1961):

A Cyprus-domiciled testatrix left two wills dealing with assets in England and Cyprus; the first will was valid in both countries, the second (which revoked the first) was valid only in England. The Cyprus executor obtained a grant to the first will only, but his English attorney obtained a grant relating to both. The latter asked the court for directions as to distribution of the English estate and was ordered to account direct to the beneficiaries under the second will, not to the Cyprus executor.

Where the English PR is an executor in his own right, the case for accounting to the principal representative is even weaker, unless this is expressly authorised in the English will. In such circumstances, the right course would appear to be for the English executor to distribute the net estate in accordance with the terms of the will, or as directed by the beneficiaries, bearing in mind the rule that the devolution of *moveable* assets will be governed by the law of the last domicile – see *ante* 3.36.

6.46 ASSENTS AND TRANSFERS OF ASSETS

The word 'assent' has two meanings in this context. In general it signifies the act by which a PR converts a beneficiary's inchoate right to a legacy or share of residue into a positive interest in the relevant property. Such an assent may be either express or implied, although in the latter case, where land is concerned, an implied assent would be effectual only if it related to an equitable interest of which the PR himself were the beneficiary: *Re Edward* (1982). If there is any doubt about whether or not an assent has been made, the question is generally one of fact. Personal Representatives should beware of inadvertently assenting to a gift before they in fact wish to do so. In many cases, of course, transfer of the legal title to an asset will coincide with – and will thus constitute – an assent. Indeed, it is better if the legal title does not long remain divorced from the equitable right to an asset. The significance of an assent is that, until it is given, the property affected by it remains at the disposal of the PR for administration purposes. Once assented, it belongs, either in law or in equity, to the beneficiary.

As well as being used in the wider sense outlined above, the term 'assent' also describes the document by which PRs transfer the title of real and leasehold property to a beneficiary – see s. 36 AEA. Reference has already been made to the vesting assent by which the title of settled land is transferred to the tenant for life – see *ante* 6.26. See *post* 7.7 for a reference to the need in the case of land for PRs to assent in their own favour as trustees at the end of the administration period, where they are continuing in that role.

6.47 TAXATION DURING THE ADMINISTRATION

Personal Representatives must settle all tax liabilities before distributing the estate. In the case of IHT it may be necessary to submit Form D-3

(Corrective Account) where there have been changes in the value of assets and liabilities since the original account was submitted on application for a grant. When the tax liability has been finally settled and paid, a certificate of discharge should be applied for under s. 239 IHTA. The Board of Inland Revenue is bound to issue such certificates in all cases involving payment of IHT on death, when satisfied, of course, that proper accounts have been submitted and the right amount of tax has been paid.

6.48 PRs' LIABILITY FOR CGT

On death, all the deceased's assets are deemed to have been acquired by the PRs at the market value on the date of death. There is an uplift in value, but no charge to the tax: s. 62(1) TCGA. Death wipes out any capital gain which existed pre-death.

Allowable losses in excess of chargeable gains in the period from the previous 6 April to the date of death can be carried back to the three earlier tax years (later years to be taken first), if by so doing the gains of those earlier years can be reduced to the amount of the annual exemption: s. 62(2) TCGA. But there is no carry forward of the deceased's unused losses to the PRs.

Sales during the administration period may give rise to a liability for CGT. PRs pay CGT at the rate of 25%. Normal deductions for sale expenses are allowed from the proceeds and, in addition, there is a scale of expenses allowable under s. 38(1)(b)TCGA for the costs of establishing title to the assets sold; this scale is set out in the Inland Revenue Statement of Practice SP7/81 and if the actual expenditure is higher, that can be claimed instead. The basis of the Revenue practice is *IRC* v *Richards' Executors* (1971) where a deduction was allowed for the expenses in obtaining a grant of representation as a necessary step to establish title to the assets, including the cost, not only of obtaining the grant itself, but also of making investigations and valuations and preparing the Inland Revenue account.

Personal Representatives have an annual allowance (£5,800 for 1992/93 and allowable in full for the broken period from the date of death) which is exempt from CGT in the tax year of death and in the following two tax years. Thereafter, there is no exemption – a powerful incentive to carry out sales during the first three tax years. If any sales have to be made after this period has expired, it may be better to transfer the asset to the beneficiary and allow him to carry out the sale. All outstanding CGT should be paid before the estate is distributed.

6.49 PRs' LIABILITY FOR INCOME TAX AND NATIONAL INSURANCE CONTRIBUTIONS

The PRs must make a return of income and gains for the period from 6 April to the date of death; full allowances will be admissible despite the

163

broken period. As regards their responsibility for earlier years, see note 1 to this chapter.

During the administration period, PRs are liable for IT at the basic rate on all income received by them, which will be satisfied either by deduction at source under, or by direct assessment under, Schedules A and D, for which purpose Form 1 covering untaxed income and gains for each tax year needs to be submitted to the Revenue. They are neither entitled to allowances nor liable to any higher rate of tax, either that for individuals under s. 1 ICTA or that for trustees under s. 686.

Where a general legatee is entitled to interest (e.g. when the legacy is paid more than 12 months after the date of death) or where interest is payable on the statutory legacy under intestacy, payment should be made gross and the beneficiary will be assessed direct under Schedule D Case III.

A specific legatee is entitled to income arising on the subject-matter of the legacy from the date of death; where such income has been received by the PRs and handed over to the legatee, it will be assessed on the legatee for the tax year(s) in which it arose. The legatee should get a tax deduction certificate from the PRs.

Residuary legatees may have either an absolute interest or a limited interest for IT purposes. In the former case, sums paid to the beneficiary in any year are deemed to be net income up to the amount of the net residuary income available in that year and must be grossed up. Any payment in excess of the net residuary income is deemed to be capital. When the administration is complete, the assessments based on payments made during the administration are revised, so that the beneficiary is deemed under s. 697 ICTA to have received the full net residuary income for each tax year. Limited interest beneficiaries also have to gross up income payments received during the administration. When this is complete, the total of such payments (plus income in hand at the end) is deemed to accrue from day to day at a uniform rate over the period from the date of death to the date of the conclusion of the administration, again necessitating revision of the original assessments: s. 695 ICTA.

National Insurance contributions should not normally present any difficulty. If the deceased was an employer, his PRs will be liable in the same way that he would have been in respect of any outstanding matters. If he was an employee, no liability will attach to lifetime earnings received after death. If he was self-employed, any outstanding liability will be dealt with in the income tax return to the date of death.

6.50   PRs' RESPONSIBILITIES FOR VALUE ADDED TAX

This matter has already been touched upon – see *ante* 3.23. Personal Representatives carrying on a business must inform the Commissioners within 21 days and will become responsible in the same manner as a registered person. Their liability to tax will be limited to the extent of the assets of the deceased over which they have control: Reg.63 VAT (General) Regulations 1985.

6.51   SOLICITORS' BILL OF COSTS

Unless the estate solicitors' bill of costs has been submitted and paid as soon as the grant is issued – which is reasonable in cases where no further legal work is thought likely to occur – payment of the solicitors' bill will probably be the last item dealt with in the administration before preparation of the accounts. It should be said that the vast majority of such bills are reasonable and are paid without question. If, however, the PR is not satisfied with the figures he should, in the first place, discuss them with the solicitors. If a satisfactory solution is not then reached, an application to the Law Society for certification should be requested (a solicitor cannot be *compelled* to submit his bill for certification, although the Legal Services Ombudsman has suggested that beneficiaries should have a right to require this to be done); in the mean time, the bill should remain unpaid. It is only the client who can request certification, not the beneficiary, where, for instance, a professional executor has been acting. This procedure produces a fair result. The alternative course of having the bill taxed by the court under s. 70 Solicitors' Act 1974 can be recommended only where large sums are involved. For a case in which the sums involved *were* large, see *Maltby v D J Freeman & Co* (1978); the estate was worth about £1.8m. It appears that the solicitors involved were instructed only to obtain probate for the executors, for which service their bill was £11,175. The Law Society certified that a more appropriate charge would be £8,500, a sum upheld by Walton J. after the executors had asked for the bill to be taxed. Reference may be made to s. 1 Supreme Court (Non-Contentious probate costs) Rules 1956, SI 1956 No. 552 for the principal heads used by solicitors in calculating their bills for probate work. In case the above is taken to imply that legal costs need especial attention I should add that it is not only the solicitor's bill which needs to be carefully reviewed before payment. No agent's bill should be paid unthinkingly; payment of an unjustified sum will lay the PRs open to an accusation of *devastavit* – see *post* 14.1.

6.52   ACCOUNTS

When the PRs have finally established residue, they are in a position to prepare administration accounts for approval of the beneficiaries. Where the administration has been prolonged it is desirable to do interim accounts; otherwise the accounts at the end of the day can be excessively cumbersome. It may be found convenient to write up such interim accounts to 5 April, coinciding with the end of the tax year. As to the form they should take, it should be borne in mind that in most cases they will be going to members of the public without knowledge either of accountancy or law. There is no set form; it is desirable to avoid jargon and to state all items simply and clearly. In simple cases a single sheet will suffice to show the original assets and liabilities and what has happened to them. In more complex cases the principles of double-entry book-keeping should be followed. It will often be helpful to attach to the accounts a numbered series of explanatory notes. The accounts should, of course, be carefully checked for accuracy and completeness, but there is no need for an external audit unless the PRs choose to exercise the discretionary power to order this under s. 22(4) TA. There is also provision in s. 13(1) Public Trustee Act 1906 for either a PR or a beneficiary to require accounts to be investigated and audited by a solicitor or public accountant or, alternatively, by the Public Trustee himself.

Personal Representatives are entitled to have their accounts approved by the residuary beneficiaries. Until they have such approval they may also withhold assent of the residuary assets. They are also *probably* entitled to a formal release on handing over those assets to the residuary legatee (*Snell*, p. 295) whereas trustees are not: see *post* 9.13. Personal Representatives are entitled to be indemnified out of an estate for all proper expenses incurred, and this indemnity is a charge on both income and capital. Proper expenses in this context include the costs of actions relating to the estate, where rightly incurred. Until their accounts are approved, PRs cannot be sure that they will not incur further expense in respect of which they will be entitled to this indemnity; hence the need to exercise caution in completing the distribution of the estate, if necessary making a partial assent only.

6.53   APPROVAL OF THE ACCOUNTS

Personal Representatives should obtain beneficiaries' approval by means of signature to a suitable form of words either endorsed on the accounts or clearly referable to them; the cautious approach is to ask individual beneficiaries to confirm at the same time that their interest in the estate is unencumbered, i.e. has not been assigned or charged. If a PR becomes aware that a beneficiary may be insolvent, it will be prudent also to make bankruptcy searches before making payment. In addition to this, receipts are taken for the actual assets transferred and cash payments made.

Sometimes accounts are approved by most residuary beneficiaries, but not by all; the PRs are then in a difficult position. Should they hold out for universal approval, or should they pay out those who have approved? The practical answer must depend upon their assessment of the worth of the objections (if any) raised by the minority. If there is a risk that such objections may entail a revision of the administration and the figures shown in the accounts, then a total distribution to any beneficiary must seem dangerous. If on the other hand, the objections raised are not such as to require a retracing of steps and entail no risk of, say, an administration action, then distribution to the approving majority is justifiable – equally so if it appears that lack of approval is not due to any real objection to the conduct of the administration but is the result of mere lethargy or indi erence on the part of the beneficiary.

6.54   PAYMENT INTO COURT

If, after full discussion, a beneficiary persists in refusal to approve accounts, there are two alternative routes out of the impasse. Firstly, the beneficiary himself may start an administration action for examination of the accounts and the conduct of which he complains. Secondly, the PR pays the outstanding fund into court, in accordance with s. 63 TA as amended, which is the appropriate action whenever a PR or trustee finds that he cannot get a discharge from the beneficiary, but it does involve the fund in extra expense and should not, therefore, be lightly undertaken. Where a beneficiary is simply missing, for instance, PRs should pursue all possible lines of enquiry before considering payment into court – including the instruction of one of the firms which specialise in missing person investigations. Sometimes missing persons may be reached through a government department such as the Department of Health and Social Security; it is understood that a sealed letter addressed to the beneficiary will be forwarded by the Department (without responsibility), if its records enable this to be done. Otherwise it may be appropriate to apply to the court for leave to distribute on the basis that a missing person is dead; this would be an application for a 'Benjamin' order, authorising PRs to distribute on a specified basis. (For an example of the making of such an order, see *post* 7.32.) If there is doubt about *who* is actually entitled to a fund, the proper course is not to pay into court but to issue an originating summons with a view to getting the court's guidance. This is a course of action which may be followed in any situation where the PRs have a problem which they feel unable to solve without the court's help, e.g. a question concerning construction of the will, or, less happily, where PRs find themselves in dispute with the beneficiaries. Where such an application is successful, costs of all parties are likely to be ordered to come from the estate; an unsuccessful application may result in the PRs having to pay their own costs, if not those of the other parties.

In non-contentious situations there is the power given to the court by s. 48 AJA 1985 to make an order authorising PRs and trustees to act in accordance with a written opinion given by a barrister of at least ten years' standing on a question of construction of a will or trust instrument. Such an order can be made in chambers, thus saving the expense of a full hearing in open court; it will not be made where a dispute exists which the court considers should be argued before it. This novel procedure could be useful in cases where there is some doubt about the correct course to take, Counsel having nevertheless advised with reasonable confidence, but some beneficiaries either decline to approve the proposed solution (while not actively opposing it) or are unable to approve it, e.g. because of lack of capacity.

The costs of payment into court are less if the county court is used, and this is permissible where the sum involved is £30,000 or less. The smaller the amount involved, the less attractive this course will be. One might suggest that the minimum sum should be £500 and that any lesser sum should be dealt with by the PRs at their discretion, the risk of doing so being covered by a joint and several indemnity from the known and available beneficiaries backed up, perhaps, by an indemnity insurance policy.

6.55 BENEFICIARIES UNDER AGE

Obviously it is impossible to obtain effective approval of accounts from those who are either infants or who lack the necessary mental capacity to deal with such matters. Nor, if it comes to that, can either of these classes of persons give PRs a satisfactory receipt for the assets to which they are entitled. In the case of infants a good discharge for a vested legacy or share of residue can be obtained by appointing trustees of the fund in accordance with s. 42 AEA. The professional PR will normally, however, retain such legacy or share, whether vested or contingent, in his own hands, without formality; for the investment of such funds, see *ante* 6.25. Where infants take shares of residue, their parents can be invited to approve the administration accounts on their behalf on the understanding that the infants themselves will be asked to confirm such approval when they come of age.

6.56 MENTAL INCAPACITY

An adult beneficiary may be incapable, by reason of mental disorder, of managing his own affairs; such a person is known as a 'patient' – see s. 94(2) Mental Health Act 1983. The proper solution in such cases is for an application to the Court of Protection for an order appointing a receiver. Directions given by the court to the PRs concerning the disposal of the beneficiary's share provide the discharge which is otherwise unobtainable. Normally, the application will be made by a close relative – a personal application is possible, or the matter can be dealt with by the family solicitor. The nearest relative is also the first choice to act as receiver, but if no such person is willing to act, a close friend may be appointed or an officer of a local authority or, exceptionally, a solicitor or manager of a bank trustee department branch. In the latter event, remuneration may be allowed – normally a receiver is expected to act gratuitously, like an executor or trustee. In the last resort and where no other acceptable person is willing to act, the Official Solicitor may be appointed. For further and expert guidance, see *Heywood & Massey*. There is sometimes reluctance on the part of the patient's nearest relatives to agree to an application for appointment of a receiver; it is felt that some kind of stigma attaches to it. This rather understandable sentiment must be overcome by the persuasive power of the family's advisers. It is really quite unsatisfactory for dealings with the patient's assets to be virtually blocked for an indefinite period. Unauthorised dealings are to be shunned. Sometimes an attempt is made to use a power of attorney under the 1971 Act but such a power becomes void when its donor loses capacity and its use is therefore a pointless and potentially dangerous exercise – both for the donee and for third parties, such as banks, who may be tempted to rely on its non-existent validity. Personal Representatives may properly retain funds due to an incapacitated beneficiary for a limited period whilst an application to the Court of Protection is arranged and prepared; once it becomes clear that no such application will be made they should consider their other recourse, i.e. a payment into court under s. 63 TA as amended.

6.57 ENDURING POWERS OF ATTORNEY

A more streamlined procedure may be available if the beneficiary has anticipated trouble by taking advantage of the Enduring Powers of Attorney Act 1985. A power constituted in accordance with the provisions of this Act is not revoked by the subsequent mental incapacity of the donor, though registration of the document with the Court of Protection is mandatory as soon as the donee becomes aware that the donor is becoming or has become mentally incapable of managing his affairs. Once this has happened it may be too late to consider the execution of a power of attorney of this kind, although *Re K, Re F* (1988) indicates that the level of understanding required of a donor of an enduring power need not be of the highest; such a power is not rendered invalid because of the donor's incapacity for managing his affairs at the date of its execution, provided the donor then understood the nature and effect of the enduring power.

An enduring power must be in the form prescribed by the Enduring Powers of Attorney (Prescribed Form) Regulations 1990 SI 1990/1376. Such a power, if properly made, will authorise the donee to approve administration accounts on behalf of the donor and to give a valid receipt for distributions from the estate of which the donor is a beneficiary. It also, incidentally, authorises the donee to exercise all powers and discretions vested in the donor as trustee – s. 3(3) of the Act – but recommendations are afoot for restrictive legislative amendments to this remarkable intrusion into the rule '*delegatus non potest delegare*' – see *ante* 5.49.

The Protection Division of the Public Trust Office at Stewart House, 24 Kingsway, London WC2B 6JX handles the administrative arrangements for the Court of Protection in respect of receiverships and enduring powers of attorney.

PART II

TRUSTS, TRUSTEES AND BENEFICIARIES

7 Trusts (1)

7.1 IMMENSE AND VARIED USAGE OF THE TRUST

If we were asked what is the greatest and most distinctive achievement performed by Englishmen in the field of jurisprudence I cannot think that we should have any better answer to give than this, namely the development from century to century of the trust idea.

So wrote the great legal historian of the nineteenth century, Francis Maitland (*Selected Essays*, p. 129). When one surveys the immense variety and value of the current usage of the trust concept, one can only agree with the views he expressed. At one end of the scale the small legacy fund held in trust for an infant until he becomes 18; at the other end the billion pound pension fund. In between, countless private trusts (the Inland Revenue has estimated that there are at least 60,000 discretionary trusts in existence), charitable trusts (in 1991 turnover was estimated at £15 billion per annum) and unit trusts, to say nothing of the many insurance policies and family homes held on trust.

7.2 USE OF TRUST IN FOREIGN JURISDICTIONS

The trust, being of English origin, has also taken root in those parts of the world which were, at one time, members of the Empire upon which the sun never set. So one finds the trust to be well-known and well-used in such countries as the USA, Canada, Australia, New Zealand, to say nothing of small territories such as Bermuda and the Bahamas, now much in use as tax havens. Civil law countries such as France and Germany do not know the trust as such, although roughly comparable concepts exist (the *fondation* and the *stiftung*, for instance) with limited scope. The Roman concept of *fideicommissum* has been developed in such countries to validate the transfer of property from A to B in trust for C, the trust to be implemented on the happening of a specified event, e.g. A's death. Failure of the trust results in the property belonging to B absolutely, a conclusion quite at odds with the English law of trusts – see *post* 7.4. Scotland, with a jurisprudence derived from Roman Law, might also be a stranger to the trust but its proximity to England has resulted in its developing a trust law of its own, similar to but not identical with the English law of trusts. The Hague Convention of the Law Applicable to Trusts and on their Recognition requires civil law countries to recognise trusts – it does not impose trust law upon them – and this should ease the task of English trustees whose trusts have connections in civil law countries. The

Convention applies only to trusts created voluntarily and evidenced in writing; it was adopted by the Hague Conference on Private International Law in October 1984 and by the UK in the Recognition of Trusts Act 1987.

7.3 DEFINITION OF A TRUST

This is difficult; the Hague Convention states:

> the term 'trust' refers to the legal relationships created – *inter vivos* or on death – by a person, the settlor, when assets have been placed under the control of a trustee for the benefit of a beneficiary or for a specified purpose.

A better definition is that used by Professors Sheridan and Keeton in *The Law of Trusts*, and cited with approval by *Snell*:

> A trust is the relationship which arises wherever a person called the trustee is compelled in equity to hold property, whether real or personal, and whether by legal or equitable title, for the benefit of other persons (of whom he may be one and who are termed beneficiaries) or for some object permitted by law, in such a way that the real benefit of the property accrues, not to the trustee, but to the beneficiaries or other objects of the trust.

It will be seen from this very full definition that the essential elements of the trust are (a) the existence of property of some kind in the name of or held to the order of a trustee(s) and (b) the existence of a beneficial interest in such property belonging to persons or objects called beneficiaries, of whom the trustee himself may be one.

7.4 EXPRESS TRUSTS AND RESULTING TRUSTS

Express trusts are created as the result of a positive decision by a settlor or settlors; such trusts may be created informally, even by word of mouth and unwittingly, as in *Paul* v *Constance* (1977) where there was evidence that the sole legal owner of a bank account had made it clear that the money in the account belonged jointly to himself and his lady friend. As Scarman LJ remarked, one does not expect the technical language of the equity lawyer to be used by the ordinary man in the street. In this case, the words 'The money is as much yours as mine' were enough to enable the court to infer the creation of a trust. It is, of course, more sensible to have a trust embodied in a formal deed drawn by a lawyer; this avoids dispute in the future, but it is not an essential element in the event. A trust created by will must, however, comply with the terms of s. 9 WA. With regard to trusts of land, care must be taken; s. 53(1)(b) LPA says:

> a declaration of trust respecting any land or any interest therein must be manifested and proved by some writing signed by some person who is able to declare such trust or by his will.

Note that it is not the declaration itself which must be in writing; what is required is written evidence that the declaration has been made. In the case of a professionally drawn document then, of course, the settlement deed is the evidence. Note also that the sub-section refers not only to land but also to interests in land and therefore covers mortgages and equitable interests in land as well as leases. The absence of such written evidence makes the trust unenforceable but not void.

In *Re Vandervell's Trusts (No. 2)* (1974) Megarry J. classified resulting trusts as either presumed or automatic. The former arises out of a gratuitous transfer of property by A to B without any indication that a gift was intended. The property in question is held on a resulting trust by B for A. The latter arises as the consequence of a transfer of property from A to B linked to an incomplete disposition of the beneficial interest; for instance, A tells B to hold the property on trust for C for life but fails to say what is to happen to it when C dies. In these circumstances, the property must automatically result or 'spring back' to A or A's estate when the life interest ends.

In the 'presumed' category it should be noted that, in the circumstances described, there may be a presumption that a gift was intended – the so-called 'presumption of advancement', which applies in cases where transferor A is under an equitable obligation either to support or to make provision for transferee B. A will be either B's husband or father; the presumption does not operate in the reverse direction from B (wife) to A (husband). Where it is a case of making provision for B, A will be either father of, or in *loco parentis* to B. Like other presumptions, the presumption of advancement may be rebutted; it is said nowadays to be weaker than it was as between husband and wife, especially in respect of purchases of matrimonial homes.

7.5 CONSTRUCTIVE TRUSTS

Constructive trusts are dealt with in more detail in ch. 8; it will suffice to say here that they have a different character from trusts of the express or resulting kind which are enforced because, quite independently of the court, a person has been constituted trustee by a declaration of trust or a transfer of property creating a trust. Constructive trusts are remedial in character and are imposed by the court in circumstances where Equity holds it to be unconscionable for a person to hold property entirely for his own benefit. For instance, where a matrimonial home has been bought in the name of one spouse alone but both spouses have contributed to its value; the legal owner will be trustee of the property for both spouses, both of them having a beneficial interest in the home. Similarly, where a trustee has made use of his office to make a private profit for himself, a constructive trust will be imposed so that the profit in question is held on trust for the beneficiaries.

7.6 TRUSTS AND ESTATES

There is a strong similarity between the position of a PR and that of a trustee. The former may be regarded as being a trustee for the beneficiaries under the will, but it is a mistake to treat the two offices as identical. Different periods of limitation apply to them and their powers of administration do not coincide, e.g. the statutory power of appropriation is available only to PRs. It is important for other reasons also to be able to identify the moment at which the PR changes hats and becomes trustee. For instance, the two are treated differently for tax purposes, and the machinery provided in the TA for a trustee to retire without an application to court is not available to a PR.[1] See also *post*, 10.2.

7.7 WHEN DOES ADMINISTRATION FINISH AND TRUSTEESHIP BEGIN?

The moment of transition from the administration of an estate to a trusteeship depends on circumstances. Generally one can say that, when residue is ascertained and the PRs bring in their accounts, then the work of administration is finished. As an example of this, consider *Re Claremont* (1923); the facts were that an executor had filed a residuary account (for the purposes of the now long-defunct legacy duty) – a comparable situation nowadays would be the preparation by an executor of his final administration accounts – and it was held that in these circumstances there was a presumption that the administration was at an end with the executor holding the assets as trustee and the residuary legatees having become beneficiaries under a trust. In *Re Cockburn* (1957) Danckwerts J. had this to say:

> 'Whether persons are executors or administrators, once they have completed the administration in due course, they become trustees holding for the beneficiaries either on an intestacy or under the terms of the will and are bound to carry out the duties of trustee, though in the case of personal representatives they cannot be compelled to go on indefinitely acting as trustees, and are entitled to appoint new trustees in their place. . . . It seems to me that, if they do not appoint new trustees to proceed to execute the trusts of the will, they will become trustees in the full sense.'

Some doubt was thrown on this passage by the decision of Pennycuick J. in *Re King* (1964):

> The testatrix died in 1939, having appointed two executors C and H, and the administration of the estate was prolonged until 1952. Meanwhile, H had died in 1951. In 1953 C, the surviving executor and trustee appointed J to be a trustee jointly with himself. C died in 1958 and his will was proved by two executors, one of whom died in 1959, leaving his other executor as sole surviving PR of the

testatrix by representation. In 1959 J appointed A a trustee of the will of the testatrix jointly with himself. J died in 1963 leaving A as sole surviving trustee of the will of the testatrix. The question which then arose was about the identity of the persons in whom the legal estate in the properties of the estate scheduled in the 1953 appointment was vested. Was it vested in the surviving PR on the one hand, or in the surviving trustee on the other? There had never been any formal assent vesting the properties belonging to Mrs King's estate in her trustees. It was held that when the replacement trustee was appointed the title was held by C as PR and the statutory vesting of title under s. 40 TA did not apply, and accordingly the title vested in C's surviving executor as the surviving PR of the estate of the testatrix.

The above decision was not, it seems, in accordance with then current conveyancing practice. It needs to be borne in mind when new trustees are appointed in cases involving land. The safe course where a trust is involved is for PRs to execute a written assent of land to themselves on completion of the administration period, which will obviate the risk of their becoming trustees of the pure personalty while remaining PRs of the land. Lack of a written assent will not, however, prevent transmission of the *beneficial* interest by an implied assent where the sole PR is also the sole beneficiary of the land – *Re Edward* (1982) – see *ante* 6.46.

7.8 TRUSTS AND POWERS

Just as it is important to be able to distinguish between cases where an estate is being administered by PRs and cases where a trust is being administered by trustees, so it is vital to be able to distinguish between cases where a trust is imposed and cases where a power has been bestowed. This is because a trust is said to be mandatory – it must be carried out – whilst a power is discretionary – the holder of the power has the option to exercise or not to exercise it. So, if trustees fail to carry out a trust – for instance, to allocate a trust fund amongst a specified class – the court will carry it out for them; but, if the holder of a power decides to do nothing when given the power to choose who shall benefit, the court will not exercise the power for him and the fund will go to those entitled in default of appointment.

Unfortunately, the distinction between trusts and powers is not as clear-cut as might be expected; an instrument which appears to confer a power may, in fact, have created a trust. In the leading case of *Burrough* v *Philcox* (1840) a testator gave property to his two children for their lives and empowered the survivor to dispose of it by will 'amongst my nephews and nieces or their children, either all to one of them, or to as many of them as my surviving child shall think proper'. The surviving child failed to exercise the power and the court decided that there was a general intention to benefit the class of nephews and nieces which the court would carry into effect by ordering that the property be divided equally between the objects

– invoking the maxim 'equality is equity'. In other words the court treated the power as a trust.

There is one useful guideline in such circumstances; if there is what appears to be a power, is there also a gift over expressly in default of exercise of the power? If there is, then the power is a mere power – see, e.g., *Re Mills* (1930). If there is not, then *probably* the power is a trust power, but not necessarily so – *Re Weekes'* (1897). A *general* power – i.e. a power to appoint to anyone, including the appointor himself – cannot be a trust power.

7.9 POWER OF APPOINTMENT GIVEN TO THE DONEE IN A FIDUCIARY CAPACITY

It should be added that whilst a private person is under no obligation to exercise a power or even to consider exercising it, a trustee to whom a power is given must consider its exercise from time to time. In the hands of a trustee the power is a fiduciary power and creates an obligation. Similarly trustees have various administrative powers, such as the power to invest trust funds; these too, where relevant, should be considered from time to time. Section 155 LPA says that a person to whom any power is given may, by deed, release it or contract not to exercise it; this provision does not apply to powers coupled with a duty, such as those given to trustees: *Re Eyre* (1883) and see also *post* 13.11. A power should only be exercised with the sole purpose of benefiting the objects of the power, otherwise the exercise runs the risk of falling foul of the doctrine of fraud on a power: see *Re Brook* (1968) where a power was exercised in favour of objects of the power but with a view to a partition of the fund between such objects *and* the donee of the power; the appointment was invalid.

7.10 CAPACITY TO MAKE A TRUST

Anyone over the age of 18 and having the capacity to manage his own affairs can create a trust; as to the degree of capacity required, see *ante* 1.9. It is possible for an infant to make a trust, even if it may not be a desirable practice; however, such a trust will be voidable at the election (not to be confused with the kind of election referred to in 6.42 *ante*) of the settlor when he reaches 18 or shortly after. Where a person lacks capacity and his affairs are in the hands of the Court of Protection, not only can the Court make a will for him (see *ante* 1.10), it also has wide powers to make orders in respect of the patient's property, including a power to settle it – s. 96(1)(d) Mental Health Act 1983. Such settlements may be varied later on under s. 96(3) if, for instance, there has been a substantial change in the circumstances.

7.11 THE THREE CERTAINTIES FOR THE CREATION OF A TRUST

On the basis of Lord Langdale MR's judgment in *Knight* v *Knight* (1840), *Snell says*:

For the creation of a trust three things are necessary:
(a) the words must be so used that on the whole they ought to be construed as imperative;
(b) the subject-matter of the trust must be certain; and
(c) the objects or persons intended to have the benefit of the trust must be certain.

7.12 CERTAINTY OF WORDS

There is no special form of words but, as stated above, they must result in an imperative direction to the trustee. Precatory words (words praying or expressing a desire that a thing be done) will generally not do, although, as *Snell* remarks, at one time the Chancery Court was very ready to infer a trust from such words. The leading case which established the modern attitude on the subject is *Re Adams and the Kensington Vestry* (1884) where a testator gave his estate to his wife absolutely 'in full confidence that she will do what is right as to the disposal thereof between my children, either in her lifetime or by will after her decease'. The Court of Appeal held that the wife took the property absolutely and without strings. Since then few cases have been reported in which precatory words were allowed to create a trust. Nevertheless, some of the old decisions may still be used in an effort to support such an outcome. To avoid the risk of this happening it is sensible to add the proviso that any precatory words used are not to create a trust or legally binding obligation. (Most of the cases in which such words were discussed arose out of wills.)

In *Re Steele* (1948) where the same formulation of precatory words was used as had been held to be an imperative trust in an earlier case, that earlier decision was followed in preference to the modern cases.

A trust may be created not only by a formal document or by an informal statement, but also through the interpretation of an act done by the putative settlor:

In *Re Kayford Ltd* (1975) a mail-order company, being in financial difficulties, decided to protect its customers by opening a separate banking account for them called 'Customers' Trust Deposit Account'. Money sent in by customers of the company was paid into this account. In liquidation proceedings it was held that the money in this account was held in trust for the customers and was not an asset of the company. In this case the court was satisfied that the action taken by the company was a sufficiently certain act of creation to make an enforceable trust. The liquidators did not contend that what the company had done was fraudulent preference, but it has been argued that its unilateral declaration of trust contravened provisions now contained in s. 107 Insolvency Act 1986.

7.13 CERTAINTY OF SUBJECT MATTER

Since any form of property may be settled, including choses in action, it follows that the variety of subject-matter available for settlement is great. Whatever it is, it must be described with reasonable certainty so that there is no difficulty in identifying it, otherwise the trust will fail; for instance, a reference in a will to the 'bulk' of the testatrix's estate, as in *Palmer* v *Simmonds* (1854), was insufficiently certain. Sometimes an initial uncertainty may be capable of resolution; in *Re Golay* (1965):

> a gift to allow a beneficiary to receive a 'reasonable income' during her lifetime was upheld on the grounds that the words used imputed an objective yardstick which could be applied in quantifying the amount to which the life tenant was entitled.

It is possible for the subject-matter to be clearly established so far as the property is concerned but the shares in the property are not defined with precision; this form of uncertainty will also cause the trust to fail unless, perhaps, the court can be persuaded that the equality is equity maxim should prevail (as in *Burrough* v *Philcox, ante* 7.8).

7.14 CERTAINTY OF OBJECTS

Assuming that the settlor has achieved certainty of intention and certainty of subject-matter, it is still possible for a trust to fail because the objects of the trust – that is, the beneficiaries – are not defined with sufficient certainty. It must be possible to find out who they are. Certainty in this context means linguistic or conceptual certainty; the fact that it may be difficult to trace some of the beneficiaries is not usually a fatal flaw, although a really serious problem of this kind may mean that the trust is 'administratively unworkable'; see, for instance, *R* v *District Auditor ex p. West Yorkshire Metropolitan County Council* (1985) where the local authority tried to create a discretionary non-charitable trust for the inhabitants of West Yorkshire and it was held to be unworkable and therefore void. Although the test of conceptual certainty applies to all trusts, it is applied more strictly in the case of 'fixed trusts', that is, trusts in which the settlor has fixed the shares which beneficiaries are to take in the trust instrument: for example, to A for life, then to B's children in equal shares. The trustees have no power to vary the size of the interests taken by A and the members of the class of remaindermen. In such trusts, the description of the beneficiaries must be sufficiently clear to enable the trustees to make a complete list of them. If the descriptive words used are too vague to enable this to be done, the trust fails. It would, for instance, be impossible to interpret a gift to 'my friends' with enough certainty to make it possible to compile a complete list of those intended to benefit, unless the gift is so phrased as to remove any doubts over quantum.

In *Re Barlow* (1979) the testatrix died leaving valuable paintings. The will included a direction to sell the paintings, but any members of her family and any friends of hers who wished to do so could purchase any of them at probate value or at the much lower prices shown in a catalogue prepared in 1970, whichever was more advantageous to family and friends. Held (a) that the use of the word 'friends' did not make the gift void for uncertainty, as it could be construed as a series of individual gifts to persons answering, on any reasonable basis, the description and (b) that the word 'family' which would normally be restricted to statutory next-of-kin, could in this instance be construed as extending to blood relations, as the deceased had left no issue.

7.15 *McPHAIL v DOULTON*

Until 1971 the same rule was applied in the case of discretionary trusts – it had to be possible to make a complete list of all the objects of the trust. This may still be the case in trusts of this kind where the settlor's intention is that, failing selection by the trustees, all possible objects should share; if this is so, then clearly it must be possible to make a complete list. But it is thought that this is not likely to happen very often nowadays, when the fashion is for trusts to include very large classes of discretionary objects. As a result of the decision of the House of Lords (by three to two) in *McPhail* v *Doulton* (1971) the certainty test for discretionary trusts was relaxed. Briefly, the facts were that a trust deed set up by Bertram Baden in favour of certain employees and their relatives and dependants contained the following clause:

The trustees shall apply the net income of the Fund in making at their absolute discretion grants to or for the benefit of any of the officers and employees or ex-officers and ex-employees of the Company or to any relatives or dependants of any such persons in such amounts at such times and on such conditions (if any) as they think fit . . .

It was accepted that it would be impossible for the trustees to make a complete list of all possible objects of this clause; did this mean that the trust failed for uncertainty? No, said the majority of the House of Lords, holding that the test of certainty in such trusts was the same as the one to be applied in the case of mere powers: can it be said with certainty that any given individual is or is not a member of the class? This was the test applied to the certainty of the objects of a power in *Re Gulbenkian* (1970), an earlier decision of the House of Lords.

The McPhail case was referred back to the High Court for a decision on whether it was possible to apply this test to the words of the clause as set out above. The litigation finally came to an end in the Court of Appeal under the title *Re Baden (No. 2)* (1973) where it was held that the class of objects was conceptually certain. It is not, it seems, necessary to be able to prove of everybody that they are within or without the class; according to Megaw LJ the test is satisfied if a substantial number of objects can be said with certainty to qualify and it does not matter that, as regards a substantial number of others, they cannot be said to be either in or out. Obviously, in such a case as the Baden trust, it would be quite difficult, perhaps impossible, for any given person to be able to prove that he was *not* a relative of a former employee.

7.16 ADMINISTRATIVE UNWORKABILITY

Reference was made *ante* 7.14 to the concept of administrative unworkability; this certainly applies to discretionary trusts but not, apparently, to mere powers. In *Re Manisty* (1974) Templeman J. held that such powers could not be invalidated simply on the grounds of size, the duties of a trustee in such cases being less stringent than in trusts of the same character. But might a very wide class of large numbers of people be void for 'capriciousness'? There is no general rule in English law that a capricious gift is void, but it remains to be decided whether such a rule exists in the case of mere powers.

7.17 INCOMPLETELY CONSTITUTED TRUSTS

Sometimes a settlor changes his mind in midstream, so to speak, and decides that he will go no further with the creation of a settlement. The question then is whether the imperfect transaction can be enforced against the settlor either by the intended beneficiaries or by the trustees on their behalf. The equitable maxims, 'Equity will not assist a volunteer' and 'Equity will not perfect an imperfect gift' may be prayed in aid. Unless valuable consideration has been given to the settlor in exchange for his agreement to create a trust the court will not require him to carry out his promise if he fails to do so; valuable consideration in this context means money or money's worth. Marriage settlements are enforceable in the same way as settlements for valuable consideration by the parties to the marriage and their issue.

A voluntary trust is only completely constituted and therefore enforceable if either the settled property has been effectively conveyed to the trustees or if the settlor has declared himself to be a trustee of it. This is the so-called 'complete and perfect rule', and reference to the judgment of Turner LJ in *Milroy* v *Lord* (1862) can hardly be avoided:

'... in order to render a voluntary settlement valid and effectual, the settlor must have done everything which according to the nature of the property comprised in the settlement, was necessary to be done in order to transfer the property and render the settlement binding upon him.'

A little later on Sir George Jessel MR said in *Richards* v *Delbridge* (1874):

'The principle is a very simple one. A man may transfer his property without valuable consideration, in one of two ways: he may either do such acts as amount in law to a conveyance or assignment of the property, and thus completely divest himself of the legal ownership, in which case the person who by those acts acquires the property takes it beneficially, or on trusts, as the case may be, or the legal owner of the property may, by one or other of the modes recognised as amounting to a valid declaration of trust, constitute himself a trustee, and, without an actual transfer of the legal title, may so deal with the property as to deprive himself of its beneficial ownership, and declare that he will hold it from that time forward on trust for the other person.'

7.18 THE MEANING OF A 'COMPLETE AND PERFECT' GIFT

Both the above judgments were referred to by Upjohn J. in *Re Wale* (1956), an interesting case and one which illustrates the dangers of allowing the legal title to settled assets to remain in names other that those of the trustees. It is not always easy to discern whether a settlor has, in fact, done all that is required of him to divest himself completely of the legal ownership of the settled property.

In *Re Wale* (1956) Elizabeth was entitled to two parcels of investments, lot 'A' which were in her own name and lot 'B' which were in the name of her husband's executors. In 1939 she made a voluntary settlement of both lots in favour of her daughter but never took any steps to transfer either parcel of shares. She died in 1953, having left her estate to her two sons and having appointed her daughter as one of her executors. It was held (a) that the deceased had had an *equitable* interest in lot 'B', which had been validly assigned to the settlement trustees, so that the daughter was entitled under the settlement, but (b) that lot 'A' passed to the sons under the will. As the deceased had held the legal title to the lot 'A' shares, they could not pass to the settlement trustees without formal transfers and the imperfect gift could not be cured by the daughter's appointment as an executor under the rule in *Strong* v *Bird*, since the deceased's donative intent had not been maintained until her death.

In *Re Rose* (1952)[2] a Mr Rose executed two transfers of shares on 30 March 1943, one in favour of his wife and the other in favour of trustees. The transfers were stamped on 12 April 1943 and registered in the company's books on 30 June 1943. Mr Rose died on 16 February 1947. The crucial date for estate duty purposes was 10 April 1943. If it could be said that the gifts were complete before that date they would avoid being subject to duty. The Court of Appeal held that, as the deceased had done everything in his power by executing the transfers to transfer his legal and beneficial interest in the shares to the transferees, the transferees thenceforth became the beneficial owners of the shares and the shares were therefore not dutiable. It follows that if, for instance, Mr Rose had changed his mind after executing the transfers and had attempted to rescind, the transferees would have been able to bring an action to protect their interests in the shares.

If the donor has put the donee in a position to complete his title to the gift without help from the donor the 'complete and perfect' rule is satisfied subject to the condition that, if, as happened in *Re Fry* (1946), the transfer formalities include the prior consent of the UK Exchange Control authorities (a form of control that was abolished in October 1979), the transfer is not complete unless that consent has been first obtained by the donor.

The principle established in *Re Rose* (1952) was followed in *Mascall* v *Mascall* (1985) where it was held that there was a completed gift of registered land once the donor had executed the transfer form and sent it and the Land Certificate to the Stamp Office. In *Jaffa* v *Taylor* (1990) the court held that physical delivery of a chattel (in this case, a painting) to the trustees was not essential for the constitution of a valid trust.

7.19   RULE IN *STRONG* v *BIRD* (1874)

This rule is an exception to the maxim 'Equity will not perfect an imperfect gift'; where a donor has made an incomplete gift during his life and has appointed the donee his executor, the vesting of the subject-matter of the gift in the executor on death of the donor will perfect the gift. There must be evidence of an intention to make an immediate gift initially and, as has been seen in *Re Wale* (1956), also evidence of a continuing intention to make the gift until death occurs, a point that cropped up again in *Re Gonin* (1979) and was sufficient to defeat an alleged gift in favour of a donee administrator. The judge in *Re Gonin* expressed the opinion *obiter* that the rule did not apply to administrators, as distinct from executors, despite a clear decision to the contrary in *Re James* (1935). The logic of the rule seems to require that the subject-matter of the gift should vest in a donee appointed by the donor, i.e. an executor, not in someone appointed by the court as is an administrator; it applies only to a specific item of property – not, for example, to cash. It was used to perfect an incomplete gift into a marriage settlement in *Re Ralli* (1964):

> Helen owned a reversionary interest in her father's estate expectant on her mother's death. Her marriage settlement included a covenant to bring this reversionary interest into the settlement but Helen never took any steps to assign her interest. Eventually the children of Helen's sister, Irene, became the beneficiaries of the marriage settlement. Helen died in 1956 and her mother in 1961, by which time Irene's husband had become the sole surviving trustee both of the marriage settlement and of the father's will. Buckley J. held that Helen's

interest in her father's estate belonged to the marriage settlement under the rule in *Strong* v *Bird*, since the imperfect gift of the reversionary interest became complete the moment that Irene's husband became the owner of it in both capacities.

The rule in *Strong* v *Bird* bears a close analogy to the rules for *donationes mortis causa* – see *ante* 2.21 – though in a more relaxed way, as what is at stake with a *dmc* is the delivery of control rather than the delivery of title.

7.20 IMPERFECT GIFTS AND NON-VOLUNTEERS

Equity has no objection to the enforcement of an imperfect gift by someone who has given valuable consideration to the donor, in which case, of course, it is not strictly a gift. 'Valuable consideration' in this context means money or money's worth or marriage. So far as marriage is concerned, any promised transfer of property into a settlement must be made on or before the marriage or, if afterwards, in pursuance of an ante-nuptial agreement. However, not everybody who is named as a beneficiary in a marriage settlement is entitled to enforce it; only beneficiaries within the so-called 'marriage consideration' can do this and may do so, in fact, even after the covenant has become statute-barred. Such beneficiaries are the respective spouses and their issue. It is clear, for instance, that next-of-kin other than issue of the marriage cannot enforce such a settlement; in *Re Plumptre* (1910):

> A marriage settlement was made for the benefit of the husband and wife, their issue and, failing such issue, the wife's next-of-kin. As events turned out, the next-of-kin were the surviving beneficiaries but were not allowed to enforce a covenant in the settlement to settle after-acquired property.

A volunteer-beneficiary who is actually a party to the deed containing such a covenant would be able to enforce it at common law, but it is not usual in practice for the beneficiaries to be parties, settlements usually being made between the settlor on the one hand and the trustees on the other. The trustees themselves would not have been permitted to sue under a covenant of the kind described above, even had it not been statute-barred, because that would indirectly have been a way of circumventing the rule against enforcement by volunteers; in *Re Kay* (1939) trustees were directed not to take action to enforce a covenant to settle made in favour of volunteers.

7.21 THE RULE AGAINST PERPETUITIES

For generations the great landowners did their best to tie up their property and to prevent its alienation for the longest possible period of time; conversely, as a matter of policy, English law has restricted their right to do this. For, as Lord Nottingham LC observed in 1683:

'. . . such perpetuities fight against God, by affecting a stability which human providence can never attain to, and are utterly against the reason and policy of the common law.' (*Duke of Norfolk's Case*.)

To implement this policy, the courts evolved the rule against perpetuities, finally settled in its modern form by the decision in *Cadell* v *Palmer* (1833). This modern form is now subject to statutory intervention in the shape of s. 163 LPA and the PAA; it may be stated as follows:

(a) any future interest in property real or personal is void from the outset if it may possibly vest after the perpetuity period has expired and, for this purpose,

(b) the perpetuity period consists of a life or lives in being together with a further period of twenty-one years and any period of gestation where such exists.

The first part of the rule is satisfied so long as a beneficiary's interest is definitely established within the perpetuity period, i.e. vested in interest, even if not also vested in possession. So, where there is a life interest to A, remainder to B provided he reaches the age of 21 and B attains that age during A's lifetime, B's interest is vested in him without qualification on his 21st birthday, even though he is not entitled to possession of the property until A dies. [3]

7.22   THE MEANING OF 'LIVES IN BEING'

The perpetuity period starts running at the date of the gift (if *inter vivos*) and at the date of death (if testamentary); whose are the lives in being which define the length of the period (plus twenty-one years)? Such lives may be expressly stated in the trust instrument; in the past it was not uncommon for what was called a 'Royal lives' clause to be used, the period expiring twenty-one years after the death of, say, the last surviving descendant now living of his late Majesty King George VI. Otherwise, one looks to the gift itself to provide the requisite lives:

'The only lives worth considering are those which are implicated in the contingency upon which the vesting has been made to depend.' (*Megarry & Wade* p. 251)

So, in a gift by will (coming into operation before 16th July 1964) to A for life, remainder to such of his grandchildren as reach 21, the lives used for the common law perpetuity rule are A and any children and grandchildren of his who are alive at the date of the gift; although the children are not directly involved in the gift, their presence is obviously essential to the implementation of the gift in remainder. But if this gift is analysed, it can be seen that it is *possible* (unless there was at the testator's death a grandchild already over 21, in which case the class must close at the death of the life tenant under the rule in *Andrews* v *Partington*, as to which see *ante* 6.30,31 and *post* note 4 to this chapter) that an interest may vest outside the perpetuity period, because A could have another child (not a life in being) and that child could himself have a child whose interest might vest more than 21 years after the death of the last surviving life in being at the date of the gift. Not very likely, perhaps, but possible and the common law rule deals with possibilities, however remote. Equally, it foolishly assumes that anyone may have a child at any age, whatever the physical impossibility involved.

7.23   POSSIBILITIES, NOT ACTUALITIES

Where, as in the foregoing example, the perpetuity rule is broken, the gift which is involved in the breach is void from the start. So a fault in draftsmanship may invalidate the creation of a trust which has otherwise safely overcome the other risks described earlier – lack of capacity, lack of certainty and incomplete constitution. Moreover, the perpetuity defect may not be observed straight away but may lie in wait, an unexploded and undetected device, only to blow up in the face of the trustees many years later:

> In *Re Drummond* (1988) a settlement had been made in 1924 upon three daughters for life with power to appoint to children and issue and in default of appointment to each daughter's children at 21, but in case there should be no such children, the share of a daughter so dying was to be distributed amongst such of the daughters as should *then be living* and the issue of any of them who might then be dead, such issue to take their parent's share at 21 or earlier marriage.
>
> One of the daughters died childless in 1984 and in the High Court it was considered that there was a possibility, taking 1924 as the standpoint, that (for example) a daughter might die leaving a child aged two, who might later die at 19, leaving a child to eventually reach 21. Inevitably that grandchild of a daughter might attain a vested interest more than 21 years after the dropping of the lives in being (the settlor and his three daughters), making the gift over bad for perpetuity.[4]
>
> The Court of Appeal reversed this decision, taking the view that the words 'daughters as should then be living' referred to the dates of death of each of the daughters and thus the gift to issue of any of the daughters who might then be dead could only take effect as a gift to issue *then living*. So such a gift must vest within the perpetuity period and was valid.

7.24   PERPETUITIES AND ACCUMULATIONS ACT 1964 (PAA)

The harshness of the common law rule against perpetuities has been reduced somewhat by the 1964 Act, but not without adding further problems of its own. The main provision is certainly beneficial. Where it is seen that a gift may or may not vest within the perpetuity period as defined by the common law rule, one treats it as valid for the time being. Then one sits down to 'wait and see' what happens – s. 3(1). In the example given in

7.22 *ante* it is just as possible for the gift to vest within the period of the modern rule as outside it. If, however, the gift is such that it must vest within the common law period (for example, if all interests must vest within the period of a royal lives clause), well and good – the gift is valid at common law and there is no room for the intervention of the 1964 Act. If there is a possibility of its vesting outside the common law period, the disposition is to be treated as if there were no perpetuity rule until it becomes apparent that, even with the benefit of the new law, the gift is bound to vest outside the period. If at the outset the gift is bound to vest outside the common law period, then it fails at the start. The Act, incidentally, applies only to instruments taking effect after 15 July 1964; hence, it was irrelevant in the case of *Re Drummond* – see *ante* 7.23.

It will be seen that the 1964 Act does not do away with the common law rule; it merely grafts further rules on to it; in particular, it is still necessary to apply the common law rule in the first place to see whether there is a possibility of an interest vesting outside the period. *Then*, if such possibility exists, one applies the provisions of the Act.

7.25 LIVES IN BEING UNDER THE 1964 ACT

It is unfortunate that, when making the useful provision for 'wait and see' for an interest that might break the common law rule, the 1964 Act then went on to provide its own list of lives in being. Reference should be made to s. 3 PAA for the statutory list of lives, which Professor Hayton has described as 'arbitrary and both over-inclusive and under-inclusive'. Nevertheless, the statutory list must be used when applying the wait and see rule; for an example see *post* 7.27. Either the old rule should have been abolished as far as the defined lives in being were concerned, or the wait and see rule should have been allowed to make use of defined lives from the old rule. We now seem to have the worst of both worlds. Perhaps it should be mentioned that, where no lives in being of any kind are available, the perpetuity period is 21 years. However, s. 1 PAA allows a fixed period of years not exceeding 80 to be specified; this is a useful alternative to the Royal Lives clause already mentioned.

7.26 AGE REDUCTION

Where a gift might offend the rule because it vested at an age greater than 21, s. 163 LPA provided that the age of 21 should be substituted. Section 4(1) PAA replaces this provision by providing that there shall be substituted the age which, if specified, would preserve the gift from being void.

Take the case of a gift by will to the children of John if and when they become 25. If the gift comes into operation before 16 July 1964, the age would be reduced at the outset to 21 for all members of the class (assuming that John did not already have a child over 25 at the date when the gift became operative). If it comes into operation after 15 July 1964 and at the time the gift is made John has no children (or he has children but they are all under four), it is possible for the vesting date to be after the end of the common law perpetuity period (the life or lives in being plus 21 years) and one therefore applies the 'wait and see' principle – see *ante* 7.24. If, when John dies (his only wife having predeceased), he leaves two children, aged 10 and two, the 10-year-old's interest will clearly vest within the period, but that of the younger child will not. The latter's age of vesting is therefore reduced to 23 and the gift is saved. (In this example it is assumed that there are no other statutory lives to extend the period, in this case, the lives of the grandparents of John's children.)

7.27 CLASS REDUCTION

Sections 4(3) and (4) PAA preserve 'class gifts' – see *ante* 6.29 – which cannot be saved either under s. 3 ('wait and see') or s. 4(1). Formerly, the rule was that, unless every member of the class obtained a vested interest within the perpetuity period, the whole gift was void:

> Take the case of a gift to all the children of John to attain 21, provided that if any child of John dies under 21 leaving children who attain 21, such children will take the share which their parent would have taken. If John is alive when the gift takes effect and it takes effect before 16 July 1964, the whole gift is bad. It is perfectly possible for a child who fails to reach 21 himself to leave a child who attains 21 more than 21 years after the death of John and any children who may have existed at the outset.

The amended rule provides that, in such circumstances, the class is closed at the end of the perpetuity period; those members of the class who have, by then, got their vested interests (by whatever route) take the gift, to the exclusion of those who have not.

> Thus in the foregoing example, suppose that the gift takes effect under a will in 1970 when John is alive (his parents and his wife's parents having predeceased) and has one child, A, aged 18. That child dies in 1971. Two more children are subsequently born before the deaths of John and his wife in 1975, B in 1972 and C in 1974. B dies in 1991 at the age of 19, leaving a child (John's grandchild) aged one. At the outset the gift infringed the common law perpetuity rule. The available lives in being under the 1964 Act are John, his wife and his first child. John was the last to die and the perpetuity period under the 1964 Act runs out in 1996. If C's interest is to vest at all, it will do so in 1995; on the other hand, the grandchild's interest cannot vest earlier than 2011. C will therefore take to the exclusion of the grandchild.
>
> Note that the statutory lives in being under the new Act (which include the children's mother) could also have included the donor and grandparents of the donees, had they not already been dead.

7.28 PRESUMPTIONS AGAINST PROCREATION

Section 2 PAA also states a presumption (in connection with perpetuity questions; as to the determination of beneficial interests, see *post* 13.5) that a male cannot have a child below the age of 14 and that a female can only have children between the ages of 12 and 55; these presumptions apply also to the possibility of having a child by adoption, legitimation or other means. But evidence may be adduced to the effect that a specified person is or is not capable of having children by natural means at any age.

7.29 INTERESTS CONTINGENT ON SURVIVING AN UNBORN SPOUSE

Under the old law a gift to A (a bachelor) for life with remainder to any wife he may marry for life, with remainder to such of their children as survive them both is bad at the outset, as regards the gift to the children, because the wife need not turn out to be a person living at the start of the gift and could live more than 21 years after A's death. Section 5 PAA provides that if A's unborn spouse survives him for less than 21 years, the gift is good under the 'wait and see' rule. If she survives beyond that period, the children living at the end of 21 years from A's death take vested interests, regardless of whether they die later during the widow's remaining years.

7.30 POWERS OF APPOINTMENT AND THE PERPETUITY RULE

A distinction has to be drawn between general and special powers. A general power enables its holder to appoint the property involved to anyone, including himself. A special power is one which restricts its exercise in some way, either by designating a class or classes of persons as beneficiaries or by excluding some person or persons or object of the power. (See s. 7 PAA for the definition of a special power for the purposes of the rule against perpetuities.)

A general power is valid if acquired within the perpetuity period appropriate to the case; it does not have to be *exercised* within that period, except where it is exercisable by will only. Dispositions created by the exercise of a general power are valid if they vest within the perpetuity period, which runs from the date on which it is exercised.

A special power is void if it may be exercised outside the appropriate perpetuity period and dispositions created by such an exercise must vest within that period to be valid. It is therefore necessary to read into the original gift the terms of any subsequent exercise of a special power created by that gift in order to find out whether it does or does not offend the rule against perpetuities.

For the exercise of special powers the old law had a built-in principle of 'wait and see', because in reckoning up the limitations from the date when the power had been created it was permissible to use the facts of the actual appointment, rather than a hypothesis of them.

Suppose that T dies in 1963 leaving property to A for life with power to appoint to his children. A's first child is born in 1987 and in 1992, when the child is five years old, A makes an appointment to him by deed, if and when the child reaches 25. This is a perfectly good appointment, requiring no age reduction under s. 163 LPA, because by taking into account events subsequent to 1963, the appointee's interest must vest, if it vests at all, within A's lifetime plus 21 years, even supposing that A died the day after making the appointment. Had the same appointment been made in 1985 when the child was three, the appointment would have been bad under the old law but would have been saved by an age reduction to 21 under s. 163 LPA.

Turning to the new law, the new 'wait and see' principle is an enlarged concept for special powers, because of the facility for using the statutory lives, which in the case of special powers additionally include the life of the donee of the power and the lives of the appointees or potential appointees.

Suppose that T dies in 1975 leaving property to A for life, with power to appoint to his children. A's first child is born in 1989 and in 1992, when the child is three, an appointment is made by deed in favour of that child if and when he reaches 25. As the appointment is bad under the old law and cannot be rescued by the repealed s. 163 LPA, we are allowed to 'wait and see' in the statutory sense of that term. Suppose that A dies in 1993 when the child is four. The appointment is good without any age reduction. Note the important difference here from the old law, which insisted upon contemplation of the possibility of A's death immediately after the appointment. If instead we suppose that A died in 1992 immediately after making the appointment, the child's interest would vest in 2013 at the age of 24 (instead of 25) under the new age reduction rule.

7.31 THE RULE AGAINST EXCESSIVE ACCUMULATION OF INCOME

This is a statutory rule; there are six (alternative) permitted periods during which income may be accumulated:

(a) the life of the settlor (the only life that can be selected); or
(b) 21 years from the death (starting immediately on death) of the testator or settlor; or
(c) the minorities of any persons (beneficiaries or not) living or conceived at the death of the testator or settlor; the total period cannot exceed 18 years plus a gestation period (21 years for pre-1970 cases); or
(d) the minorities of beneficiaries who would be getting the income if they were 18 (21 for pre-1970 cases) – this type of accumulation can arise at any time and at different times for different beneficiaries, even if they were unborn when the trust started.

The above periods are provided for by s. 164 LPA. The following periods are added by s. 13 PAA:

(e) 21 years from the date of the *inter vivos* disposition; or
(f) the minorities of any persons (beneficiaries or not) in being at the date of the settlement.

7.32 OTHER ASPECTS OF ACCUMULATION

A direction to accumulate for longer than the common law perpetuity period (or for more modern instruments, the statutory perpetuity period) is completely void except, it appears, where the settlor is a company – *Re Dodwell & Co Ltd's Trust* (1979) – and where the trust is a charitable one – see *post* 12.8.* A further provision for accumulation is found in s. 31(2) TA and this may be used in addition to any of the periods referred to above. Thus, if a testator directs accumulation for a period of 21 years from his death and at the end of that period, the beneficiary turns out to be a minor, accumulation can continue under s. 31(2): see *post* 10.14 and 10.16.

The accumulation rules apply as much to powers to accumulate as they do to directions to accumulate. Powers or directions which are within the perpetuity period but which exceed the authorised accumulation periods are void as to the excess accumulation but are valid otherwise. An interesting illustration of this is contained in *Re Green* (1985):

The testatrix died in 1976, having by her will made in 1972 left her estate in trust for her son, Barry, who had been shot down in a bombing raid in 1943 and never heard of since. The testatrix never gave up hope that her son might still be alive and accordingly directed that the income of her estate was to be accumulated until 2020 and if by that date he had not made an appearance, the capital and accumulations were to be used to endow an animal charity; she also specified that the period from the date of her death to 2020 was to be the perpetuity period for the purposes of the trust. It was held that -
(a) income could accumulate until 1997, i.e. 21 years after death;
(b) the accumulation could be stopped by the charity at any time once it had been set up;
(c) the gift over to charity was not too remote, since, although no period 'consisting of a fixed period of years not exceeding 80' had been stated in the form of a period of years, a term of 44 years had been unambiguously identified, which was sufficient compliance with the wording of the 1964 Act;
(d) the trustees could proceed on the assumption that Barry had predeceased the testatrix and had died a bachelor, without prejudice to his right to follow the assets should he unexpectedly turn up – this last ruling is a 'Benjamin' order – see *ante* 6.54.

7.33 RULE AGAINST INALIENABILITY

It is a fundamental rule of English law that property should not be inalienable; hence the rule against perpetuities already discussed, which

---

*But note that charitable income must be expended or invested for charitable purposes, taking one year with another – see *post* 12.9.

prevents trust interests from vesting outside the perpetuity period. It is equally improper to make an immediate gift which is subject to a permanent restriction on alienation. Such trusts are commonly called purpose trusts, because their objective is the implementation of a purpose rather than the benefit of human beings. In such cases the rule against perpetuities is inapplicable because there is no gift of a future interest to which the rule could be applied. There is no objection to a *charitable* purpose trust continuing indefinitely; all other trusts for purposes are void, even if restricted to a perpetuity period, with certain exceptions mentioned below.

7.34 THE BENEFICIARY PRINCIPLE

A further objection to non-charitable purpose trusts lies in this principle; as Sir William Grant MR remarked in *Morice* v *Bishop of Durham* (1804), a case which concerned a gift upon trust for 'such objects of benevolence and liberality as the Bishop of Durham shall most approve of',

> 'Every other [i.e. non-charitable] trust must have a definite object. There must be somebody in whose favour the court can decree performance.'

Closely allied with unenforceability is the court's reluctance to cope with uncertainty as to the way in which the trust is to be administered – the difficulty, for example, of taking on the role of the Bishop of Durham should he fail to carry out his trust. As was said by Lord Eldon in that same case:

> 'As it is a maxim that the execution of a trust shall be under the control of the court, it must be of such a nature that it can be under that control; so that the administration of it can be reviewed by the court; or, if the trustee dies, the court itself can execute the trust; a trust, therefore, which, in case of maladministration could be reformed; and a due administration directed; and then, unless the subject and the objects can be ascertained upon principles familiar in other cases, it must be decided that the court can neither reform maladministration nor direct a due administration.'

So a trust is void unless there are human beneficiaries to enforce it; in the case of charitable trusts the Attorney-General is charged with the task of enforcement: see *post* 12.6. Section 15(4) PAA expressly excludes purpose trusts from its ambit. Another example of a non-charitable purpose trust arose in *Re Astor* (1952):

> The settlement was expressly stated to be restricted to a period of lives plus 21 years; the objects were various non-charitable purposes, including the mainten-ance of good relations between nations and the preservation of the independence and integrity of newspapers. Roxburgh J. held the trust to be void, both in respect of the beneficiary principle and on the grounds of uncertainty.

7.35   THE ANOMALOUS CASES – TOMBS AND ANIMALS

Notwithstanding the general disapproval of non-charitable purpose trusts, there are a few recognised exceptions to the overall ban. Trusts for the maintenance of a particular grave, vault or monument are acceptable – *Re Hooper* (1932) – and are valid for 21 years. Trusts for specific animals, a very popular form of bequest, are also allowed; such trusts are a 'concession to human weakness or sentiment'. There are difficulties in such cases about the perpetuity period. The animals themselves cannot be lives in being for the purpose of the rule. There is a tendency to gloss over this factor; see, e.g., *Re Haines* (1952) where Danckwerts J. took judicial notice of the fact that 16 years was a long life for a cat (therefore within the perpetuity period of 21 years). Cats, in fact, can live for much longer than 16 years.

7.36   GIFTS TO CLUBS, SOCIETIES AND OTHER UNINCORPORATED ASSOCIATIONS

Such gifts have to be held in trust, the club or society having no separate legal existence. It follows that the rules against perpetuity, inalienability and the beneficiary principle apply to such gifts; particular trouble is caused when the gift is said to be for a purpose, as in *Re Grant* (1980) where the gift was for the purposes of the (non-charitable) Chertsey Labour Party Headquarters. The rules of the local Party Headquarters were such as to make its property inalienable, and the gift failed. Where there are no strings attached to a gift, so that it is freely alienable, there is no problem; see, e.g. *Re Prevost* (1930) where there was a gift to the trustees of the London Library for general purposes. If such a gift can be construed as for the benefit of members of the club or society and there is no restriction on their right to dispose of it, the fact that the gift is described as for purposes is no objection – *Re Lipinski* (1976). It is even possible for a gift which appears to be primarily a gift for purposes to be validated by treating it as a gift for ascertainable individuals, as in *Re Denley* (1969) where a plot of land was transferred to trustees to hold, for a specified perpetuity period, 'for the purpose of a recreation or sports ground primarily for the benefit of the employees of the company'. Goff J. upheld the gift as one for the benefit of the employees; there was no breach of the beneficiary principle and the trust was one which the court could control.

7.37   THE INSOLVENT SETTLOR

It is not unknown for those engaged in business ventures to take steps to protect their personal fortunes and their families by putting funds into trust and so out of reach of their creditors. As Jessel MR remarked:

'If I succeed in business, I make a fortune for myself. If I fail, I leave my creditors unpaid. They will pay the loss.' (*Re Butterworth* (1882))

But this tactic is not necessarily going to succeed. Section 42 Bankruptcy Act 1914 and s. 172 LPA provided for the avoidance of settlements of this kind within specified periods of years since their creation. The relevant legislation is now in the Insolvency Act 1986.

7.38 BANKRUPTCY – SS. 339–42 INSOLVENCY ACT 1986

Where an individual (there are corresponding provisions for corporate insolvency) is adjudged bankrupt and he has at a relevant time entered into a transaction at an undervalue, the trustee in bankruptcy may apply to the court for an order under s. 339; the court may make such order as it thinks fit for the purpose of restoring the position of the bankrupt to what it would have been if the transaction had not been entered into. Under s. 339(3) a transaction at an undervalue is either any gift or a transaction in consideration of marriage or any transaction for a consideration 'significantly less' in money or money's worth than the value being provided. Relevant time, in the case of transactions at an undervalue, generally covers a period of five years ending with the date on which the bankruptcy petition is presented, but within not more than two years unless the individual was insolvent at the time the transaction took place or became insolvent as a result of it: s. 341. Although an order made under s. 339 may affect anyone holding the property disposed of by the transaction at an undervalue, no order will be made so as to prejudice the interest of a purchaser in good faith without notice from someone other than the bankrupt: s. 342(2).

7.39 TRANSACTION DEFRAUDING CREDITORS – SS. 423–5 INSOLVENCY ACT 1986

Section 423 replaces s. 172 LPA: where a person (which term includes corporations) enters into a transaction at an undervalue (defined as above) and the court is satisfied that his intention in doing so was either to put the assets disposed of beyond the reach of a present or future creditor or of otherwise prejudicing the interests of a claimant against him, the court may make an order restoring the position to what it would have been if the transaction had not been entered into and protecting the interests of those who have been adversely affected by the transaction. There is no time limit affecting applications to the court under this section. Neither is there any requirement that the debtor/transferor should be adjudged bankrupt or that (as was the case under s. 172) he must be shown to have intended, when entering into the transaction, to defraud his creditors. The court must, however, be satisfied that the transaction complained of was intended either to put assets out of the reach of some person with a claim against him or of otherwise prejudicing the interests of such a person with regard to such a claim. There is similar protection in s. 425(2) for a purchaser in good faith without notice to that referred to in connection with s. 342(2) above but the beneficiaries of a settlement which is attacked under either s. 339 or s. 423 do appear to be in a rather vulnerable position.

8 Trusts (2)

8.1 GENERAL CONSIDERATIONS IN MAKING A TRUST

It was suggested in chapter two that, before making a will, it was desirable to establish both the current circumstances of the testator and his wishes as regards his testamentary dispositions. The same requirements apply to a prospective settlor, with the important proviso that, before handing assets over to the trustees of a new settlement, it is essential for the settlor to satisfy himself that financially he and his family remain securely based for the foreseeable future.

Very often, a settlement is made in order to save inheritance tax from having to be paid at a later date. This is a laudable objective, but there is surely no point in taking a tax-saving exercise of this kind to the point where the settlor and his dependants might find their standard of living curtailed to an unpleasant degree. The first step for a private individual who contemplates making a trust, whether in favour of individuals or for charitable purposes, must be to assess the consequences, not only the potential saving in tax but also the impact on future living costs and funding requirements.

So far as tax saving and tax planning are concerned, it also has to be borne in mind that, although there will always be taxes, the rules are changed every year and that a sensible move in year one may turn out to be disadvantageous in year two, simply because the current Chancellor of the Exchequer has altered the law. For instance, at the time of writing, there is in progress a Revenue review of the taxation of trusts (see note 3 to 8.4 *post*). How this will be concluded, one cannot tell. There is no more certainty as regards the future in tax matters than there is in anything else.

8.2 THE CAKE THAT IS GIVEN CANNOT BE EATEN BY THE GIVER

In any event, a potential settlor must be reminded that, if a trust is to be effective as a tax-saving exercise, it must be irrevocable for inheritance tax as well as income tax. The benefit given cannot be retrieved and the donor must so arrange his affairs that he can live in reasonable comfort without it. Furthermore, he must realise that, even if he acts as a trustee (not advisable – see *post* 8.10) his power to do as he pleases with the settled property is at an end. This is a fact which many settlors find hard to swallow.

Provided the settlor has stripped himself and his spouse of any conceivable interest in the gifted property, his continuing presence on the scene as a trustee will not in itself be treated as the retention of an interest for income tax purposes, since a purely fiduciary role cannot be regarded as a beneficial interest for tax purposes. (The ban in the income tax legislation on the inclusion of the settlor's wife or husband in the settlement does not extend to provision for a widow or widower.) At one time, whether or not the settlor was a trustee, if the trustees chose to discharge out of the funds settled the lifetime CTT then exigible, the Revenue took the view that by removing from the settlor any liability for the tax, he had retained an interest in the settlement for income tax purposes; a view they no longer hold – SP1/82. Different considerations apply to CGT; the settlor is alone liable for that tax and the trustees must not be empowered to meet his CGT liability, although they can acquire held-over relief without introducing the income tax complication. But there are three other risks for the settlor who installs himself as a trustee of his own settlement: (a) accidental enjoyment of the gifted property, thus creating a gift with reservation – see *post* 8.10; (b) the receipt of director's remuneration from a company in which the trust has a shareholding – also *post* 8.10; and (c) the control he might be said to retain over family company shares put into the settlement, bearing in mind the extraordinarily wide definition of 'director' for tax purposes.

8.3   INCOME TAX CONSEQUENCES OF MAKING A SETTLEMENT

The best advice to give to the prospective settlor is that he should carefully exclude himself and his wife from any possibility of ever obtaining an interest in the settlement funds, which means (a) that the settlement must not be capable of being revoked or diminished by the settlor or anyone else; (b) that in no way can income or capital be steered back to the settlor or his spouse or his infant children by the exercise of a power of appointment or any other means; and (c) that neither deliberately nor accidentally may the settlor retain an interest in the income or capital of the settled property. There is otherwise the danger that the undistributed income (and sometimes the whole of it) will remain that of the settlor, although there are exceptions. [1]

There have for many years been elaborate provisions in the Income Tax Acts to make it difficult for the settlor and spouse to benefit themselves and their infant children out of any funds settled or to get those funds back into their own hands. For settlements made after 13 March 1989 a harder edge has been given to these provisions by the introduction of s. 674A into ICTA. Whereas previously the anti-avoidance provisions had tended to concentrate upon the undistributed and accumulated income of the settlement, s. 674A attacks both distributed and undistributed income; all of it will stay in the settlor's hands, unless he has stripped himself absolutely of the capital from which that income arises. This new provision reaches out not only at settlements made after 14 March 1989 but also at those made before that date in respect of any income arising from 6 April 1990 if the spouse can benefit from it. The purpose of s. 674A is more easily understood if it is recalled that the Finance Act 1988 took the important step of destroying the income tax advantage of non-charitable covenants and also heralded the introduction of independent taxation for husband and wife as from 1990/91. What could no longer be achieved by covenant could still be secured by a transfer of capital to trustees, making the income irrevocably payable to the chosen beneficiary but retaining the reversion to the capital. Section 674A, introduced by the Finance Act 1989, put a stop to this, although the gate is still left open for the settlor to retain an interest, in a limited number of cases. [2]

8.4 THE DANGEROUS WIDTH OF 'SETTLOR' AND 'SETTLEMENT'

These expressions are widely defined in the income tax legislation:

In *Thomas* v *Marshall* (1953) the taxpayer paid money into National Savings Bank accounts opened in the names of his unmarried infant children and also purchased Defence Bonds for them. It was held by the House of Lords that these arrangements constituted a 'settlement' within the meaning of what is now s. 670 ICTA and that the interest from the bank accounts and Defence Bonds must be treated as the father's income. Note that under s. 663(4) small sums not exceeding £100 a year paid to the child as the result of a parental gift are disregarded as from 1991/92 (previously £5).

The way round this problem of children's income is to set up an express trust giving the child an absolute interest in the income and allowing the income to accumulate, a practice which appears to be acceptable to the Revenue.[3] A more sophisticated view of the word 'settlement' appears from *Butler* v *Wildin* (1989):

The two taxpayers were an architect and his brother (a chartered accountant), who incorporated a company, the shares in which were partly allocated to their four infant children, the cost being met from the children's own resources. The company was in the business of development and eventually it started to pay dividends to the children. The Revenue rejected an income tax repayment claim on their behalf because the income had to be treated as that of the parents under s. 663 ICTA. The taxpayers had arranged for the shares to be allotted to the children at trifling cost and they were the organisers of the development programme from which the company was making its money. It was held that the only limitation on the width of the definition of 'settlement' was that it must contain an element of bounty and that there could be no doubt on this score, as the children's contributions were minuscule and their exposure to risk was virtually non-existent.

8.5   SETTLEMENTS ON OWN CHILDREN – SS. 663–5

These have always occupied a compartment of their own in the income tax legislation. The overriding rule is (a) that no income must be fed back to the settlor or spouse or applied for the maintenance of the infant children and (b) that to the extent that there is any undistributed income or income accumulations, any application of capital for an infant child's benefit must be treated as the settlor's income. The settlement must be irrevocable but a retained interest is permitted if restricted to the determination of the children's interest by bankruptcy or assignment. Having clambered its way through the restrictions of ss. 663–5, the settlement then has to survive the more general obstacles of s. 673 and (for higher rates) s. 685; or if made after 13 March 1989, of s. 674A and s. 685.

8.6   SETTLOR AND SPOUSE – THE DANGER IF MONEY PASSES BETWEEN THEM AND TRUSTEES

Whatever kind of settlement is involved, any movement of capital by way of loan or repayment of loan between the trustees and the settlor, or settlor's spouse, is liable to be treated as the settlor's income, unless the loan is made in a year when there is no undistributed or accumulated income and is repaid before any such income arises: s. 677 ICTA. There are relieving provisions but s. 677 continues to be a trap for the innocent as well as the guilty and its breadth may make it desirable to expressly forbid any monetary traffic between trustees and settlor (or spouse):

> In *De Vigier* v *IRC* (1964) the trustees, who were the settlor's wife and a solicitor, administered a contingent accumulation settlement and wished to take advantage of a rights issue on one of the trust investments, but there was no cash on the trust account and no power to borrow. The settlor's wife accordingly paid £7,000 into the trust banking account, which sum was later repaid to her. The House of Lords confirmed that the settlor was taxable on the grossed up equivalent of £7,000. Exactly the same position would arise today and could be cured under s. 677(5) only by re-lending the money to the trustees.

If the trustees are participators in a close company and that company has made payments to the settlor (or spouse), there must be a matching payment by the trustees to the company, otherwise the settlor will have the payments added to his income: s. 678. (A close company is one which is under the control of five or fewer participators, or of participators who are directors; in the latter case, no restriction numerically: s. 414(1) ICTA.)

8.7 INHERITANCE TAX CONSEQUENCES OF MAKING A TRUST

For the above purpose there are three principal types of private trust – interest in possession trusts, discretionary trusts and accumulation and maintenance settlements. The creation of the first of these is treated as a gift by one individual (the settlor) to another (the beneficiary who is given the interest in possession and whose estate is thereby increased); it therefore qualifies as a PET – ss. 3A(1)(c) and 3A(2) IHTA. There will be no IHT payable on the making of the trust if the settlor survives for seven years or more. If he dies within that period then a charge will arise under s. 3A(4), but in the meantime there is an assumption under s. 3A(5) that the gift will prove to be an exempt transfer. Primarily, this liability will fall on the trustees under s. 199(1)(c), although the life tenant is also liable (if the trustees fail to pay the tax), not only under s. 199(1)(c) as one who is beneficially entitled to an interest in possession, but also under s. 199(1)(b) as a person whose estate has been increased by the transfer; the settlor's PRs could be caught under s. 199(2)(a), as limited by s. 204(8), if the others fail to pay up.

A transfer to an accumulation and maintenance settlement (see *post* 8.11) is also a PET. The liability for IHT if the settlor dies within seven years falls upon the trustee under s. 199(1)(c); also, if the tax remains unpaid, upon any person for whose benefit any of the income or capital is applied under s. 199(1)(d). There is again a residual liability for the settlor's PRs: s. 199(2)(a) and s. 204(8). For transfers to non-privileged discretionary settlements, see *post* 8.9.

Whatever the type of trust, the trustees are responsible for submitting an account under s. 216(1). Their liability to IHT is limited to the property they have received, accounted for or had available to them as trustees, or would have had but for their neglect or default: s. 204(2). Trustees who receive PETs should do their sums and work out their maximum potential liability in the event of the settlor's death within seven years; if they risk being short of cash to settle such liability, they should seriously consider insurance.

Once the trust is up and running, the liability for IHT on subsequent events (except where an interest in possession is terminated, for which see *post* 8.18) is determined by the settled property rules in s. 201. As one might expect, the trustees are primarily liable under s. 201(1)(a) but if the tax remains unpaid, discretionary beneficiaries can be liable under s. 201(1)(c), if they have had any money out of the trust. If the trustees happen not to be resident in the UK, the settlor of an *inter vivos* trust can be liable under s. 201(1)(d).

8.8 MEANING OF INTEREST IN POSSESSION

Normally there will be no difficulty in deciding which trust falls into which category for IHT, but there may be borderline cases, especially in drawing the distinction between the interest in possession trust and the discretionary trust. There is no definition of 'interest in possession' in the legislation, and its meaning has to be got from an Inland Revenue Press Notice of 12 February 1976 and from the leading case of *Pearson* v *IRC* (1981):

The Press Notice:
An interest in possession in settled property exists where the person having the interest has the immediate entitlement (subject to any prior claim by the trustees for expenses or other outgoings properly payable out of income) to any income produced by that property as the income arises; but a discretion or power, in whatever form, which can be exercised after income arises so as to withhold it from that person negatives the existence of an interest in possession. For this purpose, a power to accumulate income is regarded as a power to withhold it, unless any accumulations must be held solely for the person having the interest or his personal representatives.

On the other hand, the existence of a mere power of revocation or appointment, the exercise of which would determine the interest wholly or in part (but which, so long as it remains unexercised, does not affect the beneficiary's immediate entitlement to income) does not in the Board's view prevent the interest from being an interest in possession.

Pearson v *IRC*:
In 1964 the settlor made a settlement; there was a power of appointment for discretionary objects and subject to the exercise of this power, the trustees were empowered to accumulate such income as they thought fit for 21 years. There was then a gift of both capital and income to such of the settlor's children as should reach 21 or marry under that age and, if more than, in equal shares absolutely.

By February 1974 all three of the settlor's children had reached 21. In 1976 the trustees appointed the sum of £16,000 on trust for one child, Fiona, for life. The Revenue then claimed that as a result of this appointment, Fiona had become entitled to an interest in possession where no such interest had previously existed and that a charge to CTT (a tax which had come into operation on 27 March 1974) arose as a result. The amount involved was quite trivial. The Revenue's assertion that no interest in possession had before existed was based on two factors, (a) the existence of the power to accumulate for 21 years from 1964 and (b) a provision in the settlement entitling the trustees to charge all expenses to income, including those which would normally be charged to capital.

Both the High Court and the Court of Appeal took the view that neither of these aspects of the settlement prevented Fiona, when 21, from enjoying an interest in possession; it was common ground that the power of appointment did not affect its existence one way or the other. However, the House of Lords, by a bare majority, took the other view and held that the power to accumulate prevented an interest in possession from coming into existence. 'Their right [i.e. the children's] to anything depended on what the trustees did or did not do'. On reaching 21 they did not get a *right* to the present enjoyment of anything; hence no interest in possession.

The Revenue's view, as expressed in the Press Notice, therefore prevailed; the question about the power to pay all expenses out of capital did not have to be answered, although opinions were expressed *obiter* that such a power was administrative in character and would not in itself prevent the existence of an interest in possession.

However, it seems that the Revenue adheres to its view that such a power should be restricted to expenses properly payable out of income. It may, therefore, be prudent to avoid extending it to capital expenses where there is a risk that it may convert an interest in possession trust into a discretionary trust. According to some authorities, the discretionary trust regime is now such as to pose fewer dangers than the earlier version, so the disadvantage in the adoption of the Revenue's view is correspondingly reduced. Also, the Scottish case of *Miller* v *IRC* (1987) indicates that an interest in possession is not easily eliminated by such provisions; the trustees had power to use income at their discretion for various purposes, including replacement of capital depreciation. It was held that the trustees' powers were administrative only and that the interest in possession was unaffected.

8.9 DISCRETIONARY TRUSTS

The creation of a discretionary trust, as defined in s. 58 IHTA (where the various exceptions are set out), cannot be a PET and will be a lifetime chargeable transfer. If any tax is payable it is the liability of the settlor (as transferor) under s. 199(1)(a) and the trustees under s. 199(1)(c); the beneficiaries (who have received any benefits) are potentially liable under s. 199(1)(d) but only if the tax remains unpaid: s. 204(6). The responsibility for delivering an account rests with the settlor under s. 216. Who pays the tax (settlor or trustees) is important in deciding the amount of the chargeable transfer, which will have to be grossed up if the settlor foots the bill. If the settlor's death supervenes within seven years, the reduced lifetime rate will be brought up to the full rate of tax, subject to taper relief under s. 7(4), but if the recalculation of the tax produces a lower bill than the one already paid, s. 7(5) blocks the chance of a refund. The trustees will be primarily liable for the extra tax under s. 199(1)(c) and secondarily the PRs of the settlor under s. 199(2)(b) and the beneficiaries under s. 199(1)(d), as in the case of the first instalment of tax.

The initial charge for IHT on the setting up of the discretionary settlement is often more eloquently described as an entry charge. During the continuation of the settlement, there is a further charge to tax every ten years, often called a periodic charge. Additions to the settlement funds will incur both an entry charge and a proportionate periodic charge at the next (or first) 10-year anniversary. Withdrawals from the settlement funds (or total termination of the discretionary trust) will incur a proportionate periodic charge, calculated from the previous 10-year anniversary (or from the start of the settlement), otherwise known as an exit charge. Tax is always computed at lifetime rates and the 10-yearly charge is at 30% of those rates, making for 1992/93 an effective rate of 6%, subject to reduction by the nil band, business and agricultural reliefs and the time reduction if the charge occurs inside the 10-year period. Theoretically, after about 33 years the trust will have paid the full 20% lifetime tax on the assets held for that period. So the IHT discretionary trust regime is not nearly as oppressive as it seems at first sight and if the gift that the settlor wants to make is pregnant with non-business gains, the advantage of the application of holdover relief is not to be despised – see *post* 8.14.

Liability for the IHT during the life of the trust falls upon the trustees under s. 201(1)(a) and if tax remains unpaid, those who have benefited from the trust can be made to pay under s. 201(1)(c). The settlor of an *inter vivos* trust may be liable too, if the trustees are non-resident.

8.10   IHT AND RESERVATION OF BENEFIT

For both income tax (see *ante* 8.3) and CGT (see *post* 8.14), there are ample reasons for excluding the settlor and spouse (but not the settlor's widow or widower) as actual or potential beneficiaries under the discretionary trust. For IHT it seems that the Revenue takes the view that in all cases where the settlor is a discretionary beneficiary he must be treated as having reserved a benefit in the entire fund, though there is no objection to the inclusion of the other partner to the marriage, whether as spouse or as widow or widower. Therefore, if the settlor is included, the settled fund will be chargeable on his death, no matter how many years he survives.

There are no decisions on this point but it would obviously be a bold settlor (and a wealthy one) who decided to challenge the Revenue's view. The reservation of an interest should be carefully distinguished from the kind of settlement where the settlor makes a contingent gift or carves out a limited interest, which is followed either by a resulting trust for himself or by an express gift over to himself, on the failure or expiration of the interest given.

The appointment of the settlor as trustee does not in itself amount to a reservation of benefit but, if there is provision for him to be paid for his services, then there will be such a reservation: *Oakes v Stamp Duties Commissioners of New South Wales* (1954), where it was also held that payments for the education of the settlor's children did not amount to a reserved benefit under the NSW estate duty legislation. There will, however, be a reservation of benefit where a settlor who is a paid director of a family company settles shares in that company *unless* it can be shown that his directorial fees are a genuine payment for work done in that capacity. Often a settlor who has built up a family business is reluctant to give up control when settling shares of this kind. The risk factors inherent in this situation are plain to see, and regular consultations with professional advisers are desirable both as regards the conduct of the trust and the tax implications of such conduct.

8.11 ACCUMULATION AND MAINTENANCE TRUSTS – S. 71 IHTA

Section 3A(1)(c) permits the creation of this favoured[4] class of trusts as a PET, so there will be no entry charge unless the settlor dies within seven years. In addition, so long as the trust operates within the limits imposed by s. 71, the discretionary trust regime with its exit charges and periodic charges will not apply: s. 58(1)(b). To qualify for this favourable treatment, three requirements must be satisfied at the start:

(a) s. 71(1)(a) – one or more persons will [= bound to[5]], on or before attaining a specified age not exceeding 25, become entitled to, or to an interest in possession in, the settled property; and

(b) s. 71(1)(b) – no interest subsists in the settled property and the income from it is to [= must] be accumulated so far as it is not applied for the maintenance, education or benefit of such a person; and

(c) s. 71(2) – *either* (i) not more than 25 years have elapsed since the day on which the settlement was made or (if later) since the time when the settled property began to satisfy the two requirements of s. 71(1), *or* (ii) all the persons who are or have been beneficiaries are, or were, either grandchildren of a common grandparent, or children, widows or widowers of such grandchildren who were themselves beneficiaries but died before becoming entitled as mentioned in s. 71(1)(a).

Where different parts of a trust fund of this kind are held for the benefit of different beneficiaries, the rules apply severally to each part.

8.12 INTERACTION OF SS. 31 AND 32 TA (SEE *POST* CHAPTER 10)

A straightforward trust in favour of A, if and when he reaches the age of 18, will qualify as an accumulation and maintenance settlement, always assuming, of course, that A is under 18 when the trust is made. So will a trust in favour of the children of A contingently upon their reaching the age of 25, again assuming that such children are under 18 at the date of the settlement. Such cases will be controlled by s. 31 TA and if the age contingency selected is higher than 18, it is essential to exclude the operation of the section, since otherwise the children will acquire interests in possession under s. 31(1)(ii) at 18, thereby bringing to an end the operation of s. 71 IHTA.[6]

The existence of a power of appointment which *may* deprive the beneficiaries of an interest in possession on or before 25 will prevent the requirement in s. 71(1)(a) from being satisfied. The mere existence of a power of advancement, such as that available under s. 32 TA, will not in

205

itself breach that requirement. If, however, it is exercised in such a way as to deprive a beneficiary of the right to an interest in possession on or before the age of 25, the trust no longer qualifies as an accumulation and maintenance trust, and a charge to IHT will result.

8.13 OTHER ASPECTS OF ACCUMULATION AND MAINTENANCE TRUSTS

In addition to the exoneration from the IHT discretionary trust regime, s. 71(4)(a) ensures that there is no charge for IHT either when a beneficiary becomes entitled to an interest in possession or if he dies before reaching the specified age. But there will be a PET if his interest in possession is reduced in size by an increase in number of the class of which he is a member. For this reason, it is desirable for a trust to contain an express class-closing provision when the first member of a class to acquire an interest in possession does so.

A trust cannot sail under the s. 71 flag until there is a living beneficiary, so if no children have yet been born, a peg life (such as a young nephew) will have to be inserted. On the other hand, if there is one living beneficiary and he dies without attaining an interest in possession, the door of s. 71 will be kept open until another one comes along.

If a beneficiary acquires his interest in possession by becoming entitled to the income of the trust property at, say, 25, it will be quite usual for the trustees to have power to appoint the capital to him at some later age and when they do so, there will not be any charge to IHT, since he already has an interest in possession.

8.14 CAPITAL GAINS TAX – CONSEQUENCES OF MAKING A TRUST

Under s. 70, TCGA there will be a liability to CGT (or an allowable loss) if chargeable assets are settled. Settlor and trustees are 'connected persons' and under s. 18(3) any allowable loss will be deductible only from a gain on a subsequent disposal to the same trustees. Generally speaking, holdover relief on lifetime gifts was abolished for disposals made after 13 March 1989. However, a settlement by an individual of *business* assets, as defined by s. 165(2), may attract holdover relief, if the settlor so elects: s. 165(1); but as regards subsequent dispositions, where the business assets transferred are individual items rather than blocks of shares, then, unless the trustees or the life tenant are going to run a business which uses those assets, there will be no repetition of the business relief. A transfer into settlement which is also a chargeable transfer for IHT – typically the setting up of a discretionary trust which does not qualify as an accumulation and maintenance trust – will also attract holdover relief on all assets, not just business assets; furthermore this relief will be available to the trustees themselves when they make capital distributions from the discretionary trust: s. 260(1). When non-business assets are involved, the attraction of holdover relief in a discretionary trust may be more appealing than the undoubted merits of the privileged accumulation and maintenance trust, where holdover relief is restricted to business assets.

The rate of CGT payable by the trustees after a settlement has been set up is 25% if there is a life interest in possession, but 35% for any part of the trust which is of a discretionary nature, i.e. where income can be accumulated or has to be accumulated or is payable at the discretion of the trustees (for this purpose the simplest accumulation and maintenance trust and the most complex discretionary trust are in the same boat). The annual exemption for trusts is £2,900 (for 1992/93) and there are elaborate anti-fragmentation rules where a settlor has made more than one settlement.

Section 77, TCGA applies special rules to settlements in which the settlor or the settlor's spouse either has an interest or the possibility of an interest. These rules require that the gains of the trustees, after offsetting allowable losses, should be taxed as the settlor's own gains as if they formed the highest part of his chargeable gains. These is no annual exemption for the trustees and the only exemption available is that of the settlor, if not already used up on his personal gains. [7]

With assets that are privately owned, the great cleansing agent from CGT liability is death, providing a fresh start for the succeeding beneficiaries without any charge for CGT. For settled property, the death of the life tenant similarly leads to revaluation without any charge to CGT, whether or not there is a continuing trust. The lifetime termination of an interest in possession under the settlement (followed by a continuing trust) will result neither in a charge to CGT nor in revaluation, possibly with unfortunate consequences for the ultimate remainderman.

To illustrate the points in this paragraph, the trust fund is settled upon L for life with remainder to R if and when he attains 25. L dies when R is aged 15. The fund is revalued on L's death but there is no chargeable gain: s. 72(1). When R reaches 25 he becomes absolutely entitled as against the trustees, and there is a charge under s. 71(1) on the increase in value since the revaluation on L's death. Suppose instead that R is already 25 when L dies; the assets are revalued but the chargeable disposal that would otherwise arise under s. 71(1) is negated by s. 73(1). Suppose yet another alternative: L's interest is terminated not by his death but by his surrender of his interest to R aged 15. There is no charging provision that can operate until R reaches 25 when s. 71(1) will create a chargeable disposal based upon the original acquisition cost of the trustees.

8.15   THE TEST FOR THE RESIDENCE OF A TRUST FOR INCOME TAX

While it is not difficult for UK source income to be taxed at source, if a trust is in receipt of overseas income and the trustees are all resident abroad, there will be no means of assessing the foreign income, unless, of course, the beneficiary entitled to the income is resident in the UK.

In the long run in a fixed interest trust the residential status of the beneficiary is more important than the residence of the trustees. In *Williams* v *Singer* (1921) the trust fund consisted of Singer sewing machine shares, an American company who paid the dividends direct to the beneficiary domiciled and resident in France. The trustees, in whose names the shares were registered, were all domiciled and resident in the UK but the Revenue's attempt to assess them was dismissed by the House of Lords on the basis that the person charged to tax is neither the trustee nor the beneficiary as such, but the person in actual receipt and control of the income which it is sought to reach. In *Archer-Shee* v *Baker* (1927) the UK resident beneficiary was the sole life tenant of a New York trust consisting entirely of overseas investments. The taxpayer life tenant, who had been assessed on the gross income arising, contended that under the law at the time the assessment should be on the net income remitted to the UK, which was nil. The House of Lords held that the entitlement was to the actual dividends as they arose, on the assumption that New York trust law coincided with our own.

If the beneficiaries have discretionary interests or are non-resident, the vulnerability of the trustees becomes important. In 1989 there was a remarkable decision by the House of Lords in *Dawson* v *IRC* that the overseas income could not be assessed unless all the trustees were resident in the UK. The Revenue's reaction was swift, and as the result of s. 110 FA 1989, the current rules can be stated as follows:

(a)   UK source income is always liable to UK income tax, no matter where the trust is resident.

(b)   Non-UK source income is liable to UK income tax, if the trust is UK resident. For a trust to be non-resident, all the trustees must be non-resident, unless at the time when the funds are provided (i) the settlor or testator is resident, ordinarily resident and domiciled outside the UK *and* (ii) the body of trustees includes at least one resident trustee and at least one non-resident trustee.

(c)   A non-resident discretionary trust is not only liable for UK basic income tax on UK source income but also for additional rate income tax under s. 686 ICTA. There is a practical difficulty for the English Revenue to collect such tax, since unlike the basic rate tax, there is no deduction at source and the Revenue would not normally have the information upon which they could issue an assessment. They can, however, bring pressure to bear, if a UK beneficiary of the discretionary trust to whom payments are made, seeks repayment of tax suffered on UK source income, as the Revenue can then refuse to countenance repayment unless the offshore trustees submit returns and pay the additional rate tax: Inland Revenue Concession B18.

8.16   IHT AND THE EFFECT OF THE FOREIGN ELEMENT ON TRUSTS

For assets in a settlement to be exempt from IHT as excluded property, two conditions must be satisfied: (a) the assets must be situated outside the UK and (b) the settlor or the testator or the intestate must not have been domiciled in the UK when the settlement was made or when the testator or intestate died: s. 48(3). There are no statutory rules to determine where an asset is located for IHT purposes, and reference has to be made to judicial decisions, mostly in the field of the conflict of laws: see *Dicey and Morris*[8] and *ante*, 3.37.

Certain British Government securities are granted exemption from taxation if beneficially owned by a person neither domiciled nor ordinarily resident in the UK. In the case of settled property, if the life tenant is so circumstanced, there will be no IHT on his death; if the trust is a discretionary one, the securities will also qualify as excluded property if it can be shown that all known persons for whose benefit the capital or income can be applied are persons neither domiciled nor ordinarily resident in the UK: ss. 6(2) and 48(4).

If a settlor is domiciled abroad (or is *deemed* to be domiciled abroad) at the inception of the settlement the trust fund is normally permanently exempt from IHT on its foreign assets, irrespective of subsequent changes in the settlor's domicile or in the domicile of the beneficiaries. [9] For the meaning of *deemed* domicile, see *post* 13.20.

8.17   RESIDENCE OF TRUSTS FOR CGT PURPOSES

If the trustees or a majority of them are not resident or ordinarily resident in the UK, there is no liability on them for CGT; furthermore, professional UK trust administrators will be treated as non-resident trustees, provided that the settlor (or testator or intestate) is at the inception domiciled and resident or ordinarily resident outside the UK. Neither the trustees nor the beneficiaries (whatever the latter's domicile or residence) will be liable for CGT, if the following requirements of s. 69 TCGA are met:

(a)   The majority of the trustees must *at no time* during the year of assessment be resident or ordinarily resident in the UK. This requirement is satisfied if there is a sole UK professional trustee as in (c) below. If an English bank is trustee along with two individual trustees (one UK resident and the other not), the requirement is satisfied, but not if the English bank has only one co-trustee, who is UK resident.

(b)   The administration of the trust must ordinarily be carried on outside the UK. It will be deemed to be so carried on if the administration is in the hands of a UK professional trustee as in (c) below.

(c)   A person, such as a bank, carrying on a business which consists of or includes the management of trusts, and acting as trustee of a trust in the course of that business, counts as a non-resident trustee, despite the fact that he is administering the trust in the UK, but only if at the inception of the trust the whole of the settled property was provided by a settlor or testator or intestate then domiciled and resident or ordinarily resident outside the UK. In addition,

209

in the case of an *inter vivos* trust, the settlor must remain domiciled and resident or ordinarily resident abroad; while a change to a UK residence or domicile will not disturb the professional trustee's artificial non-resident status, it will expose the UK beneficiaries of the trust to the possibility of a claim for CGT under s. 87 TCGA (see below).

Section 87 TCGA applies if the settlor always has been domiciled and either resident or ordinarily resident in the UK or has become so since the inauguration of the settlement. Primarily, therefore, it is aimed at UK settlors and testators who appoint foreign trustees. If the trust has any beneficiaries, both domiciled and resident in the UK, and they receive capital payments (very broadly defined) from the offshore trustees, a proportion of the trustees' capital gains will be attributed to those beneficiaries, including the capital gains in the portfolio of a non-resident company owned by the offshore settlement.

8.18 THE TRUST DEED

It has already become apparent from surveying the taxation aspects of *inter vivos* trusts that the trust is an extremely flexible instrument, allowing the beneficial interests it contains to be tailored to meet the circumstances of the case. A settlor will have a basic choice between a fixed interest settlement, in which the beneficial interests are spelled out and cannot be varied by the trustees, and a discretionary trust where the trustees are given power to choose who shall benefit from a range of objects delineated by the settlor. In all cases, of course, the drafter must work within the parameters of the rules against perpetuities and against excessive accumulations and must ensure that the three certainties are satisfied. The IHT regimes of the two types of trust are very different. In a fixed-interest trust, the person who for the time being is entitled to an interest in possession is treated as though he were the owner of the trust fund: s. 49 IHTA. This, of course, is a fiction, since a life tenant in no way is the owner of the trust fund from which he derives his income. If more than one person is entitled in this way to the trust fund, it is apportioned between them: s. 50 IHTA, which also contains elaborate provisions for determining the attributable shares of capital as between an annuitant and the beneficiary entitled to the surplus income. The result of the fiction is that, when a life tenant or other income beneficiary dies, the fund in which he had an interest passes on his death for IHT purposes and is aggregated with the rest of his property, the trustees being liable for the tax on the settled property under s. 200(1)(b) IHTA, as are the remaindermen under s. 200(1)(c) and (d). If his interest terminates otherwise than on death, there is a PET which becomes chargeable on the death of the former life tenant within seven years; the trustees are primarily liable under s. 199(1)(c) and, if the tax is not paid, the subsequent beneficiaries (including advanced beneficiaries) are liable under ss. 199(1)(b) or 199(1)(c); also the PRs of the deceased former life tenant under s. 199(2)(a), if the tax cannot be collected in due time. There is, of course, no assurance that the rate of IHT that happens to be ruling at the time when the PET is made will still apply when death supervenes.

Whatever type of trust is chosen, it may be created either *inter vivos* or by will; in the latter case the requirements of s. 9 WA must be complied with. In the former case, although a trust of moveable property may be created with complete informality, the sensible course is to have the terms embodied in a formal document.

8.19   CONSULTING THE POTENTIAL TRUSTEE

A potential trustee will hope to be informed and consulted about the contents of the trust deed. As no one can be compelled to act as a trustee against his will, the selected trustee at least needs to be given the option of saying yes or no to the proposition. In addition he will, if a professional, expect to have the chance of considering the document in draft form. In some cases, of course, the trustee (or one of two or more) is the solicitor responsible for drawing up the document. The main concern must be to ensure, so far as is possible, that the proposed trusts are practicable, that there are no gaps in the beneficial interests and no opportunities for confusion during the term of the trust. It is true that the court has power to rectify a settlement where words have been wrongly added or omitted or miswritten and where words were mistakenly thought to bear a meaning different from that which they actually bear (there is now, fortunately, a similar power of rectification applicable to wills – see *ante* 2.30). In *Re Butlin* (1976), for instance, Brightman J. granted rectification of a settlement made nearly 30 years before. The power is, however, exercised sparingly, especially in the case of voluntary settlements, and clearly it is unwise to take any less care over the creation of a settlement because of the possibility of going to court later on to get things put right.

8.20   POWERS OF ADMINISTRATION AND MANAGEMENT

A prospective trustee will want to see that he is given adequate powers of administration and management over the trust. The modern policy is to provide very wide powers – safe enough where a professional trustee is appointed. Examples of such powers are:

(a)   *Investment*. The TIA is quite inadequate and cumbersome to operate (see chapter 11). It is helpful if what are called 'beneficial owner' powers of investment are inserted. Power to buy land and buildings, to improve them and to allow them to be occupied by beneficiaries rent-free[10] should be included, as should a power to invest in non-UK assets and in non-income-producing property, thus circumventing the inconvenient rule emanating from *Re Power* (1947). So far as non-income producing assets are concerned, consider excluding them from the interest given to a life tenant; if acquired during the course of the trust, again the life tenant may be excluded, giving rise to a PET under s. 52(1) IHTA.

(b) *Insurance.*

(i) Life. Trustee may wish to insure against the possibility of having to pay IHT on the death of the settlor within seven years of the creation of the settlement. Unless an express power to do so is included this is not possible.

(ii) Fire etc. It has already been pointed out (see *ante* 2.5 and 3.21) that the statutory power to insure is in an unsatisfactory state; an express power to insure is therefore desirable.

(c) *Power to allocate additional assets* as between capital and income at discretion. This is useful in dealing with, e.g. capital distributions, where the correct destination is often far from clear (see *ante* 5.23).

(d) *Remuneration of trustees.* If a trust corporation is to act, its fees should be authorised. Unless this is done it will be necessary to seek authority from the beneficiaries, which may be difficult – perhaps impossible. Even if a trust corporation is not to act initially it is reasonable to include a power for one appointed at a later date to charge remuneration. There should also be a 'professional charging clause' which authorises a solicitor or accountant who acts as trustee to charge his profit costs as well as his expenses. Such a clause does *not* authorise the fees of a trust corporation. Where a family company is involved, director/trustees should be authorised to retain fees received, otherwise they may find themselves having to act gratuitously – *Re Keeler* (1981).

(e) *Power to 'export'* a trust and to change its 'proper law' – see chapter 13.

(f) *Power to provide maintenance and advancement* outside the limits imposed by ss. 31 and 32 TA – see chapter 10. Typically by removing the proviso to s. 31(1) and by removing the restriction in s. 32(1)(a) of advancements to one-half of the presumptive or vested share.

(g) *Power to accumulate income.* There is no *implied* power to accumulate and the only statutory power is in s. 31 TA, which will not be available in every case. Bear in mind the six (alternative) permitted periods for accumulation – see *ante* 7.31

(h) *Directions which negative legal and equitable apportionment* are a convenience administratively.

(i) *An express trust for sale, coupled with a power to postpone sale and to retain existing assets* at the absolute discretion of trustees; particular reference may be made to assets which the settlor *wishes* to remain undisturbed – e.g. shares in unquoted companies. In this connection it is helpful for the trustees to be absolved from responsibility for the conduct and management of such companies, if the settlor is happy that this should be the case. See *Bartlett* v *Barclays Bank Trust Co Ltd* (1980), *ante* 5.30. Power may also be usefully added to allow beneficiaries to live in and to use trust assets[10].

(j) *Power to delegate investment management* and to place investments and other assets in the names of nominees. Where private trustees are acting this device can be especially convenient, and it avoids having to go to the length of appointing a custodian trustee (see chapter 12).

(k) *Power to appropriate assets* towards beneficial interests without the consent of the beneficiaries.

(l)   *Power to pay settlor's IHT* arising on creation of settlement – see *ante* 8.2.
(m)   *Power to release or restrict the future exercise of all powers given to the trustees* in the trust instrument (see *post* 13.11) and to delegate the exercise of discretionary trusts and powers (see *Re Hay* (1982), *post* 9.29).

8.21   COSTS AND EXPENSES

These are the responsibility of the settlor but he may expressly authorise the trustees to defray them from the trust fund when it is constituted, and there would not appear to be any tax risk in such a provision. They may include CGT, IHT and solicitors' costs and disbursements. A declaration of trust in any form of writing (other than a will) is liable to stamp duty of 50p; the transfer of property to the trustees is exempt from stamp duty, provided the instrument effecting the transfer is duly certified in accordance with The Stamp Duty (Exempt Instruments) Regulations 1987. For IHT an account of the settlement must be delivered by the settlor to the Revenue under s. 216(1)(a); the tax is primarily his liability but, if he does not pay, the Revenue may call upon the trustees to do so: s. 199(1)(c). It is sensible, therefore, for trustees to seek confirmation that any tax liability arising on creation of the settlement has been assessed and paid. Under s. 218, professional persons involved in the making of a settlement when the settlor is UK-domiciled but the trustees will be non-resident must notify the Revenue of the names and addresses of settlor and trustees and the date of the settlement – what *Ray* calls a 'snooper's charter'. Any CGT liability arising is the responsibility of the settlor, as is that for solicitors' costs and disbursements. It should be borne in mind that, until the trust instrument is executed and the trustees have accepted office (which they should signify by executing the document themselves), they have no status in the matter other than, possibly, as agents of the settlor. Moreover, if the trust is a voluntary settlement (without any marriage consideration) it will not be enforceable until completely constituted – see *ante* 7.17.

Once the trust deed is complete (i.e. executed by all parties and dated) it remains in the hands of the trustee or trustees. If more than one trustee is appointed it may be left with one of their number or it may be deposited with a bank: s. 21 TA. In any event each trustee should have his or her own authenticated working copy. Newly appointed trustees must at once take possession of the settled property and check that the legal title is in their names; if this cannot be the case as, for instance, when an equitable interest is settled, they must ensure that proper notice to the holders of the legal title has been given and acknowledged.

8.22   IMPLIED, RESULTING AND CONSTRUCTIVE TRUSTS

This chapter and the previous one have so far been concerned with express trusts – that is, trusts arising as the result of a purposeful act by the settlor

213

even though, on occasion, he may have been unaware that what he was doing was to create a trust – *Paul* v *Constance* (1977) (see *ante* 7.4). There is, however, a sort of alternative society of trusts, created with no formality and, in the case of constructive trusts, imposed by operation of law rather than by the conscious act of a settlor. Such trusts give rise to property interests which may not be at all apparent on the surface but which anyone involved in the administration of estates and trusts needs to be able to recognise. Resulting and constructive trusts are particularly relevant in any discussion of interests in matrimonial and quasi-matrimonial homes.

Although s. 53(2) LPA carefully excludes resulting, implied and constructive trusts from the operation of s. 53(1), there is no separate category of implied trusts. The use of the term seems to be superfluous – there are express trusts on the one hand, implied, resulting and constructive trusts on the other. Nevertheless, the statutory phrase is often used as an omnibus term and seems to be deeply embedded in the legal subconscious.

Resulting trusts, as we have seen in 7.4, arise from a transfer of property which is in some way imperfect. Constructive trusts, on the other hand, are imposed on someone by operation of law – that someone becoming, in effect, a trustee by *force majeure*: As *Oakley* remarks in *Constructive Trusts*, p. 1, a constructive trust is imposed by the court as a result of the conduct of the trustee and therefore arises quite independently of the intention of any of the parties.

Although, in America for instance, the constructive trust can be treated simply as a remedy for unjust enrichment, in this country it remains an institution rather than a remedy, albeit an institution that is remedial in character. But 'there is no general doctrine of unjust enrichment recognised in English law' Lord Diplock in *Orapko* v *Manson Investments* (1978).[11] As we have seen from the examples in 7.5, constructive trusts can arise in a variety of situations but the type of particular interest to us is the one which is imposed upon a property owner where it would be inequitable for him to claim to be entitled to the whole beneficial interest, usually centring around the ownership of the home.

8.23 CONSTRUCTIVE TRUSTS AFFECTING THE HOME

This type of trust appears to have been developed during the latter part of this century, initially to deal with property disputes between husband and wife; later on, it was extended to cover similar disputes between unmarried couples. Now that ss. 23 and 24 Matrimonial Causes Act 1973 give the court absolute discretion to vary matrimonial property rights on divorce, the use of a constructive trust in such cases is unnecessary, although the case law will usually be an essential guide for situations other than matrimonial disputes, e.g. on the death or bankruptcy of a spouse, and see *Midland Bank* v *Dobson* (1986) discussed *post* 8.26.[12]

The classical approach to this sort of problem may be found in the judgment of the House of Lords in *Gissing* v *Gissing* (1971):

The facts in this case were that the matrimonial home was in the sole name of the husband, there being no express trusts as to the respective interests of husband and wife. The wife had spent some money on having a lawn laid down and claimed also that she had made indirect contributions towards the value of the home because she had paid children's school fees and had bought furniture with her own money. The House of Lords refused to award her a share of the home on the grounds that her financial contributions were not referable to the acquisition of the house, the spouses not having formed any intention to this effect at the date the home was acquired. It should, perhaps, be emphasised that a *direct* financial contribution in such circumstances will raise a presumption of a resulting trust in favour of the contributor so as to give him or her a proportionate interest in the property. In general terms, the following words of Lord Diplock are as good a summary of the traditional view as it is possible to get:

'A resulting, implied or constructive trust – and it is unnecessary for present purposes to distinguish between these three classes of trust – is created by a transaction between the trustee and the *cestui que trust* in connection with the acquisition by the trustee of a legal estate in land, whenever the trustee has so conducted himself that it would be inequitable to allow him to deny to the *cestui que trust* a beneficial interest in the land acquired. And he will be held so to have conducted himself if by his words or conduct he has induced the *cestui que trust* to act to his own detriment in the reasonable belief that by so acting he was acquiring a beneficial interest in the land.'

The *Gissing* case concerned an application under s. 17 MWPA by the wife, after divorce, for a determination of her interest in the property. A similar application arose in *Pettitt* v *Pettitt* (1970), this time by the husband. The wife had bought a cottage with her own funds and it was conveyed into her name alone. The husband made various improvements to the property and he also did some work in the garden. The House of Lords held that the work he did inside and outside the house gave him no beneficial rights in the property. Lord Upjohn pointed out that the respective interests of the spouses in the property must depend upon what they agreed in this respect at the time of its acquisition (hence the importance, especially for those who are not married to each other, of expressly stating in the Land Registry Transfer Form or the conveyance, the terms of beneficial ownership, if there is to be a sharing arrangement; see also *ante* 5.39). The *Pettitt* case prompted the passing of s. 37 Matrimonial Proceedings and Property Act 1970, which provides that if a spouse contributes to the improvement of an asset belonging to either or both of them, the spouse so contributing shall be treated as having acquired a share or an enlarged share of an extent agreed between them or, in default of such agreement, as may be determined by the court in any proceedings in which the question of ownership may arise. The section applies to any asset, moveable or immoveable, but only between husband and wife and between engaged couples, see *post*, 8.30.

8.24   CASE LAW SINCE *GISSING* AND *PETTITT*

After *Gissing* and *Pettitt*, there was a tendency to extend the imposition of constructive trusts into the area of unjust enrichment; the words of Lord Diplock in *Gissing* ('whenever the trustee has so conducted himself that it would be inequitable to allow him to deny to the *cestui que trust* a beneficial interest') being used in isolation from the rest of his speech as authority. In *Hussey* v *Palmer* (1972), for instance, Lord Denning said:

'By whatever name it [a constructive trust] is described, it is a trust imposed by law whenever justice and good name and good conscience require it. It is a liberal process, founded upon large principles of equity, to be applied in cases where the legal owner cannot conscientiously keep the property for himself alone, but ought to allow another to have the property or the benefit of it or a share in it.'

Hussey v *Palmer* was not a dispute about matrimonial or quasi-matrimonial property. The plaintiff in the case had been invited by her daughter and son-in-law to live with them. She paid £607 for a new bedroom in their house. The arrangement did not work and, after just over a year, Mrs Hussey left and claimed repayment of the £607. The majority of the Court of Appeal went further and said that she was entitled to a proportionate interest in the property by way of a resulting or constructive trust. This decision was not followed in *Re Sharpe (a bankrupt)* (1980) where Browne-Wilkinson J. decided that a loan to the bankrupt by his aunt for their common home (in his name) gave her, not a proprietary interest, but an irrevocable licence to remain there, which had the effect of imposing a constructive trust binding upon the owner and, consequently, upon the owner's trustee in bankruptcy. But as appears from *Ashburn Anstalt* v *Arnold* (1989) where it was relevant to consider the position of a contractual licensee, the reasoning in *Re Sharpe* was discredited by the Court of Appeal, their view being that a contractual licence would not automatically give rise to a constructive trust in favour of the licensee, although it might do so in cases where it would be against conscience to hold otherwise.

8.25   CONSTRUCTIVE TRUSTS – SOME CASES ON COHABITATION

In *Eves* v *Eves* (1975):

a man and a woman living together as man and wife bought a house which was conveyed into the sole name of the man. He told his companion that, had she been over 21, it would have been put into their joint names as it was to be their joint home. The purchase price was provided by the man but the lady did a lot of heavy work in the house and the garden. The Court of Appeal held that she was entitled to a quarter share in the property; the majority view was that there had been an agreement between the parties that she should have a share in the house in return for the work she did to improve it, a view which accords with the principles enunciated in *Gissing* and *Pettitt*. Lord Denning's minority view was that, where two parties acquire a property by their joint efforts for their joint benefit, the court may impose a constructive trust to produce a just solution to a dispute about ownership; 'it would be most inequitable for him to deny her any share in the house'.

Lord Denning's bold approach to the use of the constructive trust as a solution to property disputes has not been adopted in more recent decisions. *Grant* v *Edwards* (1986) gave the Vice-Chancellor the chance to reiterate the principles applicable to the joint acquisition of a home, as laid down by Lord Diplock in the *Gissing* case:

(a)   If the legal estate in a joint home is vested in only one of the parties, the other party, in order to establish a beneficial interest, has to establish a constructive trust by showing that it would be inequitable for the legal owner to claim sole beneficial ownership. To prove this, the other party must show (i) that there was a common intention that both should have a beneficial interest and (ii) that the other party has acted to his or her detriment on the basis of their common intention.

(b)   The common intention can be proved either by direct evidence or by inference from the parties' actions.

(c)   Quantification of the size of the respective interests may be established by reference to both direct and indirect contributions.

In this case the unmarried parties moved into a house bought by the male partner with the help of a mortgage. The female partner made very substantial indirect contributions towards the mortgage repayments. She had been told by her partner that the property would not be put in her name because this would prejudice her in matrimonial proceedings between her and her husband. This holding out was regarded by the Court of Appeal as evidence of common intention that the lady should have a share in the house and she had acted to her detriment in reliance on this 'holding out'; she was entitled to a half share in the house.

In some circumstances, application of the above principles can produce an untoward result:

In *Ungurian* v *Lesnoff* (1990) the defendant, a Pole, gave up her flat and career in Poland in order to live with the plaintiff in London in a house which was registered in the plaintiff's sole name. This relationship lasted for four years, during which the defendant did a considerable amount of work by way of improving the property. Then the parties separated, the defendant stayed in the house and the plaintiff claimed possession. As was remarked in [1990] *Conv* 224, the case illustrated the problems inherent in raising equitable interests on oral evidence. The defendant's evidence about the intentions of the parties had to be translated from the Polish; the plaintiff brought no evidence. Vinelott J. concluded, however, that the common intention resulted in the acquisition of a licence to reside in the property (or a substituted property) during her life. Following *Bannister* v *Bannister* (1948), this made the defendant tenant for life under the SLA – manifestly not a very convenient outcome.

8.26 CONSTRUCTIVE TRUSTS – THE MORTGAGE CASES

Two recent cases involving banks as mortgagees have given the court further opportunity to put limits upon the way in which a beneficial interest in property may be acquired informally, thus giving rise to a constructive trust in favour of the owner of such an interest. In *Midland Bank plc v Dobson & Dobson* (1986):

> A matrimonial home was bought in 1953 and conveyed into the sole name of the husband. The wife never made any direct contribution towards the repayment of the mortgage; the husband defaulted on mortgage repayments to the bank, which sought possession. The wife claimed that there had been a common intention that she should have a beneficial interest in the property; this was accepted by the Court of Appeal but it was also held that this, in itself, was not sufficient to give her such an interest. There must also be some evidence that the claimant had been induced to act to her detriment in pursuance of the joint intention, and no such evidence existed.

In *Lloyds Bank* v *Rosset* (1991):

> The facts were that a husband and wife decided to buy a semi-derelict property. The purchase money was got from the husband's family trust, the trustees insisting that the property should be conveyed into his sole name. It was the intention of both husband and wife that the renovation should be a joint venture. The builders moved in and the wife spent nearly every day on the property helping them. Unknown to the wife, the husband had got a loan from the bank to help meet the costs of the repairs. The husband and wife moved in, but later, as a result of matrimonial dispute, the husband left. The loan was not repaid and the bank sought possession. The wife resisted this, on the grounds that she had a beneficial interest under a constructive trust which was an overriding interest under s. 70(1)(g) LRA. The House of Lords held that the wife's activities in connection with renovation of the property were not enough to give her a beneficial interest in the property, whatever the intentions of the parties may have been. It was quite natural that the wife should have done all she could to speed the work along, irrespective of any expectations she might have about getting an interest in the property. The following words of Lord Bridge are especially significant:
>
> 'In the situation where there is no evidence to support a finding of an agreement or arrangement to share, however reasonable it might have been for the parties to reach such an arrangement if they had applied their minds to the question, and where the court must rely entirely on the conduct of the parties, both as the basis from which to infer a common intention to share the property beneficially and as the conduct relied on to give rise to a constructive trust, direct contributions to the purchase price by the partner who was not the legal owner, whether initially or by payment of mortgage instalments, will readily justify the inference necessary to the creation of a constructive trust. But, as I read the authorities, *it is at least extremely doubtful whether anything less will do.*' [emphasis supplied].

Those words of Lord Bridge make it clear that Lord Denning's liberal approach to the acquisition of beneficial interests via the constructive or resulting trust is now dead. A more flexible route may be found in the equitable doctrine of proprietary estoppel (below).

8.27 PROPRIETARY ESTOPPEL

This must not be confused with estoppel at common law, which precludes someone who has previously asserted a certain state of affairs from subsequently denying that such a state exists. Equitable estoppel was developed to supplement the common law variety. It is based, as one might guess, on the existence of unconscionable or inequitable conduct. Under the equitable head there are a number of different varieties, including proprietary estoppel, which may be described shortly as 'estoppel by encouragement or by acquiescence' (*Hanbury*, p. 850). Such an estoppel is based on the presumption that an owner of land who requests or even allows another to spend money on his land in the expectation that the spender will be allowed to remain on the land has created an equity coupled with a licence in favour of the spender which is binding on the owner and his successors in title. In *Jones* v *Jones* (1977):

> The defendant's father had bought a house into which the defendant had moved. He paid his father one-quarter of the cost and he was given to understand that the house was to be his. However, it was never conveyed to him. Eventually the title devolved on the father's widow (the son's stepmother), who brought proceedings for possession. The County Court awarded the son a quarter share of the property with three-quarters to the widow (thereby creating a statutory trust for sale) and an entitlement on her part either to rent from the son or the sale of the house. On appeal by the son, the Court of Appeal held that the father's conduct had produced an equity in favour of his son which, in effect, gave him the right to remain in the property during his life, which could not be defeated by the statutory trust for sale.*

The use of the doctrine of proprietary estoppel to provide residential security was demonstrated in *Pascoe* v *Turner* (1979):

> The plaintiff and defendant lived together in the plaintiff's house. In 1973 the plaintiff left the defendant but she continued, with his permission, to live in his house and he, on several occasions, referred to the house and its contents as belonging to her. Relying on these statements, the lady spent small sums on improvements. Going back on his earlier promises, the plaintiff sought possession of the property. The court held that, in the circumstances, the equity in favour of the defendant could only be satisfied by the transfer to her of the freehold of the house.

---

*It was also held that no rent was payable by the son as tenant in common in occupation. On this subject see *Megarry & Wade* p.419 and *Snell* p.689.

It is difficult not to feel that, in this case, the court was punishing the plaintiff for bad behaviour. Note the slender margin of reasoning between a case such as this (an imperfect gift backed by estoppel) and the informal declaration of trust established in *Paul* v *Constance* (1977) (see *ante* 7.4). The ultimate limit of proprietary estoppel is perhaps to be seen in *Greasley* v *Cooke* (1980):

> The defendant, employed as a maid in a widower's house, became the mistress of one of his four children. She acted as unpaid housekeeper to the family for many years, on the basis, she said, that she had been encouraged to believe that she could stay in the house for the rest of her life. Eventually an action was brought by surviving members of the family for possession of the property. The court held that an equity in favour of the defendant had been raised, which should be satisfied by her being given a licence to stay in the house as long as she wished to do so. It was not necessary for her to prove that she had spent money on the house, or even to prove that she was prejudiced in any way by relying on the promises made to her. The bare assurance that she could stay in the house was sufficient to raise the equity in her favour.

8.28   THE RELATIONSHIP OF THE CONSTRUCTIVE TRUST TO PROPRIETARY ESTOPPEL

The recent case of *Re Basham* (1986) illustrates well the very extensive power of the court to satisfy an equity raised by the doctrine of proprietary estoppel in any way it thinks fit. In this respect, the remedy provided by this doctrine is more satisfactory than the one available under a constructive trust; it is now quite clear that a claim under a resulting or constructive trust can only rest upon an application of the traditional rules of property law. The facts in *Basham* were as follows:

> The plaintiff was the stepdaughter of the deceased, who died intestate. For some 30 years the plaintiff had worked for the deceased for nothing, helping to run his public houses and a service station. She claimed to have done this because the deceased had promised that he would leave his estate to her when he died. This he failed to do. The plaintiff relied on the doctrine of proprietary estoppel, which was stated by the judge in the following terms:
> 'Where one person (A) has acted to his detriment on the faith of a belief, which was known to and encouraged by another person (B), that he either had or is going to be given a right in or over B's property, B cannot insist on his strict legal rights if to do so would be inconsistent with A's belief.'
> Finding in the plaintiff's favour, the court made it clear that expenditure of money is not the only kind of detriment giving rise to an estoppel of this kind. Neither is it necessary for A to have been in occupation of B's land. The equity arising in favour of the plaintiff was in the nature of a constructive trust (a view which has not escaped criticism* – was it really necessary to introduce this link

---

*See the casenote by Jill Martin in [1987] Conv 211.

between proprietary estoppel and constructive trusts?). As to the way in which the equity should be satisfied, the court decided that the plaintiff should take the whole of the deceased's net estate, the costs of the defendants to come out of the estate.

The practical consequences of the modern application of the resulting trust, constructive trust and doctrine of proprietary estoppel can be significant. It cannot be assumed without question that, because the legal title to a property is vested in one spouse or another (or in one partner of any informal relationship) that the entire beneficial interest is likewise vested. The existence of an equitable interest in such property may affect the devolution of property on death, the creation of *inter vivos* trusts and tax planning. It may also have its effect upon commercial transactions such as the borrowing of money on mortgage; see, for instance, *Williams and Glyns' Bank Ltd* v *Boland* (1981), in which a resident wife's equitable interest in the matrimonial home was held to be an overriding interest for the purposes of s. 70(1)(g) LRA and so binding on a mortgagee, irrespective of lack of notice of the interest. This was a case where a presumed resulting trust in favour of the wife was firmly established by the wife's substantial contribution to the purchase price; contrast the cases noted *ante* 8.26 where the issue was not nearly so clear cut.

8.29   CO-OWNERSHIP OF LANDED PROPERTY AND S. 30 LPA

It is possible, though unusual, for an equitable joint tenancy for life to be created under the SLA. This exception apart, and aside from party walls, co-ownership of landed property must exist behind a trust for sale, either express or statutory: see *ante* 5.39. The difficulty about co-ownership is that the parties are rarely, if ever, in the mood at the time when the arrangement is inaugurated to ask their lawyer to specify what is to happen should they be unable to agree at some time in the future upon the mode of occupation or other use to which the property should be put or upon the appropriate time to sell it or the effect of their differing contributions to mortgage repayments or improvements to the property. So what happens if a dispute arises? The answer may depend upon the form which the trust for sale takes:

(a)   More often than not, the conveyance or transfer to joint owners contains an express trust for sale. The normal principle with trusts for sale of land is that if the trustees cannot unanimously agree to postpone sale, the land must be sold, even though the majority of the beneficiaries wish to retain it: *Re Mayo* (1943). Words to the contrary can be introduced into the instrument of transfer, but it is not usual to do so.

(b)   If a trust for sale is not expressly stated, under the statutory trust for sale imposed by s. 34(2) LPA the trustees are obliged by s. 26(3) to consult the beneficiaries (usually themselves) regarding the exercise of any powers (sale, leasing and so on) and to give effect to the wishes of the majority, according to the value of their combined interests. Section 26(3), when it applies (and it does not apply where there is an express trust for sale), puts *Re Mayo* into reverse; if the majority by value are in favour of retention, the trustees cannot sell. It is important to note that a statutory trust for sale can arise where there is a purchase in the name of one person, but the purchase money comes from more than one person (see *Bull v Bull* below), thus creating a resulting trust in favour of the person whose name does not appear on the legal title. (There are situations in which the presumption of a resulting trust is rebutted by a presumption of advancement – see *ante* 7.4.)

(c) Section 30 LPA provides that if trustees for sale (whether express or statutory) or a consenting party refuse to exercise their powers of sale or management or consent, *any person interested* (which includes a trustee in bankruptcy but does not include the trustees, unless themselves beneficiaries) may apply to court for the position to be regularised and the court may make such order as it thinks fit. The court's power is unfettered by considerations of s. 26(3) and it will not compel a sale if it will help breach an agreement by the parties not to sell or if it will defeat the original purpose of the trust. Thus, in *Bull v Bull* (1955) mother and son contributed unequally to a purchase in the son's name alone as a home for both of them, the effect of which was to create a statutory trust for sale in favour of the two of them as tenants in common. The son, who had made the greater contribution, applied for an order to evict his mother, which was refused by the Court of Appeal who held that she could not be turned out without her consent. If it was desired to sell the property with vacant possession, the son must appoint a co-trustee and apply to the court under s. 30 LPA to ascertain whether, because of the mother's refusal to move, the court would grant an order that she must leave.

(d) In the absence of fraud or mistake, an express declaration of the beneficial interests in the documentation holds sway over the intentions of the parties and displaces any question of resulting or constructive trusts. In *Goodman v Gallant* (1986) a house in the sole name of the husband belonged in equity to the husband and wife in equal shares. The husband (Goodman) left his wife and was eventually replaced by Mr Gallant. The husband sold his half share to Mrs Goodman and Mr Gallant, the legal title to the property being conveyed to them jointly upon trust for sale for themselves as beneficial joint tenants. Later Mrs Goodman served Gallant with a notice of severance of the joint tenancy and asked the court to declare that she was not only entitled to her original half share but also another quarter share as the result of her husband's conveyance. It was held by the Court of Appeal that as the conveyance contained an express declaration of a beneficial joint tenancy, it followed that the subsequent severance must leave Mrs Goodman with only a half share.

(e) Where the breakdown of a marriage is involved, the application should be made, not under s. 30 LPA, but under the Matrimonial Causes Act 1973, as was held in *Williams v Williams* (1976). Where, as between husband and wife, the object of the exercise is to determine existing rights without seeking to alter them or create new ones, an application to court can be made under s. 17 Married Women's Property Act 1882.

(f) Section 30 LPA provides the machinery not only for the resolution of disputes between parties such as mother and son or brother and sister, but also for persons who are living together outside the marriage bond. The courts have shown no reluctance to take into account the underlying objective, where it exists, of providing a home for the parties and any children; for example by suspending the sale until alternative accommodation can be found. But s. 30 cannot be used to vary the original terms of the trusts. In *Turton* v *Turton* (1988) an unmarried couple purchased a house in 1972 for £8,500 with an express trust for sale for a beneficial joint tenancy. In 1975 when the house was worth £10,000 the parties separated. The beneficial joint tenancy was severed in 1982. In 1987 when the property was worth £35,000 the county court judge made an order for sale and directed that the woman's half share should be one half of the 1975 value when the purpose of providing a joint home had ceased. It was held by the Court of Appeal that she was entitled to a half share of the actual proceeds, as the termination of the relationship had no bearing on the nature of the beneficial interests as determined at the outset of the trust for sale.

(g)   In many cases of cohabitation there is no co-ownership to latch on to. The non-owning party then has the task of imputing a trust or inferring one from the circumstances: see the cases discussed *ante* in 8.25.

The Law Reform Committee's 23rd Report (1982) recommended that s. 30 LPA should be extended to the type of case where a trustee, not being a beneficiary, wishes to apply to court to question the trustees' decision to postpone sale.

Under s. 336 Insolvency Act 1986, if the co-owners are husband and wife and an application is made under s. 30 LPA by the trustee in bankruptcy, the interests of the creditors must be balanced against the needs and resources of the non-bankrupt co-owner and the children, but after a year has elapsed, the creditors' interests become paramount. Normally, it should not be expected, therefore, that the court will delay the sale for more than a year.

8.30   ENGAGED COUPLES

The presumption of advancement (see *ante* 7.4) can apply to an engaged couple once the marriage takes place:

In *Moate* v *Moate* (1948) the husband-to-be purchased a house in the name of his fiancée, subject to mortgage. After the marriage, the husband paid the mortgage instalments on the wife's behalf, the final payment being made 16 years later. The following year the wife started divorce proceedings and the husband asked for determination of the ownership of the house. It was held that the presumption of advancement applied both to the original purchase as well as the supplementary gifts of the mortgage instalments.

Section 2(1) Law Reform (Miscellaneous Provisions) Act 1970 (the Act which also abolished actions for breach of promise) extends s. 37 Matrimonial Proceedings and Property Act 1970 (see *ante* 8.23) and other rules of law relating to the property rights of husband and wife to couples whose engagement has been called off. Thus, if a man purchases a property in his own name and his fiancée helps with improvements to it, her contribution will qualify her for an interest in the property just as if they had been husband and wife. Quite how far this statutory innovation goes is not clear, but it certainly has its limitations; in *Mossop* v *Mossop* (1988):

> An engaged couple lived together for four years in a property in the man's name, to which he was the sole contributor. When they split up, the woman tried to obtain a property adjustment order under s. 24 Matrimonial Causes Act 1973, such as would have been available, had the parties been married and subsequently divorced. Her application was rejected on the ground that s. 24 could not be used without an antecedent decree of divorce, nullity or judicial separation.

9 Trustees and their duties

9.1 CAPACITY TO ACT AS TRUSTEE

Lord Hardwicke remarked, in *Knight* v *Earl of Plymouth* (1747), that trusteeship 'if faithfully discharged, [is] attended with no small degree of trouble and anxiety [so that] it is an act of great kindness in any one to accept it'. It is certain that the office of trustee should not be taken up without considerable thought. It entails heavy responsibilities and personal liability for mistakes made, however innocently committed. A further disadvantage is that, unless expressly authorised, a trustee is not entitled to be paid for his work; he is, however, able to claim to be refunded his expenses, including the fees[1] and expenses of any agent properly employed by him – see *ante* 5.45. The subject of trustees' remuneration is discussed in more detail below.

Anyone, except an infant, may be a trustee; s. 20 LPA says that the appointment of an infant to be a trustee in relation to any settlement or trust shall be void. Section 1(6) says that a legal estate in land is not capable of being held by an infant. But infants can become trustees of pure personalty under resulting and constructive trusts.

> In *Re Vinogradoff* (1935), a lady transferred stock into the joint names of herself and her granddaughter, who was four years old. The lady died and the little girl held the stock on a resulting trust for the estate.

If an infant, or any incapacitated person, is appointed a trustee he may be removed and replaced under s. 36(1) TA. Corporations may be appointed trustees; they are considered in more detail *ante* 2.8 and *post* chapter 12.

9.2 ACCEPTANCE AND DISCLAIMER OF OFFICE

Having duly reflected upon the pros and cons and having made up his mind to accept, the embryo trustee can signify acceptance either expressly or by implication. It need hardly be said that acceptance by any mode should not be signified until a complete picture of the trust has been obtained; there is always a risk, in the case of any trust, that, by intermeddling with its administration, a trustee will be regarded as having accepted office by implication. This is of particular importance in the case of transferred trusts where one may often find that records of the previous administration leave a lot to be desired. Execution of the trust instrument will be regarded as signifying acceptance of office in the case of a new settlement – see *ante*

8.21. Where a trust is set up by will, and the executors are also named as trustees, proving the will implies acceptance of office as trustee. Conversely, renunciation of office as executor in such circumstances raises a strong presumption that the trusteeship is also being declined.

A trustee who has decided not to accept appointment should disclaim, preferably by deed, as this makes the position perfectly clear but a disclaimer may be implied. In *Re Clout and Frewer's Contract* (1924):

> An executor/trustee survived the testator for nearly 30 years, taking no steps to administer either the estate or the trust. It was held that he had disclaimed; consistent apathy or inactivity may amount to a disclaimer.

9.3 APPOINTMENT OF TRUSTEES

Trustees may be appointed (a) by the settlor in the trust instrument, (b) under an express power in the trust instrument, (c) under statutory powers, (d) by the court, (e) in the case of charitable trusts, by the Charity Commissioners (see *post* 12.17), (f) by the beneficiaries. When a new trust is created deliberately the settlor will usually either appoint himself as trustee, or nominate another person or persons to act. If by some mischance no trustees are nominated or, being nominated, they refuse to act, an awkward situation can arise in the absence of any power to appoint in the trust instrument – the only option is to ask the court to appoint. In the case of a will trust the executors will usually be appointed trustees also.

If there is an express power to appoint in the trust instrument it is usually given to the settlor. Sometimes he also reserves to himself the power to remove trustees, although such extension may be questionable on principle. Trustees should be prepared to take an independent line irrespective of the views held by the settlor, and a power of removal in such circumstances may well give him a virtual power of veto.

9.4 STATUTORY POWERS OF APPOINTING TRUSTEES

Section 36(1) TA:

> Where a trustee, either original or substituted, and whether appointed by a court or otherwise, is dead, or remains out of the United Kingdom for more than twelve months, or desires to be discharged from all or any of the trusts or powers reposed in or conferred on him, or refuses or is unfit to act therein, or is incapable of acting therein, or is an infant, then, subject to the restrictions imposed by this Act on the number of trustees, –
> (a) the person or persons nominated for the purpose of appointing new trustees by the instrument, if any, creating the trust; or
> (b) if there is no such person, or no such person able and willing to act, then the surviving or continuing trustees or trustee for the time being, or the personal representatives of the last surviving or continuing trustee;

may, by writing, appoint one or more other persons (whether or not being the persons exercising the power) to be a trustee or trustees in the place of the trustee so deceased, remaining out of the United Kingdom, desiring to be discharged, refusing, or being unfit or being incapable, or being an infant, as aforesaid.

This sub-section is subject, like the rest of the powers in the statute, to a 'contrary intention' expressed in the trust instrument: s. 69(2). It does not apply to PRs, who may, however, be removed and replaced by the court – see *ante* 3.50.

9.5 REPLACEMENT OF TRUSTEES

It will be noticed that this important sub-section lists seven different ways in which an existing (or dead) trustee may be replaced; indeed, in some cases, he may be *removed* and replaced – e.g. where a trustee has been outside the UK for more than 12 months. In such cases the replaced trustee has no say in the matter.

> In *Re Stoneham* (1953), a son of the settlor who was one of two trustees had been out of the UK for more than 12 months and his co-trustee made an appointment replacing him. The son protested but the court held that he could be replaced without his consent.

Note, however, that the absence from the UK must be uninterrupted. A trustee who returns to the UK, if only for a very short time, will not have been out of the UK for the required period for the purposes of this provision.

The provision for the replacement of dead trustees applies to testamentary appointments where a trustee (not being the sole trustee) has predeceased the testator: s. 36(8). A disclaiming trustee comes under the head of a trustee who refuses to act. There are no recent cases about unfitness to act, but it seems to mean *moral* decrepitude (so bankruptcy would not necessarily be included), e.g. a serious criminal conviction might well make a trustee unfit to act under the sub-section. 'Incapable of acting', on the other hand, means physical or mental unfitness. Appropriate reference to the mental health authorities is necessary, if the incapable trustee also has a beneficial interest.

Section 36(2), not reproduced here, deals with cases where a trustee has been removed under an express power in the trust instrument; where this has happened, and there is no express power to appoint a new trustee in the trust instrument (or such power exists but is not exercised) the provisions of s. 36(1) apply and may be used to appoint a new trustee in place of the one removed.

9.6 NUMBER OF TRUSTEES

It will be noted that under s. 36(1) one *or more* other persons may be appointed in place of the outgoing trustee; there is no restriction upon the number of trustees of pure personalty or of charitable trusts (unless such a restriction appears in the trust instrument) but there should not be more than four trustees of a settlement of land, whether or not on trust for sale. Where more than four are appointed, the first four named are to act – s. 34(2) TA. Even in a trust of pure personalty it is not sensible to appoint more than two or three trustees; the Law Reform Committee has suggested that there should be no more than four trustees of non-charitable trusts in all cases where the settlor does not otherwise provide.

If there is a stipulation in the trust instrument as to a minimum number of trustees, this should be strictly observed, except, it seems, where the Public Trustee is appointed. He may act alone, even if the trust instrument insists on two or more trustees: *Re Moxon* (1916).

9.7   MAKING THE APPOINTMENT

Section 36(1) says that, if there is someone named in the trust instrument with power to appoint new trustees, then that person makes the appointment; if there is no such person, or if such person declines to act, then the appointment is made by the continuing trustee or trustees.

If all the trustees are dead, then the PRs of the last surviving trustee make the appointment under s. 36(1)(b). By s. 36(4) an appointment by PRs does not require the approbation of non-proving executors, but by s. 36(5) executors who are unanimously renouncing (or a sole renouncing executor) can make the appointment of a new trustee without thereby accepting the office of executor, although the status of the new trustee as the result of an appointment under either s. 36(1)(b) or s. 36(5) cannot be authenticated until a grant of administration with the will annexed is obtained: *Re Crowhurst Park* (1974).[2] Mention may be made here of s. 18(2) TA, which authorises the PRs of the last surviving or continuing trustee to carry on the business of the trust until such time as a new trustee or trustees are appointed: see *ante* 3.14.

The appointment must be in writing and should be done by deed; if there is land, a deed is essential to take advantage of the implied vesting declaration under s. 40 TA – see *post* 9.18. If a refusing or retiring trustee is willing to do so, he may act as if he were a continuing trustee for the purpose of exercising the statutory power under s. 36: s. 36(8). But not if he is being removed against his will – *Re Stoneham, ante* 9.5.

9.8   THE APPOINTMENT OF ADDITIONAL TRUSTEES

The rules for the appointment of additional trustees where there is no vacancy are set out in s. 36(6):

Where a sole trustee, other than a trust corporation, is or has been originally appointed to act in a trust, or where, in the case of any trust, there are not more than three trustees (none of them being a trust corporation) either original or substituted and whether appointed by the court or otherwise, then and in any such case –

(a) the person or persons nominated for the purpose of appointing new trustees by the instrument, if any, creating the trust; or

(b) if there is no such person, or no such person able and willing to act, then the trustee or trustees for the time being;

may, by writing appoint another person or other persons to be an additional trustee or additional trustees, but it shall not be obligatory to appoint any additional trustee, unless the instrument, if any, creating the trust, or any statutory enactment provides to the contrary, nor shall the number of trustees be increased beyond four by virtue of any such appointment.

The restriction to four trustees needs to be read in the light of s. 37(1)(b). We have already seen, *ante* 3.8, that there is a limit of four PRs for the same part of an estate. For trustees, s. 37(1)(b) provides that a separate set of trustees, not exceeding four, can be appointed for any part of the trust property held on trusts 'distinct from those relating to any other part or parts of the trust property'. This provision may be useful, for instance, where the existing trustees are having difficulty with the beneficiaries of one particular settled fund, or where a particular fund requires specialised attention, e.g. a literary estate, or where it is desired to export a particular fund out of several and to appoint new non-resident trustees.

There is the slightly curious restriction in s. 36(6) – 'none of them being a trust corporation' – which precludes the appointment of any additional trustees where a trust corporation is already on the scene. The Law Reform Committee has recommended the abolition of this restriction; and would also want to amend s. 36(6) to enable the persons with power of appointing new trustees to be able to appoint themselves, which they can do under s. 36(1) but not under s. 36(6). For the appointment by PRs of trustees of an infant's *vested* legacy, see *ante* 6.21.

9.9 APPOINTMENT BY BENEFICIARIES

It might be thought that, where all the beneficiaries of a trust are ascertained and *sui juris*, they should be able to remove uncongenial trustees and appoint others in their place, but this is not so. *Re Brockbank* (1948) is a good illustration of the true position:

The testator had made a will appointing his son-in-law and his solicitor to be his trustees. The son-in-law retired in favour of his son. In turn, the son wished to retire in favour of Lloyds Bank, and the beneficiaries were in favour of this course. However, the solicitor/trustee refused to co-operate, and the court refused to compel him to agree to the change. It would not tell the trustee how to exercise his discretionary power of appointment in such a case.

The most that the beneficiaries can do is to exercise their powers of persuasion on the person or persons with the power of appointment. If they are all ascertained and *sui juris* then they may, indeed, go to the trustees and compel them to hand over the fund (see *post* 13.2) but this is rather a drastic step to take and may have adverse tax consequences. It is, of course, sensible to inform and consult adult beneficiaries about a proposed appointment before executing it.

9.10   APPOINTMENT BY THE COURT

As a last resort, it may be necessary to ask the court to make the appointment. Section 41 TA says that the court *may* (the power is discretionary), whenever it is expedient to appoint a new trustee or trustees and it is difficult or impossible to do so in any other way, make an order appointing a new trustee or trustees either in substitution for or in addition to an existing trustee or trustees. Like s. 36, this provision does not apply to PRs.

It seems that the court cannot make use of s. 41 to intervene where there is either a statutory or express power available and capable of being used to appoint. Where such a power is being misused, the court could no doubt be asked to exercise its inherent jurisdiction to put matters right. Under s. 42, where the court has appointed a corporation to be a trustee, it may also authorise it to charge for its services.

9.11   WHO SHOULD BE A TRUSTEE?

It has been observed that some people are temperamentally unsuited to being a trustee and it is definitely not an office which just anyone can fill satisfactorily; integrity, common sense, willingness to spend time and trouble on the trust, ability to get on well with co-trustees and beneficiaries are obvious qualifications. Knowledge of trust law and practice is not essential, since advice on these subjects should be available from the trust solicitor. If the trust is likely to be of long duration, then consideration should be given to the appointment of one of the perpetual professional trustees, such as the clearing banks and the Public Trustee. The testator or settlor can, of course, appoint whom he likes, but will do well to bear in mind the elementary principles mentioned above.

Trustees should not be appointed simply because they are relatives or friends; to do that may simply be a recipe for disaster, especially where discretionary trusts are concerned.

In *Turner* v *Turner* (1984) a discretionary settlement had been made in 1967, of which the trustees were the settlor's elderly father and a neighbouring farmer and his wife, none of whom had any experience or understanding of trust matters. They made three appointments in favour of the beneficiaries between 1967 and

1976. The were of a contradictory nature and in the end two of the trustees (the settlor's father having emigrated to Australia) asked the court for directions. The three trustees had never met, had left the settlor to make all the decisions and had signed whatever was prepared for them by the settlor's solicitor. In these circumstances the court had jurisdiction to put aside the purported exercises of the power and made the appropriate order. See also *post* 9.32

There are a number of old rules which, probably, are now more honoured in the breach than the observance – for instance, that a beneficiary should not be appointed. However, it cannot be wrong to try to follow the policy of the court when making an appointment, it considers the wishes of settlor and beneficiaries, whether the personal interests of the trustee will conflict with his fiduciary duties and, most importantly, whether the proposed new trustee's appointment will promote or impede the execution of the trust: see *Re Tempest* (1866) where a proposed trustee was rejected by the Court of Appeal on the grounds of his possible hostility to the trust and its beneficiaries.

In *Re Northcliffe's Settlements* (1937) the Court of Appeal held that there is no principle which would prevent a bank from being appointed a trustee of a settlement merely because one or more of the beneficiaries were customers of the bank, even though their accounts were overdrawn; also no importance was to be attached to the possibility that the bank might, in course of time, become sole trustee or that it was also the banker of the settlor's executors. The view that a bank might exercise its powers under discretionary trusts so as to favour unduly the beneficiary, whose account might be overdrawn, likewise received no support from the Court of Appeal.

Although a single individual can act as a trustee on his own, there are both technical and practical disadvantages to this; the opportunities for fraud, neglect and prejudice are greatly increased when such an appointment is made, and there must always be the risk of death, when the trust will be left, temporarily at any rate, in the hands of the dead trustee's PRs. Although a sole trustee may *hold* land, there must be either a trust corporation or two or more individuals to give a valid receipt for the proceeds of land held on trust for sale (s. 2(2) LPA) and for capital money arising from settled land (s. 94(1) SLA). Unless the proposed trust is of very modest size, prudence will usually suggest the appointment of a trust corporation, with or without one or two personal co-trustees; or two or more individuals, including a representative of either the legal or the accountancy professions.

9.12 THE RETIREMENT OF TRUSTEES WITHOUT REPLACEMENT

A trustee cannot be compelled to remain in office, but he needs to be able to choose an available route out of it. There may be an express power which can be used, but it is more likely that reliance will be placed on the statutory powers found in ss. 36 and 39 TA. Section 39, unlike s. 36, authorises retirement without replacement, provided the following conditions are observed:

(a) there must remain to act either two or more individual trustees or a trust corporation; and
(b) the continuing trustees must consent to the retirement; and
(c) the consent of anyone named in the trust instrument as having the power to appoint new trustees is obtained; and
(d) the retirement is effected by deed.

Section 39 is also unlike s. 36 in that it does not authorise retirement from part of the trusts. If there is neither an express power to authorise retirement nor the feasibility to make use of the statutory powers, then the trustee may still be able to retire either through the agency of the beneficiaries (assuming them to be all ascertained and *sui juris*) or as a last resort, by authority of the court.

9.13 THE POST-RETIREMENT RESPONSIBILITIES OF A TRUSTEE

It is fair to add that the act of retirement by a trustee is of the same measure of importance as is his acceptance of office; whichever way he goes about it, the administration of the trust will, in future, be dealt with by others. A trustee who intends to retire should be satisfied that he is leaving the conduct of the trust's affairs in safe hands; if he has notice of or even suspects that a breach of trust is contemplated and retires in order to avoid complicity he runs the risk of being saddled with responsibility for the breach jointly with the trustees who continue to act. See *Head* v *Gould* (1898); the question asked in such cases is whether the trustee retired in order to facilitate a breach of trust.

A retiring trustee will, of course, remain liable for breaches of trust committed during his term of office and for debts incurred and contracted – notably those to the Revenue – until the relevant periods of limitation expire. It is sensible for a retiring trustee either to see that such debts are discharged or to obtain a specific release from liability. There seems to be no way in which a retired trustee can now be made liable for taxation due in respect of the trust after he has ceased to act, unless, indeed, he be also either the settlor or a beneficiary or unless the reason for his retirement is the export of the trust.[3] There is an additional risk in cases where *part* of a trust is exported that UK trustees of the resident funds may find themselves liable for tax arising in respect of the overseas funds; see *post* 13.23.

While a trustee will, in practice, often get a formal release from his beneficiaries when winding up a trust it seems to be settled that he is not entitled to one, either from the beneficiaries or from the continuing trustees, upon retirement: see *Tiger* v *Barclays Bank Ltd* (1951); neither is he entitled to an indemnity, except in respect of costs and expenses properly incurred.

9.14 THE REMOVAL OF TRUSTEES

We have seen in 9.3 that there may be an express power of removal, and it was apparent in 9.4 and 9.5 that, provided a replacement was envisaged, a trustee could be forcibly retired in five situations: (a) remaining out of the UK, (b) refusing to act, (c) unfitness to act, (d) incapable of acting and (e) infancy. The court's inherent jurisdiction (already referred to) empowers it to remove trustees as well as to appoint them, although, 'the principles on which this power is exercised are somewhat vague' (*Hanbury*, p. 478). In addition, s. 41 TA clearly envisages the removal of a trustee as a corollary to the court's appointment of a replacement. *Parker and Mellows* point out (p. 262) that removal by the court presents some difficulty, and go on to say:

> The court's primary concern is to protect and enhance the interests of the beneficiaries. So that where the trustee is convicted of dishonesty, or by becoming bankrupt or otherwise shows that he is not fit to be in charge of other people's property, the court will remove him. Nevertheless, removal by the court does involve, at least to the outside world, some moral stigma, and difficulties arise where an application is made to remove a trustee, not because he has done anything wrong, but because he cannot agree or get on with his co-trustees.

Although one might suspect that the removal of trustees would be the sort of subject likely to give rise to frequent applications to court, there is remarkably little recent case material about it, the last relevant report being the *Stoneham* case (see *ante* 9.5 and 9.7). A later case, *Jones* v *A-G* (1974) was concerned with the removal of a charitable trustee by the Charity Commissioners in accordance with the powers given to them by s. 20 Charities Act 1960. The reason for the absence of litigation on this subject is probably that most trustees at risk of being forcibly removed by the court are advised to retire voluntarily, and do so.

9.15 DELEGATION AS AN ALTERNATIVE TO RETIREMENT OR REMOVAL

Either retirement or removal of a trustee may be avoidable, if the impediment is temporary, by making use of s. 25 TA, which, as we saw in 5.45, empowers a trustee (and the term includes a PR and a tenant for life under the SLA – s. 25(8)) to delegate, by a power of attorney, for a period not exceeding twelve months 'all or any of the trusts, powers and discretions vested in him'. A trust corporation may be the donee of such a

233

power. Written notice of its execution, or intended execution, must be given to the other trustees, if any, and to any other person having the power to appoint a new trustee (s. 25(4)). The donor of the power is liable for the acts and defaults of the donee as if they were his own (s. 25(5)).

Use of this authority will be convenient where a trustee is inaccessible for a limited period; where he is going to be unable to carry out his duties for, say, more than one year it would seem better for him to retire outright – and, if he declines, for him to be removed after the required period of absence.

Note also s. 3(3) Enduring Powers of Attorney Act 1985 which enables the donee of a power of attorney in the prescribed form to exercise all powers and discretions exercisable by the donor as trustee – see *ante* 6.57.

9.16 DUTIES OF TRUSTEES

A trustee's first and primary duty is to carry out the provisions of the trust instrument. Subject to this, he must secure and control the trust property.

9.17 DUTY ON APPOINTMENT

The duties of a trustee on taking up his appointment differ somewhat according to the circumstances; if he is taking over an existing trust it is necessary for him to investigate its previous history and, in particular, to correct any breaches of trust which may become apparent as a result of his enquiries. Not to do so will make the new trustee liable for such breaches as though they had been effected or acquiesced in by him personally. *Parker and Mellows*, p. 268, say that a new trustee is not expected to act like a bloodhound straining to sniff out some breach of trust; on the other hand he is under a duty to question anything which appears out of order. Perhaps the most basic enquiry is into the state of the trust fund itself – can it in its present form be traced back to the original trust assets? In the absence of proper accounts (and private trustees are not always punctilious about these) such an enquiry may not be easy. If there is a discrepancy, how has it occurred? If capital has gone, has it gone rightly to a beneficiary entitled to capital – perhaps by way of advancement? Has the trust income been either properly disposed of or accumulated in accordance with an available power? Are the trust's tax affairs in order? Whilst a new trustee may reasonably ask the beneficiaries to confirm that they are satisfied with the present state of the trust fund he should not allow such a confirmation to deter him from investigating the past history of the fund.

To carry out an investigation of the above kind the newly-appointed trustee must have access to and take possession of what may loosely be described as the 'trust papers'. Corporate trustees should note that internal memoranda and correspondence may come within the general description of documents to be handed over. Discovery of an apparent breach of trust by previous trustees places upon the shoulders of their successors the responsibility of demanding an explanation; if this is unsatisfactory it may be necessary, in the end, to take proceedings for the recovery of any loss sustained by the trust as a result of the breach. Failure to take such action may result in the newly-appointed trustee becoming personally liable for the loss.

The new trustee should make a special point of searching the trust papers for any notices of incumbrances by the beneficiaries upon their interests.

9.18   OBTAINING CONTROL OF THE TRUST ASSETS

Trustees should exert control over the trust assets by having them placed in their names at the earliest possible moment. In this connection, s. 40 TA may be of some help because it provides for any *deed* appointing a new trustee (or discharging a trustee without replacement) to operate as if it contained a declaration vesting any estate or interest in land and any personal property in the new and continuing trustees. This vesting declaration does not apply to those cases which contain a requirement that the landlord's permission to any assignment must be obtained and such permission had not been obtained before execution of the deed. Neither does it apply to mortgages of land, which should be separately transferred, nor to stocks and shares, which should be transferred and reregistered (as should also, for instance, building society share and deposit accounts). Although a transfer of registered land is not strictly necessary it seems desirable, otherwise the deed of appointment itself must be registered with the Land Registry. Where choses in action, other than stocks and shares, such as debts or equitable interests are held in trust, notice of the change in the trusteeship should be given in writing to the debtor or fund-holder without delay. Where PRs, having completed their administration, are continuing to hold land as trustees without having executed an assent in favour of themselves as trustees, s. 40 cannot normally apply on a subsequent change of trusteeship – see *ante* 7.7.

The duty of the *first* trustees to be appointed is less onerous in two ways – firstly, the documentation in existence is minimal, principally consisting of the trust instrument and any expression of wishes placed with it by the settlor. Secondly, there is no past history to investigate. The trustees are, however, under the same obligation to take possession of the settled assets and to have them registered in their joint names. [4]

Documents of title are best deposited under joint control, e.g. deposited in the names of all the trustees with the trust bankers. [5] However, this will not be necessary where the trust instrument authorises one out of several trustees to have control of such items, which will usually be the case where a trust corporation is appointed. There is also precedent for trust deeds and securities to be left in the custody of one trustee – *Re Sisson* (1903) – in the absence of 'special circumstances'. Trustees who deposit trust property with a banker have statutory backing and may pay the banker's charges for safe custody – s. 21 TA. Bearer securities in a trust *must* be deposited with a banker – s. 7.

9.19   DUTY TO ACT JOINTLY AND UNANIMOUSLY

Whatever the position as regards deposit of the trust deeds and securities, where there is more than one trustee they each have a duty to act personally and jointly and to give joint receipts. 'There is no law that I am acquainted with which enables a majority of trustees to bind a minority' (Jessel MR in *Luke v South Kensington Hotel Co* (1879)); so, only a *joint* exercise of their powers will be valid and only a receipt from all the trustees will discharge a purchaser of trust property. There should generally be no question of one out of several trustees acting as 'leader' and making decisions which are then acquiesced in, more or less gracefully, by the rest – see *Turner v Turner, ante* 9.11 and *post* 9.32. As is said in *Underhill* p. 553, although a trustee may listen to the opinions of others, he must exercise his own judgment. It is therefore of prime importance for trustees to keep in touch with each other and to keep a full and intelligible record of trust business and of joint decisions taken. (Trustees may be inclined to keep such a record separate from any further record, whether in correspondence or otherwise, of their *reasons* for taking decisions – see *post* 9.25 and 9.26.)

Exceptions to this rule may occur; the trust instrument may authorise one trustee to act alone in a matter such as the deposit of documents, or it may authorise a majority of trustees to make decisions (which a majority of charity trustees can do without such authorisation – see *post* 12.17). It is generally recognised that one out of several trustees may receive income because of the practical impossibility of the alternative (the other trustees must, over a period of time, ensure that the income in question is being duly collected and credited to the trust bank account). Lastly, where a power of delegation exists, such power may be exercised in favour of a co-trustee but s. 25(2) TA bans the delegation of the statutory power to the only other co-trustee, unless the donee is a trust corporation – see *ante* 5.45 and 9.15.

What is to be done where trustees find it impossible to carry out their duty to act jointly because of an irreconcilable and persistent difference of opinion? One suspects that, in many cases, this results in a policy of unjustifiable, rather than masterly, inactivity. This is not a satisfactory state of affairs because the administration of most trusts requires, in varying degrees, *positive* thinking; if the impasse continues it must, eventually, be detrimental to the trust and can only be resolved by an application to the court.

9.20   THE DUTY OF CARE

As a general rule a trustee sufficiently discharges his duty of care if, in managing trust affairs, he takes all those precautions which an ordinary prudent man of business would take in managing similar affairs of his own; this standard was laid down by Jessel MR in *Speight* v *Gaunt* (1883) and approved by the House of Lords:

> In this case the trustee had employed a broker for the purpose of investing £15,000 in corporation stocks. The broker appropriated the purchase price for his personal use and then went bankrupt, not having delivered the securities for which the money had been paid. The beneficiaries claimed that the trustee should refund the loss to the trust fund. The Court of Appeal rejected this claim; a trustee investing funds is justified in employing a broker to buy securities if he follows the usual and regular course of business adopted by ordinary prudent men in making such investments.
>
> 'If,' as Jessel MR said, 'a trustee has made a proper selection of a broker, and has paid him the money on the bought-note, and, by reason of the default of the broker, the money is lost, it does not appear to me in that case that the trustee can be liable.'

This leading case is useful in that it reminds us that a trustee is not expected to *guarantee* the value of the trust fund of which he has custody; neither is he expected to insure the beneficiaries against loss. Only if he has failed, in some way, to carry out the duties which he takes on with the office, and such failure amounts to a breach of trust, will he be liable to indemnify the fund against any loss arising as a result of the breach (see ch. 14).

9.21   STANDARDS OF CARE FOR PROFESSIONAL TRUSTEE

There are, however, standards of care and standards of care, and some standards are pitched at a higher level than others; this is particularly so where the trustee is a professional. In *Re Waterman's Will Trusts* (1952) Harman J. said that 'a paid trustee is expected to exercise a higher standard of diligence and knowledge than an unpaid trustee', and this view was reiterated by Brightman J. in *Bartlett* v *Barclays Bank Trust Co Ltd* (1980) – see *ante* 5.30:

> 'I am of opinion that a higher duty of care is plainly due from someone like a trust corporation which carries on a specialised business of trust management . . . a professional corporate trustee is liable for breach of trust if loss is caused to the trust fund because it neglects to exercise the special care and skill which it professes to have.'

The relevant standard of care required of a trustee is of some importance in cases where a trustee asks to be relieved from liability for breach of trust under s. 61 TA – see *post* 14.19; the relevant standard in the case of a

237

non-professional trustee (say, a member of the settlor's family) will be that stated by Jessel MR in *Speight* v *Gaunt*. The standard expected of a professional man, e.g. a solicitor, will be higher. See, for instance, *Re Rosenthal* (1972), where a solicitor/trustee was refused relief in respect of the incorrect allocation of an estate duty payment. The standard expected of a trust corporation such as a bank will be higher still – the actual level perhaps depending upon the quality and extent of the expertise which it has advertised itself as possessing. According to the Law Reform Committee's 23rd Report, 'Professional trustees, such as banks, are under a special duty to display expertise in *every* aspect of their administration of the trust'; it must be difficult to achieve such a standard of perfection. A settlor may, of course, reduce the impact of the duty of care upon a trustee by indemnifying trustees against the consequences of a breach of trust, unless committed in bad faith; a trustee contemplating such consequences in the case of a large, complicated trust may well insist that the trust instrument contains such a clause (perhaps a dubious protection – see *post* 14.20).* Where a trustee, professional or otherwise, is most likely to come unstuck is in the exercise of his powers of delegation (see ch. 10) and of his powers of investment (see ch. 11).

9.22 DUTY TO INFORM AND ACCOUNT

Lindley LJ in *Low* v *Bouverie* (1891) said:

> 'The duty of a trustee is properly to preserve the trust fund, to pay the income and the corpus to those who are entitled to them respectively, and to give all his *cestuis que trust*, on demand, information with respect to the mode in which the trust fund has been dealt with, and where it is.'

Trustees have the further obligation to advise a beneficiary of his interest in the trust (see *Hawkesley* v *May* (1956)) though not, it would seem, until he comes of age. In practice trustees will advise the parents of infant beneficiaries of the interests belonging to their offspring. It must be a moot point whether trustees have a duty to inform the possible beneficiaries of a discretionary power or trust, as they have no tangible interest but merely the right to be considered by the trustees as they exercise their discretion. In my view, information should generally be provided in such circumstances, if only to give the possible objects of the discretion the opportunity to consider the way in which the trustees are carrying out their duties. [6]

Payments must, of course, be made to the right persons, and any error in this respect, however extenuating the circumstances (e.g. if done under legal advice), amounts to a breach of trust. The position of the trustees is hardly different from that of PRs who commit a *devastavit* by making

---

*See the article by William Goodhart QC, 'Trustee Exemption Clauses and the Unfair Contract Terms Act 1977' in *Trust Law and Practice*, July/August 1986, 43.

wrong payments – see *ante* 6.2. Both PRs and trustees who have acted honestly and reasonably may ask the court to excuse them from the consequences of the breach under s. 61 TA as mentioned above; but if trustees find themselves in real doubt about the proper destination of either capital or income, the sensible course is to apply to the court for guidance.

9.23   THE DUTY IS TO INFORM, NOT ADVISE

It should, perhaps, be added that, although trustees have an obligation to inform beneficiaries of their interests, they are under no further obligation to *advise* them about the extent and nature of such interests, still less of ways in which they may be disposed of. In view of the House of Lords' decision in *Hedley Byrne & Co* v *Heller & Partners* (1964), the less trustees volunteer by way of advice, whether to the beneficiaries or to an intended assignee, the better their prospects of remaining unscathed. This is not to suggest that trustees should maintain a grim silence at all times, but rather that they should exercise a certain restraint when writing and talking to beneficiaries; if the latter are in any doubt as to their rights under the trust, or if they are contemplating any dealing in their interests, they should be referred to their own personal legal advisers. Information given to third parties should be qualified by a warning that responsibility for the data provided will not be accepted; such data should never be supplied to third parties without the express written authority of the beneficiary concerned.

In this connection, trustees not infrequently receive directions from beneficiaries as to the way in which their interests shall be satisfied. Apart from taking the obvious precautions of ensuring that such directions are in writing (as required by s. 53(1)(c) LPA, if an assignment is intended) and are authentic, some care needs to be taken to distinguish between the simple authority for payment on the one hand and the outright assignment on the other. The former may be revoked or amended at will, the latter only with the consent of the assignee. In some cases, this distinction is not easy to make but the appearance of the word 'irrevocable' in an otherwise informal authority should make the trustee-recipient reflect. A formal deed of assignment is the property of the assignee but it must, of course, be produced to the trustee, who should record it and take a copy for his own use. *Underhill* suggests, p. 544, that he should also obtain an acknowledgment for production and an undertaking for safe custody.

9.24   KEEPING AND SUPPLYING ACCOUNTS

A trustee must:

(a)   keep clear and accurate accounts of the trust property; and

(b)   at all reasonable times, at the request of a beneficiary, give him full and accurate information as to the amount and state of the trust property and permit him or his solicitor to inspect the accounts and vouchers, and other documents relating to the trust, including counsel's opinions. *

In theory, a beneficiary must pay for accounts and copies of trust documents supplied to him by the trustee; in practice, a professional trustee will usually regard the cost of supplying such items as part of the service for which he charges his fees. Only in an exceptional case would a beneficiary be expected to pay personally for accounts.

No special form of accounts is prescribed. The trustee may, under s. 23(1) TA, employ agents to prepare them (see ch. 10). Whether or not this is done, there is a separate power in s. 22(4) to have the trust accounts audited by an independent accountant; this power should normally not be exercised more than once every three years. Both these courses are optional and trustees have considerable latitude as to the way in which they carry out their duties in this respect. The professional trustee will be expected to maintain a high standard of accounting and to prepare accounts for the beneficiaries without prompting; the intervals between the dates on which accounts are produced is a matter for separate judgment in each case. In a large trust where frequent capital transactions take place, annual accounts will be desirable; income beneficiaries should, in any event, receive a full statement of income receipts and payments at least once every twelve months in addition to a certificate showing tax deducted from the income to which they become entitled – see *ante* 6.26. Section 13(1) Public Trustee Act 1906, mentioned *ante* 6.52, applies to trust accounts as well as to the estates of deceased persons.

Should accounts be sent to *all* beneficiaries, i.e. not only to those with interests in possession but also to those with future interests? Again much depends on the circumstances; whilst trustees must always be prepared to provide accounts to any beneficiary on request, it is suggested that they need not *volunteer* them, as a general rule, to beneficiaries who are not immediately interested in the trust fund, provided they are ready to do so. There appears, incidentally, to be an obligation to supply accounts to the possible object of a discretionary trust, notwithstanding the fact that he has no interest in possession, which supports the view (*ante* 9.22) that such objects are entitled to be informed of their connection with the trust fund. Again it seems reasonable for trustees not to volunteer accounts in such circumstances, but to be prepared to provide them on request.

9.25   DISCLOSURE OF INFORMATION GENERALLY

As regards disclosure of information generally (as distinct from the provision of trust accounts) reference should be made to *Re Londonderry's Settlement* (1965):

Underhill, p. 580. This passage quoted by permission of the publishers, Butterworth & Co (Publishers) Ltd.

This was concerned with a discretionary settlement made in 1934; the trustees were given power to appoint both capital and income to members of a specified class in such shares as they should appoint. In exercising this power they had to get the consent of certain other persons known as the 'appointors'. In 1962 the trustees decided to bring the trust to an end by appointing all the capital to members of the specified class; amongst those appointed shares were the settlor's daughter and her children. The former was dissatisfied with the amounts allocated to her and her family and asked for copies of the trustees' minutes, the documents prepared for their meetings, correspondence between the trustees, appointors and beneficiaries and between the settlor, one of the appointors and the trustees' solicitors. The trustees supplied her with copies of the appointments they had made and of the trust accounts but nothing else; they then issued a summons seeking determination of the nature and extent of their duty to disclose. Plowman J. held that they were bound to disclose all the documents asked for and the trustees appealed.

In the Court of Appeal some criticism was voiced of the trustees' action in appealing, but Salmon LJ spoke up for them, pointing out that, as they were dissatisfied with the judgment in the court below they were perfectly entitled to appeal. Salmon LJ also said that beneficiaries have a proprietary interest in, and a right to see, all trust documents. The problem was to reconcile that rule with the rule that trustees are not obliged to disclose to beneficiaries their reasons for exercising a discretionary power. The decision of the Court of Appeal was that Plowman J.'s order should be set aside; the trustees were not bound to disclose any or any part of documents relating to the deliberations about the way in which they should carry out their discretionary function and they were not bound to disclose correspondence except that which took place between them and the appointors on the one hand and the trustees' solicitors on the other.

This is a useful decision for trustees (it also applies to PRs) in that it emphasises their right to preserve from beneficiaries details of their reasons for reaching a decision, whether it concerns a power of appointment over capital, a power of maintenance or any other matter lying under their discretion. It seems a sensible rule for, as Salmon LJ pointed out:

> 'Nothing would be more likely to embitter family feelings and the relationship between the trustees and members of the family, were trustees obliged to state their reasons for the exercise of the powers entrusted to them.'

Nevertheless it still leaves open the question of what are and are not trust documents. Probably no general answer can be provided and each case must be decided in the light of its own facts and its own merits. To quote from Salmon LJ's judgment again:

> 'The category of trust documents has never been comprehensively defined. Nor could it be – certainly not by me. Trust documents do, however, have these characteristics in common: (1) they are documents in the possession of the trustees as trustees; (2) they contain information about the trust which the beneficiaries are entitled to know; (3) the beneficiaries have a proprietary interest in the documents and, accordingly, are entitled to see them.'

This definition has to be read, of course, against the background of the non-disclosure rule where the exercise of discretion is involved.

9.26 AFTERTHOUGHTS ON *RE LONDONDERRY*

As a postscript to the above perhaps I might refer readers to an interesting note by R E Megarry QC (as he then was) in [1965] 81 LQR 192 entitled 'The Ambit of a Trustee's Duty of Disclosure', where he suggested that, when exercising a discretionary power, trustees were under an obligation to exercise it *discreetly* and that this duty is perhaps the basis of the rule that reasons do not have to be disclosed. Certainly it is just as possible for a trustee to be over-communicative as to be the reverse, and both deviations from the norm are liable to have unfortunate consequences.

One should, perhaps, leave this particular subject with a reminder that the general rule about beneficiaries being entitled to inspect trust documents may not be the whole story where trustees are accused of breach of trust. In some cases, assuming that proceedings are put in train, there will be the usual order for discovery of documents and any written material which is relevant to the action will have to be disclosed, including documents which include references to the trustees' reasons for the decision they have taken. Professional trustees should bear in mind that their internal memoranda are likely to be discoverable in this sort of situation.

9.27 DISCRETIONARY SETTLEMENTS

The discussion in chapter 8 of trusts with an interest in possession and the simpler kind of children's settlements revealed legal rules with a strong statutory flavour of ss. 31 and 32 TA. There is no special trust legislation for discretionary settlements in the wider sense (whether by deed or will), sharply distinguished though they may be from interest in possession trusts and from the privileged trusts under ss. 71–9 IHTA. Nevertheless, they require trustees to answer different and, perhaps, more difficult questions from those normally asked and, for this reason, deserve a certain amount of special attention.

Commonly, the structure of a discretionary settlement is this; the trust property is held by the trustees upon the following trusts:

(a) a power to distribute the income, at their discretion, amongst a specified class of objects during the trust period, which is usually based on the 80-year period permitted by s. 1(1) PAA. Usually there will also be a power to accumulate income, instead of distributing it, for a period of 21 years from the date of the settlement: s. 13(1) PAA.

(b) a power to appoint capital at any time during the trust period amongst a specified class of objects – this may well be identical with the class for income distributions.

242

(c)   a 'long-stop' clause directing the destination of the trust fund if the trustees do not exercise their power of appointment over the capital and income.

For IHT purposes the line to be drawn between discretionary trusts and interest in possession trusts is crucial – see *ante* 8.8. So far as the practical problems are concerned, there is a similarity to those discussed in connection with maintenance (see *post* 10.17) and advancement (*post* 10.24), but the range of available decisions is greater. Whereas an advancement is made in respect of a beneficiary's quantified absolute or contingent share, a possible object of a discretionary trust has no right to any part of the trust fund (except the right to be considered by the trustees, called a *spes*) and he may, with equal propriety, receive either everything or nothing. Thus, potential objects under the overriding powers of appointment envisaged in (a) and (b) above have no beneficial interest to which they can point, whereas the beneficiaries under (c) are entitled to have the trust executed in default of the exercise of those powers.

It will readily be understood that, in a discretionary trust, an additional burden of some weight is thrown upon the trustees. The exercise of the usual discretionary powers, such as investment and advancement, requires the application of an intelligent, balanced and knowledgeable mind. When a trustee also has to weigh in the balance the various competing interests of the members of a specified class of beneficial 'objects' (it is wrong, in the context, to call them 'beneficiaries') his responsibilities are very seriously increased. Because of this, the advisability of appointing at least one trustee able to exercise a dispassionate judgment over an extended number of years is increased. Continuity of office and freedom from bias are the usual attributes of trust corporations, and they are particularly well suited for office in discretionary trusts.

Discretionary trusts were first used as a means of avoiding estate duty; since then, they have been brought within the tax-gatherer's net, the Revenue's object being to try to ensure that funds in a discretionary settlement should suffer the same amount of capital tax as they would if individually owned. The present tax regime is not, however, too rigorous and it may even be advantageous – see, e.g. *Sherring*, ch. 15. Apart from tax advantages, a discretionary settlement will always appeal to a settlor who cannot make up his mind, and will also be useful where it is necessary to protect a spendthrift family from their own worst selves.

9.28   THE DISTINCTION BETWEEN TRUSTS AND POWERS

This is relatively easy to define but not so easy, in practice, to identify. There is no doubt that a trustee is under an obligation to carry out a trust and, if he does not, the court will enforce it. He need not exercise a power, although he is under an obligation to *consider* exercising it. Unfortunately, as already discussed *ante* 7.8, there is a half-breed known as a 'trust power', which must be treated as if it were an express trust and exercised accordingly. In practice the distinction is probably not of as much consequence as might be thought. Granted that a trustee must *consider* all trusts and powers contained in the trust instrument, it is unlikely that he will overlook the need to exercise a power in the nature of a trust. Having said that, one can only add, not helpfully, that whether a power is a mere power or a power in the nature of a trust will often depend entirely upon construction of the words used by the settlor. There are two general principles: (a) that a general power of appointment cannot be a trust power; (b) if a gift over in default of appointment exists then, equally, there cannot be a trust power. Otherwise, each case has to be tackled individually.

9.29 'CERTAINTY OF OBJECTS' IN DISCRETIONARY SETTLEMENTS

As was seen *ante* 7.14 and 7.15, in settlements which provide fixed shares for the beneficiaries it is vital that the trustee should be able to draw up a complete catalogue of the beneficiaries, especially if they are having to carry out a trust in default of appointment. But no such rigid rule applies to the possible objects under a power of appointment (unless it belongs to that peculiar class of trust powers described above); it is good enough if the potential beneficiary who is to receive payment is clearly identifiable as a member of the class described. The House of Lords decision in the *McPhail* case has put the trusts in a discretionary settlement on the same footing as its powers.

It is clear that trusts and powers drawn in very wide terms, of which the *McPhail* case is a typical example, must create problems for the trustees, even if they do not have to compile a complete list of objects. Some comments on their proceedings in such cases are made at the end of this chapter. The courts have shown that they are not unaware of the difficulties which trustees face in considering the exercise of their discretion. In *Re Hay* (1982) the Vice-Chancellor confirmed that a very wide (even gigantic) class of objects is not in itself invalid, though a *trust* (as distinct from a power) in favour of such a class may be void simply because it is administratively unworkable – see the *West Yorkshire* and *Manisty* cases, *ante* 7.14 and 7.16. Lord Wilberforce's suggestion in the *McPhail* case that a trust in favour of all the residents of Greater London would be void for this reason is a graphic example.* But, assuming that there is no flaw of this sort, the trustees should first of all take a kind of bird's eye view of the class of objects, simply to get an understanding of the area it covers, in human terms. Having applied their minds to the size of the problem, the trustees

---

*See *Administrative Unworkability*, I M Hardcastle, [1990] Conv 24.

may then consider individual cases, although they are not required to make exact calculations between deserving claimants. *Re Hay*, incidentally, also makes the point that trustees may not normally use a power of appointment as a means of delegating their discretion to others – it must be exercised in favour of its objects; but a settlor could authorise his trustees to delegate in this fashion (see below).

9.30 CONTENTS OF A DISCRETIONARY SETTLEMENT

In addition to the comments already made concerning the content of a trust deed, *ante* 8.20, the following points may be of particular interest in the case of a discretionary settlement:

(a) *The perpetuity period*, taking advantage of the 80–year period as being the latest possible time for the vesting of any interests, including those appointed by the trustees. Charitable gifts are not necessarily immune – see *post* 12.8.

(b) *Accumulation of income*. There is no general power to accumulate income, except under s. 31(2) TA, and an express power should therefore be included. Exactly how long trustees may retain income and still exercise their discretion over its distribution appears to be undecided (see *post* 9.31) but the safe course is to reach an annual decision at least. It is usual to include a power to accumulate income for 21 years from the date of the settlement. It is important to be aware of the difference between a trust to distribute income (no alternative) and a power to distribute or retain (discretionary); in the latter case a further power to accumulate is necessary.

(c) *Powers of appointment*. Consideration should be given to the inclusion (i) of a power to add or subtract from the list of potential beneficiaries, (ii) a power to exercise discretionary powers by delegation to other trustees and (iii) a power for the trustees to augment their existing powers, whether administrative or dispositive.

(d) *Powers of management*. Note particularly the need for wide investment powers, including power to purchase residences for use by beneficial objects,[7] to invest overseas, to invest in non-income producing assets. Powers to allow beneficial objects to 'use' assets, to lend money to them[8] and to appropriate assets in their favour can also usefully be included. In exercising their powers, whether administrative or dispositive, the trustees must be constantly on watch to ensure that they do not unwittingly convert a discretionary interest into an interest in possession or vice versa, with undesired tax consequences.

(e) It is emphasised that the mere existence (whether exercised or not) of powers that are capable of disturbing a beneficiary's right to income (ordinary trust administration fees and expenses excepted) could stand in the way (i) of establishing an accumulation and maintenance settlement under s. 71 IHTA, because it could not be said with certainty that a beneficiary would attain an interest in possession by the age of 25; and (ii) of setting up an interest in possession trust. Therefore, if either of these measures is to be taken, the trustees must be careful to exclude the application of the offending powers (e.g. a power to pay life policy premiums out of income) to the new trusts they are creating.

(f)   *Power to export*, i.e. power to retire in favour of non-resident trustees coupled with the power to change the proper law of the settlement – see *post* 13.16 *et seq*. The power to move the trust to a different jurisdiction and to change the trustee may be vested in a 'Protector' (a variant on the traditional role of the person of that name whose task it was to put a brake upon the barring of an entail in an SLA settlement), who might have a less constrained view of the political or economic situation requiring such a move to be made.

(g)   *The residual fixed-interest gift*, which acts as a kind of 'long-stop' if the trustees do not wholly exercise their powers. The settlor and settlor's spouse should be excluded from possible benefit, whether under this heading or elsewhere, though it is in order to include the settlor's *widow* – see *ante* 8.3, 8.10 (IHT) and 8.14 (CGT).

(h)   *Appointment of new trustees*. Often a power is reserved for the settlor; this is unexceptionable, but a power for him to remove trustees can be abused and should not be accepted.

9.31   ADMINISTRATION OF A DISCRETIONARY SETTLEMENT

'A settlor or testator who entrusts a power to his trustees must be relying on them in their fiduciary capacity so they cannot simply push aside the power and refuse to consider whether it ought in their judgment to be exercised.' (*per* Lord Reid, *Re Gulbenkian* (1970))

Perhaps the most important requirement where any discretionary trust or power is involved is that the discretion must be *consciously* exercised. Moreover, the process is a continuous one. Having once, for instance, exercised their discretionary power to invest the trust fund as they think fit, trustees cannot rest on their laurels; they must *review* the exercise of their discretion at regular intervals. The same principle applies to those trusts where the trustees have the power to allocate either income or capital or both amongst a specified class. An initial decision is made, for instance, to pay the income to A. The passage of time tends to give this decision an air of permanence, with the result that a *de facto* fixed-interest trust is created. Decisions relating to a discretionary power over income should be reviewed annually *at least*; in fact, it is a good rule to review all possible discretionary powers every year – some of them, e.g. investment powers, will often need to be looked at more frequently. Inactivity can amount to a breach of trust. Do not forget that for investment powers statutory duties are imposed: see *post* 11.6 and 11.12.

It is true that a discretion will not lapse merely because it is not exercised, though there is a risk that, eventually, the funds over which the discretion is exercisable will devolve as though the discretionary power did not exist. This is particularly so in the case of income. Trustees have no general power to accumulate income. They should, therefore, make a definite decision either (a) to allocate it amongst the beneficial objects or (b) to accumulate, if given an express power to do so. It is true that the length of time during which income can be uncommitted seems to be an extremely flexible one:

Re Gulbenkian No. 2 (1970) – here there was a *power* of appointment over income; the trustees' discretion did not lapse during a 12-year period, but there was the justification that the trustees had been awaiting the outcome of the litigation in the first *Gulbenkian* case (for a case where there was no such justification, see the *Allen-Meyrick* decision in note 9 to this chapter). This case also held that an object of a discretionary trust or power is able to renounce his right to be considered as a potential beneficiary, if he does so by deed or for valuable consideration.

In *Re Locker* (1977) there was an exhaustive discretionary *trust* to distribute income amongst a class of individuals and charitable and other institutions at the trustees' discretion. 'Paying too deferential a respect to the settlor's subsequent wishes', the trustees failed to carry out their trust from December 1965 to April 1968. Goulding J. said that it was common ground that it was the duty of the trustees to distribute the trust income within a reasonable time after it came into their hands. As the trustees wanted to repair their breach of duty, the judge allowed them to do so, provided they exercised their discretion only in favour of persons who would have been valid objects had it been exercised at the proper time.

Notwithstanding the leeway allowed to the trustees in these cases, it is surely better practice to exercise a discretion over income at annual intervals, if not more frequently. It is worth noting that in an exhaustive discretionary trust, if all the possible objects were *sui juris*, they could collectively terminate the trust, although individually they are powerless. To talk of a non-exhaustive discretionary trust is a confusion in terms, as it follows that such a trust will merely empower the trustees to appoint income, and their duty then is to consider the exercise of the power; if there is a genuine decision to pay nothing, not only are the objects individually powerless to complain, they are also collectively powerless. In this type of situation, if the income is still unapplied after a reasonable time, the succeeding provisions of the trust instrument will have to take effect: *Re Allen-Meyrick* (1966).[9]

9.32   THE SETTLOR

He or she often sets out his or her wishes in the form of a letter to the first trustees of the settlement. This is extremely useful, but it is *not* binding on the trustees and it is wrong to tell the settlor that the trustees will inevitably follow such guidance. In my view, settlors should be told that, once having effectively created the settlement, the trustees and noone else are responsible for its conduct, and that they must have a free hand. A settlor who is unwilling to concede this principle should perhaps not make a settlement at all. The case of *Turner* v *Turner* (1984) – see *ante* 9.11 – illustrates the dangers of allowing a settlor to control the conduct of the trust. There the court set aside deeds of appointment which, at the direction of the settlor, the trustees had signed without understanding that the decision that lay behind them was a matter for their discretion.

With the abolition of estate duty the risks involved where the settlor is also a trustee disappeared, but in 1986 the introduction of PETs brought with it the gift with reservation rules, under which it is not inconceivable for a settlor to fail to achieve his virtual exclusion from the enjoyment of the gifted assets and property substituted for them: sch. 20, para.5, FA 1986. The safety-first course must be for the settlor not to be one of the trustees.

9.33   DATA

'Any trustee would surely make it his duty to know what is the permissible area of selection and then consider responsibly, in individual cases, whether a contemplated beneficiary was within the power and whether, in relation to other possible claimants, a particular grant was appropriate.' (Lord Wilberforce in *McPhail* v *Doulton* (1971)).

Any fact which has a bearing upon the way in which the trustees should exercise their discretion is relevant. They need to be *fully* informed, and the time to start collecting data is when the settlement is made. How often does one see cases where a discretion is being exercised with only a sketchy knowledge of the beneficial objects' backgrounds and real requirements (to rely on a beneficiary's own view of his needs can be dangerous). In these circumstances, it is useful to have as one trustee someone with knowledge in depth of the family history and circumstances – the family solicitor, for instance. To require detailed knowledge of *all* the beneficial objects of a discretionary settlement is asking too much, and probably impossible in many cases; in practice, the *probable* objects are confined to a number which it is not difficult to describe in some depth, and trustees are not expected to be able to go further than that: see *ante* 9.29.

The settlor's views have already been referred to; a letter expressing his wishes may usefully be updated from time to time. The trust instrument itself may provide guidance. The ages, marital status, sex, family commitments, educational standards and progress, careers and prospects, financial status (present and prospective) are others. An eye must be kept on the fiscal implications of activity on the one hand and non-activity on the other. The total equation is complex, and being a trustee of a discretionary trust is no sinecure – a very good reason for appointing a professional in such cases. The main requirement is that a trustee should consciously and conscientiously exercise the discretion given to him; having done so, it is prudent for trustees to record their decisions, to publish them as and when this is necessary, but *not* to publish their reasons also unless it is entirely impracticable to withhold them: see *ante* 9.25. To give the reason for a decision as well as the decision itself dangerously increases the area over which an argument can occur.

9.34 DUTY NOT TO PROFIT FROM THE TRUST

'It is an inflexible rule of a court of equity that a person in a fiduciary position is not, unless otherwise expressly provided, entitled to make a profit' – Lord Herschell in *Bray* v *Ford* (1896). This inflexible rule is, in fact, a part of a much wider rule that a trustee should not place himself in a position in which his duty as trustee and his personal interest may conflict, although it seems that if a trustee is put into this position by the settlor, the rule is not broken:

> In *Sargeant* v *National Westminster Bank* (1990) the trustees held three farms on trust for sale under their father's will for the benefit of themselves and their deceased brother's estate. They occupied the land under agricultural tenancies granted by their father and they wanted to purchase one of the farms (there was power in the will for them to do this despite their fiduciary capacity) at a price which would discount the existence of the tenancy and to sell the others also subject to the tenancies. The PRs of the brother objected, but the Court of Appeal held that there was no infringement of the self-interest rule; this did not apply where the PRs or trustees had been put into the 'conflict situation' by the testator or settlor. The PRs were, however, under the usual obligation to get the best price for the freeholds subject to the tenancies.

Both this rule and the rule against making an unauthorised profit apply not only to trustees and PRs, but also to other persons acting in a fiduciary capacity, such as partners in a business, the directors of companies and solicitors: see, e.g. *Guinness plc* v *Saunders* (1991) where the sum of £5.2m paid to a director in breach of his fiduciary duty was ordered to be repaid.

9.35 REMUNERATION OF TRUSTEES

In trusts, the most general application of this 'inflexible' rule is that a trustee is not permitted to take any remuneration for his services to the trust unless he is expressly authorised to do so in the trust instrument. Clauses authorising remuneration are construed strictly. In their absence a trustee may ask the beneficiaries for authority to extract remuneration from the trust fund; he will be wise to take such authority in the form of a deed, with an indemnity against the consequences of acting upon the authority. It will only be safe to take such an authority from beneficiaries of full capacity with absolute interests in the trust fund. In some cases (e.g. where the beneficiary is either youthful or elderly) it will be wise to require a beneficiary to take separate advice before executing the deed.

9.36 REMUNERATION AUTHORISED BY THE COURT OR BY STATUTE

Otherwise, recourse may be had to the court for authority to charge; the court has an inherent jurisdiction to provide this – *Re Duke of Norfolk's Settlement* (1982):

> In this case a trust of land had been made in 1958; a trust corporation was appointed trustee and was authorised to charge its 1958 scale of fees. The trustee asked the court to authorise payment for work it had done in connection with the redevelopment of the land and to authorise it to take a higher scale of fees in the future. The Court of Appeal held that it had the inherent jurisdiction both to authorise remuneration initially and to increase remuneration already authorised. In deciding such applications as this, the crucial question was what would be the best course to take in the interests of the beneficiaries? It was of great importance to the beneficiaries that a trust should be well administered and this might make it desirable for the court to exercise its jurisdiction in favour of a trustee.

As we have seen in 9.10, s. 42 TA permits the court when appointing a corporation to authorise charges for its services.

An unscrupulous trustee might seek to mitigate his lack of remuneration by delegating the work of the trust, so far as this is possible. The statutory power to delegate is wide and authorises a trustee to pay for the services of an agent – see *ante* 5.45. But this is not a proper course to take in such circumstances, bearing in mind the primary rule that a trustee is expected to act personally. The question of remuneration is one which should be considered by the trustee *before* appointment, not after. If lack of it is a stumbling-block – as it certainly will be for a professional trustee or a trust corporation – then the appointment should be turned down.

Some trustees have statutory authority to charge fees for their work; the Public Trustee is in this happy position, as are custodian trustees (see 12.1, 12.4 *post*).The Law Reform Committee has come down against the idea of a similar statutory authority for all professional trustees to take their fees out of their trust funds.

All trustees have authority to reimburse themselves for expenses incurred 'in or about the execution of the trusts or powers' for which they are responsible: s. 30(2) TA.

9.37 INDIRECT PROFIT-TAKING

What of indirect profit-taking? The early case of *Keech* v *Sandford* (1726) illustrates the application of the rule:

> A trustee was holding a lease in trust for an infant. Renewal for the benefit of the infant was refused. The trustee then got the lease renewed for himself. The court decided that he held the lease as constructive trustee for the infant. The lease

which he had got arose out of his fiduciary status – he could not obtain a personal benefit from this situation, however proper his behaviour might have been; as the Lord Chancellor observed, the trustee was the one person of all mankind who might *not* have the lease in these circumstances.

Another problematical situation arises when trustees are also directors of companies as a result of their holding office as trustees; do any fees which they receive on account of their directorships belong to the trust?

> In *Re Francis* (1905) holders of shares in a company were entitled to appoint themselves directors. Such shares were held by trustees on behalf of a trust; when they procured their appointment as directors, the court held that they must account to the trust for the fees they received.

But the trust instrument may authorise such directors to retain fees received for their services; if it is possible that this kind of situation may occur, a settlor will wish to consider whether an appropriate clause to this effect should be inserted. The rule does not apply where the trustees were directors before becoming trustees.

The court may authorise a trustee to retain his director's remuneration:

> In *Re Keeler* (1981), although the trust instrument authorised the trustees to act as directors of a family company and to charge for professional services, it did not authorise them to keep directors' fees. Goulding J. said that a trustee who was a director was required to use the effort and skill which a prudent man of business would use in dealing with his own investments. The trustees who were actively engaged in running the company would be allowed to keep a proportion of the directors' fees they received over and above what was deemed to be earned as a result of their general duty as trustees.

As has been mentioned, the rule against profiting from a trust applies also to others acting in a fiduciary capacity:

> In *Boardman* v *Phipps* (1967) the profit in question was made, not by a trustee, but by the trust solicitor. The trust held 8,000 shares out of 30,000 in a private company. One of the trustees who was an accountant felt that the company was badly managed and that there was scope for increasing the value of the shares. The trustees had no power to acquire the rest of the shares for the trust (although they could have applied to the court for authority to do this). However, the trust solicitor, Boardman, and a beneficiary set out, successfully, to acquire the non-trust shares and did so. They presided over a reorganisation of the company, as a result of which the value of all the shares was greatly increased. Subsequently another beneficiary formed the view that the profits made by Boardman and his partner in the affair belonged to the trust. The House of Lords, by a bare majority, agreed with him. Although it was accepted that Boardman had acted in good faith throughout, he must account for the profits he had made. His connection with the trust meant that he was a fiduciary; he was, however, entitled to generous payment for the work and skill used in the reorganisation of the company. The 'inflexible' rule was applied in what must be thought of as marginal circumstances.

Another example of the application of the rule which underlines the fact that its limits are difficult to define is to be found in *Reading* v *Attorney-General* (1951):

> A staff-sergeant in the British Army was bribed to allow contraband goods to pass safely through the streets of Cairo. About £20,000 was taken from the sergeant as money obtained in this way and he petitioned the court for it to be returned. His argument was that even if the money had been improperly earned, the British Government had no right to it. The House of Lords, in finding against the NCO, said that he was in a fiduciary relationship with the Crown and must therefore account for profits improperly made as a result of that.

Of this case, it has been remarked that the status of a fiduciary is easily acquired, if it is necessary for it to exist in order that the right result may be arrived at.

9.38   PURCHASE OF TRUST PROPERTY BY TRUSTEES

The rule is that a purchase of trust property by a trustee is not forbidden but is always[10] liable to be set aside at the request of a beneficiary and may be regarded as an offspring of the rule that a trustee must never place himself in a position in which his own personal interest and his duty as a trustee are in opposition – see *ante* 9.34. Clearly, it is impossible to avoid such a conflict of interest in a case where a trustee seeks to buy a trust asset from himself. However fair and above-board the transaction may appear to be, there must always be a suspicion that justice has not been done, and any beneficiary has an absolute right to apply to have the sale set aside within a reasonable time after the facts have been discovered. If such a transaction is set aside, the trustee is generally entitled to have the purchase price refunded, with interest. Because of the risk involved, a purchaser *from* a trustee who has bought trust property is bound to be extremely cautious, if on notice of the previous transaction (as he is almost bound to be if buying unregistered land); indeed, since the trustee has only a voidable title in these circumstances it may be almost impossible for him to convey it. It is possible, of course, for the beneficiaries to authorise a transaction of this kind (provided they are all ascertained and *sui juris*) but a purchaser from a trustee may not be prepared to accept this as a safeguard. The only completely safe solution is for the trustee to apply to the court for authority to make the purchase.[11] Personal Representatives can come up against the self-dealing rule just as much as trustees – see *ante* 5.3.

9.39   DUTY TO BE EVEN-HANDED

A trustee should hold the scales evenly between beneficiaries, not favouring one against another, or one class of beneficiaries against another class. This means that a trustee is required, in some situations, to perform an almost impossible balancing act. Beneficiaries with interest in income will want the trustee to maximise the dividend receipts from investments. Beneficiaries with capital interests will want maximum capital appreciation. Somehow, the trustee must steer a course between these two extremes. This is not always easy to do, and beneficiaries tend to believe that the course taken has not been in their favour. This was one aspect of *Nestle* v *National Westminster Bank* (1992) (see *post* 11.10):

> The plaintiff complained that the trustee's investment policy had favoured the life tenants at her expense (she was the remainderman). In giving judgment in the High Court in favour of the trustee, Hoffman J. said that he did not care too much for the traditional image of a trustee holding the scales equally between life tenant and remainderman - it was too mechanistic. He thought that it would be better to say that a trustee must act fairly in making investment decisions as between different classes.

The Law Reform Committee has, in fact, recommended that the rules of equitable apportionment which we discussed *ante* 6.44 should be replaced with a new statutory duty to hold a fair balance between income and capital beneficiaries.

9.40 EVEN-HANDEDNESS AS DISTINCT FROM EQUALITY

The duty to be even-handed is not confined to investment; it may apply throughout the administration of a trust or estate. In *Lloyds Bank* v *Duker* (1987):

> There was a dispute about the disposition of a holding of 999 shares (out of 1,000) owned by a testator in a private company. The residuary estate was divisible between the widow (who took over one-half) and five other beneficiaries. The widow took the view that she was entitled to have transferred to her a proportionate share of the private company shares - 574 out of the 1,000 issued. The other beneficiaries objected to this on the grounds that a majority holding, which was what the widow would get as a result, was worth a great deal more per share than the minority holdings which were all that they would be entitled to on a proportionate distribution. The court took the view that a distribution of the kind called for by the widow would not be fair, in the circumstances, and ordered that the entire holding should be sold on the open market, the widow having the right to be a buyer at such a sale. The proceeds would, of course, be distributed in accordance with the size of the residuary interests.

Normally, an indefeasible interest entitles the beneficiary concerned to the satisfaction of his interest in specie but, as the above case indicates, only if it can be achieved without the mutilation of the interests of others.

10 Powers of trustees

10.1 SIMILARITIES WITH POWERS OF PRs

Sections 68(17) and (19) and 69 TA ensure that wherever the context of the Act and the terms of the trust instrument permit, any powers conferred upon trustees apply also to PRs. Examples are to be found *ante* in 3.21 (insurance), 3.25 (notices for claims), 5.4 (power to compromise) and 5.45 (use of agents), as well as statutory powers of maintenance, advancement and investment. The strongest common feature limiting the powers of both is the rule against conflict of duty and interest, including the ban on unauthorised profits.

10.2 DIFFERENCES FROM POWERS OF PRs

As we have already seen – *ante* 6.35 (power of appropriation) – while PRs may make free use of the statutory powers accorded to trustees, the AEA is exclusively the province of the PRs, a typical example being their power of assenting – see *ante* 6.46. Personal Representatives have sweeping statutory powers of selling and mortgaging and leasing not possessed by trustees, unless given to them via the LPA when they are acting as trustees for sale of land. The differences do not end with their powers – see *ante* 7.6.

Where there is more than one PR or trustee, there is a striking difference to be observed between the two functions. Except in the case of the transfer of registered stocks and shares and a conveyance (in the broadest sense of the term – s. 2(2) and 3(1) AEA) of landed property, the authority of PRs is joint and *several* – one PR out of two or more may exercise the power of sale and bind his fellow PRs. Joint trustees must, on the other hand, act jointly – one cannot bind all, unless it is expressly authorised in the trust instrument.

The Law Reform Committee has recommended (October 1982) that PRs should be placed under a duty to act unanimously (subject to any contrary provision in the will, where this is relevant) when disposing of property from the deceased's estate.

10.3 LANDED PROPERTY

So far as settled land is concerned, it will be held either on trust for sale or in accordance with the SLA. In the former case, the trustees in whom the land is vested are under an obligation to sell, but 'a power to postpone sale shall, in the case of every trust for sale of land, be implied unless a contrary intention appears' – s. 25(1) LPA. The provisions of the SLA are looked at more closely in chapter 11; suffice to say here that land which is held under this Act should be vested in the tenant for life, who has a power of sale – s. 38(1) SLA. Trustees for sale of land have all the powers of a tenant for life under the SLA – s. 28(1) LPA. In the case of both land held on trust for sale and under the SLA, there must be at least two individual trustees or a trust corporation to provide a valid receipt to a purchaser – s. 27(2) LPA and s. 94(1) SLA respectively. These restrictions have no application (a) to a sole PR or (b) to a land transaction where no capital money is involved.

10.4 PURE PERSONALTY

Where personal property is held on trust for sale, (a) there is no requirement, as there is for land, that there should be at least two individual trustees to give a valid receipt and (b) there is no power to postpone sale in the absence of express provision. If there is neither a trust to sell nor a power of sale, a power to sell will be implied. Alternatively, s. 1(1) TIA will apply; this empowers trustees to invest property in their hands, whether in a state of investment or not, in any of the investments authorised by the Act and, by implication, authorises them to carry out sales for this purpose.

10.5 SELLING BY AUCTION OR PRIVATE TREATY

Section 12(1) TA gives trustees wide scope for carrying out sales, including the power to sell either by auction or by private contract, as the trustees think fit. Whatever method is used, there is one overriding duty – to obtain the best price possible. Failure to observe this rule may result in the beneficiaries applying to the court for an injunction to prevent the sale taking place. In *Buttle* v *Saunders* (1950):

> The trustees had agreed to sell a freehold reversion at a certain price. A beneficiary then offered more for the property. The trustees declined to accept this higher offer, believing that they were bound morally to stick to the agreement made in the first place. The court said that the overriding duty to get the best price for the beneficiaries prevailed over the moral obligation.

As *Snell* observes, this is an indication that there is a fiduciary duty to 'gazump'. There may be occasions where a lower price should be accepted, perhaps on the principle of a bird in the hand being the more attractive proposition. The duty to get the best price on sale is echoed by a corresponding duty to invest for the greatest financial benefit – *Cowan* v *Scargill* (1985), discussed *post* 11.11.

10.6 POWERS OF DELEGATION

Generally speaking, a trustee is expected both to take decisions about the trust and to administer it himself; it has been pointed out already (*ante* 9.19) that, where there are several trustees, each one must be active in the trust's affairs. There are now, however, considerable opportunities for delegation of day-to-day work. We have already looked at s. 23(1) TA (*ante* 5.45 and 9.24) giving authority for the appointment and payment of agents generally; also s. 23(2) facilitating the appointment of agents to take care of overseas assets. Section 23(2), unlike s. 23(1), allows the delegation of discretions as well as ministerial powers. Section 23(3) specifically authorises trustees to appoint a solicitor to receive money on behalf of the trust (but they are warned not to leave it in his hands for long). There may, of course, also be an express power of delegation in the trust instrument.

Note that s. 23 does not require trustees and PRs who make use of its provisions to demonstrate a *need* to delegate; in this connection the Law Reform Committee have recommended that the reference in s. 23(1) to payment of an agent should be expunged and that a new provision should be inserted entitling a trustee to be reimbursed for the costs of delegation *reasonably incurred*, 'taking into account the trustee's knowledge, qualifications and experience and the level of remuneration received by him'.

10.7 DELEGATING THE DECISION-MAKING POWER

Section 23(1) only authorises the delegation of work arising out of decisions taken by the trustees – it does *not* authorise delegation of the decision-making process itself. Trustees who leave decisions to agents (in the absence of express authority in the trust instrument to do so) are in breach of trust and will be liable for any loss arising out of the breach. Trustees who leave decisions to beneficiaries are equally at fault, although there can be no objection – indeed, it is a practice to be encouraged – to a problem being discussed between trustees and beneficiaries, provided it is made clear that the decision has to be taken by the former and that this is their responsibility alone. Reference has, however, been made (see *ante* 9.15) to the statutory authority for delegation by a trustee of all or any of his trusts, powers and discretions by means of a power of attorney for a period of not more than 12 months. This authority would, for instance, enable a trustee to delegate his power of investment to, say, a stockbroker or merchant bank for not more than a year at a time, bearing in mind the important fact that he will remain liable for the investment decisions taken by his attorney during this period.

10.8 LIMITATIONS ON A TRUSTEE'S STATUTORY INDEMNITY

While s. 23(2) provides a very strongly worded power of delegation where overseas assets are concerned, the indemnity is a thin one – 'shall not, by reason *only* of their having made such *appointment*, be responsible for any loss arising thereby', which suggests that the trustee's standard of supervision might well be higher because of the remoteness of the foreign agent, even to the extent of cross-checking progress with a second source of information in the foreign territory. The indemnity in s. 23(3) is particularly weak because of the awful warning about leaving money in the hands of the agent for any length of time.

But s. 23(1) is the sphere where the trustee or PR is likely to run into the most trouble; it absolves them from responsibility for the default of an agent appointed in accordance with its provisions, provided he was employed in good faith. We have seen (*ante* 5,46) how Maugham J. in *Re Vickery* (1931) linked the standard of care required of the trustee with the expression 'through his own wilful default' in s. 30(1), construing the latter phrase by reference to *Re City Equitable Fire Insurance Co* (1925), not a trust case, where it was defined as either an intention to commit a breach of duty or recklessly proceeding without caring, whether an act is a breach of duty or not; this is a far cry from Equity's pre-1926 notion that a trustee's duty required not only careful selection of the agent but careful monitoring of his subsequent performance. To exempt a trustee from liability except in cases where he actually intends to commit a breach of a duty or does not care one way or the other would seem to be excessively generous. The Law Reform Committee interpret s. 30(1) as meaning that a trustee should only be liable for the acts of some other person where the trustee has 'connived' at such acts (whereas, under s. 23(1), a trustee is vicariously liable for the acts of an agent not employed 'in good faith'). It would be better, surely, if the former equitable meaning of 'wilful default', i.e. failure to maintain an acceptable standard of care, were applied in cases arising under s. 30(1).

Re Lucking (1968) may be cited as an example of delegation by one trustee to another, where liability for a loss resulting from failure by the trustee to supervise the affairs of a private family company was confined to that trustee:

> The trust was of a majority holding of shares in the company. There were two trustees, Mr Lucking (who was a director and substantial minority shareholder) and another. Mr Lucking was instrumental in the appointment of an old friend of his to be managing director who misappropriated funds, so indirectly causing a loss to the trust fund. Mr Lucking was held liable for the loss, applying the standard of the ordinary prudent man of business. The other trustee was not liable; his responsibility was not personal and he was entitled to rely on Mr Lucking to supervise the company's affairs.

Section 30(1) does not deal only with a trustee's responsibility for agents; it also clears a trustee (in the absence of wilful default) from responsibility for the acts of his co-trustee. Neither *Lucking* nor *Bartlett* v *Barclays Bank Trust Co Ltd* (1980) – see *ante* 5.30 – are concerned with the appointment of agents, but they both illustrate the nature of the difficulties that can arise if trustees fail to go through a proper process of delegation and subsequent supervision.

The fact that trustees are given some protection by the *Vickery* view of s. 23(1) and 30(1) does not mean that they should carry out their duties in this respect with anything less than the required standards of diligence and care. Not only should they take care only to appoint agents in whom they have good reason to be confident, they should also exercise continuous and intelligent control over their activities. In particular, they should not leave funds in agents' hands for longer than is reasonable and they should not hesitate to discharge agents who prove unsatisfactory in practice. Again, one has to remember that a higher standard of care is expected of professional trustees than of those of the lay variety.

The Law Reform Committee has recommended that s. 23(1) should be amended so that a trustee should only escape responsibility for the default of his agent where:

(a) it was reasonable for him to employ the agent;
(b) he has taken reasonable steps to ensure that the agent is competent;
(c) he has taken reasonable steps to ensure that the agent's work has been done competently.

It would seem sensible for trustees to adopt these recommendations forthwith as a code of conduct in respect of their employment of agents.

10.9 OTHER POWERS OF DELEGATION

Reference has already been made to the power given to the donee of an Enduring Power of Attorney to execute the powers and discretions vested in the donee as trustee: see *ante* 6.57.

As mentioned *ante* 5.47, a further and useful power to delegate is contained in s. 29(1) LPA; this authorises trustees for sale of land to revocably delegate, in writing, their powers of management to any adult beneficiary entitled for the time being to the net rents and profits of the land. Having exercised this power, the trustees are not responsible for the acts or defaults of the person to whom they have delegated the management. Such a person must, however, act as a trustee; it seems, therefore, that the same considerations of character and ability must arise where delegation of this type is envisaged as where the appointment of a new trustee is being reviewed.

10.10 EXPRESS POWERS OF DELEGATION

Finally, on the subject of delegation, it may be noted here that current practice is for settlors to give trustees wider powers of delegation than are available to them under the statutory rules already outlined; this is particularly the case in large funds with respect to the making of investment decisions, as illustrated in *Steel* v *Wellcome Custodian Trustees Ltd* (1988):

The Wellcome Trust is a group of charities, mainly involved in medical research. The trust had been almost entirely invested in Wellcome Foundation Ltd. The total value of the trust was about £3 billion. The trustees asked the court to give them beneficial owner powers of investment and also to authorise them to delegate the power of making investments to expert advisers. The trustees were to be liable for loss resulting from the delegation only if they failed to take reasonable care in choosing the agents or in fixing or enforcing the terms of their engagement. They would also be liable if they failed to make the agents take remedial action in respect of breaches of the agreement of which they, the trustees, had notice (or should have had notice as reasonably prudent men of business). Otherwise, the trustees were free of liability for the actions of their investment advisers. As Hoffman J. remarked 'In practice it is inevitable that the day-to-day investment decisions concerning a fund of this size would have to be delegated to advisers. ' He went on to say that although the courts have always been reluctant to relieve paid trustees (which the trustees were in this case) from liability for breach of trust, he did not think that it would be fair, in a case where practical necessity required delegation, to insist that the trustees should be insurers of the acts of their investment advisers.

10.11 POWERS OF MAINTENANCE AND ADVANCEMENT

These two extremely important discretionary adjuncts of trust administration may be distinguished as follows: *maintenance* is primarily concerned with the defraying of day-to-day expenses out of income (but see *post* 10.20 for the court's power to order provision to be made for an infant out of either income or capital). *Advancement* is, in the main, the use of trust capital for a permanent, non-repetitive purpose; the concept has already been discussed in connection with advancement by way of portion (*ante* 6.41) and intestacy (*ante* 4.11). The statutory power of advancement discussed below is, however, extremely broad in scope – permissive might be the modern word – and there is, in practice, little to restrain trustees from exercising it as they think fit.

Fully discretionary trusts, the trustees of which have power at will to determine the destination of either income or capital or both, have been discussed *ante* 8.9 *et seq.* and 9.27 *et seq.* The remainder of this chapter is concerned with the exercise of powers of maintenance and advancement in trusts where the settlor has dictated the extent and size of the beneficiaries' interests though he may have done this on fairly broad lines, giving a life tenant a power of appointment or, in the case of a contingent accumulation settlement, giving the trustees power to suspend the vesting of the capital.

10.12 READ THE TRUST INSTRUMENT FIRST

In the case of both maintenance and advancement, the statutory powers in ss. 31 and 32 TA are extremely significant; they are probably consulted by trustees more often than any other statutory provision. Neither section applies to instruments coming into operation before 1 January 1926, and neither applies where the trust instrument expresses an intention to the contrary – s. 69(2) TA. It is, therefore, of great importance to inspect the trust instrument *before* applying the statutory powers. A contrary intention need not be spelt out in so many words – it may be inferred, as in *Re McGeorge* (1963):

> A testator devised certain land to his daughter and declared that the 'devise . . . shall not take effect until after the death of my wife should she survive me'. In his judgment, Cross J. pointed out that, by deferring enjoyment of the devise until after the widow's death, the testator had expressed the intention that the daughter should not have the intermediate income. Section 31 therefore, did not apply.

In *Re Erskine's Settlement Trusts* (1971) the rather paradoxical result was that an *invalid* direction to accumulate was held to be a sufficient 'contrary intention' to exclude s. 31.

10.13 THE STATUTORY POWER TO MAINTAIN

Section 31(1) TA reads:

> Where any property is held by trustees in trust for any person for any interest whatsoever, whether vested or contingent, then, subject to any prior interests or charges affecting that property–
> (i)   during the infancy of any such person, if his interest so long continues, the trustees may, at their sole discretion, pay to his parent or guardian, if any, or otherwise apply for or towards his maintenance, education or benefit, the whole or such part, if any, of the income of that property as may, in all the circumstances, be reasonable whether or not there is–
> (a)   any other fund applicable to the same purpose; or
> (b)   any person bound by law to provide for his maintenance or education; and
> (ii)   if such person on attaining the age of eighteen years has not a vested interest in such income, the trustees shall thenceforth pay the income of that property and of any accretion thereto under subsection (2) of this section to him, until he either attains a vested interest therein or dies, or until failure of his interest;
> Provided that, in deciding whether the whole or any part of the income of the property is during a minority to be paid or applied for the purposes aforesaid, the trustees shall have regard to the age of the infant and his requirements and generally to the circumstances of the case, and in particular to what other income, if any, is applicable for the same purposes; and where trustees have notice that the income of more than one fund is applicable for those purposes, then, so far as practicable, unless the entire income of the funds is paid or applied as aforesaid or the court otherwise directs, a proportionate part only of the income of each fund shall be so paid or applied.

Trust instruments quite frequently amend the above by omitting the words 'may, in all the circumstances, be reasonable' and replacing them with 'the trustees may think fit' and by omitting the whole of the proviso.

It should be borne in mind that 'infancy' now ends when a person reaches 18, as indicated in the amended version of s. 31(1) shown above. Where, however, the trust instrument was signed before 1 January 1970, s. 31 must be read as if it contained the age of 21 and for this purpose, in the case of a will and codicil, it is the date of the will that counts, not that of the updating codicil; if the age of 21 has to be applied because of this rule, the trustees are allowed to pay the income direct to the beneficiary between the ages of 18 and 21 – FLRA Sch. 3, paras. 1(2), 5(1) and 5(2).

It is only the statutory age that may be affected by the date of the trust instrument. Where the trust instrument (no matter what its date) refers expressly to a relevant age, such as 21, it is not affected by the statutory change in the age of majority. Generally, the receipt of a parent or guardian (or of a married infant – s. 21 LPA) will be a good discharge to the trustees, when applying income under s. 31(1).

10.14   THE TRUST TO ACCUMULATE IN S. 31

Section 31(2) goes on to provide that, during the infancy of a beneficiary, if his interest so long continues, the trustees shall (it is a trust, not a power) accumulate income not applied for maintenance purposes. On reaching the age of 18 (or marrying under that age) the beneficiary may become absolutely entitled to accumulations so made if either (a) his interest in the income during infancy was vested or (b) he has become absolutely entitled to the property from which the income was produced. In all other cases the trustees are to hold the accumulations as an accretion to the capital of the property from which they arose. During infancy, accumulations can be applied as though they were income of the current year.

Section 31 applies to a contingent interest only if it carries the intermediate income – s. 31(3). Reference has already been made to the need to inspect the trust instrument in order to find out whether it expresses a 'contrary intention', and reference is also necessary when considering whether a gift carries the intermediate income. Until a trustee is satisfied that both these hurdles can be jumped, exercise of the statutory power should be deferred. The law relating to the intermediate income of contingent gifts is not exactly straightforward and it will, in many cases, be prudent to take advice.

10.15   GIFTS THAT CARRY THE INTERMEDIATE INCOME

As maintenance may be allowed only out of income which is carried by the gift, it is vital to know when this is the case and when it is not. In the first place, s. 31(3), which prohibits the use of income where the gift does *not* carry it, applies only to contingent gifts; so, a vested gift (or a vested gift subject to divestment) will always carry the income it produces, subject, of

261

course, to any prior interest in the property and subject also to any contrary intention expressed by the settlor, as where enjoyment of the gift is expressly deferred (*Re Geering* (1964)).

Gifts with an age contingency attached can sometimes turn out to be vested subject to divesting, owing to the operation of the rule in *Phipps* v *Ackers* (1842). This rule, which applies indiscriminately to real and personal property, and to settlements as well as wills, is invoked if a gift governed by an age contingency is followed by an *express* gift over (the natural process of falling into residue on failure of the gift will not suffice) to another person, if that age is not attained. The rule is based upon the principle that the specific gift over sufficiently indicates that the testator or settlor intended the first beneficiary to have everything except the specific interest given to the succeeding beneficiary, in other words, the immediate interest subject only to the possibility of being divested of it by dying under the specified age.

In *Brotherton* v *IRC* (1978) by a settlement made in 1942 one moiety of the trust fund was directed to go to the settlor's son if and when he should attain 30, but if he should die under that age, then upon the trusts of the other moiety. The other moiety was to be held on similar trusts for the settlor's daughter. So long as the son or the daughter should be under 22, income was to be accumulated, and between the ages of 22 and 25 they were to be deprived of their right to call for payment of the income under s. 31(1)(ii). The son and daughter were assessed to surtax on the income arising in their respective 22nd years, on the footing that, in so far as the settlement directed accumulation beyond their 21st birthdays, it was void under s. 164 LPA. The Court of Appeal held that the children had vested interests subject to divesting under the rule in *Phipps* v *Ackers*, which meant that the undisposed of income belonged to them instead of reverting to the settlor. The court rejected the view that the directions in the settlement deed regarding the destination of income under the age of 25 affected the gift of capital so as to make it contingent.

It has to be said that the rules for establishing whether or not income is carried in the case of contingent gifts are not very coherent; some are found in case law, some in statute law. A single comprehensive code would be a great advantage. The statutory rules for gifts by will are found in s. 175 LPA; income is carried in the following situations:

(a)   A contingent or future *specific* devise or bequest of any property, real or personal (wider than the rule before 1926); included are deferred specific devises and deferred specific bequests, e.g. a gift to X after the death of Y (Y not being a life tenant).

(b)   A contingent *residuary* devise of freehold land (it did not do so before 1926); as to contingent residuary bequests, see below.

(c)   A *specific* or *residuary* devise of freehold land to trustees upon trust for persons whose interest are contingent or executory (i.e., to arise in the future) – again this is wider than the pre-1926 rule. This should include a deferred residuary devise, even if no trustees are mentioned, because obviously the gift will have to be held in trust.

In all these cases the income is carried from the date of the testator's death, *unless it is otherwise expressly disposed of*. The omissions from this list are

(a) contingent residuary gifts of personalty or of blended realty and personalty, but these types of gift have always carried the intermediate income as a general rule, (b) contingent general legacies (including pecuniary legacies), and (c) deferred general legacies (including pecuniary legacies):

(a)   Exceptionally a residuary gift of personalty will not carry the intermediate income if enjoyment of the gift is deferred, no matter whether the gift is vested, vested subject to divesting, or contingent; for example, a gift to X after the death of Y (or to X after the death of Y, if X attains 25), Y being an annuitant.
(b)   The intermediate income is carried by contingent *testamentary* general legacies where there is either:
    (i)   A contingent general legacy to an infant child of the testator (or to an infant to whom he stood in *loco parentis*) where no other fund is designated for the infant's maintenance and where the contingency concerns the attainment of majority or earlier marriage; or
    (ii)   A contingent general legacy to an infant (not necessarily a child of the testator) where the will shows an intention that the income should be used for his maintenance or education (*Re Selby-Walker* (1949) – a future pecuniary legacy which carried the intermediate income because the trustees had been given a discretionary power to apply the legacy for the legatee's education); or
    (iii)   A contingent general legacy where the will directs it to be set aside for the benefit of the legatee (*Re Medlock* (1886)).
(c)   The typical example of a deferred general legacy is a pecuniary legacy payable on the death of a life tenant. Usually it will be vested or will have vested in the life tenant's lifetime and if so, will carry interest from the moment of the life tenant's death. Even if it is still subject to an age or other personal condition, one would expect the intermediate income to be carried *sed quaere*.

Contingent pecuniary legacies within category (b) above are a particular trap for trust administrators and the basic rule about such legacies is that, apart from the exceptions noted, they do *not* carry the intermediate income unless the testator directs that they shall – he can make his own rules about this. All the rules set out above relate to testamentary gifts; gifts contained in *inter vivos* settlements will carry the intermediate income unless there are either prior interests which take precedence or an expression of contrary intention by the settlor.

Having determined that a gift carries the intermediate income, there may be a separate question of deciding the date from which the interest on the vested or contingent legacy starts to run – see *ante* 6.22 and 6.24 and the notes thereto.

10.16   THE INTERPRETATION OF S. 31(2)

Where there is a class gift to infants, from the income of which maintenance may be allowed, trustees should treat each presumptive share as a separate entity for this purpose. So, in a gift to the infant children of X, three in number, annual income £900, maintenance may be allowed in each case up to a limit of £300. Any of the income of a presumptive share which is not used for maintenance must be accumulated in the name of the infant and may be used in later years for his maintenance – s. 31(2). Accumulations which remain unused when the infant reaches 18 (or marries under that age) become payable to the beneficiary if either he had a vested interest during his infancy or if he becomes entitled at 18 (or upon earlier marriage) to the property from which the accumulations arose. In all other cases unused accumulations of income are added to the capital of the gift and devolve as capital. So, if, for instance, a beneficiary is given an interest in property which is to vest in him absolutely at 25, he becomes entitled at 25 not only to the original gift but also to the accumulated income added to the capital whilst he was an infant. If he fails to reach the age of 25, the original gift plus accumulations go to the alternative donee. One curious feature of this aspect of the section is that a beneficiary who is entitled to a vested interest in income only – i.e. has a vested life interest – can have income used for his maintenance during his infancy but, if he should die before 18 (not having married), any accumulations made during his infancy do not belong to his estate but go with the capital to the next person entitled. In this respect, the statutory rule turns a vested interest into a contingent one (*Stanley* v *IRC* (1944)), with the result that it becomes a contingent accumulation settlement subject to the additional 10% rate of IT and the 35% rate of CGT.

> In *Stanley* v *IRC* (1944), where the infant beneficiary had a vested life interest, the Court of Appeal held that the beneficiary was, in fact, for all practical purposes in precisely the same position under s. 31(2)(ii) as if his interest in the income unapplied for maintenance were contingent. The infant did not during infancy enjoy the surplus income. It was not his in any real sense. The title to it was held in suspense to await the event, and if he died during infancy his interest in it was destroyed. The effect of the section was to engraft on the vested interest originally conferred on the infant a qualifying trust of a special nature which gave him a title to the *income* of the accumulations if and only if he reached his majority or married earlier, the accumulations themselves reaching him as capital. Consequently, the accumulated income never became part of the infant life tenant's income for tax purposes, neither when it arose nor when he became entitled to the income of the accumulations and the main fund on attaining majority or earlier marriage.
>
> Thus, the life tenant gets the accumulations on majority or earlier marriage as capital under s. 31(2)(i)(a) but if he dies beforehand, the accumulations will be added to capital under s. 31(2)(ii) and will not go to his estate.
>
> Annuities under trusts are not often met with these days but it is worth mentioning that if the infant is entitled, not to a life interest in a fluctuating fund, but to a vested annuity, the annuity accumulations are bound to go to his estate under s. 31(4).

The statutory inversion just discussed is subject to a contrary intention; this is illustrated by *Re Delamere* (1984):

> There was a revocable appointment of income in favour of six infants 'in equal shares absolutely'. The question arose whether in the event of an appointee's death under 18 his share of accumulated income belonged to his estate or accrued over to the other shares. The Court of Appeal held that the use of the word 'absolutely' was inconsistent with s. 31(2) and that the accumulations would belong to the minor's estate; so he had had a vested and indefeasible interest in the income until such time as the trustees might revoke the appointment. It followed that the infants had acquired interests in possession for IHT purposes – see *ante* 8.8.

Generally, a trust to accumulate income (either express or imported under s. 31(2)) not used for maintenance purposes will prevent an infant from having an interest in possession, normally a beneficial outcome in view of the privileged status for most trusts of this kind, so far as IHT is concerned (see *ante* 8.11 and 8.12), but there must be weighed against this a higher rate of CGT (see *ante* 8.14) and additional income tax (see *post* 10.19).

10.17 CONSCIENTIOUS EXERCISE OF DISCRETION

It is important to have constantly in mind that income for maintenance is provided at the *discretion* of the trustees unless, exceptionally, the settlor directs them to provide it. They should not, therefore, allow themselves to lapse into a routine whereby income is paid over automatically.

> In *Wilson* v *Turner* (1883) the trustees had power to apply the whole or part of a child's income for or towards his maintenance or education, either directly or by payment to the child's parent or guardian and without seeing to its application or requiring an account. What they did was to pay the whole of the income to the child's father, although they had no request from him for this to be done and they had no evidence that the income was required for the child's maintenance. It was clear that the trustees had made no attempt to assess the situation and had, in fact, not exercised the discretion given to them on the subject of allowing maintenance. The father's estate was ordered to refund the income to the beneficiary.

Having made up their minds, on the basis of proper evidence, to allow maintenance, trustees should review their decision at intervals of not more than one year. In so doing, they should check whether the circumstances of the child and its parents remain the same. Changes in financial status and requirements will need a rethinking of the original decision. Whether maintaining or accumulating, they must, in any event, make a note to consider the position a month or two before the beneficiary attains his majority (see *ante* 10.13) and even where an express power is being used, some change in the previous arrangement may well be required.

Section 31 is quite helpful to trustees about the factors they should take into account in exercising their discretion to allow maintenance. In fact, the discretion extends also to education and 'benefit' – and, as will be seen when discussing advancement, this last word has a very wide meaning in this context. The power may be exercised, notwithstanding the existence of other sources of finance, although such other sources should not be disregarded. In particular, if there is more than one trust fund available for maintenance, so far as is practicable, a proportionate part of the income of each fund should be used. Trustees are directed to have regard to the age of the infant, his requirements and the circumstances generally. There is the overall admonition that the trustees should do what is reasonable.

One way in which a trustee can draw a helpful analogy in cases concerning maintenance is to consider himself to be somewhat in the position of a rich and reasonably generous uncle of the infant beneficiary. Rich but, it should be added, of a prudent disposition and not given to scattering largess unconcernedly. Given the required knowledge of the infant's parents and general circumstances, would this rich, affectionate but prudent uncle think it desirable to use part or all of the income for the child's maintenance, education or benefit – or might he not rather think that the infant would be better served by accumulation of the income for use later on?

It is, unfortunately, inevitable that an infant's parents must be asked some rather personal questions if trustees are to exercise their discretion properly; moreover, such questions must be repeated at intervals, since, as has already been pointed out, it is not reasonable for trustees to exercise their discretion and not subsequently to review it. Trustees cannot, however much they may be tempted to do so, overlook the fact that the primary responsibility for maintaining a child belongs to its parents. Establishing that it is reasonable for a trust fund to share this responsibility often requires a considerable amount of tact and diplomacy.

10.18 STATUTORY CONVERSION OF A CONTINGENT INTEREST INTO A VESTED ONE

We have seen in 10.16 how s. 31 is capable, albeit infrequently, of converting a vested interest into a contingent one. Of more frequent occurrence is the reversal of this process. Under s. 31(1)(ii), in the absence of a contrary intention expressed in the trust instrument, if by the time the infant has reached his majority (earlier marriage does not count for this purpose) he has not become indefeasibly entitled to the income, the trustee *must* start to pay the income to him in his own right without regard to outstanding contingencies such as the need to reach a higher age than majority, or the possible defeat of his interest by the exercise of a power of appointment or revocation. Payment of the income (which includes the income of the accumulated income fund as well as that of the main fund) will continue until either the contingency is satisfied or the power is no longer exercisable, or the beneficiary's prior death. The effect of this direction to the trustee is to convert the beneficial interest into an interest in possession for IHT purposes.

In *Swales* v *IRC* (1984) an appointment was made by trustees of capital, not to a minor, but to an adult. It was implicit in the exercise of the power of appointment that the appointee could not attain a vested interest until her child had attained 21, which he did in 1976, six years after the appointment had been made. The Revenue therefore claimed CTT (the forerunner of IHT but having the same rules) on the basis that a settlement without an interest in possession had terminated with the vesting of the fund in the appointee absolutely. It was held that although the appointee had had only a contingent interest in capital between 1970 and 1976, the trustees were bound to pay her the income under s. 31(1)(ii) and that she therefore already had an interest in possession before becoming entitled to the capital.

What is to happen to the accumulated income fund itself, if the beneficiary has less than an absolute interest in both capital and income after attaining his majority or marrying earlier? The answer is that the destination of the accumulated income fund must remain in abeyance until that of the main fund has been determined, when they will devolve together.[1] For the exceptional case of the vested life interest, see *ante* 10.16.

In the case of class gifts, where there may be a failure of the interest of existing members and the introduction of new members, it is vital to keep separate track of the shares of capital of individual members and their entitlement to income unapplied for their maintenance. The application of legal apportionment must also be kept in mind – see *Re Joel* (1967) *ante* 5.21.

10.19 TAX CONSIDERATIONS

If the infant has an indefeasibly vested interest in capital as well as income, both the trust income and the trust capital gains and losses are those of the infant himself; and the corpus and accumulated income are part of his estate for IHT purposes. There is complete transparency, and for tax purposes the trustee is in the same position as a nominee.

In all other infancy situations, there is a discretionary trust running which imposes IT on the trustees at the additional rate of 10%: s. 686 ICTA. The exercise of the power of maintenance will convert the trust income into the infant's income for IT purposes, enabling his parents or guardians to obtain repayment, unless the infant's other income is already in the 40% bracket. Thus, if £650 is applied in the tax year, the trustees will issue a tax certificate for a gross amount of £1,000 and if the infant's personal allowance and his other sources of income permit, up to £350 will be recoverable. The trustees will also be assessable for capital gains on the trust assets, again at the rate of 35%, but with a maximum annual exemption of £2,900 (from 1992/93). The IHT position will depend upon whether the trust falls under the discretionary trust regime or is in the privileged category – see *ante* 8.11.

In the case of an *inter vivos* settlement in favour of the settlor's own children, the application of income or capital for the benefit of his children may have dire consequences for the settlor's income tax position – see *ante* 8.5.

If the discretionary trust becomes a fixed interest trust (for example, between the ages of 18 and 25 under s. 31), the IT and CGT rates of the trustees will switch from 35% down to 25%; and in the case of a privileged discretionary trust, there will be no charge to IHT: s. 71(4)(a) IHTA. The alteration in these circumstances of the beneficiary's interest from that of a contingent interest in income and capital to that of a vested interest in the income will not give rise to any CGT charge but later, if the capital vests in him at 25, there will be a deemed disposal under s. 71(1) TCGA, a section which can apply only where a beneficiary becomes indefeasibly entitled to both capital and income. In these circumstances, however, holdover relief in respect of capital gains on non-business assets will *not* be available because the deemed disposal referred to in the previous sentence is not one in respect of which there is an exemption from charge to IHT by reason of s. 71(4) IHTA; therefore s. 260(3) TCGA does not apply*. To ensure that holdover relief will be available in such cases one must avoid a provision which will give the beneficiary a life interest at age 18 (or any other before the age at which he takes the capital), whether under s. 31 TA or otherwise. If this precaution is taken there is, when the entitlement to capital arises, an exemption from any charge to IHT by reason of s. 71(4) IHTA; s. 260(3) TCGA will apply, and holdover relief will be available. But where the trust property consists of business assets as defined by s. 165 TCGA, holdover relief will be available in any event. Generally, the presence or absence of such relief is a matter of some consequence to the trustees as they may be faced at this juncture with having to pay CGT not only on any gain produced by the trust assets during the trust period, but also on any gains in respect of which CGT was held over on creation of the trust.

10.20 MAINTENANCE UNDER COURT ORDER

Under its inherent jurisdiction over trusts, the court has power to order provision to be made for an infant out of the income of property held in trust for him, where neither s. 31 nor an express trust to maintain is

---

*See also 8.12, footnote 6.

available to the trustees. In the very old case of *Barlow* v *Grant* (1684) there is a reference to the use of capital for maintenance, but it must be very doubtful whether this would now be an acceptable proposition. Section 53 TA empowers the court, 'with a view to the application of the capital or income thereof for the maintenance, education or benefit' of an infant beneficially entitled to property, to authorise its sale but this can be done only if the proceeds are to be *applied* for the infant's maintenance, education or benefit; resettling the funds is an application: *Re Meux* (1958); an outright payment to the infant would not be made.

10.21 ADVANCEMENT

One of the principal objects of putting money into trust is to tie it up for a long period of time, during which the beneficiaries are unable to get their hands on it. This state of affairs is seldom wholly satisfactory to the beneficiaries, who adopt all sorts of ingenious devices to try to persuade the trustees to hand over the trust fund before the trust has run its course. One means by which this end may sometimes be quite legitimately achieved (in part, at least) is by an advance of capital under the power of advancement conferred on trustees by s. 32 TA*.

Section 32 reads:

(1) Trustees may at any time or times pay or apply any capital money subject to a trust, for the advancement or benefit, in such manner as they may, in their absolute discretion, think fit, of any person entitled to the capital of the trust property or of any share thereof, whether absolutely or contingently on his attaining any specified age or on the occurrence of any other event, or subject to a gift over on his death under any specified age or on the occurrence of any other event, and whether in possession or in remainder or reversion, and such payment or application may be made notwithstanding that the interest of such person is liable to be defeated by the exercise of a power of appointment or revocation, or to be diminished by the increase of the class to which he belongs:

Provided that—

(a) the money so paid or applied for the advancement or benefit of any person shall not exceed altogether in amount one-half of the presumptive or vested share or interest of that person in the trust property; and

(b) if that person is or becomes absolutely and indefeasibly entitled to a share in the trust property the money paid or applied shall be brought into account as part of such share; and

(c) no such payment or application shall be made so as to prejudice any person entitled to any prior life or other interest, whether vested or contingent, in the money paid or applied unless such person is in existence and of full age and consents in writing to such payment or application.

---

*From an article by the late J Willcock on the statutory power, first published in the *Journal of The Institute of Bankers* in 1956.

(2) This section applies only where the trust property consists of money or securities or of property held upon trust for sale calling in and conversion, and such money or securities, or the proceeds of such calling in and conversion are not by statute or in equity considered as land, or applicable as capital money for the purposes of the Settled Land Act, 1925.

(3) This section does not apply to trusts constituted or created before the commencement of this Act.

It is important to remember that s. 32, in addition to being confined to trusts which began after 1925, is also excluded, unlike s. 31, in cases to which the SLA applies. Where a testator made a will before 1926 but died after 1925, the section applied. It also applies to trusts created by a *general* (but not a special) power exercised after 1925, even if created before 1926. The section can be excluded, like s. 31, by the expression in the trust instrument of a contrary intention – s. 69(2). The following discussion of the exercise of powers of advancement is based upon s. 32 but the all-important principles to be followed when making use of the statutory power are generally applicable to express powers as well. One should add, by way of warning, that any express power of advancement in a trust instrument should be carefully read and construed before being acted upon.

In *Henley* v *Wardell* (1988) the testator, who died in 1981, had by his will, made in 1960, given his trustees a power of advancement 'to the intent that the powers given to trustees by s. 32 TA shall be enlarged so as to permit my trustees in their absolute and uncontrolled discretion to advance at any time the whole of any expectant or presumptive share to any of my children or any infant beneficiary under this my will for his or her benefit during his or her minority'. The income of the estate was split between the widow and a company that had obtained its interest by assignment. In 1983 the trustees by way of advancement under s. 32, knowing that the assignee company objected but dispensing with their consent on the basis that 'uncontrolled' did not merely permit the payment of the whole rather than one half of the expectant interest but removed also the need for the consents of those with prior interests. The judge, in holding that the advancement was invalid without such consents, observed that it was unlikely that the testator had intended that the trustees should be able to make advances to the children without the consent of his wife.

Making a decision about the advancement of capital – and about the *mode* of advancement – is one of the subtlest acts of the trustee, and also one of the most crucial. A misjudgment which concerns maintenance out of income is serious, but at least the capital remains; make a mistake about advancement and both capital and income disappear, probably for good.

10.22   THE MEANING OF 'BENEFIT'

The trustee's task has not been made less onerous by the use of the alternative word 'benefit' in the wording of the statutory power. 'Advancement' is generally held to mean a payment for the purpose of helping a beneficiary to make a start in life or career or to consolidate himself once a start has been made. It is some 'substantial preferment': see *ante* 6.41. Advances to help pay the cost of education are common enough. Payments for ephemeral needs, such as living expenses, do not constitute 'advancement'. 'Benefit', on the other hand, is much wider in meaning:

> In *Re Moxon* (1958) Danckwerts J. said: 'It seems to me that the word "benefit" is the widest possible word one could have and that it must include a payment direct to the beneficiary, but that does not absolve the trustees from making up their minds whether the payment in the particular manner which they contemplate is for the benefit of the beneficiary.'

Later on, in *Pilkington* v *IRC* (1964) (see *post* 10.25) it was said that the phrase 'advancement or benefit' means 'any use of the money which will improve the material situation of the beneficiary':

> In *Re Clore* (1966) Pennycuick J. remarked: 'The improvement of the material situation of a beneficiary is not confined to his direct financial advantage . . . it includes the discharge . . . of certain moral or social obligations on the part of the beneficiary.'

'Benefit' can include resettling the funds advanced (see *post* 10.25), handing the money over to the beneficiary *simpliciter* (*Re Powles* (1954), an express power case[2]) and making a charitable donation to which the beneficiary was morally committed, as happened in the Clore case above. This very width of meaning is perhaps a danger since there is a tendency for trustees to think that there are no bounds at all to the exercise of their discretion. This is not true; in all cases they must consider whether it will truly be for the beneficiary's benefit to make the advance, e.g. is he a spendthrift?

10.23 THE NEED FOR CONSENTS

The trustees must also consider the interests of other beneficiaries affected by their decision, bearing in mind that the statutory power to advance may be exercised in favour of a beneficiary with only a contingent interest or a vested interest liable to be divested. In this connection it will be recalled that anyone with a prior life *or other interest* must consent *in writing* to a proposed advance, and it is not always easy to decide whether or not a prior interest exists.

> In *IRC* v *Bernstein* (1961) the settlement contained a direction for the income to be accumulated during the settlor's lifetime for the benefit of those who would eventually take the capital. The capital was separately disposed of, after the settlor's death, to his wife or failing her to their children. The Revenue sought to argue that under what is now s. 673(2) ICTA the settlor had retained an interest, since there was the possibility that the trustees might advance capital to his wife

under s. 32 TA out of the main fund. The Court of Appeal held that the direction to accumulate, suggesting the need to preserve the capital intact, negated the statutory power. The point was also made that the gift of the income accumulations was a separate and prior gift to that of the main fund and that the children (there were none as yet) therefore had prior interests, which effectively blocked the exercise of the power of advancement. On this point it was not necessary to express an opinion, and the Court refrained from doing so.

Sometimes it is impossible to get the necessary consent because, although the prior interest can be seen, it is as yet unfulfilled, as when its beneficiaries are unborn, making an advance under s. 32 impossible. In the case of an express power of advancement, it was held in *Re Winch* (1917), where the prior interests were those of unborn children, that the power of advancement was exercisable only in favour of those *next* entitled to the capital, i.e. the unborn children, thus precluding an advance to the subsequent beneficiary.[3]

The requirement of consent in writing is rigid. In *Re Forster* (1942), a case on an express power of advancement, it was held that not even the court could dispense with it, even though it was impossible to contact the life tenant, who was an enemy alien. (In general, the court cannot authorise trustees to dispense with requisite consents, except where there is statutory provision to the contrary, as where execution of a trust for sale is ordered under s. 30 LPA – see *ante* 8.29.)

10.24 GUIDELINES IN CONSIDERING ADVANCEMENTS

(a) Whether or not the proposed payment is for the beneficiary's 'advancement' or 'benefit' within the meaning outlined above, is it truly to his advantage to use the capital of his trust fund thus? Are there, perhaps, other funds which should be used – particularly, in the case of an infant, those of his parents? The fact that an advancement may incidentally benefit other persons besides the beneficiary will not necessarily invalidate it -see *post* 10.25.

(b) An advancement should not usually be retrospective in nature. In particular, it is usually wrong to reimburse a third party for money already spent on behalf of the beneficiary, because it is of no benefit to the beneficiary himself. An exception can be justified where the beneficiary has incurred debts and may find it difficult to discharge them but it is well to make it clear to him (and to his creditors also, if possible) that the exception is not going to be repeated. Another exception may occur where trustees have agreed to a particular course of action, e.g. an educational plan covering several years, and feel able to reimburse debts incurred through implementation of this plan.

(c) Equally, trustees should not commit themselves too far ahead, at least not without reserving to themselves the right to withdraw. An advancement should be made in the light of the circumstances prevailing at the time it is carried out, and this means a fresh enquiry. Prior commitment is inconsistent with this rule. Particular difficulty is encountered when asked to advance funds for payment of school fees in advance under one of the advantageous schemes available for this purpose. In practice, trustees feel able to agree to help in such cases where they are satisfied that there is no risk of the parents acquiring additional wealth in the near future and where any refund of the commuted fees will accrue to the trust fund from which the advance has been made.

(d)   Reference is made above to the need to consider an advancement in the light of the prevailing facts. Trustees must also calculate the current value of the trust fund (where the statutory power is being used, the total value of past advancements must be added back) before deciding what is the maximum available sum for advancement, bearing in mind the very important limitation overall to one half of the beneficiary's presumptive or vested share. Suppose that the trustees have made this calculation, have then advanced the maximum capital sum and that, later on, the remaining fund increases in value so that a recalculation throws up a larger maximum advanceable sum; can the trustees make a further advance? This question was put to the court in *Re Marquess of Abergavenny's Estate Act Trusts* (1981)[4], in connection with an express power of advancement, and the answer was 'no'. Once the power has been fully exercised, it expires and cannot be revived. The safe course, therefore, whether one is dealing with an express power or the statutory one, is always to retain *some* proportion of the maximum advanceable sum in hand during the life of the trust.

(e)   Notwithstanding the very wide meaning accorded to the word 'benefit', trustees should not wash their hands of the matter when the advance leaves them if it has, in fact, been made for a particular purpose or motive. They have a duty in such cases to try to ensure that the purpose for which an advancement is made is duly fulfilled. If, for reasons beyond their control, this proves to be impossible, they will at least be on their guard for the future.

(f)   Where a beneficiary is an infant, the trustees will deal with his parent or guardian. Where he is of age, they should deal with him direct, notwithstanding that the parent may still – quite rightly – be concerned and under some moral responsibility to assist financially, if in a position so to do. Any payment made should be either to or with the concurrence of the adult beneficiary. Until a child is 'emancipated' from his parents he remains under their influence, and the greatest care should be taken if he seeks to benefit them by means of an advance; the trustees should, in such cases, see that the child receives truly independent advice and should, in addition, ensure that the advice received is acted on.

(g)   Consider the possible tax consequences of the proposed advance; the implications of a capital advance for IHT purposes are dealt with *post* 10.28. For CGT, any disposal of trust assets to fund the advance will result in either a chargeable gain or an allowable loss; if the former, subject to the trustees' annual exemption allowance, CGT will be payable (at basic rate if there is a life interest in possession, otherwise at the higher rate). An allowable loss may be set off against chargeable gains incurred in the year of disposal, or may be carried forward for use in future years. If the advance consists of a transfer of specific property to the beneficiary, there will be a deemed disposal by the trustees under s. 71(1) TCGA and again there will be either a chargeable gain or an allowable loss; the advanced beneficiary will be entitled to take over any unrelieved loss. Holdover relief is not available in these circumstances, unless either the asset transferred consists of agricultural or business property used by the life tenant

273

in his business, or the advancement is a chargeable transfer, which will not usually be the case.[5] Where the advancement takes the form of a resettlement there may be a charge to CGT on the basis that the new trustees have become absolutely entitled as against the old trustees under s. 71(1), even if the old trustees and the new trustees are one and the same. There is a Revenue Statement of Practice which gives some guidance – SP 7/84, based upon *Roome v Edwards* (1981) (see *post* 13.23) where the suggestion was made that the existence of separate and defined property, separate trusts and separate trustees were factors which would indicate that there was a resettlement, not just a continuation of the old settlement in another guise. But, unhelpfully, the outcome depends upon the facts of each individual case. Trustees contemplating an advance of this kind must bear the possibility of a CGT charge in mind.[6]

(h) So far as income tax is concerned, some of the peril involved in making an advance of capital and then finding that the Revenue treats it as income and taxable as such seems to have disappeared. It had been reasonably clear that payments out of capital remained capital whatever the purpose of the payment in two cases (a) in a fixed interest trust, if the payment was to persons other than the current life tenant and (b) where the trust was in favour of an infant absolutely entitled to both capital and income. The problem therefore centred round capital advancements or distributions from accumulation and maintenance settlements and discretionary trusts generally. In *Stevenson v Wishart* (1988) Knox J. held that payments of capital out of a discretionary trust to defray the nursing home expenses of one of the trust's objects were not taxable as income in that object's hands. The Court of Appeal agreed with him. Following upon that decision the Revenue has now agreed that advances, which include those under s. 32 TA or appointments under a specific power to appoint capital contained in the trust instrument, will be treated as capital in the hands of the recipient beneficiary unless they come within the following exceptions:

(i) where the power to apply capital is given with a specific proviso that it is used to augment income up to a certain figure annually, as in *Brodie's Trustees v IRC* (1933). There the trustees were directed to hold part of the estate on trust to pay the income to the widow and pay out of capital sufficient to bring the payments up to £4,000 if the income fell below that figure;

(ii) where the power contains a proviso to use capital to maintain the beneficiary in the same degree of comfort as in the past (see *Cunard's Trustees v IRC* (1946));

(iii) where the capital payments authorised really amount to an annuity, as in *Jackson's Trustees v IRC* (1942), where the will contained a direction that £250 be paid each year to each of two daughters out of the capital of the estate.

(i) Two final suggestions. Firstly, plan ahead. Trustees will find it useful to do some pre-thinking about advancement before any request for help actually reaches them and, certainly, they should not make any advance without considering the effect this will have upon future demands on the trust fund. It may not be very sensible, for instance, to engage to spend the whole available capital on education, leaving nothing for use at a later stage in the beneficiary's career – but a child with a precocious IQ may well justify the early expense; having been given a good start he may be expected to need little further help.

Trustees also need to consider that what they do on one occasion will probably be regarded as a precedent on a later occasion, and should take some care to avoid being impaled on the horns of a dilemma of their own creation. Secondly, know the beneficiary; it seems to me impossible to be certain that an advance is going to be of 'benefit' unless a personal assessment of the person's character and ability has been made. This rule should apply all the way from childhood to old age. It may not be necessary to adhere to it where only a modest sum is involved ('modest' having a different meaning in different situations) and in some cases it will be a practical impossibility to meet the beneficiary; where this is so, trustees must do their best to inform themselves by other means.

10.25 THE *PILKINGTON* AND *PAULING* CASES

These two cases should be compulsory reading for all involved with the administration of trusts. In *Pilkington* v *IRC* (1964) a trust fund was held for the life interest of a Mr Richard Pilkington on protective trusts with remainder to his issue as he might appoint and, in default of appointment, to his children at 21. There was no provision excluding, replacing or amending s. 32 but it was provided that Richard's consent to an advancement should not cause a forfeiture of his life interest.[7] He had three children, one of them a girl called Penelope who was born in 1956. The trustees, with the intention of avoiding estate duty, desired to exercise their statutory power of advancement by applying up to one-half of Penelope's presumptive share in a transfer to a new settlement. This provided for the income to be applied for her maintenance until she was 21, then for the income to be paid to her until she was 30, when she was to take the capital absolutely. Should she die before the age of 30, any children she might leave, and who attained 21, would share the capital in her place. The trustees took out a summons asking the court whether they might lawfully make use of their s. 32 powers in such a way; they did not surrender their discretion to the court but asked whether what they wanted to do was in order:

Danckwerts J. decided in favour of the trustees; the Court of Appeal then joined the Commissioners of Inland Revenue as an extra party to the action. The Commissioners appealed and were successful. The trustees then appealed to the House of Lords. The main objection of the Court of Appeal to the proposed advance was that the statutory power could not be exercised unless the benefit to be conferred was 'personal to the person concerned, in the sense of being related to his or her own real or personal needs'. Viscount Radcliffe found it impossible to agree with this gloss on the statute. He thought that there was no maintainable reason for introducing into the statutory power a qualification of the kind produced by the Court of Appeal. Both he and Lord Reid felt some apprehension that, in declining to adopt the reasoning of the Court of Appeal, they might be opening the floodgates to any number of similar schemes but, as Viscount Radcliffe said, 'I do not believe that it is wise to try to cut down an admittedly wide and discretionary power, enacted for general use, through fear of its being abused in certain hypothetical instances. '

Rather strangely, the trustees did not get an affirmative answer to their summons from the House of Lords. Although it was made clear that the proposed exercise was in order in principle, Viscount Radcliffe agreed with the Court of Appeal that the intended resettlement offended the rule against perpetuities (i.e. in this case the rule as applied to pre-1964 instruments) by deferring for too long the final vesting date (see *ante* 7.21 *et seq.*). The 'new' settlement being effectively created through a fiduciary power in the 'old' settlement, this power was equated with a special power of appointment and the 'new' trusts had to be treated as stemming from the original trust instrument (a will) and as coming into effect as from the date of death of the testator – see *ante* 7.30. No doubt the Pilkington trustees, duly fortified, went back to counsel and produced a scheme which was within the rule against perpetuities.

Trustees may reasonably deduce from *Re Pilkington* that, provided the proposed exercise of the statutory power or of a comparable express power is generally for the benefit of the object of the power, the fact that others may benefit incidentally is not improper; furthermore, the propriety of resettling advanced funds was reasserted. A fairly extreme example of this particular kind of advancement is illustrated in *Re Earl of Buckinghamshire* (1977):

The trustees had an express power to pay or apply capital to or for the benefit of certain 'capital beneficiaries'. Walton J. held that a deed resettling property on the children of one such beneficiary was a valid exercise of the power, notwithstanding the fact that he received no personal material benefit. He was a wealthy man and the overall result was beneficial to him in the largest sense.

10.26   THE *PAULING* CASE

Re Pauling (1964) is quite a different cup of tea to *Re Pilkington*. The history of the events which gave rise to the action is a fascinating one. It is also, as the court said in its judgment, 'a sorry story, and one which reflects no credit at all on any of the parties to it'. The facts are too thick on the ground to be capable of succinct explanation here but, reduced to the bare essentials, the case concerned a series of improper advances made over a period of six years from 1948 to 1954. This was due in part to a misunderstanding of the express power of advancement contained in the settlement, in part to its plain misuse, but largely because the trustees were charmed, persuaded and cajoled by the father of the objects of the power into allowing the trust capital to be 'frittered away . . . in the ordinary living expenses of the family'.

Perhaps two examples from the transactions complained of will serve to illustrate the kind of impropriety into which the trustees honestly but foolishly fell. In 1947 it was decided that the family residence should be in the Isle of Man; as it was impossible to apply the settlement funds in such a purchase, a scheme was devised by which the trustees would advance funds to the two eldest children, Francis and George, who were then both over 21. The money so advanced would be used to buy the house, which would then be settled on their mother for life, with remainder to the sons. It was recommended that they be separately advised but they disclaimed any desire for this. A memorandum was signed by the children asking the trustees to apply the proposed advances (up to £10,000 was envisaged) along the lines already described. Later in 1948 a house in the Isle of Man was bought for £8,450. Before this happened, however, the trustees knew that none of the funds to be advanced were to be settled and, shortly before completion of the purchase, in October 1948, they wrote to solicitors in the Isle of Man instructing them to convey the property into the names of the parents, Commander and Mrs Younghusband. The trustees never obtained the consent of Francis and George to this complete reversal of the original plan and there was no evidence that they ever did consent. Subsequently the property was mortgaged for £5,000 which was apparently spent as income, and when in 1956 it was sold for less than the amount of the mortgage the children entirely lost their £8,450.

'Long before the purchase of the house was completed the children's father . . . conceived the idea that the power of advancement conferred by clause 11 of the settlement could be used for the purpose of raising further sums up to one-half of each child's presumptive share in the capital of the trust fund, which sums could then be used for paying off his wife's overdraft, and for living expenses.' An example of the way in which this interesting theory was carried into practice is found in advances totalling £3,260 made in 1949 on account of the daughter's presumptive share. In theory, these payments were to pay for the purchase of furniture and improvements at a house in Chelsea bought (ill-advisedly) for the daughter but (providentially) put into her name. The daughter did request the trustees to make the various advances, but only £300 was actually spent on furniture, the rest going to the mother's account (presumably for living expenses). The Court of Appeal did not think that the trustees really believed that the various written requests they received from the daughter were genuine; they merely wanted some documents which would provide them with some justification for making what were, in fact, singularly ill-founded advances.

One sympathises with the trustees of the Younghusbands' marriage settlement. The judge at first instance, who saw the witnesses, got the impression 'of a united family determined to extract from the bank by hook or by crook the money necessary to continue its extravagant way of life.' The trustees were certainly subjected to consistent and persuasive attack; however, trustees are often subjected to this kind of pressure and, particularly if they are professionals, should be strong-minded enough to withstand it. A great deal can be learned from *Re Pauling*; the following list summarises the main lessons which it contains:

(a) If trustees resolve to advance funds for a particular purpose or from a particular motive they cannot wash their hands of responsibility for seeing that the stated objective is carried out.

277

(b) *Any* request for an advance should be thoroughly tested for reasonableness and validity.

(c) Care should be taken to avoid falling into a routine pattern of making advances with the result that little or no thought is given to later transactions. Every proposition should be inspected with the same assiduous care.

(d) Requests from and consents of young adult objects of the power of advancement should be treated with extreme caution, a point that has already been touched upon in 10.24, point (f). Until they are 'emancipated' from their parents they must be assumed to be subject to undue influence from that quarter. When a person does become 'emancipated' is partly a question of law and partly a matter of fact. It may be deferred for a long time in some cases, e.g. a spinster living at home. An 'unemancipated' adult should have *independent, professional* advice before trustees can safely rely on his or her concurrence in a transaction in breach of trust – whether this takes the form of a purported advancement or otherwise.

(e) The court will be slow to relieve a paid trustee under s. 61 TA, particularly where the trustee is also a banker (as in *Re Pauling*) and has placed himself in a position where his duty as trustee conflicts with his interest as a banker; such a trustee should be particularly careful about making advancements which might be applied directly or indirectly in reducing a customer's indebtedness to the bank. Finally, a paid trustee should not expect to be forgiven simply because he relied on misleading or inadequate advice (see also *post* 14.19).

10.27 BRINGING AN ADVANCEMENT INTO ACCOUNT

It will be recalled that money paid or applied by trustees for advancement or benefit has to be brought into account when the beneficiary becomes absolutely entitled: s. 32(1)(b), *ante* 10.21. The process is somewhat analogous to the requirement that advancements be brought into hotchpot on an intestate distribution, *ante* 4.10. The traditional method in s. 32 cases has been to bring the advance into account at its historical value, i.e. its value when paid or applied. There is now indirect authority for the use of an alternative method, which is to bring the advance into account as a fraction or percentage of the total fund; this method was one approved by the court in *Re Leigh's Settlement Trusts* (1981) for use in bringing the value of appropriated (not advanced) assets into account. The two methods are compared in the following simple example:

The trustees of a fund worth £100,000 and held for the life interest of A, remainder to B and C in equal shares absolutely, resolve to exercise their statutory power of advancement in favour of B to the extent of £20,000 in 1983, no previous advances having been made. In 1993 the life tenant dies and the fund (now worth £160,000) becomes distributable to B and C; B has to bring his advance into account against the gross fund before the calculation of any IHT.

A. *The traditional method:*	£	£ B's share	£ C's share
Value of fund	160,000		
Advance	20,000		
	180,000	90,000	90,000
Less advance	20,000	20,000	
	160,000	70,000	90,000

B. *The new method:*
Percentage of fund remaining for
distribution, 20% having been
advanced in 1983　　　　　80%　　30% for B, i.e.　　50% for C, i.e.
　　　　　　　　　　　　　　　　3/8ths = £60,000 5/8ths = £100,000

The theory behind the new method is that it produces a fairer result in times of high inflation; in the example given above, for instance, it may be assumed that B's advance, if sensibly invested, should have appreciated in monetary value over the ten years since it was made. Even if not so invested, B had the use of £20,000 ten years before the distribution date, a considerable advantage in itself. The use of this alternative method is not, apparently, widespread and its attractions are less obvious when the rate of inflation is low. There is no direct authority for its use in s. 32 advancement cases, but it would seem that advancing trustees who feel that it will be fairer all round than the traditional method and who make a decision to use it, having carefully reviewed the alternatives, will not be held by the court to be at fault, especially as the Law Reform Committee (1982 Cmnd.8733) has made the following recommendation:

33. Trustees should no longer be bound to use the cash basis of accounting when bringing advances and appropriations into account, but should be permitted to account for such sums at their value at the time of advance multiplied by any increase in the retail price index up to the time of the final division.

The alternative method has no relevance to hotchpot on intestacy, where the statutory rule must apply – see *ante* 4.10.

Where hotchpot applies in the administration of an estate, either under the express terms of a will or through the application of the doctrine of ademption of legacies by portions (see *ante* 6.40) or under an intestacy, a problem can arise in apportioning income and capital gains as between those beneficiaries who have been advanced during the deceased's lifetime and those who have not.[8] For trustees who have made advancements during the currency of a trust the position should be different. On the death of the life tenant or on the coming of age of a member of a class there is an ascertained fund which can be notionally carved up when the distributable event occurs, thus enabling subsequent income and capital gains to be attributed where they properly belong.

10.28   ADVANCEMENT AND IHT

Bringing advancements into account may be complicated by the impact of IHT; as the life tenant of a fixed-interest trust is treated as the owner of the trust fund for IHT purposes, it follows that an advance from such a fund to, for instance, a remainderman, will be treated as a gift by the life tenant to the remainderman in question. Originally such transactions were excluded from the definition of a PET but, since 17 March 1987, that definition has been widened to include not only the creation of such trusts, but also the ending of a life interest in the fund: ss. 3A(2) and 3A(7) IHTA. So if an advance is made, no immediate liability for IHT arises. But, if the life tenant dies within seven years of the advance date, it will be treated as a chargeable lifetime transfer by the deceased person and will be included in the IHT calculations resulting from his death.

The primary liability for IHT payable as the result of a 'failed' PET is that of the trustees of the settlement; see *ante* 8.7. It therefore behoves the trustees, when the advancement is made, to ensure that the beneficiary (or his parents) are aware of the potential liability and that sufficient funds are retained to cover it, bearing in mind that the rate of tax applicable will be that in force when the life tenant dies and that the rate of tax will be calculated by adding the original value of the PET (frozen at its value at that time) to the life tenant's accumulator as it stood on the day when the PET was made. It must take up its position in the accumulator in chronological order, if need be, ranking after an earlier PET that has also become chargeable. The maximum rate of tax will not necessarily be 40%; it will be the rate in force when the life tenant dies, subject to taper relief, if that relief is still in force. The trustees may need to insure against the liability and deduct the cost from the amount advanced, unless the trust instrument authorises this form of insurance.

There remains the question of apportioning the IHT payable on the death of the life tenant amongst the advanced and unadvanced beneficiaries. If the old estate duty decisions are anything to go by, the IHT on settled property is a charge spread over all the assets, so that whoever takes part of the fund, be he a deferred pecuniary legatee or a remainderman, must suffer a proportion of the charge. The following is an example of the apportionment required:

The trustees of a fixed-interest settlement held for the life interest of A, remainder to B, C and D in equal shares, have made the following advances:
In 1983, £5,000 to B
In 1985, £6,000 to C
In 1987, £7,000 to D
In 1993 the life tenant dies and the fund, worth £102,000, suffers an IHT liability of £10,000.

Value of fund	£102,000			
Advances	18,000	B's share	C's share	D's share
	120,000	40,000	40,000	40,000
Less advances	18,000	5,000	6,000	7,000
	102,000	35,000	34,000	33,000
Less IHT in proportion to the actual distribution entitlement	10,000	3,432	3,333	3,235
	£92,000	£31,568	£30,667	£29,765

It will be noticed that the 'traditional' method of bringing into account, at historical values, has been used in this example. The proportionate distribution after IHT is in accordance with the principle enunciated in *Re Tollemache* (1930); any liability arising in respect of the last advance (made within seven years of death) is ignored in calculating the distribution, the advances being brought in at their gross values as originally made. The liability arising out of the failed PET falls on the advanced beneficiary's share, unless defrayed by insurance or a reserve. As Clauson J. pointed out in the *Tollemache* case, the object of the provision requiring advancements to be brought into account was to produce equality of participation, not to produce equality 'in shouldering the imposts' (in those days, estate duty).

As was said by Plowman J. in *Re Turner* (1968) the *Re Tollemache* principle applies only to a case where an advance has to be brought into account against a fund which bears its own duty. *Re Tollemache* is, therefore, not relevant to hotchpot on the death of a lifetime donor because the sum to be brought into account on his death will normally be brought in against the net residue of the estate, i.e. after payment of the testamentary expenses including the inheritance tax. (The sum brought into account on such an occasion will also be net of any IHT which the donee incurs – see *ante* 6.41.)

281

11 Investment of trust funds

11.1 THE PRIMARY DUTY

'It is the duty of a trustee to make the fund productive to the beneficiaries by its investment on some proper security' (*Lewin*, p. 314). The last words have an old-fashioned ring but the general meaning of the quotation is clear enough. Trustees are under an obligation to invest funds in their care and neglect this duty at their peril; by 'invest' in this context is meant the purchase of an income-producing asset – *Re Power* (1947), see *post* 11.15. Leaving money on deposit with a banker does not constitute an investment, although there are times, of course, when to do this is perfectly justified; s. 11(1) TA authorises trustees to leave money in a bank account whilst seeking an investment, and a building society deposit is an authorised investment under the TIA Sch. 1, Part II, para.12 (a share account with a building society is, however, a wider-range investment).

Having established the primary duty, there is guidance about the way in which the conscientious trustee should carry it out in *Re Whiteley* (1886) in the words of Lindley LJ:

'The duty of a trustee is not to take such care only as a prudent man would take if he had only himself to consider; the duty rather is to take such care as an ordinary prudent man would take if he were minded to make an investment for the benefit of other people for whom he felt morally bound to provide.'

In *Cowan* v *Scargill* (1985), a case concerned with the way in which a pension fund should be invested, Megarry V-C made the general point about trust investment that the trustees' duty to the beneficiaries was paramount; where the object of the trust was to provide financial benefit (which would usually be the case), trustees should use their investment powers so as to produce the best return, having regard to the risks involved. When making investment decisions, trustees should put aside their own personal interests and views. (This case is considered below in connection with 'ethical' investment.)

11.2 WIDE INVESTMENT POWERS DO NOT INCLUDE SPECULATION

It is important for a trustee to remember that he is not dealing with his own money (although the investment clause may well say that he may act as though he is). This means that he should not speculate. Precisely what is and what is not speculation will always be open to debate, and a trustee can pursue an 'active' investment policy without offending against the principle. On the other hand, a trustee who purchases an asset with little or no intrinsic value but with possibilities of profit from an advantageous movement of the laws of supply and demand is clearly taking a risk which he may find it difficult to justify later on. Other kinds of unorthodox 'investment' may be fashionable for a time but are often subject to political interference and to the vagaries of national and world economic forces. Works of art may seem attractive acquisitions to trustees hard-pressed to maintain the value of their funds in times of high inflation but they are peculiarly susceptible to changes in taste. Apart from being inherently unstable, such assets are often difficult – and perhaps impossible – to realise at short notice; generally speaking, a trust fund is best invested in assets which will always, so far as can be seen, command a ready sale on the open market. A further consideration for the investing trustee is that he must take into account the interests of *all* the beneficiaries; in the situation of a life interest followed by a gift in remainder a balance must be struck between the natural desire of the life tenant for the best income and the equally natural desire of the remainderman for maximum capital appreciation. Achieving and retaining this balance is perhaps the most difficult aspect of the subject under discussion, though it may be mitigated if the life tenant's idea of the best income is concerned with dividend growth rather than dividend yield.

Trustees generally have much wider powers of investment now than was the case, say, 30 years ago. Not only does the TIA (discussed below) provide considerable scope for investment in equities but it is now (and has been for some decades) customary for new trust instruments to confer very wide powers upon trustees. As the possibilities have increased, so has the responsibility and the opportunity for error. At the same time the public has become more knowledgeable about investment generally and thus more capable of challenging the investment performance of trust funds. Much is expected of trustees – sometimes more than can reasonably be expected, as was the case in *Nestle v National Westminster Bank*, below. There is a tendency to expect trustees to *guarantee* the value of the funds in their care; a tendency which was anticipated and refuted by Lindley LJ in *Re Whiteley, op. cit.*:

> 'Whilst on the one hand the Court ought not to encourage laxity and want of care, on the other hand the Court ought not to prevent people from becoming trustees by converting honest trustees into insurers of the moneys committed to their care.'

To purchase an *unauthorised* investment is, of course, a breach of trust and the trustee will be responsible for any loss which results from it; see *post* 14.5 for an example. Furthermore, if an authorised investment were sold to permit the purchase of an unauthorised one, the trustee could be made to repurchase the former holding and to provide out of his own pocket any loss incurred as a result of this transaction. Strict attention to the appropriate authority for the purchase of an investment is therefore quite essential. Provided this authority is complied with, the purchase is *prima facie* good but it may still be possible for the beneficiaries to show that the trustee was at fault in that he did not properly fulfil either the general duty of care already referred to (see *ante* 11.1) or the statutory duty imposed by s. 6(1) TIA, *post* 11.6. Reference must again be made to the fact that in this field, as in others, higher standards are expected of the paid trustee than of the layman, see *ante* 9.21.

11.3   TRUSTEE INVESTMENTS ACT 1961 (TIA)

Section 1(1) reads:

> A trustee may invest any property in his hands, whether at the time in a state of investment or not, in any manner specified in Part I or II of the First Schedule to this Act or, subject to the next following section, in any manner specified in Part III of that Schedule, and may also from time to time vary any such investments.

The sub-divisions of Schedule 1 (headed 'Manner of Investment') are broadly as follows:

PART I – NARROWER-RANGE INVESTMENTS NOT REQUIRING ADVICE
Savings certificates and Savings Bank deposits (excluding quoted stocks on the National Savings Register) which, while they may be highly susceptible to inflation (if not index-linked), are immune from any loss in their nominal value.
PART II – NARROWER-RANGE INVESTMENTS REQUIRING ADVICE
These correspond, in the broadest sense, to the old trustee range of fixed-interest securities; they include mortgages, building society deposits and debenture and loan stocks of UK companies.
PART III – WIDER-RANGE INVESTMENTS
These are stocks and shares of UK companies (including investment trust companies), building society share accounts and units of authorised UK unit trusts.

When contemplating an investment in a UK company, whether under Part II or Part III, it is very important to bear in mind two things:

(a)   it will not be authorised unless quoted on a recognised investment exchange – primarily, in this country, the Stock Exchange – and
(b)   it will also be unauthorised (i) if the company's issued and paid up share capital is less than £1 million and (ii) if it has not in each of the five years immediately preceding the calendar year in which the investment is made paid a dividend on all the issued shares, excluding shares issued after the dividend has been declared and shares which by their terms of issue did not rank for dividend in that particular year. It has not been unknown for company directors with

substantial shareholdings to waive payment of dividends declared in their favour, thus bringing into play the second head of exclusion and depriving the company of its trustee status. Purchase of stock or shares in a company which has lost this status will be unauthorised and will expose the trustee to a claim for breach of trust.

Section 1(3) provides that the powers conferred on trustees by the section shall not be limited by any provision contained in an instrument (not being an enactment or an instrument made under an enactment) made before 3 August 1961. It is helpful to remember that s. 1(1) can be applied to assets specifically settled without a power of sale; in *Re Pratt* (1943) it was held that s. 1(1) TA empowered trustees to sell such assets for the purpose of making investments authorised by the Act, the wording of that sub-section being identical with that of s. 1(1) TIA.

11.4 SPLITTING THE FUND INTO TWO PARTS

Narrower-range investments may be made without observance of any special formality, apart from the need to get advice, see *post* 11.12, but a wider-range investment may be bought only after the fund has been divided into two parts, equal in value at the time of division: s. 2(1). These two parts are then designated narrower-range and wider-range. Either part may be invested in investments of the first category, but only the wider-range part may be invested in wider-range investments. Once divided, the fund is not revalued or divided again. It is interesting to note, however, that withdrawals from the fund, for whatever purpose, may be taken from either part, at the discretion of the trustee: s. 2(4). There is no rule that each part must be reduced by the same proportion. On the other hand, transfers between the two parts must be self-compensating in the sense that one part does not benefit in this way without making a transfer of similar value to the other part. If, for instance, a wider-range investment is acquired in the narrower-range part it must either be sold and the proceeds used to buy a narrower-range investment or it must be transferred to the wider-range part and a transfer of equal value made in the opposite direction, i.e. from wider-range to narrower-range: s. 2(2).

11.5 SPECIAL RANGE INVESTMENTS

The statutory powers briefly outlined above are intended to be read in conjunction with any special powers of investment conferred upon the trustees: s. 3(1). Such special powers may derive from the trust instrument itself, from the court or from other statute law, e.g. under s. 10(3) and (4) TA. Any investment retained or acquired under a special power is not included in the division between narrower and wider-range parts but is carried to its own special range part: s. 3(3) and Sch. 2. There it remains until it is either sold or transferred to a beneficiary. If it is sold, the proceeds of sale may be used to purchase other special range investments. If not so used, the proceeds are transferred in equal shares to the narrower and wider-range parts: Sch. 2, para.3. In the other direction, special range investments may be bought with funds from either narrower or wider-range moneys, at the discretion of the trustees – rather on the same principle of allowing them complete freedom over the source of funds for withdrawals. Authorised narrower-range investments, incidentally, should never find their way into the special range part: s. 3(3).

The principles of the TIA impose upon trustees who make use of the wider-range a duty to keep a careful record of all investment transactions carried out under its authority, clearly allocating all investments *and cash capital* to the appropriate range, narrower, wider and special. A misdescription in carrying out this requirement could well result in an investment being unauthorised, and the consequences of this kind of error can be serious – see *ante* 11.2.

11.6 DUTY OF TRUSTEES IN CHOOSING INVESTMENTS

Although the TIA was enacted with the best of intentions, it was, in practice, already out of date when it arrived. The great majority of modern wills and trust deeds incorporate an investment clause which gives trustees the widest possible powers (so-called 'beneficial owner' powers) which enable them to invest in any form of property at their absolute discretion and as though they were in every respect the personal owners of the trust funds. The 1961 Act, therefore, is increasingly irrelevant in most respects; the Law Reform Committee, in its 23rd Report (1982) described the TIA as 'tiresome, cumbrous and expensive in operation', preferring a system which divided investments into those which can be made without advice and those which can be made only with advice but otherwise freeing trustees from the fetters of the TIA. In one respect, however, the Act is of universal significance; s. 6(1) reads:

> In the exercise of his powers of investment a trustee shall have regard–
> (a) to the need for diversification of investments of the trust, in so far as is appropriate to the circumstances of the trust;
> (b) to the suitability to the trust of investments of the description of investment proposed and of the investment proposed as an investment of that description.

This subsection applies to *all* powers of investment, however derived, and therefore needs to be firmly borne in mind by trustees making use of express powers as well as by those proceeding under the TIA or some other statutory power.

11.7 DIVERSIFICATION

So far as the first consideration is concerned, diversification is a common-sense precaution which should always be under review. The risk involved in having all one's eggs in one basket is self-evident. It is true that exceptions to the rule can always be produced to prove the contrary, but a trustee who declined to diversify and whose trust fund then suffered a loss would find it more difficult to prove that he had exercised his discretion with the required standard of care. In the equity sector diversification should be applied broadly so that as many different sectors of commerce and industry are represented as is feasible in the context of a particular trust and, more narrowly, within a particular sector by the choice of several representative companies. Diversification amongst numerous securities may not be possible; the size of the trust fund may inhibit it. A small fund will be better served by having its equity content confined to a unit trust or investment trust company with a proven record and a largely general portfolio, whereas larger funds can go for direct investment in companies. It is sensible not to rely on only one unit trust or investment trust management team if the size of the fund permits investment in two or three. Diversification should not be carried too far. A multiplicity of holdings is difficult to manage effectively and the number should therefore be restricted to a reasonable maximum – 20 or 25 holdings of equities should be ample at any given time to produce a desirable level of diversification and still ensure that each holding is given individual attention.

11.8 CHOOSING THE TYPE AND THE CHOICE WITHIN THE TYPE

The second head of s. 6(1) is perhaps a little less easy to discuss. It is clear that a trustee must, in the first place, consider whether a proposed investment is suitable in general terms. Broadly speaking, one has fixed-interest securities (including mortgages) on the one hand and equities and land on the other. Within each main category there are sub-divisions, such as gilt-edged stocks, local authority stocks, commercial debentures and loan stocks, ordinary stocks and shares, investment and unit trusts; to which one might add two kinds of investment that have come to the fore in recent years: index-linked stocks and convertible company stocks that pay fixed dividends or fixed interest pending conversion. A trustee must, before doing anything else, decide what balance he proposes to establish between the main classes of investment. In making this all-important assessment he should have in mind (a) the special requirements of the trust which he is dealing with, and (b) his assessment of the immediate prospects for fixed-interest securities and equities. Having got so far, he can then make the further decision as to the desirable constitution of each main class. This is the first part of head (b) in s. 6(1). Lastly he decides what *actual* investment should be chosen to represent the *type* of investment allocated to each main class. This is the second part of head (b). The allocation of resources between fixed-interest securities and equities, once made, is not immutable; the trustee should keep it under review at all times. The relative merits of these two basic classes of investment are always on the move and the trustee must be alert enough to alter the balance of his portfolio in the light of such changes. The choice of the fixed-interest securities may appear to be relatively simple compared with that of equity holdings but, in fact, selection of the right investment in this category is by no means easy; the options tend to be quite numerous and the relative income yields, gross and net redemption yields and, possibly, index-linked yields must all be considered.

11.9   LIFE INTEREST TRUSTS

One of the truisms of this subject is that each trust has to be considered on its own merits, so far as investments are concerned. There is no doubting this precept but there is also one general principle which will at least be applicable to many trusts having a life interest in possession. A trustee must, as a rule, hold the scales evenly between capital and income; so far as income is concerned, he may not expect to maintain its purchasing power in the hands of the life tenant in times of surging inflation, but it should be possible to achieve some improvement in the actual yield over the years, and this is worth aiming for. Turning to the capital side, a trustee should try to arrange that the original value (in real terms) of the fund is sustained *at the time the life interest comes to an end*. If he can manage to produce a real profit (not just a monetary one), so much the better. It is important to be able to form a view about the period over which a trust is likely to extend both in order to judge the maximum spread of redemption dates and because a trust with only a short life to run is not likely to be suitable for investment in equities. This particular aspect of the investment equation will be complicated by any need to provide capital during the interim, e.g. for advancements. It is also important, when a trust nears the end of its life, to consider any impending liability for IHT and to provide for its liquidation out of investments that may be sold without loss.

The suggested dual objective of gradual improvement in annual yield coupled with an eventual capital profit is, of course, liable to infinite variation in particular cases (investment of trust funds for infants has already been discussed, *ante* 6.21 to 6.25). In some life interest cases, income will be of little or no importance and all the emphasis will be on capital performance. In others, a higher than average yield is imperative from the start; where this is the case, the life tenant must be warned that the scope for further improvement is limited. In no case, however, can a trustee contemplate with equanimity a negative performance; in this respect, the history of undated gilt-edged stocks since the war is both depressing and instructive.

It may be helpful to conclude this part of the discussion, which has primarily related to stock exchange investment, by referring briefly to *Nestle* v *National Westminster Bank plc* (1988), a case that was not reported at first instance, and *Cowan* v *Scargill* (1985).

11.10   THE *NESTLE* CASE

The facts were:

In 1921 a Mr Nestle made a will which bequeathed an annuity of £1,500 to his widow, the residue of the estate to his two sons on protective trusts in equal shares and a remainder to the sons' children. The testator died in 1922 and the predecessor of the bank administered the estate and the subsequent trust until the survivor of the two sons died in 1986. At that point, the sole grandchild brought an action against the bank for failure to manage the trust investments with sufficient skill, thereby causing loss to the trust fund and to her as the sole beneficiary in remainder.

During the course of the argument there was a discussion about the proper way to fund the annuity to the widow (who died in 1960). The view expressed earlier, *ante* 6.18, was put forward on behalf of the bank. The plaintiff clearly took the view that there should have been much greater emphasis throughout on investment in equities, and that, had this been done, the value of the fund at the end of the day would have been vastly greater than it actually was.

The equity argument would, of course, have upset the balance of the trust fund, if implemented. The plaintiff, in fact, argued that the bank had paid too much attention to the needs of the two life tenants and not enough to her entitlement to the capital. As was remarked above, holding the scales fairly between different classes of beneficiary is probably the most difficult aspect of trust investment practice. A further complication was the fact that both life tenants were non-resident. Hoffman J., incidentally, took the view that this traditional image of a trustee holding the scales between life tenant and remainderman was too mechanistic in its imagery and that a better way of stating the principle was to say that a trustee must act fairly in making investment decisions as between different classes of beneficiary (a view which is reminiscent of the Law Reform Committee's recommendation in its 1982 report that the present rules of equitable apportionment should be replaced by a duty to hold a fair balance between capital and income).

In the end, Hoffman J. dismissed the claim against the bank as being entirely without merit; he went on to say: 'Trustees like the bank act for reward and therefore owe duties of professional skill, but the engagement into which they enter is not one of insurance. They do not guarantee results. Possibly for a suitable premium such a guarantee could be obtained, but I very much doubt it . . . In my view the bank had acted conscientiously, fairly and carefully throughout the administration of the trust and the action must therefore be dismissed.'

This decision not only emphasises the fact that trustees are not insurers of the trust funds in their hands but also makes the point that there is no duty to produce guaranteed results, whether in line with the retail price index, the Footsie index or anything else, and this principle applies to all trustees, professional or not. It is reasonable to have a trust investment *objective* and, of course, the overall duty of care applies but, provided that a trustee can show that such a duty has been fulfilled he should be safe from a punitive action of the kind brought against the National Westminster Bank. The Court of Appeal dismissed an appeal by the beneficiary (*The Times*, 11 May 1992); members of the court did not adopt Hoffman J.'s view of the bank/trustee's conduct of the trust – indeed, they were somewhat critical. But, as Leggatt LJ pointed out, the bank's engagement was as a trustee; as such it is to be judged not so much by success as by absence of proven default. The importance of preservation of a trust fund will always outweigh success in its advancement.

11.11   THE SCARGILL CASE

This was quite a different type of case to *Nestle*, but is equally interesting in the light it throws upon the right approach for trustees to take for investment decisions:

The dispute which came before the court concerned the investment policy for the Mineworkers' Pension Scheme. There appear to have been ten trustees altogether, five from the National Coal Board and five from the NUM. The latter did not wish to adopt an investment policy put forward for approval unless it was amended so that there would be no increase in overseas investment and no investment in industries in direct competition with the coal industry. The court was asked to decide whether the dissenting trustees were entitled to take the views on investment as just described.

In giving judgment, the Vice-Chancellor said:

The law on the duties of trustees was that they should exercise their powers in the best interests of the present and future beneficiaries of the trust, holding the scales impartially between different classes of beneficiary.

and: A power of investment . . . had to be exercised so as to yield the best return for the beneficiaries, judged in relation to the risks of the investment in question, and the prospects of the yield and capital appreciation both had to be considered . . .

and: . . . in considering what investments to make, trustees had to put on one side their own personal interests and views; they might hold strong social or political views, they might be firmly opposed to an investment in South Africa . . . or . . . in companies concerned with alcohol, tobacco or armaments. . . . Yet if, under a trust, investments of that type would be more beneficial to the beneficiaries than some others, the trustees must not refrain from making such investments by reason of the views they held.

The Vice-Chancellor then held that the five dissenting trustees would be in breach of trust if they failed to concur in the investment policy put forward for their approval. A rather similar attempt to introduce a greater moral element into the investment decisions of the Church Commissioners was made recently by the Bishop of Oxford, which likewise failed (*Bishop of Oxford* v *Church Commissioners* (1991) – see further below).

The 'best return' principle, to which Megarry V-C referred to above, has the advantage of clarity and it is surely easier to judge whether or not a trustee has managed investments with a reasonable degree of skill if such a principle is adopted as the standard. This is not to say that 'ethical' investment is impossible; where there is nothing to choose between an ethical and a non-ethical security, the former may be safely chosen under the 'best return' principle. A trust instrument may direct the trustees to take ethical considerations into account; there are, for instance, a number of unit trusts offering ethical or 'socially responsible' investment policies, and there is an Ethical Investment Research Service which will advise on ethical investment problems.

In the *Bishop of Oxford's* case, Nicholls VC seems to have accepted that, where the proportion of 'excluded investments' (i.e. those rejected on ethical grounds) was relatively small in relation to the whole, there can be little objection to the taking by the trustees of the ethical line when making investment decisions; in that case, the Church Commissioners' own exclusions ruled out some 13% by value of listed UK companies. The Bishop would have excluded a further 24%; clearly this was thought to be going too far. It is of interest to note that the Charity Commissioners themselves have accepted the fact that the prospective financial return is not in all cases the sole consideration for charity trustees – p. 10 of their 1987 Report. The Comissioners also take the view that charity trustees should not invest in companies which pursue activities which are directly contrary to the purposes or trusts of their charity; an obvious example would be that of a medical research charity faced with a recommendation to invest in a tobacco company.

11.12 INVESTMENT REVIEW – THE STATUTORY OBLIGATION

The duty to invest is rarely performed once and once only during the life of a trust. It is essential that all trust portfolios be reviewed and reconsidered at regular intervals. Section 6(3) TIA imposes a statutory duty to review investments made under the Act, and there must be an overall duty to review trust investments, however acquired. Trustees should form their own views about the length of such intervals, but in no case, it is suggested, should they be greater than 12 months. (There may be occasions, of course, when some event affecting a particular stock or share, e.g. a take-over bid, will prompt a professional trustee to look at *all* trusts in which he holds office in order to review the affected holdings.) Trustees are positively enjoined by the TIA to take advice before reaching an investment decision. They may not make a Sch. 1, Part II or III investment without first obtaining and *considering* advice from 'a person who is reasonably believed by the trustee to be qualified by his ability in and practical experience of financial matters' – see s. 6(2) and (4); the definition is wide enough and vague enough to cover anyone with pretensions to being an investment expert. However, where the powers of a trustee are exercised by an officer or servant who is competent to give this advice, as in the case of a trust corporation, there is fortunately no need to seek advice elsewhere, and where there are two or more trustees one of the number can give the advice required by s. 6(2) to the other or others – s. 6(6), which covers the position of a trust corporation giving advice to its co-trustees; the advice should either be given in writing or so confirmed – s. 6(5). Review of the portfolio may disclose the fact that an investment has become unauthorised, for whatever reason. This circumstance will obviously require consideration. If the trustee decides that, nevertheless, the holding should be retained, s. 4 TA protects him so far as lack of authorisation is concerned.

Quite apart from the statutory provisions regarding advice it is obviously sensible for the non-specialist to consult the expert both when buying or selling a trust investment and when reviewing the trust portfolio. It should be remembered that the trustee is expected to *consider* the advice he gets – he should not adopt it without thought. The trustee can do a good deal to make a review a worthwhile exercise by doing his homework before consulting the expert; if he does the job thoroughly it may not be necessary to refer to the investment specialist at all, so saving time and expense.

11.13   INVESTMENT REVIEW PROCEDURE

It is suggested that, on the review date, the trustee should adopt the following pattern of thought and action:

(a)   Have the beneficiaries' circumstances changed since the previous review date, necessitating a reconsideration of trust investment policy?

(b)   Revalue each holding and recalculate annual income from each holding. Compare capital value and annual yield with:
  (i)   capital value and annual yield on the previous review date; and
  (ii)   capital value and annual yield at the commencement of the trust; and
  (iii) *Financial Times* Actuaries All-Share Index and Yield at present and on previous review date (equities only).

(c)   Consider individual equity holdings:
  (i)   progress since previous review;
  (ii)   prospects;
  (iii) size – too large or too small in relation to:
    (1)   investment in company's special field;
    (2)   total equity content of portfolio;
  (iv)   current yield and current profit over acquisition price.

(d)   Consider individual fixed-interest holdings. Is there scope for switching into stock of comparable date but with higher yield, or into stock with similar yield but greater capital appreciation potential? (Reference may usefully be made to *Winfield and Curry*, pp. 102–4 on 'Anomaly Switching' and 'Policy Switching'.)

(e)   Is there scope for transactions to negative taxable capital profits, such as a sale at close of business on one day and repurchase when business opens on the next ('bed and breakfasting')? It is equally possible to use this method to create a taxable profit in order to absorb an unused CGT loss.

(f)   Consider the data revealed in (a) to (e) above, with particular reference to s. 6(1) TIA. Bear in mind also that there may well be other assets in the trust, such as land, policies, chattels, which need to be considered on a review of the investment portfolio.

(g)   In the absence of special provision in the trust instrument, gearing is not permitted, in other words the investment base cannot be expanded by mortgaging one asset to buy another. In the realm of settled land, there is power to mortgage in order to raise portions or to carry out improvements and other specified purposes connected with the well-being of the settled land. In the case of other trusts, there is power under s. 16 TA to mortgage any of the trust property for trust purposes, but this does not enable the PR or trustee to raise money by mortgage in order to acquire further land as an investment or, for that matter, any other type of asset: *Re Suenson-Taylor* (1974).

What the trustee decides to do in the light of the data revealed by his enquiries depends upon (a) the policy he is following in the trust under review, and (b) the view he takes of the general investment scene. It is essential for a trustee to keep abreast of the current thinking about future trends for both fixed-interest and equity shares. He may form his own view of these matters but it must be an intelligent one. A trustee cannot administer a trust in a vacuum; the success or failure of his management of the investments will depend to some extent upon his being able to anticipate future economic, political and financial developments. It is true that he can employ agents to do his thinking for him but (unless expressly empowered to delegate or unless he expressly delegates his investment powers for 12 months under s. 25 TA) the trustee must take the decisions. A good deal depends upon his having a clear picture of the trust's needs and of the way in which these can be satisfied now and later on. A trustee who is not also an investment expert will find it helpful to read *Winfield and Curry*, chs. 21 and 22 when he takes office.

11.14   THE ACCRUED INCOME SCHEME

In a trust with a life interest, this can be a worrisome feature on the purchase, sale or appropriation of fixed-interest securities. For its impact on the administration of estates, see *ante* 5.22. It does not apply to pension fund trusts and charitable trusts: s. 715(1)(d) and (k) ICTA. The initial transfer of fixed-interest securities to the trustees of a private trust will be a transfer for the purposes of the Scheme and interest must be apportioned accordingly (transfer in this context includes the moment in time when PRs become trustees). But the termination of a life interest and the fruition of a contingency such as the attainment of majority are not transfers, although apportionment may be necessary for a quite different reason: see *ante* 5.21. Transfers to and from bare trustees and nominees are non-events so far as the Scheme is concerned; transactions carried out by such persons are treated as though executed by the principal: s. 720(1) and (2) ICTA. Transfers resulting from a change of trustee are ignored also, but where non-resident trustees of an English trust are appointed (see *post* 13.15 *et seq.*) the Scheme is applied for fixed interest securities on the transfer of such securities, accrued income being treated as that of a resident beneficiary: s. 742(4) to (7).

The *de minimis* relief for PRs referred to in 5.22 does not apply to trustees. Where the Scheme applies, the rate of tax for trustees is the sum of the basic and additional rates – 35% for 1992/93. Such tax, when paid, is charged to capital. Where, for instance, trustees sell a security *cum dividend* and are credited by the broker with the gross interest accruing from the previous dividend date to the date of sale, it is only reasonable that the tax on that accrued income should come out of capital, since the proceeds of sale, income as well as capital, will be credited to capital without apportionment: see *ante* 5.21. What should be done with a rebate amount, where trustees *purchase* fixed-interest stock, is not so straightforward, as the following illustration shows:

Trustees of a life interest buy £25,000 12.5% Exchequer stock 1999, which pays interest on 26 March and 26 September. Date of purchase, 25 May. Accrued interest is £503.42. This is the rebate amount, on which the trustees are entitled to relief. Interest is received on the following 26 September:

Gross	1,531.25
Tax	382.81
Net	1,148.44

Relief on the rebate amount is £503 at 25% = 125.75
The statutory income of the life interest in this stock is £1,028 (1,531 − 503); the trustees have received £1,148.44 + £125.75 = £1,274.19. Should the life tenant get the actual interest net payment of £1,148.44 and no more, or should he get the £125.75 on top of this as well? Some trustees may take the view that, sooner or later they are going to have to pay tax under the Scheme on a sale and should keep the relief as a reserve for this purpose. Other trustees will take the view that the £125.75 relief is part of the £382.81 tax deducted from the September interest and that the life tenant should get the increased amount resulting from the relief. The life tenant will agree with this view. But is it fair that, on a sale, the tax payable comes out of capital (see above) whilst on a purchase the tax rebate goes to income?*

---

*The author is indebted to Tony Sherring for this example, and, indeed, for detailed guidance on both passages in the text concerning the Accrued Income Scheme.

11.15   INVESTMENT IN LAND

Neither the TA nor the TIA empowers trustees to invest in the purchase of landed property, a state of affairs which in the opinion of the Law Reform Committee's 1982 report should be changed. Unless another statutory route is available, a purchase of real or leasehold property as an investment is possible only if either (a) there is an express power in the trust instrument, or (b) the beneficiaries, being all ascertained and *sui juris*, authorise it (see *post* ch. 13), or (c) the trustees apply to the court for the necessary authority (*post* ch. 13). Most modern trust instruments do, in fact, authorise the purchase of land (including any buildings on it) because a 'beneficial owner' clause (see *ante* 11.6) will cover this type of investment. Care still needs to be taken, however, because of the rather restricted interpretation of the word 'invest' in *Re Power* (1947); in that case Jenkins J. decided that an express power to invest in the purchase of land did not authorise the purchase of a property for a beneficiary to live in because any property so acquired would not produce income and the production of income was an essential element in the definition of an 'investment'. (He was also concerned about the fact that, when such a purchase was made, part of the price paid would be for vacant possession and was presumably not something one would pay when making an investment.) *Re Power*, although not much liked, is a real stumbling-block where a clause authorises 'investment' and no more. Fortunately, the lesson has been learned and a properly drawn clause will include, in addition, either a power to 'apply' capital (more extensive in meaning than 'invest') or a power to invest in non-income producing assets or an express power to apply capital in the purchase of property for occupation or use by a beneficiary. Property so bought will normally be held on trust for sale and there should be an express power to spend money on improvements: see *ante* 8.20(a); this will avoid any technical difficulties such as are described *post* 11.19.

11.16   THE RELEVANCE OF SLA POWERS TO TRUSTEES FOR SALE

Reference was made above to an alternative statutory route, and here one has in mind the application of capital money in accordance with the provisions of the SLA. This statute applies where any land is held in trust for persons by way of succession: s. 1(1); but *not* to land held upon trust for sale: s. 1(7). The distinction between (a) land and the proceeds of sale of land held in accordance with the SLA and (b) land held on trust for sale is crucial and must, of course, be considered and resolved from the start. In both cases the comprehensive powers given to a tenant for life under the SLA are available; thus:

Section 19(1) says that the person of full age who is for the time being beneficially entitled under a settlement to possession of settled land for his life is the tenant for life of that land and the tenant for life under that settlement. A previous provision, s. 9(2), entitles such a person to call for the settled land to be vested in him and it is usually sensible to do this. In ss. 38–93 the Act goes on to provide the tenant for life with virtual powers of life and death over the settled land, reducing the trustees to the status of depositaries of capital money and holders of the personalty investments representing it. Section 73 (mode of investment or application of capital money) and s. 84 (mode of application of capital money for improvements) are of particular interest in the present context. Section 73(1) says that capital money may be invested or otherwise applied (*inter alia*) in payment for any improvement authorised under s. 84 and in the purchase of freehold and leasehold land, the latter with 60 or more years unexpired. 'Authorised improvements' are elaborated in s. 84 and Schedule 3, but note that where agricultural property is concerned – see s. 73(1)(iv) – the expression 'improvements' may mean nothing more than 'repairs': see *Wolstenholme and Cherry*, vol.3, p. 163.[1]

Section 28(1) LPA gives trustees for sale of land all the combined powers of a tenant for life and the trustees of a settlement (including the more extensive powers conferred upon the latter during a minority by s. 102 SLA, even if no minority exists). Personal Representatives holding land on trust for sale are included by the definition of a trust for sale in s. 205(1)(xxix) LPA, but they also get the same powers by another route – see *ante* 5.2.

11.17 TRUSTEES FOR SALE WHO NO LONGER HOLD LAND

Where the SLA applies directly there is never any problem (except of a practical nature) about the use of its provisions concerning the application of capital money, but their use by trustees for sale is hampered by the decision in *Re Wakeman* (1945), the effect of which is to deny such trustees the use of SLA powers *if they no longer hold land upon trust for sale.* There may also be difficulty, on occasion, in identifying proceeds of sale of land where they have been mixed with pure personalty; it is only such proceeds which may be applied by trustees for sale of land in accordance with the combined powers referred to above.

The Court of Appeal decided in *Re Wellsted* (1949) that provided the trustees for sale are still holding some land after they have sold Blackacre, they can apply the proceeds of sale of Blackacre to meet the cost of a new property, whether it is being acquired as an income-producing asset or for occupation. The 'proceeds of sale' as mentioned in s. 28(1) LPA are properly said to exist so long as they can be traced. The court did not go so far as to overrule the *Wakeman* decision. Thus, if Blackacre is the only property held and it is desired to sell it and replace it with Whiteacre, the fact that the proceeds of sale are clearly traceable will be of no help, since the powers under s. 28(1) will have dropped off.

11.18   THE POSITION OF A TENANT FOR LIFE UNDER THE SLA

A tenant for life under the SLA is in a strong position – perhaps an impregnable one – to dictate events, for s. 75(2) says that the investment or other application of capital money by the trustees shall be made according to the direction of the tenant for life. It is true that the subsection then goes on to say that, in default of such direction, the trustees may exercise their discretion (and they should not overlook the need to consider its exercise in appropriate cases) but, even so, s. 75(4) emphasises that any investment or other application shall not during the subsistence of the beneficial interest of the tenant for life be altered without his consent. The positions of tenant for life and trustees are reversed if the former wishes to have dealings with the settled land for his own benefit or wishes to sell or exchange his own land to the trust; the powers are then exercised by the trustees in the name and on behalf of the tenant for life: s. 68.

> In *Re Pennant* (1969) the testator, who died in 1958, devised realty to his widow during widowhood with remainders over. The will was proved by the three executors, one of them being the widow. In 1960 the three executors, who had not executed any vesting assent under ss. 6 and 8(4) SLA in respect of part of the realty, sold this part to the widow, giving a receipt for the purchase money as PRs. Upon the widow's death in 1966 the question arose whether *her* PRs could make title to the land, bearing in mind that the 1960 conveyance showed a sale by executors to one of their own number. It was held that the land was settled land from the testator's death despite the absence of a vesting assent and that the conveyance was in order as being a sale of settled land to the tenant for life by the trustees of the settlement under s. 68.

Any attempt in the trust instrument to limit the tenant for life's powers is void: s. 106. The trustees cannot prevent the *bona fide* exercise of his discretion, and s. 97 protects them accordingly, although they are at liberty to refer the matter to court under s. 93. In *England* v *Public Trustee* (1968) a beneficiary entitled in remainder complained that the trustee had done nothing to prevent the tenant for life from selling some property too cheaply, but the Court of Appeal dismissed the claim. However, the trustees should satisfy themselves that what the tenant for life is proposing to do is authorised, either by the Act or by the settlement, and they can, at their discretion, seek independent advice as to title and form with regard to a proposed conveyance or mortgage. Otherwise their only recourse would appear to be to ask the court to restrain a tenant for life where they believe that he is not carrying out his statutory duty to have regard for the interests of *all* parties entitled under the settlement, bearing in mind that he is a trustee of the land under s. 16 and a trustee of his powers under s. 107. This was done in *Re Hunt's Settled Estates* (1905), applying s. 53 SLA 1882, the forerunner of s. 107, where a tenant for life was proposing to buy property which was undesirable though within his powers.

The Settled Land trustees do have a discretion to exercise with regard to the improvements described in Part II of Schedule 3, as, subject to any alternative provisions in the trust instrument, they may require the capital cost to be replaced by instalments paid by the tenant for life out of the income of the settled land: s. 84(2). In all cases where capital money is to be spent on improvements the trustees should obtain a certificate that the work has been properly done and that the amount due is properly payable: s. 84(2)(i).

11.19 TRUSTEES FOR SALE – LEASING, IMPROVING, REPAIRING AND BUYING LANDED PROPERTY

As mentioned above, 11.16, trustees for sale have all the powers of both a tenant for life and trustees under the SLA, including the power to grant leases, subject to the statutory restrictions as to length – 999 years for building and forestry leases, 100 years for mining leases and 50 years for all other leases: s. 41 SLA. 'Lease' includes an agreement for a lease. Reference should be made to one of the standard works on the law of landlord and tenant for guidance as to the contents of an appropriate lease for trust property.* (Some comments are made on rent review clauses, see *post* 11.43.)

Trustees for sale may, however, find themselves holding land for occupation by a beneficiary and unless the trust instrument sensibly spells out the respective obligations of occupant and trustee as to repairs and maintenance, there may well be arguments about who is to pay for what. Generally, a tenant for life under the SLA is not liable for 'permissive waste', i.e. failure to repair, unless the terms of the interest which he enjoys impose such liability on him; and a beneficiary occupying a property held on trust for sale will be in the same position. If the trust instrument itself does not dictate the respective liabilities of beneficiary and trustee for sale, the trustee will be well-advised to seek an agreement about this with the beneficiary at the start of the occupation period; a course that becomes even more essential if the trust instrument does not confer any right to occupation or even empower the trustee to permit occupation.[2]

Where trustees for sale have to lay out money on property, they may allocate the liability in accordance with Schedule 3 of the SLA, if relevant, (see *ante* 11.16 and 11.18) or in accordance with directions given in the trust instrument. Alternatively, they may instead rely on the general principle that ordinary repairs should be paid for out of income and improvements should be paid for out of capital: *Re Hotchkys* (1886). (In addition, if trustees exercise their discretion to pay for work done out of income which

---

*E.g. *Hill and Redman*, but *Landlord and Tenant*, J M Male, M & E Handbook Series, is a useful introduction to the subject.

could have been paid for out of capital, they will not be out of order: *Re Gray* (1927).) It is assumed that both a tenant for life under the SLA and trustees for sale will always take the sensible precaution of obtaining competitive estimates for work of any substance before actually instructing contractors to start operations.

When buying a property it should be second nature to obtain, before *any* commitment is entered into, a full report and valuation from a qualified surveyor employed independently of either vendor or beneficiary (if the property is intended for the latter's occupation). The surveyor should be told that he is advising trustees and should be asked to end his report with a specific recommendation to them to purchase the property for the trust fund at a specified price. Trustees should bear in mind that, although such a report, valuation and recommendation will constitute a powerful argument in support of a decision to acquire a property, they are still required to make up their own minds about the proposition and should not blindly accept even the most plausible advice. Personal inspection by the trustees is recommended; if this is impracticable they should ask someone in whom they have confidence (again *not* the beneficiary, where he is an interested party) to inspect the property on their behalf – independently of the surveyor whose professional services are retained.

11.20 MORTGAGES

Whereas land has considerable attractions as a trust asset, a mortgage has few. Yet a mortgage is an authorised narrower-range investment under the TIA and may be secured on freehold property in England and Wales or Northern Ireland and on leasehold property in those countries of which the unexpired term at the time of investment is not less than 60 years. Case law adds two further requirements: (a) that it should be a first legal mortgage, and (b) that it must not be a contributory mortgage. The disadvantage of land, either as an asset or as security for a mortgage, is that the market for sale is liable to contract or even to disappear altogether at what may be an inconvenient moment (the early 1990s saw both falling land values and defaulting mortgagors on a wide front); values, especially of investment properties, are likely to be adversely affected by political interference. On the other hand, the advantage of putting money into land and the bricks and mortar on top of it (provided the price is right) is obvious; whatever happens, short of an uninsurable disaster, there will be something tangible to show for the money spent. Quoted stocks and shares, by comparison, are susceptible to wasting diseases which may turn out to be fatal. It is difficult to summon up enthusiasm for mortgages as trust investments and one suspects that nowadays they only find their way into a portfolio either as a means of selling off a 'difficult' property, where part of the purchase money is left outstanding, or as a means of helping a beneficiary.

As regards difficult sales, s. 10(2) TA authorises trustees to leave not more than two-thirds of the purchase money outstanding on a mortgage of the property being sold, but note that if the property is leasehold it must have at least 500 years to run, a little difficult to reconcile with the TIA power to make mortgage advances on leasehold property with only 60 years to run. They need not obtain advice before doing so and are protected from any liability which might arise through the fact that the security was insufficient at the date of the transaction. The only trouble about this particular provision is that a really difficult property will only be sold on condition that a larger proportion of the sale price than two-thirds is left outstanding. A 'beneficial owner' clause will be sufficient authority in such a case. The trustees must negotiate the best terms as to periodic repayments that they can get and endeavour to sell only to a purchaser who they have good reason to believe will carry out his covenants under the mortgage.

When it comes to helping a beneficiary, *Underhill* (p. 534) says that trustees should not invest on mortgage merely to accommodate one of their beneficiaries where it is not reasonable to do so. Notwithstanding the generally unattractive nature of the asset, it will sometimes be reasonable to lay out a *proportion* of a trust fund for this purpose. It would be unwise to tie up a large part of a fund in a mortgage, but a fairly modest exercise need not be wrong and may be regarded as part of the fixed-interest element in the portfolio. Whatever express investment powers may be available, trustees should have recourse to the provisions of s. 8(1) TA and should be guided by it. *Underhill* develops the statutory provisions into a very helpful list of seven 'precautions' for trustees proposing to advance money on mortgage – pp. 536–7; trustees who take them should be in a good position to defend themselves later if the matter goes sour. It is important to remember that trustees are not necessarily in order in advancing two-thirds of the value placed upon the proposed security by the independent valuer. In the first place, the valuer may recommend a lesser proportion. In the second place, if the proposed mortgage is an improper one, e.g. because the security is of a speculative nature or because the mortgagor's financial prospects are suspect, no adherence to the rules will save the trustees from being accused of misjudgment and breach of trust.

11.21 BASIC PRINCIPLES

It may be appropriate at this point to recapitulate certain basic principles which a trustee should observe *when* investing and *after* having invested. Firstly, a reminder that trustees proposing to invest – whether in stocks and shares, land, mortgages or some more esoteric form of property – should always bear in mind the provisions of s. 6(1) TIA. Secondly, an investment, once made, needs constant attention. This rule applies to all forms of assets; those of a tangible nature – land, mortgaged lands, works of art, and so on

– need, in addition to being *considered* at regular intervals, regular inspection. Trustees may delegate this latter responsibility if they wish, but should on no account overlook its existence. Lastly, trustees should never forget that what they are investing is not their money but someone else's, and speculative decisions are, therefore, quite inappropriate.

11.22 INVESTMENT IN LAND – SECURITY OF TENURE

These days fewer estates and trusts will contain tenanted residential properties held as investments, such properties having fallen greatly in number over the past 50 years. Nevertheless, they do still turn up from time to time. Properties occupied for business purposes and tenanted farms are also encountered. In all these cases, PRs and trustees will deal with problems not found within the normal ambit of landlord and tenant law – problems arising out of the fact that the tenant is given a measure of protection from eviction and protection from being overcharged for rent. The law is extensive and labyrinthine and all that can be done here is to sketch in its most important features.

11.23 RESIDENTIAL TENANCIES

The story begins in 1915 when the Increase of Rent and Mortgage Interest (War Restrictions) Act was passed; fortunately, one does not have to go back that far. The legislation was consolidated in the Rent Act 1977, which forms the basis of the present law, subject, however, to the very important provisions of the Housing Act 1988.

Under the 1977 Act, a tenancy of a dwelling-house or of part of a dwelling-house was a regulated tenancy (i.e. it was either a contractual tenancy with rent protection or a statutory tenancy receiving both rent protection and security of tenure) unless, as in the case of expensive properties, the annual value exceeded a specified limit. In the case of most tenancies granted before 15 January 1989, the limits within which the rateable value of the dwelling-house must fall if the tenancy is to be protected are defined by the complex provisions of s. 4(1)-(3) of the Act. As from 15 January 1989 no more regulated tenancies can be created, with certain very limited exceptions.

Ground rent leases are excluded from Rent Act protection, but long tenancies of this kind (originally granted for over 21 years) get some protection under Part 1 of the Landlord and Tenant Act 1954. Furthermore, tenants of houses (not flats) held on long leases at low rents may purchase either the freehold or an extended lease under the provisions of the Leasehold Reform Act 1967. To complete this list of non-Rent Act protection, the Landlord and Tenant Act 1987 gives tenants of blocks of flats (a) a right of first refusal when their landlord wishes to dispose of his interest (Part I), (b) a right to have managers appointed (Part II) and (c) a right to compulsorily acquire their landlord's interest (Part III).

11.24 EXCLUSIONS FROM REGULATED TENANCIES

While pre-15 January 1989 regulated tenancies continue under the protection of the Rent Act 1977, it is as well to note the exclusions from that form of protection:

(a) A tenancy containing a genuine element of payment for board and attendance is excluded. The provision of a continental breakfast can constitute 'board' – *Otter* v *Norman* (1989).

(b) The existence of a 'resident landlord' or the sharing with him of essential living accommodation will prevent the tenant from being protected (see *post* 11.29).

(c) The tenancies under items (a) and (b) above receive 'restricted contract' protection, giving some rent protection but very little security of tenure. No new restricted contracts can be set up on or after 15 January 1989. The resident landlord exemption continues for the purpose of excluding the creation of the new type of tenancy under the Housing Act 1988, known as an assured tenancy.

(d) In addition to the exclusions noted in 11.23 above, business and agricultural tenancies are outside Rent Act protection and have their own special form of protection.

The pre-15 January 1989 regulated tenancy would have commenced life as a contractual tenancy, and during the term of the tenancy, the tenant is a protected tenant, protected for possession by the tenancy and protected for rent by the fair rent provisions of the Act; only when the contractual term has expired and the tenant stays on by virtue of the protection given him by the Act does he become a *statutory* tenant; for instance, when served with a notice to quit which the court does not enforce or where the statutory right of succession to the premises is exercised.

11.25 LICENSEES ARE NOT PROTECTED

Only tenants, as distinct from licensees, are protected, but calling a tenancy a licence will not help the landlord to evade the Rent Act. Thus in *Walsh* v *Griffiths-Jones* (1978) two persons signed a printed form headed 'licence' giving them the right to occupy a flat for three months but it was held that they owned a joint tenancy.

In *Street* v *Mountford* (1985), Mr Street owned a property in Boscombe and granted Mrs Mountford the right to occupy two furnished rooms in it at £37 a week. The agreement ended with a declaration by Mrs Mountford that she understood she was not getting a tenancy protected under the Rent Act. Later on, she succeeded in getting a fair rent registered and Mr Street then asked the court to say that she was a licensee, not a tenant. The Court of Appeal agreed with Mr Street, but the House of Lords allowed Mrs Mountford's appeal. Where residential accommodation is granted for a term at a rent with *exclusive possession*, the landlord providing neither attendance nor services, the grant is a tenancy. 'The court should be astute to detect and frustrate sham devices and artificial transactions whose only object was to disguise the grant of a tenancy and evade the Rent Acts.'

'Exclusive possession' in these cases is a matter of fact; an occupier of a property who is found not to be a lodger is not necessarily in exclusive possession – see *Brooker Settled Estates Ltd* v *Ayers* (1987).

11.26 SECURITY OF TENURE UNDER THE RENT ACT

One joint tenant out of two or more is as much entitled to protection as the plurality of them – *Lloyd* v *Sadler* (1978). Pre-15 January 1989 furnished tenancies, i.e. tenancies in which the provision of furniture by the landlord is a significant factor, are generally protected in the same way as unfurnished ones.

Neither a protected tenant nor a statutory one can be evicted without a court order. If the court considers it reasonable to do so, an order for possession may be made against a protected tenant if either (a) suitable alternative accommodation is available with equivalent security of tenure or (b) the circumstances come within one of a number of prescribed 'Cases' as set out in the Act, Sch. 15, Parts I and II. Part I Cases give the court a discretion; for instance, if the tenant fails to pay rent or fails to fulfil some other contractual obligation or is behaving unsatisfactorily, so as to cause a nuisance to neighbours, or is using the premises for an improper purpose, e.g. as a thieves' kitchen. Part II Cases are mandatory – the court has no option but to order possession where the landlord can prove his facts – e.g. that the property has been let by an owner-occupier who notified the tenant that he might require it again as a residence for himself or for a member of his family then living with him; other cases in this category are short lettings of holiday homes and the situation where the landlord acquired the property for retirement purposes and has now retired.

Protected shorthold tenancies were introduced by s. 52 Housing Act 1980 and have never been particularly popular because of the restriction upon the rent which could be charged. From 15 January 1989 a new version of the shorthold tenancy, the assured shorthold tenancy, has replaced it: see *post* 11.31.

11.27 SUCCESSION RIGHTS UNDER HOUSING ACT 1988

Under the Rent Act 1977, on the death of the tenant, the spouse (if residing in the dwelling at the moment of death) or other members of the deceased's family (if they had been residing with the deceased for at least the previous six months) could continue in possession as a statutory tenant. On the death of the first statutory tenant to succeed in this way, a second transmission was permitted.

Under the Housing Act 1988, as from 15 January 1989, the only occasion on which there will be a statutory succession on death, so as to give a statutory tenancy to the successor, is where (a) the deceased tenant was the original tenant (that is, not himself a successor) and (b) there is a surviving spouse (or 'a person who was living with the original tenant as his or her wife or husband') occupying the premises as a residence. Other members of the tenant's family or a spouse (in the broad sense) *of the successor* can no longer take a statutory tenancy by succession but will take instead a new assured periodic tenancy (see *post* 11.30). The conditions to be satisfied before a succession can occur include residence of two years (previously six months) with the deceased in the dwelling-house.

11.28 RENT PROTECTION UNDER RENT ACT 1977

Since 1965 it has been possible to register a fair rent for a protected contractual tenancy or a statutory tenancy, thereby making it a regulated tenancy and imposing a rent limit, being the registered rent or the contractual rent, whichever is lower. The contractual rent may be limited to that payable under a previous regulated tenancy of the same premises, provided that it ended not more than three years before the current tenancy began. A protected tenant, while retaining his statutory rights of security of tenure and rent regulation, may enter into an agreement for a higher rent under s. 51 of the Act. Once a fair rent has been registered by the Area Rent Officer (subject to a right of appeal to a Rent Tribunal) no variation is possible during the next two years, unless there is a change in the condition of the premises.

11.29 RESIDENT LANDLORD EXEMPTION

It will be recalled from 11.24 *ante* that the existence of a resident landlord will prevent the tenant from being protected under the Rent Act 1977, the prerequisite of this exemption being a tenancy granted on or after 14 August 1974 of a dwelling in the same building (not a purpose-built block of flats) as the one in which the landlord lives; a typical example being a two or three-storey house which is divided into two or more flats with the landlord residing in one of them. (Independently of this rule, the sharing of essential living accommodation with a landlord also excludes a protected tenancy, even though the tenant is in exclusive occupation of the other part of his accommodation – a kitchen is living accommodation for this purpose, a bathroom or WC is not.) Whether the building is shared or the living accommodation is shared, the tenant's protection is of the 'restricted contract' variety, i.e. the limited measure of security and rent protection given to rights of occupancy which fall short of the tenancy of a separate dwelling.

For the resident landlord concept to apply, the landlord himself (in the case of joint landlords, it need be only one of them) must reside, throughout the tenancy, in another dwelling in the same building. Normally a PR or trustee will be unable to reside in the property himself so as to preserve the exemption after the death of the landlord, but continuity can be maintained if a beneficiary goes into occupation as resident landlord. Breathing space is provided by a two year 'disregard' period, during which a new resident landlord may be found. If none has been established by the end of the period, the tenant will become protected. Where, however, the contractual tenancy does come to an end during the 'disregard' period, the PRs are immediately entitled to possession. In effect, the vesting of the property in the PRs on death entitles them to be treated as quasi-resident landlords during the 'disregard' period. Personal Representatives should therefore consider their rights as against a 'restricted contract' tenant well before the end of the period. A rent tribunal may postpone the effect of a notice to quit to such a tenant, and where this results in the notice taking effect after the end of the 'disregard' period a statutory tenancy will ensue, unless a new resident landlord has been found and installed during the period.

The alternatives open to the PRs are either to vest the property in a beneficiary who is able to take up residence (in which case they ought to appropriate it at a value close to its vacant possession value) or to sell it to a purchaser who is desirous of taking the deceased landlord's place as resident landlord. It was held in *Williams* v *Mate* (1982) that if there is an assent by the executor in favour of trustees, the executorship period and the trustee period are not mutually exclusive but can be added together in calculating the two-year 'disregard' period.

Under the Housing Act 1988, no new restricted contracts may be established from 15 January 1989. However, the resident landlord exemption continues to be relevant for preventing the tenant from claiming an assured tenancy – see below.

11.30 ASSURED TENANCIES

Subject to a few exceptions, the Housing Act 1988 replaces regulated tenancies with assured tenancies, but only for tenancies created on or after 15 January 1989. Generally, the new version seems to apply to the same tenancies as did the Rent Act. An assured tenancy cannot be brought to an end except either by a court order (there are both mandatory grounds and discretionary grounds) or by the landlord exercising an express power in a fixed-term tenancy. Basically, an assured tenancy is not subject to rent control, but there is some restriction of the landlord's power to increase the rent of *periodic* tenancies; in such cases, the landlord has first to serve a notice to the tenant in the prescribed form and the tenant may refer the notice to a rent assessment committee; there is no system of registration of rent.

11.31 ASSURED SHORTHOLD TENANCIES

Another creation of the Housing Act 1988, replacing the protected shorthold tenancy (*ante* 11.26). The new type is for a fixed period of six months or longer (no maximum). Before the tenancy is created, the prospective landlord must serve a notice upon the prospective tenant in the prescribed form. At the end of the fixed term, the landlord wishing to recover possession must give the tenant at least two months' notice. Provided the landlord has done this and that no further assured tenancy has come into being the court must make an order for possession – s. 21(1) and (2). It is obviously an advantage for landlords to have the virtual certainty of recovery of possession at the end of the fixed term; on the other hand, during the term itself, the tenant has the right to apply to a rent assessment committee if he considers that the agreed rent is excessive. In this respect, an assured shorthold tenancy seems less attractive to a landlord than a fixed-term assured tenancy under the Act.

11.32 COUNCIL HOUSES AND HOUSING ASSOCIATIONS

To complete the story of residential tenancies, it may be helpful to refer very briefly to the Housing Act 1985, Part IV, which gave to local authority tenants both security of tenure and the so-called 'right to buy'. The security provisions instituted a different regime from that established by the Rent Act 1977, discussed above, but is now not dissimilar to the protection given to assured tenancies by Part I of the Housing Act 1988. In any event, privatisation of council estates will mean that existing secure tenants become assured tenants.

Housing Associations established under the Housing Associations Act 1985, as amended in Part II of the Housing Act 1988, may grant assured tenancies unless they are of the fully mutual variety (limiting membership of the association to its tenants). Registered Housing Associations are eligible for loan or grant aid.

11.33 PROTECTION FROM EVICTION ACT 1977

This statute makes it a criminal offence to evict anyone lawfully occupying a property as a residence, whether as a protected or statutory tenant or under an unprotected lease, contract or licence – s. 1(2). Recourse to the court for an order for possession is therefore essential in such cases – s. 2; to succeed in an application for possession, the landlord must be able to show that he is entitled to re-enter under the terms of the lease or contract. Where the property is occupied unlawfully by a trespasser or squatter, the owner is entitled to make peaceable entry on the land without recourse to the court; however this is inadvisable, since the use of *any* force may make him criminally liable under s. 6 Criminal Law Act 1977. There is one exception; s. 6(3) states that it is a defence to any proceedings to prove that the accused was 'a displaced residential occupier' – someone who was occupying premises, went away and on returning found them occupied by a trespasser. Otherwise, summary proceedings for possession against squatters may be taken under RSC O.113 and CCR O.26 in the High Court and County Court respectively.

11.34 BUSINESS TENANCIES – SECURITY OF TENURE

Security of tenure for tenants of business premises is provided in Part II Landlord and Tenant Act 1954 which, in essence, allows a business tenancy to continue indefinitely until ended in accordance with the statutory procedure; s. 23(1) describes the tenancies to which Part II applies. As in residential cases, licences to occupy business premises are not protected; neither is there any statutory control over the rent to be paid on the initial grant of a business tenancy – it is entirely a matter to be settled by negotiation in the open market between landlord and tenant.

'Business' in this context means any trade, profession or enterprise with some element of commerce in its make-up; for instance a members' tennis club and a block of furnished bed-sitters have been held to be business premises for the purpose of the Act, whereas a Sunday School has not. A flat used by a medical school to house students is occupied for business purposes – *Groveside Properties Ltd* v *Westminster Medical School* (1983). The existence of living accommodation does not exclude the premises, provided there is a significant business 'presence' – in *Cheryl* v *Saldanha* (1978) the tenant lived in a service flat which he used for business purposes, installing office equipment and using business notepaper bearing the flat's address. The Court of Appeal decided that Part II of the Act applied.

Premises used for the purposes of an agricultural business are dealt with *post* 11.36.

As remarked above, a business tenancy will go on indefinitely until either landlord or tenant does something to end it. So far as the landlord is concerned, this something will be the service of notice in the prescribed form under s. 25(1) to end the tenancy, not less than six months and not more than 12 months from the date of the notice; the prescribed form is set out in statutory instruments, but it has been held that a form *substantially* correct is effective. The date of expiry must not be before the date upon which the tenancy can be ended contractually. Such a notice requires the tenant to notify the landlord in writing within two months whether or not he is willing to go and the landlord must say whether he would approve an application to the court for a new tenancy. If the tenant is not willing to go, he must first serve a counter-notice on the landlord within two months of the s. 25(1) notice (no prescribed form) that he is not willing to give up possession and he must then apply to the court for a new tenancy not less than two months and not more than four months after receiving the landlord's notice, assuming that the landlord is not prepared to offer a new tenancy. It may be noted here that an application to court on behalf of a deceased business tenant's estate may be made by his PRs after they get their grant.

On the tenant's side, he may end the tenancy by serving notice to quit on the landlord or by surrendering his lease. He may also forfeit it, or lose it because of forfeiture of a superior tenancy, subject to an application for relief under s. 146 LPA. Otherwise the tenancy will continue until the landlord himself makes the first move as outlined in the previous paragraph. However, a tenant for a fixed term may himself serve notice in prescribed form on his landlord asking for a new tenancy to begin not earlier than the date on which the existing tenancy expires and, failing a positive response from the landlord, may apply to the court for a new tenancy. It is important to ensure that any notice or counter-notice under the 1954 Act is properly served upon the recipient. It is also important for a tenant to observe any relevant time limits, since failure to do so will almost certainly deprive him of the right to a new tenancy.

11.35   THE GRANT OF A NEW BUSINESS TENANCY

The court is bound to grant a new tenancy unless the landlord can establish to the court's satisfaction that one or more of seven statutory grounds for refusal exists: s. 30 of the 1954 Act. If the landlord fails in this respect, and failing agreement between the parties, the terms of the new tenancy are determined by the court, taking into account the terms of the current tenancy and all relevant circumstances: s. 35. The rent will be the rent acceptable on the open market by a willing lessor: s. 34. The duration of the new tenancy will not exceed fourteen years; there may, however, be provision for renewals. In the event of the court's turning down the tenant's application (and in other cases where the tenancy ends), the tenant will sometimes be entitled to claim compensation – broadly, where the landlord will derive additional benefit from obtaining vacant possession. Section 47 prescribes the time-limits (varying according to the manner of termination) within which the claim must be made. Such compensation is based on rateable values multiplied by a factor called a multiplier and is calculated in accordance with the Landlord and Tenant Act 1954 (Appropriate Multiplier) Regulations 1990. The statutory provisions protecting business tenants seem to be particularly prolific in producing case law – partly, no doubt, because landlords and business tenants are in a better position to finance litigation than other sections of the community – and one can only counsel PRs and trustees on either side of this particular fence to have careful regard for the minutiae of the procedure to be followed. If possible, of course, it is much better for landlord and tenant to reach an agreement between themselves rather than to have recourse to litigation.

Protection under the 1954 Act is only available if the tenant's occupation of the property is real; it must be his business, not that of someone else. On the other hand, if there are joint tenants it is not necessary that all of them should be engaged in the business: s. 41A. If the landlord's interest is held on trust, the reference in the legislation to the landlord includes his beneficiaries. Thus, one of the seven grounds upon which a landlord may successfully oppose a new tenancy (provided that his interest was purchased or created five years or more before the end of the tenancy) is that he himself wishes to go into occupation: s. 30(1)(g). If the landlord's interest is held on trust, the reference to the landlord includes the beneficiaries: s. 41(2). Thus a PR or trustee is not precluded by reason of his fiduciary position from putting forward as a ground of opposition to a new tenancy the intention of one of his beneficiaries to occupy the property, provided that the testator's death occurred at least five years before the end of the current tenancy.

In *Nozari-Zadeh* v *Pearl Assurance plc* (1987) it was held that, where premises are occupied by a limited company controlled by the tenant of the premises, an application by the tenant for a new tenancy must be struck out because the premises were not 'occupied by the tenant for the purposes of a business carried on by him' within the meaning of s. 23(1) of the Act.

In *Morar* v *Chauhan* (1985) freehold premises belonging to C were leased by his nominee trustee to M for the 10 years ending October 1983. In August 1979 the trustee transferred the legal ownership back to C, but on the same day C declared a trust of the property in favour of his children. C opposed the grant of a new tenancy to M in 1983 on the ground that the premises were required for his own business or residential purposes. The Court of Appeal dismissed the argument that C's interest had been created less than five years before; it was sufficient that his interest had existed for five years, either as beneficiary under the nominee agreement or as trustee.

11.36 AGRICULTURAL TENANCIES

The Agricultural Holdings Act 1986 consolidated the existing law relating to tenancies of agricultural land; 'agricultural' in this context has a wide meaning and covers such concerns as market gardens, livestock breeding and factory farming, but is restricted to land which is used for trade or business purposes: s. 1(4). 'Tenancy' is defined as a letting of land for a term of years or from year to year: s. 1(5). A tenancy for less than a year and licences of agricultural land are treated as tenancies from year to year: s. 2(2). Agreements for grazing or mowing for less than a year are excluded from the provisions of the Act: s. 2(3); but they must be for grazing or mowing, and nothing else. Tenancies for two years and upwards, unless terminated by notice, do not terminate on their term date but continue from year to year: s. 3(1). A tenancy for a fixed term between one and two years is outside the provisions of the Act and is therefore not an agricultural holding for the purpose of security of tenure – a loophole which the Law Reform Commission has recommended should be closed. There should be a written tenancy agreement; if there is not or it is deficient in some respect, arbitration machinery is available to correct the position: s. 6.

Landlord and tenant are free to agree the rent to be paid, subject to s. 12, which provides for arbitration in the event of disagreement. If the landlord carries out improvements, the rent may be increased, subject again to arbitration: s. 13. Once a rent has been fixed, whether by agreement or by arbitration, the subject generally cannot be reopened for a further three years: Sch. 2, para.4. Note that the landlord has the right, under s. 23, to enter the agricultural holding which is subject to the tenancy, at any reasonable time in order to view its condition and to carry out his own responsibilities under the tenancy agreement.

11.37   SECURITY OF TENURE FOR AGRICULTURAL TENANCIES

The question of security of tenure cannot arise until the tenancy terminates which, in the case of a yearly tenancy, requires a notice to quit. It is a peculiarity of fixed-term agricultural tenancies for two years or more, that they too cannot terminate at their term date without service of a notice to quit, served by either party not less than one year and not more than two years before the term date: s. 3(1). In the absence of such notice, the tenancy will continue after the term date as a tenancy from year to year. If the tenancy is for a term of between two and five years, the parties may contract out of s. 3 with the approval of the Minister of Agriculture.

In the case of a tenancy for two years or more granted on or after 12 September 1984, if the *original* tenant dies, the tenancy will not continue as a yearly tenancy but will expire at the contractual date of termination (or, if the tenant dies in the last year of the term, one year later), eliminating any question of security of tenure: s. 4.

A notice to quit an agricultural holding is invalid if it purports to end the tenancy before 12 months has expired after the end of the current tenancy year: s. 25(1). There are exceptions, as where the tenant is insolvent, s. 25(2), but normally at least 12 months' notice is required. The tenant, on receiving such a notice, may serve a counter-notice on the landlord but must do so within one month of the giving of the notice s. 26(1). The effect of giving such a counter-notice is that the notice to quit will be ineffective unless the Agricultural Land Tribunal consents to its operation. The counter-notice must refer to subsection 26(1) and the parties cannot agree to exclude the right of the tenant to serve it: *Johnson* v *Moreton* (1980). However, the requirement of the Tribunal's consent to a notice to quit is excluded in eight cases (an example of which is irreparable breach of a term of the tenancy, ineffectively raised in *Johnson* v *Moreton*): s. 26(2) and Part I of Sch. 3.

In *Johnson* v *Moreton* (1980) there was a lease of a farm for ten years under which the tenant agreed to give possession immediately on termination of the tenancy and not in any event to serve a counter-notice. The landlords served notice of intention to terminate the tenancy at the end of the 10-year term, but contrary to the undertaking in the lease, the tenant served a counter-notice. The landlords responded with a second notice to quit in the same terms as the first but this time adding that the landlords' interest had been materially prejudiced by an irreparable breach of a term of the tenancy, to wit the serving of the counter-notice despite the ban. The House of Lords held that despite the absence in the legislation of express words prohibiting contracting out, the provision requiring a notice to quit to be ineffective in face of a counter-notice was overriding.

Under s. 27, the Tribunal *must* consent, if satisfied, to the operation of a notice to quit in a further six cases set out in s. 27(3), unless it takes the view that a fair and reasonable landlord would not insist on possession: s. 27(2).

11.38   COMPENSATION ON ENDING OF AGRICULTURAL TENANCY

Part V of the 1986 Act (ss. 60–78) deals with the question of compensation on the ending of a tenancy of an agricultural holding. There may be compensation to the tenant for disturbance (excluded in a number of cases, e.g. where the tenancy is ended because of failure to pay rent), for improvements (ss. 64 and 66–9) and for tenant-right, e.g. in respect of growing crops: s. 65. Compensation may flow in the other direction, from tenant to landlord, under ss. 71 and 72, where the farm has deteriorated through failure on the part of the tenant to observe the rules of good husbandry.

11.39   AGRICULTURAL TENANT'S RIGHT TO REMOVE FIXTURES

Subject to certain conditions, a tenant whose tenancy is ended has the right under s. 10 of the 1986 Act to remove fixtures such as machinery which he

311

has added to the holding, and even buildings which he has erected on the holding, provided he does so whilst the tenancy is still in force or within two months of its ending. He must avoid causing unnecessary damage during the removal and must make good damage which cannot be avoided. Notice in writing of the tenant's intention to remove such items has to be given to the landlord, who may elect to buy the fixtures and buildings as an alternative to their removal.

11.40 DEATH OF AN AGRICULTURAL TENANT

Case G is one of the eight cases in Part I of Sch. 3 mentioned above and refers to a notice to quit given after the death of a tenant. Such notice to quit must be served not more than three months after the date upon which the landlord receives the 'relevant notice' – this is the date upon which he is notified by the deceased's PRs of the death of the tenant.

The facts in *Lee* v *Tatchell* (1990) were as follows; T, the tenant of an agricultural holding, died on 19 March 1987. A demand for rent due on 25 March was returned by T's executors with a cheque for the amount due. The landlord served notice to quit on 1 August 1987. T's executors claimed that the return of the rent demand with their cheque was 'relevant notice' and that notice to quit had not been served within the three-month period. However, the Court of Appeal decided that the landlord could not have reasonably concluded from the action taken by T's executors following his death that time had started to run for the purposes of Case G.

Generally speaking, the right to succeed a deceased agricultural tenant was abolished by the Agricultural Holdings Act 1984, but not for tenancies created before 12 July 1984. As there are many agricultural tenancies created before that date, the succession on death provisions will remain significant for years to come; they are contained in ss. 35–48 and Sch. 6 of the 1986 Act, and there is a very full and helpful discussion of them in [1985] Conv 111. Briefly, succession to a pre-1984 agricultural tenancy on the death of the tenant may be claimed by 'an eligible person' who must be a 'close relative' of the deceased, defined by s. 35(2) as (a) the surviving spouse, (b) a brother or sister of the deceased, (c) a child of the deceased and (d) a person treated by the deceased as a child of the family – a notion we have encountered before: see *ante* 4.35. Such an eligible person must apply to the Tribunal for a direction entitling him to a tenancy within three months of the date of death: s. 39(1). A person cannot be 'eligible' unless during at least five years of the seven years leading up to the date of death his principal source of livelihood was agricultural: s. 36(3). The powers of the Tribunal under this head are discretionary, so a fully-qualified 'eligible person' will not necessarily get a tenancy. There cannot be more than two 'statutory' successions to an agricultural tenancy: s. 37.[3] Note finally the right of a tenant to nominate an 'eligible person' to succeed him as tenant on his retirement on or after the age of 65: ss. 49–58. The retirement provisions, although new in the 1984 Act, apply only to pre-1984 agricultural tenancies. The nominated 'eligible person' may apply to the Tribunal for a tenancy and the Tribunal has discretion to allow such a succession to the tenancy on the tenant's retirement; such a succession will count toward the two-succession restriction under s. 37.

11.41   THE RENT (AGRICULTURE) ACT 1976

This statute is designed to give the occupier of a 'tied cottage' the same sort of protection as that available to pre-15 January 1989 residential tenancies under the Rent Act. Such a protected occupier is one who had a licence or tenancy of a dwelling-house at a low or nil rent and is employed in agriculture. Note that a gamekeeper is employed in sport, not agriculture, so is unprotected: *Earl of Normanton* v *Giles* (1980). In addition to being protected in his own right, such an employee may transmit the protection to a member of his family on his death; only one such transmission is permitted. An order for possession will only be made, at the discretion of the court, against the occupier if (a) suitable alternative accommodation is available, or (b) the local housing authority is offering suitable alternative accommodation, or (c) in circumstances similar to those in which the court has discretion to order Rent Act possession: Sch. 4, Part I. An order for possession is mandatory where (a) the landlord occupied the dwelling as his residence before letting it to the occupier and requires it for his own residence or as a residence for a member of his family, or (b) the landlord is retiring and requires the dwelling as his residence, having acquired it for that purpose. There are provisions for rent control for such dwellings *after* the contractual relationship has ended and the protected occupier has become a statutory tenant: ss. 10–16.

By s. 34(4) Housing Act 1988 a licence or tenancy made on or after 15 January 1989 is outside the terms of the 1976 Act, with certain exceptions, as where a tenancy is granted to an existing protected occupier.

11.42   VULNERABILITY OF PRs AND TRUSTEES UNDER CONTRACTS AND LEASES

It is not always appreciated how fiduciaries such as PRs (their position has already had some consideration – *ante* 6.1) and trustees are burdened with all the liabilities of a beneficial owner for any contracts or covenants they enter into in pursuance of their duties, while they are in office.

> The PR or trustee is personally liable for taxation on the trust assets, for debts incurred in running a business and for any borrowing he makes on behalf of the

trust, whether by mortgage or otherwise. If he enters into a lease or becomes the assignee of a lease, again he will be personally liable. He has, of course, a right to be indemnified out of the estate or trust fund for all liabilities properly incurred and a right of reimbursement for all expenses properly incurred. But further than this he cannot go; he cannot obtain contribution from the beneficiaries and if the fund is inadequate to cover his personal liability, he can be made bankrupt by his creditors. There must be a special contract with the beneficiaries if the right of indemnity is to extend beyond the trust estate. A *bare* trustee is in a different position; in *Hardoon* v *Belilios* (1901) an employee held partly paid shares on behalf of his employer and the company concerned went into liquidation, resulting in a demand from the liquidator for a call of £402 from the employee. It was held by the House of Lords that the employer, being *sui juris* and the beneficial owner of the shares, was bound, in the absence of any contrary agreement, to indemnify the registered holder.

Leasehold property can be a fruitful source of long-term personal liabilities for PRs and trustees, whether as landlords or as tenants. Taking their position as landlords first, it is assumed that, except in the case of tenancies of the smaller residential properties, they will be landlords under the terms of a lease granted by deed (which will, in any case, be essential for the creation of a legal leasehold estate of over three years: ss. 52 and 54 LPA). A PR or trustee *granting* a lease (as distinct from having acquired the reversion by devolution or assignment) will remain liable under the landlord's covenants throughout the term of the lease, unless there is provision for this liability to be restricted to the period during which the landlord retains the reversion. In spite of the fact that an assignee of a reversion should provide the assigning landlord with an indemnity against this liability, PRs and trustees may consider it only prudent to include such a restricting provision in any leases which they grant.

Greater difficulties arise if the PRs or trustees find themselves in the position of lessees:

(a) The original lessee is liable by virtue of privity of contract for all breaches of covenant throughout the term of the lease, even after assignment, a factor which makes the estate of an original lessee who dies particularly vulnerable. This is a *known* contingent liability, and no amount of advertising under s. 27 TA will eliminate it. The obvious danger areas are the future breach of repairing covenants and failure to pay rent. The latter liability could extend to rent arrears incurred by a subsequent assignee, including a default in meeting additional rent payable under the operation of a rent review clause. The creation of a reserve fund under s. 26 TA will protect the PR or trustee as such, but not in his personal capacity – see *Re Owers* discussed at 5.38 *ante*. The Law Commission (Working Paper No. 95, 1986) has tentatively recommended that the privity of contract principle be abrogated.

(b) If a PR or trustee enters into a brand new lease he will be liable for the duration of the lease, not only in his representative capacity but also in his personal capacity before and after he winds up the estate or trust, unless he can persuade the freeholder to accept a limitation on those liabilities.

(c)   On the other hand, an assignee of the lease is liable only for breaches committed while he holds the lease. He has privity of contract only with his assignor, and his privity of estate with the lessor on matters touching and concerning the land does not render him liable for antecedent breaches unless, as in the case of a covenant to repair, a continuing breach has been perpetrated; nor is he liable for the acts of subsequent assignees.

(d)   A PR or trustee who purchases an existing lease will also make himself personally liable by virtue of privity of estate. The liability will not extend backwards or forwards outside his ownership of the lease but this could be cold comfort in respect of past but continuing breaches of a covenant to repair.

(e)   The eventual sale of a leasehold interest will not erase any accumulation of contingent liabilities, although, through the operation of the indemnity given by the purchaser under s. 77 LPA, an extra link in the chain of possible contributors will be provided.

11.43   RENT REVIEW CLAUSES

It has already been suggested (*ante* 11.19) that one of the standard works on the law of landlord and tenant should be consulted as to the contents of the normal well-drawn lease, but a few words on the subject of rent review clauses may not come amiss, since they are commonly found in leases of commercial property and are frequently the subject of litigation. Such clauses will normally specify the timetable to be followed for an effective rent review; failure to adhere to such a timetable may deprive the landlord of the right to uplift the rent to the current level, at any rate where 'time is of the essence', a factor which may be inferred from other terms in the lease, or it may be expressly stated (which is better), as in *Weller* v *Akehurst* (1981).

> In that case, the rent review date was 1 July 1979 and the lessor could determine the revised rent payable from that date by a notice in writing delivered not less than two clear quarters before the review date. In fact, the lessor's notice was dated 25 January 1979. As time was of the essence, the court held that the rent must remain at its previous level for the next seven years; this was £850 a year, compared with the £2,500 which the lessor had hoped to get under the rent review, and the mistake over the timetable was an expensive one.

Although the general principle nowadays seems to be that time stipulations in rent review clauses are not of the essence, it is much safer to diarise such clauses well in advance and to adhere to the timetable laid down.

11.44   INVESTMENT IN LAND – REVIEWS

Reference has already been made (see *ante* 11.21) to the importance of regular consideration and inspection of land held as a trust asset, and it is hoped that the preceding brief review of the law which protects tenants

315

from eviction and overcharging will have emphasised the need for PRs and trustees to diarise certain salient dates *in advance* e.g. the end of the 'disregard' period after the death of a resident landlord (11.29), the end of a business or agricultural tenancy (11.34 and 11.37) and, where the terms of a lease so provide, the approach of a rent review date (11.43).

12 Special types of trust and trustee

12.1 THE PUBLIC TRUSTEE

'There shall be established the office of public trustee' says s. 1(1) Public Trustee Act 1906, from which the following details are also taken:

The Public Trustee is a corporation sole, with perpetual succession, and is appointed by the Lord Chancellor, holding office during pleasure: s. 8.

The Public Trustee is a trust corporation (see *ante* 2.8) and is the father-figure of the modern corporate trustee.

Taking one year with another, the Public Trustee balances his incoming fees with his outgoing expenses and, indeed, is under an obligation to do so: s. 9. This obligation is fulfilled through the agency of a series of Treasury Orders which in times of inflation become an annual event; by this means the Public Trustee's fees for acting as executor, administrator and trustee are updated and promulgated irrespective of trust instrument and beneficiaries. Beneficiaries of estates and trusts administered by the Public Trustee have the satisfaction of knowing that they are indemnified by the State against loss caused by breach of trust: s. 7 of the Act.

Although the Public Trustee may decline to accept any business offered to him he may not do so solely on the grounds that its value is too small: s. 2. He may, if he thinks fit, accept a trust which involves the management or carrying on of any business, but only for a period not exceeding 18 months and with a view to sale, disposition or winding up and if satisfied that it can be carried on without risk of loss: r.7 Public Trustee Rules 1912.

The Public Trustee may not act as trustee of a 'foreign' settlement – that is, one of which the proper law is other than English, e.g. a Scottish trust as in *Re Hewitt* (1915); this means also that he may not act as executor of a testator domiciled outside England and Wales.

The Public Trustee may act as a custodian trustee, an office created by s. 4 of the Act (see *post* 12.4), but may not accept any trust which is *exclusively* for religious or charitable purposes: s. 2(5); neither may he deal with the administration of an insolvent estate: 2(4).

The Public Trustee may be appointed a judicial trustee (see below). In the administration of any trust or estate he is authorised to 'take and use professional advice and assistance in regard to legal and other matters, and may act on credible information, though less than legal evidence, as to matters of fact': r.26 Public Trustee Rules 1912. This guidance is, perhaps, useful as a precedent for other trustees as well.

The Public Trustee has one function which gives him some extra status *vis-à-vis* other trustees in that, in accordance with the aforesaid Rules, rr.31–7, he controls any investigation and audit of a trust applied for in accordance with s. 13(1) of the Act – and may, in default, carry out such an audit himself.

317

12.2 PUBLIC TRUSTEE'S NEW ROLES

In 1972, a Committee of Enquiry recommended that the work of the Public Trustee Office should be run down and that eventually it should be closed; the Public Trustee survived this attack and, in 1986, was given a bigger role to play. The Public Trustee and Administration of Funds Act 1986 merged the offices of Public Trustee and Accountant General of the Supreme Court, both of which could henceforth be held by the same person. It also conferred on the Public Trustee the functions expressed to be conferred by Part VII, Mental Health Act 1983 on a judge with regard to the property and affairs of patients under the Act. The result is that the Public Trustee is now in charge of funds held in Court and carries out the functions of the Court of Protection for the appointment of receivers and management of patients' affairs and also for Enduring Powers of Attorney. This is in addition to the office's traditional role as executor and trustee. The Public Trustee's realm is called the Public Trust Office and the address is Stewart House, 24 Kingsway, London WC2B 6JX.

12.3 JUDICIAL TRUSTEES

Section 1 Judicial Trustees Act 1896 empowers the court, at its discretion, to appoint a person, called a judicial trustee, to be a trustee of any trust, either jointly with any other person or as sole trustee and, if necessary, in place of all or any of the existing trustees. In this context 'trustee' includes in its meaning under s. 1(2) 'executor' and 'administrator', so the court can, if it thinks fit, remove an executor and replace him with a judicial trustee.[1] Section 1(3) provides that 'any fit and proper person' may be appointed, including a trust corporation, the trust solicitor, a beneficiary and an official of the court (which term includes the Official Solicitor). The appointment, control and discharge of a judicial trustee by the court are all effected under the Judicial Trustee Rules 1983:

> Remuneration may be allowed, not exceeding 15% per annum of the capital value of the trust, plus disbursements: r.11. In particular, where a solicitor is acting he may also act as the trust solicitor and be allowed as part of his remuneration all proper costs for professional work done by him in that capacity. A trust corporation would presumably ask the court to allow it to charge its current published scale of fees. The court maintains control over the judicial trustee by requiring the submission of an annual account: rr.9,12 and 13, and may give directions to him as and when required: r.8 (a request for directions can be made quite informally). It should be borne in mind that an appointee who is not already an official of the court becomes one automatically by virtue of the appointment.

The appointment of a judicial trustee may be recommended as a less drastic remedy than an application to have an estate or trust administered in court, where every administrative move has to be sanctioned in advance by the court. Because judicial trustees are nearly always appointed in chambers, it is difficult to judge to what extent and for what reasons use has been made of the Act. Typically, an application is made where there is an insoluble breach between an executor and beneficiaries, accompanied perhaps by an internal family feud and litigation (a judicial trustee was appointed for the estate of Caleb Diplock). This sort of background makes the prospect of office rather unattractive. Nevertheless, it seems to be one in which the professional trustee should be prepared to serve.

12.4 CUSTODIAN TRUSTEES

Custodian Trusteeship is another statutory office created by s. 4 Public Trustee Act 1906 and we have already seen, *ante* 12.1, how the Public Trustee may act in that capacity. Under the Public Trustee Rules 1912 – much amended, principally by the Public Trustee (Custodian Trustee) Rules 1975, themselves also the subject of subsequent amendment – other trust corporations, certain special corporations, Regional Health Authorities, local authorities and other bodies are also entitled to act as custodian trustees: see *ante* 2.8. Appointment to the office of custodian trustee is made (a) by order of the court or (b) by the testator or settlor or (c) by the person or persons having power to appoint new trustees. The duties and limitations on the responsibilities of a custodian trustee are described in s. 4(2) of the 1906 Act:

> The basic requirement is that responsibility for the conduct of the trust's affairs is divided between *managing* trustees on the one hand and the *custodian* trustee on the other. As their title implies, the former are the active partners who exercise all powers and discretions, whilst the latter plays a passive role. Trust property is transferred to the custodian trustee, who has custody of all securities and documents of title relating to the trust property. All sums, whether capital or income, payable to or out of the trust property should be paid to or by the custodian trustee, who may, however, allow dividends and other income to be paid to the managing trustees or as they may direct. 'The custodian trustee shall concur in and perform all acts necessary to enable the managing trustees to exercise their powers of management or any other power or discretion vested in them...unless the matter in which he is requested to concur is a breach of trust or may impose on him a personal liability...': s. 4(2)(d). He may, if in good faith, accept as correct written statements of fact received from the managing trustees and may act on legal advice obtained by the managing trustees independently of the custodian trustee: s. 4(2)(h). In view of the specialised knowledge which a trust corporation would usually be presumed to have, it would be difficult in practice for such a custodian trustee to disclaim awareness of a potential breach of trust in carrying out the directions of the managing trustees.

The advantage in appointing a custodian trustee lies in the fact that the trust capital is protected from possible loss through dishonesty on the part of the managing trustees and, the custodian trustee necessarily being of a perpetual nature, the trust property remains vested in one title-holder however many changes of personnel occur amongst the managing trustees. A trust corporation appointed to act in this capacity has the further advantage of being statutorily empowered to charge fees not exceeding those which the Public Trustee is authorised to charge, at the relevant time, for this type of service: s. 4(3). Alternatively, remuneration may be authorised by settlor or beneficiaries in the usual way: see *ante* 8.20, 9.35. A possible disadvantage is that, once created, a custodian trusteeship can only be brought to an end either by an order of the court: s. 4(2)(i), or by the winding up of the trust itself with the result that both sets of trustees are discharged of their offices. Whether this or some other factor has inhibited use of the concept, it appears never to have really 'caught on' except, perhaps, in the case of pension funds, where it is fairly common for individual managing trustees to be appointed but for the trust fund itself to be vested in a corporate trustee.

12.5   CHARITABLE TRUSTS

'The charity law is not in chaos. What has happened is that charity law is of long standing . . . Originally it was designed to deal with rogues and crooks misusing charitable funds.
(Sir Michael Havers, Attorney-General, House of Commons, 18 April 1983)

Charitable trusts are big business; there were over 170,000 registered with the Charity Commissioners at the end of 1990; these figures do not tell the whole story, because not all charities are registered (see *post* 12.15) and it has been suggested that there are no reliable statistics as to the totality of charities in the UK. Their total annual turnover is said to be in the region of £17 billion, representing 4% of the gross national product. The total value of their invested funds is not known, but it must be vast. One might hope, in view of the great size of the sector, that the law relating to charitable trusts would be clear, logical and up to date. Alas, this is not so; the administrative side is taken care of by the Charities Acts 1960 and 1992. The all-important question of what is or is not charitable in law is answered by reference to a mass of case law plus the decisions of the Charity Commissioners in response to applications for registration. There is, therefore, lots of evidence about the meaning of charity but, to use a homely metaphor, it is not frightfully easy to see the wood for the trees. Should there be a statutory definition? The Nathan Committee, back in 1952, recommended it but no government since then has had the courage to grapple with this dangerous idea. The trust concept has traditionally been used as a vehicle for charitable purposes; since the nineteenth century it has become common for charitable corporations to be set up. The latter type of entity may be more suitable and it has been suggested that serious consideration should be given to the creation of a specifically charitable corporate entity which would, in time, be the only legal vehicle for charitable purposes. *

12.6   THE IMPORTANCE OF BEING CHARITABLE

Why is it so important to be able to say whether or not a trust is for charitable purposes? Most of the trusts discussed in this book are private ones for the benefit of stated human beneficiaries, and in the absence of such beneficiaries, a private trust must fail: see *ante* 7.34. Trusts for purposes, as distinct from trusts for persons fall foul of this principle; charitable purpose trusts do not. So far as enforcement goes, the Attorney-General is ultimately responsible, on behalf of the public, through the Crown. Day-to-day control is vested in the Charity Commissioners. Not only are charitable trusts exempted from the principle that the quantum of the beneficiary's interest must be capable of definition, *ante* 7.13; they are also exempt from the rule requiring certainty of objects (*ante* 7.14), provided that the donor has made it clear that the gift is for charitable purposes and that a general charitable intent can be seen to exist over and above the specific charity which the donor had in mind. The elements of uncertainty will then be cured by the preparation of a scheme – see *post* 12.16. It is essential in all cases, however, that the objects or purposes of the trust be exclusively charitable; if it is possible for the funds to be applied for non-charitable purposes, then, generally, the trust will fail, unless such purposes can be treated as subsidiary to the main charitable purposes. *Re Coxen* (1948) is an example of this approach; a fund of £200,000 was provided for a specific charitable purpose but, additionally, there was also a trust for the spending of not more than £100 each year on a dinner for the trustees after they had met on trust business. It was held that this provision was ancillary to the main charitable purpose and was, therefore, acceptable, although non-charitable in itself.

12.7   DANGERS OF BEING EITHER CHARITABLE OR BENEVOLENT

The most notable examples of failure to satisfy the need to be exclusively charitable are those cases where a charitable purpose has been coupled to a non-charitable one; e.g. a trust for 'charitable or benevolent' purposes, as in Caleb Diplock's will: see *post* 14.27. Charitable *and* benevolent purposes are usually all right, since it is assumed that the purposes must be charitable, even if also benevolent, the operative words being construed

---

*See *Charity Corporations: The Framework for the Future* – Jean Warburton, [1990] Conv 95.

conjunctively. But this construction will not inevitably be adopted. An independent benevolent purpose is not necessarily charitable; see *A-G of the Bahamas* v *Royal Trust Co* (1986) where, in a gift 'for any purposes for and/or connected with the education and welfare of Bahamian children and young people', the words 'education and welfare' were construed *disjunctively*. The word 'welfare' had too much weight in this context to be treated as a simple adjunct of 'education' and therefore the funds *could* be applied for welfare purposes, which would not necessarily be charitable. The gift therefore failed. The Charitable Trusts (Validation) Act 1954 has been used in the past to validate provisions like the one just described, but it only applies to instruments coming into force before 16 December 1952 and is now lacking in practical significance.

12.8 PERPETUAL TRUSTS

Unlike non-charitable purpose trusts (see *ante* 7.33), charitable trusts may continue indefinitely, but they are still subject to the rule against perpetuities in the sense that the initial charitable gift must vest within the perpetuity period (*ante* 7.21), subject to 'wait and see' where the 1964 Act applies (*ante* 7.24). A gift over from one charity to another is, however, valid outside the perpetuity period; this facility has been used to create perpetual non-charitable trusts. In *Re Tyler* (1891) a gift to the London Missionary Society (a charity) was made subject to a condition that, in the event of the Society's failing to maintain a family vault, the fund was to pass to the Bluecoat School (another charity). There was no obligation, as such, to maintain the vault but the incentive was there.

12.9 FREEDOM FROM TAXATION

English charities which satisfy the legal requirements as outlined above and below (as to definition) get the following relief from taxation:

INCOME AND CORPORATION TAX: non-charitable bodies, whether incorporated or not, are liable for corporation tax on their income and gains. The investment income of charities is exempt under s. 505 ICTA. The investments and loans qualifying for this exemption are widely defined in Sch. 20, but there is an escape clause permitting unlisted items (e.g. unquoted equities) to be treated as qualifying provided that there is no tax avoidance at stake. The income must be expended or invested for charitable purposes, taking one year with another. Section 505 also exempts trading profits, provided that they are applied solely for the purposes of the charity *and* (a) the trade is carried on in pursuance of the charity's primary purpose (such as an educational charity running a school) or (b) the work is mainly done by beneficiaries of the charity (such as a charity to provide work for the disabled). Fund-raising activities such as bazaars and jumble sales may be exempt under ESC C4. But it is easy to run into a situation where there is no clear exemption, e.g. the selling of greetings cards, and the sensible thing to do then is for the charity, if its constitution so provides, to set up its own trading company which covenants to pay the whole of its taxable profits to the charity. Any payment by the company under such a profit-shedding covenant (as it is known) must be made under deduction of tax, leaving it to the charity to recover the tax: ss. 339(7) and 505(2) ICTA – see also SP 3/87. Charities also benefit from what has become the rare privilege of being able to receive covenanted income which is tax deductible for the donors for both basic and higher rates: s. 660 ICTA; and, in the case of corporate donors, the covenanted sums are tax deductible for corporation tax: s. 339(8) ICTA. For employees there is a payroll deduction scheme, offering similar advantages: s. 202 ICTA. There is also the Gift Aid scheme enabling individuals and companies to make one-off tax deductible donations, provided the gift is not less than £400 (originally £600).

TAXATION OF CAPITAL GAINS: s. 257 TCGA provides that gifts to charity by an individual result in a 'no gain, no loss' situation. Charities themselves are not liable to CGT on gains made, provided they are applied for charitable purposes: s. 256 TCGA.

INHERITANCE TAX: immediate and unconditional transfers by an individual (or by a life tenant as the result of the termination of his interest in possession) to a charity, whether *inter vivos* or on death, are exempt transfers of value: s. 23 IHTA, a section which contains anti-avoidance measures for the type of gift which is not clear-cut. Distributions from trusts without an interest in possession are exempted by s. 76. Payments *out of* charitable trusts are exempt under ss. 24(6) and 58(1)(a).

STAMP DUTY: conveyances, gifts and leases to charities are exempt under s. 129 FA 1982, provided that the document carries a denoting stamp.

VALUE ADDED TAX: unfortunately there is no general relief for charities from VAT either for the goods and services they buy or for the goods and services they provide. Certain transactions are outside the scope of VAT altogether, including donations of cash by the public on flag days, house-to-house collections, TV appeals and church collections; conversely, goods or services supplied by the charity will be outside its purview, unless the activity amounts to a business (in the very broad VAT sense of the term), in which case the sale will be standard-rated, zero-rated (as in the case of the sale of goods donated by the public) or exempt, according to the nature of what is supplied. For purchases, the zero-rated category includes medical aids supplied to a charity and the cost of its fund-raising advertisements. For ticket sales, the exempt category includes lotteries and fund-raising events which are not held by it as part of a series. Bearing in mind that the tax on purchases can be recovered only against standard-rated or zero-rated supplies and even then, only if the charity is registered for VAT, it is usually the larger kind of charity with trading activities that is likely to become involved in VAT, usually by setting up a separate trading company and seeking registration of it. For further details reference should be made to the relevant Customs & Excise leaflets and the VAT (Charities) Order 1987.

COMMUNITY CHARGE: under the old rating system charities were entitled to relief of one-half of the charge for properties which they occupied wholly or mainly for charitable purposes. The position for the community charge seems to be more flexible and at the discretion of the local council, so that there may be an abatement of up to 100%.

12.10   WHAT IS CHARITABLE?

The advantages to a trust of having charitable status in law have been briefly described above; how is this desirable state of affairs attained? The question to be asked is whether the trust is for charitable purposes; in answering this question, it is usual to refer first to the preamble to the Charitable Uses Act 1601 (The Statute of Elizabeth), which contained a list of accepted charitable objects. Both statute and its preamble have been repealed but the latter is still used by the courts as a guide. A more modern source of reference is the well-known classification of Lord MacNaghten in *CIT* v *Pemsel* (1891):

'Charity in its legal sense comprises four principal divisions: trusts for the relief of poverty; trusts for the advancement of education; trusts for the advancement of religion; and trusts for other purposes beneficial to the community, not falling under any of the preceding heads.'

This classification is not a precise one and neither can it be regarded as exclusive; other purposes have been held to be charitable, from time to time, as being within the spirit of the preamble to the 1601 Act. Moreover, Pemsel's case celebrated its centenary last year and ideas about the meaning of charitable purposes do not stand still; the Charity Commissioners are said to take a 'generous view' about this (Annual Report, 1985). There may be overlapping between different categories; nevertheless the classification is a useful starting-point for any attempt to analyse and understand the large number of decisions which define the boundaries of charity in law.

12.11   TRUSTS FOR THE RELIEF OF POVERTY

In *Re Coulthurst* (1951) Lord Evershed MR said:

'Poverty, of course, does not mean destitution. It is a word of wide and somewhat indefinite import, and, perhaps, it is not unfairly paraphrased for present purposes as meaning persons who have to "go short" in the ordinary acceptation of that term, due regard being had to their status in life and so forth. '

Trusts for charitable purposes under this heading are not subject to the otherwise universal rule that there must be at least some element of benefit to the public at large. *Re Scarisbrick* (1951) is an example of this exception; a testatrix gave half her residuary estate to a clan of needy relatives of her children. This was accepted as a charitable purpose; the fact that an immediate distribution was contemplated was no objection, but a gift to needy *specified individuals* would not, it appears, qualify as charitable. Another example of a trust for the relief of poverty is found in *Dingle* v *Turner* (1972), which was in fact a trust for the benefit of past employees of a company, E Dingle & Co. The House of Lords held this to be charitable. The favourable treatment given to trusts for poor relations and poor employees has been extended to other closed classes, e.g. a trust for aged, infirm etc. actors: *Spiller* v *Maude* (1881). It is an anomaly which is difficult to justify and one which will not be extended.

12.12 TRUSTS FOR THE ADVANCEMENT OF EDUCATION

Education here is not confined to formal instruction in a classroom; in fact, it has been interpreted quite broadly. In *Re Shaw's Will Trusts* (1952):

> The widow of George Bernard Shaw provided in her will for the teaching, promotion and encouragement in Ireland of self-control, elocution, oratory, deportment, the arts of personal contact, of social intercourse, and the other arts of public, private, professional and business life. This was, rather oddly, held to be charitable.

George Bernard Shaw himself was not so lucky, posthumously, that is; his attempt to have his residuary estate devoted to researching into the advantages of a new 40-letter alphabet was rejected by Harman J. in *Re Shaw* (1957):

> '. . . if the object be merely the increase of knowledge, that is not in itself a charitable object, *unless it be combined with teaching or education*' [emphasis supplied].

While football may be for the advancement of education, politics may not:

> In 1972 the Football Association set up a trust to provide facilities for pupils at schools and universities in the UK to play association football; after a long battle, this was held to be charitable by the House of Lords in *IRC* v *McMullen* (1981). The basis of the decision was the idea that the provision of sporting facilities contributed to a balanced education; as Lord Hailsham said: 'I reject any idea which would cramp the education of the young within the school or university syllabus . . . or render it devoid of pleasure in the exercise of skill.' It should be added that generally, trusts for sport and nothing else are not charitable, except in the limited ways permitted by the Recreational Charities Act 1958.
>
> Political purposes are not charitable, because the courts cannot or will not decide whether or not a particular political policy is for the public benefit. Concealing a political purpose behind an educational front will not work. In *McGovern* v *A-G* (1982) the organisation Amnesty International failed to secure registration; although some of its objects were charitable, its political objectives were not. But the fact that a trust for the advancement of education involves, incidentally, the provision of conferences of a political nature does not prevent

its being held charitable – *Re Koeppler's Will Trusts* (1986). By the same principle, the incidental political affiliation of students' unions does not prevent them from having charitable status: *A-G* v *Ross* (1986).

12.13 TRUSTS FOR THE ADVANCEMENT OF RELIGION

Before one can decide whether a trust is charitable under this heading, one has to establish what is meant by religion in this context. In *Re South Place Ethical Society* (1980) Dillon J. said: 'Religion, as I see it, is concerned with man's relations with God'. Subject to this all-important requirement, it seems that the essential elements are faith, in the sense of spiritual belief, supported by worship. Any form of the Christian religion is acceptable, including some very minor sects, such as the Unification Church (the 'Moonies'). As between different religions, the law stands neutral, but 'any religion is at least likely to be better than none' said Cross J. in *Neville Estates Ltd* v *Madden* (1962) (a doubtful proposition). It does seem that non-Christian religions will be accepted as charitable, provided they can satisfy the primary conditions. Certainly a gift for promotion of the Jewish religion was upheld in *Straus* v *Goldsmid* (1837). Whether the religion has to be monotheistic seems doubtful but there has to be *some* public benefit element; in *Gilmour* v *Coats* (1949):

> A trust for an order of cloistered and contemplative nuns, although for the advancement of religion, produced no benefit to the public at all, Greene MR remarking: 'they are to be paid, not to do good, but to be good'. However, the public benefit requirement can be satisfied quite easily; Browne-Wilkinson VC held that a trust for the saying of masses for members of the testatrix's family was charitable in *Re Hetherington* (1989), the public benefit being the 'edifying and improving effect on members of the public who attend'.

But a vast number of ancillary religious activities have been accepted as charitable, including, at the extreme limits of the category, a trust for the ringing of church bells on 29 May each year to celebrate the restoration of the monarchy: *Re Pardoe* (1906). Trusts for the repair and maintenance of churches and graveyards are charitable. The repair of churches was the only religious item mentioned in the 1601 Act, and it might be better in these days, in our predominantly secular society, if the religious category was confined to that objective.

12.14 OTHER PURPOSES BENEFICIAL TO THE COMMUNITY

It is impossible to define what type of purpose trust will qualify as charitable under this heading. The fact that it is of benefit to the public is not enough in itself; it has to be within the 'spirit and intendment of the preamble to the 1601 Act':

In *Incorporated Council of Law Reporting for England and Wales* v *A-G* (1972) Russell LJ suggested that, if a purpose was shown to be beneficial, it was *prima facie* charitable, but that this status might not be admitted if there were a particular objection to this being done – for example, that the purpose was primarily political.

Whatever the logical basis for admission to this category, it remains impossible to define; a few examples will have to suffice to illustrate its scope:

(a) Relief of the sick: trusts in support of hospitals are charitable – *Re Smith* (1962).

(b) Relief of the aged: trusts for the provision of housing for the elderly (*probably* over 60) are charitable, even if they have to pay something towards the cost – *Joseph Rowntree Memorial Trust Housing Association* v *A-G* (1983).

(c) Protection of animals: trusts for animals generally (not specific ones) are charitable on the grounds that it is good for humans to be kind to them – *Re Wedgwood* (1915).

(d) Village halls, community centres, Women's Institutes: these are specifically catered for by the Recreational Charities Act 1958, but there is a condition under the Act that the facilities must be provided in the interests of social welfare.

(e) Cremation: this is a charitable purpose – *Scottish Burial Reform & Cremation Society Ltd* v *Glasgow Corporation* (1968).

(f) Lifeboats: trusts for the relief of human suffering and distress are charitable. So the RNLI is charitable – *Thomas* v *Howell* (1874). (But care is needed when making disaster appeals: see *post* 12.17.)

This short list only scratches the surface of purposes held to be charitable under this head; the author was tempted to add *Loscombe* v *Wintringham* (1850) – encouragement of good domestic servants – but decided that this might be 'politically incorrect'.

12.15 CHARITABLE TRUSTEES AND THE CHARITY COMMISSION

All charitable trusts, apart from 'exempt charities', are subject to supervision and control by the Charity Commissioners for England and Wales. [2] 'Exempt charities' are defined in Charities Act 1960 Sch. 2. They include universities, charities which are 'excepted' by order, various national museums, Friendly Societies, property administered by the Church Commissioners and other places of worship. Small charities without a permanent endowment do not have to register with the Commissioners. 'Charity', for the purposes of the Act, means 'any institution, corporate or not, which is established for charitable purposes': s. 45(1), a definition which covers both charitable trusts and charitable

327

companies. A registered charity with a gross income of over £5,000 a year must now publish the fact that it is so registered on notices and advertisements seeking funds and on its cheques and invoices: s. 3 Charities Act 1992. 'Charity trustees' means 'the persons having the general control and management of the administration of a charity': s. 46 of the 1960 Act.

There is a Chief Charity Commissioner and four others and at least two of the five must be lawyers. They are appointed by the Home Secretary. Their address is 14 Ryder Street, London SW1Y 6AH and there are branches in Liverpool and Taunton. Although the Attorney-General is ultimately responsible for the enforcement of charitable trusts (representing the Monarch as *parens patriae*) the Charity Commissioners have considerable powers of their own for the control and regulation of registered charities and, in some situations, exercise a concurrent jurisdiction with that of the High Court: s. 18 of the 1960 Act, as amended by s. 13 of the 1992 Act.

Section 1(3) Charities Act 1960 says that the Commissioners shall have the general function of promoting the effective use of charitable resources by encouraging the development of better methods of administration, by giving trustees information or advice on any matter affecting the charity and by investigating and checking abuses. Apart from the exempt and excepted charities, all charities should be registered with the Charity Commissioners, and charity trustees are under an obligation to apply for registration, if the trust for which they are responsible is not already either registered or exempt or excepted. A leaflet, R.E.4, can be obtained which explains the procedure.

After registration, any change either in the trusts (including termination) or in the particulars entered on the register should be notified to the Commissioners. The register is open to the public: s. 4(7). Copies of entries about local charities are sent to relevant local authorities who may maintain their own indexes; if they do, these too are open to the public: s. 10. 'An institution shall for all purposes other than rectification of the register be conclusively presumed to be or have been a charity at any time when it is or was on the register of charities': s. 5(1) and see *Re Murawski* (1971) for an example of its retrospective operation. The Charity Commissioners are sole judges of any application for admission to the register, but an appeal either for or against registration may be brought in the High Court, at the cost of expense and delay, of course. (References are to the 1960 Act.)

Under s. 6 of the 1960 Act the Commissioners have power to institute enquiries with regard to charities or a particular charity. Section 7 gives them power to require any person having charity documents in his possession to produce them, and s. 54(2) of the 1992 Act makes it a criminal offence for any person to alter, suppress, conceal or destroy a document which he is required to produce to the Charity Commissioners. The 1992 Act also contains extended and very detailed provisions (ss. 19–27) as to the provision and audit of charity accounts; there is an overriding duty to keep accounting records which will, at any time, show the financial position of the charity. There must be an annual statement of account, in prescribed form: s. 20. Small, unregistered charities are exempt from these provisions, as are exempt charities but they are, however, still subject to the general obligation imposed on all charities by s. 32 of the 1960 Act to keep proper books of account, and to preserve them for at least seven years. Part II of the 1992 Act deals with the control of fund-raising, especially professional fund-raising; regulations may be made. Part III deals with public charitable collections, for which the approval of either a local authority or the Commissioners must be obtained; again, regulations may be made.

In addition to the more extensive statutory requirements imposed by the 1992 Act, the numbers of monitoring and investigative staff employed by the Commission have been substantially increased, and failure to manage a charity efficiently should be checked more thoroughly than in the past. At the same time, computerisation of the register is taking place, which should make the contents more accessible and facilitate the supervision of the very large number of charities for which the Commissioners are responsible. Apart from the leaflet R.E.4 previously mentioned, the Charity Commissioners publish other leaflets describing their services and the duties of charity trustees. These are free and are a useful general introduction to the practical side of this particular field of trust work.

Section 23 of the 1960 Act gives the Commissioners power to make orders authorising charity trustees to take any action 'expedient in the interests of the charity', which is for use in solving problems of an administrative or managerial nature and is akin to s. 57 TA, see *post* 13.7. It is said to be used most frequently to give authority for sales of land where the power of sale is either vague or non-existent. Section 24 provides for the Commissioners to give *any* charity trustee, including exempt ones, their opinion or advice on 'any matter affecting the performance of his duties'. Charity trustees should not hesitate to draw upon the experience and knowledge thus made (readily) available to them; this service, like the other services provided by the Commissioners, is free (at the moment; the 1989 White Paper on Charities proposed that free advice should be abolished). Apart from this attractive feature, charity trustees who act in accordance with advice from the Commissioners are protected from claims for breach of trust. Non-charity trustees may reasonably feel a little envious.

12.16 SCHEMES AND THE CY-PRÈS DOCTRINE

One of the most important functions of the Charity Commission is to make 'schemes' of various kinds; in 1990 they prepared over 700 such schemes, which have the effect of altering, in one way or another, the terms of the charitable trust to which the scheme applies. In some cases the scheme will involve a change in the administrative provisions; in others, a change in the actual object or purpose of the trust. Schemes of the second category are cy-près schemes – the Norman-French expression meaning 'as near as possible'; the circumstances in which cy-près schemes may be made are now listed in s. 13(1) Charities Act 1960:

(a)   where the original purposes, in whole or in part, (i) have been as far as may be fulfilled; or (ii) cannot be carried out, or not according to the directions given and to the spirit of the gift; or

(b)   where the original purposes provide a use for part only of the property available by virtue of the gift; or

(c)   where the property available by virtue of the gift and other property applicable for similar purposes can be more effectively used in conjunction, and to that end can suitably, regard being had to the spirit of the gift, be made applicable to common purposes; or

(d)   where the original purposes were laid down by reference to an area which then was but has since ceased to be a unit for some other purpose, or by reference to a class of persons or to an area which has for any reason since ceased to be suitable, regard being had to the spirit of the gift, or to be practical in administering the gift; or

(e)   where the original purposes, in whole or in part, have, since they were laid down, (i) been adequately provided for by other means; or (ii) ceased, as being useless or harmful to the community or for other reasons, to be in law charitable; or (iii) ceased in any other way to provide a suitable and effective method of using the property available by virtue of the gift, regard being had to the spirit of the gift.

Cy-près schemes fall into two main categories; firstly, where there is an *initial* failure of the gift and secondly, where the gift has taken effect but, subsequently, its objects become inappropriate or impossible. In both cases the funds may be redirected so as to fulfil the charitable purpose in a different way. It is important, however, to bear in mind that redirection in the case of initial failure is possible only if within the gift can be found a *general charitable intention*. On the other hand, if the gift has actually been applied for a charitable purpose, a cy-près scheme may be made, whether or not a general charitable intention was present in the first place. A recent example of initial failure, followed by a cy-près scheme, is *Re Woodhams* (1981):

The testator left money to two music colleges to pay for scholarships for British boys from Dr Barnardo's and the Church Of England Children's Society Homes; the colleges declined the gifts on the grounds that the restrictions on the award of the scholarships were impracticable. There was, therefore, an initial failure. The court found a general charitable intention to promote musical scholarships and approved a scheme on the same lines as the original gifts, minus the restrictive terms.

It should be borne in mind that charitable trustees themselves have no power to vary the terms and objects of their trust, unless there is an express provision to this effect in the trust instrument. The proper procedure is for the trustees to apply to the Commissioners for a scheme. Under s. 18(1)(a) of the 1960 Act they have the same powers as the court in this respect. If the trustees' problem is of an administrative nature, s. 23 (mentioned towards the end of 12.15) is available.

As regards small charities, see ss. 43 and 44 of the 1992 Act, replacing the provisions of the Charities Act 1985, which is repealed. Under s. 43, charities whose gross income is £5,000 a year or less and which do not hold land on charitable trusts may resolve either (a) to transfer the charity property to another similar charity or charities, or (b) to modify their charitable objects. Under s. 44, charities with a gross income of £1,000 a year or less and a permanent endowment which does not include any land, may resolve that capital be spent on the charity's objects. In both cases, the approval of the Charity Commissioners is needed.

12.17 CHARITY TRUSTEES, THEIR POWERS AND REMUNERATION; DISASTER FUNDS

Under s. 20 of the 1960 Act (as amended by the 1992 Act) the Charity Commissioners have extensive powers to act for the protection of charities; in particular, where they are satisfied that there has been misconduct or mismanagement, they may remove any trustee or officer. Under s. 20(3) a charity trustee may also be removed if he has been convicted of a felony, or is a bankrupt, or is incapable of acting because of mental disorder, or refuses to act or is outside England and Wales or cannot be found. Section 20(4) empowers the Commissioners to appoint a person to be a charity trustee in place of one removed; also where there is no trustee, or it is thought desirable for an additional trustee to be appointed.

In general terms, both the duties and powers of charity trustees do not differ from those of non-charitable trustees; one distinction, however, is that, usually, a majority of the former may bind the minority: see *Re Whiteley* (1910). Another possible difference arises out of the view of the Commissioners that charity trustees may delegate investment management, provided they retain overall control: see their 1978 Report at para.10.[3] So far as investments generally are concerned, note s. 38 of the 1992 Act, enabling regulations to be made varying the proportion which may be invested by charities in the wider-range under the TIA: see *ante* 11.4; also s. 39 enabling regulations to be made extending the powers of investment of charitable funds. Section 29 Charities Act 1960 requires a charity to get the consent of the Commissioners in order to borrow on the strength of its permanent endowment or to sell or lease its land; in other respects, charity trustees holding land have the SLA powers of a tenant for life and the trustees of the settlement.

For the most part, charity trustees appear to conduct their affairs on sound lines. In their report for 1975, the Commissioners said that they get complaints and criticisms only in respect of a very small proportion of charities: 'the danger of misconduct is greater when one person is able to achieve a dominant role' – para.76. This is a feature not confined to charitable trusts. In their 1981 Report, the Commissioners remark that all complaints were carefully investigated and 'as in previous years, many were found to be based on misunderstanding' – para.106. Again, this is a feature commonly found in non-charitable trusts. The same report, incidentally, contains valuable guidelines prepared by the Attorney-General for the assistance of persons responsible for making disaster appeals – see Appendix A to the Report.

> In these disaster cases, the crucial decision is whether to make the fund charitable; if this is done, substantial tax advantages accrue, but distributions must be made in accordance with charitable principles. This will mean restricting benefit to what is appropriate for an individual's needs. No such restriction applies to non-charitable funds, if the terms of the disaster appeal permit unlimited benefit, but, of course, the tax advantage is lost. The other disadvantage of the non-charitable route is that if there is any surplus left over there may be the problem that arose in *Re Gillingham Bus Disaster Fund* (1958) of paying the money back to the original donors; in the case of a charity, application could be made for the surplus to be dealt with cy-près, and if the original purpose had failed altogether, a cy-près application would still be available, provided there were a general charitable intention, failing which s. 14 Charities Act 1960 could be called in aid.

The Commissioners' views on the remuneration of charity trustees seem to be a little old-fashioned; 'only in very special cases will we agree to register as a charity an institution whose governing instrument provides for the remuneration of charity trustees': 1981 Report, para.64. Their views on this aspect of charity administration do not seem to have changed much since then, despite criticism. The Commissioners are known to be unhappy about the standard of trusteeship generally – the Chief Commissioner expressed concern in the 1989 Report which also contains a full exposition (paras. 87–95) of the Commissioners' reasons for opposing the payment of trustees. Nevertheless, one way of raising standards would be to accept the appointment of paid professional trustees in appropriate cases.

12.18   OFFICIAL CUSTODIAN FOR CHARITIES

Both personal property and land may be transferred to this official by charity trustees, and his position is the same in all respects as that of a custodian trustee appointed under s. 4 Public Trustee Act (*ante* 12.4), except that his services are free. The advantages of making use of these services are, primarily, continuity of title whatever changes of personnel take place amongst the charity trustees, and the fact that he can pay dividends over without deduction of tax. However, this useful service to charities is to disappear. Section 29(1) of the 1992 Act says boldly:

'The Official Custodian shall, in accordance with this section divest himself of all property to which this sub-section applies. '
Section 29(2) excludes land from the operation of s. 29(1). As regards land, s. 32(1) requires the approval of the Commissioners to the disposition of land to a 'connected person', e.g. a trustee or donor to the charity; otherwise s. 32(3) to (7) contain detailed instructions to charity trustees regarding the way in which they should go about selling or leasing land.

12.19   PENSION FUND TRUSTS

There are a number of ways in which persons resident in the UK can achieve financial security (if not wealth) in their declining years; in the first place, the state pays an old age pension to those who have paid national insurance contributions during their working lives. There is also a state earnings-related scheme (SERPS) – this may, however, be contracted out of. Individuals may make their own private arrangements for a pension via a life company or some other commercial source. It is probably fair to say, however, that the majority of UK pensions, apart from the basic state pension, are financed by company occupational pension schemes;[4] such schemes will almost invariably by organised in the form of a trust. The historical reason for this is simply that the Revenue would only allow tax relief to such schemes if they took the form of an irrevocable trust. Without Revenue approval, the many substantial tax advantages arising out of the allowance of contributions against taxable income and the freedom from income and capital taxes of the invested funds would not be available. The Revenue's Superannuation Fund Office, recently renamed the Pension Scheme Office (PSO), has published a memorandum, IR12, which contains guidance as to the way in which its approval of occupational pension schemes may be obtained. There is a Registrar of Pension Schemes, with whom such schemes are registrable.

12.20   SUITABILITY OF THE TRUST AS A PENSION VEHICLE

Like many unit trusts and a considerable number of charitable trusts, pension fund trusts tend to be of great value; the total invested in such trusts was recently estimated to be well over £260 billion. Apart from the vast size of the larger ones, the other current notable feature of them is that they have been much in the news, for two main reasons – (a) the question of who owns 'surplus funds', highlighted by the Hanson Group take-over of Imperial Tobacco, and (b) the gross mismanagement of the Maxwell Group pension funds. As a result of these events, a good deal of criticism of the trust concept as a vehicle for pension funds has been published; it has been suggested, for instance, that the failure of some such trusts to protect their members' interests indicates that pension funds have outgrown their origins and that a new, tailor-made legal format should be provided for them – by statute, one presumes.

Such criticism is wide of the mark; it is not the trust concept itself which has failed the pension fund members, but the use made of it. A trust of any kind is only as good as (a) the contents of the trust instrument and (b) the trustees who administer it. It seems clear (with the benefit of hindsight) that occupational pension funds generally have been too much under the thumb of the employers who have set them up; such employers direct the drafting of the trust instrument in the first place, then often appoint their own representatives as trustees.

Even if the trustees are drawn from the ranks of the employees, problems remain. Firstly, new trustees must have adequate training to protect beneficiaries. Even more important, all trustees need on occasions to disagree with the company line, where conflicts of interest arise. They cannot operate effectively under the fear, not just of being sacked as trustees, but of losing their jobs as well. The presence of an experienced and independent co-trustee can go a long way to resolving this conflict of interest that is generally inherent in occupational pension schemes.

The terms of the trust instrument are likely to be flexible enough to permit over-emphasis upon the interests of the employer, an extreme example of which occurred not long ago when a stores group pension fund bought from the company a vacant site for £2.4 million in order to assist the company's finances; all to no avail, as the company failed and the pension fund was left with a site which produced no income and which was dropping in value. The purchase was, no doubt, authorised but this kind of transaction cannot be in the best interests of the members. In other cases it is not unknown for a large proportion of a fund's investments to be in the employer's business. Apart from breaking the basic rule that not all one's eggs should be in one basket (see *ante* 11.7), the result, so far as the members are concerned, can be quite disastrous if the company goes into liquidation, since the claim of the pension trustees for any pension fund deficit will rank only *pari passu* with those of the company's creditors.

The Social Security Act 1990, Sch. 4 makes provision for self-investment to be limited to 5% of a fund's investments and for a pension fund deficit to be treated as a debt of an employer, although the debt will merely rank as an unsecured debt and will not have any preference. Regulations to apply the first of these provisions came into force on 9 March 1992, undoubtedly as a result of the Maxwell disaster, a good example of shutting the stable door after the horse has bolted. The second provision came into force on 30 June 1992.

12.21 WHO OWNS THE SURPLUS IN A PENSION FUND?

Reference was made above to a situation where the employer goes into liquidation; when this happens or when, for instance, the employer company is taken over, it may be found that the company pension fund is in surplus, that is, the fund's assets exceed what it is estimated, on an actuarial basis, will be needed to pay present and future pensions. The existence of such a surplus is one tempting factor so far as a predator is concerned. To whom does this surplus belong?

In *Mettoy Pension Trustees Ltd* v *Evans* (1990) the terms of the trust gave the employer a discretion to apply such a surplus for the provision of further benefits to the pensioners and then claw back anything remaining for the company itself. The company went into liquidation and the liquidator asked the court whether he could exercise the discretionary power just described. Warner J. declared that the power was fiduciary; it could not be exercised by the liquidator, whose main duty was to take care of the creditors' interests and it was, therefore, exercisable by the court. One factor which influenced the judge to make this decision was the fact that the beneficiaries (the members) of the pension fund were not volunteers but had rights in the trust of a contractual and commercial origin – in other words, rights derived from the fact that they were, or had been, employees of the company.

This very significant point does indeed distinguish the pension fund trust from the ordinary run of private family trusts, large or small. The destination of a fund's surplus was also in point in the case of *Imperial Group Pension Trust Ltd* v *Imperial Tobacco Ltd* (1991):

The court was not asked any questions about the actual ownership of the surplus, but it was clearly in the minds of the fund's members that Hanson plc, which had got control of Imperial Tobacco, wanted access to this surplus. In giving judgment, Browne-Wilkinson VC said that the pension scheme trust deed and rules themselves were to be taken as being impliedly subject to the limitation that the rights and powers of the company, i.e. Imperial Tobacco, could only be exercised in accordance with the implied obligation of 'good faith'.

This does not mean, it seems, that an employer must ignore its own interests in reaching a decision concerning a pension fund, but that it must always exercise its powers in a way which does not conflict with its overall obligation of good faith towards pension fund members. This obligation obviously falls short of saying that a surplus in a pension fund *belongs* to members, although this is what some commentators on the current pension funds scene believe should be the case. And indeed if that view were to be written into the legislation, companies might become far less generous in funding their pension funds, since while they would have to make good deficits, they could never recover surpluses. It has even been suggested that in these circumstances final salary pension schemes as we know them would disappear.[5]

12.22 PRESENT STATUS OF PENSION FUND TRUSTS

Do recent developments in this field mean that a quite separate code of law is developing for pension fund trusts? There is judicial authority to the effect that the principles applied to such trusts are the same as those for private trusts; in *Cowan* v *Scargill* (1985), Megarry VC said:

> 'I can see no reason for holding that different principles apply to pension fund trusts from those which apply to other trusts. Of course, there are many provisions which are not to be found in private trusts and to these the general law of trusts will be subordinated. But subject to that, I think that the trusts of pension funds are subject to the same rules as other trusts. '

This cannot be gainsaid, but recent applications of these principles to pension funds do tend to show that the pension fund trust (like the unit trust and the charitable trust) is developing its own rules and practice and that these are quite distinct from the rules and practice applied to the traditional family trust. Thus, a family trust may have to balance the rights of current and future generations, whereas pension funds are relatively indifferent whether the return is capital or income. The sheer size of some pension funds will, for instance, justify relaxation of normal, cautious rules with regard to investments, especially as sophisticated advice is a *sine qua non* in such cases; the spread of investments available in a very large fund may justify the purchase of an investment which would be too risky to be included in a small fund.[6]

12.23 REGULATORY PROVISIONS FOR PENSION FUNDS

Apart from the relaxed attitude of the law with regard to investment matters and the unusual position of the beneficiary/members referred to above, not at all the same as that of the beneficiaries of a private trust, there is a steadily increasing corpus of regulatory provisions:

(a) *Small self-administered pensions schemes (SSASs)*: these are schemes with fewer than twelve members, usually designed to serve the key personnel of the typical family company. The members will probably be the company directors and will themselves act as trustees. The rules for the operation of these schemes were laid down in the legendary Memorandum 58, issued by the SFO (now the PSO). New regulations came into force in 1991 (Memorandum 109). Self-investment after 5 August 1991 is restricted to 25% of the contribution for the first two years, rising to 50% thereafter. There has to be one independent trustee, called a 'pensioneer trustee', either a skilled individual or a corporation – typically, a trust corporation. The pensioneer trustee has to give an undertaking to the PSO that he will block a premature, improper attempt to bring the scheme to an end in a way that would involve abuse of the tax privileges enjoyed by such schemes.

(b)   Members' complaints: disgruntled beneficiaries of a private family trust who are in dispute with the trustees can do no more, in the last resort, than sue the trustees for breach of trust – an expensive course of action. Pension fund members may have recourse, initially, to the Occupational Pensions Advisory Service (OPAS) – that is, if neither the management committee nor the trustees of the fund are prepared to deal with the complaint in the first place. If OPAS cannot resolve the problem, then there is (since April 1991) a Pensions Ombudsman; he has certain statutory powers which enable him to demand production of documents and attendance at a hearing. He can deal only with individual complaints. Any decision of his is binding on both sides to a dispute, subject (a very important exception) to an appeal to the court on a point of law.
(c)   Information: obviously it was thought that the standard rule for trustees as regards supplying information to beneficiaries (see *ante* 9.25) was not good enough for pension funds. The Occupational Pension Schemes (Disclosure of Information) Regulations 1986 impose their own very comprehensive rules on pension fund trustees in this respect.

Reference has already been made to the new regulation covering self-investment, restricting it to 5% of the fund, except for SSASs, which have their own rules. It seem inevitable that there will be further intervention by the State into this highly important sector of the trust world. One innovation which would surely be advantageous to pension fund members generally would be the mandatory appointment of at least one fully independent trustee, for which trust corporations would be the obvious choice. Already, such a trustee must be appointed when a company goes into liquidation. *All* pension fund trustees should, of course, be aware of their duties and be prepared to exercise them honestly and sensibly; in this connection, the booklet published by the DSS, *Pension Trust Principles; the Occupational Pensions Board Guide for Pension Trustees*, is required reading. In the long run it may be that a statutory framework, something akin to that which applies to charitable trusts, should be constructed, with Pension Fund Commissioners to regulate and control pension funds, which would be registered with them in the same way as charities are registered with the Charity Commissioners. The latest news is that an independent commission is to examine UK pensions legislation and recommend reforms.

12.24   UNIT TRUSTS

Reference has already been made to the flexible nature of a trust, and this characteristic is well illustrated by the development of the unit trust. The concept first appeared in the nineteenth century but, in its present form, dates from 1931. At the end of 1990, according to the Unit Trust Year Book 1991, UK unit trust funds totalled £46.3 billion; in terms of size, therefore, such trusts are a very significant feature. On the other hand, because the office of trustee in this field is largely confined to the London and Edinburgh offices of a relatively small number of substantial banks and insurance companies, unit trust work is not a subject with which the average practitioner in estates and trusts is likely to have much contact.

A unit trust is established between a manager on the one hand and a trustee on the other. The trust deed will provide for the trustee to hold the trust assets on behalf of such persons as subscribe for shares (the 'units') in them. The fund is then held for such subscribers (the 'unitholder') in proportion to the number of units they hold. Generally speaking, the manager is responsible for the active administration of the fund and the trustee for its safe-keeping and for ensuring that the fund's affairs are conducted within the limits prescribed by the trust deed: see *post* 12.27. For authorised or recognised unit trusts the trustee must also ensure observance of (a) the Scheme Particulars[7] and (b) The Financial Services (Regulated Schemes) Regulations 1991, (termed 'The Regulations' in the following passages).

12.25   DISTINCTIVE FEATURES OF A UNIT TRUST

Compared with the ordinary family trust, there are two features in the unit trust which stand out as idiosyncratic. In the first place, the beneficiaries, i.e. the unitholders, *buy* their way into the trust by purchasing units from the manager. Secondly, there is the existence of the manager himself; the introduction of this alien figure into the structure of the trust is, initially, confusing. Trustees, as we saw in Chapter 11, are generally responsible for investing trust funds but, in a unit trust, the manager performs this all-important function. In one sense, therefore, the trustee of a unit trust does not control its destiny, although his supervisory role is a crucial one. The relative positions of manager and trustee are somewhat similar to those of managing and custodian trustees: see *ante* 12.4. The manager's role is to promote and execute the trust, while the trustee acts as custodian of the assets and ensures that the manager observes both letter and spirit of the trust deed (and, for authorised or recognised unit trusts, the Scheme Particulars and The Regulations), both parties having a fiduciary relationship with the beneficiaries or unitholders.

An authorised unit trust is a 'collective investment scheme' within the meaning of ss. 75–95 Financial Services Act 1986 and the regulations made under the Act. Under s. 75 the essential elements of such a scheme are:

(a)   the contributions of participants in the scheme and the income and profits arising therefrom are pooled; and

(b)   the pooled property is managed on behalf of the participants by a scheme operator, who alone has day-to-day control.

Even where these elements are present, the result may not be a scheme within the meaning of the Act; for instance, where such arrangements are not operated by way of business, or where the participants actually *own* their shares of the property in the pool and may withdraw it at any time: Personal Equity Plans (PEPs) are examples of the latter type of arrangement. It is vital to be able to distinguish between arrangements which are schemes within the Act from those which are not.[8] If the former, then s. 76 prohibits the issue of any advertisement inviting the public to participate, unless the scheme is either authorised or recognised; a recognised scheme is one approved under ss. 86–90, constituted outside the UK, but affording similar protection to the investors as an authorised scheme. There are exceptions to the rule against advertising, e.g. under s. 76(3) the Securities and Investment Board (SIB), which exercises the functions of the Secretary of State under the Act, may make regulations exempting specified schemes, a power which has been exercised in The Financial Services (Promotion of Unregulated Schemes) Regulations 1991.

12.26 WHO MAY CARRY ON UNIT TRUST BUSINESS?

It is a basic provision of the 1986 Act that no one shall carry on investment business in the UK unless either authorised to do so or exempt from authorisation: s. 3. Investment business includes unit trust work and generally, therefore, only authorised persons may promote and operate such arrangements – or even give advice regarding them. Those who are exempted from authorisation include the Bank of England, s. 35; recognised investment exchanges, s. 36; and the Public Trustee, s. 45(1)(e). Perhaps the most important exemption is that given to persons carrying on investment business in other member countries of the European Community, s. 31; schemes operated by such persons may be marketed in the UK subject to two months' notice to the SIB, s. 86(2). Note that s. 44 confers exemption upon appointed representatives of authorised persons; this is not a reference to *employees* of authorised persons who will be working in the course of their employment under the authorised banner of their employer, but to independent agents acting under contracts to carry on investment business for a principal (for example, the self-employed representatives of an insurance company) and for whose acts such principals accept liability as if the agents were employees.

So far as authorisation to carry on investment business is concerned, the main channel for obtaining this coveted prize for both managers and trustees of unit trusts will be through the Investment Managers Regulatory Organisation (IMRO), which is a self-regulating organisation recognised as such by the SIB.

Having been authorised to carry on investment business in the form of a Collective Investment Scheme, or unit trust, the intended manager and trustee of the scheme must then apply for authorisation of the particular scheme which they wish to promote: s. 77. Such applications are made to the SIB, accompanied by a copy of the trust deed, the Scheme Particulars and a certificate signed by a solicitor stating that the trust deed complies with the statutory requirements as to content: s. 78(1). Sub-sections (2) to (6) of s. 78 specify such requirements, of which perhaps the most significant are (a) the manager and trustee must be persons independent of each other and (b) they must be incorporated bodies with places of business in the UK and authorised to carry on investment business. The SIB may require additional information to be supplied; its powers of authorisation are discretionary and, in the event of a refusal, there is little available to the applicants by way of right of appeal. There is a time limit of six months, during which period the SIB must advise the applicants of its decision.

Unregulated schemes generally may be promoted, but only by authorised persons, to specified types of investor, such as established customers of the promoter with whom the latter has a written agreement and where the customer is regarded as being an 'experienced investor' – see the Conduct of Business Rules, 1.06. These rules, which are made by the SIB, are binding upon authorised persons and are extensive in scope and complexity.

12.27 DUTIES OF UNIT TRUST MANAGER AND UNIT TRUST TRUSTEE

The respective duties of manager and trustee are summarised in The Regulations (see *ante* 12.24) as follows:

1. It is the duty of the manager to manage the property of the scheme and it is his right and duty to make decisions as to the constituents of that property from time to time in accordance with (a) the trust deed and (b) these and any other regulations made under s. 81 of the Act and (c) the most recently published scheme particulars.
2. It shall be the duty of the trustee to take reasonable care to ensure that the scheme is administered by the manager in accordance with 1. above.
3. The manager shall on the request of the trustee forthwith supply the trustee with such information concerning the management and administration of the scheme as he may reasonably require.

The general body of the law relating to the duties of trustees applies as much to unit trust trustees as it does to those responsible for a family trust, but the special circumstances in which the former find themselves both detract from and add to their functions in practice. Whilst, in the past, it might have been truly said that the trustee's role was reactive rather than active, the new regime introduced by the 1986 Act has surely increased their responsibilities. Nevertheless, the following summary* of their functions is still felt to be a valid one; but reference should also be made to Part 7 of The Regulations, which spells out their duties.

---

*Based upon a lecture by Mr P S Roots to The Association of Corporate Trustees on 3 March 1982.

(a) Before accepting office in the first place, the trustees will satisfy themselves as to the character and status of the proposed manager.

(b) Having accepted office, they take control of the unit trust's funds. Physical control of documents of title may be delegated to a third party, and such party may also be the registered holder. If that party is an associate bank of the trustee, the trustee remains liable for the third party's acts and omissions – otherwise, apparently, not. (The trustee will, however, be liable under general trust law concerning delegation see *ante* 10.8.)

(c) They then supervise the administration, see that dealings in the trust property are properly conducted and units in it are created and liquidated in accordance with the trust deed. Regulation 7.09.2 directs trustees to take reasonable care to ensure that the manager calculates issue and redemption prices in accordance with statute: see Part 4 of The Regulations relating to pricing and dealing. The trustee will supervise also the manager's investment dealings, checking that these are within his powers as provided by the trust deed, the Scheme Particulars and The Regulations; that authorised limits in any one stock are not exceeded; that advertised investment policy is followed; and that there is no improper dealing by the managers, who, it should be remembered, are themselves acting in a fiduciary capacity *vis-à-vis* the unitholders.

(d) The trustee is responsible for distributing the trust income to the unitholders at the intervals prescribed by the trust deed.

(e) LAUTRO (Life Assurance and Unit Trust Regulatory Organisation) Rule 6.20(2) requires the manager to submit to the trustee any advertisement identifying and promoting an authorised unit trust before the advertisement is issued. The trustee must therefore approve promotional literature drafted by the manager, checking that statements made are true and that the general approach is not misleading. The marketing of investments is strictly controlled under the 1986 Act and by the Conduct of Business Rules – see *ante* 12.26; see chapter 5 of *Vaughan* for further details of these Rules.

(f) The trustee is responsible for maintaining the register of unitholders but, generally, the task is delegated to a specialist registrar or to the fund manager himself.

(g) If the manager proposes an amendment to the terms of the trust deed, the trustee is responsible for checking this, with the assistance of the trust solicitors. If satisfied that all is well, they will certify that the proposed change is not detrimental to the interests of unitholders. The SIB will also have to see and approve any proposed supplemental deed to make sure that authorisation is not affected.

(h) The Regulations 7.16.10 (conflicts of interest – best execution) warns managers, trustees and their associates not to deal as principals in respect of trust property, but this prohibition is not absolute, for instance, where the transaction involves quoted securities dealt in on the Stock Exchange.

(i) The Regulations 7.17.1 lists six occasions upon which the trustee *may* serve written notice of removal on a manager, but they do not seem to be either mandatory or exhaustive. Where a manager is removed the trustee must appoint a replacement, after written notice to the SIB. Both managers and trustees may retire, provided that replacements are available who will be acceptable to the SIB, which again, in such circumstances, must be given previous notice in writing of the proposed change.

12.28   DEBENTURE AND LOAN STOCK TRUSTS

Where debenture or loan stock is being issued to a miscellaneous class of persons, especially if it is being issued to the general public, it is desirable to interpose a trust corporation between the company and the debenture or loan stockholders; the listing requirements of the Stock Exchange make such an appointment essential. The trustee will be the party who accepts and holds the security offered by the company and he will then become a watchdog, not only over the value of the security, but also over the company's observance of restrictions imposed by the debenture or loan stock deed on any further borrowing. His prime duty is to the stockholders, but as the health of the company is often locked up with the health of their security, he may have to perform a balancing act, especially if asked to waive a breach by the company (or by a charging subsidiary) of the restrictions imposed by the trust deed. A draconian decision to declare the stock repayable might, in some instances, damage the interests of the stockholders, rather than stabilise them.

In recent decades the larger companies have become fond of issuing unsecured loan stock (with or without conversion rights into the ordinary capital), so that the sole security for the issue is the company's ability to repay. The policing functions of the trustee in this situation become all the more relevant, as the unsecured issue will invariably contain a clause regulating the ceiling for total borrowings, whether secured or unsecured, of the company and its subsidiaries. Against this background, the observance and sometimes the waiving of those limits becomes a sensitive task, even with the co-operation of the company's directors and auditors.

With the admixture of company law, insolvency law and accountancy and audit practices to contend with, the trustee's judgment can be taxed more severely than with any other form of specialised trusteeship, and there may be enormous sums at stake.

12.29   TRUSTEE FOR INSURANCE COMPANIES

An insurance company, especially one from overseas operating in the UK, may be required by the Department of Trade, for the protection of UK policyholders, to set up a reserve fund and have it held by a trust corporation on behalf of the insurance company. The trustee is fundamentally a custodian of the assets, not concerned with their value or with changes in them, provided that the exchange does not conceal a release to the company, which must always have the prior consent of the Department of Trade.

12.30 DISCRETIONARY SETTLEMENTS FOR EMPLOYEES UNDER THE IHTA

Section 86 IHTA defines an employee trust as one which gives the benefit of the settled property to a class of persons comprising all or most of the persons employed by or holding office with the company concerned and their dependants and relations, although it is permissible to include also charitable purposes. An approved profit sharing scheme (see *post* 12.31) also qualifies as an employee trust. If the settlor is the company, it must be a close company and the trust beneficiaries must not include participators with a stake of 5% or more in the company: s. 13 IHTA. If the settlor is an individual, while the company whose shares he is settling need not be a close company, the trustees must be given more than one half of the company's ordinary shares and have majority voting power; also the class of beneficiaries must exclude 5% participators: s. 28 IHTA. If these conditions are observed, there is no initial charge for IHT or CGT when the trust is set up either in lifetime or by will, and no 10-year anniversary charge. A close company settlor who makes a payment into the trust should be able to claim it as a deduction for corporation tax purposes. This type of trust, which can be used to purchase shares on the death of a shareholder and thereby prevent them from getting into the wrong hands, is nevertheless not popular, because of the stringent conditions imposed.

A discretionary settlement on employees, although failing to meet the requirements of the IHTA, may still be advantageous for a company wishing to develop the concept of wider share ownership for employees in a more flexible manner than is permitted by the statutory schemes. There is no certainty, however, that the contributions (especially the initial contribution) of the company to employee benefit trusts (EBTs) of this kind will be deductible; hence the introduction in 1989 of the employee share ownership trust: see *post* 12.35.

12.31 APPROVED PROFIT SHARING SCHEMES (INTRODUCED IN 1978)

This type of scheme, which operates under s. 186 and Sch. 9 and 10 ICTA, must be open to all employees of five years' service or more (see also IR96). The trustees of the scheme obtain the shares (which must be fully paid up) by subscription, or by purchase on the open market, and allocate them to the employees in accordance with the scheme's profit sharing formula. The value of the allocation must not exceed 10% of emoluments in the range from £30,000 to £80,000 but at the lower end £3,000 is permitted for emoluments of under £30,000. The shares must be quoted or be in a company that is not controlled by another. The dividends are paid to the employee in the normal way from the moment of appropriation. The employee will never have to pay any income tax on his allocations of profit, provided that the shares are not released to him until the expiration of five years. If he eventually sells the shares there will be a chargeable disposal based on the appropriation price. The scheme is attractive to the employee, because he never has to put any of his own money in. The cost to the company will be deductible for corporation tax purposes as part of the remuneration package.

12.32 APPROVED SAYE-LINKED SHARE OPTION SCHEMES (INTRODUCED IN 1980)

This scheme, which must be open to all employees of at least five years' service, is laid down in s. 185 and Sch. 9 ICTA (see IR98) and enables them to buy the company's ordinary shares at a favourable price by regular savings out of taxed income. The shares, which must be fully paid up, must be quoted or be in a company not controlled by another or be in a subsidiary of a quoted non-close company. The contributions under the SAYE plan must not exceed £250 (formerly £150) a month. The option to buy the shares is granted at the start of the SAYE plan and the option price must not be manifestly less than 80% (formerly 90%) of the value of the shares at that time. The time for exercising the option will normally be five or seven years later on the maturity of the SAYE plan. No income tax is payable either when the option is granted or when it is exercised; CGT will arise only if the shares are eventually sold.

There is no requirement of trustees for this scheme, which has not proved to be particularly popular.

12.33 APPROVED SHARE OPTION SCHEMES (INTRODUCED IN 1984)

Again, one has to burrow into the extensively amended s. 185 and Sch. 9 ICTA for the latest details of these schemes, which are aimed primarily at middle and senior management, since the employer is able to cater for his employees on a selective basis; for detailed notes see IR100. The value of the shares available under the option (which must be the fully paid up ordinary shares of the company) must not, after adding the effect of previous options, exceed £100,000 at the time when the option is granted; or four times the amount of remuneration, if that produces a greater figure. An option over unquoted shares is not admissible unless in a subsidiary of a quoted company or in a company which is not controlled by another company. At least three years but no more than 10 must expire before an option can be exercised without incurring an income tax liability, and this must be followed up by another three year wait before the next option can be exercised. The exercise price must not be manifestly less than 100%

(85% from 1 January 1992) of the value at the time when the option is granted. Liability for income tax is eliminated altogether, provided that the price of the option plus the exercise price is within the 100% or 85% limit; if not, there is an immediate charge for income tax. The option holder may have a financing problem when the time comes for exercising his option, and in the case of unquoted shares, he may have a problem too in finding a market, if he wants to sell the shares after exercising the option; this is where an employee benefit trust, *ante* 12.30, may be able to assist. On disposal CGT is chargeable in the normal way.

There is no statutory requirement of trustees for these schemes.

12.34 UNAPPROVED SHARE OPTION SCHEMES

The rules are to be found in ss. 135–140 ICTA and ss. 77–89 FA 1988:

(a)   If an option is capable of being exercised more than seven years after it has been granted, income tax is charged on the difference between (i) the market value of the shares at the date of the grant and (ii) the option price plus the exercise price.

(b)   If, when the option is exercised, the market value of the shares is more than the combined option price and exercise price, the profit is liable to income tax. If subsequently the shares are sold, any further increase in value will be chargeable to CGT.

(c)   For shares acquired before 26 October 1987, there is a further charge for income tax on any subsequent appreciation in value (i) between the date of acquisition and the seventh anniversary of the acquisition; (ii) between the date of acquisition and the date of a subsequent sale; and (iii) between the date of acquisition and the date of the lifting of special restrictions attached to the shares. The charge arises on the earliest of the happening of these three events. The market value at 26 October 1987 may be substituted if it gives a smaller tax charge, provided that the company is not a 'dependent subsidiary', i.e. a company whose business is almost exclusively with other members of the group who holds 51% or more of its shares. There are a number of exceptions to these rules.

(d)   For shares acquired after 25 October 1987, the income tax charge on the growth in the value of the shares after the date of acquisition applies only to shares in a dependent subsidiary. The charge arises on the earlier of two events (i) seven years after the date of acquisition; or (ii) the disposal of the shares. The reason for concentrating so much attention on a dependent subsidiary is that it is so easy to manipulate an increase in the value of its shares when its trade is mostly on an inter-group basis.

(e)   If the eventual disposal of the shares is not caught for income tax by the foregoing rules, a charge to CGT will arise instead.

Much of the terror in these rules has disappeared with the scaling down of the top rate of income tax to the same levels as for CGT. An unapproved scheme has the great merit of possessing flexibility as compared with the statutory schemes. Yet another option is the 'phantom' share scheme which gears increases in remuneration to the notional allocation of shares to the employee.

Once again, there is no essential role for a trustee in these schemes.

12.35 EMPLOYEE SHARE OWNERSHIP TRUSTS (ESOTs) (INTRODUCED IN 1989)

The relevant legislation is contained in ss. 67–74 and Sch. 5 FA 1989, ss. 31–40 FA 1990 and s. 85A ICTA. The trust, which also goes under the name of QUEST (qualifying employee share ownership trust), can be set up by a company (quoted or not) and must have a minimum of three trustees, at least one of whom is a trust corporation or a professional person; the other two must be non-director employees selected by a majority of the employees. The trust instrument, in defining the beneficiaries, must include all employees (of 20 hours a week or more) with a specified number of at least one but not more than five years' service. The company's contributions are bound to qualify as a deduction for corporation tax, provided that the trustees spend them on the acquisition of the company's shares, or on repaying borrowings connected with share purchase, or on the payment of expenses, or on distributions to the beneficiaries. Length of service and salary level may be taken into account but otherwise shares must be issued to the beneficiaries on similar terms. The trustees must not hold on to the shares for more than seven years. Failure to observe these rules will result in a 35% income tax charge. For disposals on or after 20 March 1990 a form of roll-over relief is available to a shareholder who sells his shares in the company to the trustees; and from 1 April 1991 a company can claim a corporation tax deduction for the costs of setting up an ESOT.

This type of trust ought to be attractive, especially to unquoted companies, who will often not qualify for the other statutory schemes, but there seems to be a lack of interest.[9]

13 Variation of trusts

13.1 BACKGROUND

The beneficiaries of a trust sometimes become unhappy about its continuing in its original form; they would prefer either that the trusts be changed or that they be brought to an end. The saving of tax liable to be imposed on them in the future is a powerful incentive to the search for an 'arrangement' by which the beneficiaries and the trustees alter the basis of the trust as established by the settlor. In other cases the objective is not to alter or end the beneficial interests in the trust fund, but to enable the trustee to do some unauthorised thing – such as the purchase of a house as a residence for a beneficiary, the payment of a fee to a trustee, the purchase of a non-income-producing asset, or the appointment of non-resident trustees. The term 'variation of trusts' is applied here to all such cases and this chapter is concerned with the ways in which such otherwise unauthorised departures from the charted course may safely and sensibly be effected.

13.2 THE RULE IN *SAUNDERS* v *VAUTIER* (1841)

Where property is given to an adult beneficiary absolutely, any purported restriction on his enjoyment of it is inconsistent with the gift and the beneficiary can call upon a trustee in whom the property is vested to transfer it to him 'without strings'. The same rule applies where two or more adult beneficiaries are, between them, absolutely entitled to the entire beneficial interest in trust property – and this further application of the rule will take in cases where the beneficiaries are entitled, either in succession or as objects of a discretion (see *Re Smith* (1928)) provided they are *collectively* entitled to the *complete* interest in the fund. It follows that, where these circumstances exist, the beneficiaries may contrive to bring the trust to an end and a trustee is unable to prevent them from doing so. 'A man who is *sui juris* may do what he likes with his own property' – *Snell* p. 234.[1]

The rule may be used to circumvent the effect of the decision in *Re Brockbank* (1948) which makes it clear that, even where beneficiaries are absolutely entitled between them to the whole trust fund, they still have no right to dictate the way in which the trustees should exercise a discretionary trust or power. Moreover, the court will not intervene in such cases so long as the discretion is being exercised honestly. Where there is an irreconcilable difference of opinion between beneficiaries and trustee, their only recourse is to the rule in *Saunders* v *Vautier* – to bring the existing trust to an end and to replace it with another – if they so wish. To do so may have expensive consequences so far as CGT and IHT are concerned.

13.3   CO-OPERATION OF TRUSTEES AND BENEFICIARIES

Whilst beneficiaries cannot force a trustee to administer a trust in accordance with their wishes, they can combine with him amicably to authorise a variation of trusts, whether this is of an administrative nature or one which affects the beneficial interests themselves. As a working rule, it is reasonable for the former to be promoted by the trustee himself and for the latter to be in the charge of the beneficiaries, it being the primary duty of a trustee to administer the trusts set out in the trust instrument. In either case, unless the transaction is both simple and of no great substance financially, it is desirable for it to be embodied in a proper deed of arrangement executed under seal by beneficiaries and trustee(s). This document will normally contain a joint and several indemnity by the beneficiaries in favour of the trustee which will need to take particular care to ensure that beneficiaries suspected to lack complete understanding of the matter (e.g. young adult and very old beneficiaries) are fully aware of the implications, so far as they personally are concerned; where such beneficiaries exist, one should try to arrange that they have independent professional advice (beneficiaries are not always willing to be so guided). If it is thought necessary to refer specifically to the costs involved, the usual course is to direct payment from the trust fund. The trustee may well want to have express directions in the deed about the allocation of his liability for any CGT and IHT arising from the transaction. Such an arrangement will, of course, only be feasible where *all* beneficiaries are ascertained, are of full capacity and are willing to co-operate.

13.4   USING THE STATUTORY POWERS TO ALTER THE TRUSTS

It is often possible to carry out what is, in effect, a variation of trust by the exercise of the trustee's powers, either an express power in the trust instrument, or a statutory power such as that contained in s. 32 TA – see *ante* 10.21. Modern trust instruments frequently contain very extensive powers for the advancement, release and resettlement of capital. Such flexibility will often remove the need for either a deed of arrangement or an application to court – provided, of course, that the trustees are agreeable to making use of such discretionary powers. If they decline to do so, the court will not interfere with this negative exercise of the discretion so long as the trustees have applied their minds to the problem fairly and honestly.

13.5 DIFFICULTIES IN DETERMINING THE BENEFICIAL INTERESTS

To say that a variation of trusts may safely be carried out with the approval of all the beneficiaries may sometimes raise a question about the extent of the beneficial interests. These are not always precisely definable, as for instance, in the case of a protective trust set up under s. 33 TA:

> Such a trust is used when it is desirable to protect a spendthrift beneficiary from himself. Should such a person (known as the 'principal beneficiary') do, or attempt to do, or suffer anything which would have the effect of depriving him of the right to receive any part of the trust income, his interest ceases and a discretionary trust begins.

One of the discretionary objects in such a case is the wife or husband for the time being of the principal beneficiary. It is clearly not possible to establish whether or not some such spouse may come into existence until after that beneficiary is dead. Strictly, a s. 33 protective trust can therefore never be varied except with the help of the court. (Participation by a 'principal beneficiary' in a deed of arrangement may, in itself, precipitate the discretionary trust and thus defeat the object of the exercise – a further reason for particular care in such cases.) A similar problem occurs when any *future* spouse is a possible beneficiary. Where it is a question of forecasting the birth of a beneficiary there is a rebuttable presumption that a female either under the age of 12 or over the age of 55 is incapable of bearing a child, but this is only for the purpose of applying the perpetuity rule. If trustees wish to break a trust on the footing that a beneficiary is past childbearing age, the onus of the decision is upon them, after seeking suitable medical or other evidence; in a borderline case, especially where the trustees cannot get protection by insurance, an application to court is possible.[2] Even if the problem of possible childbearing is overcome, there remains the question whether an elderly beneficiary might decide to adopt a child, as there is no legal upward limit for becoming an adopter. The practical solution is insurance, unless s. 42(5) Adoption Act 1976 is applicable.[3] Again for perpetuity purposes only, there is a rebuttable presumption that a male is capable of fathering a child at any age from 14 onwards. Section 2 PAA gives the court discretion to make such order as it thinks fit in cases where the statutory presumptions concerning motherhood or fatherhood are contradicted by subsequent events, but this discretion can be applied only where there are legal proceedings and where the question at issue is one of perpetuities or calling a halt to accumulations under the rule in *Saunders* v *Vautier*.[4]

13.6 THE RISK OF BEING SUED

The rest of this chapter mostly considers cases where the intervention of the court is either essential or desirable; a trustee can always take a risk and proceed without a complete authority from either beneficiaries or court – perhaps in reliance upon personal indemnities backed up by insurance from a reputable source – but, except where the risk is small, the protection offered is substantially in excess of the maximum liability and will remain so, and the indemnities will, in practical terms, be successfully enforceable at the crucial moment, this is not a course which has much to recommend it. A variation of trust may be regarded as a breach of trust for which the trustee cannot be sued. If he decides to select a course which is not entirely free from this sort of risk he needs to be very clear-headed about it, and to have in mind the fact that an action for breach of trust may be brought within six years of the date on which the right of action accrued, but such right of action does not accrue to a beneficiary entitled to a future interest *until that interest falls into possession;*[5] thus in the *Nestle* case, *ante* 11.10, the remainderman was able to sue for breaches of trust alleged to have extended over several decades, by which time, had the action been successful, the cost of repairing the breach would have gone through the roof. Hence the need for a cautious approach. Beware the enticing suggestion of Selwyn LJ, as reported by Lindley MR in *Perrins* v *Bellamy* (1899) that the main duty of a trustee is to commit *judicious* breaches of trust!

13.7   INHERENT JURISDICTION AND S. 57 TA

The court has always had the power under its inherent jurisdiction to authorise trustees to effect, in an emergency, an unauthorised transaction on the grounds that it was necessary to 'salvage' trust property. This branch of the inherent jurisdiction has been superseded by s. 57 TA which enables the court to authorise trustees to carry out any transaction which is, in the opinion of the court, expedient. 'Expediency' is regarded as having a wider meaning than 'emergency'. The object of s. 57 was to ensure that trust property is managed as advantageously as possible in the interests of the beneficiaries. The section does *not* assist in the variation of beneficial interests. Although it is still available for use in cases where such a variation is not sought, it is generally the practice to use the Variation of Trusts Act 1958: see below. There is one circumstance, however, where it will be better to proceed under s. 57 rather than the 1958 Act, and that is where one or more *sui juris* beneficiaries will not approve the variation proposed. The court cannot provide approval under the 1958 Act on behalf of such beneficiaries because, as will be seen, they are not within the classes of persons for whom the court can use its jurisdiction. There is no such restriction in connection with s. 57 and it appears that the court could override a dissenting beneficiary if it thought that the proposed transaction was 'expedient' and in the interests of the beneficiaries as a whole. Section 57 may be more appropriate for cases involving charitable trusts because of the absence in their case of any of the classes of person on whose behalf the court exercises its jurisdiction under the 1958 Act; an alternative being the use of s. 23 Charities Act 1960: see *ante* 12.15. Section 57 does, of course, give the court a *discretion*; normally it will be the trustees who make the application and, no doubt, an application which was thought by the court to be frivolous would prevent them from getting their costs out of the trust fund. As to costs, see *ante* 4.48.

Section 57 was used in *Mason* v *Farbrother* (1983) to enable the court to approve a wide investment clause for the CWS Employees' Pension and Death Benefit Scheme; it would have been quite impossible to get consents from all the beneficiaries of this Scheme. Note that, so far as applications for wider investment powers are concerned, it is no longer necessary for trustees to produce 'special reasons' why such powers should be authorised by the court: *Trustees of the British Museum* v *A-G* (1984).

13.8   SECTION 64 SLA

This section[6] enables the court to sanction any scheme for the termination or variation of a trust of settled land and land held on trust for sale: see *Re Simmons* (1956) holding that s. 28(1) LPA imports s. 64 SLA. It may not apply to a trust for sale where all the land has been sold: see *ante* 11.17. Section 57 TA never applies either to settled land or to its capital money – see sub-section (4). Section 64 SLA is wider in scope than s. 57 TA:

In *Re Downshire* (1953) the Court of Appeal held that the words in s. 64(1) to the effect that any transaction which in the opinion of the court would be for the benefit of the settled land or the person interested under the settlement, were wide enough to enable the court to authorise the tenant for life to agree a scheme with the trustees and other *sui juris* beneficiaries which would change completely the existing beneficial interests.

As with s. 57 TA there may be cases where s. 64 SLA will look more attractive than the 1958 Act, and s. 64 has the particular advantage of enabling the court to authorise a change in beneficial interests as well as desirable, but unauthorised, administrative actions; however, the practice since the 1958 Act was passed seems, from the evidence of the law reports, to be to use that statute in preference to the earlier legislation. An application to court under s. 64 is within the province of the tenant for life of settled land (or, applying s. 23, the trustees of the settlement where there is no tenant for life) and of the trustees where land is held on trust for sale. The section was used in *Raikes* v *Lygon* (1988) to authorise the transfer of property from one trust to another for use as a maintenance fund, even though certain potential beneficiaries of the second trust were not beneficiaries of the first.

13.9 VARIATION OF TRUSTS ACT 1958

This was described, on its introduction to the legislature, as a 'dull bill'. Dull it may have seemed to the majority of members, but it has had far-reaching consequences and will continue to be significant to trustee and taxation experts. Section 1(1) of the Act reads as follows:

1. Jurisdiction of courts to vary trusts
(1) Where property, whether real or personal, is held on trusts arising, whether before or after the passing of this Act, under any will, settlement or other disposition, the court may if it thinks fit by order approve on behalf of–
  (a) any person having, directly or indirectly, an interest, whether vested or contingent, under the trusts who by reason of infancy or other incapacity is incapable of assenting, or
  (b) any person (whether ascertained or not) who may become entitled, directly or indirectly, to an interest under the trusts as being at a future date or on the happening of a future event a person of any specified description or a member of any specified class of persons, so however that this paragraph shall not include any person who would be of that description, or a member of that class, as the case may be, if the said date had fallen or the said event had happened at the date of the application to the court, or
  (c) any person unborn, or
  (d) any person in respect of any discretionary interest of his under protective trusts where the interest of the principal beneficiary has not failed or determined,
any arrangement (by whomsoever proposed, and whether or not there is any other person beneficially interested who is capable of assenting thereto) varying or revoking all or any of the trusts, or enlarging the powers of the trustees of managing or administering any of the property subject to the trusts:
Provided that except by virtue of paragraph (d) of this subsection the court shall not approve an arrangement on behalf of any person unless the carrying out thereof would be for the benefit of that person.

The exclusion to (b) is not easy to understand but it has been held to apply to a person who, if the future date or event were to coincide with the date of the application to court, would be capable of providing his own consent to the carrying out of the proposed arrangements:

In *Re Suffert* (1961) a trust fund was held on protective trusts for the applicant, a spinster of 61, during her life, with remainder to her children and, if she had none, to her statutory next of kin. At the time of the case the applicant had three next of kin, but only one of them had consented to the proposed arrangement. Buckley J. refused to approve it on behalf of the other two because they fell within the terms of the exclusion to s. 1(1)(b).

It follows that a single dissenting beneficiary who is *sui juris* may successfully prevent an arrangement from taking effect and that the proposals must be approved by all those who have capacity to agree (if they lack capacity, s. 1(1)(a) applies), before the expense of going to court is incurred. This rule applies even if there is great practical difficulty in getting consents, as where members of a class are both numerous and difficult to trace:

> In *Knocker* v *Youle* (1986) application was made to the court under s. 1(1)(b) asking it to approve a proposed variation of trust on behalf of the numerous issue of four sisters of the settlor. Such issue had a contingent interest in the trust fund, but it was a very remote one. Warner J. held that s. 1(1)(b) did not apply at all to persons with contingent interests and that he could not, therefore, approve the variation on behalf of the sisters' issue; even if it did so apply, no approval could be given on behalf of the adult members of the class in view of the excluding words in the second part of s. 1(1)(b). The broader proposition that s. 1(1)(b) can never apply to contingent interests leads to the conclusion that it applies only to persons with no present interest of any kind in the trust – for instance, the future husband of a principal beneficiary in a protective trust where that beneficiary's initial interest has ended, thus excluding the husband from consideration under s. 1(1)(d).[7]

In any event, the trustees in *Knocker* v *Youle* were left with the difficult, perhaps impossible, task of getting individual consents from numerous descendants of the four sisters, a number of them being resident overseas.

13.10 THE INVOLVEMENT OF THE TRUSTEES IN A VARIATION UNDER THE ACT

The consent of the trustees to an arrangement is not essential. The court will listen to their views with respect but will not regard them as the last word on the subject. The general rule seems to be that the trustees should not make the application themselves, at least where it is one to vary the beneficial interests. One rather curious feature of the Act is that the court may approve an arrangement *by whomsoever proposed*, which appears to open the gate for any casual busybody to apply to the court with proposals affecting a settlement with which he has no other connection. No doubt such a case would be stifled at or shortly after birth; note that it is perfectly possible for the settlor to put up an application – as in *Re Clitheroe* (1959) – and in any application, if the settlor is living, he should be given the chance to express his views: RSC O 93, r 6(2). In *Re Druce* (1962) Russell J. said:

> 'In general, the trustees should not be the applicants in applications to vary beneficial trusts, unless they are satisfied that the proposals are beneficial to the persons interested and have a good prospect of being approved by the Court, and further, that if they do not make the application no one will.'

On the other hand, an application by trustees for approval of some new administrative provision, e.g. a wider power of investment, is quite in order. Until the statutory powers of investment are updated (see *ante* 11.6), trustees do not have to show 'special reason' for asking the court to give them wider investment powers: *ante* 13.7.

How should a trustee react when, as does happen, a beneficiary asks him to discuss and advise on a variation of the beneficial interest in a trust? It is suggested that, whilst there can be no possible objection to a preliminary talk of a general nature, it should be pointed out to the beneficiary that a proposal of this kind should be discussed between and formulated by the beneficiaries themselves. Their proposals, in draft form, can then be submitted to the trustees for comment. This is a sensible rule in all cases, whether or not there is to be an application to court. The beneficiaries should be separately advised from the trustees; in practice, the same firm of solicitors may advise all parties to the application, but there will need to be separate representation in court. In particular, separate counsel will normally be instructed on behalf of (a) beneficiaries who are not *sui juris*, (b) beneficiaries who are *sui juris*, (c) the applicant, and (d) the trustees. Where leading counsel is instructed on behalf of the applicant, it is desirable for another leading counsel to be instructed on behalf of infant beneficiaries. The trustees' role is essentially a neutral one, but they are expected to provide full information about the trust to the other parties involved *and* to the court, and to look after the interest of those possible beneficiaries who are not otherwise represented, e.g. unborn beneficiaries and infants whose chances of attaining any interest under the settlement are small.

13.11   THE EXERCISE OF POWERS OF APPOINTMENT AND THE 1958 ACT

The court will not approve an arrangement which has been facilitated by the exercise of a power of appointment which amounts to a fraud on that power. 'Fraud' in this context does not connote dishonesty but reflects the fact that an appointment was made for some purpose other than that of benefiting the objects of the power. Only if the power was exercised with the *sole* purpose of benefiting its objects is it safe from being defined as fraudulent; it should be added that the fact that a non-object may benefit incidentally from the exercise is not necessarily fatal – it is the purpose or motive of the appointor which is the crucial factor: see *Re Brook* (1968), *ante* 7.9. Where a proposed arrangement involves the exercise of a power, the possibility of its being vitiated by this doctrine must therefore be considered. If the matter is being dealt with out of court the trustees will need to take particular care to avoid the risk that a deed of arrangement may be set aside in the future on the grounds that it is tainted by fraud on the power. Where a power of appointment is an inescapable factor in an arrangement, the risk may be avoidable by releasing the power and relying upon the gift over in default of appointment. Unfortunately, some powers cannot be released unilaterally by their donees. Powers conferred upon trustees in their fiduciary capacity come into this category and so do powers of appointment which their donees are under a duty to consider exercising throughout their existence.

In *Re Wills* (1964) the power of appointment embraced both charitable and non-charitable objects and the question arose as to whether the trustees could make a partial release of the power to the extent that it concerned non-charitable beneficiaries, thus turning the trust into a purely charitable one. It was held that the trustees, having been given the power by virtue of their office, could neither release it nor contract not to exercise it. That case also advanced the proposition that even in the case of a purely personal power of appointment, a gift over in default of appointment would preclude the donee from releasing it, but this runs counter to earlier decisions: see *Hanbury*, p. 180.

Unless the trust deed expressly authorises the donee of a power to release it, it may be necessary to seek the authority of the court for its release in cases where the proposed arrangement makes this a necessity.

13.12 THE 'BENEFIT' REFERRED TO IN THE PROVISO TO S. 1(1)

The court may approve a proposed arrangement under s. 1(1)(a), (b) and (c) only if it is satisfied that it is for the 'benefit' of the person or persons on whose behalf the court's approval is sought. Generally this question of 'benefit' is for the parties other than the trustees to prove – though, in their watch-dog capacity, they may well be required to comment and they are, in any event, entitled to be heard. If the trustees themselves are making the application, e.g. for some new administrative provision, they must, of course, be able to show where the benefit lies in their proposals. Generally, it seems, 'benefit' in this context means 'cash'. However, it sometimes seems to mean rather the opposite:

In *Re Remnant* (1970) the children of two sisters had interests under a will trust which contained a forfeiture clause in respect of any child practising Roman Catholicism. The children of one sister were Catholic, the children of the other were Protestant. In the interest of family harmony, Pennycuick J. accepted that the deletion of the forfeiture provision would be for the benefit of the children, although this clearly deprived the Protestant children of the prospect of benefiting in the material sense from a forfeiture of the Catholic children's interests.

It is clear from the foregoing case that, although the court will consider the original purpose and intentions of the settlor, they are certainly not regarded as sacrosanct. But there is a limit to what the court will accept:

Great powers of advocacy were used in *Re Robinson* (1976) to persuade Templeman J. that the advent of CTT had made such a change that the possible effects of a death after the approval of the arrangement should be disregarded. However, the judge did not take that view – he started with the principle that 'all these schemes should, if possible, prove that an infant is not going to be materially worse off . . . one may . . . have to take a broad view, but not a galloping, gambling view.'

Where it is a question of deciding whether an arrangement will produce a 'benefit' for a patient within the meaning of the Mental Health Act 1983, the answer is determined by the Court of Protection – but the approval of the Chancery judge is still required:

> Where a settlement of a patient's property has been made on his behalf in accordance with s. 96(1) of the 1983 Act, the court may order a variation of such a settlement as it thinks fit, if either a material fact was not disclosed when it was made or if there has been a substantial change in circumstances since then.

13.13 THE ARRANGEMENT MUST 'VARY' OR 'REVOKE', NOT UNDERMINE

Assuming that the question of 'benefit' has been answered to the satisfaction of the court, is there then any limit to the kind of arrangement which it may approve on behalf of members of the four classes specified in s. 1(1) of the Act? It will be remembered that the subsection refers to 'any arrangement . . . varying or revoking all or any of the trusts . . .'; any proposal put to the court for approval must, therefore fall within one or other of these terms. This means that an arrangement which would replace existing trusts with entirely different ones would not pass the test; see, e.g. *Re T's Settlement Trusts* (1964), where Wilberforce J. commented that the proposal put to him fell outside the jurisdiction of the court under the Act because, although it was presented as a variation, it was in truth a completely new resettlement. The dividing line between 'variation' and 'resettlement' is, however, a thin one and Megarry J. in *Re Ball* (1968) was prepared to give the proposal before him the benefit of the doubt:

> 'If an arrangement changes the whole substratum of a trust, then it may well be that it cannot be regarded merely as varying that trust. But if an arrangement, while leaving the substratum, effectuates the purpose of the original trust by other means, it may still be possible to regard that arrangement as merely varying the original trusts, even though the means employed are wholly different and even though the form is completely changed.'

Imbedded in the substratum of the trust may be found the settlor's intentions, which will not be lightly disregarded by the court:

> In *Re Steed* (1960) there was a statutory protective trust for the testator's housekeeper for life with remainder as she might by deed or will appoint. There were other indications in the will that while the trustees could give her capital they should always keep back enough to provide adequate means for her.

In fact, the testator had been apprehensive that the housekeeper's brother and his family would sponge upon her, a view shared by the trustees. The housekeeper exercised the power of appointment in her own favour (which she could do without causing a fraud on the power, as this was a general power) and applied under the Act for approval of an arrangement which would delete the protective trusts, thus making her the sole beneficiary. She was aged 53 and unmarried, and therefore the only other possible beneficiary was a future husband, a spectral spouse as the Court of Appeal described him, and he came under paragraph (d), which did not require his benefit to be considered. But it was the arrangement as a whole that had to be approved and the court was not prepared to confine itself to the narrow question of approval on behalf of the spectral spouse. Looking at the scheme of the will as a whole, why was the protective trust there at all? Only because the intention had been to ensure proper provision for the housekeeper. The variation contemplated was one which so cut at the root of the testator's wishes that the court could not approve it.

13.14 OTHER STATUTORY AVENUES FOR VARIATION BY THE COURT

(a) Under s. 24 Matrimonial Causes Act 1973 the court has power to vary any ante-nuptial or post-nuptial settlement made on the parties to a marriage when granting a decree of divorce, nullity of marriage or judicial separation. An order may also be made extinguishing or reducing the interest of either party under such a settlement, even if there are no children. The court has a very wide discretion in such cases and the word 'settlement' is interpreted broadly, e.g. as including joint interests in the matrimonial home. Note that under s. 37 of the same Act the court may be able to review a trust or other disposition made by a spouse with the idea of defeating a subsequent claim in divorce proceedings.

(b) The function of the Charity Commission, acting as a court, to vary charitable trusts: see *ante* 12.16.

(c) The anti-avoidance provisions of the Inheritance (Provision for Family and Dependants) Act 1975: see *ante* 4.43.

(d) Section 53 TA provides that where an infant is beneficially entitled to any property, the court may make an order to deal with the assets with a view to their application for the maintenance, education or benefit of the infant, e.g. to sell an infant's reversionary interest and resettle the proceeds for his benefit.[8]

13.15 THE EXPORT OF TRUSTS

This subject is dealt with here because the removal of an English trust to foreign parts, even if only as far as the Channel Islands, may involve an application to the court under the 1958 Act, especially if it is desired to change the governing law of the trust. Of course, the trust instrument itself, if capably drafted, will have foreseen the possibility that export may be desirable and will include a provision authorising the English trustees to retire in favour of non-resident trustees and to transfer to the new trustees the trust assets, perhaps also allowing for the substitution of foreign law for English law as the law governing the trust (the proper law as it is sometimes called). Such a provision may safely be acted on, and there can be no arguments later from the beneficiaries or the Revenue to the effect that such an action was unauthorised.

13.16 EXPORTING A TRUST WHERE THERE IS NO EXPRESS POWER TO EXPORT IT

Two courses are available to the English trustees. Firstly, a new settlement is set up in the country where the trust is to be administered in future. The English trust is then wound up and the assets are fed into the new non-resident settlement, with or without the use of the 1958 Act, depending upon the width of the trustees' powers and the need for approval on behalf of beneficiaries who are not *sui juris*, if the proper law is changed.

This is what was done in *Re Seale* (1961) (where the family had emigrated to Canada many years before) and what was unsuccessfully proposed to be done in *Re Weston* (1969); the latter case provides a cautionary tale to would-be exporting trustees. There, the family was being uprooted at short notice to go to Jersey purely for tax purposes, which persuaded the Court of Appeal to consider not merely the financial benefit to the infants or unborn children, but also their educational and social benefit, and led them to reject the application, especially as there was no assurance that the move to Jersey would be permanent.

The alternative to setting up a new trust simply involves the appointment of new non-resident trustees of the existing English trust and the transfer of the assets to them, with or without a court application (otherwise than under the 1958 Act), as occurred in *Re Whitehead* (1971). The litigation in that case also provided an affirmative answer to the question whether s. 36(1) TA permits the appointment of non-resident trustees.

Either method can be effective and the choice between them will depend largely upon the suitability of the existing trust instrument to a new life in the overseas territory which has been chosen. If this is a country where English trust law is understood and is enforceable by the local courts, then the existing trust structure can be retained unchanged and a simple appointment of new non-resident trustees will suffice.[9]

13.17 WHEN THE COURT'S APPROVAL OF THE EXPORT OF A TRUST IS REQUIRED

Whichever method of the two previously described is used (in the absence of a suitable power in the trust instrument) an application to the court for its approval may well be desirable. The appointment of non-resident trustees of an English trust is not prohibited, but such an appointment is proper only in exceptional circumstances, because it necessarily prevents the English courts from exercising any further control over the conduct of the trust. One cannot do better than to quote the words of Pennycuick VC in *Re Whitehead supra*:

'. . . the law I think has been quite well established for upwards of a century, that there is no absolute bar to the appointment of persons resident abroad as trustees of an English trust. I say 'no absolute bar' in the sense that such an appointment would be prohibited by law and would consequently be invalid. On the other hand, apart from exceptional circumstances, it is not proper to make such an appointment. That is to say, the court would not, apart from exceptional circumstances, make such an appointment; nor would it be right for the donees of the power, apart from exceptional circumstances, to make such an appointment out of court. If they did, presumably the court would be likely to interfere at the instance of the beneficiaries. There do, however, exist exceptional circumstances in which such an appointment can properly be made. The most obvious exceptional circumstances are those in which the beneficiaries have settled permanently in some country outside the United Kingdom and what is proposed to be done is to appoint new trustees in that country.*

Where the court itself would appoint non-resident trustees the trustees themselves may safely do so. Where the court would *not* appoint non-resident trustees but nevertheless English trustees go ahead and do so, the appointment is not void, but voidable at the instance of the beneficiaries. If the latter have all approved the non-resident appointment, the risk to the former trustees must be very small. The only other interested party could be the Inland Revenue, but it seems extremely doubtful whether the Revenue could claim to have an interest which would enable it to apply for the non-resident appointment to be upset.

But if there is doubt about the court's attitude to the appointment of non-resident trustees, it will be sensible for the trustees either to apply to the court themselves for directions or to require the beneficiaries to do so, as in *Re Whitehead supra*. If all the beneficiaries are permanently resident in the country where the trust is to be domiciled in future, then there is little doubt but that the court would appoint trustees resident there and the expense of an application to court can be avoided. In other cases trustees will be well-advised to leave the decision to the court except, one supposes, in cases where all the beneficiaries are ascertained and *sui juris* and authorise the non-resident appointment by the execution of a deed of arrangement: see *ante* 13.3.

If a new non-resident settlement is being created with altered provisions or a change in the proper law and the express powers are not sufficiently comprehensive to dispense with the consents of incapacitated and unascertained beneficiaries, the required application under the 1958 Act will cover also the introduction of non-resident trustees.[10]

---

*Some recent unreported cases suggest that the court may now take a more relaxed view than that expressed by Pennycuick VC.

13.18   THE CHOICE OF NON-RESIDENT TRUSTEES

The considerations to be taken into account when deciding on the identity of new non-resident trustees do not differ from those affecting other new appointments: see *ante* 9.11 and 9.13. The retiring trustees will want to be satisfied that the proposed new trustees have the knowledge, experience and probity needed to conduct the affairs of the trust efficiently and in accordance with the law and the terms of the trust. In countries with an Anglo-Saxon tradition – e.g. North America and Australasia – professional trust administrators, both corporate and otherwise, are easy to find and not difficult to vet. Tax havens such as the Channel Islands, Isle of Man and Bermuda are equally well provided with potential trustees. Elsewhere the search for suitable candidates may well be more difficult and it may also appear that the courts of the country of import lack the ability to control any trustees over whom they have jurisdiction. However, demand traditionally produces supply, and countries which attract trusts from this country will presumably develop the facilities to service them. In the Cayman Islands, for instance, the English non-statutory law of trusts is applied, supplemented by local legislation. For a review of the leading tax havens of the world, see *Tolley's Tax Havens 1990*.

13.19   TAXATION AND THE VARIATION OF TRUSTS

Since many, if not most, variations of trust are carried out in order to save tax it is not likely that the tax aspects of such a transaction will be overlooked. There will not, of course, normally be any tax implications where the variation is of an administrative nature, e.g. where wider powers of investment are sought. The important exception to this statement occurs where UK-resident trustees retire in favour of non-resident trustees. The tax implications on that occasion are very significant and are discussed below.

   Where the variation is entirely within the UK, for instance in a case involving the ending of an English trust and the distribution of the funds amongst the beneficiaries, the normal rules relating to CGT and IHT will apply. Where persons become absolutely entitled as against the trustees, there will be a charge to CGT under s. 71(1) TCGA and since 14 March 1989, holdover relief has been severely restricted: see *ante* 8.14. If the variation involves the relinquishment of a life interest, the transfer will be exempt initially but become chargeable to IHT if the life tenant fails to survive for seven years. Under ss. 17 and 142–4 IHTA variations within two years of a testator's or intestate's death may provide IHT advantages, provided an election is made to the Revenue within six months of the date of the variation instrument: see *ante* 4.24 *et seq.* Under s. 62 TCGA there are similar provisions enabling the variation to take effect as if the deceased himself had made it.

13.20 TAXATION ON THE EXPORT OF A TRUST – IHT

Domicile is a vital factor in determining whether foreign assets are out of reach of IHT: see *ante* 8.16, but a word must be added about the special rules for determining domicile for IHT purposes:

> Although under the general law an individual may be domiciled abroad, he will be deemed to be domiciled in the UK if at any time during the three years before the settlement was executed (or before the individual's death in will and intestacy cases) he was domiciled in the UK.
>
> He will also be deemed to be domiciled in the UK if he was resident in the UK in not less than 17 of the 20 tax years ending with the tax year in which he executed the settlement (or ending with the tax year in which he died, in will and intestacy cases). Residence is determined as for income tax purposes but without regard to any dwelling-house available in the UK for his use.
>
> These rules as laid down in s. 267 IHTA have no application to (a) exempt government securities, (b) the National Savings exemption for those of Channel Islands or Isle of Man domicile, (c) fiscal domicile under a double taxation convention affecting IHT, (d) trusts coming into being before 10 December 1974 or assets put into trusts before that date.

Probably there is not much point in most cases in exporting a trust in order to avoid IHT; although the Revenue may have practical difficulties in collecting the tax, they will not abandon it without a fight: see *Re Clore* (1982) and *IRC v Stannard* (1984). Moreover, if the offshore trustees fail to pay the tax, any UK beneficiaries or the settlor may be liable for the tax under s. 201 IHTA.

13.21 TAXATION OF OFFSHORE TRUSTS – CGT

As we saw *ante* in 8.14, there is a penalty for a settlor who retains an interest for himself or his spouse in a domestic trust. Similar provisions were introduced for offshore trusts by s. 89 and Sch. 16 FA 1991 (see now s. 86 and Sched 5, TCGA). Thus, if a settlor retaining such an interest is domiciled and resident (or ordinarily resident) in the UK and the non-resident trustees have realised gains by disposals of settled property originating from the settlor, those gains will be treated as forming the highest amount on which he is chargeable to CGT for the year. Before this legislation was introduced it was only too easy for an English taxpayer to settle assets offshore with himself as a beneficiary, extracting only the income and allowing the capital gains to accumulate free of CGT, so long as the trustees did not remit to him any payments representing the proceeds of the capital gains (thereby attracting a liability to tax under s. 80 FA 1981, for which see *ante* 8.17).

Provided that the settlor has not retained any interest (which will automatically be the case if the trust arises on death), an offshore trust and its beneficiaries will be clear of any liability to CGT if the settlor and the trustees satisfy the tests under s. 69 TCGA for domicile and residence outlined *ante* in 8.17. For the trust created *inter vivos*, this immunity drops off the moment the settlor ceases to be domiciled and resident (or ordinarily resident) outside the UK, and in the case of a will trust or intestacy will never exist at all unless the deceased died domiciled and resident (or ordinarily resident) outside the UK. The exemption of these cases from CGT is not so surprising, because they are foreign in their origin and it is in our own interests to encourage the foreigner to bring his trust business here.

The export of an English trust is a very different matter and the new legislation contained in FA 1991 has transformed the picture. Before the new Act, which came into play on 19 March 1991, a liability for CGT would arise only if gains were made by the non-resident trustees and they then proceeded to make payments out of those gains to beneficiaries domiciled and resident in the UK.

13.22 EXPORTING A TRUST ON OR AFTER 19 MARCH 1991 – CGT

Even before the new legislation there were hazards over CGT for the retiring trustees. Firstly, under s. 79 FA 1981 if the retiring trustees had held-over gains, they would become liable to the tax on those gains; liability under this head is now automatically taken care of under the new exit charge (see below). Secondly, although they will no doubt ensure that all CGT liability up to the date of retirement is settled before the funds leave their hands (along with all other outstanding liabilities and expenses) they may still be liable for CGT arising out of gains made by the new non-resident trustees during the remainder of the current tax year. Section 2 TCGA provides that the tax is levied if a person is resident in the UK in any part of the tax year; there is a concession under which the tax year may be split between a period of residence and one of non-residence (ESC D2) but this does not apply to trustees. The retiring resident trustees who retire on, say, 1 July 1992 may therefore find themselves being served with a bill for CGT in respect of a gain made by the new non-resident trustees on 1 January 1993.

If the export of the trust takes place on or after 19 March 1991, ss. 83–7 FA 1991 (now ss. 80–4 TCGA) impose an exit charge whenever the trustees of a settlement become neither resident nor ordinarily resident in the UK, no matter which of the methods of export, as discussed *ante* 13.15 *et seq.*, is adopted. There is a deemed disposal and deemed reacquisition of the trust assets for CGT purposes – rather similar to the charge which arises under s. 71(1) TCGA when a person becomes absolutely entitled to a trust asset as against the trustees. The retiring trustees must arrange that liability arising under this head is settled before they part with the funds. If the settlor has reserved an interest, the liability will fall on him.

In addition to the exit charge under the new law, there continues the liability of beneficiaries domiciled and resident in the UK under ss. 80–2 FA 1981 (now ss. 87–90, TCGA) for capital payments derived from gains made by the offshore trustees. If the trust takes the form of a discretionary settlement it should not be difficult, however, for the trustees to exhaust the gains in payments to beneficiaries who are either domiciled outside the UK or resident and ordinarily resident outside the UK.

While the new law may act as a severe deterrent to the export of a trust pregnant with gains, if the gains are minimal or the assets consist mainly of cash or gilts, the saving of future gains tax may still be an added consideration in deciding to export it.

13.23 THE DANGER FROM CGT OF PARTIALLY EXPORTING A TRUST

We have already seen, *ante* 10.24 (para.(g)), how the creation of a sub-trust by way of advancement may lead to the unexpected result (a) of creating a deemed disposal of all the assets resettled, which is the last thing the trustees want in an English situation, or (b) of avoiding the deemed disposal but instead saddling the old trustees with liability for future capital gains in the resettled funds, which is the last thing the old trustees want in an export situation. The horns of this particular dilemma were exposed in the House of Lords' decision in *Roome* v *Edwards* (1981):

> In 1955 the resident trustees of an English trust had appointed part of their trust fund on separate trusts from the main fund and then continued to act as trustees of both funds until 1972. In that year the beneficiaries of the main fund assigned their interests to two Cayman Islands companies and new trustees, resident in the Islands, were appointed. One company then assigned its interest to the other, so that the latter then became 'absolutely entitled as against the trustee' under s. 71(1) TCGA. Because the resident and non-resident trustees were deemed to be treated as a single and continuing body of persons under s. 69(1) ibid. the CGT arising on the deemed disposal in the Cayman Islands was chargeable on the resident trustees of the appointed fund.

See also *Swires* v *Renton* (1991), *ante* 10.24 n.6. It is imperative therefore for trustees exercising a power (under whatever name it runs) which results in a 'hiving-off' from the original fund, to know whether what they have created is a completely separate settlement or one which remains part and parcel (for CGT purposes) with its parent trust; guidance is available from the Revenue in SP 7/84 and there is a very full discussion of the treatment of non-resident trusts for CGT purposes in *W and S-B*, 20.43 to 20.55.

13.24   TAXATION OF OFFSHORE TRUSTS – INCOME TAX

The offshore trustees are, of course, liable for income tax on UK source income. If they are all non-resident, the trust itself will become non-resident and will no longer be liable for tax on non-UK source income: see *ante* 8.15. If any beneficiary of the trust is domiciled and resident (or ordinarily resident) in the UK and has a right to any income from the offshore trust, he will be liable to income tax on it, irrespective of its source; if his domicile is foreign, he will be taxed only on a remittance basis. The position of a beneficiary under an exported discretionary settlement is governed by s. 740 ICTA, the broad effect of which is:

> Any beneficiary, but only if he is both domiciled and ordinarily resident in the UK, is liable for income tax on any discretionary benefits made available to him. His receipts are chargeable to the extent that they represent past or present income arising to the offshore trustees, but if the amount of the benefit exceeds available income, the balance of the assessment will be carried forward to be set against the income of future years. If the beneficiary, although ordinarily resident in the UK, is not domiciled there, he will be exempt on benefits from the trust, provided that they are not remitted or constructively remitted, to the UK.

It is still possible for a settlor to make a settlement in which he retains an interest without ruining his income tax and CGT situation (see *ante* 8.3 and 8.14), for example, a contingent accumulation settlement with reverter to himself if the beneficiary dies under 25. If, however, such a trust is exported it will fall under the axe of s. 739 ICTA:

> Sections 739–45 ICTA concern a transfer of assets in consequence of which, either directly or through associated operations, the income becomes payable to persons resident or domiciled out of the UK, the usual example of such persons being the non-resident trustees of a foreign trust. The settlor is not caught by the provisions unless he is ordinarily resident in the UK. A second condition of liability is that he (or his spouse) has power to enjoy, whether forthwith or in the future, any of the trust income. A third condition of liability is that it was the settlor or spouse who made the transfer of assets to the offshore trustees, either alone or in conjunction with associated operations, but 'associated operations' are so widely defined as to bring together the creation of the settlement and its subsequent export.

13.25   RISKS OF A PREARRANGED TIMETABLE FOR AVOIDANCE SCHEMES

Most variations of trusts designed to rearrange beneficial interests are motivated by a wish to reduce future taxation. Where the proposed arrangements are (a) artificial to some degree and (b) consist of a series of transactions, consideration needs to be given in advance of the operation to the possible application by the Revenue of the *Ramsay* principle. This was evolved by the House of Lords in the leading case of *W T Ramsay Ltd* v *IRC* (1982):

The appellant company had made a chargeable gain for the purposes of corporation tax; it wished to avoid paying the tax arising out of this gain by establishing an allowable loss. It bought from a company specialising in such matters a ready-made scheme which was to create, out of a neutral situation, two assets, one of which would decrease in value and would be sold to create a loss, thus cancelling out the realised gain on the other. It was held that if such schemes, when looked at as a whole, resulted in neither gain nor loss to the taxpayer, the courts could hold that they were unavailing; they should simply be disregarded as artificial and fiscally ineffective.

How far this decision has laid to rest the ghost of the Duke of Westminster (*IRC* v *Duke of Westminster* (1936)) is unclear, but it does give clear warning that the courts may look behind the form of a transaction and consider its substance as well. The new approach was stated by Lord Wilberforce in the following terms:

'It is the task of the court to ascertain the legal nature of any transaction to which it is sought to attach a tax or a tax consequence, and if that emerges from a series, or combination of transactions, intended to operate as such, it is that series or combination which may be regarded.' He added that the principle of the Duke of Westminster's case did not compel the court to look at either documents or transactions in blinkers. So a prearranged series of transactions may be looked at as a whole, the position of the taxpayer at the end of the series, in real terms, being compared with that at the start. The *Ramsay* plan was clearly artificial, having no commercial purpose and effecting no change in the taxpayer's position in reality.

This new approach to such matters was followed in *IRC* v *Burmah Oil Co Ltd* (1982) and in *Furniss* v *Dawson* (1984):

In the latter case the shareholders in D Ltd (who were members of the Dawson family) received a cash offer for their shares from another English company, W Ltd. In order to obtain deferment from CGT, the Dawson family incorporated a company in the Isle of Man called Greenjacket and exchange their shares in D Ltd for Greenjacket shares – a paper for paper transaction then having no CGT consequences. Greenjacket then sold their holding of D Ltd, at the same price they had paid for them, to W Ltd for cash. The Special Commissioners, the High Court and the Court of Appeal were unanimous in their opinion that the two steps in the transaction, the exchange of shares and the subsequent sale, should be regarded as separate transactions. The House of Lords were of one mind in reversing this decision. In the case of a tax saving scheme no distinction was to be drawn between a series of preordained steps (despite the absence of a contractual obligation to carry them out) and a similar series of steps which the participants were legally obliged to fulfil. If there was a preordained series of transactions, or a single composite transaction, and it was possible to detect a step having no business purpose other than tax avoidance, this inserted step was to be disregarded and the transactions viewed as a whole. The introduction of Greenjacket on the scene had a business effect, but no business purpose other than a deferment of tax.

13.26 RESTRICTING THE *RAMSAY* PRINCIPLE

As remarked in *W and S-B*, the requirements in *Furniss* v *Dawson* are not easy to apply in practice, and in *Craven* v *White* (1988) the House of Lords, by a majority, decided to give the taxpayer the benefit of the doubt:

> In that case White was trying to dispose of his shares in a supermarket company, and to facilitate a merger with one possible purchaser, the shares were exchanged for shares in a Manx company. Subsequently the shares were purchased from the Manx company by a quite different purchaser. It was apparent from these facts that there was no preordained series of transactions, as it was three weeks after the transfer to the Manx company before any contract was concluded with the eventual purchaser. Nor was it a single composite transaction. It is worth noting that the transactions both in this case and in *Furniss* v *Dawson* took place before the law was altered so as to defeat paper for paper exchanges made in contemplation of tax avoidance: see s. 137 TCGA.

A very elaborate scheme designed to avoid CTT in respect of the death of Earl Fitzwilliam in 1979 has recently been held by the Court of Appeal to succeed because 'there was a real possibility that the proposed scheme would not go through' even though the steps taken were artificial in the extreme – *Fitzwilliam (Countess)* v *IRC* (1992). On the other hand, in *Hatton* v *IRC* (1992) Chadwick J held that a less elaborate scheme, also designed to save CTT, fell within the *Ramsay* principle because there was 'when the first transaction was entered into, no practical likelihood that the remaining transactions would not take place'. It has been suggested that it is relatively straightforward for the professional adviser to ensure that, in practice, the *Ramsay* principle will not apply to tax-saving schemes of this kind; 'straightforward' is, perhaps, not the *mot juste* in this context.

13.27 ASSOCIATED OPERATIONS

It seems that the Revenue takes the view that the *Ramsay* principle can be applied to all taxes, not to CGT alone (as in the *Ramsay* case itself). It has, for instance, been used to torpedo a stamp duty saving scheme: *Ingram* v *IRC* (1986). In IHT cases the Revenue has an additional weapon in the 'associated operations' provisions found in s. 268 IHTA. Associated operations are summarily described in Revenue booklet IHT 1 as follows:

> There are rules to prevent the avoidance of tax where a gift is made by a number of transactions, referred to as 'associated operations', even though one or more of these is not by itself a transfer of value. Broadly, operations may be

'associated' if they affect the same property or form a chain of linked operations. They may take place at different times, or be a number of steps taken at the same time. They do not necessarily have to be made by the same person, and the omission to do something can be an 'operation'.

Such a chain can be looked at as a whole to discover the substance of the affair for IHT purposes; the resemblance to the *Ramsay* principle is clear:

In *IRC* v *Macpherson* (1989) the trustees of a discretionary settlement made an agreement for the custody of pictures which reduced their value, closely followed by an appointment of an interest in the same pictures to the custodian's son. The agreement amounted to a depreciatory transaction under what is now s. 65(1)(b) IHTA, unless, as the trustees argued, it could be regarded as a commercial arrangement under ss. 65(6) and (10). The House of Lords held that there had been associated operations; the overall effect of the agreement and the appointment was to confer a gratuitous benefit, which took effect and created a charge to tax at the date of the final event in the series, i.e. the appointment.

It has been said that the associated operations provisions will not be used to attack inter-spouse transfers, normally exempt from IHT, except in 'blatant cases', as where a transfer by husband to wife is made on condition that the wife should at once use the money to make gifts to third parties. And at least there is authority for the negative proposition that death itself is not an associated operation (although making a will can be): *Bambridge* v *IRC* (1955) – a decision on the rather differently worded definition of associated operations for the purposes of what are now ss. 739–42 ICTA.

13.28   TRUST BUSTING

By revoking all the trusts of the limited interests a trust can be terminated by an application under the 1958 Act, but the use of that legislation is essential only if approval is required on behalf of incapacitated or unascertained beneficiaries. If all the beneficiaries are *sui juris* and can agree on a scheme (thereby driving up to a *Saunders* v *Vautier* situation, see *ante* 13.2), court costs can be saved and distribution allowed to proceed under a deed of arrangement. The main tax problem with trust breakings is CGT (especially since the severe restrictions imposed on holdover relief by FA 1989), because by terminating the trust in advance of its natural conclusion by death, the exemption under s. 62(1) TCGA is lost. With IHT, as a general rule, if there is a problem at all, it is a matter of guarding against a claim in the event of death within seven years of the termination of the trust. The following simple examples will give a better idea of the considerations to be borne in mind (it is assumed that the trustees are UK resident and remain so):

(a)   L has a life interest in the trust fund. The trustees have an express and unlimited power to pay capital to her. If they wind up the trust by paying the capital to her, the enlargement of her life interest is exempt from IHT under s. 53(2) IHTA but there is a deemed disposal of the capital under s. 71(1) TCGA.

(b)   A trust fund is settled on L for life with remainder to R. R makes a gift of his reversion to L. As the reversion was not acquired for money, it is excluded property under s. 48(1) IHTA and therefore under s. 3(2) the gift does not constitute a transfer of value. The enlargement of L's life interest is exempt under s. 53(2). The assignment of R's equitable interest is exempt from CGT under s. 76(1) TCGA.

(c)   A trust fund valued at £200,000 is settled on L for life with remainder to R. R purchases L's life interest for £80,000, which is its open market value. Under s. 51 IHTA, L's interest comes to an end and by virtue of ss. 3A(7) and 52(2) there is a PET of the whole fund, subject to a deduction of £80,000. The trustees must also allow for a claim under s. 71(1) TCGA, since R has become entitled to the whole fund as against the trustees.

(d)   A trust fund is settled on L for life with remainder to R. The fund is worth £200,000 and L buys the reversion from R for its open market value of £120,000. The enlargement of L's life interest is exempt under s. 53(2) IHTA but the total value of her estate (inclusive of the settled property) has diminished by £120,000, being the purchase money paid to R. It has diminished, because under s. 55 IHTA the reversion purchased by L is not part of her estate. L has therefore made a PET of £120,000 to R, for which the trustees must make provision. There is also a claim under s. 71(1) TCGA.

(e)   Life tenant and remainderman partition the fund between them on an actuarial basis, thus ensuring that each receives full consideration for what he gives up. Suppose that the fund is worth £200,000 and the split is £80,000 to the life tenant, £120,000 to the remainderman. The remainderman's disposition of his reversion is of excluded property with no IHT consequences. The enlargement of the life tenant's interest in the £80,000 into an absolute interest is exempt under s. 53(2) IHTA. The interest in the £120,000 has been terminated for a consideration of £80,000 but by s. 52(2) the amount of that consideration is not deductible. Hence there is a PET of £120,000, for which the trustees must make provision, in addition to attending to the claim under s. 71(1) TCGA on the whole fund. This makes sense from the Revenue's point of view, because had the fund been left alone, tax would have become chargeable on £200,000. Instead they will get tax on £120,000 if the life tenant dies within seven years and on £80,000 in the life tenant's estate on her death.

As in all matters of this kind, the trustees should be alert to ensure that parties with competing interests are independently advised, especially young beneficiaries who may still be under parental influence and elderly beneficiaries who might too readily subscribe to the views of their children.

13.29   THE DIFFICULTY OF DISTINGUISHING NOMINEE PROPERTY FROM SETTLED PROPERTY

The above discussion of the variation of trusts has been based on the presumed existence of a genuine settlement as distinct from a bare trust or nomineeship, normally terminable at the will of the principal; in the latter case, however, CGT can pose problems. Sections 60 and 68 TCGA separate settled property from property held by a nominee or bare trustee, but are not free from difficulty and have given rise to legal decisions:

(a)   A minor's interest is not turned into an interest in settled property if the sole handicap to his absolute ownership is the fact of his infancy. A deemed disposal under s. 71(1) cannot arise unless his interest is defeasible, e.g. by dying under a given age. See ss. 71(3) and 73(1).

(b)   Under s. 60(1) it is provided that there is a bare trusteeship if two or more persons are jointly entitled. It has been held that where two persons hold land upon trust for sale for themselves as tenants in common, the expression 'jointly' includes this form of concurrent ownership also: *Kidson* v *Macdonald* (1974).

(c)   Section 60(2) declares that a bare trusteeship includes the case where the beneficiary has the exclusive right (subject only to satisfying any outstanding charge, lien or other right of the trustees to resort to the assets for payment of duty, taxes, costs or other outgoings) to direct how that asset shall be dealt with. It was held in *Stephenson* v *Barclays Bank Trust Co* (1975) that this provision was not apt to cover the payment of outstanding annuities and that the residuary legatees could not be said to have an absolute interest until such time as an annuity fund was set up. This is an awkward decision for the more familiar situation where deferred legacies take effect on the death of a life tenant. The whole fund, having been revalued on the death of the life tenant under s. 72(1), will have to be revalued all over again when the legacies are satisfied in order to assess tax under s. 71(1) on any gains subsequent to the life tenant's death. But it is understood that the Revenue will not take the point if the legacies can be cleared within three months of the life tenant's death, thus leaving s. 73(1) to operate in the normal way.

(d)   In *Booth* v *Ellard* (1980) the taxpayer and 11 other members of a family company transferred some of their shares to trustees for 15 years, during which time, in order to preserve effective control by the family, each bound himself to restrictions on his right to dispose of his shares or to deal with his beneficial interest, income being distributed in proportion to their respective shareholdings. It was held by the Court of Appeal that on transfer to the trustees, the shares became nominee property under s. 60, not settled property. Where there was a plurality of beneficial owners the requirements of s. 60 were twofold: (i) their respective interest must be concurrent and not successive, and (ii) they must be qualitatively the same. Both these conditions were satisfied. Individually the shareholders had limited freedom of manoeuvre, but collectively they had power to end the trust: cf. *ante* 13.2.

(e)   There are circumstances, however, in which the difficult nature of the assets will prevent a nominee situation from arising. Under s. 72(5) TCGA a settled share properly set up under the terms of the trust instrument, without any recourse to the income of the other settled shares, is treated as a quite separate settlement, so that if there are two settled shares, the termination of one of the life interests has no CGT consequences for the other settled share. In *Pexton* v *Bell* (1976) the will envisaged separate settled shares for four daughters but the trustees left the fund in undivided form and it was held that s. 72(5) applied so as to create a deemed disposal of a fraction of the settled property corresponding to the life tenant's interest in the trust income. But in *Crowe* v *Appleby* (1976) the fund consisted of realty and was incapable of division. X was life tenant of one share and Y was life tenant of another share, Z being absolutely entitled on her death. It was held by the Court of Appeal (a) that on Y's death there was a deemed disposal of her share, as in *Pexton* v *Bell*, but (b) that Z could not become absolutely entitled during X's lifetime until the realty was sold, when there would be a deemed disposal and a chargeable gain under s. 71(1) as regards his share.

(f)   The point in *Pexton* v *Bell* has been put on a statutory basis in s. 73(2). The conclusion is that while shares of income from an undivided fund are on the same footing as the income from properly constituted settled shares, when it comes to deciding whether there has been a deemed disposal under s. 71(1), the inability to divide up the fund, as in *Crowe* v *Appleby*, will mean that, although the settlement is at an end as regards a particular beneficiary, that beneficiary cannot be said to have become absolutely entitled.

It is of interest that IHT is entirely free from this problem. If, for example, a settlor executes a declaration of trust giving himself a life interest with remainders over, it is a non-event for IHT purposes; the settlor simply exchanges one interest in possession for another. But that same transaction will result under s. 70 TCGA in a chargeable disposal of all the assets in the settlement.

14 Breach of trust

We have left undone those things which we ought to have done;
And we have done things which we ought not to have done
(Book of Common Prayer)

14.1 INTRODUCTION

Most deceaseds' estates and most trusts are administered to the entire
satisfaction of their beneficiaries; the question of breach of trust does not
arise. But, from time to time, PRs and trustees make mistakes; occasionally, these mistakes are deliberate ones. In such cases the beneficiaries
have their remedy, which is to sue the peccant PR or trustee for breach of
trust; additionally, PRs may be sued for *devastavit* – wasting the estate
assets. Breach of trust and *devastavit* overlap; there is no doubt that a PR
acts in a fiduciary capacity, and an act which would be a breach of trust by
a trustee – say, making an unauthorised investment – will also be a breach
of trust if done by a PR. If the result of the unauthorised investment is a
loss to the estate, the PR will also have committed a *devastavit*. The ambit
of breach of trust is, however, wider than that of *devastavit*. A PR who
profits from the estate in some unauthorised way – for instance, by using
knowledge acquired as PR to make a profit for himself – will have
committed a breach of trust, but there will be no *devastavit* unless the estate
has actually depreciated in value as a result of his act. Trustees and PRs are
personally liable for any loss caused by a breach of trust or *devastavit*, and
the liability is unlimited; this potential liability is something to consider
very carefully before accepting office in either capacity. There may also be
criminal liability under s. 1(1) Theft Act 1968; in this context, 'borrowing'
may be theft – see s. 6(1) of the Act.

14.2 THE INFINITE VARIETY OF BREACHES OF TRUST

The term breach of trust covers an infinite variety of situations; it is
impossible to list all the ways in which one may be committed. A few
examples may serve to illustrate its scope:

(a) Making an unauthorised investment, or inexcusable delay in making
     authorised changes of investment.
(b) Paying trust funds to the wrong person.
(c) Taking an unauthorised fee or profit.
(d) Failure to consider the exercise of a discretionary power.

(e) Exercising such a power carelessly – e.g. making an improper advance of capital.
(f) Failure to supervise agents.

14.3 THE USE OF AN INJUNCTION

Beneficiaries who have reason to suspect that a breach of trust is to be committed do not have to wait until it is committed before taking action. They can go to the court and ask the court to issue an injunction to restrain the trustees from committing the breach.

14.4 THE QUESTIONS RAISED BY A BREACH OF TRUST

Once it is appreciated that a breach of trust has occurred, a number of questions may need to be answered:

(a) Is the trustee (or PR) liable for the breach?
(b) If so, what is the measure of his liability?
(c) Does he have a right of contribution from co-trustees or a right of indemnity from co-trustees and beneficiaries?
(d) Is the beneficiary barred from action against the trustee by lapse of time or, alternatively, because he consented to the breach or instigated it?
(e) Is the trustee entitled to relief from the consequences of the breach under s. 61 TA?
(f) What if the trustees are men of straw?

14.5 PROFITS AND LOSSES – IS THERE ANY RIGHT OF SET-OFF?

Multiple breaches of trust may produce a combination of profits and losses. The position in this respect, so far as the beneficiaries are concerned, is one of 'Heads I win, Tails you lose'; a profit on one unauthorised transaction cannot be set off against a loss on another. A breach of trust which results in a profit to the trust fund ensures that the trustee has no liability, but the profit remains in the trust. If he has also committed a breach of trust resulting in a loss, he must restore the trust fund to the position it would have been in had he not committed the loss-making breach:

Example: the trustees agree upon an exchange of BP shares at £3 into ICI at £10. Mistakenly, Shell shares are sold at £5 each and the proceeds invested in Glaxo at £7. When the mistake is discovered, BP shares have risen to £4, ICI have risen to £12, Shell have risen to £6 and Glaxo have risen to £9. It is arguable that the trustees must buy back the Shell shares and find out of their own pockets the increase in price, at the same time compensating the trust for the additional cost of the ICI shares but without being allowed any offset for the profit on the sale of BP and Glaxo. (See *Dimes* v *Scott* (1828) and *Re Massingberd* (1890).) The rule against offsetting one transaction against another is described by *Hanbury* as 'harsh though logical'.

Whether you have in the above example an unauthorised sale and an unauthorised purchase (two transactions) or the one unauthorised exchange is perhaps a matter for debate, but on the latter basis the courts have allowed the rules to be modified where both breaches of trust can be treated as part of one transaction. In *Bartlett* v *Barclays Bank Trust Co Ltd (No. 1)* (1980) see *ante* 5.30 – the company had indulged in property development, one venture being a disaster and the other a success. Brightman J. discussed the rule against set-off, as outlined above:

> 'The relevant cases are, however, not easy to reconcile. All are centenarians and none is quite like the present. . . . I think it would be unjust to deprive the bank of the element of salvage in the course of assessing the cost of the shipwreck.'

Thus it seems that a set-off may be allowed to a trustee, not only where profit and loss arise out of the same transaction (as in *Fletcher* v *Green* (1864)) but also where they arise out of the same course of conduct which constitutes the breach of trust, as in the *Bartlett* case.

14.6 THE EXTENT OF THE TRUSTEE'S RESPONSIBILITY

Subject to the right of set-off in the limited circumstances in which it may be allowed, the obligation of the defaulting trustee is to place the trust fund in the same position that it would have been in, had no breach been committed. The obligation is to make complete restitution without regard to the common law principles, to be found in the realm of contract and tort, regarding causation and remoteness of damage. In *Bartlett* v *Barclays Bank Trust Co (No. 2)* (1980):

> The problem in this second dose of litigation was to determine just how much Barclays must pay from their own pocket to repair the breach of trust. The total shareholding in the company had been sold in September 1978 but Barclays sought to argue that as some of the shares had become vested absolutely in the beneficiaries in January 1974, their duty, in the case of those beneficiaries, was to restore the value in 1974 when they had only a minority interest, amounting to much less than their share of the proceeds in 1978. It was held that the obligation of a defaulting trustee was essentially that of effecting restitution to the trust estate, and until such restitution had been made the default continued. It was immaterial that a settled share of the funds had become distributable at some time antecedent to the making good of the fault; moreover, a beneficiary, properly advised, would never have sold his shareholding on its own and without regard to its value as a proportion of the company's underlying assets.

There is a statutory exception to the absolute liability of the trustee:

> Suppose that a trustee improperly advances £10,000 on the mortgage of a property when pursuant to s. 8 TA (see *ante* 11.20) he should have advanced only

373

£8,000 and that after default by the mortgagor the security has to be realised for only £5,000. The security is deemed under s. 9 TA to be an authorised investment for the smaller sum, and the trustee is liable to make good only £3,000 plus interest. Were it not for the statutory exception, the trustee would have to add £5,000 of his own to the dud investment, so that he could start all over again by making a proper investment of £10,000.

It would appear that in investment matters the proper approach, apart from the above statutory exception, is to assume that when a trustee makes an improper investment he commits his own funds to indemnifying in full the trust fund against the consequences of his action.

14.7 INTEREST ON COMPENSATION

Where a trustee is required to restore a loss to the trust fund he is normally also required to pay interest on the sum involved. Until recently the standard rate for this purpose was 4%. The rate came up for consideration in the second of the two Barclays Bank cases *supra*, where it was decided that the rate should be that allowed from time to time on the court's special account (formerly the court's short-term investment account). In other cases, a rate of 1% above that of the London clearing banks' base rate has been adopted. In all cases, the question of what rate of interest should be paid by the trustee is at the discretion of the court; generally, the interest is simple, but may be compound where the trustee has been guilty of fraud or misconduct. In such cases also, a higher rate of interest may be charged. Where it is considered that the trustee has received more than the normal rate awarded, as where he has used trust funds to trade for himself, the beneficiaries may claim what he has actually received.

14.8 LIABILITY OF TRUSTEES *INTER SE*

The liability of trustees for a breach of trust is joint and several, so that all at fault are liable and each trustee who is at fault is individually liable for the entire loss caused by the breach. This rule applies not only to formally appointed trustees but also to constructive trustees such as those persons who have knowingly received trust property in breach of trust.

In *Re Bell's Indenture* (1980), trustees misappropriated the whole of a trust fund with the knowledge and help of the trust solicitor, who thus became a constructive trustee and was liable for the breach of trust equally with the formally-appointed trustees. His partner, who had no knowledge of the misappropriation, was not liable, as the trust solicitor had no implied authority to accept office as a constructive trustee so as to make his partner also liable either as a constructive trustee or under ss. 10 and 11 of the Partnership Act 1890. The case is also authority for the rule that, in calculating the value to be replaced by the defaulting trustees, no allowance was to be made for tax (estate duty in this case) which would have been payable if the assets had not been misappropriated.

A beneficiary may sue all the trustees at fault or just one; having obtained judgment, he may levy execution against all trustees at fault or any one of them. The relationship between the trustees as to contribution and indemnity (see below) is no concern of the beneficiary.

14.9 TRUSTEE'S LIABILITY IS PERSONAL

A trustee is liable for his own faults, not for those of his co-trustees. This is now a statutory rule: see s. 30(1) TA. So, if Jones and Robinson are trustees and Jones makes an unauthorised profit out of his office, Jones alone is liable to the beneficiaries. However, the position is not always straightforward. Suppose that Robinson knew that Jones was making an unauthorised profit and stood idly by. Is this a case of 'wilful default', the statutory term found in s. 30(1)? If it is, then Robinson is equally liable for the breach of trust with Jones. Similarly, where Jones has been allowed to retain control over trust funds to the exclusion of Robinson and has made off with them. 'Wilful default' has been defined as an active commission of a breach of duty, or recklessness in the sense of not caring whether or not an act or omission is or is not a breach of duty: *Re City Equitable Fire Insurance Co Ltd* (1925), a definition which was adopted for the purposes of s. 30(1) in *Re Vickery* (1931). See *ante* 10.8.

In the second of the Barclays Bank cases, *ante* 14.6, Brightman J. defined wilful default as including a passive breach of trust, not requiring conscious wrongdoing, and dissented from the view expressed above. It would seem that a trustee is outside the protection of s. 30(1) and will make his co-trustee's acts his own acts, thereby becoming jointly and severally answerable, in three instances:

(a) Where he hands over trust assets to his co-trustee without seeing to their proper application.

(b) Where he permits his co-trustee to receive trust assets without making due enquiry as to how he has dealt with them.

(c) Where he turns a blind eye to a breach of trust either already committed by his co-trustee or contemplated.

Apart from the possible existence of an express indemnity clause in the trust instrument reducing the area of the trustee's responsibility for the acts of his co-trustees, the greatest danger to the trustee who adopts an attitude of passivity is when he retreats too far into the background and fails to participate sufficiently in the exercise of discretion. The innocent trustee in *Re Lucking* (1968), *ante* 10.8, escaped liability precisely because he did not fall into the category of a passive trustee; he was quite entitled to rely upon his co-trustee as being the trust's representative on the board of the company.

In *Re Miller* (1978) the active trustee, T, made it his business to keep a check on the trust's controlling interest in a private company but neglected to pass on any information to the other two trustees, V and W, who for their part never took any interest in the affairs of the trust. The shares in the company became valueless but without any negligence on the part of T, apart from his failure to keep V and W informed. V and W were clearly in breach of duty but Oliver J. held that, since T himself had not been negligent, it could not be claimed that their failure had led to the loss in the value of the trust fund. There must be a causal connection between the act constituting the breach and the damage suffered by the beneficiaries. *Re Lucking* (1968), see *ante* 10.8, was followed on the point that trustees are not under a duty in this situation to install themselves or a nominee on the board.

14.10 BREACHES OF TRUST BEFORE APPOINTMENT AND AFTER RETIREMENT

Generally speaking, a trustee is responsible only for breaches committed while he is actually in office, but he may be liable for one committed before his appointment if he fails to make reasonable enquiries as to the conduct of the trust before his appointment and does not discover the existence of a breach of trust for which the previous trustees should be made accountable. A newly appointed trustee will, of course, also be liable if he *does* discover the existence of an earlier breach of trust and does nothing to have it put right. Also, generally speaking, a trustee is not responsible for breaches committed after his retirement (although he remains liable for those committed during his term of office, unless released from such liability by the continuing trustees and/or the beneficiaries). A retired trustee may, however, be liable for a subsequent breach of trust if he retired in order to facilitate its commission. It has to be shown, for a retired trustee to be liable in this way, that he was aware that the particular breach that did occur would happen if he retired: *Head v Gould* (1898), in which Kekewich J. pointed out that to be liable it must be shown that the retired trustee was, in effect, guilty of being an accessory before the fact.

14.11 CONTRIBUTION AND INDEMNITY

The general rule is that trustees liable for a breach of trust should share the burden equally. So, if one paid more than his share, he could claim a contribution from the others. In certain cases, the right to contribution is replaced by a right to indemnity. There appear to be three types of situation in which indemnity will be relevant:

(a) Where a breach of trust is committed under advice from a trustee who is a solicitor, the solicitor/trustee must indemnify his co-trustees. However, it has to be shown that the co-trustees relied substantially upon the solicitor's advice and did not make an independent judgment. *Re Partington* (1887) was concerned with an improper investment by two trustees, one of whom was a solicitor. The court found that the other trustee was greatly influenced by the solicitor's advice and was entitled to an indemnity. By contrast, in *Head* v *Gould* (1898), the co-trustee was an active participator in the breach and failed in her attempt to get an indemnity against her solicitor/co-trustee.

(b)   Where a trustee is also a beneficiary and has committed a breach of trust for which he and his co-trustee are jointly to blame, then, provided that the beneficiary/trustee has benefited exclusively from the breach, he must indemnify his co-trustee against the consequences to the extent of his beneficial interest before the rule as to contribution outlined above is put into effect between the two trustees. [1]

(c)   Where one trustee has misappropriated trust funds, or is alone morally guilty for the breach, then he is required to indemnify his co-trustees against liability.

The above rules have now been superseded by statute, though no doubt they will continue to be taken into account by the court when exercising its jurisdiction under the Civil Liability (Contribution) Act 1978, which gives the court a discretion in relation to the amount to be recovered against two or more defendants who are liable for a breach of trust. The amount recoverable shall be 'such as may be found by the court to be just and equitable having regard to the extent of that person's responsibility for the damage in question'. It seems clear that this will enable a much more flexible approach to be made to questions of contribution and indemnity between trustees.

14.12   DEFENCES TO BREACH OF TRUST (1) – CONSENT

A beneficiary who requests, instigates or consents to a breach of trust cannot afterwards complain about it or seek to make the trustee liable for any loss which it causes. This was established in *Fletcher* v *Collis* (1905):

> In this case the trustee, with the consent of the two life tenants, sold the trust assets and handed the proceeds to one of the life tenants. Later, the remaindermen made the trustee replace the lost funds. The question before the court was whether the life tenants were entitled to the interest arising out of the replaced funds, or whether this should belong to the trustee until the life tenancies came to an end. The Court of Appeal held that the second alternative was the correct one; where a beneficiary has consented to a breach of trust he cannot subsequently make the trustee personally liable to account to that beneficiary for any loss arising out of the breach.

Moreover, if the consenting beneficiary has not only consented but has actually derived some benefit from the breach, the court may, if it thinks fit, order him to indemnify the trustee to the extent of his beneficial interest:

s. 62(1) TA. Under this section, while the instigation or request of the beneficiary may be either oral or written, a consent must be in writing:

> The section can be invoked not only by the current trustees but also by former trustees, as appears from *Re Pauling (No. 2)* (1963) where Coutts & Co, who had been held liable in the earlier litigation for improper advancements, claimed the right to impound the life tenant's interest and opposed the family's proposal for the appointment of new trustees in place of the bank, on the ground that Coutts would thereby lose the right to an impounding order. It was held that neither under the court's inherent jurisdiction to impound (which is not quite as extensive as s. 62) nor under s. 62 itself, would the right to an impounding order be prejudiced by the appointment of new trustees.

14.13   WHAT IS A RELIABLE CONSENT?

Not every consent, request or instigation to commit a breach can necessarily be relied on by the trustee; he will have to be sure that the beneficiary who gives such consent is of full age and capacity and knew all the facts about the proposed breach and its consequences, and that the beneficiary was a free agent and not acting under undue influence or duress. Provided these conditions are satisfied, a consent given *after* the event – in effect, a ratification – will be effective. The subject of undue influence in this context was raised in *Re Pauling* (1964) – see *ante* 10.26:

> In that case the trustee had relied upon consents received from young adult beneficiaries to make some dubious advances from capital. There was an especial problem with a daughter still living at home and undoubtedly influenced by her parents. It is well, therefore, to take particular care in such cases to see that beneficiaries receive independent advice before giving consent to a breach of trust; the same principle would no doubt apply in the case of the elderly and, indeed, anyone whose personal judgment in such matters may be doubtful. The words of Wilberforce J. (in the court below but mentioned without dissent in the Court of Appeal) are, however, of some comfort:
> '. . . the court has to consider all the circumstances in which the concurrence of the *cestui que trust* was given with a view to seeing whether it is fair and equitable that, having given his concurrence, he should afterwards turn round and sue the trustees: that, subject to this, it is not necessary that he should know that what he is concurring in is a breach of trust, provided that he fully understands what he is concurring in, and that it is not necessary that he should himself have directly benefited by the breach of trust.'

14.14   DEFENCES TO BREACH OF TRUST (2) – LIMITATION OF ACTIONS

There is no time limit to an action by the beneficiary against the trustee, if the trust property or its proceeds are still in the trustee's possession, or if he has previously received the trust property and converted it to his own use or if he has been an actual party to a fraudulent breach of trust: s. 21(1) Limitation Act 1980. A trust includes the estate of a deceased person and constructive and resulting trusts as well as express trusts. Trustees include PRs.

As an exception to the foregoing, s. 21(2) limits the liability of any trustee, who is also a beneficiary, in any action for the recovery of trust property in his hands *after* the end of the limitation period (see 14.15 and 14.16 below) to the *excess* over his proper beneficial share, provided he acted honestly and reasonably in distributing the trust funds .[2]

14.15   THE LIMITATION PERIOD FOR TRUSTS

Subject to the above provision, s. 21(3) limits the right of beneficiaries to bring an action for breach of trust to a period of six years from the date upon which the right accrued. Such a right does not accrue to a beneficiary with a future interest, e.g. a remainderman after a life interest – until that interest falls into possession. So, in a case where there is a life interest to A, remainder to B, and the trustee commits a breach of trust in 1970 and the life interest continues until 1990, B will have until 1996 to bring an action (he could, of course, bring one at an earlier date, but he may well not discover the existence of the breach until the life interest ends). In general, however, the limitation period starts from the date of the breach and not from the date of the loss. Under s. 28 of the 1980 Act, time does not start to run against a beneficiary who is an infant or is otherwise incapacitated until either the disability ends or the beneficiary dies.

14.16   LIMITATION PERIOD FOR DECEASEDS' ESTATES

Under s. 22 a beneficiary who makes a claim against a PR for a breach of trust or *devastavit* relating to pure personalty must bring it within 12 years from the date upon which he became entitled to his interest in the estate, which in the case of immediate gifts will be the date of death. For landed property (including equitable interests and the proceeds of land held upon trust for sale), the action must be brought within 12 years of the date upon which his right of action accrued, i.e. the date of the breach: ss. 15 and 18. So far as creditors of an estate are concerned, the normal limitation rules apply; proceedings in respect of contract or tort must be brought within six years of the date when the cause of action arose: ss. 2 and 5. For covenants the period is 12 years: s. 8. It will be recalled that actions both for and against a deceased person are not, in general, affected by his death: see *ante* 5.9 *et seq.*, but an action by a creditor against a PR for *devastavit*, for example, where the PR has distributed the estate without regard to the creditor's debt, is barred after six years from the date of distribution: s. 2.

379

14.17   ACTIONS BASED ON FRAUD, CONCEALMENT OR MISTAKE

Section 32 of the 1980 Act (which applies to both PRs and trustees) provides that, where an action is based upon fraud or deliberate concealment or relief for the consequences of a mistake, the period of limitation will not start until the plaintiff has discovered the fraud, concealment or mistake or might with reasonable diligence have discovered it. Deliberate concealment does not require dishonesty, merely unconscionable conduct by not disclosing the breach of trust, either knowingly or recklessly. In the second of *Barclays Bank* cases, see *ante* 14.6, the Barclays Bank Trust Co was successfully able to plead the Limitation Act against the life tenant because it had never at any stage attempted to gloss over the chain of events.

14.18   DEFENCES TO BREACH OF TRUST (3) – LACHES AND ACQUIESCENCE

If no limitation period applies, as in cases covered by s. 21(1) *ante* 14.14, unreasonable delay or negligence in bringing a claim by the beneficiary *may* defeat it – technically, a delay of this kind which is sufficient to defeat an equitable remedy is known as 'laches': 'Equity aids the vigilant and not the indolent.' The application of this doctrine is at the discretion of the court, which will ask itself what hardship has been done to the defendant trustee by the delay. Where such delay would make it practically unjust to provide a remedy, the lapse of time will be a very material factor in the court's decision. Where there is no statutory limitation period there is, in theory, no maximum period for a claim against a PR or trustee, although 20 years has been mentioned as a reasonable guide: *Weld* v *Petre* (1929). It seems clear that where the 1980 Act provides a limitation period, it will not be possible for the trustee to plead laches.

To be distinguished from laches is the principle of acquiescence. If the trustee can show acquiescence in the breach of trust by the beneficiary, he may have a defence independently of the running of time. Within the statutory periods, the trustee will not be able to use the beneficiary's delay in bringing his claim unless that delay is coupled with acquiescence or some other inequitable factor. Note s. 36(2) of the 1980 Act: 'Nothing in this Act shall affect any equitable jurisdiction to refuse relief on the ground of acquiescence or otherwise.'

The beneficiary's concurrence or acquiescence in the breach of trust will be of no avail to the trustee, unless the beneficiary is *sui juris* and fully apprised of the surrounding facts, but he need not benefit from it nor be aware that the circumstances constitute a breach of trust – see the words of Wilberforce J., *ante* 14.13.

14.19 DEFENCES TO BREACH OF TRUST (4) – STATUTORY RELIEF FROM COURT

Section 61 TA may be of such importance to PRs and trustees in cases where beneficiaries bring an action against them that it is worth quoting in full:

Power to relieve trustee from personal liability
If it appears to the court that a trustee, whether appointed by the court or otherwise, is or may be personally liable for any breach of trust, whether the transaction alleged to be a breach of trust occurred before or after the commencement of this Act, but has acted honestly and reasonably, and ought fairly to be excused for the breach of trust and for omitting to obtain the directions of the court in the matter in which he committed such breach, then the court may relieve him either wholly or partly from personal liability for the same.

'Honestly' in this context means 'in good faith'; whether or not a trustee has acted reasonably depends on the circumstances of the individual case. Whilst it may be thought reasonable in some cases to act under legal advice, doing so will not necessarily be enough to make the court grant relief to the trustee. In *National Trustees Co of Australasia* v *General Finance Co of Australasia* (1905) the trustees followed the advice of their solicitors, which turned out to be wrong. The court refused relief to the trustees. No doubt the court had in mind the fact that the trustees were professionals. There is no doubt that the court will be less likely to relieve a professional trustee than a lay trustee, and will be especially reluctant to relieve a professional trustee which advertises itself 'as being above ordinary mortals' – *Bartlett* v *Barclays Bank Trust Co, ante* 5.30 and 14.5. In that case the court held that the bank had acted honestly but not reasonably; the same comment was made in *Re Rosenthal* (1972) where the defendant PR was a solicitor. Even if a trustee under attack can satisfy the court that he acted both honestly and reasonably, he still has to persuade the court that he ought fairly to be excused, and the court may feel some compunction about denying the beneficiaries their undoubted right to be compensated for a breach of trust. Nevertheless, a PR or trustee who has to defend himself against a claim will invariably add a plea for relief under s. 61 to his defence, so that, if the worst comes to the worst, he can ask the court to exercise its discretion in his favour.

The sort of situation where there would be a *prima facie* case for applying s. 61 TA is the one that occurred in the remarkable case of *Eaves* v *Hickson* (1861). There the trustees had distributed the trust fund to the children on the basis of a forged marriage certificate produced to them by the children's father, the effect of which was to include in the distribution his illegitimate children. This was before s. 3 Judicial Trustees Act 1896 introduced for the first time the relieving power now contained in s. 61 TA. The trustees were held to be responsible for

381

the wrongful distribution, but the matter did not end there as the father was also held to be responsible, as a constructive trustee, for the breach of trust. Thus, a complete stranger to the trust can become accountable, as a constructive trustee, to the beneficiaries for a breach of trust, although he has never had any trust property in his possession or had access to it.

14.20 DEFENCES TO BREACH OF TRUST (5) – INDEMNITY CLAUSES

It is not uncommon these days to find that a will or trust deed contains a clause indemnifying the PR or trustee from the consequences of a breach of trust. Liability for breach of trust will be excluded, for instance, except where there is an absence of good faith, or wilful fraud exists. An argument has been put forward ((1980) Conv 333) that such clauses are unreasonable within the meaning of the Unfair Contract Terms Act 1977; can this be so, since the relationships between testator and executor or between settlor and trustee can hardly ever be contractual? These indemnity clauses do not seem to have been brought to the attention of the courts as yet; it may be that, when they are, the courts will use their inherent jurisdiction to prevent them from taking effect. It seems especially likely that this would be done where the PR or trustee seeking their benefit is a professional (and it is professional PRs and trustees who mostly seek the protection of such clauses).*

14.21 PROPRIETARY REMEDIES

So far, the discussion of breach of trust has been confined to personal actions against PRs and trustees. But such actions may not be profitable; the defendant may have only small personal resources. In such a situation it will be worth considering the alternative proprietary remedies, which involve tracing and reclaiming the trust property from the possession of third parties.

14.22 FOLLOWING THE ASSETS AT COMMON LAW

At common law, the legal owner of property who is deprived of possession has the right to follow it and claim it no matter in whose hands it ends up, so long as the property in question is identifiable in either its original or a converted state. But the common law remedy is not available where the property has become mixed with other property; once its separate identity is gone, the right to follow is lost.[3] Another serious defect from the point

---

*See the article by Paul Matthews 'The Efficacy of Trustee Exemption Clauses in English Law', [1989] Conv 42.

of view of a beneficiary wanting to recover trust property is that common law does not recognise equitable interests in property; the beneficiary seeking to follow under common law would therefore have to join the trustee in as a third party and this could be inconvenient, or even impossible.

14.23 WRONGFUL DISTRIBUTION IN THE ADMINISTRATION OF AN ESTATE

The vulnerable position of a PR who overpays the beneficiaries has already been referred to – *ante* 6.2. If a PR distributes assets to the wrong people, those who have not been paid or have been underpaid (whether they are creditors, legatees or intestate beneficiaries) have two rights of recourse: (a) a claim against the PR, a remedy which they must exhaust first, but failing that, (b) a direct claim in equity against the wrong recipients. These are both personal claims; they also have the proprietary remedy of tracing. The direct claim in equity against the wrong recipients, which has been described as a relic of the ecclesiastical courts' jurisdiction over deceaseds' estates, is firmly in place under the modern law but there are dicta in *Ministry of Health* v *Simpson* (1951) indicating a reluctance to extend the remedy to beneficiaries under trusts as distinct from estates.*

The direct claim in equity against an overpaid beneficiary will fail if there was a sufficiency of assets to pay the latter at the time. So, if there are two legacies, each of £2,000, and one of them is paid in full when the assets are worth £5,000, the other legatee who has to go short because of a subsequent fall in the value of the estate, will have to confine himself to his remedy against the PR. He cannot claim against the other legatee, who received no more than his due at the time. The claim does not carry interest and if it fails through the insolvency of the overpaid beneficiary, there is still the proprietary remedy of tracing available.

14.24 TRACING IN EQUITY

To provide the beneficiaries of estates and trusts with a more satisfactory remedy than that available at common law, Equity developed the remedy of tracing property where a fiduciary relationship exists. Its overwhelming advantage is that, being a proprietary remedy, it will be good against the wrongful owner's trustee in bankruptcy; the disappointed beneficiary or creditor is chasing his own assets and if he establishes his equitable title to them, they will have to be isolated from the bankrupt's estate and will not be available to the bankrupt's creditors.

---

*See, for instance, *Re Montagu* (1987) at page 271, quoted with approval in *Agip (Africa) Ltd* v *Jackson* (1991), below.

In such a situation, the owner of an equitable interest in the property may trace it into anyone's hands with a view to recovery, the only exception being property held by a purchaser for value without notice of the trust. The remedy is not only available to beneficiaries of deceaseds' estates and formally constituted trusts; it can be invoked in all cases where there is a fiduciary relationship, as in agency cases and between directors and their companies. In *Sinclair* v *Brougham* (1914) the directors of a building society carried on an *ultra vires* banking business; the House of Lords held that there was a fiduciary relationship between the directors and the depositors and the latter could therefore trace their deposits in equity.

A noteworthy modern example is *Chase Manhattan Bank* v *Israel-British Bank (London)* (1981) where the plaintiff bank mistakenly made a double payment of $2 million to another New York bank for the account of the defendant bank in London. The duplicated payment was paid under a mistake of fact. The court held that Chase Manhattan retained an equitable property in it and that the defendant bank (now in liquidation) owed a fiduciary duty to the plaintiff. The payment was therefore capable of being traced in equity and so recoverable in priority to the ordinary creditors in winding-up proceedings. The result seems right, but at the cost of straining the concept of a fiduciary relationship.

For a recent case, see *Agip (Africa) Ltd* v *Jackson* (1991) where the Court of Appeal confirmed the judge's finding in the court below that since there had been an initial breach of fiduciary duty by the plaintiffs' chief accountant (he had falsified a payment order), equitable tracing was possible against anyone in possession of the plaintiffs' property other than a *bona fide* purchaser without notice.

The use of this tracing remedy may also be helpful in reservation of title cases, enabling the vendor to trace the proceeds of a subsale by the purchaser.

In *Aluminium Industrie Vaassen BV* v *Romalpa Aluminium Ltd* (1976) it was accepted by the Court of Appeal that the defendant/buyer was an agent and bailee for the plaintiff/vendor, thus producing the fiduciary relationship which is an essential prerequisite to tracing. It will not always be possible to establish that it exists in retention of title cases.

The equitable remedy is not defeated by the fact that the property in which the interest subsists has been mixed with property owned by a third party. As was said in the *Diplock* case, Equity is able to draw up a balance sheet; on the right-hand side appears the mixed fund, on the left-hand side the two or more funds which constitute it. The theoretical basis of the remedy is the existence of an equitable charge over the mixed fund for the amount of trust property which it contains.

In addition to the insurmountable barrier of the *bona fide* purchaser for value of the legal estate without notice, there is also a difficulty where the trust property finds its way into the hands of an innocent volunteer. Where this has happened, tracing into a mixed fund is not possible. The most that Equity can do for the beneficiary in such cases is to allow him to share in the mixed fund with the innocent volunteer in proportion to the amounts which each has contributed to its make-up, except in the case of bank accounts, where the rule in *Clayton's Case* applies (see *post* 14.25). Where there is no mixing, there is no problem; equally, one might say that there is no problem where the trust funds have simply been dissipated, whether on the racecourse or simply in paying living expenses. Tracing is impossible, because there is nothing to trace. In these circumstances, the beneficiary has to fall back on his personal remedy against the trustee.

14.25 MIXING OF TRUST MONEYS WITH THE TRUSTEE'S OWN MONEYS

Tracing is not only a remedy against third parties. Before we look at that angle in more detail, there are tracing rules affecting the trustees themselves. Equity is at some pains to save a trustee from his own folly if he mixes trust moneys up with his own moneys. Where mixing takes place on a banking account, the trustee is presumed to draw out his own moneys first, the trust moneys being left unscathed until his own are exhausted: *Re Hallett* (1880), which is contrary to the usual rule in *Clayton's Case* (1816) whereby the first drawings out are attributable to the first payments in. But the *Hallett* rule will yield to the larger presumption against an intention to commit a breach of trust:

> In *Re Oatway* (1903) the trustee drew from a mixed account to buy an investment and then spent the rest of the money in the account on his own purposes. His executor tried to argue that in drawing out money to buy the investment he was drawing out his own money and then went on to spend the trust money. This argument was rejected and the beneficiaries were able to claim what had turned out to be a profitable investment.

But there is no presumption, in the absence of contrary intention, that subsequent deposits by the trustee of his own money are intended to become trust money: *Roscoe* v *Winder* (1915).

What if the trustee blends trust moneys belonging to two different trusts in the banking account? In this situation the rule in *Clayton's Case* is restored and withdrawals are matched with receipts on the first in, first out basis. This is also the rule for the innocent volunteer who receives trust moneys without notice of the trust and without giving valuable consideration. If non-banking assets are mixed there is a rateable apportionment between the two trusts or between the trust and the innocent volunteer.

If moneys are withdrawn from a banking account and the amount withdrawn is entirely trust money which the trustee then uses to acquire an asset wrongfully, the beneficiaries may adopt the purchase, thus securing for the trust any increase in value; or they can demand reconversion, which they may have to do if they are not all *sui juris*, in which case any gain will accrue to the trust fund and any loss will fall upon the trustee. A more difficult situation is created if the asset has been acquired partly with trust money and partly with the trustee's own money:

> In *Re Tilley* (1967) it was stated (*obiter*) that where a trustee lays out trust money towards the purchase of property, the beneficiaries are entitled, to the extent to which it was purchased out of trust money, to a proportionate charge on the property purchased and any capital gain, as well as income profit, from it. The decision itself had to cope with a fluctuating overdraft situation and came to the conclusion that if money is paid into the trustee's overdrawn account, that account will stand charged with the repayment of the trust money and the charge will extend to assets acquired with the assistance of the overdraft but there will be no right to the assets themselves, as they have been purchased by means of the overdraft facility, not by the use of trust money.

14.26 EXAMPLES OF TRACING AGAINST THE TRUSTEE

The Trust banking account has a credit balance of	£1,000
The trustee pays in £1,000 of his own money	1,000
	2,000
He withdraws for his own living expenses	1,000
The remaining balance is trust money (*Re Hallett*)	1,000
He withdraws, again for his own consumption	700
The balance is trust money	300
He pays in £1,000 of his own money	1,000
Only £300 of the new balance is trust money (*Roscoe* v *Winder*)	1,300
He pays in £1,700 of trust money	1,700
There is now £2,000 of trust money and £1,000 of the trustee's own money on the account	3,000
He expends £1,000 on the purchase of ICI stock	1,000
The balance is now trust money (*Re Hallett*)	2,000
He dissipates the rest of the money	2,000
	NIL

Under *Re Hallett* the trustee is assumed to have bought the ICI stock out of his own money, but the stock stands charged with the amount owing to the trust – *Re Oatway* – and if the ICI stock has gone up in value, the charge will encompass that profit also as well as its income: *Re Tilley* (1967).

Suppose that the trustee is in charge of two separate trust funds, each with £1,000 in their respective bank accounts. He then takes the £1,000 out of trust A's bank account and adds it to the £1,000 in trust B's bank account, thus increasing the balance on the latter to £2,000. Later, he extracts £1,000 from the account and spends it on himself. The rule in *Clayton's Case* applies, and it is assumed that the money withdrawn is that which belongs to trust B. The rule applies only where there is an active current bank account; whilst it may be relatively easy to apply where transactions are few, it could be quite impracticable in the case of a large, busy account with a multitude of daily credits and debits. Moreover, a withdrawal which is expressly earmarked as trust money is treated as such, irrespective of the fact that the rule dictates otherwise.

14.27   THE *DIPLOCK* CASE

The general basis of tracing was thoroughly discussed in the very significant case of *Re Diplock* (1948):

The testator, Caleb Diplock, had misguidedly left his large residuary estate to his executors for distribution amongst such charitable institution or institutions or other charitable *or benevolent object or objects* at their absolute discretion. The executors, acting under incorrect advice, distributed over £200,000 to 139 charities before the validity of the residuary gift was successfully challenged by the next-of-kin in *Chichester Diocesan Fund* v *Simpson* (1944). The executors[4] were unable to meet the full claim against them by the next-of-kin, who proceeded to claim for the balance against the various charities; they claimed both *in personam* (a personal claim) and *in rem* (a proprietary claim) and succeeded on both counts. The House of Lords affirmed the decision of the Court of Appeal, under the name of *Ministry of Health* v *Simpson* (1951), in so far as it related to the personal claim against the charities. The appeal against the liability *in personam* came from only one of the charities (a hospital), which had spent the money it had received on the erection of new buildings, a factor which had, in the opinion of the Court of Appeal, deprived the next-of-kin of the right to trace, leaving them only with the personal remedy. The hospital's appeal against the use of the personal remedy was unanimously rejected by the House.

It was unnecessary for the House to discuss the claim *in rem*, as it had been thoroughly examined in the Court of Appeal in case the personal claim was dismissed in the House of Lords. The result of this thorough examination was a restatement of the equitable doctrine of tracing. The points made by the Court of Appeal were as follows:

(a)   A beneficiary whose money had been mixed with that of another might trace his money into the mixed fund (or assets acquired with it), notwithstanding that the fund (or the assets representing it) were held by an innocent volunteer, provided that (i) there had been a fiduciary or quasi-fiduciary relationship between the claimant and the original holder of the money, in this case the executors, so as to give the claimant an equitable interest in the money; (ii) the claimant's money was identifiable; and (iii) the equitable remedy by way of an equitable charge over the fund did not create an injustice.

(b)   Where the money had passed to an innocent volunteer and no mixing had taken place, the innocent volunteer held it on behalf of the true owner.

(c)   Where the money had passed to an innocent volunteer and he had mixed it with money of his own, the claimant and the innocent volunteer were on the same footing and were entitled to a *pro rata* distribution.

(d)   Where the money had been paid into an active banking account of the innocent volunteer, the rule in *Clayton's Case* applied to determine the

387

ownership of the residual balance; but not where a specific withdrawal had been earmarked as trust money, for example, by paying it into a separate account and recording its origin.

(e)   But where the money received by the charity had been spent on the alteration or improvement of its landed property, the equitable remedy of a charge would work an injustice. The property may not have increased in value and may even have depreciated in value as the result of the alterations. Relief to the claimants was therefore refused. Relief was also refused in respect of claims against two charities who had used trust money to repay a loan. Neither the building alteration nor the loan repayments could satisfy the test of identifiability.

APPENDICES

APPENDIX 1:
FIRST CHECK-LIST FOR PERSONAL REPRESENTATIVES

(a) Funeral arrangements made? Relatives and friends advised?
(b) Last will (+ codicil(s)) obtained? Formal validity in order? Capacity undoubted? Copies to co-personal representatives + principal beneficiaries? Others advised of benefits?
(c) Deceased domiciled in England and Wales (if not, where? Evidence?)
(d) Copy death certificate(s) obtained? Bankers and other agents/advisors (see below) advised of death? Mail redirected? Deceased's (former) employers advised?
(e) Discovering the assets and debts. Personal papers reviewed? Deceased's 'personal log' obtained? Recent bank statements reviewed? Enquiries made * as in table below?

	IHT personal Tax accumulator†	Current assets	Current debts	Litigation, interests in other estates or trusts	Tax affairs
Accountants	*	*	*		*
Bankers	*	*	*	*	*
Estate agent		*	*		
Inland Revenue	*				*
Solicitors	*	*	*	*	*

†'Personal tax accumulator' in this context embraces chargeable gifts (including PETs) (i) made within seven years of death and (ii) in the case of a PET that has become a chargeable transfer, lifetime chargeable transfers made within the seven years preceding the date of the PET, even though themselves more than seven years old. One should also enquire whether the deceased had made any gifts with reservation (GWRs) and whether he had *received* any gifts upon which IHT might be outstanding (if the donor has predeceased) or upon which IHT is contingently payable on the future death of the donor.

All those in the above table should be asked (i) to supply all known information about the deceased's affairs and (ii) (except the Revenue) to give details of any outstanding accounts or debts.

(f) Have statutory notices for claims been published (having regard to possible claims from illegitimate relatives or from persons who might claim to have been maintained by the deceased)? Has consideration been given to the termination of any guarantees entered into by the deceased?
(g) Protecting the assets.
    (i) Land and buildings. Inspected? Secured? Fully insured? Services, e.g. electricity, gas, telephone, terminated or transferred? Rents being collected? Agents appointed?
    (ii) Personal effects secured? Fully insured? Any especially valuable items? Car insurance transferred? Are any items on hire, e.g. TV?
    (iii) Securities, policies and documents of title traced? Obtained (where possible before grant), inspected where not?

391

(iv)   Businesses:
(1)   Sole trader. Business to continue? Customers and suppliers notified? Manager appointed? Control? Insurance? Check licensing requirements and need to notify VAT authorities. Stationery to be modified?
(2)   Partnership. Partners advised? Copy of partnership agreement and last accounts obtained?
(3)   Private companies. Deceased's executive responsibility covered? Arrangements made for future financial information? Last (up-to-date) accounts obtained?

For (i), (ii), (iii) and (iv) above, provisional valuations made, accurate ones being obtained?

(h)   If death due to third party negligence, consider claim on behalf of estate and dependants? If deceased had committed a tortious act, consider claim against the estate; any insurance cover for it? Any family provision claim apparent?

(i)   If deceased had an interest in another estate or trust, have PRs or trustees been advised? If deceased was a co-fiduciary, has notice of death been given to survivors? If he was the sole fiduciary, consider action to safeguard assets.

(j)   Foreign assets. Attorneys being appointed?

(k)   Tax to date of death. Instructions given?

(l)   Schedule of assets and liabilities (plus relevant *inter vivos* gifts, interests in trusts, joint property) for preparation of probate papers? Can any assets be realised or applied before grant to assist with tax payment? Otherwise, loan arrangements made? How many copies of the grant required? Copy of statement of assets and liabilities to principal beneficiaries?

APPENDIX 2 (see 3.45 and 3.46): ASSESSMENT OF IHT

Lifetime dispositions by testator (no previous gifts):
● Gift on 1 November 1984 of £33,000 to his son.
● Gift on 1 November 1985 of £37,000 to his son.
● Gift on 1 May 1986 to a non-privileged discretionary settlement of his 4,000 shares in an unquoted family company, in which his wife also owned 1,500 and his son the remaining 4,500. The shares were worth £80 apiece for a controlling interest but only half that for a substantial minority interest. The donor paid the tax.
● Gift on 15 April 1988 of £56,000 to the son.
● Gift on 1 August 1988 of £70,000 to the above discretionary settlement. The trustees paid the tax.
● Gift on 6 April 1989 of £25,000 to the son on the occasion of his marriage.
Date of death: 15 May 1992.
Free estate, net of liabilities, is £510,000, including £160,000 of farmland which the deceased had owned, occupied and managed for the past three years, having an agricultural value of £140,000. Live and dead stock is valued at £20,000. Deceased was beneficial joint tenant with his sister of an investment property, his interest in which was worth £50,000. He was also life tenant of settled property worth £300,000, which now passes to his widow absolutely. By his will he has left £100,000

to his widow, his holding of 10% of the ordinary shares in an unquoted company (valued at £50,000) to his sister and the residue to his son.

On the initial gift to the discretionary settlement the related property provisions apply (s. 161 IHTA) and the lifetime tax is assessed on 4,000 x £80 = £320,000 but reduced to £160,000 by business property relief at 50% (s. 105 IHTA). The annual exemption for 1986/87 makes a further reduction to £157,000.

The son can claim the annual exemption for 1987/88 despite s. 19(3A) IHTA (see the January 1991 edition of the Revenue's publication IHT 1, para.5.16 and Example 3). Now that the PET has become chargeable it must be inserted into the accumulator at the date when it took effect, i.e. on 15 April 1988, thereby increasing the accumulator for the calculation of the death tax on subsequent gifts *inter vivos*. Note carefully that the effect of the PET is under s. 7(1)(b) is to extend the vulnerable period (usually only seven years before death) back to 15 April 1981 (6 April 1982 for the marriage gift), so including the chargeable transfer made on 1 November 1984, but only for the calculation of the death tax on the gifts *inter vivos*.

There now follows an assessment of the taxable part of the free estate after applying exemptions:

	£	£	£
Free estate		510,000	
Less Agricultural and Business relief at 100% on £180,000 and at 50% on £50,000 – (1) below	205,000		
Exempt part of widow's legacy 280,000/460,000 of £100,000 (s. 39A IHTA) – (2) below	60,870	265,870	244,130

(1) Business property relief applies at 100% to the hope or amenity value of the farmland, to the live and dead stock and to the minority holding of unquoted shares at 50%; agricultural property relief applies, also at 100%, to the agricultural value of £140,000.

(2) 'The appropriate fraction' under s. 39A(4) is –

The value transferred (305,000) minus sister's gift reduced by business relief (£25,000)   = £280,000
The unreduced value of the estate (£510,000) minus unreduced value of sister's gift (£50,000) = £460,000

The trustees of the settled property in which deceased had a life interest have no tax to pay because of the spouse exemption in s. 18(1) IHTA.

We now look at the deceased's lifetime cumulator and tax assessable in lifetime and on death on lifetime gifts:

Lifetime	**Gross** £	**Tax** £	**Net** £
1 Nov 84 £33,000 less annual exemption 84/85	30,000	Nil	30,000 +
1 Nov 85 £37,000 less annual exemption 85/86	34,000	Nil	34,000 + +
1 May 86 £160,000 less annual exemption 86/87	196,793	*39,793	157,000
	260,793	39,793	221,000

Gross up £221,000 at 1988/89 rates	248,750	27,750	221,000
1 Aug 88 Addition to settlement	70,000	14,000	56,000
	318,750	41,750	277,000

Less tax previously paid
*Paid by donor *39,793
**Payable by trustees **£1,957

On death – 15 May 92. The gift marked + is now over seven years old. The gift marked + + was before 18 March 1986 and being over three years old is exempt under FA 1986, Sch. 19, para.40.

Recalculation of tax on amount originally settled at 1992/93 death rate	260,793	44,317
Taper relief at 80% of £44,317		35,454
		8,863
Paid in May 1986		39,793
Tax assessable on trustees (no refund)		NIL

The failed PET of April 1988 has to be put into the cumulator which stood at that date at 260,793

Failed PET, less annual exemptions 1987/88 and 1988/89	50,000
	310,793

Tax at 1992/93 rate on £50,000 = £20,000
Less taper relief at 40% of £20,000   £12,000 to be paid by son

The additional gift into settlement in August 1988 now has to slot in after the failed PET. Tax recalculated at the 1992/93 death rate on £70,000 at 40% = £28,000, less taper relief at 20% of £28,000   70,000   22,400
Less amount paid in August 1988   1,957
          £20,443 to be paid by trustees

Failed PET of April 1989 (less marriage exemption of £5,000 and annual exemption for 1989/90) has to be put into the cumulator and tax calculated at 1992/93 rate, £17,000 at 40%, less taper relief at 20% of £6,800   17,000   £5,440 to be paid by son

          397,793

Less the November 1984 gift which now drops out of the cumulator in order to compute the remaining tax   30,000
Cumulative total at death   £367,793

FREE ESTATE IS TAXABLE AS FOLLOWS
Legacy to sister, £50,000, less business relief

at 50% = £25,000, not bearing its own tax and therefore grossed up	41,666	16,666	25,000
Non-exempt part of widow's legacy – £40,196, not bearing its own tax and therefore grossed up	65,217	26,087	39,130*
Exempt part of widow's legacy	60,870	–	60,870*
Exempt part of son's residue	205,000	–	205,000
Non-exempt part of son's residue	137,247	54,899	82,348
Total free estate	510,000	97,652	412,348
Joint property (tax payable by sister)	50,000	20,000	30,000

*See 'the appropriate fraction' as calculated in note (2) above.

PRINCIPAL EXEMPTIONS AND RELIEFS FROM IHT
(over and above the nil-rate band for 1992/93 of £150,000
for transfers made on or after 10 March 1992)

A. Exemptions available to lifetime transferors (but not on death)
(1) Lifetime payments for the maintenance of a spouse or a former spouse or of the donor's children or of the donor's dependent relatives: s. 11 IHTA.
(2) The normal expenditure out of income exemption: s. 21.
(3) Marriage exemption of £5,000 per parent: £2,500 per party to the marriage or per grandparent or remoter ancestor; otherwise £1,000: s. 22. Apply after (2) above but before (4) and (8) below.
(4) The annual exemption of £3,000: s. 19. Can be carried forward for one year.
(5) Small gifts exemption of £250 in any one year for outright gifts to any one person, if the total values of those gifts do not exceed £250. Does not apply to gifts into trusts and cannot be combined with the annual exemption.
(6) Waiver of remuneration or dividends: ss. 14 and 15.
(7) Enlargement of a life interest: s. 53(2).

B. Exemptions and reliefs available to transfers in lifetime or on death
(8) The domiciled spouse exemption: s. 18(1).
(9) The non-domiciled spouse exemption of £55,000: s. 18(2).
(10) Gifts to charities, political parties, housing associations, national, public or heritage purposes and into employee trusts: ss. 23–8. For further information about heritage property, see Appendix No. 3.
(11) Excluded property (generally exempted by s. 3(2)):
    (a) a reversionary interest, but not a purchased one or one owned (or previously owned) by the settlor or his spouse: s. 48.
    (b) exempt Government securities, if the individual with the interest in possession in them is neither domiciled nor ordinarily resident in the UK: s. 6(2).
    (c) assets located outside the UK, if the individual with the interest in possession in them is domiciled outside the UK and is not treated under s. 267 as domiciled within the UK: s. 6(1).

(d) foreign assets of an *inter vivos* settlement, if the settlor was not domiciled (or not treated as domiciled) in the UK when it was made: s. 48(3).

(e) foreign assets of a settlement created by will or intestacy, if the deceased was not domiciled (or not treated as domiciled) in the UK at the time of death: ss. 43(2), 44 and 48(3).

(12) 100% relief for (a) interests in unincorporated businesses; (b) holdings above 25% in unquoted and USM companies; (c) owner-occupied farmland; and (d) farm tenants: ss. 103 to 124B, incorporating the amendments made by s. 73 and Schedule 14 Finance (No. 2) Act 1992.

(13) 50% relief for (a) controlled holdings in quoted companies; (b) holdings of 25% or less in unquoted and USM companies; (c) assets used by a partnership or controlled company; and (d) let farmland: *op. cit.*

(14) Successive charges relief: s. 141, where the transferee is taxed again within five years.

(15) Survivorship clause: no charge to tax if the gift over takes effect within six months: s. 92.

(16) Disclaimer of an interest in settled property: s. 93.

(17) Reverter to settlor or settlor's spouse: ss. 53(3), 53(4), 54(1) and 54(2).

(18) Preservation (on death or termination of a surviving spouse's life interest) of the old estate duty exemption for settled property upon which duty was chargeable before 13 November 1974 on the death of the first spouse to die: Schedule 6, para. 2.

(19) Accumulation and maintenance trusts: s. 71. Protective trusts: s. 88. Disabled trusts: s. 89. These are three examples of trusts which are taken out of the discretionary trust regime.

(20) Double taxation relief for overseas tax. Either unilateral relief under s. 159 or in accordance with a double taxation convention under s. 158.

C. Exemptions and reliefs available to transfers on death

(21) In valuing woodlands on the death of the owner, the value of the non-agricultural trees or underwood can be left out of account (but will become chargeable on a subsequent disposal): ss. 125–30.

(22) Relief is given for a loss on sale of quoted securities, if sold within one year of death: ss. 178–89.

(23) Relief is given for a loss on sale of landed property, if sold within three years of death: ss. 190–8.

(24) Relief is given for a loss on sale of related property, if sold within three years of death: s. 176.

(25) Relief is given for a loss in value of gifted property (either a loss determined on revaluation on death or by prior sale in the donor's lifetime), where tax becomes chargeable on a PET owing to the donor's death within seven years: ss. 131–40.

(26) Alteration of dispositions under a will or intestacy, if made within two years of death: s. 142.

(27) Precatory trusts: s. 143.

(28) Variations within two years of death of discretionary trusts created by will: s. 144.

(29) Election by a surviving spouse to take capitalised value of life interest under intestacy: s. 145.

(30) Giving effect to an order under Inheritance (Provision for Family and Dependants) Act 1975: s. 146.

(31) Foreign currency accounts in the UK forming part of the estate of an individual who had an interest in possession in them (but in the case of a life tenant, only if the trust had been of foreign origin) and died domiciled (or treated as domiciled), ordinarily resident and resident outside the UK: s. 157.

(32) Statutory assumption of simultaneous death of *commorientes* where it is not legally possible to establish the order of deaths: s. 4(2). This prevents the commingling of two estates for IHT purposes.

(33) Death on active service: s. 154. See *Barty-King* v *Ministry of Defence* (1979).

(34) Relief from the higher rate of income tax for an absolute residuary legatee by deducting from his residuary income an amount equal to the IHT liability on any income paid after the date of death which also forms part of the estate for IHT purposes: s. 699 ICTA.

D. Generally

Broadly speaking, the choice when making lifetime gifts is between making (a) a lifetime chargeable transfer, making maximum use of held-over gains under s. 260 TCGA, and (b) making a PET with held-over gains limited to business assets under s. 165 TCGA. If a chargeable transfer is made in the same fiscal year as a PET, the chargeable transfer should be made first, otherwise the annual exemption will be set off against the PET and will be lost if the PET never becomes chargeable.

APPENDIX 3: HERITAGE PROPERTY

Conditional exemption for what is termed 'heritage property' may be claimed in respect of the deemed transfer of value on death for IHT purposes; the rules may be found in ss. 30–5 IHTA. A similar exemption is available for CGT purposes in respect of lifetime transfers: s. 258(2) TCGA. The effect of a successful claim for exemption is that payment of IHT is deferred until a 'chargeable event' occurs: s. 32.

Under s. 31 conditional exemption can be claimed in respect of two main classes of property:

(a) Works of art (which include pictures and books) of 'national, scientific, historic or artistic' interest.

(b) Land and buildings of outstanding scenic, architectural or historic interest plus, in the case of buildings, essential amenity land and objects historically associated with them.

The Inland Revenue must be satisfied that the property for which exemption is sought is up to the required standard. An undertaking has to be given (a) to take reasonable steps for the preservation of the property; (b) to allow reasonable access to the public; and (c) in the case of moveables, to keep them in the UK. Such an undertaking may be given by the PRs or the beneficiary, where exemption is claimed on the death of the owner.

If conditional exemption is granted, IHT will become chargeable should a chargeable event occur; this may be (a) a breach of the undertaking; or (b) a sale of the property; or (c) a further transfer of the property in respect of which conditional exemption is not granted. In a case where conditional exemption was granted on the death of the owner, IHT will be charged on the *current* value of the property, or on the net proceeds of sale if it has been sold, as if it were the top slice of the deceased's estate:

> Algernon died in 1990. His net estate was valued at £1m. This included a painting by Gainsborough worth £500,000. The Revenue gave the painting conditional exemption on an undertaking given by Algernon's son, Andrew, to whom it was given in the will. In 1992 the Gainsborough is sold by Andrew and the net proceeds of sale are £600,000. IHT becomes payable at the death rate on these proceeds as though they constituted the top slice of Algernon's estate, i.e. from £500,000 to £1,100,000.

It might have been more sensible for the son to have negotiated a sale by private treaty to one of the heritage bodies listed in Schedule 3 to the IHTA; under s. 32(4) such a sale avoids the loss of conditional exemption from IHT (as in the circumstances outlined above) and there is no charge to CGT. The owner, in return for these advantages will have to accept something less than the market value but will still be in pocket. The lost tax is written off and the public acquires a painting at a discount.

It may be appropriate to mention here that the transfer of property into a fund for the maintenance of category (b) property, as described above, is exempt from IHT provided the terms of the trust meet certain conditions: see ss. 27, 57(5) and Sch. 4. There is also relief for trust income from tax at the higher rate: ss. 690–694 ICTA; and from CGT: s. 260(2) TCGA.

The booklet, *Capital Taxation and the National Heritage*, (IR 67) is available from the Inland Revenue and is a valuable guide to this subject.

APPENDIX 4: TABLE OF DISTRIBUTION ON INTESTACY
(DEATHS ON OR AFTER 1 JUNE 1987)
(based on s. 46(1) Administration of Estates Act 1925)

Either there is a surviving spouse (S) and also

(a)   *Issue*: S takes personal chattels and £75,000 with interest at 6% per annum from date of death to date of payment *and* a life interest in one-half of the residuary estate. Subject to this life interest, the residuary estate is held on the statutory trusts for the issue.

(b)   *Parent(s) but no issue*: S takes personal chattels and £125,000 with interest at 6% per annum from date of death to date of payment and one-half of residue. The other half of the residue goes to the parent(s) absolutely (in equal shares if there are two).

(c)   *Brother(s) and sister(s) of the whole blood (or their issue) but no issue or parent(s)*: S takes personal chattels and £125,000 with interest at 6% per annum from date of death to date of payment and one-half of the residue. The other half of the residue is held on the statutory trusts for the brother(s) and sister(s) of the whole blood.

But if there are no issue, parent(s), brother(s) and sister(s) of the whole blood: the surviving spouse takes all the residuary estate.

For a definition of 'personal chattels', see 4.5.
For a definition of 'statutory trusts', see 4.6.

**Or, there is no surviving spouse but there are*:

(a)   *Issue*: they take the residuary estate on the statutory trusts.

(b)   *Parents but no issue*: he, she or they take the residuary estate absolutely (in equal shares if two).

(c)   *Neither issue, nor parent(s)*: the residuary estate is held in trust for the following persons and in this order of precedence:
1st Brothers and sisters of the whole blood on the statutory trusts.
2nd Brothers and sisters of the half blood on the statutory trusts.
3rd Grandparent(s), in equal shares if more than one.
4th Uncles and aunts (being brothers and sisters of the whole blood of a parent) on the statutory trusts.
5th Uncles and aunts (being brothers and sisters of the half blood of a parent) on the statutory trusts.

**But if there are no issue, parent(s) or any persons described in 3(c) above*: the residuary estate goes to the Crown, or the Duchy of Lancaster, or the Duchy of Cornwall as *bona vacantia*.
For adoptive, legitimated and illegitimate relationships, see 4.9.

APPENDIX 5: WILLS, INTESTACY AND FAMILY PROVISION IN SCOTLAND AND NORTHERN IRELAND

A. Scotland

(a)   Scottish common law derives originally from civil law and canon law but, since the Act of Union of 1707, English law has made some inroads. Fiscal legislation, such as the IHTA and the TCGA, generally applies throughout the UK which, of course, includes both Scotland and Northern Ireland. (The tax legislation generally almost invariably talks of domicile or residence inside or outside the UK, a concept which does not apply in other parts of the law: see *ante* 3.31.) On the other hand, the 1925 property legislation, so vitally important in England and Wales, does not apply in the other territories of the UK.

(b)   So far as wills are concerned, the WA does not apply to Scotland and the rules as to form are uncodified. Generally speaking, a Scottish will must be in writing; it will be valid if it is either:

(i)   'attested', i.e. signed on each page by the testator and on the last page by the testator and two competent witnesses (preferably independent ones, but there is no equivalent in Scottish law to s. 15 WA); or

(ii)   'holograph' – a document which is in the testator's own writing and signed by him; or

(iii)   'adopted as holograph', i.e. some other form of document to which the testator has added these words (or something similar) above his signature.

Witnesses are not required in cases (ii) and (iii); in (i) and (iii) it appears that, as in England, any form of 'writing' may be used, whether handwriting, type or print.

(c)   Note that the WA 1963 *does* apply in Scotland (and in Northern Ireland) so that, for instance, a will validly executed in accordance with English law will be accepted as formally valid in Scotland, and vice versa. There is no equivalent in Scotland to the English 'privileged' will but this hardly matters since capacity to make a will there begins at the age of 12 – see s. 2(2) Age of Legal Capacity (Scotland) Act 1991 – clearly a sign that early maturity is a natural phenomenon north of the border. So far as the mental element is concerned, Scottish law has its own rules but they appear not to differ significantly from English ones. As in England, a Scottish will is always revocable, but neither marriage nor divorce affect a Scottish will. However, there is a rebuttable presumption that a will which makes no provision for children subsequently born is revoked by such births.

(d)   Freedom of disposition in England and Wales is curtailed by the 1975 Act (*ante* 4.30 *et seq.*); this does not apply in Scotland, which has its own system by which a deceased's spouse and issue may claim their 'legal rights' in the deceased's moveable estate – such rights being subject to the valid claims of creditors and administration expenses and, in the case of intestacy (see below), to the prior rights of a surviving spouse.

(e)   The rights in question are the *jus relictae* and the *jus relicti*, in the case of the widow and widower respectively, and the *legitim* falling to issue (the 'bairns' part'). If the deceased is survived by both spouse and issue the legal rights are arrived at by dividing the moveable property into three – one-third belongs to the spouse, one-third to the issue and one-third (the 'dead's part') which passes under the will or intestacy as the case may be. If there is a spouse but no issue, or issue but no spouse, the division is into two parts, one of which will be the dead's part. Children of the deceased (including adopted and illegitimate ones) take *per capita*; issue of deceased children take *per stirpes*. There is provision for children to bring advances into hotchpot and for a choice to be made between a gift made in a will and the beneficiary's legal rights as outlined above – this is the Scottish doctrine of 'approbate and reprobate', the equivalent in England being the doctrine of election (see *ante* 6.42, 43).

(f) Intestacy: as stated above, the 1925 property legislation does not apply to Scotland and Scottish rules relating to distribution on intestacy are largely to be found in the Succession (Scotland) Act 1964. After creditors have been paid and administration expenses taken, the estate of an intestate is distributed as follows:

(i) a surviving spouse is entitled to 'prior rights' as follows:

    (1) the deceased's interest in the dwelling-house, with its furniture and plenishings (the equivalent to 'personal chattels' in England but not usually any car) up to a value of £12,000. If the interest in the house exceeds £65,000 in value, the spouse is entitled to take this sum but no more.

    (2) the surviving spouse is also entitled to £20,000 out of the rest of the estate (where there are issue), £35,000 if there are no issue.

(ii) Subject to the surviving spouse's prior rights, the rest of the estate devolves as follows on:

    (1) issue of the deceased *per stirpes*, adopted and illegitimate children included;

    (2) if there is a surviving spouse but no issue, the remainder devolves on the brothers and sisters of the deceased (or their descendants) or the deceased's parents;

    (3) if there is a surviving spouse, but no issue and no brothers or sisters (or descendants thereof) or parents, the spouse takes all. Alternatively, if there is no surviving spouse but there are issue of the deceased surviving, then such issue take the whole estate, regardless of the existence of any other surviving relatives.

(g) Trusts: there are substantial differences between the trust law of Scotland and that for England and Wales; it would be pointless, in the space available, to try to deal even with the main features of Scottish trust law. There is, however, one fundamental difference from the English law of trusts which is worth mentioning here: Scottish law does not regard the trust as an instance of concurrent legal and equitable ownership but rather as a form of legal ownership qualified by the rights of parties (beneficiaries) having *jura crediti* (personal rights) against the trustee. *Trusts* by Norrie and Scobbie (1991) can be recommended as a useful source of information about trust law in Scotland.

B. Northern Ireland

(a) Here the law relating to the making and revocation of wills is still largely governed by the WA 1837; as mentioned above, the WA 1963 applies but the WA 1968 does not, neither do ss. 17 to 22 AJA 1982. So far as revocation by subsequent marriage is concerned, the Wills (Amendment) Act (NI) 1954 added a provision similar to that formerly contained in s. 177 LPA (it will be remembered that that

Act does not apply in Northern Ireland), so that a will expressed to be made in contemplation of marriage is not revoked by the said marriage when it takes place. Privileged wills enjoy the same status as they do in England. Capacity in the sense of a sufficiency of understanding seems to be judged in the same way as in England.

(b)   As regards freedom of disposition, the 1975 Act does not apply but the Inheritance (Provision for Family and Dependants) (Northern Ireland) Order 1979 is largely based on it, and the position in the province as regards claims by a surviving spouse, children of the deceased and so on against a deceased's estate is much the same as it is here.

(c)   Intestacy: the relevant law is to be found in the Administration of Estates Acts (NI) 1955 and 1971 and in the Administration of Estates (NI) Order 1979. Section 6 of the 1955 Act says that all property of which the deceased died intestate shall, after payment of debts, duties and expenses, be distributed in accordance with Part II of the Act. Section 18 of the 1955 Act is of interest; in cases of partial intestacy, the undisposed-of property is to be distributed as if the testator had died intestate and had left no other estate; the rather unsatisfactory rules which apply in England (4.13 *et seq.*) are simply ignored. Furthermore, this reference to distribution on partial intestacy is subject to the qualification 'unless it appears by the will that the PRs are intended to take beneficially the remainder of his estate' – a provision which has no equivalent here. Broadly speaking, the rules for distribution on intestacy are the same as here, the fixed net sums (or 'statutory legacies') being maintained on the same level as in England (see 4.5); in the event of there being a surviving spouse but no issue or parents, brothers or sisters (or their issue) of the deceased, the spouse takes all, as do issue of the deceased *per stirpes*, where such survive but there is no surviving spouse. The list of possible beneficiaries under a Northern Ireland intestacy is more extensive than the English one and includes great-great-great grandparents (although it is added that 'it is unlikely that they would survive the intestate').

(d)   Trusts: again, broadly speaking, the law in Northern Ireland is similar to that of England and Wales; the 1925 property legislation does not apply but the Trustee Act (Northern Ireland) 1958 fulfils much the same purpose as the 1925 TA. There are some differences: s. 1(1) says that a trustee may . . . invest trust funds in the manner in, and subject to the conditions upon, which a trustee in any part of Great Britain is by the law for the time being in force in that part entitled to invest trust funds in the absence of any enlargement or restriction of his powers of investment. Section 19 contains a power to insure which is rather better than that found in the same section of the 1925 Act. Section 57 is an equivalent to the provisions of the Variation of Trusts Act 1958. Apart from statute law, there is one unusual feature about trust law in Northern Ireland, and that is the absence of the rules found here (and in Scotland) against excessive accumulation of income (see 7.31). The so-called Thellusson Act of 1800 never applied in Ireland, and so the income of a Northern Ireland trust may validly be accumulated (with one trifling exception) throughout the whole of the relevant perpetuity period. This fact has its attractions for settlors who wish to direct accumulation of income for longer than the English rules will permit. The PAA does not apply in Northern Ireland but the Perpetuities Act (Northern Ireland) 1966 contains similar provisions for perpetuities to those found in the English statute.

APPENDIX 6: *RE LYNALL* (1972) – AN EXERCISE IN VALUING UNQUOTED SHARES (see 5.28)

Mrs Nellie Lynall died on 21 May 1962; included in her private estate was a holding of 67,980 £1 shares in Linread Ltd, a private company. The total issued capital was £241,700, divided into £1 shares and all the shares, except for 200, were held by the family. Mrs Lynall, it can be seen, owned about 28% of the capital. There were stringent restrictions on the transfer of shares in the company's articles, including a provision for sale to members, at a 'fair value' if fixed, or at £1 if not fixed.

Linread Ltd was principally engaged in making such things as screws, bolts and rivets and was a leading manufacturer in this field. When Mrs Lynall died it was in a flourishing state. Its financial year ended on 31 July and the following comparative figures were given to the court:

	Year ended 31 July 1957	Year ended 31 July 1961
Turnover (£)	979,000	1,607,000
Profit before depreciation and taxation (£)	112,798	300,905
Profit available for dividend (£)	35,456	135,496

For 1957 and 1958 the dividends were 5%; for 1959, 10%; for 1960 and 1961, 15%. Each dividend was covered about six times. In the 10 years before Mrs Lynall's death there were no sales of shares providing any guidance as to their value on her death. In the circumstances, valuation had to proceed from first principles – or as Danckwerts J. put it in *Re Holt deceased* (1953) by means of intelligent guesswork.

If one wants to make use of *Re Lynall* to obtain general guidance on the valuation of unquoted shares it is best to refer to the report of the hearing before Plowman J. in the Chancery Division of the High Court (1969). The judge said that there were three principal factors affecting valuation: (a) the appropriate dividend yield; (b) the prospective dividend and (c) the possibility of capital appreciation. *Dymond* para.23.370 reduces this to the following algebraic formula:

$$£\frac{d}{y} + p = V$$

where d is the prospective dividend, y is the yield and p the premium (if any) for potential capital appreciation; the result is the share value, V. *Dymond* goes on to say that this formula can be applied to all unquoted shares and, for the layman at least, it is an extremely useful tool.

The trick, to put it bluntly, is to select the right dividend yield. Four expert witnesses gave evidence in *Re Lynall* and they suggested yields of 8%, 7%, 7.5% and 7.5% (it should be mentioned that at the date of death the Industrial Ordinary Share Index yielded 5.33%). There was, therefore, a fair consensus of opinion so far as that particular aspect of the matter was concerned. It is not clear from the judgment what Plowman J. decided to use as his prospective dividend figure, but it has been suggested that he produced it by splitting the difference between the company's current dividend and that which might be required to satisfy the then Surtax Office – the result being about 23%. The first part of the formula is then complete and it remains to add p – the premium for possible capital appreciation. In the *Lynall* case there was the distinct possibility of a public issue, and 50p was taken to be the premium in the case of a purchaser without special knowledge of this. If the prospective purchaser was deemed to have such special knowledge, the premium was to be £1.50. In the end, the House of Lords decreed that such a purchaser should *not* be assumed to have special knowledge, but this decision was quickly reversed by s. 51 FA 1973, which has now been replaced by s. 168 IHTA.

The complete formula in *Re Lynall* was, therefore:

$$\frac{23}{7.5} + 50p = £3.50 \text{ (approx)}$$

Reference was made above to the problem of selecting the right dividend yield and to the disparity between the suggested yields for Linread Ltd and that of the *Financial Times* Index on the date of death. As is said in *Dymond* para.23.346, the simplest way of arriving at a yield for a particular company is to look at the *Financial Times* Actuaries' Share Indices and to choose the relevant yield from the appropriate sector, but considerable care has to be taken in using this method. The constituent companies in the Actuaries Index may not have a great deal in common with the small, unquoted company with which, typically, PRs and trustees are often involved. It may be more sensible to seek out two or three quoted companies with a closer relationship to the unquoted company and to use these as the basis of comparison. Even so, allowance must be made for significant differences *and* for the disadvantage of holding shares lacking marketability and with restricted opportunities for transfer. The average 'discount' for such factors seems to vary between 20% and 30% , depending upon the severity of the restrictions upon transfer; in other words, to the comparable quoted yield one adds, say, 30% to produce the expected yield (y in the formula) for the unquoted company.

Reference is also made above to the level of dividend which might have been required in *Re Lynall* to satisfy the Surtax Office and thereby avoid the apportionment of the company's income amongst the shareholders. The apportionment legislation underwent a process of mitigation in the 1980s and was finally repealed by FA 1989 for accounting periods starting after 31 March 1989 (this even applies to close investment-holding companies, but they are not permitted to enjoy the lower rate of corporation tax). Contemporary pressure on a company to follow a more generous dividend policy is, perhaps, more likely to be exerted by shareholders; they may feel that the modernised Companies legislation (see *ante* 5.26) is of considerable value in such circumstances.

Valuing unquoted preference shares and other fixed-interest securities is a comparatively straightforward operation compared with that involved in dealing with ordinary shares. *Dymond* para.23.382 suggests that 50% above the *Financial Times* Actuaries' Index produces 'a reasonable yield for the average private company' in the case of preference shares. In the case of debenture and loan stocks the suggested 'uplift' is 20% above the index yield for this type of security. This 'rule-of-thumb' guidance will probably be adequate in cases where large sums are not at stake.

Notes

1 WILLS (1)

[1] Equity's traditional tenderness towards married women when they have been asked to act as surety for the debts of others, which some of the recent cases have treated as outmoded, seems to have been re-established by the Court of Appeal's decision in *Barclays Bank* v *O'Brien*, reported in *The Times* on 3 June 1992. There the bank had left it entirely to the husband to explain the transaction to his wife and to procure her consent to it. He misrepresented the effect of the transaction and she misunderstood it. It was held that creditors who took from married women security for their husband's debts must take reasonable steps to see that the wife understood the transaction. The case is concerned with misrepresentation, rather than undue influence, but it is evident from the judgment that the same principle applies where the distortion arises from undue influence.

2 WILLS (2)

[1] The great advantage of s. 144 IHTA is that the beneficial interests can be suitably rearranged without the compulsion (as there is with a s. 142 variation – see 4.27, *post*) of obtaining consents from the beneficiaries. For s. 144 to operate there must be an event which would otherwise be chargeable. Thus, an appointment made within three months of the testator's death would not otherwise be chargeable, because of the provision in s. 65(4) that there is to be no exit charge on events occurring during the first quarter of operation. The discretionary trust should be carefully drawn so as to permit its exercise at any stage of the administration, even during the period before probate, to overcome any suggestion on the part of the Revenue that appointments can be made only when the PRs have become trustees. Note that if probate is obtained before any appointments are made, IHT will have to be paid on a non-exempt basis, although the excess tax will be refunded with interest when eventually exempt appointments are made.

[2] The doctrine of dependent relative revocation has nothing whatever to do with one's poor relations. The phrase refers to the fact that revocation may be relative to another disposition (either existing or intended) and therefore dependent upon its effectiveness. If that other disposition never gets off the ground, the will stands as it was. The doctrine is part of a wider theme concerning conditional revocation, which stems from the closing words of s. 20 WA.

[3] There is this difference between a conditional destruction and a conditional revocation by a testamentary document: the former lets in evidence of the testator's intentions when committing the act of destruction, but not so the latter, unless the surrounding circumstances reveal an ambiguity in the interpretation of the will, thus letting in s. 21 AJA 1982: see 2.29.

[4] Another line of decisions which may have the effect of eliminating an intestacy (or in the case of an *inter vivos* settlement, avoiding a reverter to settlor) is the one which started with the celebrated rule in *Lassence* v *Tierney* (1849), otherwise known as the rule in *Hancock* v *Watson* (1902). In the latter, Lord Davey stated the rule:

> 'If you find an absolute gift to a legatee in the first instance, and trusts are engrafted or imposed on that absolute interest which fail, either from lapse or invalidity, *or any other reason* [my emphasis], then the absolute gift takes effect so far as the trusts have failed to the exclusion of the residuary legatee or next-of-kin as the case may be.'

The rule applies to both wills and *inter vivos* trusts, and reconciles a conflict between inconsistent clauses. In *Watson* v *Holland* (1985) the settler made two settlements, in each case excluding himself from any benefit, one of them upon his infant son, Timothy and Timothy's spouse and issue and the other upon his infant son, Neil and Neil's spouse and issue. In each settlement the gift over on failure of the trust was to the other children of the settlor absolutely, followed by an engrafted trust for each child similar to Timothy's and Neil's. The Revenue claimed that the settler had retained an interest under a resulting trust in the event of the failure of both settlements. It was held that in the event of the failure of the engrafted trusts, either Neil or Timothy would have had an absolute interest, under the rule in *Lassence* v *Tierney*, thus excluding the settlor from any possible benefit.

[5] It is a characteristic of the statute law in this subject to avoid giving anything other than broad guidelines in the construction of wills. Exceptions are s. 29 WA and s. 134 LPA as amended, which provide that in the case of a gift to A, but if he die without issue, to B, A's interest becomes absolute if any child or remoter issue attains 18 (even if none survive A) or if A dies leaving issue (even if none reaches 18). We now have s. 22 AJA 1982 introducing for deaths after 1982 a statutory presumption, except where a contrary intention is shown, that if there is a gift to the spouse in terms which in themselves would give an absolute interest to the spouse, but by the same instrument the testator purports to give his issue an interest in the same property, the gift to the spouse is absolute notwithstanding the purported gift to the issue. This is designed to take care of the home-made will, giving everything to the surviving spouse plus a direction that on her death what remains is to go to the children, which might otherwise be capable of at least three constructions: (a) the spouse takes absolutely, what follows being either repugnant or too vague, (b) the spouse has a life interest coupled with a general power of appointment and in default of appointment to the children, or (c) the spouse has a life interest with remainder to the children.

3 DEATH AND PROBATE

[1] The maximum amount was increased to £5,000 by the Administration of Estates (Small Payments) (Increase in Limit) Order SI 1984 No. 539.

[2] The typical temporary grant situation referred to in s. 7(3) AEA arises if the executor, who eventually proves, is interrupted from doing so by incapacity, absence abroad or the conduct of legal proceedings. So on the grant of

administration for the use and benefit of a minor, the chain would be restored when the minor came of age and took out a *cessate* grant of probate – i.e. a grant issued when a previous grant ceases to be operative because it has come to the end of its allotted span.

[3] As is said in *Dicey & Morris*, essential validity concerns such questions as whether the testator is bound to leave a certain proportion of his estate to his children or widow, whether legacies to charities are valid, to what extent gifts are invalid as infringing the rule against perpetuities or accumulations, whether substitutionary gifts are valid, whether gifts to attesting witnesses are valid, and so on.

[4] Section 4 WA 1963 provides that the construction of a will shall not be altered by reason of any change in the testator's domicile after the execution of the will.

[5] Unlike most foreign systems which tend to apply one single law, i.e. the personal law of the deceased, regardless of the nature of the assets, English law prefers the principle of scission, applying the personal law to the deceased's moveables and the asset's own local law to immoveables. So, in *Re Collens* (1986) the widow of an intestate, who had died domiciled in Trinidad, was held to be entitled to a statutory legacy (see *post* 4.5) out of his English immoveable estate, devolving as it did under the *lex situs* and not under the law of Trinidad, under which she had already benefited handsomely. If the Hague Convention on Succession (see *ante* 3.35) is adopted, the principle of scission will probably go.

[6] Premium Savings Bonds are eligible for prizes during the 12 months after death and beneficiaries may well prefer that they be held for this period and not either used for payment of tax or encashed at an early stage.

[7] Section 364 ICTA provides that loan interest (not overdraft interest) is eligible for relief under s. 353 if the loan is made to the PRs of a deceased person and the proceeds are applied in paying, before the grant of representation, the IHT payable immediately on the free estate.

[8] In a very useful series of four articles in (1991) 135 SJ, 2, 9, 16 and 30 August, Andrew Pinder reviews four areas of estate administration in which litigation is quite likely to occur – disputes over wills, family provision claims, claims to equitable interest in houses and Fatal Accidents Act claims; they may be interrelated. See also 'The Responsibilities of Trustees and Executors in Litigation' by W R Stewart-Smith in the *Trust Operations Gazette* No. 21, April 1987, obtainable from The Chartered Institute of Bankers.

4 INTESTACY, REARRANGEMENTS AND FAMILY PROVISION

[1] Family Provision (Intestate Succession) Order 1987 SI 1987 No. 799. Before 1953 the statutory legacy was £1,000, whether or not there were issue. For deaths from 1 January 1953 to 31 December 1966 the respective figures were £5,000 and £20,000; from 1 January 1967 to 30 June 1972, £8,750 and £30,000; from 1 July 1972 to 14 March 1977, £15,000 and £40,000; from 15 March 1977 to 28 February 1981, £25,000 and £55,000; and from 1 March 1981 to 31 May 1987, £40,000 and £85,000.

[2] The Lord Chancellor has power to fix the rate under s. 46(1)(i) and (1A) AEA. The rate was 4% per annum until 14 September 1977, then at 7% and now at 6% from 1 October 1983: Intestate Succession (Interest and Capitalisation) Order 1977 (Amendment) Order 1983 SI 1983 No. 1374. Under s. 46(4) the interest is payable primarily out of income and basic rate income tax must be deducted at source.

[3] Intestate Succession (Interest and Capitalisation) Order 1977 SI 1977 No. 1491 (reproduced in *W, M & S*, p. 1097) made under ss. 47A(3A) and (3B) AEA.

[4] A 'Tomlin' order is an order of the court, to which the parties to an action consent, the agreed terms being set out in a schedule to the order. It is used generally to stay proceedings, except for the purpose of carrying such agreed terms into effect. See the Practice Note issued by Tomlin J. [1927] WN 290.

5 DEALING WITH THE LIABILITIES AND THE ASSETS

[1] It is understood that a stock exchange will be regarded as 'recognized' for IHT purposes if (a) it is by law recognised as a stock exchange in its own country and (b) has a trading floor similar to that provided by the Stock Exchange.

[2] It is to be borne in mind that, independently of the accrued income scheme, the treatment of residuary income during the administration period for income tax purposes depends upon whether the residue is settled or goes out absolutely. If the residue is settled, the cash payments to the life tenant in the course of administration plus any undistributed income cash in hand on the last day of the administration period are aggregated and the total apportioned on a day-to-day basis between each tax year to decide what amounts should be certified as being the life tenant's income. The certification of income from absolute interests in residue is determined by the amount of income arising in each tax year. See ss. 695–701 ICTA and *post* 6.49.

[3] For a full and illuminating exploration of the subject consult *Eastaway and Booth*. Read also the valuable and realistic article by F A Sherring in the *Trust Operations Gazette* No. 23, June 1989, obtainable through The Chartered Institute of Bankers; and the section of Chapter 23 in *Dymond*, which deals with the valuation of unquoted shares and debentures.

[4] Under an amendment by the Companies Act 1989, which took effect from 4 February 1991, s. 459 Companies Act 1985 now applies to the conduct of the company's affairs in a manner which is 'unfairly prejudicial to the interests of its members generally or of some part of its members'. The reference to 'members generally' did not appear in the previous version; so, a restrictive dividend policy might not previously have been a ground for complaint under this section, since it affected all members and not some part of them.

[5] The way is now open for dividend policy to be questioned under s. 459 – see the previous note. On the subject of minority rights generally, there is a useful article entitled 'Minority Shareholder Oppression' in [1986] 102 LQR p. 179.

[6] I am indebted to Mr W J L Knight, author of *The Acquisition of Private Companies*, for his advice on the contents of this paragraph.

⁷ These provisions apply if the subsequent sale shows a difference of over £1,000 (or more than 5%, whichever is less). The taxpayer can also ask for these provisions to be applied where the sale is at a profit over the probate value. This will also adjust the base value for CGT; it is not an option the taxpayer is likely to exercise so long as the single IHT band of 40% applies.

⁸ See The Law Commission Working Paper No. 95 completed on 27 March 1986, containing a provisional recommendation that the privity of contract principle for leases should be abrogated.

⁹ Curiously enough, the *Re Owers* type of liability is not even mentioned in the above Working Paper.

¹⁰ Under s. 200(1)(a)(i) IHTA the PRs are liable for the tax on the severable share on the assumption that the informal settlement created by the joint tenancy arrangements is not a settlement within the meaning of s. 43(2) of the Act. The survivor in the joint arrangement is also liable under s. 200(1)(c) and the PRs have the right to obtain reimbursement of the tax under s. 211(3).

¹¹ When someone dies domiciled in the UK, owning overseas property, there may be a double charge to tax in respect of this property, to IHT here and to a similar tax in the country where the property is situate (the same result can occur in the opposite direction, of course). To avoid such a double charge, double taxation relief is available, either in the form of treaty relief under s. 158 IHTA or by way of unilateral relief under s. 159. If there is a double taxation convention with the overseas country, its provisions will supply the relief, either by stating which country shall have the right to tax the property or by providing for one country to give relief to the deceased's estate in respect of the tax levied in the second territory. The provisions of such agreements override other IHT legislation and the common law rules as regards situs. If there is no relevant double taxation agreement, then unilateral relief is granted in the UK in the form of a credit for the foreign tax liability against IHT payable here. For a list of the countries with whom the UK has double taxation agreements and for a full discussion of both bilateral and unilateral relief see *Dymond*, ch. 31.

¹² See The Law Commission's Consultation Paper No. 118, completed on 6 March 1991, *The Law of Trusts – Delegation by Individual Trustees*. The provisional proposals relate to a General Scheme concerning the normal type of trust where the trustees are not also the beneficiaries and a Special Scheme for the co-ownership of land where the beneficiaries are also the trustees. Under the General Scheme, no power could last longer than a year nor would it be possible for it to survive mental incapacity; it would be made clear that PRs would have the same power to delegate as trustees. Under the Special Scheme, the power could be of unlimited duration with the possibility that the donor's responsibility for the acts of his attorney might terminate with the onset of mental incapacity.

6 DISTRIBUTING THE ESTATE

¹ Under s. 40(1) Taxes Management Act 1970 assessments on PRs in respect of the income or chargeable gains arising *before* death can be made at any time within the

three years from the 5 April after the date of death. With regard to the Revenue's ability to backtrack for past tax liabilities, the ordinary time limit for a *living* taxpayer is six years behind the year of assessment, extended to twenty years if fraudulent or negligent conduct can be proved. In the case of a deceased taxpayer, however, the time limit remains at six years, even where fraudulent or negligent conduct on the part of the deceased can be established - s. 40(2) of the same Act – but if there has been such conduct, the six years are counted back from the date of death, not from the year when the Revenue happens to issue an assessment.

[2] Property not mentioned in the statutory order but which is nevertheless available for the payment of debts:

(a)   Property of the deceased in respect of which he gives in his will an option to purchase.
(b)   Property given by *DMC*.
(c)   Property appointed by deed in lifetime under a general power but taking effect on death.

These categories of property are liable in the last resort; it is not clear how they should be drawn on where more than one such category exists but, presumably, *pro rata*.

[3] Under s. 656 ICTA a purchased life annuity is to be treated as consisting of two elements, the capital element which increases each year and is exempt from income tax and the income element which remains taxable; but the section has no application to annuities purchased under a direction in a will, or to provide for an annuity payable out of income under a will or settlement. If the beneficiary would prefer the annuity to the capital sum, he should buy the annuity himself with the money provided by the PR to ensure that he obtains the advantage of s. 656.

[4] A simple gift of an annuity will charge it on the entire resources of the residuary estate, both income and capital, just as if it were a pecuniary legacy (which, indeed it is, payable by instalments) but the wording of the will may be such that it is charged on current income only, with or without a continuing charge on future income. The leading case on the topic is *Re Coller's Deed Trusts* (1939).

[5] Exceptionally the interest runs from the date of the deceased's death in four cases (a) if there is a direct legacy (i.e. a legacy without the interposition of trustees) to an infant child of the testator or testatrix or to an infant child to whom he or she stands *in loco parentis*, provided there is no other fund designated for the infant's maintenance and provided also, in the case of a contingent legacy, that the contingency concerns the attainment of a given age or earlier marriage; (b) a legacy in satisfaction of a debt; (c) a legacy charged on realty; (d) if the will shows an intention that the legatee, being an infant but not necessarily the testator's infant, is to be maintained or educated out of the income. This last category includes also contingent legacies. For the rate of interest see *post* 6.34.

[6] If there is a direction to invest a sum of money for an infant or to pay a sum of money to trustees for an infant, interest runs from the date when the money is set aside or from the end of the executorship year, if later. This rule, which is for both

vested and contingent legacies, applies even to a legacy to the testator's own infant child, because it is not a direct legacy as mentioned in the preceding note.

[7] For example, Mary's seafaring husband is lost at sea on an unknown date and Mary herself dies around the same time but it cannot be determined who was the survivor. Both die intestate. If the husband is older, the wife is deemed to survive by s. 184 LPA, but for distribution purposes, under s. 46(3) – and for no other purpose – she will be omitted from the devolution of the husband's free estate. If Mary and her husband had been joint beneficial owners of their matrimonial residence and their banking account, these assets would have passed to Mary as survivor by virtue of s. 184, since their intestacies are in no way concerned with the devolution of joint assets, any more than their wills would have been had they died testate.

[8] As where the two estates are each worth £149,000. Had s. 4(2) IHTA applied, there would have been no tax to pay at all, whereas under s. 141 the relief would be valueless and the combined estates might attract tax on as much as £298,000.

[9] Take the case of a husband dying in July 1992 worth £309,000, who has made chargeable lifetime transfers totalling £150,000 and who has left his whole estate to his wife, her fortune amounting to only £21,000 and with nothing in her lifetime cumulator. Her will is on similar lines. There is no survivorship clause in either will. Assuming that the husband dies first, the combined estates will be taxed on the wife's death on £330,000, upon which the tax comes to £72,000; subject to alterations in values, this will be the position on the wife's subsequent death, whether she dies 10 minutes, 10 days or 10 years after her husband. Now put in a survivorship clause and assume that the wife dies after the husband but within the period. On her death, there is no tax, as her estate falls within the nil band but the husband's estate now passes to the children under the gift over in the survivorship clause. Tax will be calculated on £150,000 in his cumulator plus £309,000, upon which the tax comes to £123,600, an increase of £51,600. The effect of the survivorship clause is to prevent the cleansing of the husband's cumulator had the wife been allowed to benefit.

[10] For a true class gift there must be a divisible subject matter. A gift of £100 to each of A's children who should attain the age of 21 (as occurred in *Rogers* v *Mutch* (1878)) is a gift to a class of children but it is not a true class gift, because there is nothing to divide. In the *Rogers* v *Mutch* situation, if A has no children at the date of the testator's death, the gift fails; and if there are children under 21, the class does not stay open until the first of the children to attain 21 does so, as it would if it were a true class gift to which *Andrews* v *Partington* applied – see 6.30. Thus the rule in *Rogers* v *Mutch* is a rule of convenience for the executor which is even more convenient than the rule in *Andrews* v *Partington*.

[11] The rule does not apply if the killer is insane but it does if the killer is convicted of manslaughter by reason of diminished responsibility, as happened in *Re Giles* (1972) where the court refused to relax the rule in favour of the deceased's wife who had killed him with a single blow from a domestic chamber pot.

[12] The Law Reform Committee (23rd Report, *The Powers and Duties of Trustees*, Cmnd 8233/1982) has recommended that the above equitable rules for apportion-

ment between capital and income should be abolished and that they should be replaced by a new statutory duty to hold a fair balance between beneficiaries generally and, in particular, between those entitled to capital and income respectively.

7 TRUSTS (1)

[1] A PR cannot retire from office except by applying to the court under the Judicial Trustees Act 1896 (see *post* 12.3) or by the less ponderous machinery provided in s. 50 AJA 1985 (see *ante* 3.50), under which the court is empowered to appoint someone to act as PR in place of an existing PR; the court may also, where there are two or more PRs, end the appointment of one or more, but not all. Removal under this new provision is not confined to cases where a PR is incapable of acting as such.

[2] This case followed another decision, by a curious coincidence also known as *Re Rose* but decided in 1949, in which the testator had made a lifetime gift of preference shares in 1944, having lodged an executed transfer with the company for registration. The testator died in 1946, two months before the transfer was eventually registered. It was held that there was a completed gift *inter vivos*.

It is also apparent from the *Rose* cases that even if the directors in their discretion refuse to register the donee, the gift is still a completed one, because it is for the donee, not the donor, to obtain their consent to registration.

[3] There was also a much older rule, abolished by the 1925 legislation, known as the rule in *Whitby* v *Mitchell*, which destroyed a gift in remainder to the issue of an unborn person after a gift of an interest in realty to the unborn person. This explains the use of the expression 'the modern rule against perpetuities' thereby distinguishing it from the old rule of which *Whitby* v *Mitchell* was part.

[4] In the lower court the judge felt unable to apply the rule in *Andrews* v *Partington* (see *ante* 6.30), which would have saved the day, as it would have restricted the class of issue to those living at the death of a daughter. The Court of Appeal with its different interpretation of the date for determining the class of issue did not need to apply the rule in order to arrive at its benevolent construction. But it is worth noting that the application of that rule to class gifts will often keep them clear of the breach of the common law perpetuity rule, as in the following examples of gifts by will:

(a) To X for life with remainder to all Y's grandchildren to attain 21. On the testator's death X and Y survive and there is a grandchild aged 22. There are obviously many possibilities of the birth of more grandchildren but, as there is a grandchild who has already attained a vested interest, the class must close at the death of X. With the class closed it is impossible for any of Y's grandchildren to attain a vested interest more than 21 years after the deaths of the lives in being at the testator's death (i.e. X, Y, the children of Y and the grandchild).

(b) To all X's children to attain 22. On the testator's death X survives together with a child of his aged 23 and twins of his aged six months. The existence of that child already past the age of vesting means that the class closes with the death of the testator. The lives in being are X and his three children and if the interests of the twins are to vest at all, they must do so in their own lifetimes.

(c) To all X's grandchildren. On the testator's death X survives together with a grandchild of his. Under another class-closing rule dealing with gifts where no contingency is attached (the rule in *Viner* v *Francis* (1789)), had there been no grandchild in existence on the testator's death, the class would have stayed open until the deaths of X and his children; so if another child is born to X after the testator's death there is the possibility of the birth of a grandchild more than 21 years after the dropping of the lives in being (X plus his children at the testator's death). But the existence of any grandchildren at the testator's death closes the class immediately.

But the class-closing rules will not always save a gift. Take again the case of a gift by a testator to all the children of X to attain 22. If X and a child of his aged 19 survive the testator, the class gift is bound to be bad at common law because it may be more than 21 years after the death of X and his child before the first child to attain 22 does so. For a pre-1964 death, it will take the application of s. 163 LPA to rescue the gift by cutting down the vesting age to 21. For a post-1964 death, the age of 22 will either be preserved by 'wait and see' or will be chopped down under s. 4 PAA.

8 TRUSTS (2)

[1] There are, however, some important loopholes in the legislation, in respect of settlements made before 14 March 1989, for the settlor who wishes to retain a reversionary interest in the capital. The settlor is not regarded as having retained an interest if the possibility of benefit to himself or spouse can arise only upon the happening of one or more of the following four events (s. 673(3) ICTA):

(a) the bankruptcy of a beneficiary under the settlement; or
(b) the assigning or charging by a beneficiary of his interest; or
(c) in the case of a marriage settlement, the death of both the parties to the marriage and of all or any of the children of the marriage; or
(d) the death under the age of 25 or some lower age of a beneficiary who would become entitled on attaining that age;

provided that prior to any of the above events there is a living beneficiary under 25 during whose life no income can reach the settlor or spouse unless that beneficiary becomes bankrupt or assigns or charges his interest. It is emphasised that s. 673 attacks only undistributed income.

A 'reverter to settlor' settlement made before 14 March 1989, e.g. to the settlor's mother for life with reverter to himself, is perfectly good as a transfer of income for basic rate purposes, but it falls foul of s. 683 for the higher rate, making the settlor liable on the income paid to his mother for tax on the difference between his top rate and the basic rate. Note that s. 683 read in conjunction with s. 685 contains the same four exceptions as s. 673(3) but without the added proviso. Section 683 is, of course, concerned only with income distributed otherwise than to the settlor or spouse.

[2] Section 674A(1) contains exceptions in favour of partnership annuities, charitable covenants and marriage settlements after the breakdown of the marriage. For the purpose of higher rate liability s. 674A(3) repeats the four exceptions noted in

the previous note but without the added proviso. Where s. 674A(3) applies, two results follow: (i) the trustees will not be liable for income tax at the additional rate – see s. 686(2)(b) but, (ii) no income tax repayment will be available for income applied for maintenance, because of the deeming provision in s. 674A(1) that the income must be treated as that of the settlor.

[3] The Inland Revenue's Consultative Document on Trusts dated March 1991 suggests that eventually s. 663 ICTA will be revised to put an end to this device – see Appendix A of that document, para. 23.

[4] Other favoured discretionary trusts include:
(a) a trust for the mentally or physically disabled under s. 89, although a more flexible instrument for the purpose may be a protective trust under s. 88; yet another alternative may be a settlement using the s. 11 exemption (lifetime gifts for family maintenance), thus eliminating the possibility of an entry charge on the death of the settlor within seven years;
(b) employee trusts, including approved profit sharing schemes and employee share ownership trusts, under ss. 13, 28 and 86. There is no entry charge and no periodic or exit charges so long as the conditions are complied with (see *post* 12.30);
(c) maintenance funds for heritage property – see Schedule 4 to IHTA and the penultimate para. of Appendix 3 of this book.

[5] *Inglewood* v *IRC* (1983), a case where the trust instrument contained a power for the trustees to revoke the contingent interests and make a fresh appointment, which meant that there was no certainty that a child attaining 21 (the specified age) would get a vested interest. The case is also authority for the proposition that the automatic inclusion in a trust of this kind of the statutory power of advancement under s. 32 TA (permitting payments to persons other than the beneficiary, if for his benefit) does not amount to a power of revocation.
Contrast the destructive powers of revocation and appointment for the s. 71 trust with their innocuous nature when hovering over an interest in possession – see *ante* 8.8.

[6] A gift to an infant contingent upon attaining 25, whether in a will or a settlement, is not uncommon. Another good reason to exclude the operation of s. 31(1)(ii) TA is to ensure that holdover relief will be available when capital and income vest at 25 under s. 260(3), TCGA. If s. 31(1)(ii) TA is allowed to remain, the beneficiary obtains an interest in possession at the age of 18, and when later he reaches 25 there is neither an occasion for a charge to IHT nor any reason to claim that it does not constitute an occasion for charge. (See also *post* 10.19.)

[7] Echoing the income tax provisions, the rules are excluded where the settlor's interest arises in the following circumstances:

(a) the bankruptcy of a beneficiary;
(b) an assignment or charge by a beneficiary of his interest:
(c) in the case of a marriage settlement, the deaths of husband and wife and the children of the marriage;
(d) the death of a beneficiary under the age of 25 or some lower age who would have become entitled on reaching that age.

414

It is also provided that a settlor cannot have an interest so long as there is some person living under the age of 25 without whose bankruptcy or charging of his interest no income or capital can be applied for the benefit of the settlor or spouse.

[8] A reversionary interest is also excluded property, irrespective of its location or the settlor's domicile, but under s. 48(1) it must not be a purchased reversion or one that is a reverter to the settlor or the settlor's spouse. But if those excepted reversionary interests are situated abroad and the reversioner's domicile is outside the UK, they too will be excluded property. Broadly speaking, the location of a reversionary interest is determined by its place of administration and, if that is outside the UK, there is no additional requirement that its underlying assets should be situated abroad; on the other hand if the place of administration is in the UK, the reversionary interest will be a UK asset, even if the underlying assets are situated abroad.

[9] There is an exception to this rule if the settlor or spouse (or widow or widower) is given an initial interest in possession prior to the commencement of a discretionary trust. The foreign assets of the trust will not be treated as excluded property on the death of the life tenant, unless he or she is domiciled abroad at the date of his or her death and the settlor was also domiciled abroad at the inception of the settlement: s. 82 IHTA.

[10] Trustees of discretionary trusts should think carefully before exercising a power in favour of an object of the trust which gives him the right to occupy a dwelling-house; the Revenue's view is that this creates an interest in possession and an exit charge will arise for IHT purposes.

[11] Perhaps there should be; Professor Hayton argues in favour of it in [1988] Conv 259.

[12] The court's discretion is not an unregulated one, as, although all the circumstances must be taken into account, ss. 25 and 25A of the Act lay down in some detail the particular matters to which the court is to have regard in exercising its powers under ss. 23 and 24, first (but not paramount) consideration being given to the welfare while a minor of any child who is under 18.

Of interest also is s. 37 of this Act which gives the spouse some protection against dispositions made with intent to defeat or affect the claim to financial relief under s. 23 or to a property adjustment under s. 24. Such dispositions may be set aside within three years of the disposition, except as against a *bona fide* purchaser for value without notice of the intention to defeat the claim; if the disposition is more than three years old the burden of proof will shift to the applicant who alleges that there was such an intent. In *Green* v *Green* (1981) the wife applied under s. 37 to set aside a conveyance on sale by the husband. The purchaser had subsequently charged the land to Barclays Bank and it was held that the discretion to set aside the conveyance did not extend to setting aside the charge.

An important aspect of the home is the spouse's right to be in it and not to be excluded or ejected or refused admission to it. If the spouse's name is on the land certificate or the title deeds, he or she has an inherent right to be there, but if possessed only of an equitable interest or no interest at all, statutory protection is needed and is offered in the guise of the Matrimonial Homes Act 1983, a curious piece of legislation (bristling with difficulties, according to *Megarry and Wade*, p. 810) which expects the non-owning spouse to go to the length of registering the occupational right by notice on the registered title (or as a Class F land charge under the unregistered system).

9 TRUSTEES AND THEIR DUTIES

[1] The 23rd Report of the Law Reform Committee (October 1982) mentions in para. 4.19 and 9.26 that some doubt exists about whether a delegate under s. 25 TA can properly be paid for his services and goes on to say that there is a strong case for removing any doubt. On the other hand, the Committee is in favour of tightening up the freedom to pay agents for their services under s. 23: see 4.6 and 9.25 of the Report.

[2] In this case there was a claim under the Landlord and Tenant Act 1954 for a certificate of refusal permitting compensation for the non-renewal of a business tenancy, but, as a subsidiary cause of action, the court had to decide upon the right of an executor, who had not proved the will, to make an appointment of new trustees under s. 36(5) TA. The deceased had died domiciled in Jersey, and his widow, who was named sole executrix, proved the will in Jersey only, as there was no reason to apply for an English grant, or so it appeared. The deceased had been tenant of land in England as sole trustee for a company, and when the landlord served a notice under the 1954 Act, the widow purported to appoint herself trustee in place of the deceased under s. 36(5). The widow could not be said to be 'intending to renounce' but it was accepted by the court that she could in any case make an appointment under s. 36(1) as the PR of the last surviving trustee, a power that can be exercised by an executor who has not proved his testator's will, whether or not he intends or is able to renounce probate. There remained, however, the question as to whether the widow's title to exercise the power could be proved without the issue of an English grant to someone or other. The court, while accepting that there are exceptions to the general rule that the contents of a will can only be proved by reference to a grant of representation, concluded that the power given to a non-proving executor by s. 36(5) did not imply an intention to breach the general rule and accordingly the appointment of the new trustee could not be recognised; nor could the claim under the 1954 Act.

[3] Under s. 80, TCGA, if a settlement is transferred to non-resident trustees after 18 March 1991 there is a deemed disposal of its 'defined assets' (i.e. assets other than UK assets used for trading in the UK and assets other than those exempt from UK tax under a double taxation agreement) immediately before it ceases to be UK resident. Under s. 82 every person who was a trustee at any time in the 12 months prior to the trust's emigration is made personally liable for the tax if it is not paid by the emigrant trustees. There is an exemption for a person who was not a trustee immediately before the emigration because of his earlier retirement but only if there was nothing in the wind at the date of his retirement for the transfer of the trust abroad. See further *post* 13.23.

[4] In some trusts it will be convenient to have stocks and shares registered in the name of a nominee, but this practice is unauthorised unless sanctioned by the trust

instrument (the Law Reform Committee has recommended that trustees generally should be able to make use of certain types of nominee).

[5] Trustees will no longer receive documents of title to company shares once the paperless share trading system known as *Taurus* becomes fully operative; title to shares will thenceforward be stored in a computer. Access to the computer in respect of a particular holding will, it is understood, be secured to the true owner. The Uncertificated Securities Regulations 1992, para. 50, provide authority for trustees to hold paperless shares which they could have held if certificated and exonerates them from liability for loss unless this is caused by their own wilful default or neglect.

[6] Reference was made in the *Financial Times* of 22 October 1977 to an order of Walton J. requiring trustees to provide information to an object of a discretionary trust, and this would seem to confirm the view that the duty to inform and account does extend to discretionary objects. There is an Australian case which confirms this – *Spellson v George* [1987] 11 NSWLR 300.

[7] The beneficiary should not be given exclusive occupation; alternatively he should be made to pay a proper rent. There is otherwise a danger that an interest in possession will be created for IHT purposes: see *Sansom v Peay* (1976) and IR SP 10/79 (although this has to be balanced against the CGT advantage of the main residence exemption).

[8] Loans should be at a proper rate of interest, as the Revenue appears to take the view that an interest-free loan would create an interest in possession in the fund.

[9] In the *Allen-Meyrick* case the testatrix had given her residue to trustees upon trust to apply the income in their absolute discretion for the maintenance of her husband and, subject thereto, to two godchildren. The trustees made some payments for the benefit of the husband, who was bankrupt, but were in disagreement over any further payments. They applied to court to surrender their discretion and also asked whether they could still exercise it in relation to past income accumulations. The trust was in effect a gift to the godchildren subject to an overriding power to appoint income to the husband and it was held (a) that the court accept a surrender only on a specific issue and not over the future and indefinite exercise of the discretion; (b) that the income accumulations belonged to the godchildren, except to the extent that the trustees had effectually exercised their discretion and, if within a reasonable time of receipt of the income that discretion had not been exercised, it ceased to be exercisable.

[10] The trustee or PR is not so much under a duty to eschew such a purchase as under a disability (in common with other fiduciaries such as agents, solicitors and company directors) which requires disclosure and authorisation if the transaction is not to be set aside. There is therefore no breach of trust in the ordinary sense, so that the usual limitation rules will not apply, leaving the trustee only with the defence of laches: see *post* 14.18 and Megarry V-C's judgment in *Tito v Waddell No. 2* (1977), where he chooses to describe this as the self-dealing rule, as distinct from the fair-dealing rule which applies when a trustee is purchasing the interest of a beneficiary.

[11] Recommendation No. 23 of the Law Reform Committee's 1982 report reads: where transactions between trusts with common trustees are envisaged, then so long as the common trustees are not beneficiaries under either of the trusts concerned, the trustees should be able to do business with one another with the common trustee playing such part as is thought fit, provided that the market value of any property dealt with has been certified by a truly independent valuer as being the proper market price for that property.

10 POWERS OF TRUSTEES

[1] The beneficiary must become absolutely entitled before he can claim the accumulations built up during his infancy. The attainment of a vested interest subject to divesting will not do. Section 31(2)(i)(b) requires that the beneficiary should become entitled to the main fund in fee simple, absolute or determinable, (for realty) or absolutely (for personalty), or for an entailed interest (for either realty or personalty). In the case of personalty, absolutely means what it says and does not include a vested interest in income and capital which is capable of being cut down by the subsequent exercise of a power of appointment or revocation: see *Re Sharp* (1973).

[2] In *Re Powles* the object of the power of advancement, Francis, having reached the mature age of 70, requested the trustees, in the words of Harman J. 'to hand the fund over to him so that he can do as he likes with it, without giving any reason beyond the fact that he would be better off with £7,000 in his pocket than if the money remained in trust.' On an application to the court to ascertain (*inter alia*) whether the trustees were entitled to hand the fund over in this way, Harman J. held that the trustees could not in the circumstances hand over the money without making any inquiry as to Francis's objects or wishes for its use. On the other hand, the judge continued, 'I am unwilling to fetter their discretion more than the words require. If they consider it to be for the general benefit of Francis to have this money, I think that they would be entitled to say "We think it better for him to have it than that we should have it", and if they come to that conclusion, who is to say to them "Nay"? - not I, certainly, because the testatrix has provided differently. I propose therefore to declare that, on the true construction of the will, the trustees may only resort to and spend or apply capital of the fund by paying it to the defendant Francis if they consider such expenditure or application will be for his general benefit. That gives scanty guidance, but it enables them to satisfy themselves not merely that he would like to have the money to jingle in his pocket, but that it will do him some good when he gets it.' One inference to be drawn from *Re Powles* is that, whilst trustees are not absolved from the obligation of making an enquiry into the motives of the advancee, once the trustees have made up their minds, their own motives are not open to enquiry.

[3] With the widely drawn power of advancement under s. 32, there is a case for arguing that, provided the necessary consents are forthcoming from the prior interests, the power can be exercised in favour of the beneficiaries at the level below those next entitled. Thus, if there is a gift to A for life, followed by a contingent gift of the capital to his children, with a gift over to grandchildren if the contingency is not fulfilled, while the *Winch* case would confine the use of the power on its

particular wording to those next entitled, i.e. the children, the statutory power should be available for the grandchildren, if A and his children consent: see the article by R T Bartlett in the *Trust Operations Gazette* No. 27, October 1991.

[4] The *Abergavenny Estate* bill was, in the words of Goulding J. 'prepared by the most eminent draftsman of his day. I have also reason to believe that he regarded the bill as one of his choicest pieces of work. Nevertheless, such is the difficulty of the conveyancer's art, the variety of supervening events, and *the ingenuity of the learned* that I have before me today a short question of construction upon one of the provisions contained in the statute'. (Emphasis supplied.)

[5] If the trust meets the requirements of s. 71 IHTA (see *ante* 8.11), advancements to the beneficiaries are exempted under s. 71(4)(a). In the case of a fixed interest trust the advancement will amount to a PET by the life tenant. Curiously enough, the position will be the same if the life interest is a protected life interest under s. 33 TA and forfeiture has occurred to bring the discretionary trust into operation. In *Cholmondeley* v *IRC* (1986) a protective trust was created in 1979 in favour of C for life with power for the trustees to advance capital to the remaindermen. Upon an advancement by the trustees to R absolutely, the Revenue claimed tax under s. 52(1), in response to which the trustees claimed that the failure or determination of the trusts of the advanced property should be disregarded under s. 88(2) which exempts from charge the failure or determination of the protected life interest. The trustees' argument failed as the removal of assets from the trust fund to implement the advancement was not a failure or determination; the life interest had merely been diminished, not determined. If these facts were repeated after 1987, C's consent to the advancement would amount to a PET.

Whereas a statutory protective trust (or an express protective trust very like it) steadfastly remains an interest in possession trust for IHT purposes even after forfeiture has occurred, yet for CGT and income tax, if forfeiture occurs, there is a discretionary trust in operation attracting the higher rate of tax.

[6] The latest case on the subject is *Swires* v *Renton* (1991) where a 1954 discretionary settlement empowered the trustees to pay or apply any part or parts of the trust fund freed and discharged from the existing trusts for the benefit of any members of a stipulated class. In 1981 the trustees executed a deed of appointment supplemental to the settlement, giving the settlor's daughter a life interest in place of her discretionary interest but empowering themselves to appoint to her an absolute interest, failing which the grandchildren were to take. The court held that the language of the deed of appointment clearly demonstrated that the trustees had not intended to create a new settlement but, rather, had intended to subject the appointed fund to new trusts grafted on to the 1954 settlement; there was therefore no deemed disposal under s. 71(1).

[7] The giving of consent will not work a forfeiture of a statutory protective trust, whether the consent is to the statutory power of advancement or to an express one: so provided in s. 33 TA. An express protective trust, if properly drawn, will normally contain an exception in favour of advancements, but even if it does not, the consent to an express or statutory power of advancement would not normally determine the life interest: *Re Rees* (1954).

[8] The income arising between the date of death and the date of distribution can be apportioned between the advanced and unadvanced beneficiaries either by charging interest on the advances (*Re Poyser* (1908) or by apportioning it in the ratio of the capital distribution (*Re Hargreaves* (1903)). The problem of price movements in the values of the assets can be overcome by revaluing them at the date of distribution (*Re Hillas-Drake* (1944)), although for CGT purposes the probate values will prevail - see *ante* 6.35.

11   INVESTMENT OF TRUST FUNDS

[1] The Agricultural Holdings Act 1948 introduced the revolutionary principle that the cost of current repairs (for example, the mending of fences) could be paid from capital money without replacement. This was confirmed in *Re Northumberland* (1951) and was reinforced by the decision in *Re Pelly* (1957) where the life tenant not only recovered out of capital the cost of the agricultural repairs but also was held to be entitled to keep in his own pocket the income tax repayment which he was able to obtain in respect of those same repairs. In the case of trustees for sale, however, the courts are not prepared to adopt such a relaxed attitude. In *Re Boston* (1956) the residuary estate was held on trust for sale and included agricultural properties. On the strength of the *Northumberland* decision the trustees started to pay income repairs out of capital and now applied to the court for confirmation that they could continue this course. They received a negative answer. Although the legislature in 1948 had not been concerned to protect capital and had thereby encroached upon the fiduciary role of the tenant for life by giving him a privilege which he could exercise for his own benefit if he so chose, there had been no general intention to facilitate the application of capital on expenditure, which up to that point had been made out of income. Where the privilege and the duty of controlling it were vested in the same persons, the paramount duty of the trustees was to protect the capital.

[2] Three further points may be mentioned: (a) it is arguable that, in the absence of specific provision, the right of a life tenant under a trust for sale is to the invested income, not to enjoyment *in specie*; (b) a gift over on ceasing to reside (usually an idle threat to a SLA life tenant's power of sale, because of s. 106 of the Act) is entirely effective behind a trust for sale; (c) because of the facility for fettering the power of sale by requiring the trustees for sale to obtain the prior consent of some other person, the trust for sale is a much better tool for tying up land than is the SLA machinery, for example by making the sale subject to the consent of a third party such as a remainderman who might be anxious not to see a cherished asset leave the family.

[3] A new tenancy granted by the landlord with the consent of the outgoing tenant to someone who, had the tenant then died, would have been eligible to succeed, counts towards the two successions that are allowed for any one family. Thus a voluntary transfer uses up part of the tenant's allowance of transmissions. If there is more than one eligible person anxious to succeed to the tenancy, there are rules for determining their priority; in particular, consideration must first be given by the Tribunal to an eligible person designated in the will of the deceased under ss. 39 and 40.

12 SPECIAL TYPES OF TRUST AND TRUSTEE

[1] Section 50(1) AJA 1985 gives the court power to appoint someone to act as PR in place of an existing PR; the court may also, where there are two or more PRs, end the appointment of one or more, but not all. Removal under this new provision is not confined to cases where a PR is incapable of acting as such. On a s. 50 application the court may appoint a judicial trustee and, conversely, on an application for a judicial trustee, the court may instead make a substitution under s. 50.

[2] Scotland has its own charitable regime, until recently of a very informal nature, but now codified in the Law Reform (Miscellaneous Provisions) (Scotland) Act 1990.

[3] Their response to the Law Reform Committee's Consultative Document on the Powers and Duties of Trustees was: 'we can see no grounds for relaxing the present constraints on a trustee delegating his trust, but in our view these do not normally prevent trustees from obtaining the services of professional investment managers or having their investments held by nominee companies controlled by such managers, subject to certain safeguards'. The only legitimate avenue for delegation of day-to-day investment decisions is under s. 25 TA: see *ante* 9.15; concerning which the Law Reform Committee in their 1982 Report recommended that s. 25 be amended to entitle trustees to remunerate the delegate. They also recommended the relaxation of the restrictions on the use of nominees.

[4] There are over 400,000 registrable occupational pension schemes in the UK, encompassing 11 million employees (out of a total UK workforce of about 29 million) and over 6 million pensioners. About 50,000 new such schemes are started every year.

[5] Barry Riley, in a *Financial Times* article, has pointed out the deceptive nature of the word 'surplus' used in this debate; as he says, it is not a pot of gold but a purely theoretical construct based upon hazy projections of future salary-linked liabilities and future investment returns. Of course, if the pension fund is being wound up, perhaps on account of the employer company going into liquidation, any deficit which exists can be accurately calculated by reference to the market cost of providing for accumulated pension benefits and the replacement of current pensions by means of purchased annuities.

[6] 'Pension funds – is a separate branch of trust law evolving?' by Ian Pittaway is very helpful on this subject: *Trust Law and Practice*, November 1990, p. 156.

With regard to investment compliance procedures, the effect of s. 191 Financial Services Act 1986 is to insist that day-to-day investment decisions must be in the hands of someone who is authorised to carry on investment business under the Act. An occupational pension fund trustee need not be authorised and can continue to exert strategic control over investment policy, provided that the details of the policy are executed by the authorised person.

[7] 'Scheme Particulars' are contained in a document which gives information, *inter alia*, about the constitution, objectives and operation of the unit trust, details of its

trustee, its investment policy and limitations thereon and arrangements for valuation of units; the requirements as to the contents of such a document are listed in Schedule 2 of the Financial Services (Scheme Particulars) Regulations 1988 and run to 11 pages of text. The trust manager is responsible for preparing the Scheme Particulars and for keeping them up-to-date; also, of course, for their accuracy. The trustee also has a duty to consider the contents of the Particulars in his general supervisory role. They must be revised as soon as there is any significant change in the matters with which it deals and, in any case, must be reviewed by the manager at 12 monthly intervals.

The advantage of the Scheme Particulars is that the content of the trust deed can be reduced to the bare minimum and that adjustments can be made to the Particulars with the minimum of fuss, subject to one notable exception: any change in investment objectives must be referred to a general meeting of unitholders.

[8] Employee share schemes are excluded, as are time-sharing arrangements, provided in the latter case that the predominant purpose is enjoyment, not investment. An obvious example, at first sight, of a collective investment scheme is a close-ended investment trust company whose shares can be bought and sold on the Stock Exchange; but under s. 75(7) no body corporate other than an *open-ended* investment company shall be regarded as constituting a collective investment scheme.

[9] The admittedly limited survey of employee benefits in 12.30 to 12.35 does not include registered schemes for Profit Related Pay (PRP) under ss. 169–184 and Sch. 8 ICTA, which seem to be gaining in popularity, after their initial introduction in the Finance (No. 2) Act 1987. It differs from the other schemes (all of them for incorporated businesses) in that it can be applied also to the businesses of sole proprietors and partnerships. The maximum PRP on which income tax exemption is given to the employee is the lower of (a) £4,000 and (b) one-fifth of the aggregate of his salary and his allocation of PRP (for profit periods beginning after 1 April 1991).

13 VARIATION OF TRUSTS

[1] While beneficiaries who are all *sui juris* can collectively put an end to the trust (subject to the protection of the trustees in taxation matters, if there are successive interests), the individual beneficiary may not have quite such extensive rights to distribution as the beneficiaries collectively. In the case of pure personalty, if the assets lend themselves to division, he can demand the transfer of his aliquot share forthwith: *Re Marshall* (1914). But this principle has no application to an undivided share of landed property or even to a share of pure personalty, if the asset is of a kind that presents problems of division, for example, mortgages or shares in a private company. *Lloyds Bank v Duker* (1987) is a notable example of a situation where individual requirements must yield to the collective will of the class of beneficiaries to which the individual belongs: see *ante* 9.40. Along the same chain of reasoning is the rule for CGT purposes that the absolute owner of an undivided share (of landed property or private company shares, for example) cannot regard his trustee as a bare trustee, if at the same time there is running a trust of another share of the same property, under which its beneficiary has a life or other limited interest: see the discussion *post* 13.29.

[2] Obviously if a female beneficiary is aged, say, 70 (as was the case in *Re Pettifor* (1966)), there is no practical problem. As was said in *Re Pettifor* with regard to the inherent jurisdiction, 'it is well established that in administration the court will allow funds to be distributed on the footing that at a certain age, normally in the late or middle fifties, a woman has become incapable of childbearing.' It should be added that that is a course which, while it will protect the trustees, will not prevent a claim against the beneficiaries if contrary to all the expectations a child is subsequently born. That case also makes it clear that the Variation of Trusts Act 1958 must not be used for the sole purpose of enabling trustees to distribute a trust fund on the footing that a woman is past childbearing. Under the 1958 Act, the court's discretion is to approve the allocation of benefits to beneficiaries who cannot speak for themselves; it cannot simply ignore their possible existence: see *Re Westminster Bank's Declaration of Trust* (1963).

[3] Section 42(5) Adoption Act 1976 provides:

> Where it is necessary to determine for the purposes of a disposition of property effected by an instrument whether a woman can have a child, it shall be presumed that once a woman has attained the age of fifty-five she will not adopt a child after execution of the instrument, and if she does so the child shall not be treated as her child or as the child of her spouse (if any) for the purposes of the instrument.

Suppose that a testator dies in 1992, having by his will made a gift to his daughter for life with remainder to her children. Any child adopted by the daughter at any age prior to her own death must qualify for the class gift because it is not 'necessary' for the purpose of interpreting the gift to assess her childbearing capability. But, if when she reaches 55 she enters into a deed of family arrangement with her children for breaking the trust, it then becomes 'necessary' to determine what should happen if she later adopts a child.

This problem does not arise if the trust instrument came into operation before 1976, because in that case an adopted child cannot be treated as the child of the adopter unless the adoption order has a date earlier than the date of the start of the trust (subject to any contrary intention appearing in the trust instrument).

[4] The problem of the coming into being of subsequent children can also arise as the result of legitimation. Under the pre-1976 law (i.e. for deaths before 1976 or settlements made before that date), legitimation had to antedate a trust disposition for the legitimated child to benefit, so the older cases are not likely to encounter this difficulty. But if we take the case of a post-1975 trust which (unusually) restricts the gift to the lawful children of X, it would be possible for an illegitimate child of X to be legitimated by subsequent marriage after the breaking of the trust. If the gift is not so restricted, there is no problem, as an illegitimate child (whether or not eventually legitimated) will qualify as a 'child' if the will or settlement is signed after 1969; if signed before 1970, the subsequently legitimated child is a problem only if the testator dies after 1975 (because of the disappearance of the rule that legitimation must come before the start of the trust). See Family Law Reform Acts 1969 and 1987 and Legitimacy Acts 1926, 1959 and 1976. But remember that these statutory rules will yield to a contrary intention appearing in the trust instrument.

[5] Section 21(3) Limitation Act 1980. There is no limitation period where the trustee has been fraudulent or has converted trust property to his own use – *ibid.* s. 21(1). See also chapter 14 *post.*

[6] As amended by the Statute Law (Repeals) Act 1969 and s. 2 Settled Land and Trustee Acts (Court's General Powers) Act 1943. Section 1 of the latter Act allows the court to authorise the treatment of management expenses for settled land or land held on trust for sale as capital outgoings where the circumstances of the income beneficiary would otherwise cause hardship.

[7] J G Riddall in a note on this case in [1987] Conv 144 argues that the word 'interest' in s. 1(1)(b) should be construed so as to bring within the paragraph those persons who might become entitled to a *vested* interest, which would, of course, have the effect of bringing into its fold anyone having a contingent interest, however remote.

[8] Another form of application to court which, while not ostensibly having the aim of varying a trust or partially revoking its provisions, may well finish up with that result is an application under s. 30 LPA for the sale of landed property held in co-ownership, which could result in an order postponing what was technically an immediate binding trust for sale. See *ante* 8.29(c).

[9] If an overseas trust company has been chosen as the new trustee, a couple of its directors should be appointed as new trustees as well, to overcome the difficulty presented by s. 37(1)(c) TA. That provision stipulates that the old trustees cannot get a discharge unless they leave behind them either at least two new individual trustees or a trust corporation. The overseas trust company will not be a trust corporation in the English sense. This point has been taken by the Revenue in a number of cases in the past with the result that for taxation purposes the transfer out of the jurisdiction becomes a nullity. Section 37(1)(c) may be mandatory and not capable of being over-ridden by an express provision in the trust instrument to the contrary.

[10] It is interesting to note that there have been cases under the 1958 Act where the English court has exercised jurisdiction to vary the trust, despite the fact that its governing law was foreign: *Re Ker* (1963), where the proper law was that of Northern Ireland; and *Re Paget* (1965) where the law of New York applied.

14   BREACH OF TRUST

[1] In *Chillingworth* v *Chambers* (1896) the plaintiff and defendant were the trustees of a will trust, of which Mrs Chillingworth was one of the beneficiaries. On her death her husband became a beneficiary. The trustees made unauthorised investments in mortgages of leasehold property, some of which were made before the wife's death and some of them afterwards. There was a deficiency of £1,580 which was made good out of the husband's interest. He then sued Chambers for an equal contribution but it was held that he must indemnify his co-trustee not merely to the extent of the benefit that he had derived from the breach of trust, but as far as his beneficial interest would go. Thus the right of contribution did not come into play until the beneficial interest was exhausted.

² Thus, the trustee, who is also a beneficiary, pays himself £6,000 as being one of the two members of a class collectively entitled to £12,000. The limitation period expires and there then emerges a third member, so he has overpaid himself £2,000. £2,000 is his maximum liability under s. 21(2), whereas under s. 21(1) he would have been liable to pay £4,000 and would have been left with the miserable task of trying to recover £2,000 from the other beneficiary to whom he paid £6,000 initially.

³ Professor Goode, in two very learned articles in [1976] 92 LQR 360 and 528, asserts that the supposed inability of the common law to allow money to be followed into a mixed fund is a myth. R A Pearce, in [1976] 40 Conv 277 at 291, seems to come to the same conclusion. He also contends that there is no need for a fiduciary relationship to exist to found a right to trace in equity (*post* 14.24), a right which is also available to a beneficial legal owner.

⁴ *Pettit* mentions (p. 453n) the belief that at least one of the executors committed suicide.

Index